CollegeBoard

CLEP®
Official Study Guide
2010

D1377426

College-Level Examination Program®

THE COLLEGE BOARD: CONNECTING STUDENTS TO COLLEGE SUCCESS

The College Board is a not-for-profit membership association whose mission is to connect students to college success and opportunity. Founded in 1900, the association is composed of more than 5,400 schools, colleges, universities, and other educational organizations. Each year, the College Board serves over seven million students and their parents, 23,000 high schools, and 3,500 colleges through major programs and services in college admissions, guidance, assessment, financial aid, enrollment, and teaching and learning. Among its best-known programs are the SAT®, the PSAT/NMSQT®, and the Advanced Placement Program® (AP®). The College Board is committed to the principles of excellence and equity, and that commitment is embodied in all of its programs, services, activities, and concerns.

For further information, visit www.collegeboard.com.

Additional copies of this book may be obtained by sending $24.95 plus $5 for postage and handling to College Board Publications, Box 886, New York, NY 10101-0886. Please allow two to four weeks for delivery. For faster delivery, call 800 323-7155 and charge your order to a credit card.

If you have questions about CLEP that are not answered in this or other publications, write to the College-Level Examination Program, The College Board, 45 Columbus Avenue, New York, NY 10023-6992.

ISBN-13 978-0-87447-853-2
ISBN-10 0-87447-853-7

Library of Congress Catalog Card Number: 9685-660

Printed in the United States of America

9 8 7 6 5 4 3 2 1

Contents

VI. Interpreting Your Scores

VII. Examination Guides

Composition and Literature

Foreign Languages

History and Social Sciences

Science and Mathematics

Business

Appendix

Introduction

This is the only *official* guide to the 34 College-Level Examination Program® (CLEP®) exams. CLEP exams are administered on computer test centers across the country.

This *Guide* has been written mainly for adults who are making plans to enroll in college, but it contains information of interest to others as well. College-bound high school students, current college students, military personnel, professionals seeking certification, and persons of all ages who have learned or wish to learn college-level material outside the college classroom will find the *Guide* helpful as they strive to accomplish their goals.

CLEP is based on the premise that some individuals enrolling in college have already learned part of what is taught in college courses through job training, independent reading and study, noncredit adult courses, and advanced high school courses. Often, their jobs and life experiences have enhanced and reinforced their learning. CLEP provides these individuals with the opportunity to demonstrate their mastery of college-level material by taking exams that assess the knowledge and skills taught in college courses.

The first few sections of this study guide explain how CLEP can help you earn credit for the college-level learning you have acquired and provide suggestions for preparing for the exams. The guides to the individual exams include test descriptions, sample questions, and tips for preparing to take the exams.

CLEP has also made available an online preparation tool that uses the real computer-based testing (CBT) software to help you prepare to test on this platform. The *Sampler* contains tutorials to familiarize you with the basic computer skills needed to take the CBT exams. However, if you are already comfortable using a computer, you can bypass those tutorials and go straight to the sections illustrating how to use the testing tools and how to answer the types of questions developed especially for the computer version of each exam. The *Sampler* also shows you what to expect on the day of the test and gives useful test-taking tips and strategies. You can find the *Sampler* at www.collegeboard.com/clep.

Use the *CLEP Sampler* to get comfortable with the computer-based format of the tests. Then, use this *Guide* to become familiar with the description and content of each exam you're interested in taking. This *Official Study Guide* contains sample questions and an answer key for each exam, as well as in-depth information about how to decide which exams to take, how to prepare to take those exams, and how to interpret your scores.

CLEP Study Materials: A Word of Warning

There are many free or inexpensive sources for CLEP preparation materials, including public or college libraries, bookstores, and educational Web sites. CLEP exams reflect the material taught in introductory college courses; check with local colleges to see what texts are being used in the subject in which you hope to study for a CLEP exam.

The College Board provides the *CLEP Official Study Guide* and individual exam guides (available for download at www.collegeboard.com/clep) to familiarize you with the types of questions on the exams and to provide important tips to help you prepare for the tests. They are not meant to help you learn all the subject matter that CLEP exams cover. We recommend that you study a textbook for the relevant course at your college to learn or review the content of the exam in which you're interested.

Many private companies offer preparation services for CLEP exams. Some companies are legitimate, but others make promises they cannot keep and sell services and products you don't need.

We have received complaints from CLEP candidates regarding the following practices (practices which we consider to be unfair or inappropriate).

- Attempts to sell preparation services for many CLEP exams at once, with sizable payment up front or on credit
- Credit agreements with companies other than the one selling the preparation material
- Contacts from salespeople to you or your family at home
- Promises that you can get college credit without enrolling in college
- Efforts to sell dictionaries or encyclopedias as part of a test preparation package

If you feel you have been cheated, we recommend that you seek the assistance of an organization such as the Better Business Bureau (www.bbb.org) or the Federal Trade Commission (www.ftc.gov).

American Council on Education (ACE)

If you still have general questions about continuing or adult education after reading this book, ACE can provide advice and information:

American Council on Education
One Dupont Circle, N.W.
Washington, DC 20036
202 939-9300
www.acenet.edu

I. The College-Level Examination Program

How the Program Works

CLEP exams are administered at 1,500 colleges and universities nationwide, and 2,900 institutions award college credit to those who perform well on them. The 34 exams allow people who have acquired knowledge outside the usual educational settings to show that they have learned college-level material so that they can bypass introductory college courses and focus on advanced course work.

The CLEP exams cover material that is taught in introductory-level courses at many colleges and universities. Faculty at individual colleges review the exams to ensure that they cover the important material currently taught in their courses. Colleges differ in the CLEP exams for which they award credit; some colleges accept only two or three of the exams while others accept all of them.

Although CLEP is sponsored by the College Board, only colleges may grant credit toward a degree. To learn about a particular college's CLEP policy, contact the college directly. When you take a CLEP exam, you can request that a copy of your score report be sent to the college you are attending or planning to attend. After evaluating your score, the college will decide whether or not to award you with credit for a certain course or courses, or to exempt you from them.

If the college decides to give you credit, it will record the number of credits on your permanent record, thereby indicating that you have completed work equivalent to a course in that subject. If the college decides to grant exemption without giving you credit for a course, you will be permitted to omit a course that would normally be required of you and to take a course of your choice instead.

The CLEP program has a long-standing policy that an exam may not be retaken within a six-month period. This waiting period provides you with an opportunity to spend additional time preparing for the exam or the option of taking a classroom course. If you take an examination of the same title within six months of the initial test date, the administration will be considered invalid, the score canceled, and any test fees will be forfeited.

The CLEP Examinations

Six CLEP examinations cover material taught in the core courses required by most colleges during a student's first two years. These courses may be offered for either three or six semester hours in general areas such as mathematics, history, social sciences, English composition, natural sciences, and humanities. The CLEP examinations appropriate for these general types of courses are College Mathematics, Social Sciences and History, English Composition with Essay, English Composition without Essay, Natural Sciences, and Humanities. Colleges may grant credit in the general area in which a satisfactory test score is earned, rather than for a specific course.

The other CLEP exams cover material directly related to specific undergraduate courses. Exam titles are similar to those of the courses. Institutions will grant credit for a specific course based on a satisfactory score on the related exam. This credit is equal to the credit awarded to students who successfully complete the course. See the Table of Contents for a complete list of all the exam titles.

What the Examinations Are Like

CLEP exams are administered on computer and are approximately 90 minutes long. Most questions are multiple-choice; other types of questions require you to fill in a numeric answer, to shade areas of an object, or to put items in the correct order. Questions using these kinds of skills are called zone, shade, grid, scale, fraction, numeric entry, histogram, and order match questions. The *CLEP Sampler* (downloadable for free at www.collegeboard.com/clep) has been developed to prepare you to take CLEP exams on the computer. It contains tutorials that will familiarize you with basic computer skills and allow you to practice answering each of the question types described above.

CLEP English Composition with Essay includes a mandatory essay section, responses to which must be typed into the computer.

Some of the examinations have optional essays. You should check with the individual college or university where you are sending your score to see whether an optional essay is required for those exams. These essays are administered on paper and are graded by faculty at the institution that receives your score.

Where to Take the Examinations and How to Register

CLEP exams are administered throughout the year at 1,500 test centers in the United States and select international sites. Once you have decided to take a CLEP examination, you must call a test center directly to register and to make an exam appointment. Some colleges administer CLEP exams only to their own students. If your college does not administer the exams, contact a test center in your area for information about its testing schedule. You will find a list of institutions that administer CLEP in a searchable database on the College Board Web site at www.collegeboard.com/cleptestcenters. If you are unable to locate a test center near you, call 800 257-9558 for more information.

Test centers set their own registration criteria. You may have to complete a form or use an online registration system. When you call to make a testing appointment, be sure to ask about the test center's registration requirements.

ACE's College Credit Recommendation Service

The College Credit Recommendation Service (CREDIT) of the American Council on Education (ACE) enables you to put all of your educational achievements on a secure and universally accepted ACE transcript. All of your ACE-evaluated courses and examinations, including CLEP, appear in an easy-to-read format that includes ACE credit recommendations, descriptions, and suggested transfer areas. The service is perfect for candidates who have acquired college credit at multiple ACE-evaluated organizations or credit-by-examination programs. You may have your transcript released at any time to the college of your choice. There is a one-time setup fee of $45 (includes the cost of your first transcript) and a nominal fee of $15 for each transcript requested after release of the first. ACE has an additional transcript service for organizations offering continuing education units.

The College Credit Recommendation Service is offered through ACE's Center for Lifelong Learning. For more than 50 years, ACE has been at the forefront of the evaluation of education and training attained outside the classroom. For more information about ACE CREDIT, contact:

ACE CREDIT
One Dupont Circle, NW
Suite 250
Washington, DC 20036

ACE's Call Center is open Monday to Friday, 8:45 a.m. to 4:45 p.m., and can be reached at 866 205-6267 or CREDIT@ace.nche.edu. Staff are able to assist you with courses and certifications that carry ACE recommendations for both civilian organizations and training obtained through the military.

If you are already registered for an ACE transcript, you can access your records and order transcripts using the ACE Online Transcript System: https://www.acenet.edu/transcripts/.

ACE's Center for Lifelong Learning can be found on the Internet at: www.acenet.edu/CLLL/index.cfm.

How Your Score Is Reported

You have the option of seeing your CLEP score immediately after you complete the exam, except in the case of English Composition with Essay, for which scores are available 2–3 weeks after the exam date. Once you choose to see your score, it will be sent automatically to the institution you have designated as a score recipient; it cannot be canceled. You will receive a candidate copy of your score before you leave the test center. If you have tested at the institution that you have designated as a score recipient, it will have immediate access to your test results.

If you do not want your score reported, you may select that as an option at the end of the examination *before the exam is scored*. Once you have selected the option to *not* view your score, the score is canceled. The score will not be reported to the institution you have designated, and you will not receive a candidate copy of your score report. You will have to wait six months before you can take the exam again.

CLEP scores are kept on file for 20 years. During this period, for a small fee, you may have your transcript sent to another college or to anyone else you specify. Your score(s) will never be sent to anyone without your approval.

II. Approaching a College about CLEP

The following sections provide a step-by-step guide to learning about the CLEP policy at a particular college or university. The person or office that can best assist you may have a different title at each institution, but the following guidelines will lead you to information about CLEP at any institution.

Adults and other nontraditional students returning to college often benefit from special assistance when they approach a college. Opportunities for adults to return to formal learning in the classroom are now widespread, and colleges and universities have worked hard to make this a smooth process for older students. Many colleges have established special offices that are staffed with trained professionals who understand the kinds of problems facing adults returning to college. If you think you might benefit from such assistance, be sure to find out whether these services are available at your college. You may also wish to obtain information from external degree colleges. Many adults find that such colleges suit their needs exceptionally well. (For more information on external degrees, please refer to page 7.)

How to Apply for College Credit

Step 1. *Obtain the general information catalog and a copy of the CLEP policy from each college you are considering. If you have not yet applied for admission, ask for an admission application form too.*

Information about admission and CLEP policies can be obtained on the college's Web site or by contacting or visiting the admissions office. Ask for a copy of the publication in which the college's complete CLEP policy is explained. Also, get the name and the telephone number of the person to contact in case you have further questions about CLEP.

Step 2. *If you have not already been admitted to a college that you are considering, look at its admission requirements for undergraduate students to see whether you qualify.*

Whether you're applying for college admission as a high school student, transfer student, or as an adult resuming a college career or going to college for the first time, you should be familiar with the requirements for admission at the schools you are considering. If you are a non-traditional student, be sure to check whether the school has separate admissions requirements that might apply to you. Some schools are very selective, while others are "open admission."

It might be helpful for you to contact the admissions office for an interview with a counselor. State why you want the interview and ask what documents you should bring with you or send in advance. (These materials may include a high school transcript, transcript of previous college work, or completed application for admission.) Make an extra effort to have all the information requested in time for the interview.

During the interview, relax and be yourself. Be prepared to state honestly why you think you are ready and able to do college work. If you have already taken CLEP exams and scored high enough to earn credit, you have shown that you are able to do college work. Mention this achievement to the admissions counselor because it may increase your chances of being accepted. If you have not taken a CLEP exam, you can still improve your chances of being accepted by describing how your job training or independent study has helped prepare you for college-level work. Tell the counselor what you have learned from your work and personal experiences.

Step 3. *Evaluate the college's CLEP policy.*

Typically, a college lists all its academic policies, including CLEP policies, in its general catalog or on its Web site. You will probably find the CLEP policy statement under a heading such as Credit-by-Examination, Advanced Standing, Advanced Placement, or External Degree Program. These sections can usually be found in the front of the catalog.

Many colleges publish their credit-by-examination policies in separate brochures, which are distributed through the campus testing office, counseling center, admissions office, or registrar's office. If you find a very general policy statement in the college catalog, seek clarification from one of these offices.

Review the material in the section of this chapter entitled "Questions to Ask about a College's CLEP Policy." Use these guidelines to evaluate the college's CLEP policy. If you have not yet taken a CLEP exam, this evaluation will help you decide which exams to take. Because individual colleges have different CLEP policies, a review of several policies may help you decide which college to attend.

Step 4. *If you have not yet applied for admission, do so as early as possible.*

Most colleges expect you to apply for admission several months before you enroll, and it is essential that you meet the published application deadlines. It takes time to process your application for admission. If you have yet to take a CLEP exam, you may want to take one or more CLEP exams while you are waiting for your application to be processed. Be sure to check the college's CLEP policy beforehand so that you are taking exams your college will accept for credit. You should also find out from the college when to submit your CLEP score(s).

Complete all forms and include all documents requested with your application(s) for admission. Normally, an admission decision cannot be reached until all documents have been submitted and evaluated. Unless told to do so, do not send your CLEP score(s) until you have been officially admitted.

Step 5. *Arrange to take CLEP exam(s) or to submit your CLEP score(s).*

You may want to wait to take your CLEP exams until you definitely know which college you will be attending. Then you can make sure you are taking exams your college will accept for credit. You will also be able to request that your scores be sent to the college, free of charge, when you take the exams.

If you have already taken a CLEP exam, but did not have your score sent to your college, you can have an official transcript sent at any time for a small fee. Fill out the Transcript Request Form included on the same page as your exam score. If you do not have the form, visit http://www.collegeboard.com/clep to download a copy, or call 800 257-9558 to order a transcript using a major credit card. Completed forms should be sent to the following address, along with a check or money order made payable to CLEP for $20 (this fee is subject to change).

> CLEP Transcript Service
> P.O. Box 6600
> Princeton, NJ 08541-6600

Transcripts will only include CLEP scores for the past 20 years; scores more than 20 years old are not kept on file.

Your CLEP scores will be evaluated, probably by someone in the admissions office, and sent to the registrar's office to be posted on your permanent record once you are enrolled. Procedures vary from college to college, but the process usually begins in the admissions office.

Step 6. *Ask to receive a written notice of the credit you receive for your CLEP score(s).*

A written notice may save you problems later, when you submit your degree plan or file for graduation. In the event that there is a question about whether or not you earned CLEP credit, you will have an official record of what credit was awarded. You may also need this verification of course credit if you meet with an academic adviser before the credit is posted on your permanent record.

Step 7. *Before you register for courses, seek academic advising.*

A discussion with your academic adviser can help you to avoid taking unnecessary courses and can tell you specifically what your CLEP credit will mean to you. This step may be accomplished at the time you enroll. Most colleges have orientation sessions for new students prior to each enrollment period. During orientation, students are usually assigned academic advisers who then give them individual help in developing long-range plans and course schedules for the next semester. In conjunction with this counseling, you may be asked to take some additional tests so that you can be placed at the proper course level.

External Degree Programs

If you have acquired a considerable amount of college-level knowledge through job experience, reading, or noncredit courses; if you have accumulated college credits at a variety of colleges over a period of years; or if you prefer studying on your own rather than in a classroom setting, you may want to investigate the possibility of enrolling in an external degree program. Connecticut, New Jersey, and New York offer external degree programs that allow you to earn a degree by passing exams (including CLEP), transferring credit from other colleges, and demonstrating in other ways that you have satisfied certain educational requirements. No classroom attendance is required, and the programs are open to out-of-state candidates as well as residents. Thomas Edison State College in New Jersey, Charter Oak State College in Connecticut, and Excelsior College in New York are fully accredited independent state colleges. If you are interested in exploring an external degree, you may contact:

Charter Oak State College
55 Paul Manafort Drive
New Britain, CT 06053-2150
860 832-3800
www.charteroak.edu

Excelsior College
7 Columbia Circle
Albany, NY 12203-5159
518 464-8500
888 647-2388
www.excelsiorcollege.edu

Thomas Edison State College
101 West State Street
Trenton, NJ 08608-1176
888 442-8372
www.tesc.edu

Many other colleges also have external degree or weekend programs. While they often require that a number of courses be taken on campus, the external degree programs tend to be more flexible than other traditional programs in transferring credit, granting credit-by-examination, and allowing independent study. When applying to a college, you may want to ask whether it offers these kinds of programs.

Questions to Ask about a College's CLEP Policy

Before taking CLEP exams for the purpose of earning college credit, try to find the answers to these questions:

1. *Which CLEP exams are accepted by the college?*

   A college may accept some CLEP exams for credit and not others—possibly not the exams you are considering. For this reason, it is important that you know the specific CLEP exams for which you can receive credit.

2. *Does the college require the optional free-response (essay) section for exams in composition and literature as well as the multiple-choice portion of the CLEP exam you are considering? Will you be required to pass a departmental test such as an essay, laboratory, or oral exam in addition to the CLEP multiple-choice exam?*

   Knowing the answers to these questions ahead of time will permit you to schedule the optional free-response or departmental exam when you register to take your CLEP exam.

3. *Is CLEP credit granted for specific courses at the college? If so, which ones?*

   You are likely to find that credit is granted for specific courses and that the course titles are designated in the college's CLEP policy. It is not necessary, however, that credit be granted for a specific course for you to benefit from your CLEP credit. For instance, at many liberal arts colleges, all students must take certain types of courses; these courses may be labeled the core curriculum, general education requirements, distribution requirements, or liberal arts requirements. The requirements are often expressed in terms of credit hours. For example, all students may be required to take at least six hours of humanities, six hours of English, three hours of mathematics, six hours of natural science, and six hours of social science, with no particular courses in these disciplines specified. In these instances, CLEP credit may be given as "6 hrs. English Credit" or "3 hrs. Math Credit" without specifying for which English or mathematics courses credit has been awarded. To avoid possible disappointment, you should know before taking a CLEP exam what type of credit you can receive or whether you will be exempted from a required course but receive no credit.

4. *How much credit is granted for each exam you are considering, and does the college place a limit on the total amount of CLEP credit you can earn toward your degree?*

Not all colleges that grant CLEP credit award the same amount for individual exams. Furthermore, some colleges place a limit on the total amount of credit you can earn through CLEP or other exams. Other colleges may grant you exemption but no credit toward your degree. Knowing several colleges' policies concerning these issues may help you decide which college to attend. If you think you are capable of passing a number of CLEP exams, you may want to attend a college that will allow you to earn credit for all or most of them. For example, the state external degree programs grant credit for most CLEP exams.

5. *What is the required score for earning CLEP credit for each exam you are considering?*

Most colleges publish the required scores for earning CLEP credit in their general catalogs or in brochures. The required score may vary from exam to exam, so find out the required score for each exam you are considering.

6. *What is the college's policy regarding prior course work in the subject in which you are considering taking a CLEP exam?*

Some colleges will not grant credit for a CLEP exam if the candidate has already attempted a college-level course closely aligned with that exam. For example, if you successfully completed English 101 or a comparable course on another campus, you will probably not be permitted to also receive CLEP credit in that subject. Some colleges will not permit you to earn CLEP credit for a course that you failed.

7. *Does the college make additional stipulations before credit will be granted?*

It is common practice for colleges to award CLEP credit only to their enrolled students. There are other stipulations, however, that vary from college to college. For example, does the college require you to formally apply for or to accept CLEP credit by completing and signing a form? Or does the college require you to "validate" your CLEP score by successfully completing a more advanced course in the subject? Getting answers to these and other questions will help to smooth the process of earning college credit through CLEP.

III. Deciding Which Examinations to Take

If You're Taking the Examinations for College Credit or Career Advancement...

Most people who take CLEP exams want to earn credit for college courses. Others take the exams to qualify for job promotions, professional certification, or licensing. Whatever the reason, it is vital to most candidates that they be well prepared for the exams so that they can advance as rapidly as possible toward their educational or career goals.

Those who have limited knowledge in the subjects covered by the exams they are considering are advised to enroll in the college courses in which that material is taught. Although there is no way to predict whether you will pass a particular CLEP exam, you may find the following guidelines helpful.

1. *Test Descriptions*

   For each exam, read the test description and the outline of "Knowledge and Skills Required" that are provided in this *Guide*. Are you familiar with most of the topics and terminology in the outline?

2. *Textbooks*

   Review the textbook and other resource materials used for this course at your college. You can find a list of suggested textbooks and free online resources for each exam at www.collegeboard.com/clepprep. Are you familiar with most of the topics and terminology used in college textbooks on this subject?

3. *Sample Questions*

   The sample questions included in this *Guide* are intended to be representative of the content and difficulty of the questions on the exam. None of the sample questions appear on any CLEP examination. You may use them to get an understanding of the difficulty level and content of the questions on an actual exam. Knowing the correct answers to all of the sample questions is not a substitute for college-level study or a guarantee of satisfactory performance on the exam.

   Following the instructions and suggestions in Chapter V, answer as many of the sample questions for the exam as you can. Check your answers against the answer key at the end of each section.
   - Were you able to answer almost all of the questions correctly? You may not need to study the subject extensively.
   - Did you have difficulty answering the questions? You will probably benefit from more extensive study of the subject.

4. *Previous Study*

Have you taken noncredit courses in this subject offered by an adult school or a private school, through correspondence, or in connection with your job? Did you do exceptionally well in this subject in high school, or did you take an honors course in this subject?

5. *Experience*

Have you learned or used the knowledge or skills included in this exam in your job or life experience? For example, if you lived in a Spanish-speaking country and spoke the language for a year or more, you might consider taking the Spanish Language exam. Or, if you have worked at a job in which you used accounting and finance skills, Financial Accounting would be an exam to consider taking. Or, if you have read a considerable amount of literature and attended many art exhibits, concerts, and plays, you might expect to do well on the Humanities exam.

6. *Other Exams*

Have you done well on other standardized tests in subjects related to the one you want to take? For example, did you score well above average on a portion of a college entrance exam covering similar skills, or did you obtain an exceptionally high score on a high school equivalency test or a licensing exam in this subject? Although such tests do not cover exactly the same material as the CLEP exams and may be easier, people who do well on these tests often do well on CLEP exams too.

7. *Advice*

Has a college counselor, professor, or some other professional person familiar with your ability advised you to take a CLEP exam?

If you answered yes to several of the above questions, you probably have a good chance of passing the CLEP exam you are considering. It is unlikely that you would have acquired sufficient background from experience alone. Learning gained through reading and study is essential, and you will probably find some additional study helpful before taking a CLEP exam. Information on how to review for CLEP exams can be found in Chapter IV and in the examination guides in Chapter VII.

If You're Taking the Examinations to Prepare for College...

Many people entering college, particularly adults returning to college after several years away from formal education, are uncertain about their ability to compete with other college students. You may wonder whether you have sufficient background for college study, and if you've been away from formal study for some time, you may wonder whether you have forgotten how to study, how to take tests, and how to write papers. You may wish to improve your test-taking and study skills before you enroll in courses.

One way to assess your ability to perform at the college level and to improve your test-taking and study skills at the same time is to prepare for and take one or more CLEP exams. You need not be enrolled in a college to take a CLEP exam. You may choose not to send your scores to an institution when you take the exam, and then later request that a transcript be sent to a college if you then decide to apply for credit. By reviewing the exam descriptions and sample questions in this *Guide*, you may find one or several subject areas in which you think you have substantial knowledge. Review at least one college textbook or other college-level resource on the subject(s) you have chosen. For some exams, it may be necessary to study more than one textbook to cover the entire scope of material covered by the exam. By doing this, you will get a better idea of how much you know of what is usually taught in a college-level course in that subject. Study as much material as you can, until you think you have a good grasp of the subject matter. Then take the exam at a test center in your area.

To find out whether you are eligible for credit based on your CLEP score, you must compare your score with the one required by the college you plan to attend. If you are not yet sure which college you will attend, or whether you will enroll in college at all, you should begin to follow the steps outlined in Chapter II. It is best that you do this before taking a CLEP exam, but if you are taking the exam only for the experience and to familiarize yourself with college-level material and requirements, you might take the exam before you approach a college. Even if the college you decide to attend does not accept the exam you took, the experience of taking such an exam will give you more confidence about pursuing your college-level studies.

You will find information about how to interpret your score in the appendix of this *Guide* and in *What Your CLEP Score Means*, a pamphlet you will receive with your score report. Many colleges follow the recommendations of the American Council on Education (ACE) for setting their required scores, so you can use this information as a guide in determining how well you did. The ACE recommendations are included in the appendix.

If you do not do well enough on the exam to earn college credit, don't be discouraged. The fact that you did not get credit for your score means that you should probably enroll in a college course to learn the material. However, if your score was close to the required score, or if you feel you could do better on a second try or after some additional study, you may retake the test after six months. Do not take the same exam sooner or your score will not be reported and your fee will be forfeited.

If you do earn the score required to earn credit, you will have demonstrated that you already have some college-level knowledge. You will also have a better idea of whether you should take additional CLEP exams.

IV. Preparing to Take CLEP Examinations

Having made the decision to take one or more CLEP exams, most people then want to know how to prepare for them—how much, how long, when, and how should they go about it? The precise answers to these questions vary greatly from individual to individual. However, most candidates find that some type of test preparation is helpful.

Most people who take CLEP exams do so to show that they have already learned the key material taught in a college course. Many of them need only a quick review to assure themselves that they have not forgotten what they once studied, and to fill in some of the gaps in their knowledge of the subject. Others feel that they need a thorough review and spend several weeks studying for an exam. Some people take a CLEP exam as a kind of "final exam" for independent study of a subject. This last group requires significantly more study than do those who only need to review, and they may need some guidance from professors of the subjects they are studying.

The key to how you prepare for CLEP exams often lies in locating those skills and areas of prior learning in which you are strongest and deciding where to focus your energies. Some people may know a great deal about a certain subject area but may not test well. These individuals would probably be just as concerned about strengthening their test-taking skills as they would about studying for a specific test. Many mental and physical skills are required in preparing for a test. It is important not only to review or study for the exams but also to make certain that you are alert, relatively free of anxiety, and aware of how to approach standardized tests. Suggestions about developing test-taking skills and preparing psychologically and physically for a test are given in this chapter. The following section suggests ways of assessing your knowledge of the content of an exam and then reviewing and studying the material.

Using the Examination Guides

The individual exam guides, available for purchase on www.collegeboard.com/clep, contain the same information you will find in this *Study Guide*. Each exam guide includes an outline of the knowledge and skills covered by the test, sample questions similar to those that appear on the exam, and tips for preparing to take the exam.

You may also choose to contact a college in your area that offers a course with content comparable to that on the CLEP exam you want to take, or read the suggested resources for each exam on www.collegeboard.com/clepprep. If possible, use the textbook and other materials required for that course to help you prepare. To get this information, check the college's catalog for a list of courses offered. Then call the admissions office, explain what subject you're interested in, and ask who in that academic department you can contact for specific information on textbooks and other study resources to use. You might also be able to find the course syllabus, which will list course materials and assignments, online at the college's Web site. Be sure that the college you're interested in gives credit for the CLEP exam for which you're preparing.

Begin by carefully reading the test description and outline of knowledge and skills required for the exam in the exam guide. As you read through the topics listed, ask yourself how much you know about each one.

Also note the terms, names, and symbols that are mentioned, and ask yourself whether you are familiar with them. This will give you a quick overview of how much you know about the subject. If you are familiar with nearly all the material, you will probably need a minimum of review; however, if topics and terms are unfamiliar, you will probably require substantial study to do well on the exam.

If, after reviewing the test description provided in the exam guide, you find that you need extensive review, put off answering the sample questions until you have done some reading in the subject. If you complete them before reviewing the material, you will probably look for the answers as you study, and this will not be a good assessment of your ability at a later date. Do not refer to the sample questions as you prepare for the exam. The sample questions are representative of the types of questions you will find on a CLEP exam, but none of the questions will actually appear on an exam, so concentrating on them without broader study of the subject won't help you.

If you think you are familiar with most of the test material, try to answer the sample questions, checking your responses against the answer key. Use the test-taking strategies described in the next chapter.

Assessing Your Readiness
for a CLEP Examination

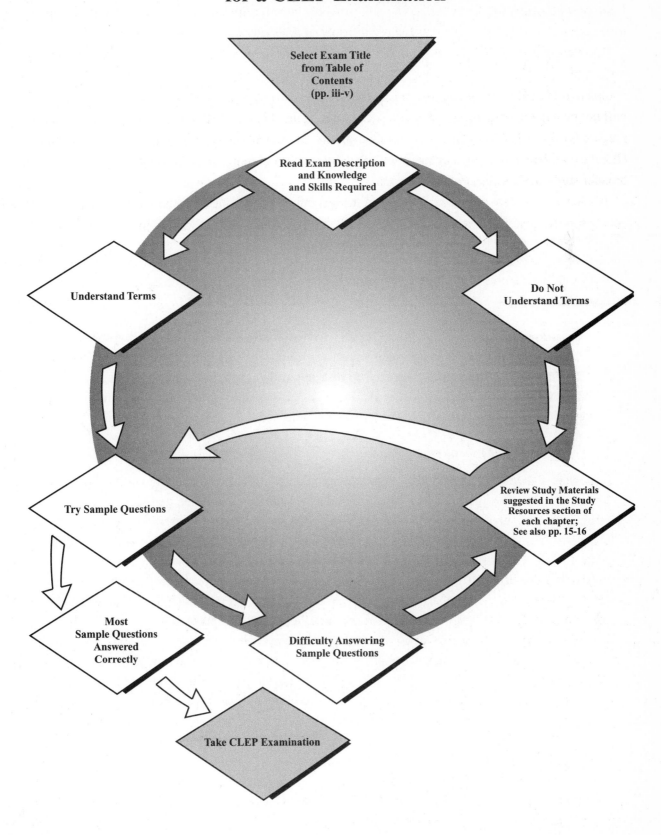

Select Exam Title
from Table of
Contents
(pp. iii-v)

Read Exam Description
and Knowledge
and Skills Required

Understand Terms

Do Not
Understand Terms

Try Sample Questions

Review Study Materials
suggested in the Study
Resources section of
each chapter;
See also pp. 15-16

Most
Sample Questions
Answered
Correctly

Difficulty Answering
Sample Questions

Take CLEP Examination

Suggestions for Studying

The following suggestions have been gathered from people who have prepared for CLEP exams or other college-level tests.

1. *Use CLEP tutorials.*

Make sure you are familiar with the computer-based format of the CLEP exams. Use the *CLEP Sampler*, which can be downloaded from the CLEP Web site, to familiarize yourself with CLEP testing software before taking the test. If you are not comfortable using a computer, you can practice the necessary pointing, clicking, and scrolling skills by working with the *Sampler.* You'll also be able to practice using the testing tools that will help you navigate throughout the test, and you'll see the types of questions you'll be required to answer.

If you don't have access to a computer, check with the library or test center at the school where you'll be testing. Many CLEP test centers and college libraries will have the *Sampler* installed on computers in public areas, so you'll be able to practice and review before your test date. The tutorials are also part of the testing software, and you'll be able to work through them before you begin your test. Check with the test center to see how much time will be allotted for your testing appointment; then you can determine how much time you might need to spend on the tutorials.

> **Remember, if you want to review *content* covered by each examination, Chapter VII of this *Study Guide* contains a complete exam description—including a content outline, a description of the knowledge and skills required to do well, and sample questions—for each subject. An answer key for each subject is also included. However, the *Study Guide* is not intended to replace a textbook. Additional study may be required.**

2. *Define your goals and locate study materials.*

Once you've determined how much preparation you'll need to do, you'll need to define your study goals. Set aside a block of time to review the exam guides provided in this book, and then decide which exam(s) you will take. Using the guidelines for knowledge and skills required, locate suitable resource materials. If a preparation course is offered by an adult school or college in your area, you might find it helpful to enroll. (You should be aware, however, that such courses are not authorized or sponsored by the College Board. The College Board has no responsibility for the content of these courses, nor are they responsible for books on preparing for CLEP exams that have been published by other organizations.) If you know others who have taken CLEP exams, ask them how they prepared.

You may want to get a copy of a syllabus for the college course that is comparable to the CLEP exam(s) you plan to take. You can also ask the appropriate professor at the school you'll be attending, or check his or her Web site, for a reading list. Use the syllabus, course materials, and/or reading list as a guide for selecting textbooks and study materials. You may purchase these or check them out of your local library. Some Web sites offer course materials and lectures online; these can be an excellent resource. Examples of these include:

- MIT OpenCourseWare (ocw.mit.edu/index.html),
- Carnegie Mellon's Open Learning Initiative (www.cmu.edu/oli/),
- and the Online Education Database (oedb.org/library/features/236-open-courseware-collections).

Most of this material is offered for free. Educational Web sites, like those offered by PBS (www.pbs.org) or the National Geographic Society (www.nationalgeographic.com), can be helpful as well. You can also find a list of suggested textbooks and online resources for each CLEP exam at www.collegeboard.com/clepprep.

Check with your librarian about locating study aids relevant to the exams you plan to take. These supplementary materials may include videos or DVDs made by education-oriented companies and organizations, language tapes, and computer software. And don't forget that what you do with your leisure time can be very educational, whether it's surfing current-events Web sites, watching a PBS series, reading a financial newsletter, or attending a play.

3. *Find a good place to study.*

To determine what kind of place you need for studying, ask yourself the following questions: Do I need a quiet place? Does the telephone distract me? Do objects I see in this place remind me of things I should do? Is it too warm? Is it well lit? Am I too comfortable here? Do I have space to spread out my materials? You may find the library more conducive to studying than your home. If you decide to study at home or in your dorm, you might prevent interruptions by other household members by putting a sign on the door of your study room to indicate when you will be available.

4. *Schedule time to study.*

To help you determine where studying best fits into your schedule, try this exercise: Make a list of your daily activities (for example, sleeping, working, eating, attending class, sports, or exercise) and estimate how many hours a day you spend on each activity. Now, rate all the activities on your list in order of their importance and evaluate your use of time. Often people are astonished at how an average day appears from this perspective. You may discover that your time can be scheduled in alternative ways. For example, you could remove the least important activities from your day and devote that time to studying or to another important activity.

5. *Establish a study routine and a set of goals.*

To study effectively, you should establish specific goals and a schedule for accomplishing them. Some people find it helpful to write out a weekly schedule and cross out each study period when it is completed. Others maintain their concentration better by writing down the time when they expect to complete a study task. Most people find short periods of intense study more productive than long stretches of time. For example, they may follow a regular schedule of several 20- or 30-minute study periods with short breaks between them. Some people like to allow themselves rewards as they complete each study goal. It is not essential that you accomplish every goal exactly within your schedule; the point is to be committed to your task.

6. *Learn how to take an active role in studying.*

If you have not done much studying for some time, you may find it difficult to concentrate at first. Try a method of studying, such as the one outlined below and on the next page, that will help you concentrate on and remember what you read.

a. First, read the chapter summary and the introduction so you will know what to look for in your reading.

b. Next, convert the section or paragraph headlines into questions. For example, if you are reading a section entitled "The Causes of the American Revolution," ask yourself, "What were the causes of the American Revolution?" Compose the answer as you read the paragraph. Reading and answering questions aloud will help you understand and remember the material.

c. Take notes on key ideas or concepts as you read. Writing will also help you fix concepts more firmly in your mind. Underlining key ideas or writing notes in your book can be helpful and will be useful for review. Underline only important points. If you underline more than a third of each paragraph, you are probably underlining too much.

d. If there are questions or problems at the end of a chapter, answer or solve them on paper as if you were asked to do them for homework. Mathematics textbooks (and some other books) sometimes include answers to some or all of the exercises. If you have such a book, write your answers before looking at the ones given. When problem solving is involved, work enough problems to master the required methods and concepts. If you have difficulty with problems, review any sample problems or explanations in the chapter.

e. To retain knowledge, most people have to review the material periodically. If you are preparing for an exam over an extended period of time, review key concepts and notes each week or so. Do not wait for weeks to review the material or you will need to relearn much of it.

Psychological and Physical Preparation

Most people feel at least some nervousness before taking a test. Adults who are returning to college may not have taken tests in many years, or they may have had little experience with standardized tests. Some younger students, as well, are uncomfortable with testing situations. People who received their education in countries outside the United States may find that many tests given in this country are quite different from the ones they are accustomed to taking.

Not only might candidates find the types of tests and questions unfamiliar, but other aspects of the testing environment may be strange as well. The physical and mental stress that results from meeting this new experience can hinder a candidate's ability to demonstrate his or her true degree of knowledge in the subject area being tested. For this reason, it is important to go to the test center well prepared, both mentally and physically, for taking the test. You may find the following suggestions helpful.

1. Familiarize yourself as much as possible with the test and the test situation before the day of the exam. It will be helpful for you to know ahead of time:

a. how much time will be allowed for the test and whether there are timed subsections. (This information is included in the examination guides and in the *CLEP Sampler.*)

b. what types of questions and directions appear on the exam. (See the examination guides.)

c. how your test score will be computed.

d. in which building and room the exam will be administered. If you don't know where the building is, get directions ahead of time.

e. the time of the test administration. You may wish to confirm this information a day or two before the exam and find out what time the building and room will be open so that you can plan to arrive early.

f. where to park your car and whether you will need a parking permit or, if you will be taking public transportation, which bus or train to take and the location of the nearest stop.

g. whether there will be a break between exams (if you will be taking more than one on the same day), and whether there is a place nearby where you can get something to eat or drink.

2. Be relaxed and alert while you are taking the exam.

a. Get a good night's sleep. Last-minute cramming, particularly late the night before, is usually counterproductive.

b. Eat normally. It is usually not wise to skip breakfast or lunch on the day you take the exam or to eat a big meal just before testing.

c. Avoid tranquilizers and stimulants. If you follow the other directions in this book, you won't need artificial aids. It's better to be a little tense than to be drowsy, but stimulants such as coffee and cola can make you nervous and interfere with your concentration.

d. Don't drink a lot of liquids before taking the exam. Leaving to use the restroom during testing will disturb your concentration and reduce the time you have to complete the exam.

e. If you are inclined to be nervous or tense, learn some relaxation exercises and use them to prepare for the exam.

3. On the day of the exam, remember to do the following.

a. Arrive early enough so that you can find a parking place, locate the test center, and get settled comfortably before testing begins. Allow some extra time in case you are delayed unexpectedly.

b. Take the following with you:

- any registration forms or printouts required by the test center. Make sure you have filled out all necessary paperwork in advance of your testing date.

- your driver's license, passport, or other government-issued identification that includes your photograph and signature, as well as a secondary form of ID that includes a photo and/or your signature, such as a student ID, military ID, social security card, or credit card. You will be asked to show this identification to be admitted to the testing area.

- a valid credit card to pay the $72 examination fee. (This fee is subject to change.) Although a credit card is the preferred method of payment, you can also pay by check or money order (payable to the College-Level Examination Program). Your test center may require an additional administration fee. Contact the test center to determine the amount and the method of payment.

- two pencils with good erasers. You may need a pencil for writing an outline or figuring out math problems. Mechanical pencils are prohibited in the testing room.

- your glasses if you need them for reading or seeing the chalkboard or wall clock.

c. Leave all books, papers, and notes outside the test center. You will not be permitted to use your own scratch paper; it will be provided by the test center.

d. Do not take a calculator to the exam. If a calculator is required, it will be built into the testing software and available to you on the computer. The *CLEP Sampler* and the pretest tutorials will show you how to use that feature. For some exams, a sample calculator is available for download via the CLEP Web site.

e. Do not bring a cell phone or other electronic devices into the testing room.

f. Be prepared to adjust to an uncomfortable temperature in the testing room. Wear layers of clothing that can be removed if the room is too hot but that will keep you warm if it is too cold.

4. When you enter the test room:

a. You will be assigned to a computer testing station. If you have special needs, be sure to communicate them to the test center administrator *before* the day you test.

b. Read directions carefully and listen to all instructions given by the test administrator. If you don't understand the directions, ask for help before test timing begins. If you must ask a question after testing has begun, raise your hand and a proctor will assist you. The proctor can answer certain kinds of questions but cannot help you with the exam.

c. Know your rights as a test-taker. You can expect to be given the full working time allowed for taking the exam and a reasonably quiet and comfortable place in which to work. If a poor testing situation is preventing you from doing your best, ask whether the situation can be remedied. If it can't, ask the test administrator to report the problem on an Electronic Irregularity Report that will be submitted with your test results. You may also wish to immediately write a letter to CLEP, P.O. Box 6656, Princeton, NJ 08541-6656. Describe the exact circumstances as completely as you can. Be sure to include the name of the test center, the test date, and the name(s) of the exam(s) you took.

Arrangements for Students with Disabilities

CLEP is committed to working with test-takers with disabilities. If you have a learning or physical disability that would prevent you from taking a CLEP exam under standard conditions, you may request special accommodations and arrangements to take it on a regularly scheduled test date or at a special administration. Contact a CLEP test center prior to registration about testing accommodations and to ensure the accommodation you are requesting is available. Each test center sets its own guidelines in terms of deadlines for submission of documentation and approval of accommodations. Only students with documented hearing, learning, physical, or visual disabilities are eligible to receive testing accommodations. Also, it is important to ensure that you are taking the exam(s) with accommodations that are approved by your score recipient institution.

Testing accommodations that may be provided with appropriate disability documentation include:
- ZoomText (screen magnification)
- Modifiable screen colors
- Scripts for the listening sections of the language exams
- Use of a reader or amanuensis or sign language interpreter
- Extended time
- Untimed rest breaks

V. Taking the Examinations

A person may know a great deal about the subject being tested but not be able to demonstrate it on the exam. Knowing how to approach an exam is an important part of the testing process. While a command of test-taking skills cannot substitute for knowledge of the subject matter, it can be a significant factor in successful testing.

Test-taking skills enable a person to use all available information to earn a score that truly reflects his or her ability. There are different strategies for approaching different kinds of exam questions. For example, free-response and multiple-choice questions require very different approaches. Other factors, such as how the exam will be graded, may also influence your approach to the exam and your use of test time. Thus, your preparation for an exam should include finding out all you can about the exam so you can use the most effective test-taking strategies.

Taking CLEP Exams

1. Listen carefully to any instructions given by the test administrator and read the on-screen instructions before you begin to answer the questions.

2. Keep an eye on the clock and the timing that is built into the testing software. You have the option of turning the clock on or off at any time. As you proceed, make sure that you are not working too slowly. You should have answered at least half the questions in a section when half the time for that section has passed.

3. Before answering a question, read the entire question, including all the answer choices. Instructions usually tell you to select the "best" answer. Sometimes one answer choice is partially correct but another option is better, so it's a good idea to read all the answers even if the first or second choice looks correct to you.

4. Read and consider every question. Questions that look complicated at first glance may not actually be so difficult once you have read them carefully.

5. Do not spend too much time on any one question. If you don't know the answer after you've considered it briefly, go on to the next question. Mark that question using the mark tool at the bottom of the screen, and go back to review the question later, if you have time.

6. Watch for the following key words in test questions:

all	generally	never	perhaps
always	however	none	rarely
but	may	not	seldom
except	must	often	sometimes
every	necessary	only	usually

When a question or answer option contains words such as "always," "every," "only," "never," and "none," there can be no exceptions to the answer you choose. Use of words such as "often," "rarely," "sometimes," and "generally" indicates that there may be some exceptions to the answer.

7. Make educated guesses. There is no penalty for incorrect answers. Therefore, you should guess even if you do not know an answer. If you have some knowledge of the question and are able to eliminate one or more of the answer choices as wrong, your chance of getting the right answer is improved.

8. Do not waste your time looking for clues to right answers based on flaws in question wording or patterns in correct answers. CLEP puts a great deal of effort into developing valid, reliable, and fair exams. CLEP test development committees are composed of college faculty who are experts in the subjects covered by the exams and are appointed by the College Board to write test questions and to scrutinize each question that is included on a CLEP exam. They make every effort to ensure that the questions are not ambiguous, that they have only one correct answer, and that they cover college-level topics. These committees do not intentionally include "trick" questions. If you think a question is flawed, ask the test administrator to report it, or write immediately to CLEP Test Development, P.O. Box 6600, Princeton, NJ 08541-6600. Include the name of the exam and test center, the exam date, and the number of the exam question. All such inquiries are investigated by test development professionals.

Answering Essay Questions

The English Composition with Essay exam is the only CLEP exam that includes a mandatory essay. Both the multiple-choice section and the essay section of the exam are administered on the computer. You are required to type your essay using a format similar to word processing.

The essay for the English Composition with Essay exam will be graded by English professors from a variety of colleges and universities who are trained by CLEP. A process called holistic scoring is used to rate your writing abilities. This process is explained in the examination guide for English Composition with Essay, which also includes graded sample essays and essay questions.

Four other CLEP exams have optional essays. Some colleges or universities may require you to take one of these optional essays as part of the American Literature, Analyzing and Interpreting Literature, English Literature, or Freshman College Composition exam. There is an additional fee of $10 for each of the optional essays, payable to the institution that administers the exam. These essays are administered on paper and are graded by the faculty of the institution that grants the credit. Therefore, you may find it helpful to talk with someone at your college to find out what criteria will be used to determine whether you will get credit. Ask how much emphasis will be placed on your writing ability and your ability to organize your thoughts, as opposed to your knowledge of the subject matter. Find out how much weight will be given to your multiple-choice test score in comparison with your free-response grade in determining whether you will get credit. This will give you an idea of where you should expend the greatest effort in preparing for and taking the exam.

Here are some strategies you will find useful in taking any essay exam:

1. Before you begin to respond, read all the questions carefully and take a few minutes to jot down some ideas or create an outline. Scratch paper will be provided at the test center.
2. If you are given a choice of questions to answer, choose the questions that you think you can answer most clearly and knowledgeably.
3. Determine the order in which you will answer the questions. First, answer those you find the easiest so you can spend any extra time on the questions you find more difficult.
4. When you know which questions you will answer and in what order, determine how much testing time remains and estimate how many minutes you will devote to each question. Unless suggested times are given for the questions, try to allot an equal amount of time for each question.

5. Before answering each question, read it again carefully to make sure you are interpreting it correctly. Pay attention to key words, such as those listed below, that often appear in free-response questions. Be sure you know the exact meaning of these words before taking the exam.

analyze	demonstrate	enumerate	list
apply	derive	explain	outline
assess	describe	generalize	prove
compare	determine	illustrate	rank
contrast	discuss	interpret	show
define	distinguish	justify	summarize

If a question asks you to "outline," "define," or "summarize," do not write a detailed explanation; if a question asks you to "analyze," "explain," "illustrate," "interpret," or "show," you must do more than briefly describe the topic.

VI. Interpreting Your Scores

CLEP score requirements for awarding credit vary from institution to institution. The College Board, however, recommends that colleges refer to the standards set by the American Council on Education (ACE). All ACE recommendations are the result of careful and periodic review by evaluation teams made up of faculty who are subject-matter experts and technical experts in testing and measurement. To determine whether you are eligible for credit for your CLEP scores, you should refer to the policy of the college you will be attending. The policy will state the score that is required to earn credit at that institution. Many colleges award credit at the score levels recommended by ACE. However, some require scores that are higher or lower than these.

Your exam score will be printed for you at the test center immediately upon completion of the examination, unless you took English Composition with Essay. For this exam, your score will be mailed to you two to three weeks after the exam date. Your CLEP exam scores are reported only to you, unless you ask to have them sent elsewhere. If you want your scores sent to a college, employer, or certifying agency, you must select this option through the examination software. This service is free only if you select your score recipient at the time you test. A fee will be charged for each score recipient you select at a later date. Your scores are kept on file for 20 years. For a fee, you can request a transcript at a later date.

The pamphlet *What Your CLEP Score Means*, which you will receive with your exam score, gives detailed information about interpreting your scores. A copy of the pamphlet is in the appendix of this *Guide*. A brief explanation appears below.

How CLEP Scores Are Computed

In order to reach a total score on your exam, two calculations are performed.

First, your "raw score" is calculated. This is the number of questions you answer correctly. Your raw score is increased by one point for each question you answer correctly, and no points are gained or lost when you do not answer a question or answer it incorrectly.

Second, your raw score is converted into a "scaled score" by a statistical process called *equating*. Equating maintains the consistency of standards for test scores over time by adjusting for slight differences in difficulty between test forms. This ensures that your score does not depend on the specific test form you took or how well others did on the same form. Your raw score is converted to a scaled score that ranges from 20, the lowest, to 80, the highest. The final scaled score is the score that appears on your score report.

How Essays Are Graded

The College Board arranges for college English professors to grade the essays written for the English Composition exam. These carefully selected college faculty consultants teach at two- and four-year institutions nationwide. The faculty consultants receive extensive training and thoroughly review the College Board scoring policies and procedures before grading the essays. Each essay is read and graded by two professors, the sum of the two grades is combined with the multiple-choice score, and the result is reported as a scaled score between 20 and 80. Although the format of the two sections is very different, both measure skills required for expository writing. Knowledge of formal grammar, sentence structure, and organizational skills are necessary for the multiple-choice section, but the emphasis in the free-response section is on writing skills rather than grammar.

Optional essays for CLEP composition and literature examinations are evaluated and graded by the colleges that require them, rather than by the College Board. If you take an optional essay, it will be sent with a copy of your score report (which includes only the results of your multiple-choice test) to the institution you designate when you take the test.

You may opt not to have your score sent to a college until after you have seen it. In this case, your essay can still be sent to the college of your choice as long as you request a transcript within 90 days after you take the exam. Copies of essays are not held beyond 90 days or after they have been sent to an institution.

VII. Examination Guides

American Literature

Description of the Examination

The American Literature examination covers material that is usually taught in a two-semester survey course (or the equivalent) at the college level. It deals with the prose and poetry written in the United States from colonial times to the present. It is primarily a test of knowledge about literary works—their content, their background, and their authors—but also requires an ability to interpret poetry, fiction, and nonfiction prose, as well as a familiarity with the terminology used by literary critics and historians. The examination emphasizes fiction and poetry and deals to a lesser degree with the essay, drama, and autobiography.

In both coverage and approach, the examination resembles the chronologically organized survey of American literature offered by many colleges. It assumes that candidates have read widely and developed an appreciation of American literature, know the basic literary periods, and have a sense of the historical development of American literature.

The test contains approximately 100 questions to be answered in 90 minutes. Some of these are pretest questions that will not be scored. Any time candidates spend on tutorials and providing personal information is in addition to the actual testing time.

An optional essay section can be taken in addition to the multiple-choice test. The essay section requires that two essays be written during a total time of 90 minutes. For the first essay, a common theme in American literature and a list of major American authors are provided. Candidates are asked to write a well-organized essay discussing the way that theme is handled in works by any two of those authors. For the second essay, candidates are asked to respond to one of two topics—one requiring analysis of a poem, the other requiring analysis of a prose excerpt. In each case, the specific poem or prose excerpt is provided and questions are offered for guidance.

Candidates are expected to write well-organized essays in clear and precise prose. The essay section is graded by faculty at the institution that requests it and is still administered in paper-and-pencil format. There is an additional fee for taking this section, payable to the institution that administers the exam.

Knowledge and Skills Required

Questions on the American Literature examination require candidates to demonstrate one or more of the following abilities in the approximate proportions indicated.

- Knowledge of particular literary works—their authors, characters, plots, style, setting, themes, etc. (about 45 to 60 percent of the examination)
- Ability to understand and interpret short poems or excerpts from long poems and prose works presented in the test (about 25 to 40 percent of the examination)
- Knowledge of the historical and social settings of specific works, their relations to other literary works and to literary traditions, and the influences on their authors (about 10 to 15 percent of the examination)
- Familiarity with critical terms, verse forms, and literary devices (about 5 to 10 percent of the examination)

The subject matter of the American Literature examination is drawn from the following chronological periods. The percentages indicate the approximate percentage of exam questions from each period.

15%	**The Colonial and Early National Period (Beginnings–1830)**
25%	**The Romantic Period (1830–1870)**
20%	**The Period of Realism and Naturalism (1870–1910)**
25%	**The Modernist Period (1910–1945)**
15%	**The Contemporary Period (1945–Present)**

Sample Test Questions

The following sample questions do not appear on an actual CLEP examination. They are intended to give potential test-takers an indication of the format and difficulty level of the examination and to provide content for practice and review. Knowing the correct answers to all of the sample questions is not a guarantee of satisfactory performance on the exam.

Directions: Each of the questions or incomplete statements below is followed by five suggested answers or completions. Select the one that is best in each case. Some questions will require you to match terms with one another or to put a list in chronological order.

1. Make me, O Lord, thy Spining Wheele
     compleate.
   Thy Holy Worde my Distaff make for mee.
   Make mine Affections thy Swift Flyers neate
   And make my Soule thy holy Spoole to bee.
   My Conversation make to be thy Reele
   And reele the yarn thereon spun of thy Wheele.

   The passage above is notable chiefly for

   (A) irony of statement
   (B) pathetic fallacy
   (C) a literary conceit
   (D) a paradox
   (E) a simile

2. In *The Federalist*, No. X, James Madison proposed that the dangers of factions be controlled by a

   (A) republican form of government
   (B) pure democracy
   (C) curtailment of individual liberty
   (D) reapportionment of property
   (E) clause for emergency rule by a minority

3. Sky Woman, Wolverine, and Turtle are all important figures in which of the following types of literature?

   (A) Puritan allegorical tales
   (B) Frontier tall tales
   (C) African American animal fables
   (D) Native American oral tales
   (E) Hispanic American magical-realist stories

Questions 4–5

     Thou ill-formed offspring of my feeble brain,
     Who after birth didst by my side remain,
     Till snatched from thence by friends, less
Line   wise than true,
  (5) Who thee abroad, exposed to public view,
     Made thee in rags, halting to th' press
       to trudge,
     Where errors were not lessened (all
       may judge).
 (10) At thy return my blushing was not small,
     My rambling brat (in print) should
       mother call,
     I cast thee by as one unfit for light,
     Thy visage was so irksome in my sight.

4. In line 1, "offspring" most probably refers to the author's

   (A) philosophy
   (B) book of poems
   (C) unwanted child
   (D) despair
   (E) intelligence

5. "My rambling brat" (line 11) is an example of

   (A) epigram
   (B) alliteration
   (C) onomatopoeia
   (D) personification
   (E) hyperbole

6. Your wickedness makes you as it were heavy as lead, and to tend downwards with great weight and pressure towards hell; and if God should let you go, you would immediately sink and swiftly descend and plunge into the bottomless gulf, and your healthy constitution and your own care and prudence, and best contrivance, and all your righteousness, would have no more influence to uphold you and keep you out of hell, than a spider's web would have to stop a falling rock.

The passage above is an example of

(A) Puritanism

(B) Transcendentalism

(C) Naturalism

(D) Realism

(E) Deism

7. Besides, what could they see but a hideous and desolate wilderness, full of wild beasts and wild men—and what multitudes of them they knew not. Neither could they as it were, go up to the top of Pisgah to view from this wilderness a more goodly country to feed their hopes; for which way soever they turned their eyes (save upward to the heavens) they could have little solace or content in respect of any outward objects. For summer being done, all things stand upon them with a weather-beaten face, and the whole country, full of woods and thickets, represented a wild and savage hue.

The passage above is from

(A) William Bradford's *The History of Plimouth Plantation*

(B) Jonathan Edwards' "Sinners in the Hands of an Angry God"

(C) James Fenimore Cooper's *The Pioneers*

(D) Washington Irving's "Rip Van Winkle"

(E) Nathaniel Hawthorne's *The Scarlet Letter*

8. All of the following are writers of the Colonial era EXCEPT

(A) Anne Bradstreet

(B) Margaret Fuller

(C) Cotton Mather

(D) Phillis Wheatley

(E) Roger Williams

9. Which of the following best describes a theme of Whitman's poem "Out of the Cradle Endlessly Rocking"?

(A) The desire of the poet to retreat to the protected life of the child

(B) The grief that overwhelmed America at Lincoln's death

(C) The celebration of America as the hope of the world

(D) The anguish of a man confronted by war

(E) The awakening of the poet to his vocation

10. Which of the following did NOT write a slave narrative?

(A) Olaudah Equiano

(B) William Wells Brown

(C) Frederick Douglass

(D) Charles Brockden Brown

(E) Harriet Jacobs

Questions 11–12

The mass of men lead lives of quiet desperation.

To be a philosopher is not merely to have subtle thoughts, nor even to found a school, but so to love wisdom as to live according to its dictates a life of simplicity, independence, magnanimity, and trust.

I had three pieces of limestone on my desk, but I was terrified to find that they required to be dusted daily, when the furniture of my mind was all undusted still, and I threw them out the window in disgust.

11. The sentences are taken from the opening pages of

    (A) *The House of the Seven Gables*, Hawthorne
    (B) "Nature," Emerson
    (C) "The Philosophy of Composition," Poe
    (D) *Democratic Vistas*, Whitman
    (E) *Walden*, Thoreau

12. The phrase "the furniture of my mind was all undusted still" can best be paraphrased by which of the following?

    (A) I had become morose and antisocial.
    (B) I had not examined my ideas and beliefs.
    (C) I needed a change of scene.
    (D) I was intellectually and emotionally exhausted.
    (E) I had become so lazy that I could not work.

Questions 13–15

Society everywhere is in conspiracy against the manhood of every one of its members. Society is a joint-stock company, in which the members agree, for the better securing of his bread to each shareholder, to surrender the liberty and culture of the eater. The virtue in most request is conformity. . . . It loves not realities and creators, but names and customs.

Whoso would be a man, must be a non-conformist. He who would gather immortal palms must not be hindered by the name of goodness, but must explore if it be goodness. Nothing is at last sacred but the integrity of your own mind. Absolve you to yourself, and you shall have the suffrage of the world.

13. The passage is excerpted from

    (A) Thoreau's "Civil Disobedience"
    (B) Emerson's "Self-Reliance"
    (C) Lowell's "Democracy"
    (D) Crèvecoeur's *Letters from an American Farmer*
    (E) Holmes's *The Autocrat of the Breakfast Table*

14. The sentence beginning "He who would gather immortal palms . . . " is best interpreted to mean which of the following?

    (A) Anyone who wishes to achieve greatness must examine society's fundamental values.
    (B) A person worthy of emulation need not be good.
    (C) A love of goodness usually stands in the way of great achievements.
    (D) Immortality is denied to the individual who opposes conventional values.
    (E) The means an individual uses to achieve a worthy goal are not important.

15. The philosophy expressed in the passage is best paraphrased by which of the following statements?

   (A) Doing deliberate evil is preferable to surrendering freedom.

   (B) The ideal relationship between the individual and society strikes a balance between total conformity and excessive nonconformity.

   (C) Society and individuality are at odds, so those seeking to be individuals must define their own terms for living.

   (D) Each individual is threatened by society but finally must compromise for the greater good.

   (E) Some people surrender their integrity to society, but they must choose to set themselves against it.

16. The founders of a new colony, whatever Utopia of human virtue and happiness they might originally project, have invariably recognized it among their earliest practical necessities to allot a portion of the virgin soil as a cemetery, and another portion as the site of a prison. . . . But, on one side of the portal, and rooted almost at the threshold, was a wild rose-bush.

   In the passage above, the images of the cemetery, prison, and rose-bush set the tone for which of the following works?

   (A) Jonathan Edwards' *Freedom of the Will*

   (B) Nathaniel Hawthorne's *The Scarlet Letter*

   (C) Herman Melville's *Typee*

   (D) Washington Irving's "The Legend of Sleepy Hollow"

   (E) Edgar Allan Poe's "The Fall of the House of Usher"

17. The "unpardonable sin" committed by Ethan Brand is

   (A) allowing one's intellectual curiosity to violate the privacy of others

   (B) any mortal transgression not followed by repentance

   (C) the attempt to improve upon God's handiwork

   (D) loss of faith in God

   (E) ambition deteriorating into a lust for power

18. Which of the following writers, born into a family of New England ministers, achieved popular success with an abolitionist novel?

   (A) Mary Wilkins Freeman

   (B) Sarah Orne Jewett

   (C) Harriet Beecher Stowe

   (D) Rebecca Harding Davis

   (E) Louisa May Alcott

19. So it came to pass that as he trudged from the place of blood and wrath his soul changed. He came from hot plowshares to prospects of clover tranquilly, and it was as if hot plowshares were not. Scars faded as flowers.

   It rained. The procession of weary soldiers became a bedraggled train, despondent and muttering, marching with churning effort in a trough of liquid brown mud under a low, wretched sky. Yet the youth smiled, for he saw that the world was a world for him, though many discovered it to be made of oaths and walking sticks. He had rid himself of the red sickness of battle. The sultry nightmare was in the past.

   The name of the central character in the work from which the passage above is taken is

   (A) Thomas Sutpen

   (B) Henry Fleming

   (C) Clyde Griffiths

   (D) Frederic Henry

   (E) Nick Carraway

20. About which of the following works did Ernest Hemingway say, "It's the best book we've had. All American writing comes from that"?

(A) *The Last of the Mohicans*

(B) *Moby-Dick*

(C) *The Scarlet Letter*

(D) *Walden*

(E) *Adventures of Huckleberry Finn*

21. "I would prefer not to" is a statement often made by a character in which of the following?

(A) "My Kinsman, Major Molineux"

(B) "The Minister's Black Veil"

(C) "Rappaccini's Daughter"

(D) "Bartleby the Scrivener"

(E) "Benito Cereno"

22. The title character of Henry James's *Daisy Miller* finally

(A) adjusts to the mores of international society in Europe

(B) chooses the life of an artist rather than marriage

(C) enters a convent in France

(D) dies as the result of a night visit to the Colosseum

(E) marries an Italian nobleman

23. Which of the following best states the theme of Stephen Crane's "The Open Boat"?

(A) Human beings are largely responsible for their own fate.

(B) By acts of courage, people may overcome inherent weakness.

(C) Nature, though seemingly hostile, is actually indifferent to human beings.

(D) Through perseverance, a world of peace and harmony will ultimately be achieved.

(E) In any struggle, the strongest are fated to survive.

24. The King and the Duke in Mark Twain's *Adventures of Huckleberry Finn* are

(A) aristocrats

(B) confidence men

(C) slaves

(D) tradesmen

(E) slave traders

25. At the end of Kate Chopin's *The Awakening,* the heroine does which of the following?

(A) Travels to a new home

(B) Walks into the sea

(C) Makes a speech

(D) Has a child

(E) Marries for the second time

26. Which of the following does NOT appear in a poem by Emily Dickinson?

(A) A fly in a still room making an "uncertain stumbling buzz"

(B) A slanted ray of late-afternoon winter sunlight

(C) A rain-filled red wheelbarrow "beside the white chickens"

(D) A train metaphorically described in terms of a horse

(E) A saddened person who "never lost as much but twice"

27. Mark Twain, William Dean Howells, and Henry James are commonly described by literary historians as

(A) transcendentalists

(B) symbolists

(C) realists

(D) romantics

(E) naturalists

28. Which of the following writers was particularly important in the development of the short story as a literary form?

   (A) James Fenimore Cooper
   (B) Harriet Beecher Stowe
   (C) Frederick Douglass
   (D) Edgar Allan Poe
   (E) Edith Wharton

29. Which of the following was a writer of feminist essays and Utopian novels who achieved widespread recognition with the publication of her fictionalized account of depression and mental breakdown?

   (A) Edith Wharton
   (B) Sojourner Truth
   (C) Lydia Maria Child
   (D) Mary Wilkins Freeman
   (E) Charlotte Perkins Gilman

30. Which of the following best describes people as they are portrayed in the fiction of Crane, Dreiser, and Norris?

   (A) Victims of original sin
   (B) Self-determining entities
   (C) Creatures shaped by biological, social, and economic factors
   (D) Beings whose biological natures are fixed, but who are able to manipulate their environments
   (E) Individuals who must be awakened to the fact that their wills are free

31. John Steinbeck's *The Grapes of Wrath* depicts

   (A) the plight of dispossessed farmers who migrate to California
   (B) prison conditions in turn-of-the-century America
   (C) a wounded soldier who tries in vain to escape the effects of war
   (D) racial problems in a small farming town in Oklahoma
   (E) a drifter and his friend who dream hopelessly of better lives

32. Which of the following statements summarizes Booker T. Washington's message in a well-known speech delivered in Atlanta, Georgia, in 1895 and later included in his autobiography, *Up From Slavery*?

   (A) Educational opportunities in the liberal arts are the key to social and economic advancement for African Americans.
   (B) Progress for both the African American and the White communities requires cooperation in developing commercial and industrial opportunities.
   (C) African Americans want to establish separate, self-sustaining communities.
   (D) The economic interests of the African American and White communities will inevitably develop separately.
   (E) African Americans demand immediate and full equality in all aspects of life that are purely social.

Questions 33–34

Let me tell you about the very rich. They are different from you and me. They possess and enjoy early, and it does something to them, makes them soft where we are hard, and cynical where we are trustful, in a way that, unless you were born rich, it is very difficult to understand. They think, deep in their hearts, that they are better than we are because we had to discover the compensations and refuges of life for ourselves. Even when they enter deep into our world or sink below us, they still think that they are better than we are. They are different.

33. In the passage, which of the following best describes the speaker's attitude toward the very rich?

   (A) He finds their cynicism alarming and unwarranted.
   (B) He believes that, because of their advantages and experiences, the rich know more than others do.
   (C) He is envious of their moral superiority.
   (D) He thinks that he understands their psychology even though he has not shared their advantages.
   (E) He finds them so different from the rest of society as to be practically unknowable.

34. The passage was written by

   (A) F. Scott Fitzgerald
   (B) John P. Marquand
   (C) John Steinbeck
   (D) Sinclair Lewis
   (E) Theodore Dreiser

35. Demands of African Americans for the franchise, civic equality, and education of youth were voiced in *The Souls of Black Folks* by

   (A) W.E.B. Du Bois
   (B) Richard Wright
   (C) Harriet Tubman
   (D) Langston Hughes
   (E) Jean Toomer

36. Which of the following writers was a part of the Harlem Renaissance, a flowering of African American literature and art during the 1920s?

   (A) Frederick Douglass
   (B) Zora Neale Hurston
   (C) Phillis Wheatley
   (D) Alice Walker
   (E) James Baldwin

37. Place the name of each of the following writers beside the region that figures most prominently in her writing.

   Sarah Orne Jewett
   Willa Cather
   Flannery O'Connor

   _____ The Great Plains
   _____ The Deep South
   _____ New England

Questions 38–39

Tree at my window, window tree,
My sash is lowered when night comes on;
But let there never be curtain drawn
Between you and me.

Line

(5) Vague dream-head lifted out of the ground,
And next thing most diffuse to cloud,
Not all your light tongues talking aloud
Could be profound.

But, tree, I have seen you taken and tossed,
(10) And if you have seen me when I slept,
You have seen me when I was taken and swept
And all but lost.

That day she put our heads together,
Fate had her imagination about her,
(15) Your head so much concerned with outer,
Mine with inner, weather.

38. The "light tongues" (line 7) are a metaphorical reference to the tree's

    (A) frivolous thoughts
    (B) inquisitiveness
    (C) large branches
    (D) imagination
    (E) leaves

39. When the tree is "taken and tossed" (line 9), the speaker sees the tree as an image of

    (A) the ruthlessness of nature
    (B) his own troubled mind
    (C) the uncertainty of Fate herself
    (D) a lack of seriousness in nature
    (E) shaken but unbowed human will

40. Place the name of each of the following novels beside the war during which is set.

    The Things They Carried
    The Naked and the Dead
    For Whom the Bell Tolls

    _____ The Spanish Civil War
    _____ The Second World War
    _____ The Vietnam War

41. In *The Great Gatsby,* who is directly responsible for the death of Myrtle Wilson?

    (A) Daisy Buchanan
    (B) Jay Gatsby
    (C) Tom Buchanan
    (D) Nick Carraway
    (E) George Wilson

42. Characters with the last names of Snopes, Compson, and Sartoris figure prominently in the fiction of

    (A) Eudora Welty
    (B) Flannery O'Connor
    (C) Thomas Wolfe
    (D) William Faulkner
    (E) Robert Penn Warren

43. Which of the following poets is best known for sonnets that combine a traditional verse form with a concern for women's issues?

    (A) Edna St. Vincent Millay
    (B) Gertrude Stein
    (C) Marianne Moore
    (D) H.D.
    (E) Amy Lowell

44. Which of the following poets derived the title, the plan, and much of the symbolism of one of his or her major poems from Jessie Weston's *From Ritual to Romance*?

    (A) Wallace Stevens
    (B) T.S. Eliot
    (C) Robert Frost
    (D) Marianne Moore
    (E) Langston Hughes

45. As part of a series of dramas chronicling the lives of African Americans in each decade of the twentieth century, Pulitzer Prize winner August Wilson has written which of the following pairs of plays?

    (A) *The Crucible . . . A View from the Bridge*
    (B) *The Piano Lesson . . . Fences*
    (C) *The Iceman Cometh . . . Desire Under the Elms*
    (D) *Dutchman . . . The Slave*
    (E) *Cat on a Hot Tin Roof . . . The Sweet Bird of Youth*

46. Place the name of each of the following writers beside the genre with which he is most closely associated.

    O. Henry
    Frank Norris
    Eugene O'Neill

    _____ Drama
    _____ The short story
    _____ The novel

47. "You've just seen a prince walk by. A fine, troubled prince. A hard-working, unappreciated prince. A pal, you understand? Always for his boys."

    In which of the following modern American plays is the principal character described above?

    (A) *The Glass Menagerie*
    (B) *The Hairy Ape*
    (C) *Trifles*
    (D) *A Raisin in the Sun*
    (E) *Death of a Salesman*

48. Which of the following cities is Carl Sandburg noted for celebrating?

    (A) New York
    (B) Chicago
    (C) Los Angeles
    (D) New Orleans
    (E) Pittsburgh

49. Bigger Thomas is the central character in

    (A) Upton Sinclair's *The Jungle*
    (B) Carson McCullers' *The Ballad of the Sad Café*
    (C) Richard Wright's *Native Son*
    (D) Nella Larsen's *Passing*
    (E) Thomas Wolfe's *Look Homeward, Angel*

50. "I wish that you were my sister, I'd teach you to have some confidence in yourself. The different people are not like other people, but being different is nothing to be ashamed of . . . . Other people are . . . one hundred times one thousand. You're one times one! They walk all over the earth. You just stay here. They're common as—weeds, but—you—well, you're Blue Roses."

In the passage above from Tennessee Williams' *The Glass Menagerie*, the term "Blue Roses" is a metaphor for the young woman's

(A) favorite flowers

(B) profession as a dancer

(C) vivacious personality

(D) shyness and sensitivity

(E) unusual taste in fashion

Questions 51–54

The extraordinary patience of things!
This beautiful place defaced with a crop of
    suburban houses—
Line How beautiful when we first beheld it,
(5) Unbroken field of poppy and lupin walled with
    clean cliffs;
No intrusion but two or three horses pasturing,
Or a few milch cows rubbing their flanks on the
    outcrop rockheads—
(10) Now the spoiler has come: does it care?
Not faintly. It has all time. It knows the people
    are a tide
That swells and in time will ebb, and all
Their works dissolve. Meanwhile the image of
(15)   pristine beauty
Lives in the very grain of the granite,
Safe as the endless ocean that climbs our
    cliff.—As for us:
We must uncenter our minds from ourselves;
(20) We must unhumanize our views a little, and
    become confident
As the rock and ocean that we were made from.

51. In line 10, the word "it" refers to

(A) "The extraordinary patience of things" (line 1)

(B) "This beautiful place" (line 2)

(C) "a crop of suburban houses" (lines 2–3)

(D) "the spoiler" (line 10)

(E) "a tide . . . That swells" (lines 12–13)

52. In lines 11–14, the discussion of "the people" emphasizes their

(A) foresight

(B) dignity

(C) timidity

(D) transience

(E) greed

53. The primary contrast in the poem is between

(A) the land and the sea

(B) urban and suburban landscapes

(C) animals and people

(D) time and space

(E) nature and humankind

54. The poem is written in which verse form?

(A) Ballad

(B) Blank verse

(C) Free verse

(D) Italian sonnet

(E) Shakespearean sonnet

55. Which of the following is the first-person narrator of Harper Lee's 1960 novel *To Kill a Mockingbird*?

(A) Jem

(B) Dill

(C) Scout

(D) Calpurnia

(E) Mayella

56. Which of the following novels has as its main concern the experiences of an African American protagonist?

(A) *All the King's Men*

(B) *The Age of Innocence*

(C) *Henderson the Rain King*

(D) *Invisible Man*

(E) *The Catcher in the Rye*

57. At the end of Flannery O'Connor's "A Good Man Is Hard to Find," the grandmother does which of the following?

(A) She ponders the truth of Red Sammy's words: a good man is hard to find.

(B) She collapses in the street after being hit by a woman she has insulted.

(C) She dies after being shot by an escaped convict, the Misfit.

(D) She marries a Bible salesman who is also a con artist.

(E) She sits in a roadside diner, abandoned by the drifter she has befriended.

58. When we Chinese girls listened to the adults talk-story, we learned that we failed if we grew up to be but wives or slaves. We could be heroines, swordswomen. Even if she had to rage across all China, a swordswoman got even with anybody who hurt her family. Perhaps women were once so dangerous that they had to have their feet bound. . . .

My mother told [stories] that followed swordswomen through woods and palaces for years. Night after night my mother would talk story until we fell asleep. I couldn't tell where the stories left off and dreams began, her voice the voice of the heroines in my sleep. . . .

At last I saw that I too had been in the presence of great power, my mother talking-story.

In the passage above, the discussion of "talk-story" helps to express the speaker's

(A) acceptance of having outgrown the stories of her childhood

(B) development of her own capacity for writing through practice in storytelling

(C) sense that storytelling was a way that her mother transmitted strength

(D) desire to pursue an active life rather than tell stories like her mother

(E) confusion about her mother's ultimate purpose in telling stories

59. The characters Shug Avery, Celie, and Mister appear in which of the following novels?

(A) *The Color Purple*

(B) *The Crying of Lot 49*

(C) *Their Eyes Were Watching God*

(D) *Go Tell It on the Mountain*

(E) *Light in August*

Questions 60–61

my mamma moved among the days
like a dreamwalker in a field;
seemed like what she touched was hers
Line seemed like what touched her couldn't hold,
(5) she got us almost through the high grass
then seemed like she turned around and ran
right back in
right back on in

Lucille Clifton, "my mamma moved among the days" from
Good Women: Poems and a Memoir 1969-80. Copyright © 1987
by Lucille Clifton. Used by permission of BOA Editions, Ltd.,
www.boaeditions.org.

60. Lines 1–4 suggest that the speaker viewed the mother as

(A) reverent

(B) indomitable

(C) absentminded

(D) ineffectual

(E) unrealistic

61. The poem makes use of all of the following EXCEPT

(A) first-person perspective

(B) extended metaphor

(C) repetition

(D) simile

(E) satire

62. All of the following were written by Toni Morrison EXCEPT

(A) *Song of Solomon*

(B) *Beloved*

(C) *The Bluest Eye*

(D) *Sula*

(E) *Tell Me a Riddle*

63. The Native American author of the Pulitzer Prize-winning novel *House Made of Dawn* is

(A) N. Scott Momaday

(B) Louise Erdrich

(C) Leslie Marmon Silko

(D) Toni Cade Bambara

(E) Jack Kerouac

Study Resources

To prepare for the American Literature exam, you should read critically the contents of at least one anthology, which you can find in most college bookstores. Most textbook anthologies contain a representative sample of readings as well as discussions of historical background, literary styles and devices characteristic of various authors and periods, and other material relevant to the test. The anthologies do vary somewhat in their content, approach, and emphases; you are advised to consult more than one or to consult some specialized books on major authors, periods, and literary forms and terminology. You should also read some of the major novels that are mentioned or excerpted in the anthologies, such as Hawthorne's *The Scarlet Letter*, Twain's *Adventures of Huckleberry Finn*, and Chopin's *The Awakening*. Other writers whose major works you should be familiar with include Melville, Crane, James, Cather, Fitzgerald, Hemingway, Faulkner, Ellison, and Morrison. You can probably obtain an extensive reading list of American literature from a college English department, library, or bookstore.

Visit www.collegeboard.com/clepprep for additional American literature study resources. You can also find suggestions for exam preparation in Chapter IV of the *Official Study Guide*. In addition, many college faculty post their course materials on their schools' Web sites.

Answer Key

#	Ans	#	Ans
1.	C	33.	D
2.	A	34.	A
3.	D	35.	A
4.	B	36.	B
5.	D	37.	See below
6.	A	38.	E
7.	A	39.	B
8.	B	40.	See below
9.	E	41.	A
10.	D	42.	D
11.	E	43.	A
12.	B	44.	B
13.	B	45.	B
14.	A	46.	See below
15.	C	47.	E
16.	B	48.	B
17.	A	49.	C
18.	C	50.	D
19.	B	51.	B
20.	E	52.	D
21.	D	53.	E
22.	D	54.	C
23.	C	55.	C
24.	B	56.	D
25.	B	57.	C
26.	C	58.	C
27.	C	59.	A
28.	D	60.	B
29.	E	61.	E
30.	C	62.	E
31.	A	63.	A
32.	B		

37. Willa Cather — The Great Plains
    Flannery O'Connor — The Deep South
    Sarah Orne Jewett — New England

40. *For Whom the Bell Tolls* — The Spanish Civil War
    The Naked and the Dead — The Second World War
    The Things They Carried — The Vietnam War

46. Eugene O'Neill — Drama
    O. Henry — The short story
    Frank Norris — The novel

Analyzing and Interpreting Literature

Description of the Examination

The Analyzing and Interpreting Literature examination covers material usually taught in a general two-semester undergraduate course in literature. Although the examination does not require familiarity with specific works, it does assume that candidates have read widely and perceptively in poetry, drama, fiction, and nonfiction. The questions are based on passages supplied in the test. These passages have been selected so that no previous experience with them is required to answer the questions. The passages are taken primarily from American and British literature.

The examination contains approximately 80 multiple-choice questions to be answered in 90 minutes. Some of these are pretest questions that will not be scored. Any time candidates spend taking tutorials and providing personal information is additional to actual testing time.

Because writing about literary texts is central to the study of literature, some colleges may require candidates to take an optional essay section in addition to the multiple-choice section. The essay section is 90 minutes long and is made up of two 45-minute questions. One question asks candidates to analyze a short poem, the other asks them to apply a given generalization about literature (such as the function of a theme or a technique) to a novel, short story, or play that they have read. The essay section is still administered in a paper-and-pencil format; the essay responses are graded by the institution, not by the College Board.

Knowledge and Skills Required

Questions on the Analyzing and Interpreting Literature examination require candidates to demonstrate the following abilities.

- Ability to read prose, poetry, and drama with understanding
- Ability to analyze the elements of a literary passage and to respond to nuances of meaning, tone, imagery, and style
- Ability to interpret metaphors, to recognize rhetorical and stylistic devices, to perceive relationships between parts and wholes, and to grasp a speaker's or author's attitudes
- Knowledge of the means by which literary effects are achieved
- Familiarity with the basic terminology used to discuss literary texts

The examination emphasizes comprehension, interpretation, and analysis of literary works. A specific knowledge of historical context (authors and movements) is not required, but a broad knowledge of literature gained through reading widely and a familiarity with basic literary terminology is assumed. The following outline indicates the relative emphasis given to the various types of literature and the periods from which the passages are taken. The approximate percentage of exam questions per classification is noted within each main category.

Genre

35–45%	Poetry
35–45%	Prose (fiction and nonfiction)
15–30%	Drama

National Tradition

50–65%	British Literature
30–45%	American Literature
5–15%	Works in Translation

Period

3–7%	Classical and pre-Renaissance
20–30%	Renaissance and 17th Century
35–45%	18th and 19th Centuries
25–35%	20th and 21st Centuries

Sample Test Questions

The following sample questions do not appear on an actual CLEP examination. They are intended to give potential test-takers an indication of the format and difficulty level of the examination and to provide content for practice and review. Knowing the correct answers to all of the sample questions is not a guarantee of satisfactory performance on the exam.

Directions: Each of the questions or incomplete statements below is followed by five suggested answers or completions. Select the one that is best in each case.

Questions 1–5

CHORAGOS: Men of Thebes: look upon Oedipus.
This is the king who solved the famous riddle
And towered up, most powerful of men.
Line No mortal eyes but looked on him with envy,
(5) Yet in the end ruin swept over him.

Let every man in mankind's frailty
Consider his last day; and let none
Presume on his good fortune until he find
Life, at his death, a memory without pain.

1. Line 3 primarily suggests that Oedipus

    (A) was an unusually tall and intimidating man
    (B) became a figure of great fame and authority
    (C) waged war against the men of Thebes
    (D) was stronger and more agile than other men
    (E) proved to be a persuasive, if corrupt, politician

2. Which of the following is the best paraphrase of "No mortal eyes but looked on him with envy" (line 4)?

    (A) Even the gods were envious of him.
    (B) The gods considered him an envious person.
    (C) Everyone wished to have his advantages.
    (D) Only envious people would seek him.
    (E) Everyone longed to be immortal like him.

3. The speaker assumes that "every man" (line 6) is

    (A) averse to idolizing other men as gods
    (B) likely to underestimate his own abilities
    (C) prone to turn down a challenge too quickly
    (D) vulnerable to fate and his own destiny
    (E) capable of accomplishing great feats

4. In the context of the passage, to "Presume on his good fortune" (line 8) is best interpreted as

    (A) assume bad luck must turn to good
    (B) believe that happiness will endure
    (C) try to gain wealth and prosperity
    (D) plan for good fortune before it comes
    (E) make judgments on those who are poor or unlucky

5. The passage can best be described as

    (A) a warning against hubris or pride
    (B) a poetic rejection of bad fortune
    (C) an acceptance of catharsis
    (D) a poetic affirmation that all is vanity
    (E) God's promise of final happiness

Questions 6–11

How many thousand of my poorest subjects
Are at this hour asleep! O sleep, O gentle sleep,
Nature's soft nurse, how have I frightened thee
Line That thou no more wilt weigh my eyelids down
(5) And steep my senses in forgetfulness?
Why rather, sleep, liest thou in smoky cribs,
Upon uneasy pallets stretching thee
And hushed with buzzing night-flies to thy slumber,
Than in the perfumed chambers of the great,
(10) Under the canopies of costly state,
And lulled with sound of sweetest melody?
O thou dull god, why liest thou with the vile
In loathsome beds, and leavest the kingly couch
A watch-case or a common 'larum bell?
(15) Wilt thou upon the high and giddy mast
Seal up the ship-boy's eyes, and rock his brains
In cradle of the rude imperious surge
And in the visitation of the winds,
Who take the ruffian billows by the top,
(20) Curling their monstrous heads and hanging them
With deafening clamor in the slippery clouds,
That, with the hurly, death itself awakes?
Canst thou, O partial sleep, give thy repose
To the wet sea-son in a hour so rude,
(25) And in the calmest and most stillest night,
With all appliances and means to boot,
Deny it to a king? Then happy low, lie down!
Uneasy lies the head that wears a crown.

6. The dramatic situation suggested by the speech
   is that of a king

   (A) cast down from high estate
   (B) concerned about the poverty of his subjects
   (C) setting forth on a dangerous journey
   (D) fearful of death
   (E) restless with cares

7. The point of the scene described in lines 15–22
   is that

   (A) death is an inevitable extension of sleep
   (B) common folk are accustomed to danger even
       though the king is not
   (C) fear is best overcome by sleep
   (D) evil inevitably overtakes the weak
   (E) sleep comes to common folk even in peril-
       ous circumstances

8. In the context of the passage, "partial" (line
   23) means

   (A) biased
   (B) unsatisfying
   (C) half-waking
   (D) two-faced
   (E) favorite

9. In line 27, "low" refers to

   (A) "my poorest subjects" (line 1)
   (B) "sweetest melody" (line 11)
   (C) "rude imperious surge" (line 17)
   (D) "O partial sleep" (line 23)
   (E) "a king" (line 27)

10. The speaker's tone in addressing sleep
    changes from

    (A) confident to insecure
    (B) bitter to victorious
    (C) pleading to reproachful
    (D) outraged to sarcastic
    (E) angry to bewildered

11. With minor variations, the passage is written in

    (A) elegy form
    (B) blank verse
    (C) free verse
    (D) heroic couplets
    (E) the form of an ode

Questions 12–19

"A clear fire, a clean hearth, and the rigor of the game." This was the celebrated wish of old Sarah Battle (now with God) who, next to her devotions,
Line loved a good game at whist. She was none of
(5) your lukewarm gamesters, your half-and-half players, who have no objection to take a hand, if you want one to make up a rubber; who affirm that they have no pleasure in winning; that they like to win one game, and lose another; that they
(10) can while away an hour very agreeably at a card table, but are indifferent whether they play or no; and will desire an adversary, who has slipt a wrong card, to take it up and play another. These insufferable triflers are the curse of a table. One of these
(15) flies will spoil a whole pot. Of such it may be said, that they do not play at cards, but only play at playing at them.
Sarah Battle was none of that breed. She detested them, as I do, from her heart and soul; and would
(20) not, save upon a striking emergency, willingly seat herself at the same table with them. She loved a thorough-paced partner, a determined enemy. She took, and gave, no concessions. She hated favors. She never made a revoke, nor ever
(25) passed it over in her adversary without exacting the utmost forfeiture. She fought a good fight: cut and thrust. She held not her sword (her cards) "like a dancer." She sat bolt upright; and neither showed you her cards, nor desired to see yours.
(30) All people have their blind side—their superstitions; and I have heard her declare, under the rose,* that Hearts was her favourite suit.

*sub rosa, in confidence

12. The phrase "now with God" (line 3) reveals that Sarah Battle

(A) was a religious person
(B) had an unexpected religious experience
(C) placed devotion to God ahead of whist
(D) has decided to give up cards
(E) is no longer alive

13. In line 3, "next to" is best paraphrased as

(A) second only to
(B) besides
(C) before
(D) in addition to
(E) even more than

14. To Sarah Battle, the most significant characteristic of the triflers described in lines 5–15 is their

(A) amiable sociability
(B) generosity toward their opponents
(C) nonchalant attitude toward whist
(D) ability to keep the game in perspective
(E) inability to play whist well

15. It can be inferred from the description of Sarah Battle's behavior at the whist table that she

(A) would respect a superior opponent
(B) had an ironic sense of humor
(C) would do anything to win
(D) did not really enjoy playing whist
(E) enjoyed being catered to in whist

16. The most apparent metaphor in this character sketch is drawn from

   (A) nature
   (B) religion
   (C) finance
   (D) swordplay
   (E) gamesmanship .

17. The attitude of the narrator toward Sarah Battle is chiefly one of

   (A) sarcastic anger
   (B) affectionate respect
   (C) tolerant understanding
   (D) arrogant condescension
   (E) fearful regard

18. The passage suggests all of the following about the narrator EXCEPT that the narrator

   (A) has a sense of humor
   (B) has spent time in Sarah Battle's presence
   (C) is an excellent whist player
   (D) scorns casual whist players
   (E) sees Sarah Battle's weakness

19. Which of the following best summarizes the structure of the passage?

   (A) The first paragraph concentrates on Sarah Battle's serious side; the second, on her fun-loving side.
   (B) The first paragraph defines Sarah Battle by what she is not; the second, by what she is.
   (C) The passage interprets, in turn, what Sarah Battle would regard as "A clear fire, a clean hearth, and the rigor of the game" (lines 1–2).
   (D) The passage moves from a discussion of the refinements of whist to an explanation of what makes Sarah Battle like the game.
   (E) The first paragraph describes Sarah Battle as a gambler; the second, as a soldier of reform.

Questions 20–24

All towns should be made capable of purification by fire, or of decay, within each half century. Otherwise, they become the hereditary haunts of
Line vermin and noisomeness, besides standing apart
(5) from the possibility of such improvements as are constantly introduced into the rest of man's contrivances and accommodations. It is beautiful, no doubt, and exceedingly satisfactory to some of our natural instincts, to imagine our far
(10) posterity dwelling under the same rooftree as ourselves. Still, when people insist on building indestructible houses, they incur, or their children do, a misfortune analogous to that of the Sibyl, when she obtained the grievous boon of immor-
(15) tality. So, we may build almost immortal habitations, it is true; but we cannot keep them from growing old, musty, unwholesome, dreary, full of death scents, ghosts, and murder stains; in short, such habitations as one sees everywhere in Italy, be they hovels or palaces.

20. The first sentence of the passage serves primarily to

    (A) state a fact
    (B) express a generally accepted opinion
    (C) startle by its unorthodoxy
    (D) say the opposite of what the speaker means
    (E) present an unwarranted conclusion

21. What misfortune of the Sibyl is implied in lines 11–15?

    (A) She lived in an indestructible house.
    (B) She remained young forever.
    (C) She did not get what she asked for.
    (D) Her children lived in old houses.
    (E) She could not die but continued to age.

22. The speaker objects to "almost immortal habitations" (lines 15–16) because they

    (A) start as palaces and end as hovels
    (B) are full of unpleasant memories and gloom
    (C) are unhealthy for growing children
    (D) burden families with their upkeep
    (E) are structurally unsound

23. The speaker apparently regards changes brought about by modernization with

    (A) approval
    (B) indifference
    (C) resentment
    (D) hesitancy
    (E) bewilderment

24. The speaker's attitude toward houses in Italy is best described as one of

    (A) envy
    (B) aversion
    (C) ambivalence
    (D) enthusiasm
    (E) defensiveness

Questions 25–29

Besides the neutral expression that she wore when she was alone, Mrs. Freeman had two others, forward and reverse, that she used for all her
Line human dealings. Her forward expression was
(5) steady and driving like the advance of a heavy truck. Her eyes never swerved to left or right but turned as the story turned as if they followed a yellow line down the center of it. She seldom used the other expression because it was not often
(10) necessary for her to retract a statement, but when she did, her face came to a complete stop, there was an almost imperceptible movement of her black eyes, during which they seemed to be receding, and then the observer would see that Mrs.
(15) Freeman, though she might stand there as real as several grain sacks thrown on top of each other, was no longer there in spirit. As for getting anything across to her when this was the case, Mrs. Hopewell had given it up. She might talk her head
(20) off. Mrs. Freeman could never be brought to admit herself wrong on any point. She would stand there and if she could be brought to say something, it was something like, "Well, I wouldn't of said it was and I wouldn't of said it wasn't," or letting her
(25) gaze range over the top shelf where there was an assortment of dusty bottles, she might remark, "I see you ain't ate many of them figs you put up last summer."

25. The metaphor suggested by "forward and reverse" in the opening sentence is also suggested by all of the following words EXCEPT

(A) "advance" (line 5)
(B) "swerved" (line 6)
(C) "turned" (line 7)
(D) "retract" (line 10)
(E) "stop" (line 11)

26. What quality of Mrs. Freeman's character does the controlling image of the passage suggest?

(A) Her forbearance
(B) Her insecurity
(C) Her rigidity
(D) Her proper manners
(E) Her sense of irony

27. That Mrs. Freeman "might stand there as real as several grain sacks thrown on top of each other" (lines 15–16) suggests that she is all of the following EXCEPT

(A) plain and down-to-earth
(B) undecided in her opinions
(C) clearly visible
(D) part of the country scene
(E) closed and contributing nothing at present

28. Mrs. Freeman's remark in lines 23–24 can best be described as

(A) a cliché
(B) a paradox
(C) an equivocation
(D) a circular argument
(E) a metaphoric contrast

29. Mrs. Freeman's remarks are best described as

(A) self-protective
(B) self-censuring
(C) self-analytical
(D) aggressive
(E) contemptuous

Questions 30–34

The Child at Winter Sunset

The child at winter sunset,
Holding her breath in adoration of the peacock's tail
That spread its red—ah, higher and higher—
Line Wept suddenly. "It's going!"

(5) The great fan folded;
Shortened; and at last no longer fought the cold, the dark.
And she on the lawn, comfortless by her father,
Shivered, shivered, "It's gone!"

"Yes, this time. But wait,
(10) Darling. There will be other nights—some of them
    even better."
"Oh, no. It died." He laughed. But she did not.
It was her first glory.

Laid away now in its terrible
Lead coffin, it was the first brightness she had ever
(15) Mourned. "Oh, no, it's dead." And he her father
Mourned too, for more to come.

30. The central subject of the poem is

    (A) the indifference of fathers to the sensibilities of their daughters
    (B) facing one's own death
    (C) dealing with loss and sorrow
    (D) the cruelty of time and the seasons
    (E) the difficulty parents have in understanding their children

31. Which of the following lines most clearly presents the difference in perspective between the father and the daughter?

    (A) "And she on the lawn, comfortless by her father" (line 7)
    (B) "'Darling. There will be other nights—some of them even better.'" (line 10)
    (C) "'Oh, no. It died.' He laughed. But she did not." (line 11)
    (D) "It was her first glory." (line 12)
    (E) "And he her father/ Mourned too, for more to come." (lines 15–16)

32. The image of the lead coffin (line 14) functions to

    (A) diminish and caricature the child's sorrow at the sunset
    (B) confirm the significance of the child's feelings of loss
    (C) indicate that the sunset symbolizes the child's own death
    (D) suggest that the father is now mourning his dead child
    (E) represent the specter of death hovering over the father

33. The last two lines of the poem suggest that the father

    (A) laments his own losses, both past and future
    (B) fears that he will ultimately lose his daughter
    (C) has come to mourn the sunset in the same way that his daughter does
    (D) dreads his own inevitable death
    (E) realizes that his child faces future sorrows that he cannot prevent

34. At the end of the poem, the father's attitude toward his daughter's crying is best characterized as

    (A) patronizing and selfish
    (B) patient but stern
    (C) sympathetic and understanding
    (D) condescending and detached
    (E) good-humored but naïve

Questions 35–38

In My Craft or Sullen Art

In my craft or sullen art
Exercised in the still night
When only the moon rages
Line And the lovers lie abed
(5) With all their griefs in their arms,
I labour by singing light
Not for ambition or bread
Or the strut and trade of charms
On the ivory stages
(10) But for the common wages
Of their most secret heart.

Not for the proud man apart
From the raging moon I write
On these spindrift* pages
(15) Nor for the towering dead
With their nightingales and psalms
But for the lovers, their arms
Round the griefs of the ages.
Who pay no praise or wages
Nor heed my craft or art.

*wind-blown sea spray

By Dylan Thomas, from THE POEMS OF DYLAN THOMAS, copyright © 1946 by New Directions Publishing Corp. Reprinted by permission of New Directions Publishing Corp.

35. The negative constructions "Not . . . But" (lines 7 and 10) and "Not . . . Nor . . . But" (lines 12, 15, and 17) are a feature of the structure of the poem that emphasizes a contrast between the

(A) typical human motivations and the motivation of the speaker

(B) attitudes of the speaker toward himself and toward the lovers

(C) lovers embracing their own griefs and embracing the griefs of the ages

(D) attitude of the speaker toward the lovers and their attitude toward the speaker

(E) common craft of writing light verse and the sublime art of writing poetry

36. Which of the following is the antecedent of "their" (line 11)?

(A) "lovers" (line 4)

(B) "griefs" (line 5)

(C) "strut and trade of charms" (line 8)

(D) "ivory stages" (line 9)

(E) "wages" (line 10)

37. The phrase "the towering dead / With their nightingales and psalms" (lines 15–16) alludes to the

(A) oppressive weight of time and eternity

(B) poet's physical and spiritual future

(C) voices of nature and the supernatural

(D) artificiality and futility of human institutions

(E) great poets and poetry of the past

38. How does the speaker feel about the response of the lovers to his efforts?

(A) The speaker wishes to get vengeance by revealing the secrets of the lovers.

(B) The speaker will stop writing out of resentment for their indifference.

(C) The speaker will seek a new audience and relegate the lovers to the position of the proud man.

(D) The speaker will continue to write for the lovers regardless of their response.

(E) The speaker really writes only for himself and does not desire an audience.

Questions 39–45

Now Winter Nights Enlarge

Now winter nights enlarge
    The number of their hours;
And clouds their storms discharge
Line   Upon the airy towers.
(5) Let now the chimneys blaze
    And cups o'erflow with wine,
Let well-tuned words amaze
    With harmony divine.
Now yellow waxen lights
(10)   Shall wait on honey love
While youthful revels, masques, and courtly sights
    Sleep's leaden spells remove.

This time doth well dispense
    With lovers' long discourse;
(15) Much speech hath some defense,
    Though beauty no remorse.
All do not all things well;
    Some measures comely tread,
Some knotted riddles tell,
(20)   Some poems smoothly read.
The summer hath his joys,
    And winter his delights;
Though Love and all his pleasures are but toys,
    They shorten tedious nights.

39. In the first stanza (lines 1–12), the poet contrasts the

(A) cold weather during winter with the heat of summer
(B) experience of living alone with that of receiving guests
(C) beginning of the winter season with its ending
(D) energy of the natural world with the relative stupor of civilization
(E) stark chill outdoors with the warm cheer indoors

40. In context, lines 7–8 are best understood as a call for

(A) shocking revelations of truth
(B) stimulating intellectual debates
(C) informal discussions of religious issues
(D) poetry in honor of the natural world
(E) pleasing and compelling songs

41. In context, "leaden spells" (line 12) implies that sleep is

(A) a period of dullness
(B) detrimental to health
(C) one way to endure the night
(D) subtly bewitching
(E) an occasion for fantasy

42. Lines 13–14 suggest that winter nights are suitable times for

(A) lovers to talk less
(B) lovers to say goodbye
(C) lovers to meet
(D) talking about lovers
(E) not talking at all

43. Which of the following conclusions could one draw from lines 15–16?

  I. The charms of beauty are more overpowering than the charms of conversation.
  II. Extended conversation has its merits, but a beautiful listener may not heed it.
  III. While conversation is often entertaining, beauty only sometimes pleases.

(A) III only
(B) I and II only
(C) I and III only
(D) II and III only
(E) I, II, and III

44. In lines 21–22, "his" refers to the

    (A) lover talking with his beloved in lines 13–16
    (B) person who has none of the talents described in lines 18–20
    (C) "Love" described in line 23
    (D) summer and winter seasons, respectively
    (E) lover whose pleasures have been cut short by each season in turn

45. The speaker's attitude toward winter nights is characterized by

    (A) dread of their loneliness and cold
    (B) regret that they will never return
    (C) anticipation of the joy they afford
    (D) a fear that they will be lengthy
    (E) criticism of how wastefully they can be spent

Questions 46–51

The following was written in 1955.

About my interests: I don't know if I have
any, unless the morbid desire to own a sixteen-
millimeter camera and make experimental movies
Line can be so classified. Otherwise, I love to eat and
(5) drink—it's my melancholy conviction that I've
scarcely ever had enough to eat (this is because
it's *impossible* to eat enough if you're worried
about the next meal)—and I love to argue with
people who do not disagree with me too profoundly,
(10) and I love to laugh. I do *not* like bohemia, or
bohemians, I do not like people whose principal
aim is pleasure, and I do not like people
who are *earnest* about anything. I don't like
people who like me because I'm a Negro; neither
(15) do I like people who find in the same accident
grounds for contempt. I love America more than
any other country in the world, and, exactly for
this reason, I insist on the right to criticize her
perpetually. I think all theories are suspect, that
(20) the finest principles may have to be modified, or
may even be pulverized by the demands of life,
and that one must find, therefore, one's own
moral center and move through the world hoping
that this center will guide one aright. I consider
(25) that I have many responsibilities, but none
greater than this: to last, as Hemingway says,
and get my work done.
I want to be an honest man and a good writer.

46. Which of the following best describes the passage?

    (A) A literary tribute to the writer's profession
    (B) A detailed chronicle of the writer's past experiences
    (C) A personal statement revealing the writer's character
    (D) A critique of various philosophical outlooks
    (E) A plea for the reader to examine the meaning of existence

47. In line 15, "accident" is best understood to refer to

    (A) education
    (B) ethnicity
    (C) mood
    (D) behavior
    (E) philosophy

48. In line 23, "moral center" refers to an individual's

    (A) sense of dismay at the world's injustices
    (B) values shared with like-minded people
    (C) obsession with ethical issues
    (D) essential beliefs that govern actions
    (E) attitude about extreme views

49. The last sentence in the first paragraph (lines 24–27) suggests that the speaker

    (A) realizes he will never achieve literary fame
    (B) views life as a struggle in which only the fit survive
    (C) thinks that he is exempt from the laws followed by others
    (D) respects the writings of others more than he does his own
    (E) sees his writing as his most important contribution

50. It can be inferred from the passage that the speaker would disapprove most strongly of

    (A) crusaders who are zealously devoted to their cause

    (B) American citizens who criticize national policy

    (C) those who fail to explain the moral principles underlying their actions

    (D) young rebels who refuse to listen to wiser, more experienced advisers

    (E) those who insist that experience is the best teacher of moral values

51. The tone of the passage is best described as

    (A) cynical
    (B) flippant
    (C) reflective
    (D) agitated
    (E) nostalgic

Questions 52–58

Time to Be Wise

Yes; I write verses now and then,
But blunt and flaccid is my pen,
No longer talk'd of by young men
Line　　　　As rather clever;
(5) In the last quarter are my eyes,
You see it by their form and size;
Is it not time then to be wise?
　　　　Or now or never.

Fairest that ever sprang from Eve!
(10) While Time allows the short reprieve,
Just look at me! would you believe
　　　　'T was once a lover?
I cannot clear the five-bar gate;
But, trying first its timber's state,
(15) Climb stiffly up, take breath, and wait
　　　　To trundle over.

Through gallopade[1] I cannot swing
The entangling blooms of Beauty's spring:
I cannot say the tender thing,
(20)　　　　Be 't true or false,
And am beginning to opine
Those girls are only half divine
Whose waists yon wicked boys entwine
　　　　In giddy waltz.

(25) I fear that arm above that shoulder;
I wish them wiser, graver, older,
Sedater, and no harm if colder,
　　　　And panting less.
Ah! people were not half so wild
(30) In former days, when, starchly mild,
Upon her high-heel'd Essex smil'd
　　　　The brave Queen Bess.[2]

---

[1] a lively dance
[2] Queen Elizabeth I; the Earl of Essex was a favorite of the queen.

52. The speaker of the poem specifically addresses

　(A) an unnamed woman
　(B) lusty young men
　(C) Queen Bess
　(D) an admirer of his poems
　(E) a noble patron

53. The "entangling blooms of Beauty's spring" (line 18) are best understood as

　(A) beautiful flowers
　(B) lush gardens
　(C) lovely young women
　(D) violent passions
　(E) dangerous delusions

54. In context, lines 21–24 suggest that the

　(A) speaker's eyesight is failing
　(B) speaker's beloved is no longer beautiful
　(C) speaker has trouble choosing only one lover
　(D) speaker's attitude toward women has changed over time
　(E) speaker treats girls as though they were goddesses

55. In context, the tone of the phrase "yon wicked boys" (line 23) is best described as

　(A) self-deprecatory
　(B) mock moral
　(C) apologetic
　(D) obsequious
　(E) euphoric

56. In the last lines of the poem, the speaker suggests that the era of "brave Queen Bess" (line 32) would have been

    (A) too peaceful for him

    (B) too conscious of hierarchy and nobility

    (C) more conducive to amorous adventures

    (D) more suitable for him given his present condition

    (E) more appealing to the young people of his own time

57. The poem as a whole can best be described as

    (A) a fond remembrance of one man's youthful days

    (B) a tearful complaint about the indignities of old age

    (C) an ironic commentary on the traps beauty sets for the unwary

    (D) a dispassionate analysis of the changes that took place in an ill-fated romantic relationship

    (E) a wry reflection on the changes age has wrought in a man who once considered himself a lover

58. The speaker's attitude in the poem is primarily one of

    (A) wretchedness and despair

    (B) regret tempered by mature insights

    (C) envy of the passions of younger men

    (D) moral disapproval of young lovers

    (E) mockery of polite courtship conventions

Questions 59–64

Dr. Trench is engaged to marry Blanche, the daughter of Mr. Sartorius.

SARTORIUS: Live on your income! Impossible: my daughter is accustomed to a proper establishment. Did I not expressly undertake to provide for that?
Line Did she not tell you I promised her to do so?

(5) TRENCH: Yes, I know all about that, Mr Sartorius; and I'm greatly obliged to you; but I'd rather not take anything from you except Blanche herself.

SARTORIUS: And why did you not say so before?

TRENCH: No matter why. Let us drop the subject.

(10) SARTORIUS: No matter! But it does matter, sir. I insist on an answer. Why did you not say so before?

TRENCH: I didnt know before.

SARTORIUS [*provoked*] Then you ought to have known your own mind on a point of such vital
(15) importance.

TRENCH [*much injured*] I ought to have known! Cokane: is this reasonable? [*Cokane's features are contorted by an air of judicial consideration; but he says nothing; and Trench again addresses Sartorius,*
(20) *this time with a marked diminution of respect*]. How the deuce could I have known? You didnt tell me.

SARTORIUS: You are trifling with me, sir. You said that you did not know your own mind before.

TRENCH: I said nothing of the sort. I say that I did
(25) not know where your money came from before.

SARTORIUS: That is not true, sir. I—

COKANE: Gently, my dear sir. Gently, Harry, dear boy. Suaviter in modo: fort—*

TRENCH: Let him begin, then. What does he mean
(30) by attacking me in this fashion?

SARTORIUS: Mr Cokane: you will bear me out. I was explicit on the point. I said I was a self-made man; and I am not ashamed of it.

TRENCH: You are nothing of the sort. I found out
(35) this morning from your man—Lickcheese, or whatever his confounded name is—that your fortune has been made out of a parcel of unfortunate creatures that have hardly enough to keep body and soul together—made by screwing, and bullying, and
(40) threatening, and all sorts of pettifogging tyranny.

SARTORIUS [*outraged*] Sir! [*They confront one another threateningly*].

COKANE [*softly*] Rent must be paid, dear boy. It is inevitable, Harry, inevitable. [*Trench turns

(45) away petulantly. Sartorius looks after him reflectively for a moment; then resumes his former deliberate and dignified manner, and addresses Trench with studied consideration, but with a perceptible condescension to his
(50) youth and folly*].

*The first part of a Latin proverb meaning "gently in manner: forcibly in deed"

59. The passage is most concerned with

   (A) a plea for help
   (B) a clash of values
   (C) an argument for austerity
   (D) a denunciation of pride
   (E) an examination of marriage conventions

60. In context, the phrase "proper establishment" (line 2) means

   (A) appropriate home and standard of living
   (B) socially prominent family and friends
   (C) respectable work and business associates
   (D) access to the finest modern university education
   (E) involvement in charitable and philanthropic activities

61. The tone of Trench's responses to Sartorius in lines 5–7 ("Yes . . . herself") is best described as

   (A) reproachful
   (B) inquisitive
   (C) embarrassed
   (D) enthusiastic
   (E) courteous

62. The stage directions in lines 44–50 ("*Trench . . . folly*") suggest that

    (A) Trench is looking forward to a discussion with Sartorius

    (B) Trench is reserved and Sartorius is preparing to be aggressive

    (C) Trench is sulking and Sartorius is preparing to patronize him

    (D) Sartorius is about to compliment Trench's ethical stance

    (E) Sartorius is determined to make Trench end the engagement

63. Cokane's role in this scene is best described as

    (A) a bully

    (B) a referee

    (C) an antagonist

    (D) a legal expert

    (E) a social commentator

64. The movement of the passage is from

    (A) polite disagreement to angry disputation to possible resolution

    (B) furious confrontation to reasoned discourse to full agreement

    (C) controlled anger to open discussion to deep empathy

    (D) physical threats to dignified atonement

    (E) rational analysis to self-recrimination

Study Resources

The most relevant preparation for the Analyzing and Interpreting Literature exam is attentive and reflective reading of the various literary genres of poetry, drama, and prose. You can prepare for the test by:

1. Reading a variety of poetry, drama, fiction, and nonfiction

2. Reading critical analyses of various literary works

3. Writing analyses and interpretations of the works you read

4. Discussing with others the meaning of the literature you read

Textbooks and anthologies used for college courses in the analysis and interpretation of literature contain a sampling of literary works in a variety of genres. They also contain material that can help you comprehend the meanings of literary works and recognize the devices writers use to convey their sense and intent. To prepare for the exam, you should study the contents of at least one textbook or anthology, which you can find in most college bookstores. You would do well to consult two or three texts because they do vary somewhat in content, approach, and emphases.

Visit www.collegeboard.com/clepprep for additional literature and writing resources. You can also find suggestions for exam preparation in Chapter IV of the *Official Study Guide*. In addition, many college faculty post their course materials on their schools' Web sites.

Answer Key

1.	B		33.	E	
2.	C		34.	C	
3.	D		35.	A	
4.	B		36.	A	
5.	A		37.	E	
6.	E		38.	D	
7.	E		39.	E	
8.	A		40.	E	
9.	A		41.	A	
10.	C		42.	A	
11.	B		43.	B	
12.	E		44.	D	
13.	A		45.	C	
14.	C		46.	C	
15.	A		47.	B	
16.	D		48.	D	
17.	B		49.	E	
18.	C		50.	A	
19.	B		51.	C	
20.	C		52.	A	
21.	E		53.	C	
22.	B		54.	D	
23.	A		55.	B	
24.	B		56.	D	
25.	D		57.	E	
26.	C		58.	B	
27.	B		59.	B	
28.	C		60.	A	
29.	A		61.	E	
30.	C		62.	C	
31.	C		63.	B	
32.	B		64.	A	

English Composition

Description of the Examination

The English Composition examination assesses writing skills taught in most first-year college composition courses and, in particular, skills for college assignments requiring writing that explains, interprets, analyzes, presents, or supports a point of view. The examination does not cover some topics included in many first-year college writing courses, nor does it require knowledge of grammatical terms. However, the student will need to apply the principles and conventions expected of academic writing discourse.

Two versions of the test are offered. One is all multiple-choice, and the other is multiple-choice with an essay. In both versions, some of the multiple-choice questions are pretest questions that will not be scored. The all multiple-choice version contains approximately 90 questions to be answered in 90 minutes.

The version with the essay has two separately timed sections. Section I contains approximately 50 questions to be answered in 45 minutes. Section II contains one essay question to be answered in 45 minutes. In either version, any time candidates spend on tutorials or providing personal information is in addition to the actual testing time.

The essay is scored by college faculty who teach writing courses. Each essay is read and assigned a rating by two scorers; the sum of the two ratings is weighted and then combined with the candidate's multiple-choice score. The resulting combined score is reported as a scaled score between 20 and 80. Separate scores are not reported for the multiple-choice and essay sections.

Policies of colleges differ with regard to their acceptance of the two versions of the English Composition examination. Some grant credit only for the version with essay; others grant credit for either version. A number of schools supplement the all-multiple-choice version with a writing assignment that they administer and score themselves. Many colleges grant six semester hours (or the equivalent) of credit toward satisfying a liberal arts or distribution requirement in English; others grant six credit hours of course credit for a specific first-year composition or English course that emphasizes expository writing.

Knowledge and Skills Required

The multiple-choice questions measure candidates' writing skills both at the sentence level and within the context of passages. The current examination in English Composition places a greater emphasis on revising work in progress than did previous forms of the test.

Skills at the Sentence Level

The examination measures the candidate's knowledge of a variety of logical, structural, and grammatical relationships within a sentence; these skills are tested by approximately 55 percent of the all-multiple-choice version and 30 percent of the multiple-choice questions in the version with essay. Questions test recognition of standard written English relating to

- Sentence boundaries
- Clarity of expression
- Agreement: subject-verb; verb tense; pronoun reference, shift, number
- Active/passive voice
- Diction and idiom
- Syntax: parallelism, coordination, subordination, dangling modifiers
- Sentence variety

The following kinds of question format assess sentence-level skills throughout the test:

Identifying Sentence Errors—This type of question appears in both versions of the exam. It requires the candidate to identify wording that violates the standard conventions of written discourse.

Improving Sentences—This type of question appears in both versions of the exam. It requires the candidate to choose the phrase, clause, or sentence that best conveys the intended meaning of the sentence.

Restructuring Sentences—This type of question appears only in the all-multiple-choice version. The candidate is given a sentence to reword in order to change emphasis or improve clarity. He or she then must choose from five options the phrase that would most likely appear in the new sentence.

Skills in Context

Questions in approximately 45 percent of the all-multiple-choice version and 20 percent of the version with essay measure recognition of the following in the context of works in progress or of published prose.

- Main idea, thesis
- Organization of ideas in the paragraph or essay
- Relevance of evidence, sufficiency of detail, levels of specificity
- Audience and purpose (effect on style, tone, language, or argument)
- Logic of argument (inductive, deductive reasoning)
- Coherence within and between paragraphs
- Rhetorical emphasis, effect
- Sustaining tense or point of view
- Sentence combining, sentence variety

The following kinds of questions measure writing skills in context:

Revising Work in Progress—This type of question appears in both versions of the exam. The candidate identifies ways to improve an early draft of an essay.

Analyzing Writing—Two prose passages written in very different modes appear only in the all-multiple-choice version. The candidate answers questions about each passage and about the strategies used by the author of each passage.

The Essay

This section comprises 50 percent of the version of the exam with essay. The candidate is expected to present a point of view in response to a topic and to support this point of view with a logical argument and appropriate evidence. The essay must be typed on the computer.

Scoring the Essay

Shortly after each administration of the CLEP English Composition with Essay examination, college English faculty throughout the country score the essays. Each essay is scored independently by two different readers, and the two scores are then combined. This score is weighted approximately equally with the score from the multiple-choice section, then combined with it to yield the reported score for the test.

The college English teachers who score the essay expect that the writer has a command of English grammar and sentence structure and can use words precisely; they also expect that the essay will be organized, the ideas will be presented logically, and the examples will be pertinent. These qualitative descriptions are linked to a 6-point rubric, or scoring guide.

Each reader awards an essay a score on a scale of 1 to 6; the sum of the two independent scores ranges from 2 to 12. In addition, a score of zero is given to off-topic essays and blank responses; this score can be assigned only by the Scoring Leader (a faculty member who is a scoring expert).

CLEP

Introducing College Composition and College Composition Modular

Two new CLEP® exams launching July 1, 2010

These new exams will replace:

▷ English Composition

▷ English Composition with Essay

▷ Freshman College Composition

CLEP exams can help you satisfy your college's introductory composition requirement so you can move quickly into more advanced courses, earn additional college credit toward your degree and save money on tuition.

College Composition and **College Composition Modular** both offer a multiple-choice section, although the inclusion of an essay section may vary depending on your college's policy. Check with your academic adviser, test center or admissions office to find out which exam your college prefers.

	College Composition	College Composition Modular
Multiple Choice	50 minutes/50 questions	90 minutes/90 questions
Essay	70 minutes/2 essays	Determined by the college: 70 minutes/ 2 essays or an alternate writing assessment provided by the college

**Visit www.collegeboard.com/clep
in April 2010 to download a FREE study guide for
College Composition and College Composition Modular.**

Introducing College Composition and College Composition Modular

CLEP will introduce College Composition and College Composition Modular on July 1, 2010. These new exams will replace the English Composition, English Composition with Essay, and Freshman College Composition exams.

About the Exams

The CLEP College Composition examinations assess writing skills taught in most first-year college composition courses. Those skills include analysis, argumentation, synthesis, usage and research. Candidates will be expected to apply the principles and conventions used in college writing projects to two timed essays, and to apply the rules of Standard Written English.

Multiple-Choice Section

10% Conventions of Standard Written English

This section measures candidates' awareness of a variety of logical, structural and grammatical relationships within sentences. The questions test recognition of acceptable usage relating to the items below:

- Syntax (parallelism, coordination, subordination)
- Sentence boundaries (comma splice, run-ons, sentence fragments)
- Recognition of correct sentences
- Concord/agreement (pronoun reference, case shift and number; subject-verb; verb tense)
- Diction
- Modifiers
- Idiom
- Active/passive voice
- Lack of subject in modifying word group
- Logical comparison
- Logical agreement
- Punctuation

40% Revision Skills

This section measures candidates' revision skills in the context of works in progress (early drafts of essays):

- Organization
- Evaluation of evidence
- Awareness of audience, tone and purpose
- Level of detail
- Coherence between sentences and paragraphs
- Sentence variety and structure
- Main idea, thesis statements, and topic sentences
- Rhetorical effects and emphasis
- Use of language
- Evaluation of author's authority and appeal
- Evaluation of reasoning
- Consistency of point of view
- Transitions
- Sentence-level errors

25% Ability to Use Source Materials

This section measures candidates' familiarity with elements of the following basic reference and research skills:

- Use of reference materials
- Evaluation of sources
- Integration of resource material
- Documentation of sources (in particular, MLA, APA and Chicago Manual styles)

25% Rhetorical Analysis

This section measures candidates' ability to analyze writing, focusing on the following elements:

- Appeals
- Tone
- Organization/structure
- Rhetorical effects
- Use of language
- Evaluation of evidence

The Essays

College Composition includes an essay section that tests skills of argumentation, analysis and synthesis and measures a candidate's ability to write clearly and effectively. The first essay is based on the candidate's reading, observation or experience, while the second requires candidates to synthesize and cite two sources that are provided.

College Composition Modular includes a separate handwritten essay component that is administered and scored by the college. Be sure to check with your college regarding their College Composition Modular policy and essay requirements.

Sample Test Questions

The following sample questions do not appear on an actual CLEP examination. They are intended to give potential test-takers an indication of the format and difficulty level of the examination and to provide content for practice and review. Knowing the correct answers to all of the sample questions is not a guarantee of satisfactory performance on the exam.

Identifying Sentence Errors

Directions: The following sentences test your knowledge of grammar, usage, diction (choice of words), and idiom. Note that some sentences are correct, and no sentence contains more than one error.

You will find that the error, if there is one, is underlined and lettered. Assume that elements of the sentence that are not underlined are correct and cannot be changed. In choosing answers, follow the requirements of standard written English.

If there is an error, select the <u>one underlined part</u> that must be changed to make the sentence correct.

If there is no error, select answer (E).

Example: **SAMPLE ANSWER**

Ⓐ ● Ⓒ Ⓓ Ⓔ

<u>The other</u> delegates and
   A

<u>him</u> <u>immediately</u> accepted
 B   C

the resolution <u>drafted</u> by
         D

the neutral states. <u>No error</u>
           E

---

1. Ms. Marco found that it was easier for her

   <u>teaching of</u> children arithmetic <u>once</u>
      A   B

   <u>they had become</u> <u>familiar with</u> the idea of
        C   D

   a set. <u>No error</u>
          E

2. The bill of the Australian platypus, which

   <u>consists of</u> rubbery skin stretched over bone,
     A

   <u>and is</u> <u>more sensitive</u> than the bills of
     B   C

   <u>most other</u> animals. <u>No error</u>
      D   E

3. The rules of the contest <u>indicate that</u> a writer is
                    A

   not eligible <u>for any</u> of the prizes if <u>you have</u>
             B   C

   <u>ever received</u> payment for writing fiction or
      D

   poetry. <u>No error</u>
          E

4. Artificial "time histories" are used by

   seismologists <u>to predict</u> the response and
             A

   <u>improve</u> the resistance of <u>such structures as</u>
     B   C

   buildings, bridges, and power plants <u>to</u> damage
                           D

   from earthquakes. <u>No error</u>
            E

5. One study <u>of</u> the cries of humpback whales
           A

   <u>describe</u> a variety of sounds <u>suggesting</u> that
     B   C

   these mammals <u>may organize</u> their utterances
              D

   in a hierarchical system. <u>No error</u>
             E

6. Sculptor Isamu <u>Noguchi, who spent</u> his
               A

   childhood in Japan, <u>was later educated</u> in the
                     B

   United States and Paris, where there <u>was</u>
                          C

   <u>not many</u> other Japanese students.
      D

   <u>No error</u>.
     E

7. Dr. Turner's choice <u>of</u> the sea urchin <u>instead of</u>
               A   B

   the starfish <u>for her experiments</u> <u>were questioned</u>
            C   D

   by her colleagues. <u>No error</u>
            E

8. Dr. St. Clair <u>requested</u> a residency with the
        A
surgical team <u>at</u> County Hospital because
                    B
<u>they have</u> special facilities <u>for performing</u>
    C   D
surgery on infants. <u>No error</u>
                             E

9. <u>Among</u> the most intelligent animals
      A
<u>known to</u> us <u>is</u> the bottle-nosed dolphin,
    B   C
<u>mammals that exhibit</u> a remarkable ability to
            D
communicate. <u>No error</u>
                      E

10. People <u>have always enjoyed</u> learning about the
                  A
American <u>West, but</u> their overwhelming
                  B
<u>preference has been</u> for the <u>colorful, if often</u>
            C   D
<u>bizarre</u>, fictions that the pulp writers have so

voluminously supplied. <u>No error</u>
                                E

11. At <u>yesterday's</u> ceremony <u>more awards</u> for
            A   B
literary achievement <u>were given</u> to poets
                              C
<u>than novels</u>. <u>No error</u>
      D   E

12. <u>Although</u> Cicely Tyson <u>has inspired</u> many
        A   B
people through her portrayals of heroic women,

it is her <u>selection of</u> controversial roles that has
                C
<u>taken real courage</u>. <u>No error</u>
        D   E

13. <u>When gold was discovered</u> in California,
                A
<u>perspective</u> miners from other parts of the
        B
country <u>and from all over</u> the world <u>flocked to</u>
                C   D
the state in search of instant wealth. <u>No error</u>
                                              E

14. The package directions read that the medication

<u>can damage</u> the <u>kidneys, liver, and other</u> organs
        A   B
when <u>they are consumed</u> in large amounts
                C
<u>over an</u> extended period of time. <u>No error</u>
    D   E

15. Frequently, the pattern of seeds inside a piece

of fruit <u>evokes</u> the shape of the flower that
              A
<u>produced</u> the fruit<u>;</u> for instance, a sliced apple
    B   C
shows five seed compartments arranged in a

starburst, <u>resembling</u> the five petals of the
                D
blossom. <u>No error</u>
                E

16. Even a careful listener <u>could scarcely</u>
                                    A
distinguish liberal <u>from</u> conservative among
                          B
the speakers, for the issue had become

<u>a highly</u> emotional <u>one</u>. <u>No error</u>
    C   D   E

17. When Charles Dickens, <u>ignoring</u> the advice of
                                    A
his friends, family, and physician, persisted

<u>to give</u> public readings from his novels, his
    B
already poor health <u>deteriorated</u> <u>rapidly</u>.
                          C   D
<u>No error</u>
    E

Improving Sentences

Directions: The following sentences test correctness and effectiveness of expression. In choosing answers, follow the requirements of standard written English: that is, pay attention to grammar, diction (choice of words), sentence construction, and punctuation.

In each of the following sentences, part of the sentence or the entire sentence is underlined. Beneath each sentence you will find five versions of the underlined part. Choice A repeats the original; the other four are different.

Choose the answer that best expresses the meaning of the original sentence. If you think the original is better than any of the alternatives, choose it; otherwise, choose one of the others. Your choice should produce the most effective sentence — one that is clear and precise, without awkwardness or ambiguity.

Example: **SAMPLE ANSWER**

Laura Ingalls Wilder published her first book <u>and she was sixty-five years old then</u>.

(A) and she was sixty-five years old then

(B) when she was sixty-five

(C) being age sixty-five years old

(D) upon the reaching of sixty-five years

(E) at the time when she was sixty-five

---

18. Leny Andrade, who has been called the Brazilian equivalent of Ella Fitzgerald and Sarah Vaughan, <u>a phenomenal singer with</u> a soul-wrenching voice.

(A) a phenomenal singer with

(B) a phenomenal singer having

(C) is a phenomenal singer with

(D) being a phenomenal singer with

(E) as a phenomenal singer having

19. <u>The many and varied writings of Mary Wollstonecraft offering</u> an abundance of material to scholars who have begun to examine her impact on eighteenth-century rhetoric.

(A) The many and varied writings of Mary Wollstonecraft offering

(B) It is Mary Wollstonecraft's many and varied writings offering

(C) Offering Mary Wollstonecraft's many and varied writings were

(D) The many and varied writings of Mary Wollstonecraft offer

(E) To offer the many and varied writings of Mary Wollstonecraft is

20. <u>Supposedly daylight travelers, researchers have accidentally discovered that bumblebees can navigate outside their nests in the dark</u>.

(A) Supposedly daylight travelers, researchers have accidentally discovered that bumblebees can navigate outside their nests in the dark.

(B) Supposedly daylight travelers, researchers have accidentally discovered that in the dark, bumblebees can navigate outside their nests.

(C) Researchers have accidentally discovered that bumblebees, supposedly daylight travelers, can navigate outside their nests in the dark.

(D) That bumblebees, supposedly daylight travelers, can navigate outside their nests in the dark, researchers have accidentally discovered.

(E) Accidentally, bumblebees have been discovered by researchers to be able to navigate outside their nests, despite being considered supposedly daylight travelers.

21. <u>While cats are valued for their independence, many people have dogs for their affectionate ways</u>.

(A) While cats are valued for their independence, many people have dogs for their affectionate ways.

(B) Cats are valued for their independence, but having a dog is for its affectionate ways.

(C) Cats are valued for their independence, dogs for their affectionate ways.

(D) The reason people have dogs is their affectionate ways, cats independence.

(E) An affectionate pet is the dog, but cats are independent.

22. <u>At breakfast with reporters, the governor denied that he had an interest in running for the presidency.</u>

    (A) At breakfast with reporters, the governor denied that he had an interest in running for the presidency.

    (B) The governor who denied that he had an interest in running for the presidency at breakfast with reporters.

    (C) The governor denied that he was interested in running at breakfast with reporters for the presidency.

    (D) The governor denied that he was interested in running for the presidency; at breakfast with reporters.

    (E) At breakfast, the governor denying that he had an interest in running for the presidency to reporters.

23. Seventeenth-century Dutch painter Judith Leyster was a contemporary of <u>Frans Hals, many</u> of her paintings were once attributed to him.

    (A) Frans Hals, many

    (B) Frans Hals; many

    (C) Frans Hals, however many

    (D) Frans Hals when many

    (E) Frans Hals although many

24. Centuries ago, Greeks established an aesthetic for formal beauty <u>which has influenced artists for centuries and continue inspiring artists today</u>.

    (A) which has influenced artists for centuries and continue inspiring artists today

    (B) with influencing artists for centuries and continuing to inspire them today

    (C) that influenced artists for centuries and continues to inspire artists today

    (D) which influence artists for centuries and continued to inspire them

    (E) for influencing artists for centuries while continually inspiring today's artists

25. In describing Herman Melville's struggles with religious doubt, Nathaniel Hawthorne said that Melville could neither believe <u>nor be comfortable</u> in his disbelief.

    (A) nor be comfortable

    (B) nor being comfortable

    (C) and yet he was not comfortable

    (D) and he was not even comfortable

    (E) nor to take comfort

26. In the historic district we found an elegant old stone house with a lovely courtyard <u>restaurant, and it offers inventive cuisine this uses local ingredients mostly</u>.

    (A) restaurant, and it offers inventive cuisine this uses local ingredients mostly

    (B) restaurant, which offers an inventive cuisine that relies on mostly local ingredients

    (C) restaurant and with an inventive cuisine and mostly local ingredients

    (D) restaurant by offering mostly local ingredients in an inventive cuisine

    (E) restaurant, uses mostly local ingredients, while having an inventive cuisine

27. The booklet includes biographies of physicists Shirley Jackson and Marie <u>Curie, and frames her achievement with</u> the message: science is women's work.

    (A) Curie, and frames her achievement with

    (B) Curie, framing her achievement with

    (C) Curie and they frame their achievements with

    (D) Curie by the achievement of each of them being framed with

    (E) Curie and frames their achievements with

28. Having decided to cultivate <u>roses, the right fertilizer was what the gardener needed</u> to ensure proper growth.

   (A) roses, the right fertilizer was what the gardener needed

   (B) roses, the gardener knew that she needed the right fertilizer

   (C) roses, the right fertilizer was what the gardener was in need of

   (D) roses; the gardener's first need was for the right fertilizer

   (E) roses; the right fertilizer was, for the gardener, what she needed

29. <u>Speaking no English, Phillis Wheatley arrived in North America in 1761 at the age of eight, she</u> spoke English fluently by age ten and published her first poem when she was fourteen.

   (A) Speaking no English, Phillis Wheatley arrived in North America in 1761 at the age of eight, she

   (B) When only eight, Phillis Wheatley, speaking no English, arrived in North America in 1761, and she

   (C) Arriving in North America in 1761 speaking no English, Phillis Wheatley

   (D) In 1761, arriving in North America at the age of eight, but Phillis Wheatley

   (E) She was only eight when she arrived in North America, she spoke no English, and Phillis Wheatley

30. The effect of sugar on the energy level of this group of children is <u>greater than that of</u> other children who eat a similar quantity of sweets each day.

   (A) greater than that of

   (B) greater than that on the energy levels of

   (C) a greater level of energy than that of

   (D) greater than

   (E) greater than on

31. <u>Driving up the New England coast, picturesque seascapes and landscapes surround travelers with the scenic charm of the Northeast.</u>

   (A) Driving up the New England coast, picturesque seascapes and landscapes surround travelers with the scenic charm of the Northeast.

   (B) When you drive up the New England coast, picturesque seascapes and landscapes surround travelers with the scenic charm of the Northeast.

   (C) Driving up the New England coast, travelers are surrounded by the scenic charm of the Northeast, with its picturesque seascapes and landscapes.

   (D) While driving up the New England coast, travelers have been surrounded by picturesque seascapes and landscapes, they are the scenic charm of the Northeast.

   (E) The scenic charm of the Northeast, with its picturesque seascapes and landscapes, surround travelers driving up the New England coast.

32. After traveling to Africa, <u>the languages of Ghana became a special interest of Chuck's.</u>

   (A) the languages of Ghana became a special interest of Chuck's

   (B) Chuck became especially interested in the languages of Ghana

   (C) a special interest of Chuck's became the languages of Ghana

   (D) Chuck's special interest in Ghana's languages grew

   (E) Ghana's languages grew especially interesting to Chuck

Revising Work in Progress

Directions: Each of the following selections is an early draft of a student essay in which the sentences have been numbered for easy reference. Some parts of the selections need to be changed.

Read each selection and then answer the questions that follow. Some questions are about particular sentences or parts of sentences and ask you to improve sentence structure and diction (word choice). In making these decisions, follow the conventions of standard written English. Other questions refer to the entire essay or parts of the essay and ask you to consider organization, development, and effectiveness of language in relation to purpose and audience.

Questions 33–37 are based on the following draft of a student essay.

(1) I used to be convinced that people didn't actually win radio contests; I thought that the excited winners I heard were only actors. (2) Sure, people could win T-shirts. (3) They couldn't win anything of real value.

(4) I've always loved sports. (5) Unlike my friends, who fall asleep to "Top 40 Radio," I listen to "Sports Night with Dave Sims." (6) One night I heard Dave Sims announce a sports trivia contest with cash prizes of two thousand dollars. (7) I jump at the chance to combine my talk-show knowledge with everything my father had taught me about sports. (8) I sent in my self-addressed stamped envelope. (9) I forgot about the whole matter. (10) Then the questionnaire appeared in my mailbox ten days later. (11) Its arrival gave me a rude surprise. (12) Instead of sitting down and whipping through it, I trudged to libraries and spent hours digging for answers to such obscure questions as "Which NHL goalie holds the record for most career shutouts?"

(13) Finally, after days of double-checking answers, I mailed off my answer sheet, certain I would hear no more about the matter. (14) Certain, until two weeks later, I ripped open the envelope with the NBC peacock and read "Congratulations . . ." (15) I was a winner, a winner of more than a T-shirt.

33. Which of the following is the best way to revise the underlined portions of sentences 2 and 3 (reproduced below) so that the two sentences are combined into one?

    Sure, people could win T-shirts. They couldn't win anything of real value.

    (A) T-shirts, and they couldn't win
    (B) T-shirts, but they couldn't win
    (C) T-shirts, but not being able to win
    (D) T-shirts, so they do not win
    (E) T-shirts, while there was no winning

34. Which of the following sentences, if added after sentence 3, would best link the first paragraph with the rest of the essay?

    (A) I have held this opinion about contests for a long time.
    (B) The prizes offered did not inspire me to enter the contests.
    (C) However, I recently changed my opinion about these contests.
    (D) Usually the questions on these contests are really easy to answer.
    (E) Sometimes my friends try to convince me to enter such contests.

35. In the context of the second paragraph, which of the following is the best version of the underlined portion of sentence 7 (reproduced below)?

    I jump at the chance to combine my talk-show knowledge with everything my father had taught me about sports.

    (A) (As it is now)
    (B) I jumped at the chance to combine
    (C) Having jumped at the chance to combine
    (D) Jumping at the chance and combining
    (E) Jumping at the chance by combining

36. Which of the following is the best way to revise and combine sentences 8 and 9 (reproduced below)?

    I sent in my self-addressed stamped envelope. I forgot about the whole matter.

    (A) Having sent in my self-addressed stamped envelope, the whole matter was forgotten.
    (B) After sending in my self-addressed stamped envelope, the matter was wholly forgotten.
    (C) After my self-addressed stamped envelope was sent in, it was then that I forgot the whole matter.
    (D) After sending in my self-addressed stamped envelope, I forgot about the whole matter.
    (E) Forgetting about the whole matter after sending in my self-addressed stamped envelope.

37. All of the following strategies are used by the writer of the passage EXCEPT

(A) using an informal tone

(B) describing an experience to develop a point

(C) criticizing those whose opinions differ from the writer's

(D) building suspense by withholding the outcome until the end

(E) disproving the assumption stated in the first sentence of the passage

Questions 38–42 are based on the following early draft of a letter to the editor of a local newspaper.

(1) Our community needs more parks and play areas. (2) Living in a world where concrete surrounds us, it is important that we create places that are green and natural so that children can run and play.

(3) It is possible to do much with little expense to the city. (4) An abandoned lot can become a big patch of green grass ideal for running games. (5) And buying expensive playground equipment and strange pieces of modern art for children to climb on is unnecessary. (6) Children will climb on anything if one lets them. (7) A large concrete pipe or an old truck with its wheels and doors removed makes an imaginative plaything. (8) Simply remove any part that may be breakable or unsafe, then paint the equipment with bright colors. (9) Bury the truck or pipe a foot or two deep so that it is stable. (10) Great opportunities for fun! (11) Children can play for hours, crawling through a secret tunnel or navigating to a distant planet. (12) Neighborhood committees could contribute other discards.

(13) We should do these things because children need oases in this concrete desert we live in. (14) This may take time, but if people get together and contribute both ideas and labor, much can be done successfully.

38. Which of the following is the best way to revise the underlined portion of sentence 2 (reproduced below)?

Living in a world where concrete surrounds us, it is important that we create places that are green and natural so that children can run and play.

(A) Living in a world where concrete surrounds us, the important thing is to

(B) We live in a world where concrete surrounds us, it is important that we

(C) Being surrounded by a world of concrete, it is important to

(D) Surrounding us with a world of concrete, we need to

(E) Surrounded by a world of concrete, we need to

39. Which of the following would best replace "And" at the beginning of sentence 5?

(A) Furthermore,

(B) Instead,

(C) Despite this,

(D) Nevertheless,

(E) Excepting this,

40. The writer of the passage could best improve sentence 12 by

(A) acknowledging drawbacks to the suggestions

(B) providing specific examples

(C) including personal opinions

(D) discussing other community problems

(E) defining the idea of a neighborhood

41. In context, the best phrase to replace "*do these things*" in sentence 13 is

(A) accomplish our intentions

(B) help these children

(C) consider other options

(D) build these play areas

(E) have new ideas

42. Which is the best version of the underlined portion of sentence 14 (reproduced below)?

This may take time, <u>but if people get together and contribute</u> both ideas and labor, much can be done successfully.

(A) (as it is now)

(B) and if people get together and they contribute

(C) but if people will get together and they will also contribute

(D) but if people get together and they would have contributed

(E) however, if people get together, also contributing

Restructuring Sentences

Directions: Revise each of the sentences that follow according to the directions below it. Some directions require you to change only part of the original sentence; others require you to change the entire sentence.

You may need to omit or add certain words in constructing an acceptable revision, but you should **keep the meaning of your revised sentence as close to the meaning of the original sentence as the directions permit.** If you have thought of a revision that does not include any of the words or phrases listed, try to revise the sentence again so that it does include the wording in one of the answer choices.

Examples:

I. Sentence: Owing to her political skill, Ms. French had many supporters.

Directions: Begin with <u>Many people supported</u>.

Your new sentence will contain

(A) so

(B) while

(C) although

(D) because

(E) and

Your rephrased sentence will probably read: "Many people supported Ms. French because she was politically skillful." This new sentence contains the correct answer: (D), "because." None of the other choices will fit into an effective, grammatically correct sentence that retains the original meaning.

II. Sentence: Coming to the city as a young man, he found a job as a newspaper reporter.

Directions: Change <u>Coming</u> to <u>He came</u>.

Your new sentence will contain

(A) and so he found

(B) and found

(C) and there he had found

(D) and then finding

(E) and had found

Your rephrased sentence will probably read: "He came to the city as a young man and found a job as a newspaper reporter." This new sentence contains the correct answer: (B), "and found."

43. Should Antarctica's average temperature ever rise ten degrees, the oceans of the world would drown out all low-lying coastal regions.

Begin with If Antarctica's average temperature rises.

Your new sentence will contain

(A) should drown
(B) will drown
(C) will have drowned
(D) will result in the drowning
(E) drowning would be

44. Ms. Perry claimed that, because of special promotions by the airline industry, air travel has become "as American as apple pie."

Change that, because to that special.

Your new sentence will contain

(A) industry, making
(B) industry, which has made
(C) industry had made
(D) industry have made
(E) industry, and they have made

45. Might it not be better for this discussion to concentrate more on *Native Son* itself and less on the life of Richard Wright?

Change so that the sentence ends with a period instead of a question mark.

Your new sentence will contain

(A) might not be better
(B) not it be better
(C) will have to be better
(D) will not be better
(E) might be better

46. Luther Burbank's development of an edible pitless plum was accomplished by crossing a pitless plum tree many times with standard varieties of plum trees.

Begin with Luther Burbank.

Your new sentence will contain

(A) by many crossings
(B) frequent crossings
(C) by repeatedly crossing
(D) plum was crossed many times
(E) it was by repeated crossings

47. Most people who run in marathons have little expectation of being among the first to finish.

Begin with Few people.

Your new sentence will contain

(A) lack expectation
(B) expect to be
(C) expect their being
(D) have no expectation
(E) have much to expect

48. Because of their appeal to passions rather than to reason, poets were banned by Plato from the republic that he envisioned.

Begin with Believing that poets.

Your new sentence will contain

(A) are to be banned
(B) their banishment
(C) banned them
(D) they are banned
(E) has poets banned

49. The new ideas that influenced many American painters were brought to the United States in the 1940s by artists who left Europe during the war.

   Begin with The artists.

   Your new sentence will contain

   (A) and brought
   (B) ideas have been brought
   (C) war have brought
   (D) thus bringing
   (E) war brought

50. Posters, buttons, and balloons were considered by many campaign workers/fundraisers to be the most effective vote-getting devices.

   Change were considered to considered.

   Your new sentence will contain

   (A) balloons in the light of
   (B) balloons would be
   (C) balloons that
   (D) balloons the
   (E) balloons being the most

51. The reader is provided with an insightful and sometimes controversial analysis of African American perspectives on Reconstruction by W.E.B. Du Bois's books.

   Begin with The books of W.E.B. Du Bois.

   Your new sentence will contain

   (A) provide the reader
   (B) have provided the reader
   (C) cause the reader to be provided
   (D) are responsible for providing the reader
   (E) provides the reader

52. Madeline's seemingly innocuous announcement caused considerable consternation among her students.

   Change caused to but it caused.

   Your new sentence will contain

   (A) announcement, and it seemed
   (B) announcement seemed
   (C) announcement which seemed
   (D) announcement, seemingly
   (E) announcement, despite seeming

53. When we consider how technology encroaches on our daily life, we can understand why many works of modern art are strident and fragmented.

   Change we can understand to explains.

   Your new sentence will begin with which of the following?

   (A) Technology encroaching
   (B) On account of technology's encroaching
   (C) The fact of technology's encroachment
   (D) Due to the encroachment of technology
   (E) The encroachment of technology

54. In 1900 the Spanish language newspaper La Bandera Americana became the second newspaper established by the well-known defender of Latino rights, Nestor Montoya.

   Begin with Nestor Montoya. Your new sentence will contain

   (A) rights, established
   (B) newspaper, this
   (C) this will become
   (D) of 1900
   (E) Americana by

55. In the 1970's, Zora Neale Hurston's novels, which depict the lives of African Americans in the early 1900's, were rediscovered by scholars and critics.

Begin with <u>In the 1970's, scholars and critics.</u> Your new sentence will contain

(A) who rediscovered
(B) rediscovering her
(C) rediscovered Zora
(D) 1900's, novels
(E) depicting that

56. Most butterfly and moth wings are covered with a dense mosaic of tiny individually colored scales.

Begin with <u>A dense mosaic</u>. Your new sentence will contain

(A) which, covering
(B) scales of
(C) wings covers
(D) covers mostly
(E) scales covers

57. With Lewis Latimer's invention of the carbon filament, the electric lightbulb was finally made commercially feasible.

Begin the sentence with <u>It was Lewis Latimer who made.</u> Your new sentence will contain

(A) thus with
(B) in so doing, he thus
(C) was invented
(D) with his
(E) consequently

58. Many visitors to Hawaii are unaware that Hawaii is the only state in the United States that was once ruled by a resident monarchy.

Begin with <u>Few visitors</u>. Your new sentence will contain

(A) Hawaii, unaware
(B) being unaware of the fact
(C) are aware
(D) is aware
(E) aware, once

Analyzing Writing

Directions: Each of the following passages consists of numbered sentences. Because the passages are parts of longer writing samples, they do not necessarily constitute a complete discussion of the issues presented.

Read each passage carefully and answer the questions that follow it. The questions test your awareness of a writer's purpose and of characteristics of prose that are important to good writing.

<u>Questions 59–63</u> refer to the following paragraph.

(1) In Lovedu society, the individual was held to be inviolate. (2) The exercise of force of any kind, except in dealing with the very young infant, was never approved. (3) Even the courts of law refrained from executing their decisions, on the principle that to do so would be to coerce, and coercion should be avoided. (4) The parties involved in a case were expected to work out matters between them, aiming at a conciliatory solution and implementing the court decision through mutual agreement. (5) The culprit, if there was one, was left to pay restitution at his or her own pace. (6) Preferably, disputes were settled before they came to the point where they had to be submitted for a court decision. (7) If an individual wronged another, either deliberately or accidentally, it was the usual practice to send a conciliator to express regret and to offer a goat as a gesture of reconciliation. (8) This procedure was urged first of all, as the preferred solution, even when disagreements were brought to court. (9) Explicit condemnation was avoided as violating the individual and as not leading to rehabilitation; punishment was seen as bad because it meant vengeful retribution.

59. Which of the following best describes the relationship of sentence 1 to the rest of the paragraph?

(A) It establishes the organization for the paragraph as a whole.
(B) It establishes the basis for comparisons later in the paragraph between one kind of society and another.
(C) It demonstrates the writer's authority on the subject to be discussed in the paragraph.
(D) It presents the principle on which the behavior described in the rest of the paragraph is based.
(E) It describes the idea that will be refuted in the rest of the paragraph.

60. Which of the following best describes the function of sentence 4?

(A) It indicates the procedure by which the court's decisions were carried out.
(B) It demonstrates the laxness of the court in not executing its own decisions.
(C) It gives an example of what can happen when the courts do not exercise common sense.
(D) It alludes to the disorder that resulted from the court's decision.
(E) It forces the reader to make an independent judgment about the issues in the case.

61. In sentence 5, the effect of using the expression "if there was one" is to

(A) reveal the writer's uncertainty about the details of the sequence of events
(B) emphasize the court decision mentioned in sentence 4 by referring back to it
(C) reinforce the idea that assigning blame was not always important in the view of justice under discussion
(D) suggest the carelessness inherent in this method of dealing with injustices
(E) prepare the reader for the statement about court decisions in sentence 6

62. The function of sentence 7 is primarily to

(A) illustrate the ineffectiveness of informal methods of dealing with conflict

(B) present a specific incident that symbolizes the issues discussed in the paragraph

(C) give an example to support the generalization in sentence 5

(D) indicate the method by which the ideal described in sentence 6 would be realized

(E) prepare for the suggestion in sentence 8 that most disputes eventually ended up in court

63. The purpose of the paragraph is primarily to

(A) tell the story of a society that is not well known

(B) demonstrate the extremes of behavior arising from a specific idea

(C) describe a particular system of social interactions

(D) analyze the effects on society of dogmatic ideas

(E) propose a change in methods of administering justice

Questions 64–68 refer to the following passage.

(1) Michael Goldman wrote in a poem, "When the Muse comes She doesn't tell you to write;/She says get up for a minute, I've something to show you, stand here." (2) What made me look up at that roadside tree?

(3) The road to Grundy, Virginia, is, as you might expect, a narrow scrawl scribbled all over the most improbably peaked and hunched mountains you ever saw. (4) The few people who live along the road also seem peaked and hunched. (5) But what on earth . . . ? (6) It was a hot, sunny summer. (7) The road was just bending off sharply to the right. (8) I hadn't seen a house in miles, and none was in sight. (9) At the apogee of the road's curve grew an enormous oak, a massive bur oak 200 years old, 150 feet high, an oak whose lowest limb was beyond the span of the highest ladder. (10) I looked up; there were clothes spread all over the tree. (11) Red shirts, blue trousers, black pants, little baby smocks —they weren't hung from branches. (12) They were outside, carefully spread, splayed as if to dry, on the outer leaves of the great oak's crown. (13) Were there pillowcases, blankets? (14) I can't remember. (15) There was a gay assortment of cotton underwear, yellow dresses, children's green sweaters, plaid skirts. . . . (16) You know roads. (17) A bend comes and you take it, thoughtlessly, moving on. (18) I looked behind me for another split second, astonished; both sides of the tree's canopy, clear to the top, bore clothes.

64. Which of the following best describes the relationship between the two paragraphs in this passage?

(A) The second paragraph restates the question at the end of the first.

(B) The second paragraph offers a concrete illustration of the quotation in the first.

(C) The second paragraph takes an opposite point of view from the first.

(D) The second paragraph generalizes about the quotation in the first.

(E) The second paragraph is an elaborate contradiction of the thesis in the first.

65. Which of the following most accurately describes what happens in the second paragraph?

   (A) The speaker has a poetic vision symbolizing cleansing renewal.
   (B) The speaker has a hallucination brought on by the heat.
   (C) The speaker tries to explain how what was seen is possible.
   (D) The speaker sees a tree full of flowers and imagines they are someone's washing.
   (E) The speaker sees a large tree inexplicably covered with clothes spread to dry.

66. The descriptive details in sentences 9–15 provide a

   (A) precise visual image
   (B) picture of something unearthly
   (C) representation of a blur of color
   (D) view from a child's perspective
   (E) distorted sense of motion

67. Which of the following pairs of words best describes the speaker's reaction to the experience?

   (A) Ecstasy and fear
   (B) Dismay and wonder
   (C) Delight and fear
   (D) Disgust and disbelief
   (E) Wonder and delight

68. The main implication of the passage is that

   (A) you never know what you will see on country roads
   (B) people are resourceful in finding ways to rise above domestic tasks
   (C) inspiration or vision is often a matter of chance or caprice
   (D) the poet sees more intensely than other people
   (E) the Muse encourages only the eccentric to write

Questions 69–74 refer to the following passage.

(1) The bishop and his vicar were riding through the rain in the Truchas Mountains. (2) The heavy, lead-colored drops were driven slantingly through the air by an icy wind from the peak. (3) These raindrops, Father Latour kept thinking, were the shape of tadpoles, and they broke against his nose and cheeks, exploding with a splash, as if they were hollow and full of air. (4) The priests were riding across high mountain meadows, which in a few weeks would be green, though just now they were slate colored. (5) On every side lay ridges covered with blue-green fir trees; above them rose the horny backbones of mountains. (6) The sky was very low; purplish lead-colored clouds let down curtains of mist into the valleys between the pine ridges. (7) There was not a glimmer of white light in the dark vapors working overhead—rather, they took on the cold green of the evergreens. (8) Even the white mules, their coats wet and matted into tufts, had turned a slaty hue, and the faces of the two priests were purple and spotted in that singular light.

69. In sentences 2 and 3, the phrases "driven slantingly" and "exploding with a splash" emphasize

   (A) the severity of the weather
   (B) an otherworldly atmosphere
   (C) the narrator's irritable attitude
   (D) the beauty of simple natural objects
   (E) an unusual combination of sounds

70. One way the writer suggests strangeness is to describe

   (A) extreme emotion
   (B) eerie sounds
   (C) unexpected colors
   (D) a character's loneliness
   (E) the sensation of danger

71. The writer unifies the selection primarily through references to

    (A) action and conflict
    (B) similar sounds
    (C) passionate emotions
    (D) color and light
    (E) odors and fragrances

72. Which of the following best describes the relationship of sentence 1 to the rest of the paragraph?

    (A) It states facts that the rest of the paragraph elaborates.
    (B) It demonstrates the writer's knowledge of the geography of the Truchas Mountains.
    (C) It supplies background information about the plot and a motive for the characters' journey.
    (D) It presents an assumption that the rest of the paragraph contradicts.
    (E) It introduces a mystery that the rest of the paragraph solves.

73. In sentence 4, the function of the words "which in a few weeks would be green" is to

    (A) reveal the length of the priests' journey
    (B) emphasize the diversity of color in the meadows
    (C) establish that the spring season had not yet arrived
    (D) identify the type of vegetation in the region
    (E) create an image that suggests bounty and well-being to the priest

74. In context, the primary function of sentence 8 is to

    (A) supply critical information about the type of transportation used by the priests
    (B) demonstrate the effect of the rainwater on the mules' coats
    (C) indicate that the priests had become ill during the stormy journey
    (D) emphasize that the rain and the light changed the appearances of things
    (E) refer to a supernatural phenomenon on the trail

Sample Essays and Essay Topics

This section includes the following:

- General information about how to respond to the essay topic
- Essay writing directions as they appear in the test
- The scoring guide used to evaluate the essays
- A sample essay topic
- Three scored essays written in response to the topic
- An additional sample essay topic that may be used to practice writing essays

During the exam you will have 45 minutes to plan and write an essay on the topic specified. Read the topic carefully. You are expected to spend a few moments considering the topic and organizing your thoughts before you begin writing. It is important that you do not write on a topic other than the one specified. An essay on a topic of your own choice is not acceptable.

The essay is intended to give you an opportunity to demonstrate your ability to write effectively. Take care to express your thoughts on the topic clearly, keeping in mind that how well you write is much more important than how much you write. Be certain, however, to develop your ideas thoroughly, using specific details and supporting examples when appropriate.

You will see the following instructions when you take the essay portion of the exam:

> **Directions:** Read the essay topic and then make any notes that will help you plan your response. You will have 45 minutes to write your response. Begin typing your response in the box at the bottom of the screen. Time will begin to count down after you click on **Dismiss Directions**. Click on **Dismiss Directions** to go on to the next screen.

Scoring Guide
CLEP English Composition with Essay Examination

Readers will assign scores based on the following scoring guide. The essays must display the following characteristics in response to the assigned task.

6 A 6 essay demonstrates *a high degree of competence and sustained control* although it may have a few minor errors.

A typical essay in this category

- addresses all elements of the writing task effectively and insightfully
- develops ideas thoroughly, supporting them with well-chosen reasons, examples, or details
- is well focused and well organized
- demonstrates superior facility with language, using effective vocabulary and sentence variety
- demonstrates general mastery of the standard conventions of grammar, usage, and mechanics, but may have minor errors

5 A 5 essay demonstrates *a generally high degree of competence* although it will have occasional lapses in quality.

A typical essay in this category

- addresses the writing task effectively
- is well developed, using appropriate reasons, examples, or details to support ideas
- is generally well focused and well organized
- demonstrates facility with language, using appropriate vocabulary and some sentence variety
- demonstrates strong control of the standard conventions of grammar, usage, and mechanics, but may have minor errors

4   A 4 essay demonstrates *clear competence* with some errors and lapses in quality.

A typical essay in this category

– addresses the writing task competently

– is adequately developed, using reasons, examples, or details to support ideas

– is adequately focused and organized

– demonstrates competence with language, using adequate vocabulary and minimal sentence variety

– generally demonstrates control of the standard conventions of grammar, usage, and mechanics, but may have some errors

3   A 3 essay demonstrates *limited competence.*

A typical essay in this category exhibits ONE OR MORE of the following weaknesses:

– addresses only some parts of the writing task

– is unevenly developed and often provides assertions but few relevant reasons, examples, or details

– is poorly focused and/or poorly organized

– displays frequent problems in the use of language

– demonstrates inconsistent control of grammar, usage, and mechanics

2   A 2 essay is *seriously flawed.*

A typical essay in this category exhibits ONE OR MORE of the following weaknesses:

– is unclear or seriously limited in addressing the writing task

– is seriously underdeveloped, providing few reasons, examples, or details

– is unfocused and/or disorganized

– displays frequent serious errors in the use of language that may interfere with meaning

– contains frequent serious errors in grammar, usage, and mechanics that may interfere with meaning

1   A 1 essay is *fundamentally deficient.*

A typical essay in this category exhibits ONE OR MORE of the following weaknesses:

– provides little or no evidence of the ability to develop an organized response to the writing task

– is undeveloped

– contains severe writing errors that persistently interfere with meaning

0   Off topic (i.e., provides no evidence of an attempt to respond to the assigned topic), in a language other than English, merely copies the topic, consists of only keystroke characters, or is nonverbal.

Sample Topic 1:

There are no challenges so difficult, no goals so impossible, as the ones we set for ourselves.

Write an essay in which you discuss the extent to which you agree or disagree with the statement above. Support your discussion with specific reasons and examples from your reading, experience, or observations.

Essay A—This essay is scored a 6.

I disagree with the statement that the most difficult challenges people face are those that everybody creates for themselves. The assertion is not true, or at least not always, as I intend to show below. There may be instances where people set difficult objectives for themselves, but very often people simply have to try to address challenges they did not create, and survive or make the best of situations they have been put into by accidents such as geography, history, or ethnic and racial background. There are exceptions, but they are just that: exceptions, not the norm.

Often, especially for those coming from countries that are not dominating the world stage, succeeding in life, or simply making ends meet are major challenges, and not because those who face these challenges want to be in such situations. My parents grew up at a time when their country was undergoing major social and political transformations. World War II had just ended by the time my father was 12, the economy was in shambles, and the Nazi occupiers had been driven out of the country so the Red Army can take over. My grandfather was forced to give up his little land during the process of collectivization of agriculture. His small store was eventually confiscated as well, and the couple horses he had, along with thousands of horses throughout the country, were taken away to make room for the tractors the country was beginning to manufacture. By the time my father was drafted into the military, talk of World War II was everywhere, and the hysteria gave way only a couple of decades later. My father had to lie low all his life and not say a world against a regime that did not tolerate dissent. The kids' success in school meant they could get by within or without the messed up system the country was under. In my grandfather's words, it was important to study, because "no one can take away from you what you know."

I have also seen in this country instances where people's lives are made difficult by those in power. It is often assumed that everybody in this country shares a certain standard of living, although evidence contradicts that assumption. For many, simply getting by is a major success, not because they love struggling to make ends meet, but because they do not have a choice. When Hurricane Katrina made landfall last August, the majority of the residents of New Orleans had evacuated the city. Many had not, though: some of their own free will, others because they simply did not have the means of travel. Later on, when large portions of the city were under water, some residents tried to cross one of the bridges from New Orleans to the west bank of the Mississippi River, but were received by police shooting in the air to scare them away. The city across the river apparently did not want "the problems" of the City of New Orleans.

Certainly there are instances where people set high goals for themselves and some succeed in attaining those goals, while many fail. I have all the respect for the former, but I think focusing on the few exceptions we may miss the big picture. Succeeding in spite of all odds, being a "self-made man," going "from rags to riches," are powerful myths in this country. I am not denying the effort and successes of the Rockefellers, Carnegies, or more recently the Trumps. I do think, nonetheless, that for every person who makes it in spite of all or most odds, there are many more who do not; for every college dropout who succeeds in life, such as Bill Gates, there are thousands who will struggle through life.

People often set hard-to-reach objectives and they may fail or succeed in pursuing those objectives. I do think, though, that for many, the most difficult challenges come from outside the individual, from their position in the social hierarchy, or the time and place where they are born and try to get by.

Commentary on Essay A

This insightful response argues that life's most difficult challenges come from outside the individual and cites specific accidents of history and geography as effective support for that claim. Paragraph two offers abundant, well-chosen evidence that political constraints imposed on the writer's family in Eastern Europe after the Second World War were much more formidable than any challenges they might have chosen for themselves. To provide further development, paragraph three describes the impact of similarly harsh conditions in a more immediate place and time—New Orleans after Hurricane Katrina. Finally, in preparation for a strong but carefully measured conclusion, the essay acknowledges that some few individuals do accomplish great things despite overwhelming odds. Just as the development of this response is thorough and always sharply focused, the control of language is superior. Note, for example, skillful subordination in the third sentence of the essay and effective vocabulary in phrases such as "dominating the world stage" or "a regime that did not tolerate dissent." A few minor errors are indeed present, as is allowed by the scoring guide, but sustained control supports a score of 6.

Essay B—This essay is scored a 4.

I agree that, as individuals, we tend to set higher goals for ourselves than outside influences. Because goals are so personal, it makes it that much more challenging to attain them. Psychologically, individuals can be their own worst enemy. Goals may be set and believed in by an individual but self-doubt, a low self-esteem and societal and familial attitudes may warp personal beliefs. When this happens, an individual may lose sight of the goal and instead focus doubt on the necessary steps to achieve the goal. Conversely, an individual may battle these internal and external obstacles and rise above them to successfully reach their goal. Who better to know the self then the individual? Goals are personal since only the individual really knows what they would like to achieve, at what level to set the goal and must find a way to achieve it.

An example of successful goal-setting is my business idol; George Lucas who's educational and career history has been a real inspiration. Mr. Lucas continued to set higher goals for himself as his life developed. He has become a prolific director and businessman in the entertainment industry. He currently owns several companies including his own production company and special effects company. The reason why this is so inspiring is because he almost failed high school and had almost no prospects for the future. Before graduation, Mr. Lucas was involved in an almost fatal car crash. At this point in his life, he set a goal of becoming an excellent student both in the classroom and in life. This was quite a high goal to set due to this previous academic ability and the external opinions of family and friends. He worked to accomplish graduating

from a junior college then completing his B.A. in Film from USC, both with honors. Mr. Lucas continued to set higher and more challenging goals for himself to become an independent film producer and director and to not be affiliated with any particular movie studio. He had to pay his dues at first but finally his tenacity paid off and his creation of Lucasfilm has allowed him the goal of creative freedom in his work. I don't believe that anyone else in his family or his acquaintances would have set such goals for him. Mr. Lucas psychologically believed in himself enough, knew what he wanted to do, set the applicable goals and worked to achieve them. No one else could have done this for him.

Commentary on Essay B

Since the first paragraph in this response deals mainly with psychological reasons for failure or success in achieving goals, it does not focus sharply on the question of relative difficulty. Paragraph two, however, clearly addresses the writing task and offers an extended example to argue that self-selected goals are indeed more difficult than those imposed by others. Instead of merely summarizing the life of George Lucas, the writer chooses several specific episodes in which Lucas' own aspirations surpassed the expectations of family and friends. Thus, after a slow start, the essay does achieve competence in development, focus, and organization. Despite some errors, control of language is also adequate to support a score of 4. Syntax is sometimes flawed (see the first and last sentences of paragraph one), but the essay is free of serious grammar errors. Furthermore, several phrases (e.g., "may warp personal beliefs," "his tenacity paid off,") demonstrate vocabulary that is clearly adequate.

Essay C—This essay is scored a 2.

This statement is strongly true. One example of this is my own life. I work very hard and never give up, and am even taking this test! I am very inspired to go to college and have made it my goal to achieve, no matter what. And I have achieved goals before this, so I know that I can achieve this one too, even though it seems hard. When I was a senior at Kennedy High school I saved up money to buy a car, and that was a goal that I achieved myself.

Another example of goals is my Mom. When I was little she went to nursing school and worked very hard, some people said it was impossible because she had four small children, but she graduated and now she works in a hospital. So obviously goals can be useful. I guess when a person has achieved a few goals then they feel more confident about going out to achieve other goals, and that way even though they set higher goals, you find out that you can even achieve the harder goals that seem more impossible like the question says. You feel good about what you already have achieved, so nothing seems impossible. You go out and do it!

Commentary on Essay C

Problems with development and focus make this response seriously limited in addressing the writing task. The writer twice refers to success in achieving personal goals (saving money for a car and Mom's graduation from nursing school), but both examples are extremely thin and neither shows that self-imposed goals are any more challenging than those imposed by others. In the middle of paragraph two, the writer veers even further away from the topic with the plausible but—in this context—superfluous claim that "goals can be useful." Even though the response begins by asserting that the prompt is "strongly true," later sentences argue an entirely different point—that "nothing seems impossible" after one has gained confidence. Thus, since the response provides almost no relevant development, it earns a score of 2.

Sample Topic 2:

Nobody ever made any progress by being contented or satisfied. Discontent is vital to growth and development—whether we are talking about one person or a whole nation.

Write an essay in which you discuss the extent to which you agree or disagree with the statements above. Support your discussion with specific reasons and examples from your reading, experience, or observations.

Study Resources

Most textbooks used in college-level English Composition courses cover the topics in the outline given earlier, but the approaches to certain topics and the emphases given to them may differ. To prepare for the English Composition exam, it is advisable to study one or more college textbooks, which can be found in most college bookstores. When selecting a textbook, check the table of contents against the knowledge and skills required for this test.

To become aware of the processes and the principles involved in presenting your ideas logically and expressing them clearly and effectively, you should practice writing. Ideally, you should try writing on a variety of subjects and issues, starting with those you know best and care about most. Ask someone you know and respect to respond to what you write and to help you discover which parts of your writing communicate effectively and which parts need revision to make the meaning clear. You should also try to read the works of published writers in a wide range of subjects, paying particular attention to the ways in which they use language to express their meaning.

Visit www.collegeboard.com/clepprep for additional literature and writing resources. You can also find suggestions for exam preparation in Chapter IV of the *Official Study Guide*. In addition, many college faculty post their course materials on their schools' Web sites.

Answer Key

#	Ans		#	Ans
1.	A		38.	E
2.	B		39.	A
3.	C		40.	B
4.	E		41.	D
5.	B		42.	A
6.	C		43.	B
7.	D		44.	D
8.	C		45.	E
9.	D		46.	C
10.	E		47.	B
11.	D		48.	C
12.	E		49.	E
13.	B		50.	D
14.	C		51.	A
15.	E		52.	B
16.	E		53.	E
17.	B		54.	A
18.	C		55.	C
19.	D		56.	E
20.	C		57.	D
21.	C		58.	C
22.	A		59.	D
23.	B		60.	A
24.	C		61.	C
25.	A		62.	D
26.	B		63.	C
27.	E		64.	B
28.	B		65.	E
29.	C		66.	A
30.	B		67.	E
31.	C		68.	C
32.	B		69.	A
33.	B		70.	C
34.	C		71.	D
35.	B		72.	A
36.	D		73.	C
37.	C		74.	D

English Literature

Description of the Examination

The English Literature examination covers material usually taught in a two-semester course (or the equivalent) at the college level. The test is primarily concerned with major authors and literary works, but it also includes questions on some minor writers. Candidates are expected to be acquainted with common literary terms, such as metaphor and personification, and basic literary forms, such as the sonnet and the ballad.

In both coverage and approach, the examination resembles the historically organized survey of English literature offered by many colleges. It assumes that candidates have read widely and developed an appreciation of English literature, know the basic literary periods, and have a sense of the historical development of English literature.

The examination contains approximately 95 questions to be answered in 90 minutes. Any time candidates spend on tutorials and providing personal information is in addition to the actual testing time.

The CLEP English Literature exam also includes an optional essay section. Some schools require candidates to complete this section. Candidates should check with the school(s) of their choice to confirm whether the essay is required. This optional section requires candidates to demonstrate their ability to write clearly and effectively. Candidates respond to two of three essay topics. An essay on the first topic, a persuasive analysis of a poem, is required, and candidates are advised to spend 35 to 40 minutes on it. For the second essay, candidates choose one of two topics that presents a specific observation, position, or theme. Depending on the topic chosen, candidates choose any work by a particular author to appropriately support the claim or select works from a designated list provided. Candidates should plan to spend 50 to 55 minutes on the essay. All essays are scored by faculty at the school(s) where candidates send their reports.

Knowledge and Skills Required

The English Literature examination measures both knowledge and ability. The percentages below show the relative emphasis given to each; however, most questions draw on both.

35–40% Knowledge of:

  Literary background

  Identification of authors

  Metrical patterns

  Literary references

  Literary terms

60–65% Ability to:

  Analyze the elements of form in a literary passage

  Perceive meanings

  Identify tone and mood

  Follow patterns of imagery

  Identify characteristics of style

  Comprehend the reasoning in an excerpt of literary criticism

The examination deals with literature from Beowulf to the present. Familiarity with and understanding of major writers is expected, as is knowledge of literary periods and common literary terms, themes, and forms. Some of the questions on the examination ask candidates to identify the author of a representative quotation or to recognize the period in which an excerpt was written.

Sample Test Questions

The following sample questions do not appear on an actual CLEP examination. They are intended to give potential test-takers an indication of the format and difficulty level of the examination and to provide content for practice and review. Knowing the correct answers to all of the sample questions is not a guarantee of satisfactory performance on the exam.

Directions: Each of the questions or incomplete statements below is followed by five suggested answers or completions. Select the one that is best in each case.

1. In a pungent critique of humanity addressed to the mature imagination, the author comments on human nature by examining the life of the Lilliputians, Yahoos, and Houyhnhnms.

   The book described above is

   (A) *The Way of All Flesh*
   (B) *Through the Looking Glass*
   (C) *Gulliver's Travels*
   (D) *The Pilgrim's Progress*
   (E) *Robinson Crusoe*

2. One of the great triumphs of the play is Shakespeare's addition of the character of the Fool, who attempts to comfort his old master and is distressed and puzzled by his madness, but who also ironically emphasizes the folly and the tragedy of the old man.

   The play referred to above is

   (A) *Macbeth*
   (B) *Julius Caesar*
   (C) *King Lear*
   (D) *Othello*
   (E) *Hamlet*

Questions 3–4

For I have learned
To look on nature, not as in the hour
Of thoughtless youth; but hearing often times
The still, sad music of humanity,
Nor harsh nor grating, though of ample power
To chasten and subdue. And I have felt
A presence that disturbs me with the joy
Of elevated thoughts; a sense sublime
Of something far more deeply interfused,
Whose dwelling is the light of setting suns,
And the round ocean and the living air,
And the blue sky, and in the mind of man;

3. The lines above are written in

   (A) heroic couplets
   (B) terza rima
   (C) ballad meter
   (D) blank verse
   (E) iambic tetrameter

4. The language and ideas in these lines are most characteristic of which of the following literary periods?

   (A) Medieval
   (B) Restoration
   (C) Augustan
   (D) Romantic
   (E) Early twentieth century

5. Samuel Richardson, Henry Fielding, and Tobias Smollett are best known as eighteenth-century

   (A) novelists
   (B) dramatists
   (C) essayists
   (D) poets
   (E) critics

6. "The business of a poet," said Imlac, "is to examine, not the individual, but the species; to remark general properties and large appearances: he does not number the streaks of the tulip, or describe the different shades in the verdure of the forest. He is to exhibit in his portraits of nature such prominent and striking features, as recall the original to every mind; and must neglect the minuter discriminations, which one may have remarked, and another have neglected, for those characteristics which are alike obvious to vigilance and carelessness."

Which of the following statements most agrees with the paragraph above?

(A) Poetry is the spontaneous overflow of powerful feelings.

(B) Poetry is the precious lifeblood of a master spirit.

(C) Poetry is the just representation of general nature.

(D) Poetry should not mean but be.

(E) Poets are the unacknowledged legislators of the world.

7. An anonymous narrative poem focusing on the climax of a particularly dramatic event and employing frequent repetition, conventional figures of speech, and sometimes a refrain— altered and transmitted orally in a musical setting—is called a

(A) popular ballad

(B) pastoral elegy

(C) courtly lyric

(D) villanelle

(E) chivalric romance

Questions 8–10

They, looking back, all the eastern side beheld
Of Paradise, so late their happy seat,
Waved over by that flaming brand, the gate
Line With dreadful faces thronged and fiery arms.
(5) Some natural tears they dropped, but wiped them soon;
The world was all before them, where to choose
Their place of rest, and Providence their guide.
They, hand in hand, with wandering steps and slow,
Through Eden took their solitary way.

8. These lines were written by

(A) John Donne

(B) Edmund Spenser

(C) Christopher Marlowe

(D) William Shakespeare

(E) John Milton

9. In line 2, "late" is best interpreted to mean

(A) recently

(B) tardily

(C) unfortunately

(D) long

(E) soon

10. The people referred to as "they" in the passage were probably experiencing all the following emotions EXCEPT

(A) awe

(B) doubt

(C) suspicion

(D) regret

(E) sorrow

11. Whan that Aprill with his shoures soote
The droghte of March hath perced to the roote

The lines above were written by

(A) Geoffrey Chaucer

(B) William Shakespeare

(C) Alexander Pope

(D) William Wordsworth

(E) Ben Jonson

12. Alfred Tennyson's "Ulysses" and T. S. Eliot's
"The Love Song of J. Alfred Prufrock" are both

(A) pastoral elegies

(B) literary ballads

(C) mock epics

(D) dramatic monologues

(E) irregular odes

Questions 13–14

Our two souls therefore, which are one,
Though I must go, endure not yet
A breach, but an expansion,
Like gold to airy thinness beat.

13. The passage contains an example of

(A) an epic simile

(B) a metaphysical conceit

(C) an epic catalog

(D) an alexandrine

(E) sprung rhythm

14. The passage is from a poem by

(A) Alexander Pope

(B) Robert Herrick

(C) Samuel Taylor Coleridge

(D) Samuel Johnson

(E) John Donne

Questions 15–17

He's here in double trust:
First, as I am his kinsman and his subject,
Strong both against the deed; then, as his host,
Line Who should against his murtherer shut the door,
(5) Not bear the knife myself. Besides, this Duncan
Hath borne his faculties so meek, hath been
So clear in his great office, that his virtues
Will plead like angels, trumpet-tongued, against
The deep damnation of his taking-off;
(10) And pity, like a naked new-born babe,
Striding the blast, or heaven's cherubim, horsed
Upon the sightless couriers of the air,
Shall blow the horrid deed in every eye,
That tears shall drown the wind.

15. The speaker of these lines might best be
described as a

(A) coward

(B) man badly treated by Duncan

(C) man seeking revenge

(D) man concerned only with his own safety

(E) man troubled by moral law

16. The "horrid deed" (line 13) is compared metaphorically to

(A) a cinder or speck irritating the eye

(B) a naked newborn babe

(C) an assassination

(D) the wind

(E) the consequences of the murder of Duncan

17. These lines are spoken by

(A) Hamlet

(B) Cassius

(C) Macbeth

(D) Iago

(E) Richard III

18. Which of the following is the first line of a poem by John Keats?

    (A) "What dire offence from amorous causes springs,"
    (B) "They flee from me that sometime did me seek,"
    (C) "Thou still unravished bride of quietness,"
    (D) "I weep for Adonais—he is dead!"
    (E) "Not, I'll not, carrion comfort, Despair, not feast on thee;"

Questions 19–20

O threats of Hell and Hopes of Paradise!
One thing at least is certain—*This* life flies;
    One thing is certain and the rest is Lies;
The Flower that once has blown for ever dies.

19. In the fourth line, "blown" means

    (A) blown up
    (B) blown away
    (C) bloomed
    (D) died
    (E) been planted

20. Which of the following is the best summary of the four lines?

    (A) Do not ignore the serious aspects of life; earnest dedication is necessary for success.
    (B) Do not rely on a theoretical afterlife; you can be sure only that the present moment will pass.
    (C) Life is like a flower with roots in both good and evil.
    (D) Religious belief is essential to a happy life.
    (E) The only safe course in life is to ignore outside events and cultivate one's own garden.

21. Which of the following was written earliest?

    (A) *The Waste Land*
    (B) *The Rime of the Ancient Mariner*
    (C) *Songs of Innocence*
    (D) *The Faerie Queene*
    (E) *The Rape of the Lock*

Questions 22–23

She was alone and still, gazing out to sea; and when she felt his presence and the worship of his eyes her eyes turned to him in quiet sufferance of his gaze, without shame or wantonness. Long, long she suffered his gaze and then quietly withdrew her eyes from his and bent them towards the stream, gently stirring the water with her foot hither and thither. The first faint noise of gently moving water broke the silence, low and faint and whispering, faint as the bells of sleep; hither and thither, hither and thither, and a faint flame trembled on her cheek.
    —Heavenly God! cried Stephen's soul, in an outburst of profane joy.

22. The passage above appears in which of the following novels?

    (A) *Victory*
    (B) *A Portrait of the Artist as a Young Man*
    (C) *Tess of the D'Urbervilles*
    (D) *The Egoist*
    (E) *Sons and Lovers*

23. The passage presents an example of what its author would have termed

    (A) synecdoche
    (B) pathetic fallacy
    (C) stream of consciousness
    (D) an eclogue
    (E) an epiphany

Questions 24–25 are based on the following excerpt from Henry Fielding's *Joseph Andrews*.

Now, the rake Hesperus has called for his breeches, and having well rubbed his drowsy eyes, prepared to dress himself for all night;
Line by whose example his brother rakes on earth
(5) likewise leave those beds in which they slept away the day. Now Thetis, the good housewife, began to put on the pot, in order to regale the good man Phoebus after his daily labours were over. In vulgar language, it was the evening
(10) when Joseph attended his lady's orders.

24. Which of the following describes Hesperus (line 1), Thetis (line 6), and Phoebus (line 8) in the passage above?

(A) They are references to Greek mythology.

(B) They are references to fellow authors.

(C) They are references to Biblical heroes.

(D) They refer to figures from English folklore.

(E) They are characters in the novel.

25. In line 9, "vulgar language" means

(A) commonly spoken language

(B) elevated and archaic language

(C) ungrammatical language

(D) language laden with sexual puns

(E) language characterized by obsolete and dialectal terms

26. The "Age of Johnson" in English literature was dominated by which of the following styles?

(A) Romanticism

(B) Neoclassicism

(C) Expressionism

(D) Naturalism

(E) Abstractionism

Questions 27–29 are based on the following excerpt from Ben Jonson's "To Penshurst."

Thou art not, Penshurst, built to envious show,
Of touch, or marble; nor canst boast a row
Of polished pillars, or a roof of gold;
Line Thou hast no lantern whereof tales are told,
(5) Or stair, or courts; but stand'st an ancient pile,
And these grudged at, art reverenced the while.
Thou joy'st in better marks, of soil, of air,
Of wood, of water; therein thou art fair.

27. Lines 1–5 of the passage compare Penshurst with

(A) a more ornate house

(B) an intricate tapestry

(C) an impenetrable fortress

(D) a landscape painting

(E) an autumn evening

28. The speaker in the passage indicates that Penshurst is

(A) less well-known than other landmarks

(B) enhanced by "a roof of gold" (line 3)

(C) in need of brighter lighting

(D) falling into disrepair

(E) properly appreciated

29. The poem uses which of the following forms?

(A) Ballad meter

(B) Blank verse

(C) Elegiac stanza

(D) Rhyme royal

(E) Heroic couplets

Questions 30–32 are based on the following excerpt from Virginia Woolf's essay "Professions for Women."

I discovered that if I were going to review books I should need to do battle with a certain phantom. And the phantom was a woman, and
Line when I came to know her better I called her after
(5) the heroine of a famous poem, The Angel in the House. . . . She was intensely sympathetic. She was immensely charming. She was utterly unselfish. She excelled in the difficult arts of family life. She sacrificed herself daily. If there
(10) was chicken, she took the leg; if there was a draft she sat in it—in short she was so constituted that she never had a mind or a wish of her own, but preferred to sympathize always with the minds and wishes of others. Above all—I need not say
(15) it—she was pure. Her purity was supposed to be her chief beauty—her blushes, her great grace. In those days—the last of Queen Victoria— every house had its Angel. And when I came to write I encountered her with the very first words.

30. This passage's primary purpose is to

   (A) describe a person with a dual personality

   (B) praise the traditional role of women

   (C) describe a famous historical figure

   (D) encourage readers to take seriously the importance of literary ghosts

   (E) describe one impediment a woman writer faces in making a literary career

31. Which of the following effects does the battle metaphor have?

   I. It suggests how difficult the phantom will be to overcome.

   II. It enhances the emotional impact of the conflict described.

   III. It contributes to the mock-heroic tone of the entire passage.

   (A) I only

   (B) III only

   (C) I and II only

   (D) II and III only

   (E) I, II, and III

32. The tone of the discussion of "The Angel in the House" (lines 5–6) conveys the author's

   (A) pleasure in remembering her literary precursors

   (B) anger at people who write book reviews

   (C) remorse for the slaying of an innocent person

   (D) awareness of the power of commonly held ideas

   (E) enthusiasm about writing what she feels

Questions 33–34 are based on the following passage from Anita Desai's novel *In Custody*.

The time and the place: these elementary matters were left to Deven to arrange as being within his capabilities. Time and place, these two concerns of all who are born and all who die: these were considered the two fit subjects for the weak and the incompetent. Deven was to restrict himself to these two matters, time and place. No one appeared to realize that to him these subjects belonged to infinity and were far more awesome than the minutiae of technical arrangements.

33. According to the passage, Deven is perceived by others to be

(A) capable of arranging important details

(B) suited to performing only simple tasks

(C) unable to see the ultimate meaning of infinity

(D) obsessed with his own mortality

(E) happy in his role of organizing minor matters

34. The passage implies that Deven's perspective differs from that of the people who have given him his assignment in that he is

(A) innovative instead of fastidious

(B) intellectual instead of social

(C) philosophical instead of pragmatic

(D) cosmopolitan instead of bigoted

(E) judgmental instead of apathetic

35. What is the order, from earliest to latest, in which the following works were composed?

   I. *Hamlet*

  II. *Beowulf*

 III. *Paradise Lost*

(A) I, II, III

(B) I, III, II

(C) II, I, III

(D) II, III, I

(E) III, II, I

Questions 36–37 are based on the following poem.

Farewell, thou child of my right hand, and joy;
My sin was too much hope of thee, loved boy:
Seven years thou wert lent to me, and I thee pay,
Exacted by thy fate, on the just day.
O could I lose all father now! for why
Will man lament the state he should envy,
To have so soon 'scaped world's and flesh's rage,
And, if no other misery, yet age?
Rest in soft peace, and asked, say, "Here doth lie
Ben Jonson his best piece of poetry."
For whose sake henceforth all his vows be such
As what he may never like too much.

36. The speaker expresses all of the following thoughts EXCEPT:

(A) Life has so many trials that perhaps death should be viewed as a welcome release.

(B) Poetry can keep alive those whom fate tries to take away.

(C) Bearing the death of his son is difficult because he had high expectations for him.

(D) His son was the greatest achievement in his life.

(E) He never again wants to become as attached to anybody or anything as he was to his son.

37. The tone of the poem is best described as

(A) deferential

(B) malicious

(C) playful

(D) elegiac

(E) melodramatic

38. *Lycidas* is a poem that

    (A) adapts a heroic legend from classical mythology to the society that the writer knew best

    (B) manages in a short space to record much of English history

    (C) mourns the death of the writer's friend but also reveals personal concerns of the writer

    (D) uses an important historical event of its day to air the political views of the writer

    (E) captures the magic of the Italian Renaissance and puts it into a realistic London setting

39. In the poem "The Canonization," the intense relationship between the speaker and the lover leads the speaker to argue that they should be considered candidates for sainthood.

    The author of the poem described above is

    (A) W. B. Yeats

    (B) Elizabeth Barrett Browning

    (C) John Donne

    (D) John Milton

    (E) Gerard Manley Hopkins

40. All of the following were written in the eighteenth century EXCEPT

    (A) *Pamela*

    (B) *Jane Eyre*

    (C) *Tom Jones*

    (D) *Tristram Shandy*

    (E) *Moll Flanders*

41. Observe me, Sir Anthony, I would by no means wish a daughter of mine to be a progeny of learning. . . . But, Sir Anthony, I would send her at nine years old to a boarding school, in order to learn a little ingenuity and artifice. Then, sir, she should have a supercilious knowledge in accounts;—and as she grew up, I would have her instructed in geometry, that she might know something of the contagious countries;—but above all, Sir Anthony, she should be mistress to orthodoxy, that she might not misspell and mis-pronounce words so shamefully as girls usually do; and likewise that she might reprehend the true meaning of what she is saying.

    The speaker of the lines above, as evidenced by her characteristic language, is

    (A) Elizabeth Bennet in *Pride and Prejudice*

    (B) Hellena in *The Rover*

    (C) Mrs. Malaprop in *The Rivals*

    (D) Miss Hardcastle in *She Stoops to Conquer*

    (E) Rosalind in *As You Like It*

42. A novel that uses extensive parallels from classical Greek epic and adopts an antiheroic modernity is

    (A) *Lord Jim*

    (B) *Briefing for a Descent into Hell*

    (C) *A Tale of Two Cities*

    (D) *A Passage to India*

    (E) *Ulysses*

43. A twentieth-century absurdist play in which the characters largely talk in circles, the actions are inconclusive, and the lines "Nothing to be done" and "It'd pass the time" are repeated is

    (A) *Riders to the Sea*
    (B) *Equus*
    (C) *Waiting for Godot*
    (D) *Look Back in Anger*
    (E) *Murder in the Cathedral*

44. Mill, Carlyle, and Tennyson all experienced and wrote about

    (A) an upbringing in an agrarian environment
    (B) a personal crisis of faith
    (C) the conservatism of Victorian courtship
    (D) the benefits of modern science
    (E) the triumph of democracy

45. Which of the following novelists was raised in Southern Rhodesia (now Zimbabwe) and is known for stories about Africa and for the innovative novel *The Golden Notebook*?

    (A) Virginia Woolf
    (B) Doris Lessing
    (C) George Orwell
    (D) Margaret Atwood
    (E) E. M. Forster

46. Which of the following terms is used to describe literature that evokes a rural, simple, and idyllic life?

    (A) Pre-Raphaelite
    (B) Pastoral
    (C) Sentimental
    (D) Naturalistic
    (E) Platonic

47. In the old days she had come this way quite often, going down the hill on the tram with her girl friends, with nothing better in mind than a bit of window-shopping and a bit of a laugh and a cup of tea: penniless then as now, but still hopeful, still endowed with a touching faith that if by some miracle she could buy a pair of nylons or a particular blue lace blouse or a new brand of lipstick, then deliverance would be granted to her in the form of money, marriage, romance, the visiting prince who would glimpse her in the crowd, glorified by that seductive blouse, and carry her off to a better world.

    In this passage, the protagonist remembers herself as having been

    (A) embittered
    (B) baffled
    (C) contentedly alone
    (D) carefree
    (E) naïvely optimistic

Questions 48–50 are based on the following lines.

By heaven, methinks it were an easy leap
To pluck bright honor from the pale-faced moon,
Or dive into the bottom of the deep,
Line Where fathom line could never touch the ground,
(5) And pluck up drowned honor by the locks,
So he that doth redeem her thence might wear
Without corrival all her dignities;

48. Lines 3–7 depend for their effect on

 (A) allusion
 (B) personification
 (C) antithesis
 (D) parallelism
 (E) simile

49. The lines suggest that their speaker is

 (A) bold and reckless
 (B) pensive and melancholy
 (C) grim and indifferent
 (D) anxious and cowardly
 (E) cold and scheming

50. The lines were written by

 (A) William Shakespeare
 (B) Christopher Marlowe
 (C) John Milton
 (D) Percy Bysshe Shelley
 (E) Lord Byron

51. To anyone who questioned the effectiveness of the loyalty oaths, he replied that people who really did owe allegiance to their country would be proud to pledge it as often as he forced them to.

The excerpt above provides an example of

 (A) parody
 (B) pathos
 (C) propaganda
 (D) irony
 (E) harangue

52. An episodic narrative, usually told from the first-person point of view and detailing the misadventures, escapades, and pranks of a roguish but likable hero of humble means who survives by his wits, is known as a

 (A) mock epic
 (B) roman à clef
 (C) novel of manners
 (D) picaresque novel
 (E) romance

53. Remember that I am thy creature: I ought to be thy Adam; but I am rather the fallen angel, whom thou drivest from joy for no misdeed. Every where I see bliss, from which I alone am irrevocably excluded. I was benevolent and good; misery made me a fiend. Make me happy, and I shall again be virtuous.

The passage is from which of the following works?

 (A) John Milton's *Paradise Lost*
 (B) Mary Shelley's *Frankenstein*
 (C) Emily Brontë's *Wuthering Heights*
 (D) Robert Louis Stevenson's *Dr. Jekyll and Mr. Hyde*
 (E) Bram Stoker's *Dracula*

54. Which of the following works does NOT portray characters from Arthurian legend?

(A) *Sir Gawain and the Green Knight*

(B) *Morte D'Arthur*

(C) *The Faerie Queene*

(D) *Visions of the Daughters of Albion*

(E) *Idylls of the King*

55. The typical theater was a structure, circular or polygonal in shape, built around an open court or "pit," into which projected a rectangular raised platform. In the pit and on three sides of the platform stood the "groundlings." The more well-to-do members of the audiences paid a higher admission fee and sat in the tiers of galleries that surrounded the pit and that were partitioned off into "boxes."

The type of theater described above was first developed during the reign of

(A) Richard II

(B) Henry VIII

(C) Elizabeth I

(D) George III

(E) Victoria

56. In the nineteenth century, novels published in parts over several weeks or months were known as

(A) epistolary novels

(B) chronicles

(C) social novels

(D) vignettes

(E) serialized novels

57. To whom, then, *must* I dedicate my wonderful, surprising & interesting adventures?—to *whom* dare I reveal my private opinion of my nearest relations? The secret thoughts of my dearest friends? My own hopes, fears, reflections & dislikes—Nobody!

To Nobody, then, will I write my journal! Since to Nobody can I be wholly unreserved—to Nobody can I reveal every thought, every wish of my heart, with the most unlimited confidence, the most unremitting sincerity to the end of my life! For what chance, what accident can end my connections with Nobody? No secret *can* I conceal from No-body, & to No-body can I be *ever* unreserved. Disagreement cannot stop our affection, time itself has no power to end our friendship.

The tone of this opening entry in an eighteenth-century personal journal is best characterized as

(A) argumentative

(B) playful

(C) hesitant

(D) resigned

(E) joyful

Questions 58–59 are based on the following.

The family of Dashwood had been long settled in Sussex. Their estate was large, and their residence was at Norland Park, in the centre of
Line their property, where for many generations they
(5) had lived in so respectable a manner as to engage the general good opinion of their surrounding acquaintance. The late owner of this estate was a single man, who lived to a very advanced age, and who for many years of his
(10) life had a constant companion and housekeeper in his sister. But her death, which happened ten years before his own, produced a great alteration in his home; for to supply her loss, he invited and received into his house the family of his
(15) nephew, Mr. Henry Dashwood, the legal inheritor of the Norland estate, and the person to whom he intended to bequeath it. In the society of his nephew and niece, and their children, the old gentleman's days were
(20) comfortably spent. His attachment to them all increased. The constant attention of Mr. and Mrs. Henry Dashwood to his wishes, which proceeded not merely from interest, but from goodness of heart, gave him every degree of
(25) solid comfort which his age could receive; and the cheerfulness of the children added a relish to his existence.

58. The passage is the opening of a novel by which of the following authors?

(A) Daniel Defoe

(B) Jane Austen

(C) Charles Dickens

(D) Matthew G. Lewis

(E) Mary Shelley

59. As characterized in the passage, the "late owner" (line 7) is best described as

(A) content

(B) open-minded

(C) dutiful

(D) lonesome

(E) demanding

Questions 60–61 are based on the following poem.

What's silver and a house to me
If I with my own love agree?
Any old coat would do to cover
Line Us from the nights, alive, aglow;
(5) But all are cold who lack a lover.
Time is like the falling snow.

Though he tell me yet again
And a hundred times in vain
For his going is good reason,
(10) How can barren Reason know
Love's mysterious tide and season.
Time is like the falling snow.

He may meet another there,
Forget that I am fond and fair:
(15) Absent faces lose their colour
Lacking scope for love to grow,
Mind estranged and memory duller.
Time is like the falling snow.

One song have I at daybreak heard
(20) From the throat of the waking bird.
Tell it in my true love's chamber,
Tell him truth: *None can blow*
Fire from the fading ember:
Time is like the falling snow.

60. In line 23, "ember" represents

(A) a state of despair

(B) a newfound love

(C) a desire for happiness

(D) a remnant of love

(E) an inspiration to others

61. In the course of the poem, the tone shifts from

(A) celebration to apprehension

(B) meditation to reproach

(C) hope to anger

(D) affection to disdain

(E) reserve to confession

62. The concept of "people" better expressed by the Spanish "pueblo" is fast vanishing. The writer who returns from exile at the metropolitan centre to "write for his people"; to seek with them to "break out of identity imposed by alien circumstances," and to find a new one, must come face to face with the fact that his "people" has become the "public." And the public in the Caribbean, equally like the public in the great metropolitan centres, are being conditioned through television, radio and advertising, to want what the great Corporations of production in the culture industry, as in all others, have conditioned them to want. Returning from exile at the metropolitan centre, the writer all too often finds that he returns only to . . . another facet of exile. Yet by not returning, the writer continues to accept his irrelevance.

In the excerpt, the author is primarily concerned with

(A) describing the sacrifices required by rural living

(B) highlighting a challenge that a Caribbean writer faces

(C) advocating more tolerance among the general public

(D) denouncing the television, radio, and advertising industries

(E) defining the meaning of the term "people"

63. Then she had three years of great labor with temptations which she bore as meekly as she could, thanking Our Lord for all His gifts, and was as merry when she was reproved, scorned, and japed for Our Lord's love, and much more merry than she was beforetime in the worship of the world.

The passage is from which of the following works?

(A) Geoffrey Chaucer's *Troilus and Criseyde*

(B) William Langland's *Piers Plowman*

(C) Margery Kempe's *The Book of Margery Kempe*

(D) John Gower's *Confessio Amantis*

(E) Mary Wroth's *Pamphilia to Amphilanthus*

Directions: For the following group of questions, click on a choice, then click on the appropriate box.

64. Match each of the following poets to the work that he or she wrote.

Wilfred Owen

Rupert Brooke

Edith Sitwell

	"The Soldier"
	"Anthem for Doomed Youth"
	"Still Falls the Rain"

65. Of the following five works, which three may be categorized as dystopian novels?

A Clockwork Orange

Half a Life

Brave New World

Things Fall Apart

1984

66. Identify the poets from the list below who collaborated in producing *Lyrical Ballads* (1798).

Samuel Taylor Coleridge

Percy Bysshe Shelley

William Blake

William Wordsworth

John Keats

67. Match each of the following poets to the work that he or she wrote.

Aphra Behn

Oliver Goldsmith

Samuel Johnson

Richard Sheridan

The Vicar of Wakefield

Oroonoko

The School for Scandal

A Dictionary of the English Language

Study Resources

Most textbooks used in college-level English literature courses cover the topics in the outline given earlier, but the approaches to certain topics and the emphases given to them may differ. To prepare for the English Literature exam, it is advisable to study one or more college textbooks, which can be found in most college bookstores. When selecting a textbook, check the table of contents against the knowledge and skills required for this test.

You should also read critically the contents of at least one literary anthology, many of which are used as textbooks in English or British literature courses at the college level.

Most textbook anthologies contain a representative sample of readings as well as discussions of historical background, literary styles and devices characteristic of various authors and periods, and other material relevant to the test. The anthologies do vary somewhat in content, approach, and emphasis, and you are therefore advised to consult more than one anthology as well as some specialized books on major authors, periods, and literary forms and terminology. You should also read some of the major novels that are mentioned or excerpted in the anthologies. You can probably obtain an extensive English or British literature reading list from a college English department, library, or bookstore.

Visit www.collegeboard.com/clepprep for additional English literature resources. You can also find suggestions for exam preparation in Chapter IV of the *Official Study Guide*. In addition, many college faculty post their course materials on their schools' Web sites.

Answer Key

1.	C	36.	B
2.	C	37.	D
3.	D	38.	C
4.	D	39.	C
5.	A	40.	B
6.	C	41.	C
7.	A	42.	E
8.	E	43.	C
9.	A	44.	B
10.	C	45.	B
11.	A	46.	B
12.	D	47.	E
13.	B	48.	B
14.	E	49.	A
15.	E	50.	A
16.	A	51.	D
17.	C	52.	D
18.	C	53.	B
19.	C	54.	D
20.	B	55.	C
21.	D	56.	E
22.	B	57.	B
23.	E	58.	B
24.	A	59.	A
25.	A	60.	D
26.	B	61.	A
27.	A	62.	B
28.	E	63.	C
29.	E	64.	2, 1, 3
30.	E	65.	5, 1, 3
31.	C		(any combination
32.	D		of these numbers)
33.	B	66.	1, 4 or 4, 1
34.	C	67.	2, 1, 4, 3
35.	C		

Freshman College Composition

Description of the Examination

The Freshman College Composition examination assesses skills required in most first-year college-level writing courses. It addresses elements of language and grammar; various types of writing, both formal and informal; and limited analysis and interpretation of short passages of prose and poetry. The examination assumes that candidates know the fundamental principles of rhetoric and can apply the principles of standard written English. In addition, the exam requires familiarity with the research paper and reference skills.

The Freshman College Composition exam also includes an optional essay section. Candidates should check with the college(s) of their choice to confirm whether the essay is required. This optional section requires candidates to demonstrate their ability to write clearly and effectively. Candidates respond to two essay topics, spending approximately 45 minutes on each essay. Faculty at the receiving institutions are responsible for scoring the essays; scoring instructions (scoring guide, commentary, and sample papers) are provided by CLEP to facilitate the process.

The examination contains approximately 90 questions to be answered in 90 minutes. Some of these are pretest questions that will not be scored. Any time candidates spend on tutorials or providing personal information is in addition to the actual testing time.

Knowledge and Skills Required

Questions on the Freshman College Composition examination measure students' writing skills both at the sentence level and within the context of passages. Elements of language and grammar, different styles of writing, and limited literary analysis of short prose and poetry selections are tested.

The subject matter of the Freshman College Composition examination is drawn from the following topics. The percentages next to the main topics indicate the approximate percentage of exam questions on that topic.

20% **Ability to Recognize and Use Standard Written English**

The examination measures candidates' awareness of a variety of logical, structural, and grammatical relationships within sentences. The questions test recognition of acceptable usage relating to the following:

- Syntax (parallelism, coordination, subordination, dangling modifiers)
- Sentence boundaries (comma splice, run-ons, sentence fragments)
- Recognition of correct sentences
- Sentence variety
- Concord/agreement (subject-verb; verb tense; pronoun reference, shift, number)
- Correct idiom
- Active/passive voice
- Logical comparison
- Punctuation

Two question formats are used to measure the skills above.

- **Identifying sentence errors**—Requires candidates to identify wording that violates the standard conventions of written discourse.
- **Improving sentences**—Requires candidates to choose the version of a phrase, clause, or sentence that best conveys the intended meaning of a sentence.

65% **Ability to Recognize Logical Development**

The examination measures recognition of the following in the context of works in progress (student drafts) or of published prose:

- Organization
- Evaluation of evidence
- Awareness of audience, tone, and purpose
- Level of detail
- Consistency of topic focus (sustaining coherence between paragraphs)

- Sentence variety
- Paragraph coherence
- Main idea, thesis
- Rhetorical effects and emphasis
- Use of language
- Evaluation of author's authority and appeal
- Evaluation of reasoning
- Shift in point of view

The following kinds of multiple-choice questions measure writing skills in context:

- **Revising Work in Progress**—Candidates identify ways to improve an early draft of an essay.
- **Analyzing Writing**—Two prose passages written in very different modes and a poetry selection appear in the examination. Candidates answer questions about each passage and poem and about strategies used by the author of each selection.
- **Analyzing and Evaluating Writers' Choices**—Candidates are given a short stimulus and must answer questions about tone, attitude, ambiguity, and clarity.

15%   **Ability to Use Resource Materials**

The examination tests familiarity with the following basic reference skills. Skills are tested both in context and in individual questions.

- Evaluating sources
- Integrating resource material into the research paper
- Manuscript format and documentation
- Reference skills
- Use of reference materials

Sample Test Questions

The following sample questions do not appear on an actual CLEP examination. They are intended to give potential test-takers an indication of the format and difficulty level of the examination and to provide content for practice and review. Knowing the correct answers to all of the sample questions is not a guarantee of satisfactory performance on the exam.

Identifying Sentence Errors

Directions: The following sentences test your knowledge of grammar, usage, diction (choice of words), and idiom.

Some sentences are correct.

No sentence contains more than one error.

You will find that the error, if there is one, is underlined and lettered. Assume that elements of the sentence that are not underlined are correct and cannot be changed. In choosing answers, follow the requirements of standard written English.

If there is an error, select the <u>one underlined part</u> that must be changed to make the sentence correct.

Example: **SAMPLE ANSWER**

<u>The other</u> delegates and   Ⓐ ● Ⓒ Ⓓ Ⓔ
   A

<u>him</u> <u>immediately</u> accepted
 B   C

the resolution <u>drafted by</u>
                D

the neutral states. <u>No error</u>
                E

---

1. Hydroelectric dams work <u>on a simple</u> principle:
                       A

  <u>the greater the</u> distance that the water has
      B

  <u>to fall</u>, the more the power that <u>was generated</u>.
    C   D

  <u>No error</u>
     E

2. Alexis <u>has discovered</u> that she can express her
          A

creativity more freely <u>through</u> her <u>sketches</u>
                B   C

<u>and not in</u> her photography. <u>No error</u>
  D   E

3. <u>To learn more</u> about Hispanic culture, we
   A

invited a <u>lecturer who</u> had spoken frequently
           B

<u>with regard of</u> <u>the life of</u> early settlers in
  C   D

Santa Fe. <u>No error</u>
        E

4. Language changes <u>perpetually</u>; <u>it is</u> like a living
             A   B

stream that, <u>even as</u> it is buffeted by many
         C

forces, <u>gathers</u> new strength from thousands
      D

of tributaries. <u>No error</u>
           E

5. <u>Although</u> a lottery may seem a <u>relatively easy</u>
  A   B

way for a state <u>to increase</u> revenues, <u>they</u> may
          C   D

encourage some individuals to gamble exces-

sively. <u>No error</u>
     E

6. <u>Even when using</u> a calculator, you must have
   A

a basic <u>understanding of</u> mathematics if
        B

<u>one expects</u> to solve complex problems
  C

<u>correctly</u>. <u>No error</u>
  D   E

7. Gwendolyn Brooks was <u>widely known</u> and
                  A

highly praised for her poetry, not many people
                B

<u>realize that</u> she <u>also</u> published a novel. <u>No error</u>
  C   D   E

8. Although science offers the hope <u>of preventing</u>
                          A

serious genetic diseases, <u>there is</u> difficult ethical
                  B

questions <u>raised by</u> the <u>possibility of</u> altering
        C   D

human heredity. <u>No error</u>
           E

9. If they <u>would have</u> known how capricious the
       A

winds on Lake Winasteke are, the boys would
                     B

have sailed in the <u>larger</u> of <u>their</u> two boats.
              C   D

<u>No error</u>
  E

10. Faulkner <u>had published</u> <u>only</u> a few novels when
         A   B

critics <u>seriously began</u> to compare his work to
        C

<u>Hemingway</u>. <u>No error</u>
  D   E

Improving Sentences

Directions: The following sentences test correctness and effectiveness of expression. In choosing answers, follow the requirements of standard written English: that is, pay attention to grammar, diction (choice of words), sentence construction, and punctuation.

In each of the following sentences, part of the sentence, or the entire sentence, is underlined. Beneath each sentence you will find five versions of the underlined part. Choice A repeats the original; the other four are different.

Choose the answer that best expresses the meaning of the original sentence. If you think the original is better than any of the alternatives, choose A; otherwise choose one of the others. Your choice should produce the most effective sentence—one that is clear and precise, without awkwardness or ambiguity.

Example: **SAMPLE ANSWER**

Laura Ingalls Wilder published her first book and she was sixty-five years old then.

(A) and she was sixty-five years old then

(B) when she was sixty-five

(C) being age sixty-five years old

(D) upon the reaching of sixty-five years

(E) at the time when she was sixty-five

---

11. In 1827 *Freedom's Journal* was the first African American newspaper in the United States, it was published in New York City.

(A) In 1827 *Freedom's Journal* was the first African American newspaper in the United States, it was published in New York City.

(B) In 1827 the first African American newspaper in the United States, *Freedom's Journal*, was published in New York City.

(C) In New York City in 1827 *Freedom's Journal,* the first African American newspaper in the United States, was published there.

(D) With publication in New York City in 1827, it was the first African American newspaper in the United States, *Freedom's Journal.*

(E) The first African American newspaper published in the United States was when there was *Freedom's Journal* in New York City in 1827.

12. Astronomers have extremely sophisticated instruments, which is helpful for measuring the properties of objects in space.

(A) instruments, which is helpful for measuring the properties of objects in space

(B) instruments to help measure the properties of objects in space

(C) instruments, which are helpful for measurement of space objects' properties

(D) instruments helpful to measure the properties of objects in space

(E) instruments, a help for measuring the properties of objects in space

13. Foreign correspondents are like migrating birds, resting for a few days, then flying off again to a new place.

(A) then flying off again

(B) after which again they fly off

(C) then they fly off again

(D) when once again they fly off

(E) but soon they are flying off again

14. Arguably one of the most distinctive regional cuisines in the United States, <u>the South is noted for such specialties as</u> Brunswick stew and hush puppies.

   (A) the South is noted for such specialties as

   (B) the South has such specialties of note as

   (C) the South includes among its note-worthy specialties

   (D) southern cooking includes such noteworthy specialties as

   (E) southern cooking is including such special-ties of note as

15. Today's fashion designers must consider both how much a fabric costs and <u>wearability</u>.

   (A) wearability

   (B) is it going to wear well

   (C) if it has wearability

   (D) how well it wears

   (E) the fabric's ability to wear well

16. Because the eleven women functioned as a <u>team is why they had a successful season</u>.

   (A) team is why they had a successful season

   (B) team, which was successful this season

   (C) team, they had a successful season

   (D) team, success was for them this season

   (E) team is why their season was a success

17. Home computers themselves are becoming less expensive, but software, printers, and Internet access <u>cause the total financial cost to rise up greatly</u>.

   (A) cause the total financial cost to rise up greatly

   (B) greatly increase the total cost

   (C) highly inflate the cost totals

   (D) up the expense

   (E) totally add to the expense

18. <u>Shaheen Khan, a compassionate teacher who fascinates children with</u> tales from her native Pakistan.

   (A) Shaheen Khan, a compassionate teacher who fascinates children with

   (B) Shaheen Khan is a compassionate teacher who fascinates children with

   (C) A compassionate teacher, Shaheen Khan, who fascinates children with

   (D) A compassionate teacher, children are fascinated by Shaheen Khan's

   (E) Children are fascinated by their compassionate teacher Shaheen Khan, she has

19. <u>Due to its habitat that is lost and intense poaching, wild tigers are in a precarious position.</u>

   (A) Due to its habitat that is lost and intense poaching, wild tigers are in a precarious position.

   (B) Due to habitat loss and intense poaching, they say wild tigers are in a precarious position.

   (C) Wild tigers, being in a precarious position due to losing their habitat and intense poaching.

   (D) Wild tigers are in a precarious position due to habitat loss and intense poaching.

   (E) Intense poaching and habitat loss, which is why wild tigers are in a precarious position.

20. In the past few years, oceanographers <u>will develop</u> new instruments and techniques that identify and count marine microorganisms.

   (A) will develop

   (B) will have developed

   (C) having developed

   (D) have developed

   (E) developing

21. <u>Aviva Imhov, an organic farmer who provides</u> vegetables and fruits for shopkeepers in her village in Southeast Asia.

   (A) Aviva Imhov, an organic farmer who provides

   (B) Aviva Imhov farms organically and providing

   (C) An organic farmer, Aviva Imhov provides

   (D) Farming organically, Aviva Imhov providing

   (E) Farming organically, Aviva Imhov, who provides

22. In July, scientists from Northland College in Wisconsin announced <u>that it was noticed that the rates of destruction of the ozone layer was slowing down.</u>

   (A) that it was noticed that the rates of destruction of the ozone layer was slowing down

   (B) that the rate of destruction of the ozone layer has slowed down noticeably

   (C) a noticeably slower rate that the ozone layer is being destroyed by

   (D) the rate, by which the ozone layer being destroyed, has noticeably slowed down

   (E) the ozone layer, the rate by which it is being destroyed, has noticeably slowed down

Revising Work in Progress

Directions: Each of the following selections is an early draft of student writing in which the sentences have been numbered for easy reference. Some parts of the selections need to be changed.

Read each selection and then answer the questions that follow. Some questions are about particular sentences or parts of sentences and ask you to improve sentence structure and diction (word choice). In making these decisions, follow the conventions of standard written English. Other questions refer to the entire essay or parts of the essay and ask you to consider organization, development, and effectiveness of language in relation to purpose and audience.

<u>**Questions 23–29**</u> are based on the following draft of a student essay that discusses shopping malls in the United States.

(1) Nothing epitomizes the disposable nature of American culture more than the sight of a deteriorating and underused shopping mall. (2) Each was at one time a gleaming embodiment of state-of-the-art consumerism. (3) Luring shoppers away from the urban shopping districts. (4) Just like supermarkets a few years earlier contributed to the drop of the mom-and-pop corner grocery store. (5) But the shelf life of even the most spectacular malls seems to be alarmingly short. (6) The laws of natural selection insist that every new mall will one day be relegated to obscurity and economic barrenness; it might have been trendy once.

(7) The mall is really a microcosm of the American economy. (8) In rapid succession Americans replace possessions that have worn out or gone out of style. (9) Then they see ads for new products to replace the ones they already have. (10) Our society has come to define durable goods as those that will last about three years. (11) This has manifested itself in both a high turnover of stores in shopping malls and a rush toward obsolescence of the malls themselves. (12) These abandoned structures seldom serve to remind us of the uncertain buttresses of our economy. (13) We are too busy searching for the newer, bigger, better mall deserving of our money and affection.

23. In context, which of the following is best to do with sentence 3 (reproduced below)?

Luring shoppers away from the urban shopping districts.

(A) Leave it as it is.

(B) Combine it with sentence 2.

(C) Delete it.

(D) Add "Therefore" before "luring".

(E) Place it after sentence 7.

24. In the context of the first paragraph, which is the best way to revise the phrase "Just like supermarkets" in sentence 4 ?

(A) In the same way, supermarkets

(B) In the same manner as supermarkets

(C) Just the way supermarkets

(D) Compared to supermarkets

(E) In addition, supermarkets

25. In context, the word that would best replace "drop" in sentence 4 is

(A) waste

(B) stagnation

(C) disappointment

(D) decline

(E) lambasting

26. In context, the phrase "shelf life" (sentence 5) is

(A) ineffective because it uses a cliché

(B) ineffective because it is too informal for an analysis

(C) effective because it symbolizes the causes for economic ills

(D) effective because it satirizes human greed

(E) effective because it suggests a comparison to perishable goods

27. In context, which of the following is the best version of the underlined portion of sentence 6 (reproduced below)?

The laws of natural selection insist that every new mall will one day be relegated to obscurity and economic barrenness; it might have been trendy once.

(A) (as it is now)

(B) mall will one day be relegated to obscurity and economic barrenness, and it was even trendy once

(C) trendy mall will be obscure and bare economically

(D) mall, regardless of how trendy it once was, will be relegated to obscurity and economic barrenness

(E) mall, once trendy, becomes obscure and bare economically

28. In the context of the second paragraph, which is the best way to revise the underlined portion of sentences 8 and 9 (reproduced below) in order to combine them?

In rapid succession Americans replace possessions that have worn out or gone out of style. Then they see ads for new products to replace the ones they already have.

(A) style; then see ads for new products to replace the ones they already have

(B) style, followed by tempting ads for new products to replace the ones they already have

(C) style, only to be lured by ads for new products to replace the ones they already have

(D) style, while replacing these products with new ones seen in ads

(E) style, then considering replacing these products because of ads they see

29. In the context of the paragraph, which is the best version of the underlined portion of sentence 11 (reproduced below)?

    This has manifested itself in both a high turnover of stores in shopping malls and a rush toward obsolescence of the malls themselves.

    (A) (As it is now)
    (B) These durable goods are found in
    (C) As a matter of fact, one sees
    (D) It is no surprise, then, that we see
    (E) Our society was responsible for

Questions 30–34 are based on the following early draft of a letter to the editor of a local newspaper.

(1) Our community needs more parks and play areas. (2) Living in a world where concrete surrounds us, it is important that we create places that are green and natural so that children can run and play. (3) It is possible to do much with little expense to the city. (4) An abandoned lot can become a big patch of green grass ideal for running games. (5) And buying expensive playground equipment and strange pieces of modern art for children to climb on is unnecessary. (6) Children will climb on anything if one lets them. (7) A large concrete pipe or an old truck with its wheels and doors removed makes an imaginative plaything. (8) Simply remove any part that may be breakable or unsafe, then paint the equipment with bright colors. (9) Bury the truck or pipe a foot or two deep so that it is stable. (10) Great opportunities for fun! (11) Children can play for hours, crawling through a secret tunnel or navigating to a distant planet. (12) Neighborhood committees could contribute other discards.

(13) We should do these things because children need oases in this concrete desert we live in. (14) This may take time, but if people get together and contribute both ideas and labor, much can be done successfully.

30. Which of the following is the best way to revise the underlined portion of sentence 2 (reproduced below)?

    Living in a world where concrete surrounds us, it is important that we create places that are green and natural so that children can run and play.

    (A) Living in a world where concrete surrounds us, the important thing is to
    (B) We live in a world where concrete surrounds us, it is important that we
    (C) Being surrounded by a world of concrete, it is important to
    (D) Surrounding us with a world of concrete, we need to
    (E) Surrounded by a world of concrete, we need to

31. Which of the following would best replace "And" at the beginning of sentence 5?

    (A) Furthermore,
    (B) Instead,
    (C) Despite this,
    (D) Nevertheless,
    (E) Excepting this,

32. The writer of the passage could best improve sentence 12 by

    (A) acknowledging drawbacks to suggestions
    (B) providing specific examples
    (C) including personal opinions
    (D) discussing other community problems
    (E) defining the idea of a neighborhood

33. In context, the best phrase to replace "do these things" in sentence 13 is

    (A) accomplish our intentions
    (B) help these children
    (C) consider other options
    (D) build these play areas
    (E) have new ideas

34. Which is the best version of the underlined portion of sentence 14 (reproduced below)?

    This may take time, <u>but if people get together and contribute</u> both ideas and labor, much can be done successfully.

    (A) (as it is now)
    (B) and if people get together and they contribute
    (C) but if people will get together and they will also contribute
    (D) but if people get together and they would have contributed
    (E) however, if people get together, also contributing

Ability to Use Resource Materials

Directions: The following questions test your familiarity with basic research and reference skills. For each question below, choose the best answer.

35. When a research paper's sources are cited in parentheses in the body of the text, which of the following is necessary?

    (A) A Works Cited list should appear at the end of the paper.
    (B) An Endnotes section and a Bibliography should appear at the end of the paper.
    (C) The word *"Ibid."* should be used when the source is cited more than once.
    (D) All publication information should be included the first time the source is cited.
    (E) A period should appear at the end of the sentence preceding the citation.

36. The best way to find current data for a research paper on long-term health care facilities is to

    (A) consult a medical textbook
    (B) look in indexes to journals and periodicals
    (C) go through recent issues of newspapers and magazines
    (D) search the Internet, using "health" as key word
    (E) check in a recent almanac

37. Siegfried Sassoon. "The Old Huntsman." *The Revised College Omnibus.* Ed. James D. McCallum. New York: Harcourt, Brace and Company, 1939. 87.

    The footnote given above shows that

    (A) the author of *The Revised College Omnibus* is James D. McCallum
    (B) *The Revised College Omnibus* is a periodical
    (C) "The Old Huntsman" is technically termed a subtitle
    (D) "The Old Huntsman" is the name of a book
    (E) Siegfried Sassoon wrote a work that appears in *The Revised College Omnibus*

38. When you consult a glossary in a book, you can expect to find

    (A) a list of other books the author has written
    (B) a biographical sketch of the author
    (C) a description of characters who appear in the book
    (D) a list of the books the author consulted
    (E) definitions of technical or unfamiliar words in the book

mag·net·ic \mag-'ne-tik\ *adj* (1611) 1: possessing an extraordinary power or ability to attract <a *magnetic* personality> 2a: of or relating to a magnet or to magnetism b: of, relating to, or characterized by the earth's magnetism c: magnetized or capable of being magnetized d: actuated by magnetic attraction — **mag·net·i·cal·ly** \-ti-k(-)l \ *adv_*

39. The sentence "Mesmer exerted a magnetic appeal over his student" illustrates which of the definitions of the word "magnetic"?

   (A) 1
   (B) 2 a
   (C) 2 b
   (D) 2 c
   (E) 2 d

40. Werlau, Maria C. "Foreign Investment in Cuba: The Limits of Commercial Engagement." *World Affairs*. 22 Sept. 1997. 1 June 2002 <http://www.elibrary.com/s/edumark/getdoc.cgi>.

   The date "22 Sept. 1997" is when

   (A) *World Affairs* was first published
   (B) the researcher accessed "Foreign Investment in Cuba: The Limits of Commercial Engagement" online
   (C) events described in "Foreign Investment in Cuba: The Limits of Commercial Engagement" took place
   (D) "Foreign Investment in Cuba: The Limits of Commercial Engagement" was published in *World Affairs*
   (E) a speech by Maria C. Werlau was given

41. To find a list of printed articles relevant to a given research topic, which of the following resources would be most helpful?

   (A) An almanac
   (B) An encyclopedia
   (C) A collection of abstracts
   (D) The directory of a professional organization
   (E) The published proceedings of a professional conference

42. Zimring, Franklin. Foreword. *Partisan Politics: An American Dilemma*. By James B. Jones. Chicago: U of Chicago P, 1987. vi-ix.

   The bibliographic entry above shows that

   (A) Franklin Zimring edited *Partisan Politics: An American Dilemma*
   (B) *Partisan Politics: An American Dilemma* is a journal
   (C) the foreword to *Partisan Politics: An American Dilemma* appears on pages vi-ix
   (D) James B. Jones wrote the foreword to *Partisan Politics: An American Dilemma*
   (E) Jones and Zimring coauthored *Partisan Politics: An American Dilemma*

43. **flip-flop** n. (1600) 1. The movement or sound of repeated flapping. 2. A backward somersault or handspring. 3. *INFORMAL* reversal, as of a stand or position: *a foreign policy flip-flop*. 4. A backless, often foam rubber sandal held to the foot at the big toe by means of a thong. 5. *Electronics* An electronic circuit or mechanical device capable of assuming either of two stable states, especially a computer circuit used to store a single bit of information.—**flip-flop** v.

   All of the following statements about the word defined above are true EXCEPT:

   (A) The word can be used in formal writing.
   (B) The word was first used in the twentieth century.
   (C) The word has a specific scientific meaning.
   (D) The noun and verb versions of the word are spelled the same.
   (E) The word can refer to both a movement and an object.

Analyzing Writing

Directions: Each of the following passages consists of numbered sentences. Because the passages are parts of longer writing samples, they do not necessarily constitute a complete discussion of the issues presented.

Read each passage carefully and answer the questions that follow it. The questions test your awareness of a writer's purpose and of characteristics of prose that are important to good writing.

<u>Questions 44–47</u> refer to the following passage.

(1) The place called the Great Plains spreads southward from the upper Saskatchewan River down to the Rio Grande—a high country, a big country of vast reaches, tremendous streams, and stories of death on the ridges, derring-do in the valleys, and the sweetness and heartbreak of spring-time on the prairies. (2) Half of this geographical area was the old Nebraska Territory that lay like a golden hackberry leaf in the sun, a giant curling, tilted leaf. (3) The veins of it were the long streams rising out near the mountains and flowing eastward to the Big Muddy, the wild Missouri. (4) The largest that cut through the center of the Plains was the broad, flat-watered Platte, usually pleasant and easygoing as an October day, and below it the Republican, deceptively limpid but roaring into sudden gullywashers that flooded all the wide valley and could sweep away even the most powerful of the wilderness herds.

44. The language, style, and subject of the passage suggest that it can best be classified as

(A) a narrative episode

(B) an expository statement

(C) a descriptive piece

(D) an exclamatory tribute

(E) a rational argument

45. The effect of the second paragraph depends most heavily on the use of

(A) irony

(B) understatement

(C) reasoned argument

(D) imagery and simile

(E) dramatic exaggeration

46. As used in the last sentence, "limpid" most nearly means

(A) calm

(B) cool

(C) troublesome

(D) destructive

(E) beautiful

47. In the second paragraph, the description of the leaf suggests the

(A) barrenness of the dry land

(B) topography of the territory

(C) rich forest of the river valleys

(D) changes caused by the seasons

(E) vigor of life throughout the land

Questions 48–52 refer to the following passage.

(1) So we have to ask: are the new powers offered us by technology, powers the mass media share in, really helping us to move toward the ideal society in which we can, without metaphor, speak of a common mind? (2) It is, of course, easy to say; but of certain dangers we can already be aware. (3) One danger is that of crudity in our judgments of other people, their actions, and their achievements. (4) With so much information pouring in about the mistakes, misdeeds, and misfortunes of complete strangers, we are tempted to take the latest news at its face value and to accept uncritically the snap judgments that go with hastily delivered reports. (5) Would we want other people to sum up our problems and propensities as hurriedly as we are prepared to sum up theirs? (6) I doubt it.

(7) Another hazard which besets the mass media is what I call one-way communication. (8) If I witness a road accident on the highway, I may be in a position to help in some way—perhaps by administering first aid or telephoning for an ambulance if someone is seriously hurt. (9) But if I see on the television some horror scene from Somalia, Belfast, or Bosnia, there is little or nothing I can do to mitigate the pain of the victims. (10) Repeated experiences of this kind can hardly fail to dull my sensitivity to the misfortunes of others, or worse still, to replace a genuine compassion by a morbid and irresponsible curiosity. (11) One cannot maintain for long a sense of responsibility if one lacks the power to fulfill it.

48. The phrase "a common mind" in sentence 1 is most probably used to mean

    (A) the participation by everyone in the judicial and political decisions of a society
    (B) tolerance of every action by every member of a society
    (C) access for everyone to data banks of personal information
    (D) an informed understanding shared by all members of a society
    (E) the cooperation among nations to achieve equality for all people

49. As used in sentence 3, "crudity" is best interpreted to mean

    (A) vulgarity
    (B) inexactness
    (C) baseness
    (D) rawness
    (E) injustice

50. Which of the following best summarizes the central subject of the passage?

    (A) Technology and cultural pluralism
    (B) Inherent corruption in modern civilization
    (C) The power of hastily formed opinions
    (D) Latent dangers in modern mass communication
    (E) Human indifference

51. By shifting from the use of "we" in the first paragraph to the use of "I" in the second paragraph, the author does which of the following?

    (A) Changes from impersonal generalization to personal confession
    (B) Extends the argument through hypothetical personal example
    (C) Presents a variety of points of view
    (D) Stops editorializing and starts citing cases
    (E) Establishes a contrast between two points of view

52. According to the speaker, repeated depictions of scenes of death and disaster may produce which of the following in viewers?

    (A) Apathy
    (B) Compassion
    (C) Empathy
    (D) Disdain
    (E) Repulsion

Questions 53–57 refer to the following passage.

(1) Michael Goldman wrote in a poem, "When the Muse comes She doesn't tell you to write;/She says get up for a minute, I've something to show you, stand here." (2) What made me look up at that roadside tree?

(3) The road to Grundy, Virginia, is, as you might expect, a narrow scrawl scribbled all over the most improbably peaked and hunched mountains you ever saw. (4) The few people who live along the road also seem peaked and hunched. (5) But what on earth. . .? (6) It was a hot, sunny summer. (7) The road was just bending off sharply to the right. (8) I hadn't seen a house in miles, and none was in sight. (9) At the apogee of the road's curve grew an enormous oak, a massive oak 200 years old, 150 feet high, an oak whose lowest limb was beyond the span of the highest ladder. (10) I looked up; there were clothes spread all over the tree. (11) Red shirts, blue trousers, black pants, little baby smocks—they weren't hung from branches. (12) They were outside, carefully spread, splayed as if to dry, on the outer leaves of the great oak's crown. (13) Were there pillowcases, blankets? (14) I can't remember. (15) There was a gay assortment of cotton underwear, yellow dresses, children's green sweaters, plaid skirts. . . . (16) You know roads. (17) A bend comes and you take it, thoughtlessly, moving on. (18) I looked behind me for another split second, astonished; both sides of the tree's canopy, clear to the top, bore clothes.

53. Which of the following best describes the relationship between the two paragraphs in the passage?

(A) The second paragraph answers the question at the end of the first.

(B) The second paragraph offers a concrete illustration of the quotation in the first.

(C) The second paragraph takes an opposite point of view from the first.

(D) The second paragraph generalizes about the quotation in the first.

(E) The second paragraph is an elaborate contradiction of the thesis in the first.

54. Which of the following most accurately describes what happens in the second paragraph?

(A) The speaker has a poetic vision symbolizing cleansing renewal.

(B) The speaker has a hallucination brought on by the heat.

(C) The speaker tries to explain how the phenomenon was accomplished.

(D) The speaker sees a tree full of flowers and imagines they are someone's washing.

(E) The speaker sees a large tree strikingly covered with clothes spread to dry.

55. The descriptive details in sentences 9–15 provide a

(A) precise visual image

(B) picture of something unearthly

(C) representation of a blur of color

(D) view from a child's perspective

(E) distorted sense of motion

56. Which of the following pairs of words best describes the speaker's reaction to the experience?

(A) Ecstasy and fear

(B) Dismay and wonder

(C) Delight and fear

(D) Disgust and disbelief

(E) Wonder and delight

57. The main implication of the passage is that

(A) people should be more observant as they travel country roads

(B) people are resourceful in finding ways to rise above domestic tasks

(C) inspiration or vision is often a matter of chance or caprice

(D) the poet sees more intensely than other people

(E) the Muse encourages only the eccentric to write

Analyzing and Evaluating Writers' Choices

Directions: The following questions test your ability to analyze and evaluate writers' choices. For each question below, choose the best answer.

Questions 58–59 refer to the following poem.

> From the road looking to the hill I saw
> One hollow house hunched in the shoulder.
> Windows blinded in a level sun
> Stared with not random malice,
> Though I had not been in that place.

58. To the speaker, the house is

   (A) foreboding
   (B) quaint
   (C) majestic
   (D) cheerful
   (E) tranquil

59. That the house's windows are "blinded in a level sun" indicates that the

   (A) windows in the abandoned house are broken
   (B) setting for the poem is about noontime
   (C) sun is low on the horizon
   (D) speaker feels the warmth of the sun
   (E) word "sun" plays on the word "son"

60. The controversy was a bitter one, but reasonable compromise <u>alleviated</u> some of the ill will.

   Which of the following best captures the meaning of the underlined word above?

   (A) Spared
   (B) Delayed
   (C) Eased
   (D) Made obvious
   (E) Militated against

61. Anita <u>pays attention to</u> details.

   Which of the following substitutions for the underlined words most emphatically presents a negative picture of Anita?

   (A) is finicky about
   (B) focuses on
   (C) handles
   (D) likes to deal with
   (E) is very exact about

62. He told Henry that his package would arrive tomorrow.

   Which of the following is a correct revision of the ambiguous sentence above?

   (A) That "his" package would arrive tomorrow is what Henry told him.
   (B) He told Henry that it was his package that would arrive tomorrow.
   (C) He said to Henry "that your package will arrive tomorrow."
   (D) "Henry, your package will arrive tomorrow," he said.
   (E) "Henry," he said, "tomorrow will be arriving the package."

Questions 63–64 refer to the following excerpts.

(A) When will it all end? The idiocy and the tension, the dying of young people, the destruction of homes and of cities, the starvation, exhaustion and disease, the children parentless and lost, the endless pounding of the battle line.

(B) Yet let us begin today as though the millennium were tomorrow, and start "Village Improvement Parade" down Main Street, and turn the corner east toward the rising sun to a land of clear picture and young hearts.

(C) We assume too much, we assume what cannot be assumed. We see dots so we connect them with lines and we claim to know what the lines and dots signify.

(D) Sleep came at last, vague fumbling sleep, and his mind rolled in it, pushed and drawn and split in dreams, smoky shards of dream, reconstructions, recollections.

(E) Clevenger was guilty, of course, or he would not have been accused, and since the only way to prove it was to find him guilty, it was their patriotic duty to do so.

63. In which excerpt does the speaker's tone convey a profound urgency?

64. In which excerpt is the tone sarcastic?

Questions 65–66 refer to the following excerpt.

The two speech writers were amused by the contrast between the two speakers. The press-club president had edited her speech heavily, changing the phrases "in a nutshell" to "to summarize" and "a man needing no introduction" to "someone well known to this audience." The governor, in turn, had delivered a major policy speech without even reviewing the speech writer's text. "That was a bit of a risk," said the first speech writer. "That was bungee jumping!" said the second.

65. The two changes that the press-club president made were in an effort to avoid

(A) irony
(B) clichés
(C) sexist language
(D) metaphor
(E) jargon

66. The second speech writer makes use of all of the following in the final statement EXCEPT

(A) metaphor
(B) exclamatory tone
(C) structure parallel to that of the first speech writer
(D) hyperbole
(E) speculation

Optional Essay Section

The optional essay section of the Freshman College Composition Examination requires candidates to demonstrate their ability to write clearly and effectively. Candidates respond to two essay topics, spending approximately 45 minutes on each essay. These essays are administered on paper in test booklets. Local faculty score the essays. Below is an example of a possible essay topic.

Sample Topic

We have come to believe that successful leaders must be grand heroic figures with grand heroic egos. But this notion distorts the meaning of leadership, making it dependent on style rather than substance. In fact, leaders do not have to have a grand style in order to do their jobs well. They do not even have to have bold visions. They simply have to know how to lead.

Write an essay in which you discuss the extent to which you agree or disagree with the statement above. Support your discussion with specific reasons and examples from your reading, experience, or observations.

Study Resources

To prepare for the Freshman College Composition exam, candidates can consult books that are typically used as reference books or textbooks for first-year English composition and rhetoric courses. The books in the first group include handbooks of grammar and manuals for writing papers and research papers. They offer guidance on the various elements of writing (sentences, paragraphs, essays) as well as examples illustrating acceptable usage and punctuation.

The books in the second group generally include examples of writing, usually written by professional writers but sometimes by student writers. The books in this group suggest ways to make writing interesting, effective, and suitable to a particular purpose. They provide examples of different kinds of writing and practice in reading comprehension.

Candidates are advised to visit a local college bookstore to determine which textbooks are used by the college for English composition and rhetoric courses. When selecting a textbook, they should check the table of contents against the knowledge and skills required for this test.

Visit www.collegeboard.com/clepprep for additional literature and writing resources. You can also find suggestions for exam preparation in Chapter IV of the *Official Study Guide*. In addition, many college faculty post their course materials on their schools' Web sites.

Answer Key

#		#	
1.	D	34.	A
2.	D	35.	A
3.	C	36.	B
4.	E	37.	E
5.	D	38.	E
6.	C	39.	A
7.	B	40.	D
8.	B	41.	C
9.	A	42.	C
10.	D	43.	B
11.	B	44.	C
12.	B	45.	D
13.	A	46.	A
14.	D	47.	B
15.	D	48.	D
16.	C	49.	B
17.	B	50.	D
18.	B	51.	B
19.	D	52.	A
20.	D	53.	B
21.	C	54.	E
22.	B	55.	A
23.	B	56.	E
24.	A	57.	C
25.	D	58.	A
26.	E	59.	C
27.	D	60.	C
28.	C	61.	A
29.	D	62.	D
30.	E	63.	A
31.	A	64.	E
32.	B	65.	B
33.	D	66.	E

Humanities

Description of the Examination

The Humanities examination tests general knowledge of literature, art, and music and the other performing arts. It is broad in its coverage, with questions on all periods from classical to contemporary and in many different fields: poetry, prose, philosophy, art, architecture, music, dance, theater, and film. The examination requires candidates to demonstrate their understanding of the humanities through recollection of specific information, comprehension and application of concepts, and analysis and interpretation of various works of art.

Because the exam is very broad in its coverage, it is unlikely that any one person will be well informed about all the fields it covers. The exam contains approximately 140 questions to be answered in 90 minutes. Some of these are pretest questions that will not be scored. Any time candidates spend on tutorials or providing personal information is in addition to the actual testing time.

For candidates with satisfactory scores on the Humanities examination, colleges may grant up to six semester hours (or the equivalent) of credit toward fulfillment of a distribution requirement. Some may grant credit for a particular course that matches the exam in content.

Note: This examination uses the chronological designations B.C.E. (before the common era) and C.E. (common era). These labels correspond to B.C. (before Christ) and A.D. (anno Domini), which are used in some textbooks.

Knowledge and Skills Required

Questions on the Humanities examination require candidates to demonstrate the abilities listed below, in the approximate percentages indicated. Some questions may require more than one of the abilities.

- Knowledge of factual information (authors, works, etc.) (50 percent of the examination)
- Recognition of techniques such as rhyme scheme, medium, and matters of style, and the ability to identify them as characteristics of certain writers, artists, schools, or periods (30 percent of the examination)
- Understanding and interpretation of literary passages and art reproductions that are likely to be unfamiliar to most candidates (20 percent of the examination)

The subject matter of the Humanities examination is drawn from the following topics. The percentages next to the topics indicate the approximate percentages of exam questions on those topics.

50%   Literature
- 10%   Drama
- 10–15% Poetry
- 15–20% Fiction
- 10%   Nonfiction (including philosophy)

50%   The Arts
- 20%   Visual arts: painting, sculpture, etc.
- 5%   Visual arts: architecture
- 15%   Performing arts: music
- 10%   Performing arts: film, dance, etc.

The exam questions, drawn from the entire history of art and culture, are fairly evenly divided among the following periods: Classical, Medieval and Renaissance, seventeenth and eighteenth centuries, nineteenth century, and twentieth century. At least 5–10 percent of the questions draw on other cultures, such as African, Asian, and Latin American. Some of the questions cross disciplines and/or chronological periods, and a substantial number test knowledge of terminology, genre, and style.

Note: Although the images that accompany some of the questions in this guide are printed in black and white, any works that are reproduced in the actual test will be in color.

Sample Test Questions

The following sample questions do not appear on an actual CLEP examination. They are intended to give potential test-takers an indication of the format and difficulty level of the examination and to provide content for practice and review. Knowing the correct answers to all of the sample questions is not a guarantee of satisfactory performance on the exam.

Directions: Each of the questions or incomplete statements below is followed by five suggested answers or completions. Select the one that is best in each case.

1. Often read as a children's classic, it is in reality a scathing indictment of human meanness and greed. In its four books, the Lilliputians are deranged, the Yahoos obscene.

   (A) *Tom Jones*
   (B) *David Copperfield*
   (C) *The Pilgrim's Progress*
   (D) *Gulliver's Travels*
   (E) *Alice in Wonderland*

2. Which of the following deals with the bigotry an anguished African American family faces when it attempts to move into an all-white suburb?

   (A) Eugene O'Neill's *Desire Under the Elms*
   (B) Arthur Miller's *Death of a Salesman*
   (C) Ossie Davis' *Purlie Victorious*
   (D) Edward Albee's *Who's Afraid of Virginia Woolf?*
   (E) Lorraine Hansberry's *A Raisin in the Sun*

3. Which of the following has as its central theme a boat journey up a river in Africa?

   (A) *Lord of the Flies*
   (B) *Middlemarch*
   (C) *Catch-22*
   (D) *Heart of Darkness*
   (E) *Vanity Fair*

4. Which of the following is often a symbol of new life arising from death?

   (A) A gorgon
   (B) The minotaur
   (C) A unicorn
   (D) A griffin
   (E) The phoenix

5. The lute is most similar to the modern

   (A) guitar
   (B) piano
   (C) violin
   (D) accordion
   (E) flute

6. The troubadours of the Middle Ages are best described as

   (A) poet-musicians
   (B) moralistic orators
   (C) freelance illustrators
   (D) character actors
   (E) religious philosophers

Erich Lessing/Art Resource, NY

7. The illustration shown above is an example of which of the following?

(A) Fresco
(B) Tapestry
(C) Bas-relief
(D) Mosaic
(E) Triptych

© Werner Forman/CORBIS

9. The figurine shown above is of which of the following origins?

(A) Mayan
(B) African
(C) Inuit
(D) Celtic
(E) Ancient Greek

Réunion des Musées Nationaux/
Art Resource, NY

8. The sculpture shown above is by

(A) Henry Moore
(B) Louise Nevelson
(C) Edgar Degas
(D) Gianlorenzo Bernini
(E) Auguste Rodin

Questions 10 –12 refer to the following lines.

(A) "Where the bee sucks there suck I
In a cowslip's bell I lie . . ."

(B) "Exult O shores and ring O bells! But I with
mournful tread
Walk the deck my Captain lies, Fallen cold
and dead."

(C) "Ring out, wild bells, to the wild sky."

(D) "O! what a noble mind is here o'erthrown:
And I . . . now see that noble and most
sovereign reason,
Like sweet bells jangled, out of tune and
harsh, . . ."

(E) "Oh, the bells, bells, bells!
What a tale their terror tells
Of Despair!
. . . Yet the ear, it fully knows,
By the twanging,
And the clanging, . . .
In the jangling,
And the wrangling . . ."

10. Which excerpt contains several examples of onomatopoeia?

11. Which is from *Hamlet?*

12. Which alludes to Abraham Lincoln's death?

Questions 13–15 refer to the following image.

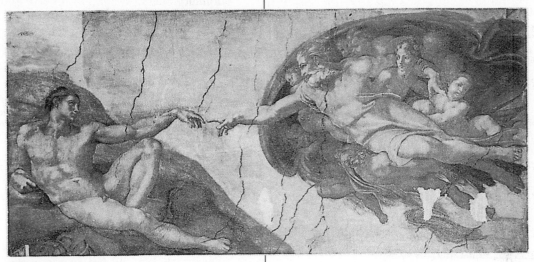

Bridgeman Art Library

13. The work pictured above is

   (A) a fresco
   (B) a stabile
   (C) a woodcut
   (D) an illumination
   (E) an etching

14. The theme of the work is the

   (A) sacrifice of Isaac
   (B) expulsion from Eden
   (C) reincarnation of Vishnu
   (D) creation of Adam
   (E) flight of Icarus

15. The work is located in the

   (A) Alhambra
   (B) Sistine Chapel
   (C) Parthenon
   (D) palace at Versailles
   (E) Cathedral of Notre-Dame

Questions 16–17 refer to the following descriptions of the stage settings of plays.

   (A) The exterior of a two-story corner building on a street in New Orleans which is named Elysian Fields and runs between the L and N tracks and the river

   (B) The living room of Mr. Vandergelder's house, over his hay, feed, and provision store in Yonkers, fifteen miles north of New York City

   (C) In, and immediately outside of, the Cabot Farmhouse in New England, in the year 1850

   (D) The stage of a theater; daytime

   (E) A room that is still called the nursery. . . . It is May, the cherry trees are in blossom, but in the orchard it is cold, with a morning frost.

16. Which is for a play by Tennessee Williams?

17. Which is for a play by Anton Chekov?

Questions 18–20 refer to the following people.

   (A) Georges Bizet, Wolfgang Amadeus Mozart, Richard Wagner

   (B) Robert Altman, Ingmar Bergman, Federico Fellini

   (C) John Cage, Aaron Copland, Paul Hindemith

   (D) Allen Ginsberg, Sylvia Plath, Gwendolyn Brooks

   (E) I. M. Pei, Ludwig Mies van der Rohe, Frank Lloyd Wright

18. Which is a group of architects?

19. Which is a group of composers of opera?

20. Which is a group of twentieth-century poets?

21. He believed that tragedy causes the proper purgation of those emotions of pity and fear which it has aroused.

   The author and concept referred to in the sentence above are

   (A) Plato . . . *hubris*

   (B) Gottfried Wilhelm Leibniz . . . *monad*

   (C) Aristotle . . . catharsis

   (D) John Locke . . . *tabula rasa*

   (E) Immanuel Kant . . . the categorical imperative

22. Which of the following composers was Picasso's closest musical contemporary?

   (A) Claudio Monteverdi

   (B) Franz Joseph Haydn

   (C) Frédéric Chopin

   (D) Igor Stravinsky

   (E) Ludwig van Beethoven

23. Which of the following satirizes the eighteenth-century doctrine "whatever is, is right" in this "best of all possible worlds"?

   (A) James Joyce's *Ulysses*

   (B) Voltaire's *Candide*

   (C) Daniel Defoe's *Moll Flanders*

   (D) Victor Hugo's *Les Miserables*

   (E) Nathaniel Hawthorne's *The Scarlet Letter*

24. Haiku is a form of Japanese

   (A) drama

   (B) poetry

   (C) pottery

   (D) sculpture

   (E) architecture

25. The terms "pas de deux," "plié," "tendu," and "glissade" are primarily associated with

(A) ballet
(B) string quartets
(C) painting
(D) theater
(E) opera

26. Which of the following terms describes a literary or dramatic form of discourse in which a character reveals thoughts in a monologue?

(A) Denouement
(B) Understatement
(C) Scenario
(D) Soliloquy
(E) Exposition

Questions 27–28 refer to the following symphony.

Mozart's *Symphony in D major, No. 35*, is divided into the following four parts.

   I. Allegro con spirito
   II. Andante
   III. Menuetto
   IV. Finale: presto

27. The parts are known as

(A) arias
(B) themes
(C) codas
(D) acts
(E) movements

28. Which two parts have the fastest tempos?

(A) I and II
(B) I and III
(C) I and IV
(D) II and III
(E) II and IV

29. *Brave New World, 1984*, and *The Handmaid's Tale* all deal with

(A) star-crossed lovers
(B) the problems of the aged
(C) extrasensory phenomena
(D) Platonic love
(E) dystopian futures

30. During his travels, his overexcited imagination invariably blinds him to reality; he thinks windmills are giants, flocks of sheep are armies, and galley slaves are oppressed gentlemen.

The sentence above describes

(A) Rasselas
(B) Robinson Crusoe
(C) Sir Lancelot
(D) Robin Hood
(E) Don Quixote

31. Which of the following, although he is sometimes called a tragic hero, is also recognized as the villain of John Milton's epic, *Paradise Lost*?

(A) Satan
(B) Gabriel
(C) Samson
(D) Adam
(E) Demigorgon

Questions 32–33 refer to the following.

(A) France during the French Revolution
(B) Russia during the Napoleonic Wars
(C) England during the Crimean War
(D) Germany during the First World War
(E) Spain during the Spanish Civil War

32. Which is the setting for most of the events in *A Tale of Two Cities*?

33. Which is the setting for events in *War and Peace*?

Bridgeman Art Library

34. The vase shown above was most likely created in

(A) South America
(B) the Pacific Islands
(C) Asia
(D) North America
(E) Africa

35. Grendel, "the mighty demon that dwelt in darkness," is a character in

(A) *The Sorrows of Young Werther*
(B) *Ivanhoe*
(C) *The Faerie Queene*
(D) *Beowulf*
(E) *The Canterbury Tales*

36. Which of the following writers is correctly matched with the literary form he or she frequently used?

(A) Saul Bellow . . . poetry
(B) Eugene O'Neill . . . the short story
(C) Walt Whitman . . . the novel
(D) Susan Sontag . . . drama
(E) Jonathan Edwards . . . the sermon

37. Choral music without instrumental accompaniment is known as

(A) improvisation
(B) a cappella
(C) atonality
(D) modulation
(E) harmony

38. *La Dolce Vita*, *La Strada*, and *8½* are films directed by

(A) Alfred Hitchcock
(B) Cecil B. De Mille
(C) Ingmar Bergman
(D) Robert Altman
(E) Federico Fellini

39. Artists associated with this nineteenth-century movement created images based on emotion, imagination, and the irrational.

Which of the following movements is referred to above?

(A) Romanticism
(B) Art Deco
(C) Art Nouveau
(D) Social realism
(E) Abstract expressionism

Questions 40–42 refer to the following periods in art and music history.

(A) Renaissance

(B) Baroque

(C) Romantic

(D) Impressionist

(E) Modern

40. To which period do Debussy and Renoir belong?

41. To which period do Leonardo and Palestrina belong?

42. To which period do Delacroix and Brahms belong?

43. Sometimes called a religion, sometimes referred to as "the religion of no religion," sometimes identified simply as "a way of life," its development can be traced from its origins in India in the sixth century B.C.E. to Japan in the twelfth century C.E. by way of China and Korea, and to the United States in the twentieth century.

To which of the following does the statement above refer?

(A) Hinduism

(B) Zen Buddhism

(C) Islam

(D) Confucianism

(E) Shintoism

44. *Giselle*, *La Bayadere*, and *Coppelia* are all

(A) ballets

(B) farces

(C) epics

(D) operettas

(E) oratorios

45. Flashback refers to

(A) the repetition of key elements of a drama

(B) a scene showing events that happened at an earlier time

(C) a rapidly changing series of images

(D) the lighting design for a play or movie

(E) the outcome of the main plot in a dramatic piece

46. Which of the following insists on the necessity of living a simple, natural, individualistic life?

(A) Henry Wadsworth Longfellow's *The Song of Hiawatha*

(B) Mark Twain's *A Connecticut Yankee in King Arthur's Court*

(C) Nathaniel Hawthorne's *The House of the Seven Gables*

(D) Henry David Thoreau's *Walden*

(E) Edgar Allan Poe's *The Raven*

Digital Image © The Museum of Modern Art/Licensed by SCALA/
Art Resource, NY

47. The painting shown above is

(A) James McNeill Whistler's *White Girl*
(B) Marc Chagall's *Around Her*
(C) Andrew Wyeth's *Christina's World*
(D) Henri Rousseau's *The Dream*
(E) Grant Wood's *American Gothic*

Questions 48–49 refer to the following descriptions of gods in Greek mythology.

(A) Son of Zeus and Hera, he is the god of fire and the forge.
(B) The god of revelry and wine, he later became patron of the theater.
(C) His daughter was born full-grown from his forehead.
(D) Euripides was the first to depict him with bow and arrow; in art, he was represented first as a youth and later as a small child.
(E) He is the god of the sun, the patron of poetry, and the ideal of male beauty.

48. Which describes Apollo?

49. Which describes Dionysus?

50. It was a school of the early twentieth century whose adherents designed buildings and objects in a functional style consistent with the era of mass production. Its use of industrial materials served as a basis for the International Style.

The school described above is known as

(A) Art Deco
(B) Bauhaus
(C) Neoclassicism
(D) the Baroque
(E) Cubism

51. **Question 51** refers to the following plays by William Shakespeare.

(A) *The Tempest*
(B) *Hamlet*
(C) *A Midsummer Night's Dream*
(D) *Macbeth*
(E) *Much Ado About Nothing*

Which two plays are tragedies?

(A) A and C
(B) A and E
(C) B and C
(D) B and D
(E) D and E

52. All of the following are percussion instruments EXCEPT

(A) the triangle
(B) the harp
(C) the gong
(D) tympani
(E) cymbals

Questions 53–55 refer to the following lines of poetry.

> Fear no more the heat o' the sun,
>   Nor the furious winter's rages;
> Thou thy worldly task hast done,
>   Home art gone, and ta'en thy wages:
> *Line*
> *(5)* Golden lads and girls all must,
> As chimney-sweepers, come to dust.
>
> Fear no more the frown o' the great;
>   Thou art past the tyrant's stroke;
> Care no more to clothe and eat;
> *(10)*   To thee the reed is as the oak:
> The scepter, learning, physic, must
> All follow this, and come to dust.
>
> Fear no more the lightning flash,
>   Nor the all-dreaded thunder stone;
> *(15)* Fear not slander, censure rash;
>   Thou hast finished joy and moan:
> All lovers young, all lovers must
> Consign to thee, and come to dust.

53. The rhyme scheme of each stanza is

   (A) aabbcc
   (B) ababab
   (C) aaaabb
   (D) abcabc
   (E) ababcc

54. The poem is addressed to

   (A) young lovers
   (B) doctors
   (C) kings
   (D) scholars
   (E) the dead

55. "To thee the reed is as the oak" (line 10) suggests that

   (A) distinctions no longer matter
   (B) little trees are as strong as big trees
   (C) all things change
   (D) ignorance causes fear
   (E) nature is unknowable

Werner Forman/Art Resource, NY

© Archivo Iconografico, S.A./CORBIS

56. The style of the statue shown above can best be described as

(A) African
(B) Mayan
(C) ancient Greek
(D) Qing Dynasty
(E) contemporary American

57. The painting shown above was created by

(A) John Constable
(B) William Blake
(C) Anthony Van Dyck
(D) Gilbert Stuart
(E) Aubrey Beardsley

58. Which is a group of novelists?

(A) Rita Dove, Marianne Moore,
    Adrienne Rich

(B) Meryl Streep, Glenn Close, Claire Bloom

(C) Toni Morrison, Doris Lessing,
    Isabel Allende

(D) Leontyne Price, Renée Fleming,
    Dawn Upshaw

(E) Diane Arbus, Margaret Bourke-White,
    Dorothea Lange

59. Two artists who used striking light and dark contrasts are

(A) Rembrandt van Rijn and Artemisia
    Gentileschi

(B) Sandro Botticelli and Sofonisba Anguissola

(C) Georges Seurat and Claude Monet

(D) Pablo Picasso and Georges Braque

(E) Michelangelo Buonarroti and Judith Leyster

Vassar College Art Gallery, Gift of Mrs. Charlotte Mahon, '11

60. The statue shown above belongs to which of the following historical periods?

(A) Ancient Egyptian

(B) Pre-Columbian

(C) Medieval European

(D) Eighteenth-century European

(E) Nineteenth-century American

61. Which is a group of composers?

 (A) Jacob Epstein, Käthe Kollwitz, Auguste Rodin
 (B) Maurice Ravel, Jacques Offenbach, Jules Massenet
 (C) Francois Truffaut, Jean-Luc Godard, Claude Chabrol
 (D) Claude Monet, Auguste Renoir, Berthe Morisot
 (E) Charles Lamb, Thomas De Quincey, John Ruskin

62. He composed in a wide variety of musical genres, including nine symphonies, 32 piano sonatas, and an opera. The composer is

 (A) Sergei Rachmaninoff
 (B) George Frideric Handel
 (C) Ralph Vaughan Williams
 (D) Gustav Mahler
 (E) Ludwig van Beethoven

63. A famous biographer and voluminous journal writer, the author was one of the most prolific in the eighteenth century. The writer is

 (A) Samuel Pepys
 (B) James Michener
 (C) James Boswell
 (D) Aphra Behn
 (E) Lord Chesterfield

64. An important structural innovation of Gothic architecture was the use of

 (A) post and lintel
 (B) catacombs
 (C) cantilevering
 (D) flying buttresses
 (E) Doric columns

65. Fagin, Pip, and Ebenezer Scrooge are characters created by

 (A) George Eliot
 (B) Elizabeth Barrett Browning
 (C) Sir Walter Scott
 (D) Edith Wharton
 (E) Charles Dickens

66. Which is a group of poets?

 (A) Percy Bysshe Shelley, S.T. Coleridge, John Donne
 (B) Henry Moore, Christo, Maya Lin
 (C) Martin Luther, John Calvin, John Knox
 (D) Sergey Eisenstein, Martin Scorsese, David Lynch
 (E) Arturo Toscanini, Pierre Boulez, Georg Solti

Questions 67–69 refer to the following excerpt from a play.

> The quality of mercy is not strain'd,
> It droppeth as the gentle rain from heaven
> Upon the place beneath: it is twice blest;
> *Line* It blesseth him that gives and him that takes:
> *(5)* 'Tis mightiest in the mightiest: it becomes
> The throned monarch better than his crown;
> His sceptre shows the force of temporal power,
> The attribute to awe and majesty,
> Wherein doth sit the dread and fear of kings;
> *(10)* But mercy is above this sceptred sway;
> It is enthroned in the hearts of kings . . . .

67. Lines 1–3 use which of the following figures of speech?

 (A) Alliteration
 (B) Simile
 (C) Onomatopoeia
 (D) Hyperbole
 (E) Apostrophe

68. Which of the following is closest in meaning to "becomes" in line 5?

    (A) Reaches
    (B) Develops
    (C) Happens
    (D) Suits
    (E) Grows

69. The lines are spoken by

    (A) Portia in *The Merchant of Venice*
    (B) Cleopatra in *Antony and Cleopatra*
    (C) Desdemona in *Othello*
    (D) Katherine in *The Taming of the Shrew*
    (E) Rosalind in *As You Like It*

70. The work of the artist Giotto strongly influenced which of the following?

    (A) Ancient Roman sculpture
    (B) Persian miniatures
    (C) Early Renaissance painting
    (D) European Romantic painting
    (E) American Colonial folk art

71. Pablo Picasso and Georges Braque are associated with which art movement?

    (A) German Expressionism
    (B) Fauvism
    (C) Futurism
    (D) Surrealism
    (E) Cubism

72. Ragtime, marching band music, and the blues all strongly influenced which form of music?

    (A) Country music
    (B) Silent film scores
    (C) Rap
    (D) Jazz
    (E) Gospel

73. Originally composed in 1928 as a ballet, this one-movement composition is Maurice Ravel's most famous. The work described is

    (A) *Bolero*
    (B) *Firebird*
    (C) *Porgy and Bess*
    (D) *Rhapsody in Blue*
    (E) *The Unanswered Question*

74. George Bernard Shaw's *Pygmalion* was the basis for which movie?

    (A) *Cat on a Hot Tin Roof*
    (B) *My Fair Lady*
    (C) *Who's Afraid of Virginia Woolf?*
    (D) *Ben Hur*
    (E) *Doctor Zhivago*

75. *A Farewell to Arms*, *The Naked and the Dead*, and *The Things They Carried* share a thematic focus on

    (A) greed and consumerism
    (B) famous shipwrecks
    (C) dignity and loss in time of war
    (D) the Great Depression
    (E) the difficulties of adolescence

76. The *Decameron* was written by

    (A) Ovid
    (B) Virgil
    (C) Giovanni Boccaccio
    (D) Dante
    (E) Sir Thomas Malory

77. Which of the following correctly pairs a novelist with a work she created?

    (A) Jane Austen . . . *The Mill on the Floss*
    (B) Emily Brontë . . . *Evelina*
    (C) George Eliot . . . *Wuthering Heights*
    (D) Fanny Burney . . . *Persuasion*
    (E) Charlotte Brontë . . . *Jane Eyre*

78. The terms "adagio," "cadenza," and "opus" are all associated with

    (A) music
    (B) theater
    (C) painting
    (D) sculpture
    (E) poetry

79. A composer and organist of the Baroque period, he created such works as the *Brandenburg Concerti*, the *Goldberg Variations*, and the *Well-Tempered Clavier*. The composer described is

    (A) Franz Joseph Haydn
    (B) Hector Berlioz
    (C) Franz Schubert
    (D) Johann Sebastian Bach
    (E) Ludwig van Beethoven

80. What is the correct chronological order of the following composers?

    I. George Frideric Handel
    II. Philip Glass
    III. Franz Liszt

    (A) I, II, III
    (B) I, III, II
    (C) II, I, III
    (D) II, III, I
    (E) III, I, II

81. Which of the following is a nineteenth-century artist who was influenced by Japanese prints and is known as both a painter and a printmaker?

    (A) Salvador Dalí
    (B) Thomas Gainsborough
    (C) Henri Matisse
    (D) Mary Cassatt
    (E) Georgia O'Keeffe

82. Born in Africa and brought to the United States as a slave as a young child, she was taught to read and write by her slaveholders and published her first poem at the age of 12. She was the first African American to publish a book and the first African American woman to earn a living from her writing.

    The poet described is

    (A) Edna St. Vincent Millay
    (B) Sylvia Plath
    (C) Phyllis Wheatley
    (D) Emily Dickinson
    (E) Marianne Moore

83. The American Civil War is the setting for a novel by

    (A) Stephen Crane
    (B) Ernest Hemingway
    (C) Booth Tarkington
    (D) John Dos Passos
    (E) Joseph Heller

84. *Tartuffe*, *The Misanthrope*, and *The Bourgeois Gentleman* are all comedies written by

    (A) Gustave Flaubert
    (B) Henrik Ibsen
    (C) Victor Hugo
    (D) Molière
    (E) August Strindberg

85. Which of the following is the most famous example of a structure built as a Christian church and later converted to a mosque?

    (A) Alhambra palace in Granada, Spain
    (B) Mosque of Selim II in Edirne, Turkey
    (C) Hagia Sophia in Istanbul, Turkey
    (D) The ziggurat in Ur, Iraq
    (E) Dome of the Rock in Jerusalem, Israel

Study Resources

Most textbooks used in college-level humanities courses cover the topics in the outline given earlier, but the approaches to certain topics and the emphases given to them may differ. To prepare for the Humanities exam, it is advisable to study one or more college textbooks, which can be found in most college bookstores. When selecting a textbook, check the table of contents against the knowledge and skills required for this test.

To do well on the Humanities exam, you should know something about each of the forms of literature and fine arts from the various periods and cultures listed earlier, in the paragraph following the examination percentages. No single book covers all these areas, so it will be necessary for you to refer to college textbooks, supplementary reading, and references for introductory courses in literature and fine arts at the college level. Two such resources are: Philip E. Bishop, *Adventures in the Human Spirit*, 5th edition, Upper Saddle River, NJ: Prentice Hall, 2007 and Henry M. Sayre, *The Humanities: Culture, Continuity, and Change*, Volumes I and II, Upper Saddle River, NJ: Prentice Hall, 2007.

In addition to reading, a lively interest in the arts— going to museums and concerts, attending plays, seeing motion pictures, watching public television programs such as *Great Performances* and *Masterpiece Theatre*, and listening to radio stations that play classical music and feature discussions of the arts—constitutes excellent preparation.

Visit www.collegeboard.com/clepprep for additional humanities resources. You can also find suggestions for exam preparation in Chapter IV of the *Official Study Guide*. In addition, many college faculty post their course materials on their schools' Web sites.

Answer Key

1.	D	44.	A
2.	E	45.	B
3.	D	46.	D
4.	E	47.	C
5.	A	48.	E
6.	A	49.	B
7.	C	50.	B
8.	E	51.	D
9.	A	52.	B
10.	E	53.	E
11.	D	54.	E
12.	B	55.	A
13.	A	56.	A
14.	D	57.	D
15.	B	58.	C
16.	A	59.	A
17.	E	60.	C
18.	E	61.	B
19.	A	62.	E
20.	D	63.	C
21.	C	64.	D
22.	D	65.	E
23.	B	66.	A
24.	B	67.	B
25.	A	68.	D
26.	D	69.	A
27.	E	70.	C
28.	C	71.	E
29.	E	72.	D
30.	E	73.	A
31.	A	74.	B
32.	A	75.	C
33.	B	76.	C
34.	C	77.	E
35.	D	78.	A
36.	E	79.	D
37.	B	80.	B
38.	E	81.	D
39.	A	82.	C
40.	D	83.	A
41.	A	84.	D
42.	C	85.	C
43.	B		

French Language

Description of the Examination

The French Language examination is designed to measure knowledge and ability equivalent to that of students who have completed two to four semesters of college French language study. It focuses on skills typically acquired from the end of the first year through the second year of college study; material taught during both years is incorporated into a single exam.

The examination contains approximately 121 questions to be answered in 90 minutes. Some of these are pretest questions that will not be scored. There are three separately timed sections. The three sections are weighted so that each question contributes equally to the total score. Any time candidates spend on tutorials or providing personal information is in addition to the actual testing time.

Most colleges that award credit for the French Language examination award either two or four semesters of credit, depending on the candidate's score on the exam.

Knowledge and Skills Required

Candidates must demonstrate their ability to understand spoken and written French. The CLEP French Language examination tests their listening and reading skills through the various types of questions listed below. The percentages indicate the approximate percentage of exam questions devoted to each type of question.

15% **Section I:**
     Listening: Rejoinders

     Listening comprehension: choosing the best responses to short spoken prompts

25% **Section II:**
     Listening: Dialogues and Narratives

     Listening comprehension: choosing the answers to questions based on longer spoken selections

60% **Section III:**
     Reading

     10% Part A. Discrete sentences (vocabulary and structure)

     20% Part B. Short cloze passages (vocabulary and structure)

     30% Part C. Reading passages and authentic stimulus materials (reading comprehension)

Sample Test Questions

The following sample questions do not appear on an actual CLEP examination. They are intended to give potential test-takers an indication of the format and difficulty level of the examination and to provide content for practice and review. Knowing the correct answers to all of the sample questions is not a guarantee of satisfactory performance on the exam.

Sections I and II: Listening

All italicized material in Section I and Section II represents what you would hear on an actual test recording. This material does not appear on the screen. During the actual test, you can change the volume by using the Volume testing tool. **The audio portions of the Listening sections of the test will be presented only one time.**

Directions for Section I: You will hear short conversations or parts of conversations. You will then hear four responses, designated (A), (B), (C), and (D). After you hear the four responses, click on the lettered response oval that most logically continues or completes the conversation. You will have 10 seconds to choose your response before the next conversation begins. When you are ready to continue, click on the Dismiss Directions icon.

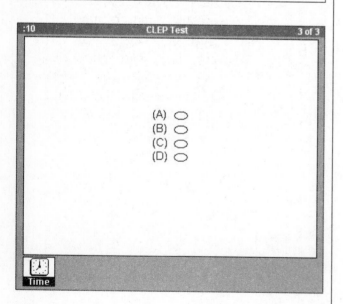

1. (Man) *Je viens de commencer à jouer dans un petit orchestre et je me sens un peu perdu.*

   (Woman)

   (A) *Ça viendra, il faut essayer d'être patient.*
   (B) *J'espère que tu le trouveras bientôt.*
   (C) *Moi non plus, je n'ai pas aimé ce concert.*
   (D) *De quel instrument joue-t-il?*

2. (Woman A) *J'aimerais bien aller dans le parc avec toi, mais il me faut faire des courses. À quelle heure voudrais-tu y aller?*

   (Woman B)

   (A) *J'ai passé des heures et des heures dans le parc.*
   (B) *J'ai fait toutes mes courses en une demi-heure.*
   (C) *Vers trois heures; tu pourrais faire tes commissions avant.*
   (D) *Vers la fin de l'après-midi, quand il n'y a plus autant de monde au marché.*

3. (Man) *Où as-tu passé tes vacances l'année dernière?*

   (Woman)

   (A) *Je préfère les vacances d'été.*
   (B) *Je suis allée en Angleterre.*
   (C) *J'ai passé l'examen d'entrée.*
   (D) *Je veux y aller l'année prochaine.*

4. (Man) *Tu as perdu ta montre? Est-ce qu'elle était précieuse?*

   (Woman)

   (A) *Non, tu n'y perdras pas grand chose.*
   (B) *Non, ces bracelets sont très bon marché.*
   (C) *Oui, tu peux me la montrer.*
   (D) *Oui, c'était un cadeau de ma tante.*

5. (Man A) *Écoute, Jean-Pierre, il faut que tu conduises très prudemment ce matin à cause de la pluie.*

(Man B)

(A) *Rassure-toi, papa, je vais faire attention.*

(B) *Je te promets, papa, je vais rentrer avant minuit.*

(C) *Sa conduite me gêne, moi aussi.*

(D) *Dommage qu'on n'ait pas de pluie; tout est si sec.*

6. (Man) *Dis, tu as vu mes lunettes quelque part? Ça fait vingt minutes que je les cherche.*

(Woman)

(A) *Vingt minutes? Mais c'est trop peu, ça!*

(B) *Oui, mes lunettes sont dans ma poche.*

(C) *Mais voyons, gros bêta, tu les portes sur le nez!*

(D) *Oui, tu as raison, ça dure au moins vingt minutes.*

7. (Woman B) *Marie, nous allons au cinéma demain. Veux-tu venir avec nous?*

(Woman A)

(A) *Mes parents aiment beaucoup les films de Truffaut.*

(B) *Je dois m'occuper de mon petit frère.*

(C) *Le cinéma est très important en France.*

(D) *C'est vrai, vous y allez avec elle.*

8. (Man A) *J'ai perdu mon portefeuille. Peux-tu régler l'addition? Je te rembourserai ma tasse de café demain.*

(Man B)

(A) *Où est ton portefeuille?*

(B) *Mais oui, sans problème.*

(C) *Qu'est-ce que tu fais au café?*

(D) *La mienne est dans ma poche.*

9. (Man) *Je viens de passer un examen difficile. J'ai presque peur de voir ma note.*

(A) *Oui, on t'a donné une note.*

(B) *Moi, je suis passé par la banque.*

(C) *Ne t'inquiète pas; ça ira bien.*

(D) *Tu ne vas pas chez lui?*

10. (Woman) *Ouf ! Quel repas copieux ! Je n'en peux plus.*

(A) *Ça ne m'étonne pas, ce n'était pas très original.*

(B) *Eh bien, essaie de nouveau, tu réussiras la prochaine fois.*

(C) *Les portions servies dans ce restaurant sont toujours énormes.*

(D) *L'essentiel, c'est de ne pas se presser.*

Directions for Section II: You will hear a series of selections, such as dialogues, announcements, and narratives. As each selection is playing, you will see a picture or a screen that says "Listen Now." Only after the entire selection has played will you be able to see the questions, which will appear one at a time. Each selection is followed by one or more questions, each with four answer choices. **You will have a total of 8 minutes to answer all the questions in this section. Note: The timer is activated only when you are answering questions.** After you read the question and the four responses, click on the response oval next to the best answer. Then, click NEXT to go on. In this section, you may adjust the volume only when a question is on your screen. It will affect the volume of the <u>next</u> audio prompt you hear. **You cannot change the volume while the audio prompt is playing.** When you are ready to continue, click on the Dismiss Directions icon.

Sélection numéro 1

Listen Now

Allo, Charles? Oui, c'est moi, Mme. Dumas. J'attends un taxi; le rendez-vous vient de se terminer. Oui, tout s'est très bien passé. Je crois bien qu'ils signeront le contrat avant peu. Quand j'arriverai au bureau, pourriez-vous me préparer leur dossier? Je veux y jeter un dernier coup d'oeil. Y a-t-il d'autres messages? Quinze? Bon, je m'en occuperai dès mon arrivée. Si M. LeBrun arrive avant moi, demandez-lui de m'attendre; je ne tarderai pas. Mais où sont tous les taxis!?

11. Avec qui Madame Dumas parle-t-elle?

   (A) Son mari
   (B) Son fils
   (C) Son patron
   (D) Son assistant

12. À quel moment de la journée de travail, cette conversation a-t-elle eu lieu?

   (A) Au début
   (B) À la fin
   (C) Au milieu
   (D) Juste avant la fin

13. Quelle expression décrit le mieux le travail de Madame Dumas?

   (A) Exigeant
   (B) Peu stressant
   (C) À mi-temps
   (D) Col-bleu

Sélection numéro 2

(Narrator) *Sélection numéro 2. Deux personnes se parlent.*

(Man) *Quel est votre emploi, Madame Robitaille?*

(Woman) *Ingénieur-chimiste, monsieur, chez Cresson.*

(Man) *Pourquoi voulez-vous changer de compagnie?*

(Woman) *Je préfère ne plus travailler pour une grande entreprise. Je voudrais avoir plus de responsabilités.*

14.

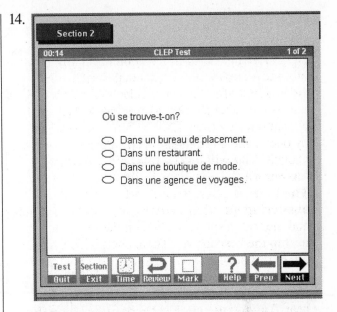

15.

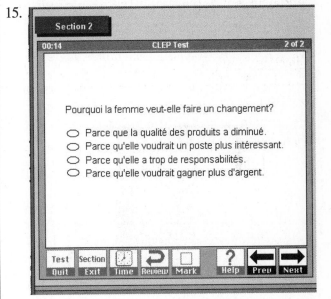

Sélection numéro 3

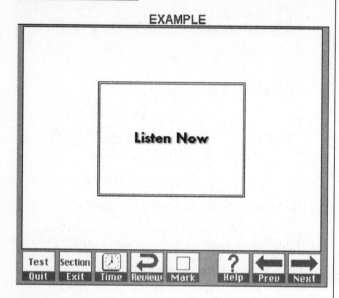

(Narrator) *Sélection numéro 3. Écoutez un bulletin météo.*

(Man) *Région parisienne—En matinée, le ciel restera couvert et les pluies seront abondantes. Dans l'après-midi, poussés par un vent d'ouest puis de nord-ouest assez violent, les nuages vont se dégager par moment, laissant passer un peu de soleil, mais il fera plus frais.*

16.

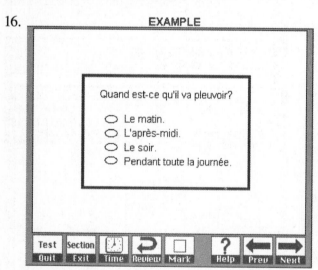

17. Comment la température évoluera-t-elle dans l'après-midi?

    (A) Il va faire plus chaud.

    (B) Il va faire plus froid.

    (C) La température va rester constante.

    (D) La température va augmenter, puis baisser.

Sélection numéro 4

(Narrator) *Sélection numéro 4. Un événement imprévu.*

(Woman) *Eh bien voilà, monsieur l'agent. Je faisais tranquillement les vitrines lorsqu'un inconnu s'est approché de moi.*

(Man) *Bon. Et après, madame, continuez . . .*

(Woman) *Alors l'homme m'a bousculée et puis il s'est sauvé. C'est à ce moment-là que je me suis rendu compte que mon porte-monnaie avait disparu.*

(Man) *Asseyez-vous là, madame, et signez votre déposition.*

18. Qui parle?

    (A) Un policier et une femme.

    (B) Un homme et sa femme.

    (C) Un assureur et sa cliente.

    (D) Un étranger et une vendeuse.

19. Où cette conversation a-t-elle lieu?

    (A) Dans une agence d'assurances.

    (B) Dans un bureau des objets trouvés.

    (C) Dans un commissariat de police.

    (D) Dans un bureau de poste.

20. De quoi s'agit-il?

    (A) D'un achat.

    (B) D'un vol.

    (C) D'une arrestation.

    (D) D'un accident.

Sélection numéro 5

(Narrator) *Sélection numéro 5. Le ministre fait une visite.*

(Woman) *Le ministre de l'Éducation Nationale, accompagné de son épouse, est arrivé ce matin dans notre ville où il assistera à l'inauguration du nouveau lycée. Il a été accueilli à sa descente d'avion par monsieur le maire ainsi que par un groupe de jeunes élèves qui ont remis à la femme du ministre un beau bouquet de fleurs.*

21. Avec qui le ministre est-il arrivé?

    (A) Avec le maire.
    (B) Avec ses filles.
    (C) Avec des enfants.
    (D) Avec sa femme.

22. Pourquoi le ministre est-il venu?

    (A) Pour passer ses vacances.
    (B) Pour un concours d'aviation.
    (C) Pour une exposition de fleurs.
    (D) Pour l'ouverture d'une école.

Sélection numéro 6

(Narrator) *Sélection numéro 6. Au petit déjeuner.*

(Man) *Oh! Tu as vu ça, Diane? Le vent a renversé le grand arbre près du garage! Et je n'ai rien entendu de la nuit!*

(Woman) *Mais Roland . . . comment se fait-il? Comme toi, j'ai dormi sans rien entendre.*

(Man) *Et le plus grave, c'est qu'il bloque la sortie du garage. Il faut que je dégage ça tout de suite.*

(Woman) *Oui. Je vais téléphoner à ton patron pour lui expliquer la situation exacte et pour lui dire de patienter.*

(Man) *Bonne idée. Dis-lui que je ne serai pas là avant midi.*

23. Que s'est-il passé?

    (A) La voiture est rentrée dans un arbre.
    (B) La voiture a été volée.
    (C) Un arbre est tombé devant le garage.
    (D) L'homme vient de couper un arbre.

24. Quand l'événement a-t-il eu lieu?

    (A) Pendant la nuit.
    (B) La veille.
    (C) Vers midi.
    (D) Pendant le petit déjeuner.

25. Qu'est-ce que la femme va dire au patron de son mari?

    (A) Que son mari s'est réveillé très tard.
    (B) Que son mari ne pourra plus aller à son travail.
    (C) Que son mari s'est gravement blessé.
    (D) Que son mari va être en retard.

Section III: Reading

> **Directions for Part A:** Each incomplete statement is followed by four suggested completions. Select the one that is best in each case by clicking on the corresponding oval. When you have decided on your answer, click NEXT to go on. When you are ready to continue, click on the Dismiss Directions icon.

26.

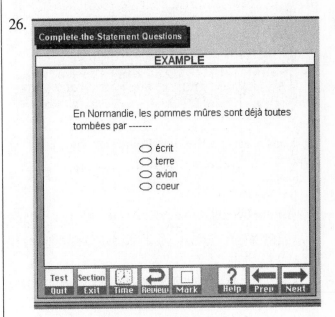

27. Dans les restaurants chics, on n'utilise pas de ------- en papier.

(A) ceintures
(B) serrures
(C) serveuses
(D) serviettes

28. Il vaudrait mieux que vous ------- à l'heure.

(A) rentrez
(B) finissez
(C) soyez
(D) partez

29.

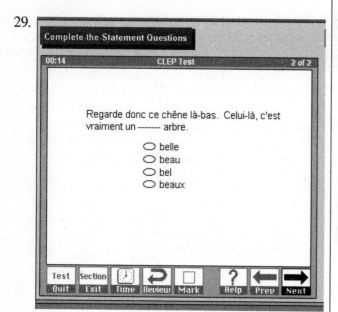

30. Vous cherchez Madame Lemierre? Vous la trouverez à l'étage -------.

(A) au-dessus
(B) par-dessus
(C) au-delà
(D) par delà

31. ------- avoir entendu la nouvelle, Martine est rentrée chez elle de toute urgence.

(A) En
(B) Pour
(C) Après
(D) Car

32. Voilà toutes les robes qu'on nous a -------.

(A) donné
(B) donnée
(C) donnés
(D) données

33.

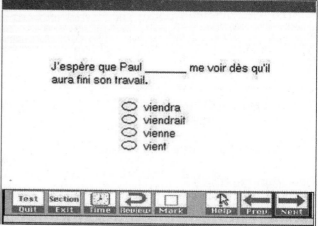

Directions for Part B: In each of the following paragraphs, there are blanks indicating that words or phrases have been omitted. As you go through the questions, the computer will highlight each blank, one at a time. When a blank is shaded, four completions are provided. First, read through the entire paragraph. Then, for each blank, choose the completion that is most appropriate, given the context of the entire paragraph. Click on the corresponding oval. Click NEXT to go on. When you are ready to continue, click on the Dismiss Directions icon.

Questions 34–40

34.

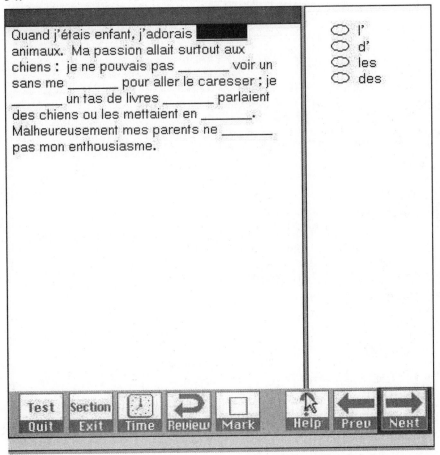

35.

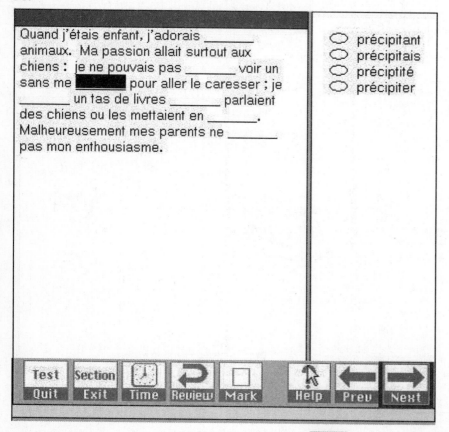

Quand j'étais enfant, j'adorais _____ animaux. Ma passion allait surtout aux chiens : je ne pouvais pas ▌▌▌▌ voir un sans me _____ pour aller le caresser ; je _____ un tas de livres _____ parlaient des chiens ou les mettaient en _____. Malheureusement mes parents ne _____ pas mon enthousiasme.

- ◯ en
- ◯ y
- ◯ lui
- ◯ le

Test Quit | Section Exit | Time | Review | Mark | Help | Prev | Next

36.

Quand j'étais enfant, j'adorais _____ animaux. Ma passion allait surtout aux chiens : je ne pouvais pas _____ voir un sans me ▌▌▌ pour aller le caresser ; je _____ un tas de livres _____ parlaient des chiens ou les mettaient en _____. Malheureusement mes parents ne _____ pas mon enthousiasme.

- ◯ précipitant
- ◯ précipitais
- ◯ préciptité
- ◯ précipiter

Test Quit | Section Exit | Time | Review | Mark | Help | Prev | Next

37.

Quand j'étais enfant, j'adorais _____ animaux. Ma passion allait surtout aux chiens : je ne pouvais pas _____ voir un sans me _____ pour aller le caresser ; je ████ un tas de livres _____ parlaient des chiens ou les mettaient en _____. Malheureusement mes parents ne _____ pas mon enthousiasme.

- ◯ dévorais
- ◯ mangeais
- ◯ dénonçais
- ◯ mordais

| Test Quit | Section Exit | Time | Review | Mark | Help | Prev | Next |

38.

Quand j'étais enfant, j'adorais _____ animaux. Ma passion allait surtout aux chiens : je ne pouvais pas _____ voir un sans me _____ pour aller le caresser ; je _____ un tas de livres ████ parlaient des chiens ou les mettaient en _____. Malheureusement mes parents ne _____ pas mon enthousiasme.

- ◯ que
- ◯ qui
- ◯ dont
- ◯ lesquels

| Test Quit | Section Exit | Time | Review | Mark | Help | Prev | Next |

39.

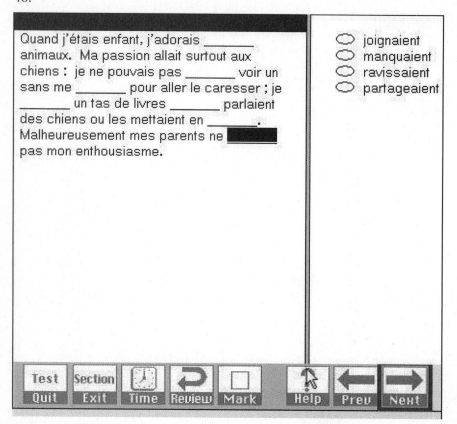

Quand j'étais enfant, j'adorais _____ animaux. Ma passion allait surtout aux chiens : je ne pouvais pas _____ voir un sans me _____ pour aller le caresser ; je _____ un tas de livres _____ parlaient des chiens ou les mettaient en ▮▮▮▮▮. Malheureusement mes parents ne _____ pas mon enthousiasme.

○ scène
○ chemin
○ plateau
○ étage

| Test | Section | | | | | Help | Prev | Next |
| Quit | Exit | Time | Review | Mark | | | | |

40.

Quand j'étais enfant, j'adorais _____ animaux. Ma passion allait surtout aux chiens : je ne pouvais pas _____ voir un sans me _____ pour aller le caresser ; je _____ un tas de livres _____ parlaient des chiens ou les mettaient en _____. Malheureusement mes parents ne ▮▮▮▮▮ pas mon enthousiasme.

○ joignaient
○ manquaient
○ ravissaient
○ partageaient

| Test | Section | | | | | Help | Prev | Next |
| Quit | Exit | Time | Review | Mark | | | | |

41.

En été, l'orage s'annonce souvent par l'arrivée à l'horizon d'un premier ▮▮▮▮ sombre. Ensuite, une masse noire absorbe graduellement le bleu du ciel. L'air vibre dans une _____ lourde. Alors, il n'y a _____ un seul souffle d'air. Le temps paraît être suspendu. Tout d'un _____, le tonnerre éclate, et il se met à pleuvoir très fort.

○ drapeau
○ nuage
○ éclair
○ maquillage

42.

En été, l'orage s'annonce souvent par l'arrivée à l'horizon d'un premier _____ sombre. Ensuite, une masse noire absorbe graduellement le bleu du ciel. L'air vibre dans une ▮▮▮▮ lourde. Alors, il n'y a _____ un seul souffle d'air. Le temps paraît être suspendu. Tout d'un _____, le tonnerre éclate, et il se met à pleuvoir très fort.

○ chaleur
○ pâleur
○ laideur
○ hauteur

43.

En été, l'orage s'annonce souvent par l'arrivée à l'horizon d'un premier _____ sombre. Ensuite, une masse noire absorbe graduellement le bleu du ciel. L'air vibre dans une _____ lourde. Alors, il n'y a ███████ un seul souffle d'air. Le temps paraît être suspendu. Tout d'un _____, le tonnerre éclate, et il se met à pleuvoir très fort.

- ◯ rien
- ◯ personne
- ◯ plus
- ◯ encore

44.

En été, l'orage s'annonce souvent par l'arrivée à l'horizon d'un premier _____ sombre. Ensuite, une masse noire absorbe graduellement le bleu du ciel. L'air vibre dans une _____ lourde. Alors, il n'y a _____ un seul souffle d'air. Le temps paraît être suspendu. Tout d'un ███████, le tonnerre éclate, et il se met à pleuvoir très fort.

- ◯ pied
- ◯ cap
- ◯ oeil
- ◯ coup

Questions 45–51

Quand j'étais petite fille, nous avons __(45)__ en Haïti pendant un an. Comme nous venions du nord, c'était un grand changement de se trouver dans un __(46)__ chaud. Aller à la plage en février! Qui l' __(47)__ cru? En fait, c'était toute une aventure pour une petite fille. J'ai appris à parler un peu le créole, la langue de ce pays. Notre domestique nous __(48)__ des mets typiques, __(49)__ que le «riz et pois». Avec mon frère et mes soeurs, on grignotait des cannes à sucre qui étaient meilleures que les bonbons. Mais ce qui était le plus impressionnant, c'était la façon __(50)__ les femmes portaient leurs affaires. Elles ne tenaient rien dans les bras mais portaient tout sur la tête dans d'immenses paniers. Elles pouvaient marcher des kilomètres sans rien __(51)__ tomber!

45. (A) conduit
    (B) habité
    (C) déménagé
    (D) emménagé

46. (A) pays
    (B) temps
    (C) paysage
    (D) siècle

47. (A) aura
    (B) aurait
    (C) a
    (D) ait

48. (A) préparait
    (B) fixait
    (C) brûlait
    (D) fabriquait

49. (A) même
    (B) tels
    (C) tant
    (D) bien

50. (A) de qui
    (B) que
    (C) qui
    (D) dont

51. (A) fait
    (B) faire
    (C) ayant fait
    (D) faisant

Directions for Part C: Read the following selections. Each selection is followed by one or more questions or incomplete statements. For each question, select the answer or completion that is best according to the selection. Click on the corresponding oval. Click on NEXT to go on. When you are ready to continue, click on the Dismiss Directions icon.

Questions 52–54

L'été dernier, j'ai revisité la maison de mon enfance. La dernière fois que je l'avais vue, c'était pour l'enterrement de ma mère alors que j'étais encore à l'université à Paris. Pendant les dix ans qui s'étaient écoulés depuis lors, elle n'avait guère changé. Elle était là, éclatante de blancheur, parmi les vignobles qui couvraient les coteaux à perte de vue. Au loin, très loin, on pouvait apercevoir le clocher du village voisin.

52. Quand l'auteur a-t-il perdu sa mère?

   (A) À l'âge de dix ans
   (B) Quand il était adolescent
   (C) Au cours de ses études
   (D) Au début de sa carrière

53. Où l'auteur a-t-il passé son enfance?

   (A) À la campagne
   (B) À Paris
   (C) Au bord de la mer
   (D) En haute montagne

54. D'après ce passage, la maison est située dans un pays où l'on fait surtout

   (A) du cidre
   (B) du vin
   (C) du fromage
   (D) des saucisses

Question 55

codec

ALIMENTATION GÉNÉRALE
FRUITS - LÉGUMES
VINS - LIBRE-SERVICE

André CUGGIA

Rue Valère-Paulin (près de la Gare)
83600 FRÉJUS · Tel 95 35 02 · Parking

55. Cette annonce vous intéresserait si vous désiriez acheter

   (A) des jouets
   (B) des livres
   (C) des pommes
   (D) des poissons

Questions 56–59

Les Français sont aujourd'hui conscients que les médias sont des entreprises commerciales, dont la vocation n'est pas de servir toute la population, mais d'accroître leur audience et leurs recettes publicitaires. La qualité de leur contenu et la véracité de l'information qu'ils délivrent ont été progressivement mises en doute.

La mise en oeuvre du nouveau paysage audio-visuel au début des années 80 n'est pas étrangère à cette perte de crédibilité. Libérée d'une partie des contraintes du passé, la télévision ne se donne presque plus de mission éducatrice ou culturelle. Guidée par les résultats des sondages, elle s'efforce de flatter les attentes des Français en faisant couler l'émotion à flots dans les émissions de variétés, les Reality shows, et autres programmes populaires.

Les Français ont de plus en plus de doutes à propos de l'influence des médias sur le fonctionnement de la démocratie. Si les enquêtes des médias permettent parfois de faire éclater la vérité, il arrive qu'elles troublent la sérénité nécessaire au fonctionnement de la justice en instruisant les procès devant l'opinion en même temps qu'ils ont lieu devant les juges ou même antérieurement.

56. D'après le texte, les Français savent que le but principal des médias en France est

    (A) de renseigner le public

    (B) de présenter des nouveautés

    (C) de gagner de l'argent

    (D) d'influencer l'opinion public

57. En ce qui concerne les médias, le public devient de plus en plus

    (A) favorable

    (B) fasciné

    (C) silencieux

    (D) sceptique

58. D'après les sondages, la majorité des téléspectateurs aimerait que la télévision

    (A) augmente le nombre d'émissions sentimentales

    (B) multiplie les émissions culturelles

    (C) reprenne son rôle d'autrefois

    (D) limite le nombre d'émissions violentes

59. D'après le texte, quel est l'effet des médias sur le travail des juges?

    (A) Ils le rendent inutile.

    (B) Ils le facilitent.

    (C) Ils l'accélèrent.

    (D) Ils le compliquent.

Questions 60–61

60. Qu'est-ce qu'on offre dans cette annonce?

    (A) Des chambres d'hôtel avec cuisine

    (B) Un voyage pour deux à St. Mandrier

    (C) Des appartements en bord de mer

    (D) Un stage de sports variés

61. Pourquoi écririez-vous à Méditerranée Holidays?

    (A) Pour réserver des chambres

    (B) Pour obtenir des renseignements

    (C) Pour louer un appartement

    (D) Pour vous abonner à un magazine

Questions 62–66

Tout à sa contemplation, Mona Lisa, appelée aussi la Joconde, n'a, comme d'habitude, rien vu ni entendu. Pendant ce temps, les gardiens du Louvre font triste mine et les conservateurs s'arrachent les cheveux. Dimanche après-midi, «Le chemin de Sèvres», un tableau du peintre Camille Corot (1796-1875), a été volé. Sur le pan de mur qu'il occupait depuis 1902, au lieu d'un coin de campagne, ne subsistent que le cadre et la vitre de protection destinée à préserver l'oeuvre. Alertée, la direction a aussitôt fermé les portes du musée pour toute la journée, retenant ainsi 10 000 visiteurs dans ses murs. Chacun a dû, pour sortir, se prêter à une fouille minutieuse, ce qui n'a pas manqué de susciter quelques commentaires acerbes, voire indignés. Hélas, la petite toile, 34 cm sur 49 cm, est restée introuvable. Une enquête a été ouverte par la section objets d'art de la brigade de répression du banditisme. Les prix des tableaux de Corot, lorsqu'ils sont vendus aux enchères, peuvent varier entre 4 200 francs et 6,43 millions de francs, selon la taille et la qualité de la toile. Derrière sa prison de plexiglas, Mona Lisa défie, elle, le temps qui passe, en souriant pour l'éternité aux hordes de touristes pressés.

62. Dans le passage, il s'agit du vol d'un tableau et

(A) des moyens de le préserver

(B) de sa récente vente aux enchères

(C) de la malhonnêteté des visiteurs du musée

(D) de la tentative d'appréhender le voleur

63. Que sait-on du tableau de Corot «Le chemin de Sèvres»?

(A) C'est le chef-d'oeuvre du peintre.

(B) Il représentait une scène rustique.

(C) Il vaut plusieurs millions de francs.

(D) Il a dû être peint entre 1875 et 1902.

64. La direction du Louvre a été obligée de considérer chaque visiteur comme

(A) suspect

(B) indifférent

(C) curieux

(D) pressé

65. D'après le passage, on peut supposer que ce qui a facilité le vol, c'est

(A) l'évidente négligence des conservateurs

(B) la taille relativement modeste du tableau

(C) l'absence complète de mesures sécuritaires

(D) le nombre et l'attitude des visiteurs

66. La conclusion qu'on peut tirer de ce reportage, c'est que le tableau volé

(A) sera recouvré à l'occasion d'une vente aux enchères

(B) n'a pas subi de dommages graves

(C) se trouve toujours au Louvre

(D) semble avoir totalement disparu

Questions 67–68

POUR VOYAGER RÉGULIÈREMENT
(CARTE 12-25)

★ **Carte 12-25 : pendant un an, voyagez à prix réduit aussi souvent que vous en avez envie.**
Nouveau : toute l'année des réductions sur le train, mais aussi l'avion ou la voiture, en France et à l'étranger : avec la Carte 12-25, la SNCF et ses nouveaux <u>partenaires</u> vous offrent le moyen de bouger toujours plus loin et toujours moins cher, aussi souvent que vous le voulez!

★ **TGV:**
· Bénéficiez d'une réduction de 50% (*) dans tous les TGV dans la limite des places offertes à ce prix.
· S'il ne reste plus de place à 50% (*), une réduction de 25% (*) vous est garantie dans tous les cas.

★ **Autres trains:**
· Bénéficiez d'une réduction de 50% (*) pour tout trajet commencé en période bleue du calendrier voyageur.
· Si votre voyage commence en période blanche, une réduction de 25% (*) vous est garantie dans tous les cas.

(*) Réduction calculée sur le prix de base. La réduction s'applique dans tous les TGV (places en nombre limité dans certains d'entre eux) et pour tout trajet commencé en période bleue du calendrier voyageurs dans les autres trains.

Exemples de prix :

Destination	Tarif A/R avec la Carte 12-25	Tarif normal sans la Carte 12-25
Paris-Deauville	146 F - 22,26 E	290 F - 44,21 E
Lille-Lyon	402 F - 61,28 E	804 F - 122,57 E
Paris-Montpellier	340 F - 51,83 E	746 F - 113,73 E

---

67. Quel avantage offre la carte?

   (A) On peut voyager sans réservation.

   (B) On paie le voyage moins cher.

   (C) On peut voyager gratuitement pendant un an.

   (D) On voyage plus loin et plus vite.

68. La carte est valable pour

   (A) le train uniquement

   (B) le TGV uniquement

   (C) le train et l'avion

   (D) le train, l'avion et la voiture

Study Resources

Most textbooks used in college-level French language courses cover the topics in the outline given earlier, but the approaches to certain topics and the emphases given to them may differ. To prepare for the French Language exam, it is advisable to study one or more college textbooks, which can be found in most college bookstores. When selecting a textbook, check the table of contents against the knowledge and skills required for this test.

Besides studying basic vocabulary, you should understand and be able to apply the grammatical principles that make up the language. To improve your reading comprehension, read passages from textbooks, short magazine or newspaper articles, or other printed material of your choice. To improve your listening comprehension, seek opportunities to hear the language spoken by native speakers and to converse with native speakers. French CDs and tapes are available in many libraries. Take advantage of opportunities to join organizations with French-speaking members, to attend French movies, or to hear French-language radio broadcasts.

Visit www.collegeboard.com/clepprep for additional French resources. You can also find suggestions for exam preparation in Chapter IV of the *Official Study Guide*. In addition, many college faculty post their course materials on their schools' Web sites.

Answer Key

1.	A	35.	A
2.	C	36.	D
3.	B	37.	A
4.	D	38.	B
5.	A	39.	A
6.	C	40.	D
7.	B	41.	B
8.	B	42.	A
9.	C	43.	C
10.	C	44.	D
11.	D	45.	B
12.	C	46.	A
13.	A	47.	B
14.	A	48.	A
15.	B	49.	B
16.	A	50.	D
17.	B	51.	B
18.	A	52.	C
19.	C	53.	A
20.	B	54.	B
21.	D	55.	C
22.	D	56.	C
23.	C	57.	D
24.	A	58.	A
25.	D	59.	D
26.	B	60.	C
27.	D	61.	B
28.	C	62.	D
29.	C	63.	B
30.	A	64.	A
31.	C	65.	B
32.	D	66.	D
33.	A	67.	B
34.	C	68.	D

German Language

Description of the Examination

The German Language examination is designed to measure knowledge and ability equivalent to that of students who have completed two to four semesters of college German language study. It focuses on skills typically achieved from the end of the first year through the second year of college study; material taught during both years is incorporated into a single examination.

The examination is administered in three separately timed sections:

- Sections I and II: Listening
- Section III: Reading

The examination contains approximately 120 questions to be answered in 90 minutes. The three sections are weighted so that each question contributes equally to the total score. Any time candidates spend on tutorials or providing personal information is in addition to the actual testing time.

Most colleges that award credit for the German Language examination award either two or four semesters of credit, depending on the candidate's score on the exam.

Knowledge and Skills Required

Questions on the German Language examination require candidates to demonstrate the abilities listed in each section below. The percentages indicate the approximate percentage of exam questions focused on each ability.

40% **Sections I and II: Listening**

15% Rejoinders
Ability to understand spoken language through short stimuli or everyday situations

25% Dialogues and Narratives
Ability to understand the language as spoken by native speakers in longer dialogues and narratives

60% **Section III: Reading**

16% Part A: Discrete sentences: Mastery of vocabulary and structure in the context of sentences

20% Part B: Short cloze passages: Mastery of vocabulary and structure in the context of paragraphs

24% Part C: Reading comprehension: Ability to read and understand texts representative of various styles and levels of difficulty (e.g., passages of about 200 words; shorter pieces such as advertisements, signs, etc.)

Sample Test Questions

The following sample questions do not appear on an actual CLEP examination. They are intended to give potential test-takers an indication of the format and difficulty level of the examination and to provide content for practice and review. Knowing the correct answers to all of the sample questions is not a guarantee of satisfactory performance on the exam.

Sections I and II: Listening

All italicized material in Section I and Section II represents what you would hear on an actual test recording. This material does not appear on the screen. During the actual test, you can change the volume by using the Volume testing tool. **The audio portions of the Listening section of the test will be presented only one time.**

Directions for Section I: You will hear statements or short conversations. Each statement or conversation is followed by a question. Each question has four answer choices, designated (A), (B), (C), and (D). After you hear the four answer choices, click on the lettered oval corresponding to the best answer.

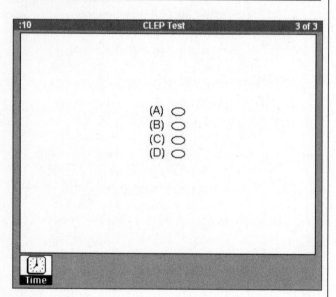

1. (MAN A) *Unsere Deutschlandreise war teuer und anstrengend, aber wir haben sehr viel Interessantes gesehen. Ich muss sagen, sie hat sich wirklich gelohnt.*

   (WOMAN) *Wie war die Deutschlandreise?*

   (MAN B)

   (A) *Billig*
   (B) *Zu kurz*
   (C) *Interessant*
   (D) *Erholsam*

2. (WOMAN A) *Entschuldigen Sie, ich suche die Vorlesung von Herrn Professor Gromann.*

   (WOMAN B) *Oh, da sind Sie hier falsch. Die ist drüben im Hörsaal sieben.*

   (MAN A) *Wo sind wohl die beiden?*

   (MAN B)

   (A) *In einem Gymnasium*
   (B) *In einem Krankenhaus*
   (C) *In einer Sportanlage*
   (D) *An einer Universität*

3. (MAN A) *Frau Schmidt, Ihr Artikel in der heutigen Zeitung ist ausgezeichnet. Könnten Sie bis nächste Woche noch einen zum selben Thema schreiben?*

   (WOMAN A) *Ja, aber ich müsste dann noch mehr Leute interviewen.*

   (MAN B) *Wer spricht hier wohl?*

   (WOMAN B)

   (A) *Zwei Journalisten*
   (B) *Zwei Schüler*
   (C) *Ein Ehepaar*
   (D) *Zwei Zeitungsverkäufer*

4. (WOMAN A) *Ich möchte bitte diesen Brief und ein Telegramm aufgeben.*

(MAN A) *Der Brief kostet drei Euro, und für das Telegramm füllen Sie bitte dieses Formular aus.*

(WOMAN B) *Wo findet das Gespräch statt?*

(MAN B)

(A) *Auf der Bank*
(B) *Im Restaurant*
(C) *Auf dem Postamt*
(D) *Im Supermarkt*

5. (MAN A) *Oh, Inge, deine schöne Vase ist kaputt! Ich werde sie natürlich ersetzen. Wo hast du sie gekauft?*

(WOMAN A) *Aber das macht doch nichts, Hans.*

(MAN B) *Was ist wohl passiert?*

(WOMAN B)

(A) *Inge hat sich verletzt.*
(B) *Inge hat Hans geärgert.*
(C) *Hans hat etwas gekauft.*
(D) *Hans hat etwas zerbrochen.*

6. (WOMAN) *Brauchen Sie sonst noch etwas?*

(MAN) *Moment mal. Käse, Schinken, ach ja! Geben Sie mir bitte auch noch fünf Scheiben Salami.*

(MAN) *Wo findet dieses Gespräch wohl statt?*

(WOMAN)

(A) *In der Küche*
(B) *Im Supermarkt*
(C) *Im Restaurant*
(D) *In der Mensa*

7. (MAN A) *Schau mal, Tante Anni. Die Fotos von deinem Geburtstag sind wirklich gut geworden.*

(WOMAN A) *Edgar, bring mir doch bitte meine Brille. Sie liegt dort drüben auf dem Tisch.*

(MAN B) *Welches Problem hat Tante Anni?*

(WOMAN B)

(A) *Sie sieht nicht gut.*
(B) *Sie hat ihre Brille verloren.*
(C) *Edgar besucht sie nicht.*
(D) *Die Fotos sind unscharf.*

8. (WOMAN A) *Ich bekomme immer wieder diese Kopfschmerzen. Können Sie mir vielleicht ein Medikament dagegen verschreiben?*

(MAN A) *Dazu muss ich Sie erst einmal näher untersuchen. Würden Sie bitte da drüben Platz nehmen?*

(MAN B) *Mit wem spricht die Frau wohl?*

(WOMAN B)

(A) *Mit einem Apotheker*
(B) *Mit einem Friseur*
(C) *Mit einem Verkäufer*
(D) *Mit einem Arzt*

9. (MAN A) *Von Angela lernten wir, dass sie und ihre Schwester Nicole Zwillinge sind, aber Nicole ist um zwei Minuten die Jüngere.*

(WOMAN) *Was erfahren wir über die zwei Schwestern?*

(MAN B)

(A) *Sie sind beide Lehrerin.*
(B) *Sie haben beide Zwillinge.*
(C) *Sie sind beide am selben Tag geboren.*
(D) *Sie haben beide den selben Vornamen.*

Section II: Listening

Directions for Section II: You will hear a series of selections, such as dialogues, announcements, and narratives. As each selection is playing, you will see a picture or a screen that says "Listen Now." Only after the entire selection has played will you be able to see the questions, which will appear one at a time. Each selection is followed by one or more questions, each with four answer choices. **You will have a total of 9 minutes to answer all the questions in this section. Note: The timer is activated only when you are answering questions.** After you read the question and the four responses, click on the response oval next to the best answer. Then, click NEXT to go on. In this section, you may adjust the volume only when a question is on your screen. It will affect the volume of the <u>next</u> audio prompt you hear. **You cannot change the volume while the audio prompt is playing.** When you are ready to continue, click on the Dismiss Directions icon.

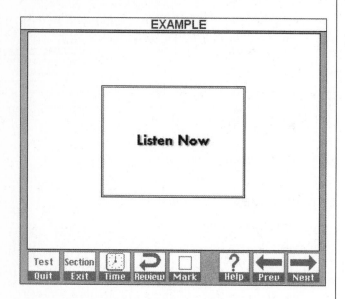

(Narrator) <u>Selection number one</u>: *You will hear a conversation between two friends.*

(WOMAN) *Tag, Michael, wie geht's dir denn?*

(MAN) *Viel besser, und in 14 Tagen werde ich schon hier aus dem Krankenhaus entlassen.*

(WOMAN) *Also sag mal. Wie ist der Unfall eigentlich passiert?*

(MAN) *Na ja, Inge und ich waren letztes Wochenende im „Big Apple" tanzen . . .*

(WOMAN) *Du hast doch nicht etwa getrunken??*

(MAN) *Nein, nein! Außerdem gibt's im „Big Apple" ja gar keinen Alkohol.*

(WOMAN) *Aber ich habe gehört, dass du gegen einen Baum gefahren bist.*

(MAN) *Na ja, ich habe doch meinen Führerschein erst seit acht Wochen, und außerdem war es schrecklich nebelig, und die Straße war nass und . .*

(WOMAN) *Also, mit anderen Worten, zu schnell gefahren! Da kannst du nur von Glück reden, dass dir nicht mehr passiert ist.*

10.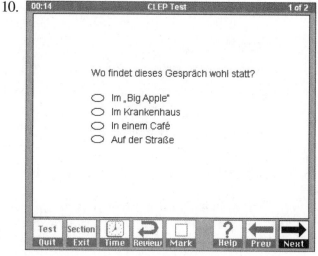

11. Wann darf Michael nach Hause?

   (A) In vier Tagen

   (B) In zwei Wochen

   (C) In vier Wochen

   (D) In vierzig Tagen

12. Wie war das Wetter an dem Wochenende, an dem Michael und Inge tanzen gingen?

    (A) Es gab ein Gewitter.

    (B) Es war windig und kalt.

    (C) Es war nass und nebelig.

    (D) Es war eine klare Nacht.

13. Was waren die Folgen des Unfalls?

    (A) Inge will im „Big Apple" arbeiten.

    (B) Inge darf nicht mehr Auto fahren.

    (C) Michael hat seinen Führerschein verloren.

    (D) Michael muss im Krankenhaus liegen.

14. Was meinte Michaels Bekannte am Ende?

    (A) Michael war betrunken.

    (B) Michael ist ein guter Tänzer.

    (C) Michael ist zu jung.

    (D) Michael ist zu schnell gefahren.

(Narrator) _Selection number two_: Listen to the following report from a German radio news magazine.

(WOMAN) _Der Bundesverband der Süßwarenindustrie hat festgestellt, dass in den skandinavischen Ländern die Menschen auch bei Minusgraden mit einem Eis in der Hand herumlaufen. Die Deutschen mögen dagegen kein Eis in der kalten Jahreszeit – deshalb geht der Verkauf von Speiseeis im Winter rapide zurück. Das soll nun anders werden. Die großen deutschen Eishersteller bieten neuerdings besondere Wintereis-Spezialitäten an. „So schmilzt der Winter", heißt es in der Werbung für Eissorten, die nur bis Ende Februar angeboten werden, wie zum Beispiel Zimtsterne, Vanilleherzen oder Apfelstrudel aus Eis._

15. Was machen Skandinavier anders als Deutsche?

    (A) Sie essen ihr Eis aus der Hand.

    (B) Sie essen Eis bei sehr kaltem Wetter.

    (C) Sie essen Eis besonders schnell.

    (D) Sie essen nur bis Ende Februar Eis.

16. Was ist das Ziel des Bundesverbands der Süßwarenindustrie?

    (A) Skandinavisches Speiseeis einzuführen

    (B) Mehr Eis in den Wintermonaten zu verkaufen

    (C) Keine Werbung für Speiseeis zu machen

    (D) Jeden Monat ein neues Speiseeis zu erfinden

17. Was machen die deutschen Eishersteller jetzt?

    (A) Sie bieten besondere Eissorten an.

    (B) Sie senken im Sommer die Preise.

    (C) Sie führen Eis in andere Länder aus.

    (D) Sie stellen mehr Gebäck als Eis her.

18. Wie lange werden Zimtsterne, Vanilleherzen und Apfelstrudel aus Eis verkauft?

    (A) Bis zum Winter

    (B) Bis zum Sommer

    (C) Bis zum Frühjahr

    (D) Bis zum Herbst

(Narrator) *Selection number three*: Listen to the following conversation between two friends.

(MAN) *Hast du eigentlich daran gedacht, dass Peter nächste Woche einundzwanzig wird?*

(WOMAN) *Ja, sicher. Aber was sollen wir ihm denn schenken?*

(MAN) *Er hat doch neulich mal erwähnt, dass er gerne einen neuen MP3-Spieler hätte.*

(WOMAN) *Ja, stimmt! Aber der kostet zu viel! Schenken wir ihm doch was anderes. Wie wär's denn mit einem Buch?*

(MAN) *Wir wissen ja gar nicht, welchen Schriftsteller er gerne liest. Außerdem hat er jetzt eine Freundin und gar keine Zeit zum Lesen. Kaufen wir ihm doch eine DVD.*

(WOMAN) *Nein, das kann man doch alles im Internet finden! Sag mal, wie viel wollen wir denn überhaupt für ein Geschenk ausgeben?*

(MAN) *Na ja, zu zweit vielleicht so zwischen fünfundzwanzig und fünfunddreißig Euro?*

(WOMAN) *Du, ich habe eine Idee! Schenken wir ihm doch einen Gutschein für ein schönes Essen mit seiner Freundin in seinem Lieblingsrestaurant.*

19. Warum wollen die beiden Peter ein Geschenk geben?

    (A) Er hat sich verlobt.
    (B) Er hat einen besonderen Geburtstag.
    (C) Er hat das Abitur bestanden.
    (D) Er hat eine neue Stelle bekommen.

20. Warum hat Peter jetzt so wenig Zeit?

    (A) Er hat einen Job in einem Restaurant.
    (B) Er schaut Filme immer im Internet an.
    (C) Er verkauft elektronische Geräte.
    (D) Er verbringt viel Zeit mit seiner Freundin.

21. Warum kaufen die beiden ihm kein Buch?

    (A) Sie wissen nicht, ob sie soviel ausgeben wollen.
    (B) Sie wissen nicht, wer sein Lieblingsautor ist.
    (C) Peter will nur im Internet lesen.
    (D) Peter liest nicht gern.

22. Wie viel Geld wollen die Freunde fürs Geschenk ausgeben?

    (A) Nicht mehr als 21 Euro
    (B) Nicht mehr als 25 Euro
    (C) Nicht mehr als 35 Euro
    (D) Nicht mehr als 53 Euro

Section III: Reading

Directions: Each incomplete statement is followed by four suggested completions. Select the one that is best in each case by clicking on the corresponding oval.

23. Meine Eltern lassen dich ------- grüßen.

    (A) kürzlich
    (B) herzlich
    (C) neulich
    (D) gut

24. Der Park liegt außerhalb des ------- Stadtzentrums.

    (A) alten
    (B) altem
    (C) alter
    (D) altes

25. Seit Monaten hofft Renate ------- einen Hauptgewinn im Lotto.

    (A) auf
    (B) für
    (C) an
    (D) zu

26. Im Kaufhof ist Ausverkauf. Hast du die ------- in der Zeitung gesehen?

(A) Anschrift

(B) Anzeige

(C) Beweise

(D) Buchstaben

27. Mit ------- willst du heute Abend Karten spielen?

(A) wer

(B) wen

(C) wem

(D) wessen

28. Ich habe in Deutschland viel fotografiert und die Filme sofort entwickeln -------.

(A) gelassen

(B) lassen

(C) lasse

(D) lasst

29. Da liegt meine Jacke. Wo ist denn -------?

(A) dein

(B) deiner

(C) deines

(D) deine

30. Da ich jedes Jahr nach Berlin fahre, ------- ich diese Stadt sehr gut.

(A) weiß

(B) kann

(C) mag

(D) kenne

31. Katharina passt gut auf ------- kleinen Bruder auf.

(A) ihr

(B) ihrem

(C) ihren

(D) ihres

Directions: In each of the following paragraphs, there are blanks indicating that words or phrases have been omitted. First read through the entire paragraph. Then, for each blank, choose the completion that is most appropriate, given the context of the entire paragraph. Click on the corresponding oval.

Ich bin schon oft von Deutschland ___(32)___ Amerika geflogen, aber nächste Woche ___(33)___ ich zum ersten Mal ein Schiff. In Bremerhaven geht es los, und fünf Tage ___(34)___ werden wir in New York ___(35)___. Ich freue mich schon sehr auf ___(36)___ Reise.

32. (A) zu

(B) nach

(C) in

(D) auf

33. (A) nehme

(B) fahre

(C) gehe

(D) reise

34. (A) erst

(B) davor

(C) lieber

(D) später

35. (A) angekommen

(B) ankommen

(C) ankommt

(D) ankamen

36. (A) diesen

(B) dieses

(C) dieser

(D) diese

Die Geschichte der Deutschen in Amerika beginnt _____(37)_____ Jahre 1683 mit der Gründung von Germantown in der _____(38)_____ von Philadelphia. Pennsylvanien war damals eines _____(39)_____ Hauptziele für deutsche Einwanderer, _____(40)_____ viele gingen auch nach New York, Virginia, Ohio und später Texas.

37. (A) zum
    (B) im
    (C) vom
    (D) am

38. (A) Höhe
    (B) Wiese
    (C) Nähe
    (D) Kirche

39. (A) der
    (B) des
    (C) dem
    (D) den

40. (A) sondern
    (B) als
    (C) wann
    (D) aber

Directions: Read the following selections. Each selection is followed by one or more questions or incomplete statements. For each question, select the answer that is best according to the selection. Click on the corresponding oval.

Ich heiße Claus. Als ich mein Studium begann und noch sehr knapp bei Kasse war, bin ich zunächst oft per Anhalter gereist. Von Oldenburg, meiner norddeutschen Heimatstadt, nach Tübingen, meinem süddeutschen Studienort, waren es ungefähr 650 Kilometer, und das konnte ich an einem Tag gerade so schaffen. Dabei bestand aber immer die Gefahr, dass ich in einen Regenschauer oder an einen zu riskanten Autofahrer geriet, und deswegen habe ich dann bald auf Mitfahrzentralen zurückgegriffen.

Mitfahrzentralen vermitteln für eine geringe Gebühr zwischen Privatleuten, die eine Mitfahrgelegenheit suchen, und anderen, die eine Mitfahrt anbieten. Meinen Fahrern musste ich jeweils auch eine bestimmte Summe zahlen. Insgesamt kostete mich die Fahrt auf diese Weise vielleicht 45 Euro, aber es war sicherer und immer noch viel billiger als die Zugfahrt, deren Preis 175 Euro betrug.

Schließlich jedoch gewann mein Umweltbewusstsein die Oberhand, und ich verdiente durch einen Job beim Rundfunk auch ein wenig Geld, so dass ich mir die Eisenbahn leisten konnte. Die Zugfahrten haben mir immer viel Spaß gemacht: Ich konnte lesen, im Speisewagen etwas essen, mich mit anderen Reisenden unterhalten oder einfach die Landschaft genießen.

41. Warum ist Claus anfangs per Anhalter gefahren?

    (A) Aus finanziellen Gründen
    (B) Aus Zeitgründen
    (C) Aus Bequemlichkeit
    (D) Aus Abenteuerlust

42. Was ist eine Mitfahrzentrale?

    (A) Eine Bahnhofshalle
    (B) Ein Autobahnrestaurant
    (C) Eine Vermittlungsagentur
    (D) Ein Reisebüro

43. Claus fuhr später immer mit dem Zug, weil er

   (A) in seinem Beruf viel reisen musste

   (B) sehr umweltbewusst war

   (C) den Mitfahrzentralen nicht vertraute

   (D) keinen Führerschein hatte

44. Claus hat an seinen Zugreisen gefallen, dass

   (A) die Züge pünktlich waren

   (B) die Züge Schlafwagen hatten

   (C) er die Landschaft schon kannte

   (D) er sich frei bewegen konnte

Portland liegt an der amerikanischen Westküste und damit so ziemlich am Ende der Welt–zumindest, wenn man einen Job in Europa sucht. Für den Medizininformatiker Henning Müller war das jedoch kein Problem. Der 28-jährige Deutsche hatte in der Großstadt im Bundesstaat Oregon nach seinem Studienabschluss ein sechsmonatiges Praktikum absolviert. Danach suchte er aber einen Arbeitsplatz in der Heimat. „Ich habe mich an den Computer gesetzt, in den Newsgroups meines Fachgebiets umgesehen und dann ein paar deutsche Jobbörsen gecheckt." Schon bald stieß Müller auf eine Doktorandenstelle an der Universität Genf. „Die passte einfach perfekt." Er bewarb sich per E-Mail – und bekam den Job.

Zielgerichtet setzt die Internetgeneration auf das Netz, um den nächsten Karriereschritt zu planen. „Bis zu 80 Prozent aller Informatikjobs werden schon über das Internet vermittelt", schätzt das Büro für Berufsstrategie in Berlin, „und die anderen Berufsgruppen ziehen nach."

In ihrer jüngsten Online-Umfrage kommen Internet-Marktforscher zu dem Schluss, dass mehr als die Hälfte der Internet-User auch die Stellenbörsen nutzt. Kein Wunder: Wer in der Samstagsausgabe der „Süddeutschen Zeitung" oder der „Frankfurter Allgemeinen Zeitung" aus mehr als 10 000 Stellenanzeigen die paar für ihn in Frage kommenden herausfiltert, braucht viel Zeit. Bei Online-Börsen dagegen genügen ein paar Mausklicks.

45. Henning Müller hatte nach dem Praktikum vor,

   (A) die amerikanische Westküste zu besichtigen

   (B) in Europa Arbeit zu finden

   (C) sein Studium zu beenden

   (D) um die Welt zu reisen

46. Wie hat Henning Müller erreicht, was er wollte?

   (A) Er las täglich die Zeitung.

   (B) Er hatte gute Beziehungen.

   (C) Er schickte eine elektronische Bewerbung.

   (D) Er wurde gleich nach dem Studium eingestellt.

47. Welche Jobsuchenden finden vor allem eine Stelle übers Internet?

(A) Mediziner

(B) Marktforscher

(C) Büroangestellte

(D) Computerfachleute

48. Was ist der größte Vorteil einer Online-Jobsuche?

(A) Es gibt mehr als 10 000 Stellenanzeigen.

(B) Mehr als die Hälfte der Bewerber bekommt eine Stelle.

(C) Man kann schnell etwas Passendes finden.

(D) Die Stellenbörsen bieten immer Samstagsausgaben an.

Wir sind ein führendes Unternehmen in der Möbelindustrie mit Fertigungsstätten an neun Standorten in Deutschland. Unsere Produkte genießen den Ruf guter Qualität und unser Marktanteil wächst ständig.

Es wird ein/e

Produktionsleiter/in

gesucht, der/die für den gesamten Fertigungsprozess verantwortlich ist. Zu den Aufgaben gehören die Leitung der Produktion unter Einhaltung der Qualitätsvorschriften, Erfüllung der Produktionsziele und die Führung des Personals.

Wir bieten viel Arbeit, aber auch kreative Mitarbeiter, Gleitzeit und ein angemessenes Gehalt an. Ein moderner Arbeitsplatz ist selbstverständlich.

Anforderungsprofil:

- Erfahrung auf dem Bereich der Holzverarbeitung
- Planungs-und Organisationsfähigkeiten
- Kenntnisse mit dem Datenbanksystem Quadratur

Idealerweise hat der Kandidat/die Kandidatin ein technisches Studium an einer Fachhochschule absolviert.

Schicken Sie bitte Ihre schriftliche Bewerbung mit tabellarischem Lebenslauf, Zeugniskopien sowie Angaben zum Einkommen und zu Ihrer Verfügbarkeit an:

Personalabteilung
Wolters & Partner GmbH
Theresienstr. 34
24943 Flensburg

Telefon: 0461- 2557117 Telefax: 0461- 2557123

---

49. Was produziert die Firma Wolters & Partner?

(A) Autos

(B) Holzspielzeug

(C) Datenbanksysteme

(D) Möbel

50. Was für eine Stelle wird angeboten?

    (A) Eine Lehrlingsstelle

    (B) Eine Halbtagsstelle

    (C) Eine führende Stelle

    (D) Eine unbezahlte Stelle

51. Was bietet die Firma dem neuen Firmenmitglied?

    (A) Ein zeitgemäßes Büro

    (B) Einen Dienstwagen

    (C) Gute Aufstiegsmöglichkeiten

    (D) Eine moderne Wohnung

52. Wie sollen sich die Kandidaten bewerben?

    (A) Sie sollen bei der Firma anrufen.

    (B) Sie sollen bei der Firma vorbeikommen.

    (C) Sie sollen der Firma eine E-Mail schicken.

    (D) Sie sollen der Firma schreiben.

Thomas Nast wurde am 26. September 1840 als Sohn eines bayerischen Militärmusikers in Landau in der Pfalz geboren. Als Sechsjähriger wanderte er mit seiner Familie nach Amerika aus. Noch nicht des Englischen mächtig, konnte sich der Knabe mit Zeichnungen auf seiner Schiefertafel verständlich machen. Schon früh durfte er eine Kunstschule besuchen, musste sie jedoch mit 15 wieder verlassen, um zum Familienunterhalt beizutragen. Nach der ersten Vorsprache bei *Leslie's Weekly* wurde er für vier Dollar die Woche als Illustrator engagiert. Im Auftrag von *Harper's Weekly* suchte Nast während des amerikanischen Bürgerkrieges die Schlachtfelder des Südens auf und schickte von dort so eindrucksvolle Skizzen nach Hause, dass er am Ende des Krieges im ganzen Land bekannt war.

Zwischen 1861 und 1884 wurde Nast immer mehr als politischer und sozialkritischer Karikaturist bekannt. Er machte mehrere politische Symbolfiguren populär, wie z.B. Uncle Sam, John Bull und die Columbia. Seinen berühmten Santa Claus hat Nast nach dem Vorbild des „Pelznikel", des Sankt Nikolaus seiner deutschen Vorfahren, gestaltet.

Durch das Scheitern eines seiner Lieblingspläne – der Herausgabe einer eigenen Karikaturzeitschrift – geriet Nast in Schulden. Als ihm daraufhin sein alter Bewunderer Theodore Roosevelt den Posten eines Generalkonsuls in Ecuador anbot, nahm er diesen Vorschlag an. Er starb am 7. Dezember 1902 – nicht ohne vorher seine Schulden beglichen und seiner Familie etwas Geld hinterlassen zu haben.

53. Warum hat Nast als Kind auf seine Schiefertafel gezeichnet?

    (A) Die Skizzen gefielen seiner Familie.

    (B) Er konnte zu wenig Englisch.

    (C) Er verdiente damit Geld.

    (D) Er wollte eine Kunstschule besuchen.

54. Warum musste der 15-jährige Nast die Kunstschule verlassen?

    (A) Der amerikanische Bürgerkrieg war ausgebrochen.

    (B) Die Lehrer hielten ihn für unbegabt.

    (C) Seine Familie hatte nicht genügend Geld.

    (D) Seine sozialkritischen Karikaturen waren unbeliebt.

55. Wodurch wurde Nast in ganz Amerika bekannt?

    (A) Durch seine Zeichnungen vom Krieg

    (B) Durch seine Symbolfiguren

    (C) Durch seine Berichte aus Ecuador

    (D) Durch seine Arbeit als Politiker

56. Welche Symbolfigur Nasts hat einen deutschen Ursprung?

    (A) Uncle Sam

    (B) Columbia

    (C) John Bull

    (D) Santa Claus

57. Was hat Theodore Roosevelt für Nast getan?

    (A) Er half ihm, seine eigene Zeitschrift zu gründen.

    (B) Er gab ihm eine angesehene Stellung im Ausland.

    (C) Er hat ihm angeboten, seine Schulden zu bezahlen.

    (D) Er hat seiner Familie etwas Geld hinterlassen.

Zimmer frei!

16qm

für ein Jahr zu vermieten
(wegen Auslandsaufenthalt)
ab Aug. oder Sep. 01, bevorzugt an †
große 4er WG, z.Zt. †††
€295,-- kalt
(möbliert oder unmöbliert)
Lage: Nähe Schloßpark
Tel. 0542/55839

---

58. Das Zimmer wird frei, weil der Bewohner

    (A) das Zimmer zu klein findet

    (B) die hohe Miete nicht bezahlen kann

    (C) das Land für ein Jahr verlassen will

    (D) ins Stadtzentrum ziehen will

59. Wofür muss der Mieter extra bezahlen?

    (A) Die Heizung

    (B) Die Möbel

    (C) Die Lage

    (D) Den Parkplatz

Study Resources

Most textbooks used in college-level German language courses cover the topics in the outline given earlier, but the approaches to certain topics and the emphases given to them may differ. To prepare for the German Language exam, it is advisable to study one or more college textbooks, which can be found in most college bookstores. When selecting a textbook, check the table of contents against the knowledge and skills required for this test.

Besides studying basic vocabulary, you should understand and be able to apply the grammatical principles that make up the language. To improve your reading comprehension, read passages from textbooks, short magazine or newspaper articles, and other printed material of your choice. To improve your listening comprehension, seek opportunities to hear the language spoken by native speakers and to converse with native speakers. If you have opportunities to join organizations with German-speaking members, to attend German movies, or to listen to German-language radio broadcasts, take advantage of them.

Visit www.collegeboard.com/clepprep for additional German resources. You can also find suggestions for exam preparation in Chapter IV of the *Official Study Guide*. In addition, many college faculty post their course materials on their schools' Web sites.

Answer Key

1.	C	31.	C
2.	D	32.	B
3.	A	33.	A
4.	C	34.	D
5.	D	35.	B
6.	B	36.	D
7.	A	37.	B
8.	D	38.	C
9.	C	39.	A
10.	B	40.	D
11.	B	41.	A
12.	C	42.	C
13.	D	43.	B
14.	D	44.	D
15.	B	45.	B
16.	B	46.	C
17.	A	47.	D
18.	C	48.	C
19.	B	49.	D
20.	D	50.	C
21.	B	51.	A
22.	C	52.	D
23.	B	53.	B
24.	A	54.	C
25.	A	55.	A
26.	B	56.	D
27.	C	57.	B
28.	B	58.	C
29.	D	59.	A
30.	D		

Spanish Language

Description of the Examination

The Spanish Language examination is designed to measure knowledge and ability equivalent to that of students who have completed two to four semesters of college Spanish language study. The exam focuses on skills typically achieved from the end of the first year through the second year of college study; material taught during both years is incorporated into a single exam.

The examination contains approximately 120 questions to be answered in approximately 90 minutes. Some of these are pretest questions that will not be scored. There are three separately timed sections. The three sections are weighted so that each question contributes equally to the total score. Any time candidates spend on tutorials or providing personal information is in addition to the actual testing time.

There are two Listening sections and one Reading section. Each section has its own timing requirements.

- The two Listening sections together are approximately 30 minutes in length. The amount of time candidates have to answer a question varies according to the section and does not include the time they spend listening to the test material.
- The Reading section is 60 minutes in length.

Most colleges that award credit for the Spanish Language exam award either two or four semesters of credit, depending on the candidate's test scores.

Knowledge and Skills Required

Questions on the Spanish Language examination require candidates to comprehend written and spoken Spanish. The subject matter is drawn from the following abilities. The percentages next to the main topics indicate the approximate percentage of exam questions on that ability.

15%   **Section I:**
Listening: Rejoinders

     Listening comprehension through short oral exchanges

25%   **Section II:**
Listening: Dialogues and Narratives

     Listening comprehension through longer spoken selections

60%   **Section III:**
Reading

     16%   Part A: Discrete sentences (vocabulary and structure)

     20%   Part B: Short cloze passages (vocabulary and structure)

     24%   Part C: Reading passages and authentic stimulus materials (reading comprehension)

Sample Test Questions

The following sample questions do not appear on an actual CLEP examination. They are intended to give potential test-takers an indication of the format and difficulty level of the examination and to provide content for practice and review. Knowing the correct answers to all of the sample questions is not a guarantee of satisfactory performance on the exam.

In addition to samples of each question type are sample computer screens showing how the directions and questions will appear to the candidate taking the test. For listening items, the script of the recording normally played by the computer appears here as italicized text.

Listening Directions: This part of the test measures your ability to understand spoken Spanish.

There are two sections in this part of the test, with special directions for each section.

The two listening sections of the test total approximately 30 minutes in length. The amount of time you have to answer a question varies according to the section and does not include the time you spend listening to the test material. Timing begins after the Section Directions are dismissed.

You can change the volume by using the Volume testing tool.

The audio portions of the Listening sections of the test will be presented only one time.

Section I Directions: You will hear short conversations or parts of conversations. You will then hear four responses, designated (A), (B), (C), and (D).

After you hear the four responses, click on the lettered response oval that most logically continues or completes the conversation.

You will have 10 seconds to choose your response before the next conversation begins.

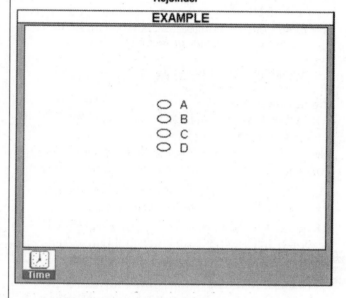

1. (WOMAN A) *¿Cómo está Ud. Señora Gómez?*

   (WOMAN B) (A) *Hace frío.*

   (B) *Bastante bien, gracias.*

   (C) *Mañana a las ocho.*

   (D) *Sí, por favor.*

2. (MAN A) *¿Cómo vino Julio?*

   (WOMAN A) (A) *Yo como con vino.*

   (B) *El vino no está bueno.*

   (C) *Vino en coche.*

   (D) *Vino en julio.*

3. (MAN A) *¿Quién llamó anoche?*

   (WOMAN A) (A) *No sé quién va.*

   (B) *Yo llamo después.*

   (C) *Viene esta noche.*

   (D) *Fue mi primo Luis.*

4. (WOMAN A) *¿Qué están poniendo dentro del cajón?*

   (MAN A)

   (A) *Está muy bien puesto.*

   (B) *Compraron las estampillas.*

   (C) *Lo están llenando con cartas.*

   (D) *Están trabajando en el sótano.*

5. (MAN A) *¿Si sigo esta calle llego a la Avenida Bolívar?*

   (WOMAN A) (A) *Bolívar fue el libertador de Venezuela.*

   (B) *Pues sí, es un señor hecho y derecho.*

   (C) *No señor, conduce al Paseo de la República.*

   (D) *Si tu mamá te lo permite, te lo consentiré.*

6. (WOMAN A) *Mozo, ¿cuánto le debo?*

   (MAN A)

   (A) *Ahora mismo le subo las maletas, señora.*

   (B) *Ud. debe marcharse en seguida.*

   (C) *Enseguida le traigo la cuenta.*

   (D) *¿Cuántos cree usted que hay aquí?*

Section II Directions: You will hear a series of selections, such as dialogues, announcements, and narratives. Each audio selection may be accompanied by a graphic or a picture.

Each selection is followed by one or more questions. **You will have a total of 12 minutes to answer the questions in this section. Note: The timer is activated only when you are answering questions.**

The questions have various formats. Some questions offer four possible responses, each with an oval to click to indicate your answer. Other questions ask you to select part of a graphic, fill out a table, or put a list in the correct order; for some of these questions, you will have to click in more than one

place to complete your response. For these questions, follow the specific directions given.

In this section, you may adjust the volume only when a question is on your screen. It will affect the volume of the <u>next</u> audio prompt you hear. **You cannot change the volume while the audio prompt is playing.**

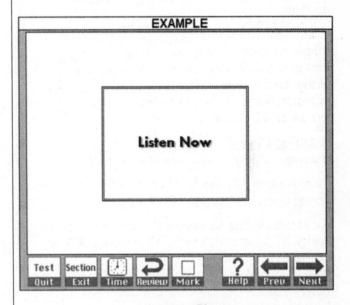

EXAMPLE

Listen Now

Test / Quit   Section / Exit   Time   Review   Mark   ? Help   Prev   Next

Listening comprehension

EXAMPLE

¿Qué debe hacer la muchacha?

○ Levantarse.
○ Esperar cinco minutos.
○ Hablar del tiempo.
○ Poner el reloj en hora.

Test / Quit   Section / Exit   Time   Review   Mark   ? Help   Prev   Next

(NARRATOR)   *En el aeropuerto.*

(MAN A)   *Señorita, ¿ya salió el vuelo 45 para Quito?*

(WOMAN A)   *Sí señor, acaba de salir.*

(MAN A)   *¡Qué lástima! ¿Y cuándo es el próximo vuelo? Tengo necesidad de llegar a Quito esta noche.*

(WOMAN A)   *Lo siento mucho, señor, pero no hay vuelos a Quito de noche. El próximo sale a las siete de la mañana y llega a Quito a las nueve.*

7. ¿Cuándo llegará el señor a Quito?

(A) Esa noche

(B) Dentro de dos horas

(C) Al día siguiente

(D) La semana próxima

(NARRATOR)   *Escuchen esta conversación entre amigos.*

(WOMAN A)   *Oye, Ricardo, espéranos. ¿Adónde vas con tanta prisa?*

(MAN A)   *Me muero de hambre, Ana. Después de un examen tan difícil, voy corriendo para la cafetería. ¿Y tú?*

(WOMAN A)   *Pues, yo te acompaño, Ricardo. Quiero tomar un refresco, por lo menos.*

8. ¿Por qué tiene prisa Ricardo?

(A) Quiere comer.

(B) Quiere ir al cine.

(C) Quiere correr.

(D) Quiere charlar con Ana.

9. ¿Qué va a hacer Ana?

(A) Va a la cafetería también.

(B) Vuelve a la residencia.

(C) Come mucho.

(D) Va a otra clase.

(NARRATOR)   *En el restaurante.*

(MAN A)   *Buenas tardes, señores.*

(WOMAN A)   *Buenas tardes. ¿Nos trae la carta en seguida, por favor? Tenemos mucha prisa.*

(MAN A)   *Aquí la tienen ustedes. Recomiendo el plato del día hoy.*

10. ¿Con quién habla la mujer?

(A) Con un invitado

(B) Con el cocinero

(C) Con su esposo

(D) Con el camarero

(NARRATOR)   *Una opinión sobre Barcelona.*

(WOMAN A)   *A mí me encanta Barcelona. Es una ciudad muy grande donde encuentras de todo: restaurantes, tiendas, actividades. Si te gusta el arte, tiene buenos y variados museos. Si prefieres la música, Barcelona tiene una orquesta sinfónica excelente y un gran repertorio de ópera. Pero a mí, lo que más me gusta es la arquitectura de la ciudad. Barcelona está situada a orillas del mar Mediterráneo y tiene unas vistas muy bonitas. Lo que no me gusta es la contaminación y lo peor de todo es el ruido de la ciudad.*

11. La ciudad tiene un hermoso paisaje porque está

(A) en las montañas

(B) cerca del mar

(C) a la orilla de un lago

(D) en el desierto

12. A la narradora, ¿qué es lo que más le gusta de Barcelona?

    (A) Los museos

    (B) Los restaurantes

    (C) La orquesta sinfónica

    (D) Los edificios

13. ¿Qué es lo peor de la ciudad?

    (A) La ópera

    (B) El ruido

    (C) Las tiendas

    (D) La playa

(NARRATOR)   *Escuchen para saber quiénes hablan.*

(MAN A)   *Señora, Ud. recibió los libros el 18 del pasado mes, y hasta la fecha no hemos recibido su pago.*

(WOMAN A)   *Lo sé, pero cuando abrí el paquete, vi que me habían mandado dos libros que no pedí.*

14. ¿Quiénes hablan?

    (A) Un profesor y su alumna

    (B) Un vendedor y su cliente

    (C) Un abogado y la acusada

    (D) Un cartero y su jefe

(NARRATOR)   *Dos estudiantes hablan.*

(WOMAN A)   *Paco, ¿qué te parecieron esos ensayos de la tarea? ¿Crees que los hiciste bien?*

(MAN A)   *No sé, Alicia. Estudié con Pedro y con Carmen, repasé mis apuntes, releí capítulos enteros, pero no llegué a contestar todas las preguntas.*

(WOMAN A)   *Yo tampoco. No tuvimos suficiente tiempo para terminar, y estoy muy preocupada.*

(MAN A)   *¿No crees que tal vez deberíamos ir a ver al profesor a ver si nos da más tiempo?*

(WOMAN A)   *Bueno, podemos intentarlo, pero me parece que nos dirá que no.*

(MAN A)   *De todos modos debemos ir a verlo pues...¿quién sabe lo que pueda pasar...? ¿De acuerdo?*

(WOMAN A)   *De acuerdo. Acudamos a sus horas de oficina mañana a las diez.*

15. ¿Qué hizo el hombre para preparar su tarea?

    (A) Asistió a una conferencia.

    (B) Repasó con otros compañeros de clase.

    (C) Buscó información en la biblioteca.

    (D) Compró un libro de referencia.

16. La mujer está muy preocupada porque no tuvo suficiente tiempo para

    (A) repasar el libro

    (B) completar sus respuestas

    (C) consultar con el profesor

    (D) estudiar con sus compañeros

17. Los estudiantes van a pedirle al profesor que les

    (A) dé otra oportunidad

    (B) suba la nota

    (C) clarifique sus dudas

    (D) cambie de clase

Some questions require you to select cells in a table grid. The question based on the next listening selection is an example of this type of question.

To choose your answers to this type of question, you will click on the cells in the table grid.

18.

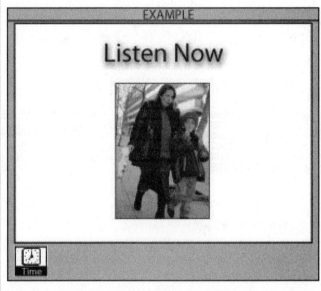

¿Qué van a pedir el muchacho y la muchacha para comer?

	El Muchacho	La Muchacha
Hamburguesa		
Papas fritas		
Pescado		
Pollo		

Click on your choices.

(NARRATOR)	Hablan dos jóvenes.
(WOMAN A)	Oigan chicos, ¡hay papas fritas en la cafetería!
(MAN A)	¡Qué rico! A mí me encantan las papas fritas con hamburguesa.
(WOMAN A)	¿Sí? Yo las prefiero con pollo.
(MAN A)	Sabes, cuando fui a Londres, comí pescado con papas fritas.
(WOMAN A)	¿Pescado?
(MAN A)	Sí, pescado frito con papas fritas es una de las comidas favoritas allá.
(WOMAN A)	Me alegro de que no estemos en Londres, porque esa combinación me parece algo rara.
(MAN A)	Pues en Londres es la comida rápida más común. ¡Ojalá la tuviéramos aquí! Pero pediré papas fritas con una hamburguesa.
(WOMAN A)	Bueno, y yo con pollo frito.

EXAMPLE

Listen Now

Time

(NARRATOR)	Una señora habla con su esposo por teléfono celular.
(MAN A)	¿Aló?
(WOMAN A)	Aló Enrique. Acabo de salir de la farmacia con Jorgito. Regresaré a casa en media hora.
(MAN A)	¿Qué pasó?
(WOMAN A)	El niño tenía una fiebre muy alta, le dolía la garganta y no podía tragar esta mañana.

(MAN A)	*¡Pobrecito! ¿Entonces, qué hiciste?*
(WOMAN A)	*Llamé al consultorio del doctor Alvarado. La enfermera me dijo que debería llevarlo a ver al médico tan pronto fuera posible. Me dio una cita inmediatamente.*
(MAN A)	*¿Y lo examinó el doctor?*
(WOMAN A)	*Sí. Pues, le recetó un antibiótico y me dijo que le diera dos píldoras como primera dosis, y luego una, tres veces al día por diez días.*
(MAN A)	*Y, ahora, ¿cómo se siente?*
(WOMAN A)	*Un poco mejor, ¡ya me pidió una galleta!*

19. ¿Quién sugirió que el niño fuera al consultorio?

    (A) La enfermera
    (B) El padre
    (C) El doctor
    (D) La madre

20. ¿Qué le recomendó el médico al niño?

    (A) Beber muchos líquidos
    (B) Quedarse en cama
    (C) Tomar medicamento
    (D) Comer galletas

Section III Reading Directions: This section measures your ability to read Spanish.

There are three parts in this section, with special directions for each part.

The Reading section is approximately 60 minutes in length.

Part A Directions: Each incomplete statement is followed by four suggested completions. Select the one that is best in each case by clicking on the corresponding oval.

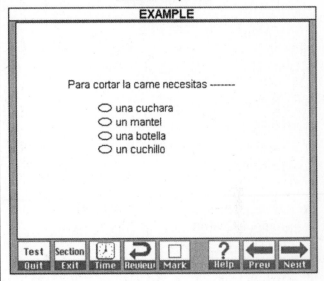

21. Dudo que ------- terminar el capítulo.

    (A) pudo
    (B) puedo
    (C) podía
    (D) pueda

22. Él se enfadó y yo no ------- dije nada.

    (A) se
    (B) le
    (C) lo
    (D) la

23. Mi padre me mandó devolver el libro a la ------- antes de que se venciera el plazo.

    (A) biblioteca
    (B) revista
    (C) página
    (D) publicidad

24. Entré en la casa sin que nadie se ------- cuenta.

    (A) da
    (B) dio
    (C) diera
    (D) daba

25. ¿Qué programa vamos a mirar esta noche? Prefiero ------- que sea alegre.

    (A) uno
    (B) un
    (C) una
    (D) alguna

26. Los señores Gómez viajan ------- por América Central.

    (A) a más tardar
    (B) a lo largo
    (C) a la orden
    (D) a menudo

27. Dicen que una de las gemelas es tan buena guitarrista ------- la otra.

    (A) que
    (B) como
    (C) de
    (D) tan

28. Era la medianoche y Susana ------- no había terminado su tarea.

    (A) ya
    (B) pero
    (C) cuando
    (D) todavía

29. A todos los profesores de esta facultad nos molesta mucho que los estudiantes no ------- a tiempo.

    (A) llegues
    (B) llegue
    (C) lleguen
    (D) lleguemos

30. Tengo que ir a la joyería para recoger -------.

    (A) la corbata
    (B) el chaleco
    (C) el arpa
    (D) la sortija

31. La tarea de matemáticas estuvo -------, pero Amalia me ayudó a entenderla.

    (A) compuesta
    (B) complacida
    (C) complicada
    (D) comprometida

Part B Directions: In each of the following paragraphs, there are blanks indicating that words or phrases have been omitted. When a blank is shaded, four completions are provided.

First, read through the entire paragraph. Then, for each blank, choose the completion that is most appropriate, given the context of the entire paragraph. Click on the corresponding oval.

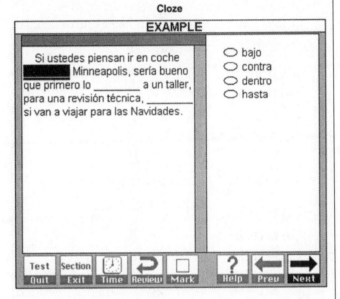

Cloze

EXAMPLE

Si ustedes piensan ir en coche ▓▓▓▓ Minneapolis, sería bueno que primero lo _____ a un taller, para una revisión técnica, _____ si van a viajar para las Navidades.

○ bajo
○ contra
○ dentro
○ hasta

El chocolate comenzó siendo una bebida de ricos pero __(32)__ se popularizó. En el Madrid del siglo XVII era tan popular que no había calle __(33)__ uno, dos o tres puestos donde se hacía y __(34)__ el chocolate. En la España de hoy, estos puestos han sido __(35)__ por chocolaterías. Las chocolaterías, que __(36)__ encontrarse en casi todas las ciudades españolas, son locales que sirven de manera casi __(37)__ chocolate a la taza.

32. (A) tarde
    (B) pronto
    (C) antes
    (D) aun

33. (A) para
    (B) con
    (C) por
    (D) sin

34. (A) vendía
    (B) vendo
    (C) vender
    (D) vendió

35. (A) ordenados
    (B) sustituidos
    (C) arreglados
    (D) olvidados

36. (A) podré
    (B) pudiera
    (C) pueden
    (D) puedo

37. (A) exclusiva
    (B) ordinaria
    (C) privada
    (D) abierta

Nunca voy a olvidar la fiesta de Año Nuevo que pasé en Lima hace unos años. Yo estaba viviendo en un barrio muy popular, y ahí, además de las fiestas, la gente tiene __(38)__ de hacer fuegos en las calles. Antes han armado muñecos con ropas viejas, periódicos, pedazos de madera y cualquier objeto inservible. Cuando se anuncia el nuevo año, se prende fuego a esos muñecos, mientras la gente se __(39)__ celebrando el Año Nuevo. Para mí fue una visión muy extraña ver todas esas cosas ardiendo en medio de la calle. Las personas actúan con bastante cuidado, felizmente, y no __(40)__ de incendios. Al día siguiente la gente recoge toda la basura y limpia la calle, para que el año __(41)__ bien.

38. (A) el antepasado
    (B) la tradición
    (C) las reglas
    (D) el costado

39. (A) abraza y sigue

    (B) abrazaban y seguían

    (C) abrazaba y seguía

    (D) abrazan y siguen

40. (A) supe

    (B) conocí

    (C) comprendí

    (D) aprendí

41. (A) comienza

    (B) comience

    (C) comenzar

    (D) comenzó

Había una vez un hombre que ___(42)___ en Buenos Aires, y estaba muy ___(43)___ porque era un hombre sano y trabajador. Pero un día se enfermó, y los médicos de la clínica le dijeron que solamente yéndose al campo podría curarse.

Sin embargo, él no quería ___(44)___, porque toda su familia residía en la ciudad.

42. (A) vivíamos

    (B) vivían

    (C) vivía

    (D) vivías

43. (A) contenta

    (B) contento

    (C) contentos

    (D) contentas

44. (A) vestirse

    (B) mudarse

    (C) sentarse

    (D) broncearse

Part C Directions: Read the following selections. Each selection is followed by one or more questions, incomplete statements, or commands.

For each question or incomplete statement, select the answer or completion that is best according to the selection. Click on the corresponding oval.

For each command, click on the appropriate area of the screen according to the directions given.

Prose

EXAMPLE

Los hermanos salieron a pasear por la noche alrededor de la plaza central. Cuando pasaron por enfrente de los portones oyeron los ladridos de unos perros que les asustaron.

¿A qué se refiere la palabra les?

○ a los perros
○ a los ladridos
○ a los portones
○ a los hermanos

Test | Section | Time | Review | Mark | Help | Prev | Next
Quit | Exit | | | | | |

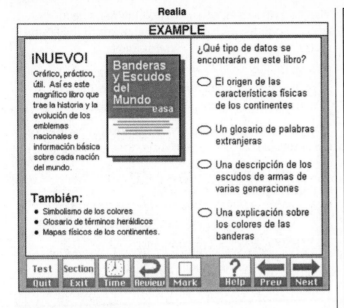

Realia

EXAMPLE

¡NUEVO!

Gráfico, práctico, útil. Así es este magnífico libro que trae la historia y la evolución de los emblemas nacionales e información básica sobre cada nación del mundo.

Banderas y Escudos del Mundo easa

También:
- Simbolismo de los colores
- Glosario de términos heráldicos
- Mapas físicos de los continentes.

¿Qué tipo de datos se encontrarán en este libro?

○ El origen de las características físicas de los continentes

○ Un glosario de palabras extranjeras

○ Una descripción de los escudos de armas de varias generaciones

○ Una explicación sobre los colores de las banderas

Test | Section | Time | Review | Mark | Help | Prev | Next
Quit | Exit

---

españa

El Centro Cultural Español le invita a un encuentro con el poeta

Ángel González

leerá su poesía
Viernes, 19 de marzo,
8:00 p.m.

Centro Cultural Español
800 Douglas Road,
Suite 170 Coral Gables, FL

RSVP 305-555-9677

Recepción prevista
tras la lectura

Aparcamiento disponible
en el garaje de
La Puerta del Sol
$4.00

Entrada por la calle Calabria
esquina a Galiano

Encuentros es un ciclo dedicado a los creadores y escritores que en España, los Estados Unidos, más concretamente en el sur de la Florida, y la zona del Caribe utilizan la lengua española como medio de expresión. Autores de diferentes nacionalidades presentan sus obras a lo largo del año mostrando la actualidad, diversidad y unidad de la literatura escrita en los dos continentes.

Querida amiga María:

Hace algún tiempo que quería escribirte, pero he estado muy ocupada con mis estudios. Tengo cuatro clases este semestre y apenas tengo tiempo para atender mis asuntos personales. No quiero que pienses que me he olvidado de nuestra amistad. Siempre recuerdo con cariño los buenos momentos que pasamos juntas cuando éramos niñas. Dentro de unos meses, cuando termine mis estudios, espero que podamos reunirnos nuevamente y conversar muchísimo. ¡Tengo tanto que contarte!

Recibe todo el cariño de tu amiga que nunca te olvida,

Emilia

45. ¿Por qué razón Emilia no le había escrito antes a María?

(A) Porque estudiaban juntas cuando eran niñas

(B) Porque sus estudios no se lo permitían

(C) Porque María se había olvidado de su amiga

(D) Porque Emilia no tenía ganas de escribirle a nadie

46. María y Emilia son dos

(A) estudiantes de la misma universidad

(B) antiguas y buenas amigas

(C) invitadas a una fiesta

(D) famosas escritoras contemporáneas

47. ¿Cuál es el tema central del ciclo "Encuentros"?

(A) Las culturas indígenas del Caribe

(B) La llegada de los españoles a la Florida

(C) La literatura contemporánea

(D) El aprendizaje del español

48. ¿Quién invita a este evento?

(A) Ángel González

(B) El Rey de España

(C) El Centro Cultural Español

(D) La ciudad de Coral Gables

49. ¿Qué se anticipa después del programa de Ángel González?

(A) Una función social

(B) La inauguración del centro

(C) Una demostración de tecnología

(D) Una exhibición de libros

Benicarló, 24 de agosto. — "Día sin sol, día perdido", parecen pensar los turistas que visitan las playas españolas, a juzgar por su paciente exposición al sol todas las horas en que es posible. Un avispado hotelero, dueño de una serie de apartamentos en la zona de playa que va desde Benicarló a Peñíscola, ha decidido hacer de esta frase su lema. Por ello ha hecho colocar grandes anuncios declarando que está dispuesto a bajar el precio a sus inquilinos por cada día sin sol. Hasta ahora, y como es tradicional en la zona, el sol no le ha hecho perder dinero porque ha lucido a más y mejor. A pesar de todo, el lema no deja de hacer efecto en los turistas que llenan sus apartamentos, tostándose muy a gusto en las playas cercanas.

50. La frase, "Día sin sol, día perdido", sirvió

(A) para confirmar el pésimo clima de la región

(B) como lema de la campaña propagandista del hotelero

(C) para desilusionar a los más fuertes tradicionalistas

(D) como serio obstáculo a todo plan de desarrollo económico

51. Benicarló y Peñíscola deben ser dos

(A) turistas

(B) hoteleros

(C) pueblos de la costa

(D) casas de apartamentos

52. Los turistas frecuentan aquella zona de España para

(A) lucir sus trajes de moda

(B) alquilar apartamentos en la sierra

(C) asistir a exposiciones

(D) aprovechar el sol y la playa

53. ¿Qué les pasaría a los clientes del hotelero los días sin sol?

(A) Podrían pintar dentro del hotel.

(B) Dejarían el apartamento.

(C) Le pagarían menos al hotelero.

(D) No le pagarían nada al hotelero.

54. El dueño de los apartamentos quedó satisfecho con su plan porque

(A) los inquilinos se resignaron a pagar la cuota extraordinaria

(B) el sol salió a lucir como nunca en la zona

(C) a los turistas les gustó pasar todo el tiempo fuera de la zona

(D) habría muchos inquilinos los días sin sol

Con una avanzada tecnología educativa, un cuerpo docente integrado por profesionales en actividad y moderno equipamiento.
Nuestros planes de estudio ofrecen salidas laborales concretas y de gran porvenir.

CARRERAS QUE SE CURSAN: PUBLICIDAD - DIRECCIÓN Y ADMINISTRACIÓN DE EMPRESAS - COMERCIO EXTERIOR - PERIODISMO - DISEÑO GRÁFICO Y PUBLICITARIO - ADMINISTRACIÓN DE SEGUROS - ADMINISTRACIÓN DE SALUD - ADMINISTRACIÓN BANCARIA - GESTIÓN AMBIENTAL - TURISMO - SISTEMAS DE DISTRIBUCIÓN.

UNIVERSIDAD DE CIENCIAS EMPRESARIALES Y SOCIALES

ABIERTA LA INSCRIPCIÓN

CENTROS DE ATENCIÓN
Rivadavia 1376 - Buenos Aires
Horario de atención : de 9 a 20 hs.
Teléfono : 555-0202

55. ¿Que tipo de profesión se puede estudiar en esta universidad?

(A) Cursos de astrofísica
(B) Cursos de medicina
(C) Estudios técnico-profesionales
(D) Estudios del área legal

56. Un estudiante interesado podrá obtener

(A) información por teléfono
(B) admisión gratuita de inmediato
(C) tecnología avanzada por teléfono
(D) actividad profesional en seguida

Some questions require you to select a part of the reading selection. Two of the questions based on the next reading selection are examples of this type of question.

57.

César Vallejo, gran escritor y antifascista feroz, nació en Santiago de Chuco, Perú, en 1892. Publicó su primer libro de poemas, *Los heraldos negros*, cuando tenía menos de treinta años. En 1920 fue acusado por actividad incendiaria y encarcelado por 112 días. Viajó a la Unión Soviética, España y París durante los años veinte, pero fue expulsado de Francia por razones políticas; se trasladó entonces a España de nuevo donde se inscribió en el Partido Comunista. En 1932 regresó a París y vivió en la ilegalidad. Murió en París en 1938. En 1939 se editaron, de manera póstuma, los *Poemas humanos*.

¿Cuál es el tema principal del texto?

○ Las ideologías políticas del siglo pasado
○ La poesía peruana del siglo pasado
○ Los viajes a varios países europeos
○ Las experiencias de una figura literaria

58.

César Vallejo, gran escritor y antifascista feroz, nació en Santiago de Chuco, Perú, en 1892. Publicó su primer libro de poemas, *Los heraldos negros*, cuando tenía menos de treinta años. En 1920 fue acusado por actividad incendiaria y encarcelado por 112 días. Viajó a la Unión Soviética, España y París durante los años veinte, pero fue expulsado de Francia por razones políticas; se trasladó entonces a España de nuevo donde se inscribió en el Partido Comunista. En 1932 regresó a París y vivió en la ilegalidad. Murió en París en 1938. En 1939 se editaron, de manera póstuma, los *Poemas humanos*.

¿Con cuál de las siguientes afirmaciones estaría de acuerdo el autor del texto?

○ César Vallejo era de una ideología política conservadora.
○ César Vallejo gozaba de buenas relaciones con la justicia.
○ César Vallejo participó en la vida política de otros países.
○ César Vallejo publicó sus obras completas mientras vivía.

To choose your answer to this type of question, you will click on a part of the reading selection. This question indicates that the answer choices are each sentence in the text.

59.

César Vallejo, gran escritor y antifascista feroz, nació en Santiago de Chuco, Perú, en 1892. Publicó su primer libro de poemas, *Los heraldos negros*, cuando tenía menos de treinta años. En 1920 fue acusado por actividad incendiaria y encarcelado por 112 días. Viajó a la Unión Soviética, España y París durante los años veinte, pero fue expulsado de Francia por razones políticas; se trasladó entonces a España de nuevo donde se inscribió en el Partido Comunista. En 1932 regresó a París y vivió en la ilegalidad. Murió en París en 1938. En 1939 se editaron, de manera póstuma, los *Poemas humanos*.	Haz clic en la oración que expresa la edad de César Vallejo al iniciar su carrera.

To choose your answer to this type of question, you will click on a part of the reading selection. This question indicates that the answer choices are the bold words in the text.

60.

César Vallejo, gran escritor y antifascista feroz, nació en Santiago de Chuco, **Perú**, en 1892. Publicó su primer libro de poemas, *Los heraldos negros*, cuando tenía menos de treinta años. En 1920 fue acusado por actividad incendiaria y encarcelado por 112 días. Viajó a la **Unión Soviética**, **España** y París durante los años veinte, pero fue expulsado de **Francia** por razones políticas; se trasladó entonces a España de nuevo donde se inscribió en el Partido Comunista. En 1932 regresó a París y vivió en la ilegalidad. Murió en París en 1938. En 1939 se editaron, de manera póstuma, los *Poemas humanos*.	Haz clic en el país que le dio asilo político a César Vallejo. Las opciones aparecen en letra **negrilla**.

To choose your answer to question 65, you will click on a part of the reading selection. This question indicates that the answer choices are each sentence in the text.

61–65.

Sin embargo, ella no hizo ninguna mención del asunto hasta después de la medianoche, en la lancha, cuando sintió como una revelación sobrenatural que había encontrado por fin la ocasión propicia para decirme lo que sin duda era el motivo real de su viaje, y empezó con el modo y el tono y las palabras milimétricas que debió madurar en la soledad de sus insomnios desde mucho antes de emprenderlo.

—Tu papá está muy triste—dijo.

Ahí estaba, pues, el infierno tan temido. Empezaba como siempre, cuando menos se esperaba, y con una voz sedante que no había de alterarse ante nada. Sólo por cumplir con el ritual, pues conocía de sobra la respuesta, le pregunté:

—¿Y eso por qué?

—Porque dejaste los estudios.

—No los dejé—le dije—. Sólo cambié de carrera.

La idea de una discusión a fondo le levantó el ánimo.

—Tu papá dice que es lo mismo—dijo.

A sabiendas de que era falso, le dije—: También él dejó de estudiar para tocar el violín.

—No fue igual—replicó ella con una gran vivacidad—. El violín lo tocaba sólo en fiestas y serenatas. Si dejó sus estudios fue porque no tenía ni con qué comer. Pero en menos de un mes aprendió telegrafía, que entonces era una profesión muy buena, sobre todo en Aracataca.

—Yo también vivo de escribir en los periódicos—le dije.

—Eso lo dices para no mortificarme—dijo ella. Pero la mala situación se te nota de lejos. Cómo será, que cuando te vi en la librería no te reconocí.

—Yo tampoco la reconocí a usted—le dije.

—Pero no por lo mismo—dijo ella—. Yo pensé que eras un limosnero.

Me miró las sandalias gastadas, y agregó—: Y sin medias.

¿Cómo sonaban las palabras de la mujer en el segundo párrafo?

○ Atemorizadas
○ Nerviosas
○ Tranquilas
○ Tristes

¿Cómo se expresa la mujer al hablar con el narrador?

○ Con felicidad
○ Con miedo
○ Con reproche
○ Con capricho

Según la mujer, ¿por qué había dejado los estudios el padre del narrador?

○ Se mudó de la ciudad.
○ Le gustaba tocar el violín.
○ Tuvo que ganarse la vida.
○ No soportaba los estudios.

¿Por quién tomó la mujer al narrador cuando lo vio en la librería?

○ Un zapatero
○ Un mendigo
○ Un librero
○ Un músico

Haz clic en la oración que indica la profesión del narrador.

Study Resources

Most textbooks used in college-level Spanish language courses cover the topics in the outline given earlier, but the approaches to certain topics and the emphases given to them may differ. To prepare for the Spanish Language exam, it is advisable to study one or more college textbooks, which can be found in most college bookstores. When selecting a textbook, check the table of contents against the knowledge and skills required for this test.

Besides studying basic vocabulary, you should understand and be able to apply the grammatical principles that make up the language. To improve your reading comprehension, read passages from textbooks, short magazine or newspaper articles, or other printed material of your choice. To improve your listening comprehension, seek opportunities to hear the language spoken by native speakers and to converse with native speakers.

If you have opportunities to join organizations with Spanish-speaking members, to attend Spanish movies, or to listen to Spanish-language television or radio broadcasts, take advantage of them.

Visit www.collegeboard.com/clepprep for additional Spanish resources. You can also find suggestions for exam preparation in Chapter IV of the *Official Study Guide*. In addition, many college faculty post their course materials on their schools' Web sites.

18.

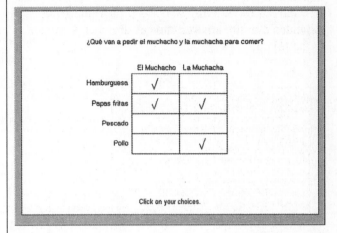

59.

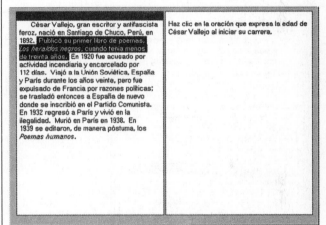

60.

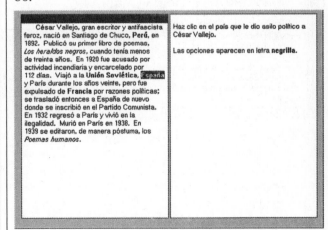

Answer Key

For some questions, the correct answer is indicated on the screens to the right.

#	Ans	#	Ans	#	Ans
1.	B	23.	A	45.	B
2.	C	24.	C	46.	B
3.	D	25.	A	47.	C
4.	C	26.	D	48.	C
5.	C	27.	B	49.	A
6.	C	28.	D	50.	B
7.	C	29.	C	51.	C
8.	A	30.	D	52.	D
9.	A	31.	C	53.	C
10.	D	32.	B	54.	B
11.	B	33.	D	55.	C
12.	D	34.	A	56.	A
13.	B	35.	B	57.	D (4th choice)
14.	B	36.	C	58.	C (3rd choice)
15.	B	37.	A	59.	To the right
16.	B	38.	B	60.	To the right
17.	A	39.	A	61.	C
18.	To the right	40.	A	62.	C
19.	A	41.	B	63.	C
20.	C	42.	C	64.	B
21.	D	43.	B	65.	On page 188.
22.	B	44.	B		

65.

Sin embargo, ella no hizo ninguna mención del asunto hasta después de la medianoche, en la lancha, cuando sintió como una revelación sobrenatural que había encontrado por fin la ocasión propicia para decirme lo que sin duda era el motivo real de su viaje, y empezó con el modo y el tono y las palabras milimétricas que debió madurar en la soledad de sus insomnios desde mucho antes de emprenderlo.

—Tu papá está muy triste—dijo.

Ahí estaba, pues, el infierno tan temido. Empezaba como siempre, cuando menos se esperaba, y con una voz sedante que no había de alterarse ante nada. Sólo por cumplir con el ritual, pues conocía de sobra la respuesta, le pregunté:

—¿Y eso por qué?

—Porque dejaste los estudios.

—No los dejé—le dije—. Sólo cambié de carrera.

La idea de una discusión a fondo le levantó el ánimo.

—Tu papá dice que es lo mismo—dijo.

A sabiendas de que era falso, le dije—: También él dejó de estudiar para tocar el violín.

—No fue igual—replicó ella con una gran vivacidad—. El violín lo tocaba sólo en fiestas y serenatas. Si dejó sus estudios fue porque no tenía ni con qué comer. Pero en menos de un mes aprendió telegrafía, que entonces era una profesión muy buena, sobre todo en Aracataca.

—Yo también vivo de escribir en los periódicos—le dije.

—Eso lo dices para no mortificarme—dijo ella. Pero la mala situación se te nota de lejos. Cómo será, que cuando te vi en la librería no te reconocí.

—Yo tampoco la reconocí a usted—le dije.

—Pero no por lo mismo—dijo ella—. Yo pensé que eras un limosnero. Me miró las sandalias gastadas, y agregó—: Y sin medias.

Haz clic en la oración que indica la profesión del narrador.

American Government

Description of the Examination

The American Government examination covers material that is usually taught in a one-semester introductory course in American government and politics at the college level. The scope and emphasis of the exam reflect what is most commonly taught in introductory American government and politics courses in political science departments around the United States. These courses go beyond a general understanding of civics to incorporate political processes and behavior. The exam covers topics such as the institutions and policy processes of the federal government, the federal courts and civil liberties, political parties and interest groups, political beliefs and behavior, and the content and history of the Constitution.

The examination contains approximately 100 questions to be answered in 90 minutes. Some of these are pretest questions that will not be scored. Any time candidates spend on tutorials and providing personal information is in addition to the actual testing time.

Knowledge and Skills Required

Questions on the American Government examination require candidates to demonstrate one or more of the following abilities in the approximate proportions indicated.

- Knowledge of American government and politics (about 55–60% of the exam)
- Understanding of typical patterns of political processes and behavior (including the components of the behavioral situation of a political actor), the principles used to explain or justify various governmental structures and procedures (about 30–35% of the exam)
- Analysis and interpretation of simple data that are relevant to American government and politics (10–15% of the exam)

The subject matter of the American Government examination is drawn from the following topics. The percentages next to the main topics indicate the approximate percentage of exam questions on that topic.

30–35% Institutions and Policy Processes: Presidency, Bureaucracy, and Congress

- The major formal and informal institutional arrangements and powers
- Structure, policy processes, and outputs
- Relationships among these three institutions and links between them and political parties, interest groups, the media, and public opinion

15–20% Federal Courts, Civil Liberties, and Civil Rights

- Structure and processes of the judicial system with emphasis on the role and influence of the Supreme Court
- The development of civil rights and civil liberties by judicial interpretation
- The Bill of Rights
- Incorporation of the Bill of Rights
- Equal protection and due process

15–20% Political Parties and Interest Groups

- Political parties (including their function, organization, mobilization, historical development, and effects on the political process)
- Interest groups (including the variety of activities they typically undertake and their effects on the political process)
- Elections (including the electoral process)

10–15% Political Beliefs and Behavior

- Processes by which citizens learn about politics
- Political participation (including voting behavior)
- Public opinion
- Beliefs that citizens hold about their government and its leaders

- Political culture (the variety of factors that predispose citizens to differ from one another in terms of their political perceptions, values, attitudes, and activities)
- The influence of public opinion on political leaders

15–20% Constitutional Underpinnings of American Democracy

The development of concepts such as:
- Federalism (with attention to intergovernmental relations)
- Separation of powers
- Checks and balances
- Majority rule
- Minority rights
- Considerations that influenced the formulation and adoption of the Constitution
- Theories of democracy

Sample Test Questions

The following sample questions do not appear on an actual CLEP examination. They are intended to give potential test-takers an indication of the format and difficulty level of the examination and to provide content for practice and review. Knowing the correct answers to all of the sample questions is not a guarantee of satisfactory performance on the exam.

Directions: Each of the questions or incomplete statements below is followed by five suggested answers or completions. Select the one that is best in each case.

1. Which of the following statements best reflects the pluralist theory of American politics?

   (A) American politics is dominated by a small elite.

   (B) Public policies emerge from cooperation among elites in business, labor, and government.

   (C) Public policies emerge from compromises reached among competing groups.

   (D) American politics is dominated by cities at the expense of rural areas.

   (E) The American political arena is made up of isolated individuals who have few group affiliations outside the family.

2. Which of the following is generally the most significant influence on an individual's identification with a particular political party?

   (A) Religious affiliation

   (B) Family

   (C) Level of education

   (D) Television

   (E) The party identification of the incumbent President

3. Which of the following committee assignments would confer the most power and influence on members of the House of Representatives?

   (A) Agriculture

   (B) Ways and Means

   (C) Veterans' Affairs

   (D) Armed Services

   (E) Education and Labor

4. Which of the following statements about *Brown v. Board of Education of Topeka* is correct?

   (A) It declared segregation by race in the public schools unconstitutional.

   (B) It established the principle of one person, one vote.

   (C) It required that citizens about to be arrested be read a statement concerning their right to remain silent.

   (D) It declared Bible reading in the public schools unconstitutional.

   (E) It declared segregation by race in places of public accommodation unconstitutional.

5. Prior to the Voting Rights Act of 1965, literacy tests were used by some southern states to

   (A) determine the educational achievement of potential voters

   (B) prevent African Americans from exercising their right to vote

   (C) assess the general population's understanding of the Constitution

   (D) hinder the migration of northerners

   (E) defend the practice of segregation

6. The practice whereby individual senators can veto federal judicial nominations in their respective states is called

(A) logrolling

(B) preferential treatment

(C) senatorial prerogative

(D) senatorial courtesy

(E) judicial selection

7. Differences between House and Senate versions of a bill are resolved

(A) in a conference committee

(B) by the rules committees of both chambers

(C) in subcommittee hearings

(D) by the president before the bill is signed into law

(E) during the bill's markup phase

8. Which of the following principles protects a citizen from imprisonment without trial?

(A) Representative government

(B) Separation of powers

(C) Due process

(D) Checks and balances

(E) Popular sovereignty

9. The passage of legislation in Congress often depends on mutual accommodations among members. This suggests that, to some extent, congressional behavior is based on

(A) ideological divisions

(B) partisan division

(C) the principle of reciprocity

(D) deference to state legislatures

(E) norms of seniority

10. Which of the following statements accurately describes the president's veto power?

 I. A president sometimes threatens to veto a bill that is under discussion in order to influence congressional decision-making.

 II. A president typically vetoes about a third of the bills passed by Congress.

 III. Congress is usually unable to override a president's veto.

(A) I only

(B) III only

(C) I and III only

(D) II and III only

(E) I, II, and III

11. All of the following issues were decided at the Constitutional Convention of 1787 EXCEPT

(A) representation in the legislature

(B) voting qualifications of the electorate

(C) the method of electing the president

(D) congressional power to override a presidential veto

(E) qualifications for members of the House and Senate

12. Which of the following statements about political action committees (PACs) is true?

(A) PACs may give unlimited contributions to the election campaigns of individual candidates.

(B) PAC spending has not kept pace with inflation.

(C) PAC activity is limited to direct contributions to political parties.

(D) Social-issue groups are the source of most PAC dollars.

(E) PACs are more likely to support an incumbent candidate than a challenger, regardless of the incumbent's party affiliation.

13. The usefulness to the president of having cabinet members as political advisers is undermined by the fact that

    (A) the president has little latitude in choosing cabinet members

    (B) cabinet members have no political support independent of the president

    (C) cabinet members are usually drawn from Congress and retain loyalties to Congress

    (D) the loyalties of cabinet members are often divided between loyalty to the president and loyalty to their own executive departments

    (E) the cabinet operates as a collective unit and individual members have no access to the president

14. All of the following are constitutional rights EXCEPT the right to

    (A) remain silent during questioning

    (B) be represented by counsel

    (C) be indicted by grand jury

    (D) be informed of the charges pending

    (E) receive a trial by jury in a criminal case

15. In the electoral history of the United States, third parties have been effective vehicles of protest when they

    (A) aligned themselves with one of the major parties

    (B) presented innovative programs in Congress

    (C) dramatized issues and positions that were being ignored by the major parties

    (D) chose the president by depriving either of the major parties of an electoral college victory

    (E) supported a political agenda that appealed especially to women

16. Which of the following best defines the term "judicial activism"?

    (A) The tendency of judges to hear large numbers of cases on social issues

    (B) The efforts of judges to lobby Congress for funds

    (C) The unwillingness of judges to remove themselves from cases in which they have a personal interest

    (D) The attempts by judges to influence election outcomes

    (E) The attempts by judges to influence public policy through their case decisions

17. High levels of political participation have been found to be positively associated with which of the following?

    I. A high level of interest in politics
    II. A sense of political efficacy
    III. A strong sense of civic duty

    (A) III only

    (B) I and II only

    (C) I and III only

    (D) II and III only

    (E) I, II, and III

18. In the last thirty years, the single most important variable in determining the outcome of an election for a member of the House of Representatives has been

    (A) incumbency

    (B) personal wealth

    (C) previous political office held in the district

    (D) membership in the political party of the president

    (E) positions on key social issues

19. Which of the following best describes the concept of federalism embodied in the United States government?

    (A) The Constitution divides power between a central government and its constituent governments, with some powers being shared.

    (B) The Constitution grants all governmental powers to the central government, which may delegate authority to state governments.

    (C) State governments join together and form a central government, which exists solely by approval of the state governments.

    (D) The central government creates state governments.

    (E) State governments are sovereign in all matters except foreign policy, which is reserved to the central government.

20. The power of the Rules Committee in the House of Representatives primarily stems from its authority to

    (A) choose the chairs of other standing committees and issue rules for the selection of subcommittee chairs

    (B) initiate all spending legislation and hold budget hearings

    (C) limit the time for debate and determine whether amendments to a bill can be considered

    (D) determine the procedures by which nominations by the president will be approved by the House

    (E) choose the president if no candidate wins a majority in the electoral college

21. Which of the following is a function of the White House Office?

    (A) Advising the president on political decisions

    (B) Heading federal departments as the president's representative

    (C) Preparing the national budget for the president

    (D) Supervising national security agencies such as the CIA and FBI

    (E) Acting as a liaison between the vice president and Congress

22. A major difference between political parties and interest groups is that interest groups generally do NOT

    (A) suggest new legislation that is supportive of their interests

    (B) try to influence the outcome of legislation

    (C) occupy a place on the ballot

    (D) concern themselves with elections

    (E) have a national organization

23. An election is a "realigning" or "critical" election if

    (A) one party controls the Congress and the other controls the presidency

    (B) voter turnout is higher than expected

    (C) it occurs during a major war

    (D) there is a lasting change in party coalitions

    (E) the same party controls both Congress and the presidency

24. Which of the following Supreme Court cases involved the principle of "one person, one vote"?

    (A) *Baker v. Carr*

    (B) *Roe v. Wade*

    (C) *Mapp v. Ohio*

    (D) *Korematsu v. United States*

    (E) *Gideon v. Wainwright*

25. The passage of broad legislation that leaves the making of specific rules to the executive branch is an example of

    (A) shared powers

    (B) delegated authority

    (C) checks and balances

    (D) executive agreement

    (E) a legislative veto

26. The redrawing of congressional districts in such a way as to give special advantage to one political party is referred to as

    (A) electioneering

    (B) gerrymandering

    (C) logrolling

    (D) apportionment

    (E) politicization

27. The details of legislation are usually worked out in which of the following settings?

    (A) A party caucus

    (B) The majority leader's office

    (C) The floor of the House

    (D) Legislative hearings

    (E) A subcommittee

28. A theoretical explanation of the operation of diverse interests in American politics is found in

    (A) the Virginia Plan

    (B) John Stuart Mill's *On Liberty*

    (C) *The Federalist*

    (D) the Declaration of Independence

    (E) John Locke's *Two Treatises of Government*

29. Which of the following best describes the jurisdiction that the Constitution gives to the Supreme Court?

    (A) Much original jurisdiction and little appellate jurisdiction

    (B) Much original jurisdiction and no appellate jurisdiction

    (C) Little original jurisdiction and much appellate jurisdiction

    (D) No original jurisdiction and much appellate jurisdiction

    (E) No original jurisdiction and little appellate jurisdiction

How People Identify With Political Parties

All Voters

	Men			Women		
	Rep %	Dem %	D-R diff	Rep %	Dem %	D-R diff
2008	43	46	+3	33	56	+22
2004	48	43	-5	40	51	+11
2000	47	42	-5	38	51	+13
1996	49	43	-6	39	53	+14
1992	45	46	+1	40	52	+12

Young Voters Ages 18–29

	Men			Women		
	Rep %	Dem %	D-R diff	Rep %	Dem %	D-R diff
2008	38	52	+14	28	63	+35
2004	44	47	+3	36	54	+18
2000	46	44	-2	37	53	+16
1996	50	44	-6	38	55	+17
1992	52	42	-10	42	50	+8

Based on registered voters who identify with or lean towards the Democratic or Republican party; 1992–2004 figures are from the surveys conducted in the 12 months prior to each election; 2008 figures are from surveys conducted Oct. 2007–March 2008.

Source: Pew Research (http://pewresearch.org/pubs/813/gen-dems)

30. According to the table above, which of the following statements is true?

    (A) In every election women between the ages of 18–29 were more likely to identify themselves as Republicans than were women of all ages.

    (B) In the 2000 election, more than one-half of all men identified themselves as Democrats.

    (C) In every election the difference in partisan identification for men is greater than the difference in partisan identification for women.

    (D) In the 1996 election, women between the ages of 18–29 were more like to identify themselves as Democrats than were men between the ages of 18–29.

    (E) In the 2008 election, more men between the ages of 18–29 identified themselves as Republicans than Democrats.

31. Which of the following activities of American labor unions is permissible by law?

(A) Engaging in strikes

(B) Denying the public access to a business

(C) Refusing a subpoena to appear before Congress

(D) Disobeying a court injunction to return to work

(E) Requiring members to make political contributions

32. Which of the following best describes the relationship between socioeconomic status and participation in politics?

(A) The lower one's socioeconomic status, the more likely it is that one will run for public office.

(B) The higher one's socioeconomic status, the greater the probability of active involvement in the political process.

(C) Adults who are unemployed have a greater personal interest in policy and tend to participate more actively in politics than do employed adults.

(D) People in the lower socioeconomic status are the most likely to vote.

(E) There is no relationship between socioeconomic status and political participation.

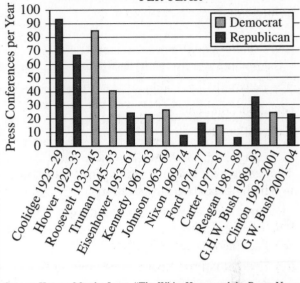

PRESIDENTIAL PRESS CONFERENCES PER YEAR

Source: Kumar, Martha Joynt "The White House and the Press: News Organizations as a Presidential Resource and as a Source of Pressure," Presidential Studies Quarterly 33, no.3 (September 2003): 669-670.

33. According to the information in the chart above, which of the following statements are true?

(A) Republican presidents held far fewer press conferences per year than Democratic presidents.

(B) The most recent presidents held fewer press conferences per year than presidents in the 1920s and 1930s.

(C) President Clinton held more press conferences per year than his predecessor.

(D) On average, President Nixon held more press conferences per year than President Johnson.

(E) President Kennedy held more press conferences per year than President Eisenhower.

34. One important change in political culture since the Second World War is that United States citizens have become

(A) less trusting of governmental institutions and leaders

(B) less likely to think of themselves as ideologically moderate

(C) less likely to support civil rights

(D) more likely to believe that their actions can influence government policy

(E) more trusting of nongovernmental institutions and leaders

35. All of the following statements correctly describe judicial appointments at the federal level EXCEPT

(A) Congress nominates and confirms all appointments to the federal judiciary.

(B) Federal judicial appointments are sent for evaluation to the American Bar Association's Committee on the Federal Judiciary.

(C) If a senator is a member of the president's party, tradition may allow the senator to exercise an informal veto over an individual being considered from the senator's state.

(D) Presidents seldom recommend for judicial appointment individuals from the opposition political party.

(E) Federal judgeships are often considered by presidents as patronage positions.

36. Which of the following agencies determines the domestic monetary policy of the United States?

(A) The Council of Economic Advisors

(B) The United States Department of the Treasury

(C) The Office of Management and Budget

(D) The Federal Reserve Board

(E) The Export-Import Bank

37. Under which of the following conditions are interest groups most likely to influence policy-making?

(A) When a problem has been dramatized by television network news

(B) When the president has made a major address on the subject

(C) When the parties in Congress have opposing positions on the issue

(D) When presidential candidates have been disagreeing with one another on the subject

(E) When the issue is a highly technical one requiring very detailed legislation

38. All of the following help to explain the president's difficulty in controlling cabinet-level agencies EXCEPT:

(A) Agencies often have political support from interest groups.

(B) Agency staff often have information and technical expertise that the president and presidential advisers lack.

(C) The president cannot dismiss appointees after they have been confirmed by the Senate.

(D) Civil servants who remain in their jobs through changes of administration develop loyalties to their agencies.

(E) Congress is a competitor for influence over the bureaucracy.

39. In the Constitution as originally ratified in 1788, the provisions regarding which of the following most closely approximate popular, majoritarian democracy?

(A) Election of members of the House of Representatives

(B) Election of members of the Senate

(C) Election of the president

(D) Ratification of treaties

(E) Confirmation of presidential appointments

40. The most likely and often the most powerful policy coalition of interests is likely to include a federal agency plus which of the following?

(A) Related agencies in the bureaucracy and a congressional committee chairperson

(B) Congress and the president

(C) An interest group and the president

(D) An interest group and a congressional subcommittee

(E) An interest group and the majority party

41. Throughout most of the twentieth century, which of the following was most likely to occur in midterm congressional elections?

(A) The party of the president typically lost seats in Congress, regardless of whether the president was a Republican or a Democrat.

(B) The party of the president typically gained seats in Congress, regardless of whether the president was a Republican or a Democrat.

(C) The Democratic Party gained seats in Congress, whereas the Republican Party lost seats.

(D) The Republican Party gained seats in Congress, whereas the Democratic Party lost seats.

(E) Voter turnout was typically higher than in presidential elections.

42. Delegates to the Republican and Democratic national conventions are primarily chosen

(A) by local party leaders

(B) in primaries

(C) in state caucuses

(D) by members of Congress

(E) by lottery

TRUST IN THE FEDERAL GOVERNMENT VERSUS YOUR OWN STATE GOVERNMENT TO DO A BETTER JOB RUNNING THINGS

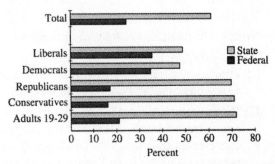

Source: *Washington Post*/Kaiser Family Foundation/Harvard University, 1995.

43. The chart above supports which of the following statements?

I. Both Republicans and Democrats have more trust in the federal government to do a better job than state governments.

II. Most groups trust their own state governments more than the federal government.

III. Democrats trust the federal government more than Republicans.

IV. Liberals believe in big government.

(A) I only

(B) III only

(C) II and III only

(D) II and IV only

(E) I, II, III, and IV

44. Which of the following political philosophers most influenced the writing of the United States Constitution?

(A) Plato

(B) Machiavelli

(C) Locke

(D) Rousseau

(E) Marx

45. The concept of responsible party government emphasizes which of the following about elections?

(A) Political parties will take positions similar to each other.

(B) Political parties will take clear, unambiguous positions.

(C) Voters will decide how to vote on the basis of how well the incumbent party satisfied them.

(D) Voters will vote mostly according to past identification.

(E) Special interest groups provide platforms and policy positions to political parties and their candidates.

46. Which of the following is a difference between the House of Representatives and the Senate?

(A) Seniority is more important in the Senate than in the House.

(B) Leadership is more centralized in the Senate than in the House.

(C) The Senate has the exclusive power to ratify treaties.

(D) The Senate has more committees than does the House.

(E) The Senate may veto laws passed by the House, but the House may not veto senatorial legislation.

47. Which of the following was a consequence of the New Deal legislation passed during the Great Depression under the administration of Franklin D. Roosevelt?

(A) States gained additional powers to pass legislation to relieve the economic problems of the Depression.

(B) The federal government became a more important agent of change than in previous presidential administrations.

(C) New presidential appointments to federal courts limited the judicial powers of the Supreme Court.

(D) Social policy became the primary concern of state governments.

(E) Presidents have been much more likely to defend their creation of emergency acts by claiming executive privilege.

48. Congressional oversight is best described as

(A) monitoring the federal bureaucracy

(B) monitoring the judicial branch and court rulings

(C) recommending and confirming federal judges

(D) regulating interstate commerce

(E) implementing public policy

49. The differences between the political attitudes of men and women are referred to as

(A) the political gap

(B) the gender gap

(C) partisan politics

(D) party loyalty

(E) the median voter theory

50. According to the Constitution, which of the following decides the presidential election outcome in the event that a single candidate does not get a majority of electoral votes?

(A) The Supreme Court

(B) The Senate

(C) The House of Representatives

(D) Both houses of Congress

(E) The sitting president

51. If the vice presidency of the United States is vacated, the Constitution stipulates that the president must

(A) appoint a new vice president with the approval of the House only

(B) appoint a new vice president with the approval of the Senate only

(C) appoint a new vice president with the approval of both houses of Congress

(D) instate the Speaker of the House as the new vice president

(E) leave the vice presidency vacant for the remainder of the term of office

52. James Madison's goal of setting power against power to minimize the concentration of authority in any one branch of government is outlined in the Constitution as a system of

(A) separation of powers

(B) checks and balances

(C) divided government

(D) national supremacy

(E) federalism

53. The declining number of marginal seats in Congress means that

(A) fewer seats are won by 55% or less of the vote

(B) there are fewer minor committee assignments in Congress

(C) redistricting no longer affects elections

(D) members of third parties are more likely to be elected to Congress

(E) fewer minorities are elected to Congress

54. The ability of the media to define the importance of particular events and issues is called

(A) preemption

(B) agenda setting

(C) investigative reporting

(D) minimal effects thesis

(E) adversarial journalism

55. The power of judicial review was established in

(A) *McCulloch v. Maryland*

(B) *Gitlow v. New York*

(C) *Dandridge v. Williams*

(D) *Miranda v. Arizona*

(E) *Marbury v. Madison*

56. Which of the following is true of both the House of Representatives and the Senate?

(A) Both chambers must approve the president's nominees for judicial and administrative positions.

(B) Both chambers employ a complex system of permanent committees to assist them in carrying out their legislative duties.

(C) Both the Speaker of the House and the Senate's president pro tempore are elected by majority vote of their respective chamber.

(D) Both chambers encourage and permit extensive discussion of important issues and proposed legislation on the chamber floor.

(E) When midterm vacancies occur in either chamber, state governors are permitted to appoint replacement members.

57. The authority of a chief executive to withhold approval from specific parts of appropriations bills passed by the legislature is known as

(A) a pocket veto

(B) a line-item veto

(C) a legislative veto

(D) an executive order

(E) an executive privilege

58. The weakening of political parties is most often traced to

(A) the single-member, winner-take-all system

(B) the growth of political action committees (PACs)

(C) Progressive Era reforms

(D) voters' increasing level of education

(E) voter apathy

59. Which of the following contemporary political ideologies posits that government power should be used to promote individual economic security and redistribute resources, but rejects the notion that government should favor a particular set of social values?

(A) Liberalism

(B) Conservatism

(C) Communitarianism

(D) Libertarianism

(E) Elitism

60. Which of the following best describes a referendum?

(A) A chief executive appoints an independent commission to investigate allegations of political corruption.

(B) A legislature repeals an unpopular law to improve the electoral advantage of incumbents.

(C) A political party caucuses to choose its candidates for a general election.

(D) Citizens vote directly on laws proposed by a state legislature.

(E) Citizens initiate the process of removing elected officials from office.

61. Which of the following is true of federal administrative agencies?

(A) All agencies are formally part of a cabinet-level department.

(B) They are seldom able to influence the formulation of national public policy.

(C) They collectively form one large institutional pyramid with a common purpose.

(D) Congress has no means of controlling administrative agencies.

(E) They have substantial influence over public policy through administrative discretion.

62. Which of the following is a check on the power of the United States Supreme Court?

(A) Congress controls the number of justices who may sit on the Court

(B) The Court has the power to enforce its decisions

(C) Cases involving a state's laws can be heard only through the Court's original jurisdiction

(D) The Court reviews all legislation after the president signs it into law.

(E) Congress cannot rewrite or repass a law that the Court has declared unconstitutional.

63. States, according to the full faith and credit clause of the Constitution

(A) can coin money if they choose, but they cannot print national currency

(B) must honor public records, acts, and judicial proceedings of every other state

(C) are not required to extradite fugitives of justice from other states

(D) can choose to suppress information on their credit rating ahead of a bond issue

(E) have the right to regulate banking and issuers of credit

64. Which of the following is most likely to weaken party leadership in the Senate?

(A) The confirmation of appointments to the Supreme Court

(B) The assignment of senators to permanent committees

(C) The use of filibuster by individual senators

(D) The removal of the president following impeachment

(E) The ratification of treaties presented by the president

65. The principal source of presidents' political influence is their

(A) constitutional authority to declare war

(B) power to convene Congress

(C) constitutional authority to execute public policies

(D) power to dictate diplomatic relations with other countries

(E) constitutional authority to grant pardons

Study Resources

Most textbooks used in college-level American government courses cover the topics in the outline given earlier, but the approaches to certain topics and the emphases given to them may differ. To prepare for the American Government exam, it is advisable to study one or more college textbooks, which can be found in most college bookstores. When selecting a textbook, check the table of contents against the knowledge and skills required for this test.

Visit www.collegeboard.com/clepprep for additional American government resources. You can also find suggestions for exam preparation in Chapter IV of the *Official Study Guide*. In addition, many college faculty post their course materials on their schools' Web sites.

Answer Key

1.	C	34.	A
2.	B	35.	A
3.	B	36.	D
4.	A	37.	E
5.	B	38.	C
6.	D	39.	A
7.	A	40.	D
8.	C	41.	A
9.	C	42.	B
10.	C	43.	C
11.	B	44.	C
12.	E	45.	B
13.	D	46.	C
14.	C	47.	B
15.	C	48.	A
16.	E	49.	B
17.	E	50.	C
18.	A	51.	C
19.	A	52.	B
20.	C	53.	A
21.	A	54.	B
22.	C	55.	E
23.	D	56.	B
24.	A	57.	B
25.	B	58.	C
26.	B	59.	A
27.	E	60.	D
28.	C	61.	E
29.	C	62.	A
30.	D	63.	B
31.	A	64.	C
32.	B	65.	C
33.	B		

History of the United States I

Description of the Examination

The History of the United States I: Early Colonization to 1877 examination covers material that is usually taught in the first semester of a two-semester course in United States history. The examination covers the period of United States history from early European colonization to the end of Reconstruction, with the majority of the questions on the period of 1790–1877. In the part covering the seventeenth and eighteenth centuries, emphasis is placed on the English colonies.

The examination contains approximately 120 questions to be answered in 90 minutes. Some of these are pretest questions that will not be scored. Any time candidates spend on tutorials and providing personal information is in addition to the actual testing time.

Knowledge and Skills Required

Questions on the History of the United States I examination require candidates to demonstrate one or more of the following abilities.

- Identification and description of historical phenomena
- Analysis and interpretation of historical phenomena
- Comparison and contrast of historical phenomena

The subject matter of the History of the United States I examination is drawn from the following topics. The percentages next to the main topics indicate the approximate percentage of exam questions on that topic.

Topical Specifications

35%	Political institutions, political developments, behavior, and public policy
25%	Social developments
10%	Economic developments
15%	Cultural and intellectual developments
15%	Diplomacy and international relations

Chronological Specifications

30%	1500–1789
70%	1790–1877

The following themes are reflected in a comprehensive introductory survey course:

- The impact of European discovery and colonization upon indigenous societies
- The nature of indigenous societies in North America
- The origins and nature of slavery and resistance
- Immigration and the history of ethnic minorities
- Major movements and individual figures in the history of women and the family
- The development and character of colonial societies
- British relations with the Atlantic colonies of North America
- The changing role of religion in American society
- The content of the Constitution and its amendments, and their interpretation by the Supreme Court
- The development and expansion of participatory democracy
- The growth of and changes in political parties
- The changing role of government in American life
- The intellectual and political expressions of nationalism
- Major movements and individual figures in the history of American literature, art, and popular culture
- Abolitionism and reform movements
- Long term democratic trends (immigration and internal migration)
- The motivations for and character of American expansionism
- The process of economic growth and development
- The causes and impacts of major wars in United States history

Sample Test Questions

The following sample questions do not appear on an actual CLEP examination. They are intended to give potential test-takers an indication of the format and difficulty level of the examination and to provide content for practice and review. Knowing the correct answers to all of the sample questions is not a guarantee of satisfactory performance on the exam.

Directions: Each of the questions or incomplete statements below is followed by five suggested answers or completions. Select the one that is best in each case. Some questions will require you to place events in chronological order.

1. In a sermon given aboard ship on the way to America, John Winthrop told the Puritans that their society would be regarded as "a city upon a hill" and that therefore they should be bonded together by love. But first he explained that there would always be inequalities of wealth and power, that some people would always be in positions of authority and that others would be dependent. His statements best illustrate the Puritans'

   (A) reaction to unsuccessful socialist experiments in the Low Countries
   (B) acceptance of the traditional belief that social order depended on a system of ranks
   (C) intention to vest political power exclusively in the ministers
   (D) desire to better themselves economically through means that included the institution of slavery
   (E) inability to take clear stands on social issues

2. The French and Indian War led Great Britain to

   (A) encourage colonial manufactures in its North American colonies
   (B) impose revenue taxes on its North American colonies
   (C) restrict emigration from England to North America
   (D) ignore its North American colonies
   (E) grant increased colonial self-government to its North American colonies

3. All of the following were common characteristics of many colonial New England families EXCEPT

   (A) a hierarchical institution in which the father represented the source of authority
   (B) a place that sheltered men from the workplace
   (C) a social institution that cared for the needy and the poor
   (D) a social institution that provided vocational training
   (E) the basic farming unit

4. Which of the following is a correct statement about the use of slave labor in colonial Virginia?

   (A) It was forced on reluctant White Virginians by profit-minded English merchants and the mercantilist officials of the Crown.
   (B) It was the first time Europeans enslaved African people.
   (C) It fulfilled the original plans of the Virginia Company.
   (D) It first occurred after the invention of Eli Whitney's cotton gin, which greatly stimulated the demand for low-cost labor.
   (E) It spread rapidly in the late seventeenth century, as African slaves replaced European indentured servants in the tobacco fields.

5. Roger Williams defended liberty of conscience on the grounds that

   (A) all religions were equal in the eyes of the Creator
   (B) the institutions of political democracy would be jeopardized without it
   (C) Puritan ideas about sin and salvation were outmoded
   (D) theological truths would emerge from the clash of ideas
   (E) the state was an improper and ineffectual agency in matters of the spirit

6. Which of the following is true of White women in the British North American colonies?

(A) They were allowed to be ordained as ministers.

(B) They were considered politically and socially equal to their husbands.

(C) They were eligible to work as teachers in public schools.

(D) They were eligible to run for political office.

(E) They were restricted in holding property and making legal contracts after marriage.

7. Which of the following was NOT a consequence of the Great Awakening in the American colonies during the mid-eighteenth century?

(A) Separatism and secession from established churches due to the democratizing effect of more accessible forms of piety

(B) The renewed persecution of people for witchcraft because of the heightened interest in the supernatural

(C) The growth of institutions of higher learning to fill the need for more ministers to spread the gospel

(D) A flourishing of the missionary spirit as an outgrowth of more intensive religious devotion

(E) The lessening of doctrinal rigor and a concomitant appreciation for more direct experiences of faith

Questions 8–9 refer to the following statement.

The present king of Great Britain… has combined with others to subject us to a jurisdiction foreign to our constitution, and unacknowledged by our laws.

8. The "constitution" referred to in the quotation above from the Declaration of Independence was

(A) the principles common to all of the colonial charters

(B) the Articles of Confederation

(C) a constitution for the colonies written by Sir William Blackstone

(D) the laws passed concurrently by the several colonial legislatures

(E) the principles the colonists believed had traditionally regulated English government

9. The protest that the king had "combined with others to subject us to a jurisdiction foreign to our constitution" referred to George III's

(A) alliance with the king of France

(B) use of Hessian mercenaries

(C) reliance on his representatives in the colonies

(D) approval of parliamentary laws impinging on colonial self-government

(E) intention to place a German prince on the throne of British America

10. By the time of the American Revolution, many American colonists had generally come to believe that the creation of a republic would solve the problems of monarchical rule because a republic would establish

    (A) a highly centralized government led by a social elite

    (B) a strong chief executive

    (C) a small, limited government responsible to the people

    (D) unlimited male suffrage

    (E) a society in which there were no differences of rank and status

11. All state constitutions drafted during the American Revolutionary era were significant because they

    (A) were based on the principle of virtual representation

    (B) included clauses that immediately emancipated slaves

    (C) provided for the confiscation and redistribution of the property of wealthy Loyalists

    (D) were the first efforts at establishing a government by and of the people

    (E) introduced the concept of checks and balances

12. *Letters from a Farmer in Pennsylvania* was written to

    (A) record the soil, climate, and profitable crops in the Pennsylvania colony

    (B) chronicle the history of William Penn's colonization efforts

    (C) argue against the power of Parliament to tax the colonists without representation

    (D) petition King George III for colonial representation in Parliament

    (E) encourage colonization of the western frontier

13. Under the Articles of Confederation, which of the following was true about the national government?

    (A) It had the power to conduct foreign affairs.

    (B) It had the power to regulate commerce.

    (C) It had a bicameral legislature.

    (D) It had an independent executive branch.

    (E) It included a federal judiciary.

14. The concept that the ultimate sovereignty of the federal government rests with the people is most explicitly stated in

    (A) the Preamble to the United States Constitution

    (B) *Common Sense*

    (C) the Fourteenth Amendment to the United States Constitution

    (D) the Bill of Rights

    (E) the Articles of Confederation

15. "There is an opinion that parties in free countries are useful checks upon the administration of the government and serve to keep alive the spirit of liberty. This within certain limits is probably true, and in governments of a monarchical cast patriotism may look with indulgence, if not with favor, upon the spirit of party. But in those of the popular character, in governments purely elective, it is a spirit not to be encouraged."

    The passage above is from a speech by which of the following presidents?

    (A) George Washington

    (B) Thomas Jefferson

    (C) John Adams

    (D) Andrew Jackson

    (E) Abraham Lincoln

16. Thomas Jefferson opposed some of Alexander Hamilton's programs because Jefferson believed that

    (A) the common bond of a substantial national debt would serve to unify the different states

    (B) the French alliance threatened to spread the violence of the French Revolution to America

    (C) the federal government should encourage manufacturing and industry

    (D) Hamilton's programs were weakening the military strength of the nation

    (E) Hamilton's programs favored manufacturing and commercial interests

17. The Embargo Act of 1807 had which of the following effects on the United States?

    (A) It severely damaged American manufacturing.

    (B) It enriched many cotton plantation owners.

    (C) It severely damaged American shipping.

    (D) It was ruinous to subsistence farmers.

    (E) It had little economic impact.

18. Henry Clay's "American System" was a plan to

    (A) compromise on the issue of extending slavery to new United States territories

    (B) foster the economic integration of the North, the West, and the South

    (C) export United States political and economic values to oppressed peoples

    (D) maintain United States noninvolvement in the internal affairs of Europe

    (E) assert the right of states to nullify decisions of the national government

19. Deists of the late eighteenth and early nineteenth centuries believed that

    (A) natural laws, designed by the Creator, govern the operation of the universe

    (B) prayer has the power to make significant changes in a person's life

    (C) the idea of God is merely the creation of people's minds

    (D) the universe was created by a natural, spontaneous combining of elements

    (E) intuition rather than reason leads people to an awareness of the divine

20. The Louisiana Purchase was significant because it

    (A) eliminated Spain from the North American continent

    (B) gave the United States control of the Mississippi River

    (C) eased tensions between Western settlers and Native Americans

    (D) forced the British to evacuate their posts in the Northwest

    (E) reduced sectional conflict over the slavery issue

21. Between the Monroe Doctrine (1823) and the outbreak of the Civil War (1861), the most important aspect of United States foreign policy was

    (A) securing access to Canadian fisheries

    (B) reopening the British West Indies to direct trade with the United States

    (C) securing international recognition

    (D) expanding the nation's boundaries

    (E) responding to Cuban independence

22. Jacksonian banking policies did which of the following?

    (A) Removed banking issues from national politics.

    (B) Stalled the westward expansion.

    (C) Ended foreign investment in the United States.

    (D) Abolished state banks.

    (E) Encouraged the expansion of credit and speculation.

23. Which of the following is true of John C. Calhoun?

    (A) He advocated a strong federal government and helped to establish the Bank of the United States.

    (B) He supported the doctrine of nullification, which declared the right of states to rule on the constitutionality of federal law.

    (C) He became a strong opponent of southern nationalism and sought federal legislation to link the West and the South.

    (D) As vice president of the United States, he helped formulate the beginnings of a new Republican Party.

    (E) He led a successful movement to include the right of concurrent majority in the Constitution of the United States.

24. Which of the following had the greatest impact on the institution of slavery in the United States in the first quarter of the nineteenth century?

    (A) Demands of Southern textile manufacturers for cotton

    (B) Introduction of crop rotation and fertilizers

    (C) Abolition of indentured servitude

    (D) Expanded use of the cotton gin

    (E) The Three-Fifths Compromise

25. The "putting-out system" that emerged in antebellum America refers to the

    (A) organizing of slave labor into efficient planting teams

    (B) production of finished goods in individual households

    (C) sending of poor children to live on farms in the Midwest

    (D) shipping of raw materials to European factories

    (E) forced migration of Native Americans from valuable lands

26. Which of the following was a major focus of antebellum reform?

    (A) Income tax law

    (B) Universal suffrage

    (C) Prison reform

    (D) Creation of national parks

    (E) Machine politics

27. The establishment of Brook Farm and the Oneida Community in the antebellum United States reflected

(A) the influence of Social Darwinism on American thinkers
(B) the continued impact of Calvinist ideas on American thought
(C) a belief in perfectionism
(D) attempts to foster racial integration
(E) the implementation of all-female Utopian communities

28. During the early stages of manufacturing, the textile mills in Lowell, Massachusetts, primarily employed

(A) native-born, single White men who had lost their farms
(B) native-born, single White women from rural areas
(C) White males from debtors' prisons
(D) recent immigrants from southern and eastern Europe
(E) African American women

29. Members of the Whig Party organized in the 1830s agreed most on which of the following?

(A) Extension of slavery into western territories
(B) Elimination of protective tariffs
(C) Endorsement of the doctrine of nullification
(D) Disapproval of Andrew Jackson's policies
(E) Disapproval of the "corrupt bargain" under John Quincy Adams

30. The issue of constitutionality figured most prominently in the consideration of which of the following?

(A) Tariff of 1789
(B) First Bank of the United States
(C) Funding of the national debt
(D) Assumption of state debts
(E) Excise tax on whiskey

31. The presidential election of 1840 is often considered the first "modern" election because

(A) the slavery issue was first raised in this campaign
(B) it was the first election in which women voted
(C) voting patterns were similar to those later established in the 1890s
(D) both parties for the first time widely campaigned among all the eligible voters
(E) a second "Era of Good Feeling" had just come to a close, marking a new departure in politics

32. The idea of Manifest Destiny included all of the following EXCEPT the belief that

(A) commerce and industry would decline as the nation expanded its agricultural base
(B) the use of land for settled agriculture was preferable to its use for nomadic hunting
(C) westward expansion was both inevitable and beneficial
(D) the Creator selected America as a chosen land populated by a chosen people
(E) the ultimate extent of the American domain was to be from the Atlantic to the Pacific Ocean

33. "Upon these considerations, it is the opinion of the court that the act of Congress which prohibited a citizen from holding and owning property of this kind in the territory of the United States north of the line therein mentioned, is not warranted by the Constitution, and is therefore void; and that neither the plaintiff himself, nor any of his family, were made free by being carried into this territory; even if they had been carried there by the owner, who intended to become a permanent resident."

The congressional act referred to in the passage above was the

(A) Kansas-Nebraska Act

(B) Missouri Compromise

(C) Northwest Ordinance

(D) Compromise of 1850

(E) Fugitive Slave Act

34. *Moby-Dick*, *The Scarlet Letter*, and *Leaves of Grass* are examples of which of the following literary traditions?

(A) American Renaissance

(B) Harlem Renaissance

(C) Realism

(D) Modernism

(E) Genteel Tradition

35. Which of the following represents William Lloyd Garrison's attitude toward slavery?

(A) Immediate emancipation and resettlement in Liberia

(B) Immediate emancipation and resettlement in the Southwest

(C) Immediate emancipation with compensation for slaveholders

(D) Gradual emancipation without compensation for slaveholders

(E) Immediate emancipation without compensation for slaveholders

M. and M. Karolik Collection
Courtesy © Museum of Fine Arts, Boston

36. The drawing above illustrates the nineteenth-century middle-class view of the

(A) home as a refuge from the world rather than as a productive unit

(B) declining influence of women in the family structure

(C) economic value of children to families

(D) importance of religious education

(E) widening role of women in society

37. Which of the following groups was most likely to adopt the Free Soil ideology?

(A) Free Blacks

(B) Northern capitalists

(C) Western frontier settlers

(D) Southern yeomen farmers

(E) Southern plantation owners

38. The 1848 women's rights convention in Seneca Falls, New York, was a protest against

(A) the use of women workers in textile factories

(B) the abuse of female slaves on Southern plantations

(C) the failure of the Democratic Party to endorse a woman suffrage amendment

(D) customs and laws that gave women a status inferior to that of men

(E) state restrictions that prevented women from joining labor unions

39. Which of the following wrote *Uncle Tom's Cabin?*

    (A) Louisa May Alcott
    (B) Herman Melville
    (C) Harriet Beecher Stowe
    (D) Richard Henry Dana
    (E) Kate Chopin

40. Which of the following was opposed by both the Free Soil Party and the Republican Party in the mid-nineteenth century?

    (A) Internal improvement in the West
    (B) Extension of slavery into the territories
    (C) Growth of textile manufacturing in New England
    (D) Unrestricted immigration from Ireland
    (E) Use of paper money

41. In the pre–Civil War era, the railroads' most important impact on the economy was that they

    (A) created a huge new market for railway equipment
    (B) created the basis for greater cooperation between Southern planters and Northern textile manufacturers
    (C) generated new employment opportunities for unskilled urban workers
    (D) involved the federal government in the financing of a nationwide transportation network
    (E) provided Midwestern farmers accessibility to Eastern urban markets

42. Which of the following was NOT an element of the Compromise of 1850?

    (A) stronger fugitive slave law
    (B) Abolition of the slave trade in Washington, D.C.
    (C) Admittance of California as a free state
    (D) Organization of the Kansas Territory without slavery
    (E) Adjustment of the Texas–New Mexico boundary

43. All of the following conditions influenced the development of American agriculture during the first half of the nineteenth century EXCEPT

    (A) settlement of the western territories
    (B) a widespread interest in conserving soil and natural resources
    (C) the trend toward regional economic specialization
    (D) the enthusiasm for land speculation
    (E) improvements in transportation by water

44. Which of the following best describes the United States position in the world economy during the period 1790–1860?

    (A) It was the leading producer of finished and manufactured goods for export.
    (B) It relied heavily on European capital for its economic expansion.
    (C) It had an inadequate merchant marine and depended largely on foreign vessels to carry its trade.
    (D) It was strengthened by the acquisition of overseas colonies.
    (E) It was severely hampered by its reliance on slave labor.

45. After the Civil War, the majority of freed slaves found work in the South as

   (A) factory workers
   (B) railroad employees
   (C) independent craftsmen
   (D) tenant farmers
   (E) domestic servants

46. Abraham Lincoln's plan for Reconstruction included which of the following?

   (A) Establishment of five military districts to prepare seceded regions for readmission as states
   (B) Punishment of Confederates through land confiscation and high property taxes
   (C) Restoration of property to White Southerners who would swear a loyalty oath to the United States
   (D) Reestablishment of state government after 10 percent of the voters in a state pledged their allegiance to the United States
   (E) Readmission of states to the Union contingent on their ratification of the Thirteenth, Fourteenth, and Fifteenth Amendments to the Constitution

47. All of the following elements of the Radical Republican program were implemented during Reconstruction EXCEPT

   (A) provision of 40 acres to each freedman household
   (B) enactment of the Fourteenth Amendment
   (C) military occupation of the South
   (D) punishment of the Confederate leaders
   (E) restrictions on the power of the President

48. Andrew Johnson's Reconstruction plan allowed for Southern states to be readmitted into the Union on the condition that they

   (A) revoke the ordinance of secession and ratify the Thirteenth Amendment
   (B) prohibit the use of the Black Codes
   (C) guarantee suffrage for all citizens, regardless of race
   (D) give land grants to emancipated slaves
   (E) punish ex-Confederates refusing to take an oath of loyalty to the United States

49. Which of the following was a renowned African American poet in New England in the late eighteenth century?

   (A) Benjamin Banneker
   (B) Lemuel Haynes
   (C) Phillis Wheatley
   (D) Gabriel Prosser
   (E) Sojourner Truth

50. During the antebellum period, the Auburn system was designed to

   (A) teach factory workers proper work habits
   (B) instill discipline in grade schools
   (C) reform criminals through solitary confinement
   (D) punish runaway slaves
   (E) cure the mentally ill

51. California was admitted as a state to the Union

   (A) as part of the Compromise of 1850
   (B) with the passage of the Wilmot Proviso
   (C) during the United States–Mexico War
   (D) with the passage of the Northwest Ordinance
   (E) when the Kansas–Nebraska Act settled the issue of western slavery

52. Which of the following wrote *Incidents in the Life of a Slave Girl*?

    (A) Frances Ellen Watkins Harper
    (B) Sojourner Truth
    (C) Lydia Maria Child
    (D) Harriet Beecher Stowe
    (E) Harriet Jacobs

53. The activities of the Freedmen's Bureau included all of the following EXCEPT

    (A) providing food, clothing, medical care, and shelter to war victims
    (B) reuniting families of freedmen
    (C) establishing a network of courts
    (D) establishing schools for freed slaves
    (E) permanently redistributing land

54. The United States completed the Gadsden Purchase in 1853 in order to

    (A) obtain Oregon
    (B) build a transcontinental railroad
    (C) relieve population pressures
    (D) obtain additional grazing lands
    (E) balance slave and free states

55. Place the following events in the correct chronological order. Place the earliest event first.

    Old Deluder Satan Act
    Establishment of grade schools
    Establishment of normal schools
    Northwest Ordinance

    [ ]
    [ ]
    [ ]
    [ ]

    Click on a choice, then click on a box.

56. Which of the following is a correct statement regarding Benjamin Franklin?

    (A) He founded the Bank of the United States.
    (B) He authored the Articles of Confederation.
    (C) He authored the Bill of Rights.
    (D) He invented electricity.
    (E) He was an important negotiator for the Treaty of Paris of 1783.

57. Which of the following was directly involved in helping slaves escape via the Underground Railroad?

    (A) William Lloyd Garrison
    (B) Harriet Tubman
    (C) Harriet Beecher Stowe
    (D) John Quincy Adams
    (E) Roger Taney

58. The acquittal of John Peter Zenger in 1735 reflected the growing colonial belief that

    (A) colonial governors should have absolute veto power over colonial assemblies
    (B) Parliament should not be involved in internal matters in the British colonies
    (C) newspaper editors should have the right to criticize public officials
    (D) Enlightenment thought should have no place in colonial culture
    (E) governors should have the right to limit the press

59. Bacon's Rebellion was

    (A) a revolt of African American slaves against treatment by their masters
    (B) the name given to a slave conspiracy in New York City
    (C) the Philadelphia version of the Boston Tea Party
    (D) a revolt by poor farmers and indentured servants
    (E) an uprising of Native Americans

60. Which of the following is true about the American victory at Saratoga in October 1777 during the Revolutionary War?

(A) It enabled George Washington to recapture New York City.

(B) It led Congress to declare independence.

(C) It caused the British to evacuate Boston.

(D) It helped convince France to enter the war.

(E) It prompted Parliament to end the war.

61. In the early seventeenth century, colonists in the Chesapeake Bay area exported which of the following to England?

(A) Cattle

(B) Tobacco

(C) Tea

(D) Cotton

(E) Coffee

62. "I do hereby grant and declare, That no Person or Persons, inhabiting in this Province or Territories, who shall confess and acknowledge One almighty God, the Creator, Upholder and Ruler of the World; and profess him or themselves obliged to live quietly under the Civil Government, shall be in any Case molested or prejudiced, in his or their Person or Estate, because of his or their conscientious Persuasion or Practice, nor be compelled to frequent or maintain any religious Worship, Place or ministry, contrary to his or their Mind, or to do or suffer any other Act or Thing, contrary to their religious Persuasion."

The excerpt above is from the charter of which of the following English colonies?

(A) Plymouth

(B) Pennsylvania

(C) Massachusetts Bay

(D) Jamestown

(E) Roanoke

63. According to the Treaty of Paris of 1783, England both recognized American independence and

(A) agreed to cancel all the prewar debts owed to the British by American citizens

(B) promised to set the western boundary of the United States at the Mississippi River

(C) retained fishing rights off Newfoundland

(D) insisted that George III remain the titular head of the former thirteen colonies

(E) agreed to the presence of British troops in the Northwest Territories for a period of ten years

64. All of the following resulted from the War of 1812 EXCEPT

(A) the decline of the Federalist Party

(B) increased domestic manufacturing

(C) the loss of Florida to the British

(D) the emergence of Andrew Jackson as a war hero

(E) heightened patriotism

65. In *Dred Scott* v. *Sandford* (1857), the Supreme Court decided that

(A) slaves could not be freed by virtue of their residence in a free state

(B) the Compromise of 1850 was supported by the Constitution

(C) Dred and Harriet Scott deserved their freedom

(D) the principle of popular sovereignty could be applied in new territories

(E) free African Americans could not be reenslaved

66. Widely read autobiographies of escaped slaves, such as *The Life and Times of Frederick Douglass*, assisted the abolitionist cause primarily by

    (A) raising money for back to Africa colonization projects in Liberia and Sierra Leone

    (B) demonstrating the inability of the federal government to stand up to pro-slave interests in the Congress

    (C) depicting slavery as benevolent and supportive of family preservation

    (D) linking American slavery to earlier slave societies in Greece and Egypt

    (E) transforming the popular understanding of slavery from an abstraction to a tangible evil

67. Which of the following best describes the significance of Shays' Rebellion and the Whiskey Rebellion?

    (A) They were early examples of colonial opposition to the British taxes imposed after the French and Indian War.

    (B) They led to the meeting of the Constitutional Convention.

    (C) They were precipitated by burdensome tax policies.

    (D) Alexander Hamilton led the armed forces that suppressed both rebellions.

    (E) They were caused by the inability of farmers to pay their debts.

68. Which of the following best explains the opposition of Thomas Jefferson and James Madison to the Bank of the United States?

    (A) Capital for the bank was raised by taxes on farmers.

    (B) The bank did not provide loans to farmers for the purchase of land.

    (C) The bank would give the president too much control over the economy.

    (D) The Constitution did not grant the Congress the right to charter a bank.

    (E) Bank speculation had led to a post–Revolutionary depression.

69. Which of the following best describes the purpose of the Hartford Convention?

    (A) To protest the impressments of American sailors into the British navy

    (B) To coordinate a federal response to the uprising of Tecumseh and the Prophet

    (C) To propose amendments to the Constitution and to avoid the secession of New England states

    (D) To select an alternate seat of government after Washington was captured by the British

    (E) To provide a plan for the incorporation of Canada into the United States

70. Which of the following were native to North America before Columbus arrived?

    (A) Horses and pumpkins

    (B) Dandelions and clover

    (C) Maize and squash

    (D) Oranges and sweet potatoes

    (E) Rice and potatoes

71. The Middle colonies differed from both the New England and Southern colonies in that the Middle colonies

    (A) had a system of staple crop agriculture

    (B) prohibited slavery

    (C) required church attendance on Sundays

    (D) were more religiously and ethnically diverse

    (E) had no history of violence against Native Americans

Study Resources

Most textbooks used in college-level United States history courses cover the topics in the outline given earlier, but the approaches to certain topics and the emphases given to them may differ. To prepare for the History of the United States I exam, it is advisable to study one or more college textbooks, which can be found in most college bookstores. When selecting a textbook, check the table of contents against the knowledge and skills required for this test.

Additional detail and differing interpretations can be gained by consulting readers and specialized historical studies. Pay attention to visual materials (pictures, maps, and charts) as you study.

Visit www.collegeboard.com/clepprep for additional history resources. You can also find suggestions for exam preparation in Chapter IV of the *Official Study Guide*. In addition, many college faculty post their course materials on their schools' Web sites.

Answer Key

1.	B	36.	A
2.	B	37.	C
3.	B	38.	D
4.	E	39.	C
5.	E	40.	B
6.	E	41.	E
7.	B	42.	D
8.	E	43.	B
9.	D	44.	B
10.	C	45.	D
11.	D	46.	D
12.	C	47.	A
13.	A	48.	A
14.	A	49.	C
15.	A	50.	C
16.	E	51.	A
17.	C	52.	E
18.	B	53.	E
19.	A	54.	B
20.	B	55.	1,4,2,3
21.	D	56.	E
22.	E	57.	B
23.	B	58.	C
24.	D	59.	D
25.	B	60.	D
26.	C	61.	B
27.	C	62.	B
28.	B	63.	B
29.	D	64.	C
30.	B	65.	A
31.	D	66.	E
32.	A	67.	C
33.	B	68.	D
34.	A	69.	C
35.	E	70.	C
		71.	D

History of the United States II

Description of the Examination

The History of the United States II: 1865 to the Present examination covers material that is usually taught in the second semester of what is often a two-semester course in United States history. The examination covers the period of United States history from the end of the Civil War to the present, with the majority of the questions being on the twentieth century.

The examination contains approximately 120 questions to be answered in 90 minutes. Some of these are pretest questions that will not be scored. Any time candidates spend on tutorials and providing personal information is in addition to the actual testing time.

Knowledge and Skills Required

Questions on the History of the United States II examination require candidates to demonstrate one or more of the following abilities.

- Identification and description of historical phenomena
- Analysis and interpretation of historical phenomena
- Comparison and contrast of historical phenomena

The subject matter of the History of the United States II examination is drawn from the following topics. The percentages next to the main topics indicate the approximate percentage of exam questions on that topic.

Topical Specifications

  35% Political institutions, behavior, and public policy
  25% Social developments
  10% Economic developments
  15% Cultural and intellectual developments
  15% Diplomacy and international relations

Chronological Specifications

  30% 1865–1914
  70% 1915–present

The following are among the specific topics tested:

- The impact of the Civil War and Reconstruction upon the South
- The motivations and character of American expansionism
- The content of constitutional amendments and their interpretations by the Supreme Court
- The changing nature of agricultural life
- The development of American political parties
- The emergence of regulatory and welfare-state legislation
- The intellectual and political expressions of liberalism, conservatism, and other such movements
- Long-term demographic trends
- The process of economic growth and development
- The changing occupational structure, nature of work, and labor organization
- Immigration and the history of racial and ethnic minorities
- Urbanization and industrialization
- The causes and impacts of major wars in American history
- Major movements and individual figures in the history of American arts and letters
- Trends in the history of women and the family

Sample Test Questions

The following sample questions do not appear on an actual CLEP examination. They are intended to give potential test-takers an indication of the format and difficulty level of the examination and to provide content for practice and review. Knowing the correct answers to all of the sample questions is not a guarantee of satisfactory performance on the exam.

Directions: Each of the questions or incomplete statements below is followed by five suggested answers or completions. Select the one that is best in each case. Some questions will require you to place events in chronological order.

1. Which of the following best describes the experiences of most emancipated slaves following Reconstruction?

   (A) They obtained land from the Freedmen's Bureau.

   (B) They were forced back onto the plantations as sharecroppers.

   (C) They established large cooperative farms.

   (D) They migrated to Northern urban areas and worked as unskilled laborers.

   (E) They were forced to migrate to marginally fertile lands in the Western territories.

2. The Reconstruction Acts of 1867 provided for

   (A) temporary Union military supervision of the former Confederacy

   (B) federal monetary support for the resettlement of African Americans in Africa

   (C) denial of property-holding and voting rights to African Americans

   (D) implementation of anti–African American vagrancy laws in the South

   (E) lenient readmission of the formerly Confederate states to the Union

3. The second Sioux war (1875–1876), in which Custer was defeated at the Battle of Little Bighorn, was caused by all of the following EXCEPT

   (A) the extension of the route of the Northern Pacific Railroad

   (B) a concentrated effort on the part of the major Protestant denominations to convert the Sioux to Christianity

   (C) the gold rush in the Black Hills

   (D) corruption within the Department of the Interior

   (E) overland migration of settlers to the Pacific Northwest

4. "This, then, is held to be the duty of the man of wealth: to consider all surplus revenues which come to him simply as trust funds, which he is called upon to administer and strictly bound as a matter of duty to administer in the manner which, in his judgment, is best calculated to produce the most beneficial results for the community—"

   The sentiments expressed above are most characteristic of

   (A) transcendentalism

   (B) pragmatism

   (C) the Gospel of Wealth

   (D) the Social Gospel

   (E) Social Darwinism

5. Reformers of the Progressive Era proposed all of the following changes in city government and politics at the turn of the century EXCEPT

(A) a large city council elected by wards

(B) civil service

(C) home rule for cities

(D) city manager and commission governments

(E) nonpartisan elections

6. The anticombination laws passed by numerous states in the late 1880s were a response to which of the following organizational innovations?

(A) The creation and growth of international cartels

(B) The development of industry-wide trade associations

(C) The joining of skilled and unskilled workers in industrial unions

(D) The formation of agricultural marketing cooperatives

(E) The use of stockholding trusts to create business monopolies

© Bettman/CORBIS

7. Which of the following constituted a significant change in the treatment of American Indians during the last half of the nineteenth century?

(A) The beginning of negotiations with individual Indian tribal groups

(B) The start of a removal policy

(C) The abandonment of the reservation system

(D) The admission of American Indians to United States citizenship

(E) The division of lands traditionally owned by Indian tribal groups among individual members

8. The late-nineteenth-century photograph shown above was intended to serve which of the following purposes?

(A) To advocate social reform

(B) To arouse anti-immigrant sentiments

(C) To encourage the purchase of cameras

(D) To document the need for prohibition

(E) To encourage immigration to the cities

9. Which of the following would have been most likely to vote for William Jennings Bryan in 1896?

(A) A Kansas farmer

(B) A Chicago industrial worker

(C) A department store clerk

(D) A university professor of economics

(E) A New York Republican Party member

10. Unionization efforts in the late nineteenth century were countered by the

(A) establishment of the eight-hour workday

(B) passage of right-to-work laws

(C) increasing use of skilled labor

(D) use of federal troops to help defeat strikes

(E) establishment of factories in foreign countries by United States corporations

11. Which of the following best states the goals of the "pure and simple unionism" advocated by Samuel Gompers?

(A) Labor unions should concentrate on increasing wages and benefits.

(B) Labor should organize industry's skilled and unskilled workers into a single union.

(C) Labor unions should compete directly with large industries in the production and distribution of consumer products.

(D) Industrial workers should form a political party to achieve their goals.

(E) The defective capitalist system should be replaced by labor cooperatives.

12. During the late nineteenth century, urban political machines were organizations that

(A) were created by native-born Americans to combat the political influence of immigrants

(B) were controlled by politicians who dispensed jobs and other patronage in return for political support

(C) worked for civil service reform to ensure sound municipal government

(D) consisted of reformers working to combat urban poverty by establishing settlement houses

(E) consisted of conservative elites seeking to maintain control of politics

13. In his interpretation of the historical development of the United States, Frederick Jackson Turner focused on the importance of the

(A) traditions of Western European culture

(B) role of women in socializing children to become good citizens

(C) historical consequences of the enslavement of African American people

(D) conflict between capitalists and workers

(E) frontier experience in fostering democracy

14. The 1896 presidential election was significant in United States history because it

(A) marked the rise of the Populist Party

(B) signaled the return of free silver coinage

(C) strengthened the image of the Republican Party as the party of prosperity and national greatness

(D) set a new pattern of vigorous two-party participation in national politics

(E) secured national Democratic Party dominance that lasted until the 1930s

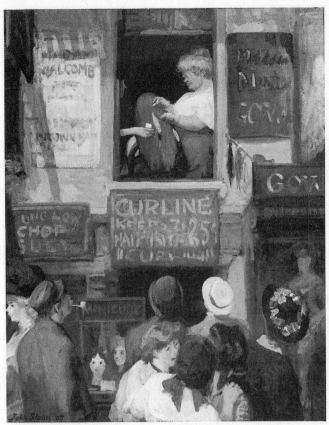

Wadsworth Atheneum Museum of Art, Hartford, CT.
The Ella Gallup Sumner and Mary Catlin Sumner Collection Fund.

15. The 1907 painting shown above is representative of the

(A) Impressionist painting of Mary Cassatt

(B) Hudson River School art of Asher B. Durand

(C) Surrealism of Giorgio De Chirico

(D) Abstract Expressionist work of Jackson Pollock

(E) Ashcan School art of John Sloan

16. In the period 1890–1915, all of the following were generally true about African Americans EXCEPT

(A) Voting rights previously gained were denied through changes in state laws and constitutions.

(B) The Federal government passed legislation protecting the voting rights of African Americans.

(C) African American leaders disagreed on the principal strategy for attaining equal rights.

(D) Numerous physical attacks on African American individuals occurred in both the North and the South.

(E) African American people from the rural South migrated to both southern and northern cities.

17. Between 1890 and 1914, most immigrants to the United States came from

(A) southern and eastern Europe

(B) northern and western Europe

(C) Latin America

(D) Southeast Asia

(E) Canada

18. Which of the following is a correct statement about the United States at the close of the First World War?

(A) It joined the League of Nations.

(B) It emerged as the world's leading creditor nation.

(C) It accorded diplomatic recognition to the Soviet Union.

(D) It repealed the amendment to the Constitution that allowed Prohibition.

(E) It received large reparations payments from Germany.

19. Which of the following is a literary work that is associated with the Lost Generation after the First World War?

    (A) Ernest Hemingway's *The Sun Also Rises*

    (B) Sylvia Plath's *The Bell Jar*

    (C) T. S. Eliot's "The Love Song of J. Alfred Prufrock"

    (D) Sinclair Lewis' *Babbitt*

    (E) Theodore Dreiser's *An American Tragedy*

20. Many Mexicans migrated to the United States during the First World War because

    (A) revolution in Mexico had caused social upheaval and dislocation

    (B) the United States offered special homestead rights to relatives of Mexican Americans serving in the armed forces

    (C) the war in Europe had disrupted the Mexican economy

    (D) American Progressives generally held liberal views on the issue of racial assimilation

    (E) the United States government recruited Mexican workers to accelerate the settlement of the Southwest

21. All of the following were among Woodrow Wilson's Fourteen Points EXCEPT

    (A) a general association of nations

    (B) freedom to navigate the high seas in peace and war

    (C) an independent Poland

    (D) a partitioned Germany

    (E) an end to secret treaties

22. A direct consequence of Henry Ford's assembly-line process was that it

    (A) raised the price of automobiles

    (B) resulted in small cuts in workers' wages

    (C) decreased the need for skilled workers

    (D) made the working environment safer

    (E) increased the number of women employed in industrial work

23. All of the following help to explain the presence of large numbers of expatriate American intellectuals in Europe during the 1920s EXCEPT the

    (A) repressive effects of Prohibition and the resurgence of conservatism in the United States

    (B) attraction of European cities, especially Paris, as centers of innovation and creativity

    (C) tradition among American writers of taking up temporary residence in Europe

    (D) claims of young American writers and critics that American culture was materialistic and hostile to the development of their art

    (E) European tradition of wealthy patrons supporting struggling American artists and writers

The Cash Register Chorus

WHAT A FRIEND WE HAVE IN COOLIDGE!

The Granger Collection, NY

24. The political cartoonist who drew the picture above probably believed that

(A) European nations were pleased with aid given them by the Coolidge administration

(B) governmental agencies were receiving too much financial support from the Coolidge administration

(C) American industrial and commercial leaders approved of the Coolidge administration's business policies

(D) consumers had benefited from the Federal Reserve Board's tight money policy from 1925 through 1928

(E) Congress was pleased by President Coolidge's accommodating stance toward pork barrel legislation

25. A number of changes took place in the intellectual life of college-educated Americans between about 1880 and 1930. Which of the following changes is LEAST characteristic of this group during this period?

(A) Expanded popularity of Freudian psychology

(B) Rise of pluralistic and relativistic worldviews

(C) More rigorous training for academic professions

(D) Growth in the influence of religious fundamentalism

(E) Increased attention to the methods and outlook of the sciences

26. In its 1932 march on Washington, the Bonus army demanded which of the following?

(A) Federal unemployment insurance for workers who had lost their jobs

(B) Federal loans to farmers, with surplus grain used as collateral

(C) Early payment to veterans of a promised reward for service in the First World War

(D) A substantial increase in the military budget

(E) A refund to investors who lost money in the stock market crash of 1929

27. Franklin D. Roosevelt was successful in securing congressional support for all of the following EXCEPT

(A) Negotiation of tariff agreements by the executive department

(B) Reduction of the gold content of the dollar

(C) Removal of the restraints of the antitrust acts to permit voluntary trade associations

(D) Adoption of processing taxes on agricultural products

(E) Reform of the judiciary to permit the enlargement of the Supreme Court

28. Franklin D. Roosevelt's farm policy was primarily designed to

   (A) reduce farm prices to make food cheaper for the consumer
   (B) increase production by opening new lands to farmers
   (C) reduce production in order to boost farm prices
   (D) use price and wage controls to stabilize farm prices
   (E) end federal controls over agriculture

29. The main purpose of the Wagner Act (National Labor Relations Act) of 1935 was to

   (A) end the sit-down strike in Flint, Michigan
   (B) settle the struggle between the American Federation of Labor and the Congress of Industrial Workers
   (C) guarantee workers a minimum wage
   (D) ensure workers' right to organize and bargain collectively
   (E) exempt organized labor from the Sherman Antitrust Act

30. Which of the following was a prominent supporter of expanding women's rights during the 1920s?

   (A) Betty Friedan
   (B) Rosa Parks
   (C) Alice Paul
   (D) Marian Anderson
   (E) Angela Davis

31. ". . . the bargaining strength of employees, under these conditions, no longer rests in organizations of skilled artisans. It is dependent upon a national union representing all employees . . ."

   The statement above best represents the views of

   (A) Emma Goldman
   (B) John L. Lewis
   (C) William Green
   (D) Bernard M. Baruch
   (E) Jane Addams

32. American participation in the Second World War had which of the following major effects on the home front?

   (A) A temporary movement of women into heavy industry
   (B) The elimination of racial segregation in the South
   (C) The growth of isolationism in the Midwest
   (D) The introduction of a system of national health insurance
   (E) A decline in farmers' income

33. "I believe that it must be the policy of the United States to support free peoples who are resisting attempted subjugation by armed minorities or by outside pressures. I believe that we must assist free peoples to work out their own destinies in their own way. I believe that our help should be primarily through economic and financial aid which is essential to economic stability and orderly political processes."

   The statement above is taken from

   (A) Woodrow Wilson's request for a declaration of war against Germany
   (B) Herbert Hoover's statement on Japanese aggression in China
   (C) Franklin D. Roosevelt's request for a declaration of war against Japan
   (D) Harry S Truman's request for funds to support Greece and Turkey against communism
   (E) an address by United Nations' ambassador Jeane Kirkpatrick on Central American conflict

34. Which of the following is true of the forced relocation of Japanese Americans from the West Coast during the Second World War?

    (A) President Roosevelt claimed that military necessity justified the action.

    (B) The Supreme Court immediately declared the action unconstitutional.

    (C) The relocation was implemented according to congressional provisions for the internment of dissidents.

    (D) The Japanese Americans received the same treatment as that accorded German Americans and Italian Americans.

    (E) Few of those relocated were actually United States citizens.

35. During the Second World War, the federal government pursued all of the following economic policies EXCEPT

    (A) rationing consumer goods

    (B) limiting wartime wages

    (C) limiting agricultural prices

    (D) selling war bonds

    (E) increasing the prime interest rate

36. The presidential election of 1928, which pitted Herbert Hoover against Al Smith, was the first presidential election that

    (A) featured a Roman Catholic as a presidential candidate

    (B) was decided by less than 1% of the popular vote

    (C) featured a Southern candidate and a Western candidate

    (D) had two candidates who were self-made millionaires

    (E) involved two candidates with strong rural constituencies

37. Following the Second World War, President Truman was unable to expand significantly his predecessor's New Deal programs primarily because of

    (A) the continuation of the Great Depression

    (B) the need to maintain a large military force in Asia

    (C) budget expenditures required to rebuild Europe

    (D) controversy surrounding the Truman Doctrine

    (E) the domination of Congress by Republicans and conservative Democrats

38. President Truman's decision to recall General MacArthur from his command of United Nations forces in Korea was primarily based on the principle of

    (A) containment of communism

    (B) limited rather than total warfare

    (C) isolationism rather than interventionism

    (D) civilian control of the military

    (E) self-determination for all free people

39. In the decade after the Civil War, the federal government's policy toward the Plains Indians focused on the

    (A) creation of a network of churches to convert them to Christianity

    (B) establishment of schools to promote tribal culture

    (C) establishment of reservations

    (D) forced migration of most Indian tribal groups to urban areas

    (E) forced migration of Indian tribal groups from the Southeast to Oklahoma

40. The purpose of the Geneva Accords (1954) was to

    (A) divide Vietnam into temporary sectors and lay the groundwork for free elections

    (B) devise plans for arms reductions between the Soviet Union and the United States

    (C) establish the boundaries for permanent North and South Koreas

    (D) establish an international peacekeeping force in the Middle East

    (E) resolve disagreements between the Guatemalan government of Jacobo Arbenz Guzmán and the United States

41. Allen Ginsberg was well-known as

    (A) a founder of the Black Panther Party

    (B) a key adviser to President Eisenhower

    (C) a poet of the Beat Generation

    (D) an anticommunist senator from California

    (E) an Abstract Expressionist painter

42. *Brown* v. *Board of Education of Topeka* was a Supreme Court decision that

    (A) was a forerunner of the Kansas-Nebraska Act

    (B) established free public colleges in the United States

    (C) declared racially segregated public schools inherently unequal

    (D) established free public elementary and secondary schools in the United States

    (E) provided for federal support of parochial schools

43. "The problem with hatred and violence is that they intensify the fears of the White majority, and leave them less ashamed of their prejudices toward Negroes. In the guilt and confusion confronting our society, violence only adds to chaos. It deepens the brutality of the oppressor and increases the bitterness of the oppressed. Violence is the antithesis of creativity and wholeness. It destroys community and makes brotherhood impossible."

    During the 1960s all the following African American leaders would probably have supported the view expressed above EXCEPT

    (A) Roy Wilkins

    (B) Martin Luther King, Jr.

    (C) James Farmer

    (D) Stokely Carmichael

    (E) Whitney M. Young, Jr.

44. Reform activity during the Progressive Era was similar to that of the 1960s in all of the following ways EXCEPT

    (A) The federal government supported civil rights for African Americans.

    (B) Reform activity was encouraged by strong and active presidents.

    (C) Many reformers advocated changes in the area of women's rights.

    (D) Governmental reform initiatives were curtailed by war.

    (E) Reform occurred despite the absence of severe economic depression.

45. What contribution did Ngo Dinh Diem make toward the escalation of hostilities between the United States and North Vietnam?

(A) He proclaimed himself commander in chief of Vietcong armies and organized guerrilla attacks on United States military installations.

(B) He was appointed by the French government to serve as a temporary president of Vietnam.

(C) He refused to carry out political reforms in South Vietnam.

(D) He advocated an alliance between himself and Ho Chi Minh to prevent United States intervention in Vietnam.

(E) He wrote articles in the Vietnamese popular press encouraging the public to support Marxism.

46. Which of the following is correct about United States involvement in the Vietnam War during the period 1956–1964?

(A) It was justified by invoking the Open Door policy.

(B) It was the exclusive responsibility of the Johnson and Nixon administrations.

(C) It came about only after a formal declaration of war.

(D) It was primarily anti-Soviet in purpose.

(E) It grew out of policy assumptions and commitments dating from the end of the Second World War.

47. Which of the following events brought the United States and the Soviet Union closest to the possibility of nuclear war?

(A) The Berlin Blockade

(B) The Cuban missile crisis

(C) The Pueblo incident

(D) The Suez Crisis

(E) The U2 incident

48. Until 1964 eligibility to vote could be restricted by which of the following means?

(A) Poll taxes

(B) Grandfather clauses

(C) Limits on woman suffrage

(D) White-only primary elections

(E) Exclusion of foreign-born citizens

49. Which of the following is true about the American Indian movement (AIM), which was founded in 1968?

(A) It sought accommodation with White society.

(B) It modeled its tactics on the Black Power movement.

(C) It issued the Declaration of Indian Purpose.

(D) It won voting rights for Native Americans.

(E) It drew its membership primarily from reservations.

50. In the twentieth century, United States Supreme Court decisions did all of the following EXCEPT

(A) end Prohibition

(B) ban official prayers in the public schools

(C) protect a woman's right to an abortion

(D) protect property rights

(E) expand minority rights

51. The "silent majority" was a term used to describe supporters of

(A) George McGovern

(B) George Wallace

(C) Richard Nixon

(D) Prohibition

(E) environmental reform

52. The military proposal popularly known as "Star Wars" was designed to

   (A) incorporate the National Aeronautics and Space Administration into the armed forces
   (B) create a satellite and laser shield to defend the United States against missile attacks
   (C) expand American space exploration efforts
   (D) construct new ballistic missiles not covered under the Strategic Arms Limitation Treaty I
   (E) increase the interest of young Americans in volunteering for military service

53. The Prairie School of architecture is best exemplified in the work of

   (A) Stanford White
   (B) Frank Gehry
   (C) Frank Lloyd Wright
   (D) Louis Sullivan
   (E) Daniel Burnham

54. The presidential debate between Richard M. Nixon and John F. Kennedy showed the importance of which of the following in presidential campaigns?

   (A) Radio
   (B) Television
   (C) Movies
   (D) Computers
   (E) The Internet

55. A major purpose of the Civil Rights Act of 1964 was to

   (A) prohibit discrimination in public accommodations and employment
   (B) create equity in Social Security benefits
   (C) standardize funding for Medicare
   (D) strengthen the women's movement
   (E) provide benefits for the disabled

56. In his book *The Fire Next Time* (1963), James Baldwin argued that

   (A) the nuclear arms race imperiled future generations
   (B) the failure of White Americans and Black Americans to overcome racism would have destructive consequences
   (C) expatriate Americans must return home in times of crisis
   (D) protest literature would not solve the problems of inequality
   (E) violence against civil rights demonstrators would escalate without federal intervention

57. The federal assistance program Aid to Families with Dependent Children (AFDC) was

   (A) established during the 1950s and continues to function today
   (B) a social welfare program created by Franklin D. Roosevelt's New Deal program and ended in the mid-1990s during Bill Clinton's administration
   (C) championed by social conservatives as a way to get poor families off welfare
   (D) a social welfare program created by Woodrow Wilson to address the needs of soldiers during the First World War
   (E) modeled after a similar program in the Soviet Union

58. The 1966 Supreme Court case *Miranda* v. *Arizona* concerned which of the following?

   (A) Segregated swimming pools

   (B) College admission quotas

   (C) Rights of citizens accused of a crime

   (D) Poll taxes

   (E) Sexual discrimination in the military

59. Senator Joseph McCarthy dominated the American media and Congress during the early 1950s. McCarthy's rise to power was aided most by

   (A) the expansion of the Democratic Party

   (B) the electoral success of the Republican Party in 1952

   (C) the support of Vice President Richard Nixon

   (D) the decision by Secretary of State Dean Acheson to hire Communist advisors

   (E) President Eisenhower's strong support of his efforts

60. The 1970s and 1980s were characterized by a shift in population from the

   (A) Southeast to the Midwest

   (B) Southwest to the Pacific Northwest

   (C) Mountain states to California

   (D) Northeast to the Southwest

   (E) Gulf Coast to the Great Lakes region

61. Sociologists Robert and Helen Lynd's *Middletown: A Study in Contemporary American Culture* (1929) is a classic community study that

   (A) analyzed the effects of cultural and economic change on a Midwestern city

   (B) described the effects of the Great Depression on Philadelphia

   (C) identified the labor unrest gripping Chicago in the early 1920s

   (D) focused on the human and economic costs of the First World War on a mid-Atlantic city

   (E) described the development of the warehouse industry in Atlanta

62. Which of the following was active in the antilynching movement?

   (A) Harriet Tubman

   (B) Ida B. Wells

   (C) Emma Goldman

   (D) Aimee Semple McPherson

   (E) Alice Paul

63. Which of the following led to the passage of the Chinese Exclusion Acts?

   (A) Public concern that Chinese immigrants would not support the war effort during the Second World War

   (B) Chinese officials wanting to restrict the flow of laborers to the United States

   (C) The existence of large numbers of Chinese immigrants working illegally in the United States

   (D) Racial prejudice towards Chinese workers in several regions of the country

   (E) The unwillingness of Chinese immigrants to become naturalized American citizens

64. The Stonewall riots which took place in New York city during the summer of 1969 were significant because they

(A) demonstrated the shift to confrontational politics by the National Organization for Women

(B) rejected radical feminism and advocated traditional roles for women

(C) encouraged the rise of a gay liberation movement calling publicly for an end to discrimination against gays and lesbians

(D) were the first indicator of a sexual revolution among young people

(E) showed increasing frustration with the slow pace of the women's movement

65. Which of the following statements best describes the impact of the growth of the Internet since the 1990s?

(A) It has greatly facilitated the exchange of information worldwide.

(B) It helped to end the Cold War.

(C) It has dramatically increased the costs of operating businesses throughout the world.

(D) It has further isolated Third World countries because they do not have access.

(E) It has made governmental censorship impossible.

66. Which of the following statements best reflects Theodore Roosevelt's beliefs about foreign policy?

(A) Trade is a crucial element in promoting alliances among nations.

(B) Maintenance of a strong navy is an effective means to promote peace.

(C) A policy of isolation is a vital element of United States foreign policy.

(D) The United States should not intervene in the affairs of other countries.

(E) The State Department should carry out a cautious foreign policy.

67. All of the following statements regarding the period in which Dwight Eisenhower served as president are true EXCEPT

(A) Eisenhower's policies steered a middle course between Democratic liberalism and traditional Republican conservatism.

(B) Growing suburbs, the baby boom, auto mania, and the development of the interstate highway system were indications of national prosperity.

(C) Eisenhower and Soviet Leader Nikita Khrushchev agreed on a massive bilateral reduction in the stockpiles of nuclear armaments.

(D) American culture in the 1950s reflected the combination of an expansive spirit of prosperity and Cold War anxieties.

(E) Eisenhower first used the term "military industrial complex" to describe the close relationship between government and military contractors.

68. President Ronald Reagan's economic program, also known as "Reaganomics," can be best summarized by which of the following statements?

(A) United States capitalism must be directed to focus on building effective social programs, increasing taxes on big business, and cutting taxes on lower-income households.

(B) The United States must increase government intervention in business regulation and economic planning.

(C) The United States capitalist system, if freed from heavy taxes and government regulations, would achieve greatly increased productivity.

(D) The United States should significantly increase government investment in social-welfare and public-school programs.

(E) The United States should decrease military spending in order to fund domestic programs.

69. During the 1950s, television shows like *The Donna Reed Show* and *Leave It to Beaver* exemplified the media's

(A) focus on the culture of Northeastern cities

(B) reflection of prevalent Cold War anxieties

(C) idealization of middle-class suburban family life

(D) idealization of the rural heartland

(E) focus on the growing generation gap in American culture

70. One of the goals of Populism was to

(A) reduce income taxes

(B) implement government ownership of the country's railroads and telegraph lines

(C) establish collectively owned farms

(D) establish a national health-insurance system

(E) obtain government subsidies in return for reduced agricultural production

71. Place the following in the correct chronological order. Place the earliest event first.

Truman Doctrine

Korean War

Gulf of Tonkin Resolution

Cuban missile crisis

```
┌─────────────────────────────────┐
│                                 │
└─────────────────────────────────┘
┌─────────────────────────────────┐
│                                 │
└─────────────────────────────────┘
┌─────────────────────────────────┐
│                                 │
└─────────────────────────────────┘
┌─────────────────────────────────┐
│                                 │
└─────────────────────────────────┘
```

Click on a choice, then click on a box.

72. The Federal Reserve system, established in 1913, has sought for much of its history to do which of the following?

(A) Stabilize the nation's money supply by expanding or restricting credit as needed

(B) Assist consumers by forcing bankers to establish nationally uniform interest rates on loans

(C) Promote confidence in the dollar by linking the value of currency in circulation directly to United States silver reserves

(D) Encourage public support for increased government spending to stimulate economic growth

(E) Lower taxes on financial transactions completed by national banks on behalf of consumers

Study Resources

Most textbooks used in college-level United States history (post-1865) courses cover the topics in the outline given earlier, but the approaches to certain topics and the emphases given to them may differ. To prepare for the History of the United States II exam, it is advisable to study one or more college textbooks, which can be found in most college bookstores. When selecting a textbook, check the table of contents against the knowledge and skills required for this test.

Additional detail and differing interpretations can be gained by consulting readers and specialized historical studies. Pay attention to visual materials (pictures, maps, and charts) as you study.

Visit www.collegeboard.com/clepprep for additional history resources. You can also find suggestions for exam preparation in Chapter IV of the *Official Study Guide*. In addition, many college faculty post their course materials on their schools' Web sites.

Answer Key

#	Ans		#	Ans
1.	B		37.	E
2.	A		38.	D
3.	B		39.	C
4.	C		40.	A
5.	A		41.	C
6.	E		42.	C
7.	E		43.	D
8.	A		44.	A
9.	A		45.	C
10.	D		46.	E
11.	A		47.	B
12.	B		48.	A
13.	E		49.	B
14.	C		50.	A
15.	E		51.	C
16.	B		52.	B
17.	A		53.	C
18.	B		54.	B
19.	A		55.	A
20.	A		56.	B
21.	D		57.	B
22.	C		58.	C
23.	E		59.	B
24.	C		60.	D
25.	D		61.	A
26.	C		62.	B
27.	E		63.	D
28.	C		64.	C
29.	D		65.	A
30.	C		66.	B
31.	B		67.	C
32.	A		68.	C
33.	D		69.	C
34.	A		70.	B
35.	E		71.	1,2,4,3
36.	A		72.	A

Human Growth and Development

Description of the Examination

The Human Growth and Development examination (Infancy, Childhood, Adolescence, Adulthood, and Aging) covers material that is generally taught in a one-semester introductory course in developmental psychology or human development. An understanding of the major theories and research related to the broad categories of physical development, cognitive development, and social development is required, as is the ability to apply this knowledge.

The examination contains approximately 90 questions to be answered in 90 minutes. Some of them are pretest questions that will not be scored. Any time candidates spend on tutorials and providing personal information is in addition to the actual testing time.

Knowledge and Skills Required

Questions on the Human Growth and Development examination require candidates to demonstrate one or more of the following abilities.

- Knowledge of basic facts and terminology
- Understanding of generally accepted concepts and principles
- Understanding of theories and recurrent developmental issues
- Applications of knowledge to particular problems or situations

The subject matter of the Human Growth and Development examination is drawn from the following categories. For each category, several key words and phrases identify topics with which candidates should be familiar. The percentages next to the main categories indicate the approximate percentage of exam questions on that topic.

10% Theoretical Perspectives
- Cognitive developmental
- Evolutionary
- Learning
- Psychodynamic
- Social cognitive
- Sociocultural

5% Research Strategies and Methodology
- Case study
- Correlational
- Cross-sectional
- Cross sequential
- Experimental
- Longitudinal
- Observational

10% Biological Development Throughout the Life Span
- Development of the brain and nervous system
- Heredity, genetics, and genetic testing
- Hormonal influences
- Influences of drugs
- Motor development
- Nutritional influences
- Perinatal influences
- Physical growth and maturation, aging
- Prenatal influences
- Sexual maturation
- Teratogens

7% Perceptual Development Throughout the Life Span
- Sensitive periods
- Sensorimotor activities
- Sensory acuity
- Sensory deprivation

12% Cognitive Development Throughout the Life Span
- Attention
- Environmental influences
- Executive function
- Expertise
- Information processing
- Memory
- Piaget, Jean
- Play
- Problem solving and planning
- Thinking
- Vygotsky, Lev
- Wisdom

8% **Language Development**

Bilingualism
Development of syntax
Environmental, cultural, and genetic influences
Language and thought
Pragmatics
Semantic development
Vocalization and sound

4% **Intelligence Throughout the Life Span**

Concepts of intelligence and creativity
Developmental stability and change
Heredity and environment

10% **Social Development Throughout the Life Span**

Aggression
Attachment
Gender
Interpersonal relationships
Moral development
Prosocial behavior
Risk and resilience
Self
Social cognition
Wellness

8% **Family, Home, and Society Throughout the Life Span**

Abuse and neglect
Bronfenbrenner, Urie
Death and dying
Family relationships
Family structures
Media and technology
Multicultural perspectives
Parenting styles
Social and class influences

8% **Personality and Emotion**

Attribution styles
Development of emotions
Emotional expression and regulation
Emotional intelligence
Erikson, Erik
Freud, Sigmund
Stability and change
Temperament

8% **Learning**

Classical conditioning
Discrimination and generalization
Habituation
Operant conditioning
Social learning and modeling

5% **Schooling, Work, and Interventions**

Applications of developmental principles
Facilitation of role transitions
Intervention programs and services
Learning styles
Occupational development
Preschool care, day care, and elder care
Retirement

5% **Atypical Development**

Antisocial behavior
Asocial behavior, fears, phobias, and obsessions
Attention-deficit/hyperactivity disorder
Autism spectrum disorders
Chronic illnesses and physical disabilities
Cognitive disorders, including dementia
Genetic disorders
Giftedness
Learning disabilities
Mental retardation
Mood disorders
Trauma-based syndromes

Sample Test Questions

The following sample questions do not appear on an actual CLEP examination. They are intended to give potential test-takers an indication of the format and difficulty level of the examination and to provide content for practice and review. Knowing the correct answers to all of the sample questions is not a guarantee of satisfactory performance on the exam.

Directions: Each of the questions or incomplete statements below is followed by five suggested answers or completions. Select the one that is best in each case.

1. The first negative emotion clearly exhibited during infancy is

   (A) fear
   (B) anger
   (C) guilt
   (D) distress
   (E) jealousy

2. According to behavioral psychologists, which of the following treatments would most likely extinguish disruptive behavior in preschool children?

   (A) Threatening to isolate them immediately after such behavior
   (B) Ignoring them so that they do not receive the reinforcement they are seeking
   (C) Punishing them immediately so they understand what they did wrong
   (D) Discouraging them but not punishing them
   (E) Reasoning with them and explaining that their behavior is wrong

3. The length of time that it takes to toilet train a child depends mostly on which of the following?

   (A) Presence or absence of older siblings
   (B) Severity of the training practices the caregivers use
   (C) Verbal ability of the caregivers
   (D) The child's feeding regimen in infancy
   (E) Age at which the caregivers begin to train the child

4. A defining characteristic of autistic children is

   (A) obsessive attachment to their mothers
   (B) lack of motor coordination
   (C) unresponsiveness to others
   (D) hyperactivity
   (E) physical abnormality

5. Anxiety over performance can positively motivate school achievement in children as long as the degree of anxiety is

   (A) very high
   (B) high
   (C) moderate
   (D) low
   (E) very low

6. According to Jean Piaget, cognitive development begins with which of the following?

   (A) Preoperations
   (B) Concrete operations
   (C) Intuitive thought
   (D) Sensorimotor activities
   (E) Formal operations

7. Social-class differences in vocabulary development result from social-class differences in the amount of

(A) maternal anxiety
(B) verbal stimulation
(C) paternal illness
(D) sibling rivalry
(E) marital discord

8. Studies in which the same people are tested at different ages are called

(A) longitudinal
(B) cross-sectional
(C) normative
(D) naturalistic
(E) experimental

9. Which of the following is most central to the concept of sensitive period?

(A) Growth spurts must occur at specific ages.
(B) Children who do not develop at the same time as their peers experience distress.
(C) A given function emerges automatically during a particular time period regardless of learning experiences.
(D) Particular experiences are especially influential at a certain time in development.
(E) Children go through a negativistic stage as a part of their cognitive development.

10. Jimmy saw his favorite candy for sale in the store. He had no money, so he planned to steal it. However, he changed his mind and decided not to do it, because stealing is wrong. According to Sigmund Freud's theory, which part of Jimmy's personality prevented him from stealing?

(A) Id
(B) Ego
(C) Superego
(D) Anima
(E) Collective unconscious

11. If reinforcement is to be most effective in the learning of a new behavior, the reinforcement should be

(A) provided as sparingly as possible
(B) administered on an intermittent schedule
(C) used primarily with high achievers
(D) delayed until the end of the learning period
(E) provided soon after the desired behavior occurs

12. In Harry Harlow's experiments, infant monkeys raised with only wire or cloth "mothers" were LEAST fearful in strange situations in the presence of

(A) the "mother" who had provided food
(B) the "mother" who had provided contact comfort
(C) the "mother" who had provided primary drive reduction
(D) other young monkeys
(E) their biological mothers

13. A sudden, loud noise made in the vicinity of a newborn infant is likely to elicit which of the following reflexes?

(A) Babinski
(B) Moro
(C) Rooting
(D) Palmar grasp
(E) Stepping

14. On which of the following types of problems would you expect a four-year-old child and a seven-year-old child to perform most similarly?

    (A) Conservation of number
    (B) Classification
    (C) Transformation
    (D) Object permanence
    (E) Superordinate concepts

15. Red-green color blindness is best described as

    (A) a sex-linked recessive trait
    (B) a sex-linked dominant trait
    (C) an autosomal recessive trait
    (D) an autosomal dominant trait
    (E) a trait resulting from chromosomal breakage

16. Over summer vacation, Gwen sees a boy she knows from school, but she is having difficulty remembering his name. Which of her memory processes is failing in this situation?

    (A) Storage
    (B) Retrieval
    (C) Encoding
    (D) Short-term memory
    (E) Sensory memory

17. Which of the following theorists did NOT develop a stage theory?

    (A) Sigmund Freud
    (B) Jean Piaget
    (C) B. F. Skinner
    (D) Lawrence Kohlberg
    (E) Erik Erikson

18. Which of the following is true of male menopause?

    (A) It is a purely physical phenomenon.
    (B) It is usually a result of too little exercise.
    (C) It is commonly a cause of work-related problems.
    (D) It is differentially damaging to the male psyche depending on age.
    (E) It is physically impossible because males do not menstruate.

19. According to psychoanalytic theory, which of the following mechanisms (and the attitude accompanying it) would be most important for healthy resolution of a little boy's Oedipus complex?

    (A) Identification with the father ("I am like Daddy.")
    (B) Object-choice of the father ("I love Daddy best.")
    (C) Identification with the mother ("I am like Mommy.")
    (D) Object-choice of the mother ("I love Mommy best.")
    (E) Projection onto the mother ("Mommy loves me best.")

20. In accounting for the rapid expansion of a child's early vocabulary, Susan Carey argued that a major role must be played by the child's own active cognitive processing. Adults simply cannot teach a child exactly what referent every word picks out. Carey coined which one of the following terms to denote this concept?

    (A) Fast mapping
    (B) Lexical conventionality
    (C) Lexical contrast
    (D) Linguistic empiricism
    (E) Metacognition

21. Heather is currently taking courses in several different academic departments and doing volunteer work to help identify and develop her interests. She also spends a lot of time thinking about her values and goals but has not chosen a career path. Heather's identity status is referred to as

    (A) fixation
    (B) identity achievement
    (C) identity diffusion
    (D) identity foreclosure
    (E) identity moratorium

22. Which of the following theorists advanced the concept of the identity crisis?

    (A) Jean Piaget
    (B) Sigmund Freud
    (C) Lev Vygotsky
    (D) B. F. Skinner
    (E) Erik Erikson

23. A researcher is evaluating the effects of three different types of parent-education programs on adolescent mothers' interactions with their toddlers. What is the independent variable in this investigation?

    (A) Adolescent mothers' interactions with their toddlers
    (B) Level of parent-child communication
    (C) Type of parent education program
    (D) Child's attachment to the mother
    (E) Child's socioeconomic status

24. Kimiko is interested in children's relationships with same-sex and opposite-sex peers. She observes children's behavior in their normal, everyday environment (for example, at school). She records each time a child speaks to or plays with another child and whether that other child is the same or opposite sex. She uses a stopwatch to record how long the children play with their peers. This research method is

    (A) a clinical interview
    (B) a structured interview
    (C) a naturalistic observation
    (D) a structured observation
    (E) an ethnography

25. The developing organism is most vulnerable to the effects of teratogens during the period of the

    (A) ovum
    (B) zygote
    (C) embryo
    (D) fetus
    (E) neonate

26. With regard to sexual maturity, females generally mature

    (A) two years earlier than males do
    (B) four years earlier than males do
    (C) two years later than males do
    (D) four years later than males do
    (E) at approximately the same age as males

27. Carolyn tripped on the carpet and fell. When she got up, she looked at her mother, who was laughing, and she laughed, too. This is an example of

    (A) empathy
    (B) sympathy
    (C) social referencing
    (D) display rules
    (E) semantics

28. Proximodistal development is exemplified by which of the following?

(A) Control of gross arm movements prior to fine motor control of the fingers

(B) Control of the lower extremities prior to control of the head

(C) Refinement of perceptual abilities prior to walking

(D) Acquisition of differential skills prior to acquisition of complex skills

(E) Maturation of neural pathways in the cerebrum prior to maturation of the neural pathways of the midbrain

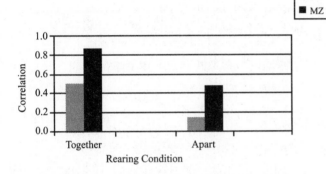

29. A researcher was interested in determining the heritability of a specific trait. He measured the trait in a group of same-sex dizygotic (DZ) twins and a group of monozygotic (MZ) twins. Half of the pairs of twins in each group were reared together, and half were reared apart. The figure above shows the correlations between the measures of the trait for the DZ and MZ twins by rearing condition. Which of the following statements most accurately interprets the heritability of the trait?

(A) Both genes and the environment influence the trait.

(B) Genetic but not environmental factors affect the trait.

(C) Environmental but not genetic factors affect the trait.

(D) Prenatal influences have stronger effects on development of the trait than do either genes or the environment.

(E) The environment influences the trait among the DZ but not the MZ twins.

30. Newborn infants were given either smooth or knobby pacifiers to suck. They were later allowed to look at both types of pacifiers. They looked longer at the type of pacifier they had previously sucked. This finding indicates that newborn infants have

(A) categorical perception

(B) intermodal perception

(C) shape constancy

(D) depth perception

(E) object permanence

31. Which of the following senses is the LEAST well developed at birth?

(A) Vision

(B) Hearing

(C) Smell

(D) Touch

(E) Taste

32. Order the types of play below from the least cognitively mature to the most cognitively mature.

   I. Cooperative play

  II. Pretend play

 III. Functional play

(A) I, II, III

(B) II, I, III

(C) II, III, I

(D) III, I, II

(E) III, II, I

33. A child explains thunder as "the clouds yelling at each other." This is an example of

(A) conservation

(B) reversibility

(C) animistic reasoning

(D) egoistic thinking

(E) logical inference

34. The stage of formal operations is characterized by

    (A) the application of logical thought to concrete objects and situations
    (B) intuitive and animistic thought
    (C) abstract thought and hypothetical problem solving
    (D) the development of transductive reasoning
    (E) the ability to conserve

35. Katie, a preschooler, sees a llama at the zoo for the first time and calls it a sheep. This is an example of

    (A) semantic overextension
    (B) chaining
    (C) fast mapping
    (D) divergent thinking
    (E) an expressive style

36. In ecological systems theory, the exosystem includes

    (A) values and beliefs of the culture in which a child is developing, such as the acceptance of violence
    (B) settings in which a child spends time, such as classrooms and neighborhood play groups
    (C) social settings that indirectly influence a child, such as parents' workplaces
    (D) connections among the different settings in which a child develops, such as the home and the school
    (E) transitions that occur over time, such as a major change in the family's economic situation

37. A theory of language development that proposes an innate language acquisition device would be classified as which of the following?

    (A) Nativist
    (B) Interactionist
    (C) Empiricist
    (D) Contextual
    (E) Functionalist

38. A child who has an IQ of 55 to 69 and delayed social development is classified as

    (A) mildly retarded
    (B) moderately retarded
    (C) severely retarded
    (D) profoundly retarded
    (E) learning disabled

39. Which of the following infant measures best predicts childhood IQ?

    (A) Performance on the Mental Scale of the Bayley Scales of Infant Development
    (B) Speed of habituation and dishabituation to visual stimuli
    (C) Age in months at which the child begins walking and talking
    (D) Percent of time spent in REM sleep
    (E) Birth weight

40. A toddler with a secure attachment to a primary caregiver would be expected to

    (A) avoid the caregiver when they were reunited after a brief separation
    (B) stay in the caregiver's lap rather than explore a new environment
    (C) cry when the caregiver left the toddler with a babysitter
    (D) have a close bond with only one parent or primary caregiver
    (E) respond equally well to the caregiver and to a strange adult

41. A boy who believes that he will become a girl if he wears his sister's clothes has not achieved the concept of

    (A) androgyny
    (B) gender stability
    (C) gender labeling
    (D) gender constancy
    (E) gender schema

42. The process by which fluid from the uterus is taken early in pregnancy to determine whether the developing fetus has a genetic anomaly is called

    (A) amniocentesis

    (B) chorionic villus sampling

    (C) positron-emission tomography

    (D) insemination

    (E) ultrasound

43. Although Elizabeth's seven-year-old son wants to stay up past his bedtime to watch a television special, she insists that he go to bed at the usual time. She explains that he will be too tired to do well in school if he does not get his rest, and she promises to record the show for him. Diana Baumrind would classify Elizabeth's parenting style as which of the following?

    (A) Nurturing

    (B) Uninvolved

    (C) Authoritarian

    (D) Authoritative

    (E) Permissive

44. Research on children without siblings reveals that they

    (A) have lower levels of self-esteem

    (B) demonstrate lower levels of prosocial behavior

    (C) do better in school

    (D) are less popular with peers

    (E) are less emotionally secure

45. The three behavioral styles identified by Alexander Thomas and Stella Chess in their early research on infant temperament are

    (A) sanguine, melancholic, choleric

    (B) easy, difficult, slow to warm up

    (C) secure, avoidant, ambivalent

    (D) emotional, sociable, inhibited

    (E) introverted, extroverted, agreeable

46. Time out is a disciplinary technique that is based on the principles of

    (A) operant conditioning

    (B) classical conditioning

    (C) observational learning

    (D) information processing

    (E) habituation

47. A mother nags her son until he cleans his room. A few weeks later, the son spontaneously cleans his room because he does not want to be nagged. The mother's nagging is an example of

    (A) positive reinforcement

    (B) negative reinforcement

    (C) vicarious reinforcement

    (D) vicarious punishment

    (E) punishment

48. Information-processing theorists argue that one of the major changes that takes place from two to five years of age is

    (A) an increase in the ability to form abstract thoughts and use logical reasoning

    (B) an increase in the complexity and power of working memory

    (C) a decrease in the complexity of schemata associated with everyday experiences

    (D) a decrease in fluid intelligence

    (E) a decrease in the storage capacity of long-term memory

49. According to research, all of the following statements comparing Head Start participants with their nonparticipating peers are true EXCEPT that Head Start participants are

    (A) less likely to become pregnant as teenagers

    (B) likely to score higher on IQ tests as adolescents

    (C) less likely to be placed in special education classes

    (D) less likely to be retained in a grade

    (E) more likely to graduate from high school

50. Keisha politely asks her teacher to please pass her the scissors but at home demands that her little brother give them to her immediately. Keisha is demonstrating her understanding of which aspect of knowledge?

   (A) Phonology
   (B) Semantics
   (C) Syntax
   (D) Pragmatics
   (E) Overregularization

51. Which of the following is the symptom most closely associated with Alzheimer's disease?

   (A) Manic-depressive behavior
   (B) Sensory impairment
   (C) Loss of ability to walk
   (D) Loss of memory
   (E) Loss of reflexes

52. One of the major criticisms of the stages of dying identified by Elisabeth Kübler-Ross is that

   (A) there are too many stages in her theory
   (B) there are not enough stages in her theory
   (C) not everyone goes through the stages in the order she describes
   (D) she does not adequately suggest how people try to cope with each stage
   (E) the stages vary by sex

53. Instruction by teachers who employ Piagetian principles is most likely to be characterized by which of the following?

   (A) Use of lecture as the dominant form of instruction
   (B) Reliance on drill and repetition
   (C) Encouragement of active experimentation
   (D) Encouragement of silent reading
   (E) Discouragement of group activities

54. According to Lev Vygotsky, the range between what a child can do alone and what a child can do with assistance is referred to as

   (A) higher mental functions
   (B) scaffolding
   (C) inner speech
   (D) egocentric speech
   (E) the zone of proximal development

55. When Frank was a child, he moved to a new house near a major airport. At first, he was unable to sleep because of the loud noise created by the airplanes. Over time, however, he was no longer disturbed by the plane noise. A behaviorist would most likely describe the change in Frank's behavior as which of the following?

   (A) Habituation
   (B) Superstition
   (C) Shaping
   (D) Operant conditioning
   (E) Response generalization

56. Which of the following grammatical morphemes would a child be likely to acquire last?

   (A) Article ("a cookie")
   (B) Plural ("two cookies")
   (C) Present progressive ("I am walking")
   (D) Simple past ("Joey walked")
   (E) Contraction ("that's Joey")

57. According to Robert Sternberg's triangular theory, which of the following are the three major components of adult love?

   (A) Friendship . . compassion . . commitment
   (B) Commitment . . intimacy . . compassion
   (C) Intimacy . . commitment . . passion
   (D) Compassion . . friendship . . passion
   (E) Compassion . . infatuation . . intimacy

58. The term "sandwich generation" refers to

(A) the current middle-adulthood generation that feels squeezed between children and aging parents, both of whom that generation must care for

(B) young adults who return to live with their parents after college or after having lived away from home for some other reason

(C) the current generation of children who are fed mostly sandwiches because their parents are working and cannot prepare meals for them

(D) the current middle-adulthood generation that survives mostly on sandwiches and fast food eaten on the run because life is too busy for sit-down meals at home

(E) a political term from the 1950s used by pacifists who felt that the federal government should generate food for poor children rather than produce nuclear weapons

59. What is the most commonly diagnosed mental disorder among individuals in very late adulthood?

(A) Schizophrenia
(B) Dementia
(C) Generalized anxiety disorder
(D) Hypochondriasis
(E) Mood disorder

60. A researcher compares church attendance between people born in the 1940s and people born in the 1960s. The groups of people are called

(A) cohorts
(B) alliances
(C) support systems
(D) reference groups
(E) cliques

61. Eighteen-month-old Michael sees his mother about to put his juice away, and he yells out, "More juice!" Michael's expression is an example of

(A) a holophrase
(B) receptive language
(C) private speech
(D) motherese
(E) telegraphic speech

62. According to psychologists, which type of aggression do adolescent girls use more frequently than do adolescent boys?

(A) Instrumental
(B) Relational
(C) Physical
(D) Emotional self-regulated
(E) Instinctive

63. According to Lawrence Kohlberg, parents can best foster their children's moral development by

(A) setting high expectations for moral behavior

(B) promptly and consistently punishing their children's misbehavior

(C) providing models of moral behavior

(D) directly teaching their children what to do when they face specific moral dilemmas

(E) exposing their children to more advanced moral reasoning by discussion of both sides of moral dilemmas

64. When there is an extremely weak relationship between two behavioral variables, the correlation coefficient will be

(A) much lower than zero
(B) close to zero
(C) close to +1
(D) close to −1
(E) much higher than +1

65. Two young boys sitting next to each other, each drawing a separate picture with his own set of crayons, are engaging in which type of play?

(A) Cooperative
(B) Independent
(C) Parallel
(D) Onlooker
(E) Associative

66. An intelligence test requires individuals to create synonyms for words from a prepared list. If change in performance on this test throughout the life span were studied longitudinally, the most likely result would be scores that

(A) steadily increase
(B) steadily decline
(C) peak in middle adulthood, then decline rapidly
(D) peak in early childhood and late adulthood, with a decline in between
(E) remain steady

67. What two developmental milestones occur around the age of one year?

(A) Walking and speaking first words
(B) Crawling and gesturing to communicate
(C) Running and climbing on furniture
(D) Throwing and catching a ball with two hands
(E) Smiling and pulling to a stand

68. In the United States, marital satisfaction is at its lowest at which stage of life?

(A) Immediately following the wedding
(B) Before children are born
(C) When children are very young
(D) When children leave home
(E) Retirement

69. An infant who is fed a balanced diet yet is not gaining enough weight would most likely be diagnosed with

(A) non-organic failure-to-thrive
(B) marasmus
(C) kwashiorkor
(D) autism
(E) Klinefelter syndrome

70. Drazen, a child with attention-deficit/hyper-activity disorder (ADHD) and oppositional defiant disorder (ODD), is likely to be rated by his peers as being in which of the following peer status categories?

(A) Average
(B) Rejected aggressive
(C) Rejected withdrawn
(D) Neglected
(E) Popular

Study Resources

Most textbooks used in college-level human growth and development courses cover the topics in the outline given earlier, but the approaches to certain topics and the emphases given to them may differ. To prepare for the Human Growth and Development exam, it is advisable to study one or more college textbooks, which can be found in most college bookstores. When selecting a textbook, check the table of contents against the knowledge and skills required for this test.

You may also find it helpful to supplement your reading with books and articles listed in the bibliographies found in most developmental psychology textbooks.

Parents and others who work with children may have gained some preparation for this test through experience. However, knowledge of the basic facts, theories, and principles of child psychology and lifespan development is necessary to provide background for taking the exam.

Visit www.collegeboard.com/clepprep for additional human growth and development resources. You can also find suggestions for exam preparation in Chapter IV of the *Official Study Guide*. In addition, many college faculty post their course materials on their schools' Web sites.

Answer Key

1.	D	36.	C
2.	B	37.	A
3.	E	38.	A
4.	C	39.	B
5.	C	40.	C
6.	D	41.	D
7.	B	42.	A
8.	A	43.	D
9.	D	44.	C
10.	C	45.	B
11.	E	46.	A
12.	B	47.	B
13.	B	48.	B
14.	D	49.	B
15.	A	50.	D
16.	B	51.	D
17.	C	52.	C
18.	E	53.	C
19.	A	54.	E
20.	A	55.	A
21.	E	56.	E
22.	E	57.	C
23.	C	58.	A
24.	C	59.	B
25.	C	60.	A
26.	A	61.	E
27.	C	62.	B
28.	A	63.	E
29.	A	64.	B
30.	B	65.	C
31.	A	66.	A
32.	E	67.	A
33.	C	68.	C
34.	C	69.	A
35.	A	70.	B

Introduction to Educational Psychology

Description of the Examination

The Introduction to Educational Psychology examination covers material that is usually taught in a one-semester undergraduate course in this subject. Emphasis is placed on principles of learning and cognition, teaching methods and classroom management, child growth and development, and evaluation and assessment of learning.

The examination contains approximately 100 questions to be answered in 90 minutes. Some of these are pretest questions that will not be scored. Any time candidates spend on tutorials and providing personal information is in addition to the actual testing time.

Knowledge and Skills Required

Questions on the Introduction to Educational Psychology examination require candidates to demonstrate one or more of the following abilities.

- Knowledge and comprehension of basic facts, concepts, and principles
- Association of ideas with given theoretical positions
- Awareness of important influences on learning and instruction
- Familiarity with research and statistical concepts and procedures
- Ability to apply various concepts and theories as they apply to particular teaching situations and problems

The subject matter of the Introduction to Educational Psychology examination is drawn from the following topics. The percentages next to the main topics indicate the approximate percentage of exam questions on that topic.

5% Educational Aims and Philosophies
- Lifelong learning
- Moral/character development
- Preparation for careers
- Preparation for responsible citizenship
- Socialization

15% Cognitive Perspective
- Attention and perception
- Memory
- Complex cognitive processes (e.g., problem solving, transfer, conceptual change)
- Applications of cognitive theory

11% Behavioral Perspective
- Classical conditioning
- Operant conditioning
- Schedules of reinforcement
- Applications of behavioral perspectives

15% Development
- Cognitive
- Social
- Moral
- Gender identity/sex roles

10% Motivation
- Social-cognitive theories of motivation (e.g., attribution theory, expectancy-value theory, goal orientation theory, intrinsic and extrinsic motivation, self-efficacy, self-determination theory)
- Learned helplessness
- Teacher expectations/Pygmalion effect
- Anxiety/stress
- Applications of motivational theories

17% Individual Differences
- Intelligence
- Genetic and environmental influences
- Exceptionalities in learning (e.g., giftedness, learning disabilities, behavior disorders)
- Ability grouping and tracking

12% Testing

- Classroom assessment (e.g., formative and summative evaluation, grading procedures)
- Norm- and criterion-referenced tests
- Test reliability and validity
- Bias in testing
- High-stakes assessment
- Interpretation of test results (e.g., descriptive statistics, scaled scores)
- Use and misuse of assessments

10% Pedagogy

- Planning instruction for effective learning
- Social constructivist pedagogy (e.g., scaffolding)
- Cooperative/collaborative learning
- Classroom management

5% Research Design and Analysis

- Research design (e.g., longitudinal, experimental, case study, quasi-experimental)
- Research methods (e.g., survey, observation, interview)
- Interpretation of research (e.g., correlation versus causation, descriptive statistics)

Sample Test Questions

The following sample questions do not appear on an actual CLEP examination. They are intended to give potential test-takers an indication of the format and difficulty level of the examination and to provide content for practice and review. Knowing the correct answers to all of the sample questions is not a guarantee of satisfactory performance on the exam.

Directions: Each of the questions or incomplete statements below is followed by five suggested answers or completions. Select the one that is best in each case.

1. Which of the following learning outcomes usually undergoes the largest loss within 24 hours of acquisition?

   (A) The learning of meaningful material
   (B) The learning of rote material
   (C) The formulation of concepts
   (D) The application of principles
   (E) The making of generalizations

2. When Robert's classmates no longer showed approval of his clowning, his clowning behavior occurred less frequently. The concept best exemplified by Robert's change in behavior is

   (A) extinction
   (B) discrimination
   (C) generalization
   (D) transfer
   (E) learning set

3. Which of the following are functions of an Individualized Education Program (IEP)?

   I. Supports classroom teachers
   II. Creates a relationship (partnership) between regular classroom and resource team
   III. Provides an instructional program to meet the needs of the individual student
   IV. Allows the school professionals to solely make decisions without consulting parents

   (A) III only
   (B) I and III only
   (C) III and IV only
   (D) I, II, and III only
   (E) I, II, III, and IV

4. In a fifth-grade class that is working on a set of arithmetic problems, which of the following behaviors would be most characteristic of the student who is a divergent thinker?

   (A) Writing down the principle used to solve the problem as well as the solution itself
   (B) Making answers far more exact than is necessary
   (C) Working as fast as possible in order to be the first to finish the assignment
   (D) Finding a variety of ways to solve each problem
   (E) Providing the correct solution to the greatest number of problems

5. To measure students' understanding of a theorem in geometry, it is best for a teacher to have the students do which of the following?

   (A) Write out the theorem
   (B) Recall the proof of the theorem
   (C) Demonstrate that they have memorized the theorem
   (D) Solve a problem that is given in the textbook
   (E) Solve a related problem that is not in the textbook

6. A child who is frightened by a dog and develops a fear of other dogs is exhibiting which of the following principles of learning?

   (A) Discrimination learning
   (B) Negative transfer
   (C) Behavior shaping
   (D) Stimulus generalization
   (E) Cognitive dissonance

7. In experimental studies of the motor development of identical twins, one twin is given practice at a particular skill early and the other twin six weeks later. The fact that it generally takes less practice for the later-trained twin to acquire the skill is evidence for the importance of

   (A) heredity
   (B) maturation
   (C) intelligence quotient (IQ)
   (D) individual differences
   (E) early experience

8. In a fifth-grade class studying the ancient Incan culture, all of the following questions are likely to stimulate pupils to think creatively EXCEPT:

   (A) Why do you suppose the clothing of the Incas was so different from today's clothing?
   (B) What weapons and tools did the Incas use for hunting?
   (C) What would be the reaction of ancient Incas toward modern Peru?
   (D) If the Incas had defeated the Spanish, how might things be different in Peru today?
   (E) If you had lived in Peru during the time of the Incas, what are the things you would have liked and disliked?

9. The psychological frame of reference that deals extensively with the effects of unconscious motivation on behavior is

   (A) behaviorism
   (B) structuralism
   (C) psychoanalysis
   (D) humanism
   (E) Gestalt psychology

10. Of the following, learning is best defined as

    (A) development that occurs without external stimulation
    (B) the process of overcoming obstacles during instinctual behavior
    (C) effort that is persistent, selective, and purposeful
    (D) the modification of behavior through experience
    (E) the gathering of data to test hypotheses

11. According to cognitive learning theorists, a new unit can be most readily learned by a class of students when the unit's concepts and terms are

    (A) recited from memory in a number of contexts
    (B) expressed as observable behavioral objectives
    (C) chosen to reflect the most up-to-date findings in the field
    (D) related hierarchically to concepts and terms mastered previously
    (E) presented in a manner that students find different and complex

12. A preschool child sees a teacher roll a ball of clay into a sausage-like shape. The teacher asks, "Is the amount of clay the same as before?" The child insists that the sausage shape consists of more clay than the ball did. According to Jean Piaget, this mistake by the child occurs principally because of which of the following?

    (A) A poorly stated question by the teacher

    (B) Erroneous earlier learning by the child

    (C) The greater attractiveness of the sausage shape

    (D) Functional retardation of the child

    (E) A lack of understanding of the conservation principle

13. A fourth-grade teacher wants her students to learn to recognize oak trees. Which of the following strategies would best lead to that goal?

    (A) Bringing oak leaves into the classroom and having students trace them

    (B) Taking the students to the park to show them oaks and other trees and pointing out the distinguishing characteristics of oaks

    (C) Giving each student one or two acorns to plant and presenting a lesson on how oak trees grow

    (D) Decorating the classroom bulletin boards with pictures of trees

    (E) Showing students a film of the major trees of North America and then giving the students a quiz on oak trees

14. Longitudinal studies of cognitive abilities during middle and later adulthood indicate which of the following declines most with age?

    (A) Speed of information processing

    (B) Size of vocabulary

    (C) Wisdom

    (D) Quality of verbal reasoning

    (E) Crystallized intelligence

15. If a test is reliable, the

    (A) results will be approximately the same if the test is given again under similar conditions

    (B) test measures what it was designed to measure

    (C) predictive validity of the test is high

    (D) objectives measured by the test are important

    (E) test scores can be interpreted objectively by anyone simply by using the test manual

16. The concept of developmental tasks refers to the

    (A) development of mental abilities, as distinguished from physical abilities

    (B) ability of the child to develop certain conceptual arrangements

    (C) behavior of the child that results from hereditary determinants

    (D) behaviors of the child that are expected at various ages

    (E) physiological development of the child

17. Which of the following correlation coefficients has the highest predictive value?

    (A) .80

    (B) .60

    (C) .00

    (D) −.70

    (E) −.90

18. Which of the following statistics is most affected by extreme scores?

    (A) Mean

    (B) Median

    (C) Mode

    (D) Rank correlation

    (E) Interquartile range

19. A certain researcher studied Stephanie's development of mathematical proof and justification from grade 1 through grade 5 by collecting videotapes, portfolios, notes, student interviews, and small-group evaluations of Stephanie over the five-year period. This type of study is referred to as

    (A) an experimental study

    (B) a case study

    (C) a matched-group study

    (D) a correlational study

    (E) a survey

20. Which of the following perspectives on teaching would most likely support the idea that instruction should emphasize a positive relationship between teachers and students?

    (A) Behavioral

    (B) Humanistic

    (C) Cognitive

    (D) Psychoanalytic

    (E) Maturational

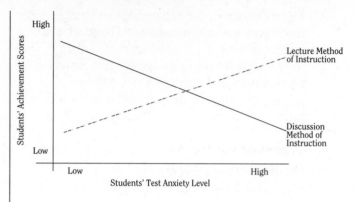

21. Assuming that the data above were collected in an experimental study, which of the following statements best describes the relationships depicted in the graph?

    (A) Differences among students in test anxiety result in different achievement levels depending on the instructional method received.

    (B) Differences among students in test anxiety result in different achievement levels independent of the instructional method received.

    (C) The effect of two different instructional methods on students' achievement is positively correlated with students' test anxiety levels.

    (D) The effect of two different instructional methods on students' achievement is negatively correlated with students' test anxiety levels.

    (E) Students' achievement levels are independent of their test anxiety levels.

22. Frank, a fifteen year old, is capable of reasoning abstractly without the use of real objects to assist him. According to Jean Piaget, Frank is in which of the following stages of cognitive development?

    (A) Concrete operations

    (B) Tertiary circular reactions

    (C) Preoperations

    (D) Formal operations

    (E) Sensorimotor

23. Decisions about the values that are transmitted in schools are best related to the teacher's role as

    (A) instructional expert
    (B) socialization agent
    (C) counselor
    (D) motivator
    (E) classroom manager

24. Using the principle of successive approximation involves which of the following?

    (A) Reinforcing responses that represent progress toward a desired response
    (B) Making a succession of trials designed to provide information about a problem
    (C) Acquiring a behavior change through imitation of models demonstrating the behavior
    (D) Averaging repeated measures for adequate assessment of a variable
    (E) Testing possible solutions until success is obtained in problem solving

25. Which of the following best characterizes the concept of a critical or sensitive period in development?

    (A) A bridge between two cognitive stages, such as the transition between preoperational and concrete-operational thinking
    (B) An age period during which a behavior must develop if it is to develop normally
    (C) An age period during which the child tends to display a certain class of behaviors, such as the "terrible twos"
    (D) An age period during which the child's sense of self-worth is especially vulnerable to social criticism
    (E) An age period during which children are influenced more by peers than by adults

26. Grace is measuring the length and width of a table in order to determine the area. What mental operation is Grace using to find the area?

    (A) Formal operational thinking
    (B) Convergent thinking
    (C) Divergent thinking
    (D) Brainstorming
    (E) Memory retention

27. Some psychologists theorize that behavioral development, like anatomical development, proceeds from the simple to the complex, from homogeneous to heterogeneous, and from the general to the specific. Which of the following terms refers to these developmental trends?

    (A) Constancy
    (B) Assimilation
    (C) Metacognition
    (D) Differentiation
    (E) Transfer

28. Paying attention to new information is important in the learning process because such attention brings information from

    (A) an external environment into the sensory register
    (B) an external environment into long-term memory
    (C) the sensory register into working memory
    (D) working memory into long-term memory
    (E) the sensory register into long-term memory

29. When a two-year-old child points to a picture of a horse in a picture book and says "doggie," the child is committing an error of

    (A) overregularization

    (B) overextension

    (C) receptive vocabulary

    (D) syntax

    (E) articulation

30. Which of the following psychological schools of thought most emphasizes perceptual organization?

    (A) Behaviorism

    (B) Classical conditioning

    (C) Humanism

    (D) Psychodynamic approach

    (E) Gestalt psychology

31. A student has to memorize a long list of nouns for a contest. Which of the following is the best strategy for the student to use to enhance recall of the words?

    (A) Grouping the words by semantic category

    (B) Spelling each of the words

    (C) Sorting the words according to length

    (D) Writing out the definition of each of the words

    (E) Determining the presence or absence of a target sound in each word

32. In an evaluation of achievement, the relationship between formative evaluation and summative evaluation is most similar to that between

    (A) skills instruction and skills practice

    (B) diagnostic examinations and final examinations

    (C) subjective data and objective data

    (D) descriptive data and inferential data

    (E) norm-referenced tests and criterion-referenced tests

33. Which of the following treatments is most common for attention-deficit/hyperactivity disorder?

    (A) Stimulant medication

    (B) Mnemonic aids

    (C) Self-esteem workshops

    (D) Psychotherapy

    (E) Motivational training

34. A person who drove a manual-transmission car for years finds that, when driving a car with an automatic transmission, he often lifts his foot to step on the clutch. This driver is experiencing

    (A) parallel distributed processing

    (B) an articulatory loop

    (C) positive transfer

    (D) proactive interference

    (E) retroactive interference

35. A parent complains that 40 percent of the questions on a classroom test were taken from 4 pages of the 70 pages covered in the material assigned in the test. The parent is questioning the test's

    (A) interrater reliability

    (B) test-retest reliability

    (C) split-half reliability

    (D) content validity

    (E) criterion-related validity

36. Joseph Renzulli's triad for identifying giftedness is best described as which of the following?

    (A) Above-average ability, task commitment, creativity

    (B) Skillful processing of verbal information, artistic expression, assertiveness

    (C) High IQ scores, academic aptitude, practical intelligence

    (D) Language fluency, analytic problem-solving ability, ethical thinking

    (E) Interpersonal intelligence, intrapersonal intelligence, logical-mathematical intelligence

37. Behavioral theories that focus on helping students develop self-management skills emphasize that it is important for students to

(A) assess their competencies

(B) improve their self-concepts

(C) increase their general knowledge

(D) develop social awareness

(E) recognize clear signals that behaviors are appropriate

38. Jacob Kounin's concept of "withitness" refers to which of the following teacher abilities?

(A) Maintaining awareness of everything that is happening in the classroom

(B) Sequentially processing classroom activities and giving feedback to students

(C) Going from one activity to another without wasting time

(D) Focusing on one thing at a time in the classroom to keep from becoming frustrated

(E) Identifying students' academic strengths and deficiencies

39. Which of the following would be the best evidence that a test intended to estimate future success in school was biased against one group of examinees?

(A) A large mean-score difference between that group and the rest of the examinees

(B) A large standard deviation in the test scores of that group

(C) A low passing rate for all examinees

(D) An 80 percent passing rate for that group

(E) An underprediction of academic achievement for that group

40. In the United States, responsible adolescents are most likely to have parents who are

(A) autocratic

(B) authoritarian

(C) authoritative

(D) permissive

(E) enmeshed

41. Which of the following is a major point in Carol Gilligan's criticism of Lawrence Kohlberg's theory of moral development?

(A) The levels of moral reasoning in Kohlberg's scheme are unrelated to social and political attitudes.

(B) Mature levels of moral reasoning may differ qualitatively between men and women.

(C) The higher levels of moral reasoning in Kohlberg's scheme apply only to children in the United States.

(D) The stages in Kohlberg's scheme deviate from those in Jean Piaget's stage theory.

(E) Chronological age is unrelated to maturity of moral reasoning on Kohlberg's scale.

42. Which of the following best illustrates metacognition?

(A) Memorizing terms and definitions from a textbook

(B) Monitoring one's comprehension while reading

(C) Listening to the radio and studying at the same time

(D) Retrieving information from working memory

(E) Retrieving information from long-term memory

43. George Miller's research finding that humans have a processing capacity of seven plus-or-minus two items applies to which of the following types of memory?

    (A) Sensory register
    (B) Explicit
    (C) Implicit
    (D) Short-term
    (E) Procedural

44. Alice maintains a messy desk in order to gain attention from her teacher. For Alice, the teacher's attention serves as which of the following?

    (A) Negative reinforcement
    (B) Positive reinforcement
    (C) Extinction
    (D) Primary reinforcement
    (E) Shaping

45. Research that investigates nature versus nurture as a basis of intelligence has found the highest correlations of IQ scores between which of the following?

    (A) Dizygotic twins raised together
    (B) Nontwin siblings raised together
    (C) Nontwin siblings raised apart
    (D) Monozygotic twins raised together
    (E) Monozygotic twins raised apart

46. Mary's score on an achievement test is 75. The normative data show an overall test mean of 50 and a standard deviation of 10. This information indicates that Mary's z score equivalent is

    (A) –2.5
    (B) –0.53
    (C) +0.53
    (D) +1.3
    (E) +2.5

47. A teacher informs parents that their child has earned a stanine score of five. The teacher is actually saying that the student's test score

    (A) is below average
    (B) is average
    (C) is above average
    (D) indicates giftedness
    (E) indicates a disability

Questions 48–49 refer to the following information.

Jodie, who is in the ninth grade, took a test that measured her ability in mathematics. The test consisted of 50 multiple-choice questions and had a completion time of two hours. It was scored from 0 to 50 points, with a mean of 27, a mode of 26, and a median of 25. Jodie's score represented her actual knowledge of mathematics and did not provide any information about how she compared with other students who had taken the same test.

48. The test that Jodie took is best characterized as

    (A) a portfolio assessment
    (B) an intelligence (IQ) test
    (C) a developmental profile
    (D) a norm-referenced test
    (E) a criterion-referenced test

49. An examination of the scores of all of the students who took the test would reveal that the score most often earned was

    (A) 15
    (B) 25
    (C) 26
    (D) 27
    (E) 50

50. A teacher rewards students for every fifth question they get right in class. Which of the following is a schedule of reinforcement that the teacher is using?

    (A) Fixed interval
    (B) Fixed ratio
    (C) Variable interval
    (D) Extinction
    (E) Differential

51. José cannot find his favorite toy. When his father talks with him about it and encourages José to think about where he last used it, José suddenly remembers the toy's location. José's thinking is thus aided by the conversation with his father. This is an example of a theory of cognitive development formulated by

    (A) Jean Piaget
    (B) Lev Vygotsky
    (C) Noam Chomsky
    (D) Carol Gilligan
    (E) Lawrence Kohlberg

52. Paul is fourteen years old, has recently broken up with his girlfriend of three weeks, and believes that no one can understand the pain he is feeling. According to David Elkind, Paul is displaying

    (A) the imaginary audience
    (B) metacognition
    (C) a personal fable
    (D) postformal thought
    (E) symbolic thought

53. Research on the use of rewards generally indicates that if a teacher continuously rewards students with candy for writing creative stories, the students'

    (A) writing abilities will keep improving
    (B) writing abilities will get worse over time
    (C) writing will not be affected in any way
    (D) interest in writing will lessen over time
    (E) interest in writing will increase over time

54. Mary enjoys reading, primarily because her father gives her a dollar for each book she reads. Mary's motivational orientation for reading is most accurately described as

    (A) mastery oriented
    (B) goal oriented
    (C) intrinsic
    (D) extrinsic
    (E) egocentric

55. Which of the following is a motivational theory in which students attempt to explain the causes of their successes and failures?

    (A) Cognitive-behavioral theory
    (B) Hierarchy of needs
    (C) Reward theory
    (D) Attributional theory
    (E) Achievement motivation

56. A student's score at the 75th percentile indicates that the student

    (A) correctly answered 75 percent of the exam
    (B) correctly answered 75 questions on the exam
    (C) scored worse than 75 percent of the test-takers
    (D) scored the same as or better than 75 percent of the test-takers
    (E) scored the same as or better than 25 percent of the test-takers

57. Five-year-old Billy rarely makes eye contact and frequently self-stimulates and repeats back the speech that he hears. Based on this information alone, it is most likely that Billy has

    (A) autistic disorder
    (B) major depressive disorder
    (C) attention-deficit/hyperactivity disorder
    (D) mental retardation
    (E) dyslexia

58. Which of the following is most likely to be used as an individually administered intelligence test?

   (A) Wechsler Intelligence Scale for Children
   (B) Differential Ability Scales
   (C) Minnesota Multiphasic Personality Inventory–2
   (D) Graduate Record Examinations General Test
   (E) Thematic Apperception Test

59. Tests such as the SAT Reasoning Test and the ACT test are most often used for which type of testing?

   (A) Diagnostic
   (B) Intelligence
   (C) Achievement
   (D) Aptitude
   (E) Projective

60. A self-regulated learner is likely to engage in all of the following EXCEPT

   (A) thinking about which learning strategies are appropriate for a given task
   (B) evaluating his or her performance while progressing through a task
   (C) thinking about multiple tasks and responsibilities simultaneously
   (D) setting realistic goals
   (E) managing study time

61. Token economies in classrooms often provide students with the opportunity to earn points for good behavior that can be exchanged for some type of reward, such as candy, free time, or toys. According to researchers, a token economy system would be most beneficial in a classroom in which students

   (A) exhibit high intrinsic motivation
   (B) typically behave well
   (C) are out of control
   (D) are especially gifted
   (E) have just begun to show minor behavior problems

62. Which of the following is NOT consistent with developmentally appropriate practice in kindergarten?

   (A) Having different learning centers in the classroom
   (B) Expecting all children to read simple words by the end of the year
   (C) Giving children time for free play during each week
   (D) Having children engaged in activities in small groups
   (E) Allowing children a rest period during the day

63. Which of the following is a gender difference that is regularly observed on achievement tests?

   (A) Boys tend to have higher average scores on reading tests than do girls.
   (B) Girls tend to have higher average scores on science tests than do boys.
   (C) Girls tend to have higher average scores on spatial reasoning tests than do boys.
   (D) There tends to be more variability among boys' scores on achievement tests than there does among girls' scores.
   (E) Girls tend to have higher average scores on math tests than do boys.

64. Learned helplessness is most likely to occur when students view the cause of their failures as

   (A) stable and uncontrollable
   (B) stable and controllable
   (C) unstable and controllable
   (D) external and controllable
   (E) internal and unstable

65. Mr. Arevola, an experienced fifth-grade mathematics teacher, is acknowledged as an excellent teacher and often acts as a mentor to young teachers. He is especially helpful by assisting newcomers to understand the difficulties that students often have with comprehension of fractions and to teach in a way that will address that issue. According to Lee Shulman, the type of teacher knowledge Mr. Arevola conveys could best be described as

(A) content knowledge

(B) process knowledge

(C) declarative knowledge

(D) pedagogical content knowledge

(E) pedagogical process knowledge

66. According to Albert Bandura, which of the following is the most powerful source of self-efficacy for a child?

(A) Physiological cues

(B) Verbal persuasion

(C) Mastery experiences

(D) Observational learning

(E) Imitation

67. Stage theories of development are best described as

(A) quantitative/continuous

(B) qualitative/discontinuous

(C) morally bound

(D) universally accepted

(E) socially determined

68. Which of the following is an example of disequilibrium?

(A) Robert has learned about different types of sharks, and he reasons that a dolphin is a type of shark because it looks similar.

(B) William has figured out that the Sun is covered by clouds at night, which causes the darkness.

(C) Dameon wonders how a caterpillar can be an insect when it appears to have more than six legs.

(D) Ricky understands that his teddy bear is not alive, because he has learned about characteristics of living things.

(E) Jon decides that sand is a liquid because it takes the shape of its container.

69. Achievement tests differ from aptitude tests primarily in that

(A) the score distributions of achievement tests tend to be linear, whereas the score distributions of aptitude tests tend to be bell-shaped

(B) achievement tests are designed to measure what students have learned, whereas aptitude tests are designed to predict how well students will perform in the future

(C) achievement tests tend to face more resistance from parents, students, and classroom teachers than do aptitude tests

(D) achievement tests are designed to measure the middle-ability population most accurately, whereas aptitude tests are designed to measure the high- and low-ability populations most accurately

(E) aptitude tests are designed to have less variability in scores than do achievements tests

70. Mr. Janis asked his class to draw a picture of a flower. Ninety percent of the class drew a picture of a rose. In terms of cognitive psychology, what would a rose be for these students?

    (A) An attribute

    (B) A concept

    (C) A prototype

    (D) A heuristic

    (E) An algorithm

71. During the final exam, Ellen started breathing really hard and her heart felt as if it would jump out of her chest. What hormone was most likely involved in this process?

    (A) Epinephrine

    (B) Dopamine

    (C) Norepinephrine

    (D) Serotonin

    (E) Cortisol

72. Jenna has just been diagnosed with an articulation disorder. Which behavior is she most likely to exhibit?

    (A) Saying "wed" instead of "red"

    (B) Speaking too slowly

    (C) Stammering while talking

    (D) Using a high-pitched voice

    (E) Speaking without emotional tone

73. Ms. Sharps has been emphasizing the use of authentic assessment in her watercolor painting class. What type of assessment is she most likely to use to grade her students?

    (A) Portfolio

    (B) Essay test

    (C) Oral presentation

    (D) Short essays

    (E) Multiple-choice tests

74. Jacquelin has always done well in school. In her fifth-grade class, she works hard and always does her homework. She often reads extra books and does extra math problems. Which of Erikson's psychosocial stages would Jacquelin best exemplify?

    (A) Trust versus mistrust

    (B) Autonomy versus shame and doubt

    (C) Initiative versus guilt

    (D) Industry versus inferiority

    (E) Identity versus role confusion

Study Resources

Most textbooks used in college-level introduction to educational psychology courses cover the topics in the outline given earlier, but the approaches to certain topics and the emphases given to them may differ. To prepare for the Introduction to Educational Psychology exam, it is advisable to study one or more college textbooks, which can be found in most college bookstores. When selecting a textbook, check the table of contents against the knowledge and skills required for this test.

You may also find it helpful to supplement your reading with books listed in the bibliographies that can be found in most educational psychology textbooks.

Visit www.collegeboard.com/clepprep for additional educational psychology resources. You can also find suggestions for exam preparation in Chapter IV of the *Official Study Guide*. In addition, many college faculty post their course materials on their schools' Web sites.

Answer Key

1.	B	38.	A
2.	A	39.	E
3.	D	40.	C
4.	D	41.	B
5.	E	42.	B
6.	D	43.	D
7.	B	44.	B
8.	B	45.	D
9.	C	46.	E
10.	D	47.	B
11.	D	48.	E
12.	E	49.	C
13.	B	50.	B
14.	A	51.	B
15.	A	52.	C
16.	D	53.	D
17.	E	54.	D
18.	A	55.	D
19.	B	56.	D
20.	B	57.	A
21.	A	58.	A
22.	D	59.	D
23.	B	60.	C
24.	A	61.	C
25.	B	62.	B
26.	B	63.	D
27.	D	64.	A
28.	C	65.	D
29.	B	66.	C
30.	E	67.	B
31.	A	68.	C
32.	B	69.	B
33.	A	70.	C
34.	D	71.	A
35.	D	72.	A
36.	A	73.	A
37.	E	74.	D

Principles of Macroeconomics

Description of the Examination

The Principles of Macroeconomics examination covers material that is usually taught in a one-semester undergraduate course in this subject. This aspect of economics deals with principles of economics that apply to an economy as a whole, particularly the general price level, output and income, and interrelations among sectors of the economy. The test places particular emphasis on the determinants of aggregate demand and aggregate supply, and on monetary and fiscal policy tools that can be used to achieve particular policy objectives. Within this context, candidates are expected to understand measurement concepts such as gross domestic product, consumption, investment, unemployment, inflation, inflationary gap, and recessionary gap. Candidates are also expected to demonstrate knowledge of the institutional structure of the Federal Reserve Bank and the monetary policy tools it uses to stabilize economic fluctuations and promote long-term economic growth, as well as the tools of fiscal policy and their impacts on income, employment, price level, deficits, and interest rate. Basic understanding of foreign exchange markets, balance of payments, effects of currency, and appreciation and depreciation on a country's imports and exports are also expected.

The examination contains approximately 80 questions to be answered in 90 minutes. Some of these are pretest questions that will not be scored. Any time candidates spend on tutorials and providing personal information is in addition to the actual testing time.

Knowledge and Skills Required

Questions on the Principles of Macroeconomics examination require candidates to demonstrate one or more of the following abilities.

- Understanding of important economic terms and concepts
- Interpretation and manipulation of economic graphs
- Interpretation and evaluation of economic data
- Application of simple economic models

The subject matter of the Principles of Macroeconomics examination is drawn from the following topics. The percentages next to the main topics indicate the approximate percentage of exam questions on that topic.

8–12% Basic Economic Concepts

Scarcity, choice, and opportunity costs
Production possibilities curve
Comparative advantage, specialization, and exchange
Demand, supply, and market equilibrium
Macroeconomic issues: business cycle, unemployment, inflation, growth

12–16% Measurement of Economic Performance

National income accounts
- Circular flow
- Gross domestic product
- Components of gross domestic product
- Real *versus* nominal gross domestic product
Inflation measurement and adjustment
- Price indices
- Nominal and real values
- Costs of inflation
Unemployment
- Definition and measurement
- Types of unemployment
- Natural rate of unemployment

10–15% National Income and Price Determination

Aggregate demand
- Determinants of aggregate demand
- Multiplier and crowding-out effects
Aggregate supply
- Short-run and long-run analyses
- Sticky *versus* flexible wages and prices
- Determinants of aggregate supply
Macroeconomic equilibrium
- Real output and price level
- Short and long run
- Actual *versus* full-employment output
- Economic fluctuations

15–20% Financial Sector

Money, banking, and financial markets
- Definition of financial assets: money, stocks, bonds
- Time value of money (present and future value)
- Measures of money supply

- Banks and creation of money
- Money demand
- Money market
- Loanable funds market

Central bank and control of the money supply

- Tools of central bank policy
- Quantity theory of money
- Real *versus* nominal interest rates

20–30%   Inflation, Unemployment, and Stabilization Policies

Fiscal and monetary policies

- Demand-side effects
- Supply-side effects
- Policy mix
- Government deficits and debt

Inflation and unemployment

- Types of inflation
    - Demand-pull inflation
    - Cost-push inflation
- The Phillips curve: short run *versus* long run
- Role of expectations

5–10%   Economic Growth and Productivity

Investment in human capital

Investment in physical capital

Research and development, and technological progress

Growth policy

10–15%   Open Economy: International Trade and Finance

Balance of payments accounts

- Balance of trade
- Current account
- Capital account

Foreign exchange market

- Demand for and supply of foreign exchange
- Exchange rate determination
- Currency appreciation and depreciation

Net exports and capital flows

Links to financial and goods markets

Sample Test Questions

The following sample questions do not appear on an actual CLEP examination. They are intended to give potential test-takers an indication of the format and difficulty level of the examination and to provide content for practice and review. Knowing the correct answers to all of the sample questions is not a guarantee of satisfactory performance on the exam.

Directions: Each of the questions or incomplete statements below is followed by five suggested answers or completions. Select the one that is best in each case.

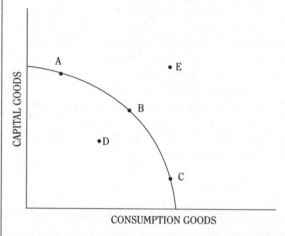

1. An economy that is fully employing all its productive resources but allocating less to investment than to consumption will be at which of the following positions on the production possibilities curve shown above?

   (A) A

   (B) B

   (C) C

   (D) D

   (E) E

2. Assume that land can be used either for producing grain or for grazing cattle to produce beef. The opportunity cost of converting an acre from cattle grazing to grain production is the

   (A) market value of the extra grain that is produced

   (B) total amount of beef produced

   (C) number of extra bushels of grain that are produced

   (D) amount by which beef production decreases

   (E) profits generated by the extra production of grain

3. Which of the following will occur as a result of an improvement in technology?

(A) The aggregate demand curve will shift to the right.

(B) The aggregate demand curve will shift to the left.

(C) The aggregate supply curve will shift to the right.

(D) The aggregate supply curve will shift to the left.

(E) The production possibilities curve will shift inward.

4. Increases in real income per capita are made possible by

(A) improved productivity

(B) a high labor/capital ratio

(C) large trade surpluses

(D) stable interest rates

(E) high protective tariffs

5. Which of the following is an example of "investment" as used in economics?

(A) A schoolteacher purchases 10,000 shares of stock in an automobile company.

(B) Newlyweds purchase a previously owned home.

(C) One large automobile firm purchases another large automobile firm.

(D) A farmer purchases $10,000 worth of government securities.

(E) An apparel company purchases 15 new sewing machines.

6. The United States Department of Labor defines an individual as unemployed if the person

(A) does not hold a paying job

(B) has been recently fired

(C) works part time but needs full-time work

(D) is without a job but is looking for work

(E) wants a job but is not searching because he or she thinks none is available

7. Assume that a country with an open economy has a fixed exchange-rate system and that its currency is currently overvalued in the foreign exchange market. Which of the following must be true at the official exchange rate?

(A) The quantity of the country's currency supplied is less than the quantity demanded.

(B) The quantity of the country's currency supplied exceeds the quantity demanded.

(C) The demand curve for the country's currency is horizontal.

(D) The supply curve for the country's currency is horizontal.

(E) There is an excess demand for the country's currency.

8. Which of the following workers is most likely to be classified as structurally unemployed?

(A) A high school teacher who is unemployed during the summer months

(B) A recent college graduate who is looking for her first job

(C) A teenager who is seeking part-time employment at a fast-food restaurant

(D) A worker who is unemployed because his skills are obsolete

(E) A person who reenters the job market after relocating

9. According to the classical model, an increase in the money supply causes an increase in which of the following in the long run?

   I. Real gross domestic product

  II. Nominal gross domestic product

  III. Nominal wages

(A) I only

(B) II only

(C) III only

(D) II and III only

(E) I, II, and III

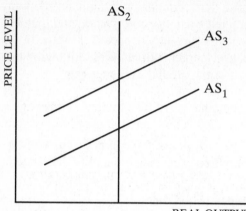

10. The diagram above shows aggregate supply curves AS_1, AS_2, and AS_3. Which of the following statements is true?

    (A) AS_2 reflects wage and price rigidity.

    (B) AS_1 reflects greater wage and price flexibility than AS_2.

    (C) AS_2 reflects greater wage and price flexibility than AS_1 and AS_3.

    (D) The shift from AS_1 to AS_3 is due to a decrease in nominal wages.

    (E) The shift from AS_3 to AS_1 is due to an increase in oil prices.

11. An increase in which of the following would cause the long-run aggregate supply curve to shift to the right?

    (A) Corporate income tax rates

    (B) Aggregate demand

    (C) Labor productivity

    (D) The average wage rate

    (E) The price level

12. As income level increases from $500 to $1,000, consumption increases from $700 to $1,100. The marginal propensity to consume is equal to

    (A) 1.10

    (B) 0.80

    (C) 0.70

    (D) 0.50

    (E) 0.10

13. In the circular flow diagram of an economy, which of the following is true?

    (A) Businesses pay wages, rent, interest, and profits to households in return for use of factors of production.

    (B) Businesses purchase goods and services from households in return for money payments.

    (C) Households pay wages, rent, interest, and profits to businesses in return for use of factors of production.

    (D) The relationship between households and businesses exists only in a traditional society.

    (E) The relationship between households and businesses exists only in a command economy.

14. Which of the following would most likely lead to a decrease in aggregate demand?

    (A) A decrease in taxes

    (B) A decrease in interest rates

    (C) An increase in household savings

    (D) An increase in household consumption

    (E) An increase in business firms' purchases of capital equipment from retained earnings

15. According to the Keynesian model, equilibrium output of an economy may be less than the full-employment level of output because at full employment

(A) sufficient income may not be generated to keep workers above the subsistence level

(B) there might not be enough demand by firms and consumers to buy that output

(C) workers may not be willing to work the hours necessary to produce the output

(D) interest rates might not be high enough to provide the incentive to finance the production

(E) banks may not be willing to lend enough money to support the output

16. If the Federal Reserve lowers reserve requirements, which of the following is most likely to happen to interest rates and nominal gross domestic product?

	Interest Rates	Nominal Gross Domestic Product
(A)	Increase	Decrease
(B)	Increase	Increase
(C)	Decrease	Decrease
(D)	Decrease	Increase
(E)	No change	No change

17. If the marginal propensity to consume is 0.9, what is the maximum amount that the equilibrium gross domestic product could change if government expenditures increase by $1 billion?

(A) It could decrease by $9 billion.

(B) It could increase by $0.9 billion.

(C) It could increase by $1 billion.

(D) It could increase by $9 billion.

(E) It could increase by $10 billion.

18. Expansionary fiscal policy will be most effective in increasing real gross domestic product when

(A) the aggregate supply curve is horizontal

(B) the economy is at or above full-employment output

(C) transfer payments are decreased, while taxes remain unchanged

(D) wages and prices are very flexible

(E) the Federal Reserve simultaneously increases the reserve requirement

19. Which of the following would increase the value of the simple spending multiplier?

(A) An increase in government expenditure

(B) An increase in exports

(C) A decrease in government unemployment benefits

(D) A decrease in the marginal propensity to consume

(E) A decrease in the marginal propensity to save

20. Assume that the reserve requirement is 25 percent. If banks have excess reserves of $10,000, which of the following is the maximum amount of additional money that can be created by the banking system through the lending process?

(A) $ 2,500

(B) $ 10,000

(C) $ 40,000

(D) $ 50,000

(E) $250,000

21. The principal reason for requiring commercial banks to maintain reserve balances with the Federal Reserve is that these balances

(A) provide the maximum amount of reserves a bank would ever need

(B) give the Federal Reserve more control over the money-creating operations of banks

(C) ensure that banks do not make excessive profits

(D) assist the Treasury in refinancing government debt

(E) enable the government to borrow cheaply from the Federal Reserve's discount window

22. The purchase of securities from the public in the open market by the Federal Reserve will

(A) increase the supply of money

(B) increase the interest rate

(C) increase the discount rate

(D) decrease the number of Federal Reserve notes in circulation

(E) decrease the reserve requirement

23. To counteract a recession, the Federal Reserve should

(A) buy securities on the open market and raise the reserve requirement

(B) buy securities on the open market and lower the reserve requirement

(C) buy securities on the open market and raise the discount rate

(D) sell securities on the open market and raise the discount rate

(E) raise the reserve requirement and lower the discount rate

24. Total spending in the economy is most likely to increase by the largest amount if which of the following occur to government spending and taxes?

Government Spending	Taxes
(A) Decrease	Increase
(B) Decrease	No change
(C) Increase	Increase
(D) Increase	Decrease
(E) No change	Increase

25. According to the Keynesian model, an increase in the money supply affects output more if

(A) investment is sensitive to changes in interest rates

(B) money demand is sensitive to changes in interest rates

(C) the unemployment rate is low

(D) consumption is sensitive to the Phillips curve

(E) government spending is sensitive to public opinion

26. Supply-side economists argue that

(A) a cut in high tax rates results in an increased deficit and thus increases aggregate supply

(B) lower tax rates provide positive work incentives and thus shift the aggregate supply curve to the right

(C) the aggregate supply of goods can only be increased if the price level falls

(D) increased government spending should be used to stimulate the economy

(E) the government should regulate the supply of imports

27. Which of the following policies would most likely be recommended in an economy with an annual inflation rate of 3 percent and an unemployment rate of 11 percent?

    (A) An increase in transfer payments and an increase in the reserve requirement
    (B) An increase in defense spending and an increase in the discount rate
    (C) An increase in income tax rates and a decrease in the reserve requirement
    (D) A decrease in government spending and the open market sale of government securities
    (E) A decrease in the tax rate on corporate profits and a decrease in the discount rate

28. According to the monetarists, inflation is most often the result of

    (A) high federal tax rates
    (B) increased production of capital goods
    (C) decreased production of capital goods
    (D) an excessive growth of the money supply
    (E) upward shifts in the consumption function

29. An expansionary fiscal policy would most likely cause which of the following changes in output and interest rates?

	Output	Interest Rates
(A)	Increase	Increase
(B)	Increase	Decrease
(C)	Decrease	Increase
(D)	Decrease	Decrease
(E)	No change	Decrease

30. Which of the following would result in the largest increase in aggregate demand?

    (A) A $30 billion increase in military expenditure and a $30 billion open market purchase of government securities
    (B) A $30 billion increase in military expenditure and a $30 billion open market sale of government securities
    (C) A $30 billion tax decrease and a $30 billion open market sale of government securities
    (D) A $30 billion tax increase and a $30 billion open market purchase of government securities
    (E) A $30 billion increase in social security payments and a $30 billion open market sale of government securities

31. Which of the following measures might be used to reduce a federal budget deficit?

    I. Increasing taxes
    II. Decreasing federal spending
    III. Decreasing interest rates

    (A) I only
    (B) II only
    (C) III only
    (D) I and III only
    (E) I, II, and III

32. Which of the following would most likely be the immediate result if the United States increased tariffs on most foreign goods?

    (A) The United States standard of living would be higher.
    (B) More foreign goods would be purchased by Americans.
    (C) Prices of domestic goods would increase.
    (D) Large numbers of United States workers would be laid off.
    (E) The value of the United States dollar would decrease against foreign currencies.

33. Which of the following policies is most likely to encourage long-term economic growth in a country?

(A) An embargo on high-technology imports

(B) A decrease in the number of immigrants to the country

(C) An increase in government transfer payments

(D) An increase in the per capita savings rate

(E) An increase in defense spending

34. Which of the following would occur if the international value of the United States dollar decreased?

(A) United States exports would increase.

(B) More gold would flow into the United States.

(C) United States demand for foreign currencies would increase.

(D) The United States trade deficit would increase.

(E) United States citizens would pay less for foreign goods.

35. If exchange rates are allowed to fluctuate freely and the United States demand for Indian rupees increases, which of the following will most likely occur?

(A) The dollar price of Indian goods will increase.

(B) The rupee price of United States goods will increase.

(C) The United States balance-of-payments deficits will increase.

(D) The dollar price of rupees will fall.

(E) The dollar price of Indian goods will fall.

36. The replacement of some portion of the federal personal income tax with a general sales tax would most likely result in

(A) greater overall progressivity in the tax structure

(B) smaller overall progressivity in the tax structure

(C) stronger automatic stabilization through the business cycle

(D) a larger budget deficit

(E) a smaller federal budget deficit

37. A deficit in the United States trade balance can be described as

(A) an excess of the value of commodity imports over the value of merchandise exports

(B) an excess of the value of merchandise exports over the value of commodity imports

(C) an excess of payments to foreigners over receipts from foreigners

(D) an almost complete depletion of the gold stock

(E) an excess of receipts from foreigners over payments to foreigners

38. Problems faced by all economic systems include which of the following?

 I. How to allocate scarce resources among unlimited wants

 II. How to decentralize markets

 III. How to decide what to produce, how to produce, and for whom to produce

 IV. How to set government production quotas

(A) I only

(B) I and III only

(C) II and III only

(D) I, II, and III only

(E) I, II, III, and IV

39. An increase in which of the following will cause an increase in the demand for a certain good?

(A) The price of the good

(B) The number of sellers of the good

(C) The price of a complementary good

(D) The cost of purchasing the good

(E) The number of buyers of the good

40. Assume that the government imposes a per unit tax on the production of a certain good. In the graphs below, P_0 indicates the price before the implementation of the tax and P_T indicates the price after the implementation of the tax. Which of the following is a graphical representation of this situation?

(A)
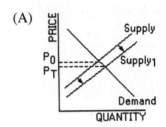

(B)
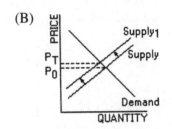

(C)
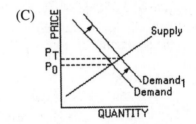

(D)
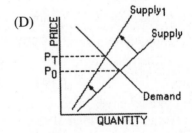

(E)
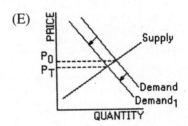

41. Which of the following groups is most likely to experience losses if inflation increases unexpectedly?

(A) Lenders
(B) Borrowers
(C) Workers with variable-wage contracts
(D) Owners of real estate
(E) People who hold noncash assets

42. Assume that last year the consumer price index (CPI) was 150 and a household's nominal income was $30,000. If the CPI this year is 160, to be as well off as last year, the household should have an increase in nominal income of

(A) $1,800
(B) $1,875
(C) $2,000
(D) $3,000
(E) $4,800

43. The natural rate of unemployment can be defined as the unemployment rate that exists when the economy

(A) is neither growing nor shrinking
(B) has zero inflation
(C) has only cyclical and structural unemployment
(D) has no trade deficit or government deficit
(E) produces at the full-employment output level

44. A fully anticipated expansionary fiscal policy will cause the price level and real output to change in which of the following ways in the long run?

	Price Level	Real Output
(A)	Increase	Increase
(B)	Increase	Not change
(C)	Not change	Not change
(D)	Decrease	Increase
(E)	Decrease	Decrease

45. If the nominal gross domestic product is $8 trillion and the money supply is $2 trillion, the velocity of money is

(A) 2

(B) 4

(C) 6

(D) 10

(E) 16

46. Which of the following is NOT true of the Federal Reserve?

(A) It serves as a lender of last resort for member banks.

(B) It supervises member banks.

(C) It provides check-clearing services.

(D) It issues traveler's checks.

(E) It controls the money supply.

47. Which of the following best describes crowding out?

(A) Competition between the government and private borrowers for loanable funds results in an increase in interest rates.

(B) Increases in the costs of inputs lead to decreases in domestic production.

(C) The Federal Reserve's open-market operations decrease the amount of funds banks have available for lending.

(D) Reductions in the government's budget deficit lead to fewer Treasury bonds being issued.

(E) The scarcity of funds forces Congress to decrease spending on critical public works programs.

48. Suppose that the economy is operating at full employment. If the government wants to discourage consumption spending, stimulate investment spending, and maintain full-employment output, which of the following combinations of monetary and fiscal policies would most likely achieve these goals?

	Monetary Policy	Fiscal Policy
(A)	Increase money supply	Increase government spending
(B)	Increase money supply	Increase personal income taxes
(C)	Decrease money supply	Increase government spending
(D)	Decrease money supply	Increase personal income taxes
(E)	Decrease money supply	Decrease personal income taxes

49. If the Federal Reserve suddenly increases the growth rate of the money supply from 4 percent to 8 percent per year, interest rates, aggregate demand, and nominal gross domestic product (GDP) will most likely change in which of the following ways in the short run?

	Interest Rates	Aggregate Demand	Nominal GDP
(A)	Increase	Increase	Increase
(B)	Increase	Decrease	Increase
(C)	Decrease	Increase	Increase
(D)	Decrease	Increase	Decrease
(E)	Decrease	Decrease	Increase

50. The United States federal government budget deficits tend to be large when which of the following is low?

(A) The interest rate on government bonds

(B) The growth rate of the economy

(C) The unemployment rate

(D) The inflation rate

(E) The international value of the United States dollar

51. Using the same amount of resources, Beeland can produce 80 tons of corn or 80 tons of wheat and Eland can produce 40 tons of corn or 20 tons of wheat. Which of the following statements is true?

   (A) The opportunity cost of producing a ton of corn in Beeland is two tons of wheat.

   (B) The opportunity cost of producing a ton of corn in Beeland is a ton of wheat.

   (C) The opportunity cost of producing a ton of corn in Eland is two tons of wheat.

   (D) Beeland has both the absolute and comparative advantage in producing corn.

   (E) Eland has the comparative advantage in producing wheat.

52. If the required reserve ratio is 0.20 and the Federal Reserve buys $200 worth of securities, the maximum increase in the money supply will be

   (A) $ 200
   (B) $ 400
   (C) $ 600
   (D) $ 800
   (E) $1,000

Assets	Liabilities
Reserves $4,000	Demand deposits $10,000
Loans $6,000	

53. The table above shows the T-account entries of a bank. If the required reserve ratio is 0.20, what is the maximum amount of additional loans that this bank can make?

   (A) $ 0
   (B) $ 2,000
   (C) $ 2,500
   (D) $ 4,000
   (E) $10,000

54. Hyperinflation is usually associated with which of the following?

   (A) An increase in labor productivity

   (B) An increase in exports

   (C) A decrease in total spending

   (D) Appreciation of the domestic currency

   (E) Rapid growth of the money supply

55. According to the short-run Phillips curve, which of the following will occur when the Federal Reserve increases the money supply?

   (A) Both the unemployment rate and the inflation rate will increase.

   (B) Both the unemployment rate and the inflation rate will decrease.

   (C) The unemployment rate will increase, and the inflation rate will decrease.

   (D) The unemployment rate will decrease, and the inflation rate will increase.

   (E) The inflation rate will increase, but the unemployment rate will remain constant.

56. Which of the following is true if there is a current account deficit in the United States balance-of-payments accounts?

(A) There is a corresponding deficit in the capital account.

(B) There is a corresponding surplus in the capital account.

(C) There is an offsetting surplus in the government's budget.

(D) There is an offsetting increase in net exports.

(E) The United States dollar appreciates in the foreign exchange market.

57. An increase in national saving will cause real interest rate and investment spending to change in which of the following ways?

	Real Interest Rate	Investment
(A)	Increase	Increase
(B)	Increase	Decrease
(C)	Increase	Not change
(D)	Decrease	Increase
(E)	Decrease	Not change

58. To raise its long-run rate of economic growth, a country should design and implement policies that do which of the following?

(A) Encourage current consumption over saving

(B) Encourage saving and investment

(C) Increase the price level and profits

(D) Promote equity through income redistribution

(E) Limit business activities to protect the environment

59. With a constant money supply, an increase in the demand for money will affect interest rates and bond prices in which of the following ways?

	Interest Rates	Bond Prices
(A)	Increase	Increase
(B)	Increase	Decrease
(C)	Increase	Not change
(D)	Decrease	Increase
(E)	Not change	Increase

60. According to the quantity theory of money, an increase in the money supply results in an increase in which of the following?

(A) Interest rate

(B) Unemployment

(C) Nominal gross domestic product

(D) The government's budget deficit

(E) The value of the dollar on the foreign exchange market

61. Which of the following policies will most likely lead to a reduction in the natural rate of unemployment?

(A) Increasing government purchases of goods and services

(B) Providing more job-training programs to help the less skilled

(C) Increasing the duration of unemployment compensation

(D) Raising the minimum wage

(E) Increasing the money supply

62. Assume that an economy produces only two goods, computers and gasoline. The quantity and price of each are given in the table below.

Year	Price of Computers	Quantity of Computers (in millions)	Price of Gasoline	Quantity of Gasoline (in millions)
2000	$1,000	5	$1	500
2004	$500	10	$2	250

If the base year is 2000, how do nominal and real gross domestic product (GDP) change between 2000 and 2004?

	Nominal GDP	Real GDP
(A)	No change	Increase
(B)	No change	Decrease
(C)	Increase	No change
(D)	Increase	Increase
(E)	Increase	Decrease

63. Assuming that the expected inflation rate is stable, an increase in interest rates will lead to

(A) an increase in bond prices

(B) an increase in the demand for money as an asset

(C) an increase in aggregate demand

(D) a decrease in private investment

(E) a decrease in capital inflows

64. A bank has demand deposits of $100,000 and actual reserves of $27,000. If the reserve requirement is 10 percent, the bank can loan out a maximum of

(A) $ 7,000

(B) $ 17,000

(C) $ 27,000

(D) $100,000

(E) $170,000

65. Which of the following is true of the long-run Phillips curve?

(A) It shows the trade-off between the price level and the money supply.

(B) It shows that lower unemployment can be gained only at the expense of higher inflation.

(C) It shows that unemployment is a monetary issue.

(D) It is vertical at the natural rate of unemployment.

(E) It is U-shaped over all possible ranges of unemployment.

66. Economics is best defined as the study of how

(A) markets allocate resources efficiently

(B) businesses make investments to maximize profits

(C) public goods and services are produced

(D) society chooses to allocate its scarce resources

(E) the invisible hand of the market works

67. Human capital refers to which of the following?

(A) The acquisition of plant and equipment by workers

(B) The amount of financial investment made by individuals

(C) The labor force requirement for sustained economic growth

(D) The education and experience of the labor force

(E) The technology available to individual workers

68. Which of the following will lower inflationary expectations?

(A) The government's announcement that it will increase spending on infrastructure

(B) The Federal Reserve's announcement that it will steadily raise the federal funds rate

(C) An increase in the value of stocks

(D) An increase in consumer and business optimism

(E) An increase in the money supply

69. An increase in national saving will affect the supply of loanable funds and the real interest rate in which of the following ways?

	Supply of Loanable Funds	Real Interest Rate
(A)	Increase	Increase
(B)	Increase	Decrease
(C)	Increase	No change
(D)	Decrease	Increase
(E)	Decrease	Decrease

70. Which of the following will cause the short-run aggregate supply curve to shift to the left?

(A) An increase in the price level

(B) A decrease in the price level

(C) An increase in trade deficits

(D) An increase in nominal wages

(E) An increase in productivity

Study Resources

Most textbooks used in college-level introductory macroeconomics courses cover the topics in the outline given earlier, but the approaches to certain topics and the emphases given to them may differ. To prepare for the Principles of Macroeconomics exam, it is advisable to study one or more college textbooks, which can be found in most college bookstores. When selecting a textbook, check the table of contents against the knowledge and skills required for this test.

There are many introductory economics textbooks that vary greatly in difficulty. Most books are published in one-volume editions, which cover both microeconomics and macroeconomics; some are published in two-volume editions, with one volume covering macroeconomics and the other microeconomics. A companion study guide/workbook is available for most textbooks. The study guides typically include brief reviews, definitions of key concepts, problem sets, and multiple-choice test questions with answers. Many publishers also make available companion Web sites, links to other resources, or computer-assisted learning packages.

To broaden your knowledge of economic issues, you may read relevant articles published in the economics periodicals that are available in most college libraries—for example, *The Economist*, *The Wall Street Journal*, and the *New York Times*, along with local papers, may also enhance your understanding of economic issues.

Visit www.collegeboard.com/clepprep for additional macroeconomics resources. You can also find suggestions for exam preparation in Chapter IV of the *Official Study Guide*. In addition, many college faculty post their course materials on their schools' Web sites.

Answer Key

1.	C	36.	B
2.	D	37.	A
3.	C	38.	B
4.	A	39.	E
5.	E	40.	B
6.	D	41.	A
7.	B	42.	C
8.	D	43.	E
9.	D	44.	B
10.	C	45.	B
11.	C	46.	D
12.	B	47.	A
13.	A	48.	B
14.	C	49.	C
15.	B	50.	B
16.	D	51.	B
17.	E	52.	E
18.	A	53.	B
19.	E	54.	E
20.	C	55.	D
21.	B	56.	B
22.	A	57.	D
23.	B	58.	B
24.	D	59.	B
25.	A	60.	C
26.	B	61.	B
27.	E	62.	A
28.	D	63.	D
29.	A	64.	B
30.	A	65.	D
31.	E	66.	D
32.	C	67.	D
33.	D	68.	B
34.	A	69.	B
35.	A	70.	D

Principles of Microeconomics

Description of the Examination

The Principles of Microeconomics examination covers material that is usually taught in a one-semester undergraduate course in introductory microeconomics. This aspect of economics deals with the principles of economics that apply to the analysis of the behavior of individual consumers and businesses in the economy. Questions on this exam require candidates to apply analytical techniques to hypothetical as well as real-world situations and to analyze and evaluate economic decisions. Candidates are expected to demonstrate an understanding of how free markets work and allocate resources efficiently. They should understand how individual consumers make economic decisions to maximize utility, and how individual firms make decisions to maximize profits. Candidates must be able to identify the characteristics of the different market structures and analyze the behavior of firms in terms of price and output decisions. They should also be able to evaluate the outcome in each market structure with respect to economic efficiency, identify cases in which private markets fail to allocate resources efficiently, and explain how government intervention fixes or fails to fix the resource allocation problem. It is also important to understand the determination of wages and other input prices in factor markets, and analyze and evaluate the distribution of income.

The examination contains approximately 80 questions to be answered in 90 minutes. Some of these are pretest questions that will not be scored. Any time candidates spend on tutorials and providing personal information is in addition to the actual testing time.

Knowledge and Skills Required

Questions on the Principles of Microeconomics examination require candidates to demonstrate one or more of the following abilities.

- Understanding of important economic terms and concepts
- Interpretation and manipulation of economic graphs
- Interpretation and evaluation of economic data
- Application of simple economic models

The subject matter of the Principles of Microeconomics examination is drawn from the following topics. The percentages next to the main topics indicate the approximate percentage of exam questions on that topic.

8–14% Basic Economic Concepts

Scarcity, choice, and opportunity cost

Production possibilities curve

Comparative advantage, specialization, and trade

Economic systems

Property rights and the role of incentives

Marginal analysis

55–70% The Nature and Functions of Product Markets

15–20% Supply and demand
- Market equilibrium
- Determinants of supply and demand
- Price and quantity controls
- Elasticity
  - Price, income, and cross-price elasticities of demand
  - Price elasticity of supply
- Consumer surplus, producer surplus, and market efficiency
- Tax incidence and deadweight loss

5–10% Theory of consumer choice
- Total utility and marginal utility
- Utility maximization: equalizing marginal utility per dollar
- Individual and market demand curves
- Income and substitution effects

10–15% Production and costs
- Production functions: short and long run
- Marginal product and diminishing returns
- Short-run costs
- Long-run costs and economies of scale
- Cost minimizing input combination

25–35% Firm behavior and market structure
- Profit:
  - Accounting versus economic profits
  - Normal profit

- Profit maximization: MR=MC rule
- Perfect competition
  - Profit maximization
  - Short-run supply and shut-down decision
  - Firm and market behaviors in short-run and long-run equilibria
  - Efficiency and perfect competition
- Monopoly
  - Sources of market power
  - Profit maximization
  - Inefficiency of monopoly
  - Price discrimination
- Oligopoly
  - Interdependence, collusion, and cartels
  - Game theory and strategic behavior
- Monopolistic competition
  - Product differentiation and role of advertising
  - Profit maximization
  - Short-run and long-run equilibrium
  - Excess capacity and inefficiency

10–18% Factor Markets

Derived factor demand

Marginal revenue product

Labor market and firms' hiring of labor

Market distribution of income

12–18% Market Failure and the Role of Government

Externalities
- Marginal social benefit and marginal social cost
- Positive externalities
- Negative externalities
- Remedies

Public goods
- Public *versus* private goods
- Provision of public goods

Public policy to promote competition
- Antitrust policy
- Regulation

Income distribution
- Equity
- Sources of income inequality

Sample Test Questions

The following sample questions do not appear on an actual CLEP examination. They are intended to give potential test-takers an indication of the format and difficulty level of the examination and to provide content for practice and review. Knowing the correct answers to all of the sample questions is not a guarantee of satisfactory performance on the exam.

Directions: Each of the questions or incomplete statements below is followed by five suggested answers or completions. Select the one that is best in each case.

1. Which of the following best states the law of comparative advantage?

   (A) Differences in relative costs of production are the key to determining patterns of trade.

   (B) Differences in absolute costs of production determine which goods should be traded between nations.

   (C) Tariffs and quotas are beneficial in increasing international competitiveness.

   (D) Nations should not specialize in the production of goods and services.

   (E) Two nations will not trade if one is more efficient than the other in the production of all goods.

2. If a retail firm plans to increase the price of a product it sells, the firm must believe that

   (A) the good is an inferior good

   (B) the price of complements will also increase

   (C) the price of substitutes will decrease

   (D) demand for the product is perfectly price elastic

   (E) demand for the product is price inelastic

3. If it were possible to increase the output of both military goods and consumption goods, which of the following statements about the economy would be true?

   (A) The economy is inefficient and inside the production possibilities curve.

   (B) The economy is inefficient and on the production possibilities curve.

   (C) The economy is efficient and on the production possibilities curve.

   (D) The economy is efficient and inside the production possibilities curve.

   (E) The economy is efficient and outside the production possibilities curve.

4. Which of the following would necessarily cause a decrease in the price of a product?

(A) An increase in the number of buyers and a decrease in the price of an input

(B) An increase in the number of buyers and a decrease in the number of firms producing the product

(C) An increase in average income and an improvement in production technology

(D) A decrease in the price of a substitute product and an improvement in production technology

(E) A decrease in the price of a substitute product and an increase in the price of an input

5. Agricultural price supports will most likely result in

(A) shortages of products if the price supports are above the equilibrium price

(B) shortages of products if the price supports are at the equilibrium price

(C) surpluses of products if the price supports are above the equilibrium price

(D) surpluses of products if the price supports are below the equilibrium price

(E) a balance between quantity demanded and quantity supplied if the price floor is above the equilibrium price

6. The market equilibrium price of home heating oil is $1.50 per gallon. If a price ceiling of $1.00 per gallon is imposed, which of the following will occur in the market for home heating oil?

I. Quantity supplied will increase.

II. Quantity demanded will increase.

III. Quantity supplied will decrease.

IV. Quantity demanded will decrease.

(A) II only

(B) I and II only

(C) I and IV only

(D) II and III only

(E) III and IV only

7. Assume that a consumer finds that her total expenditure on compact discs stays the same after the price of compact discs declines. Which of the following is true for this consumer over the price range?

(A) Compact discs are inferior goods.

(B) The consumer's demand for compact discs increased.

(C) The consumer's demand for compact discs is perfectly price elastic.

(D) The consumer's demand for compact discs is perfectly price inelastic.

(E) The consumer's demand for compact discs is unit price elastic.

8. An improvement in production technology for a certain good leads to

(A) an increase in demand for the good

(B) an increase in the supply of the good

(C) an increase in the price of the good

(D) a shortage of the good

(E) a surplus of the good

9. If the demand for a product is price elastic, which of the following is true?

(A) An increase in the product price will have no effect on the firm's total revenue.

(B) An increase in the product price will increase the firm's total revenue.

(C) A decrease in the product price will increase the firm's total revenue.

(D) A decrease in the product price will decrease the firm's rate of inventory turnover.

(E) A decrease in the product price will decrease the total cost of goods sold.

10. If an increase in the price of good X causes a decrease in the demand for good Y, good Y is

(A) an inferior good

(B) a luxury good

(C) a necessary good

(D) a substitute for good X

(E) a complement to good X

11. The demand curve for cars is downward sloping because an increase in the price of cars leads to

(A) an increased use of other modes of transportation

(B) a decrease in the expected future price of cars

(C) a decrease in the number of cars available for purchase

(D) an increase in the prices of gasoline and other oil-based products

(E) a change in consumers' tastes for cars

12. Suppose that an effective minimum wage is imposed in a competitive labor market. If labor supply in that market subsequently increases, which of the following will occur in that market?

(A) Unemployment will increase.

(B) Quantity of labor supplied will decrease.

(C) Quantity of labor demanded will increase.

(D) Market demand will increase.

(E) The market wage will increase.

13. Suppose that Pat buys all clothing from a discount store and treats these items as inferior goods. Pat's consumption of discount-store clothing will

(A) increase when a family member wins the state lottery

(B) increase when Pat gets a raise in pay at work

(C) remain unchanged when Pat's income increases or decreases

(D) decrease when Pat becomes unemployed

(E) decrease when Pat experiences an increase in income

14. The primary distinction between the short run and the long run is that in the short run

(A) firms make profits, but in the long run no firm makes economic profits

(B) profits are maximized, but in the long run all costs are maximized

(C) some costs of production are fixed, but in the long run all costs are fixed

(D) some costs of production are fixed, but in the long run all costs are variable

(E) marginal costs are rising, but in the long run they are constant

Questions 15–17 are based on the table below, which shows a firm's total cost for different levels of output.

Output	Total Cost
0	$24
1	33
2	41
3	48
4	54
5	61
6	69

15. Which of the following is the firm's marginal cost of producing the fourth unit of output?

(A) $54.00

(B) $13.50

(C) $ 7.50

(D) $ 6.00

(E) $ 1.50

16. Which of the following is the firm's average total cost of producing 3 units of output?

(A) $48.00

(B) $16.00

(C) $14.00

(D) $13.50

(E) $ 7.00

17. Which of the following is the firm's average fixed cost of producing 2 units of output?

(A) $24.00
(B) $20.50
(C) $12.00
(D) $ 8.00
(E) $ 7.50

18. Marginal revenue is the change in revenue that results from a one-unit increase in the

(A) variable input
(B) variable input price
(C) output level
(D) output price
(E) fixed cost

19. In the short run, if the product price of a perfectly competitive firm is less than the minimum average variable cost, the firm will

(A) raise its price
(B) increase its output
(C) decrease its output slightly but increase its profit margin
(D) lose more by continuing to produce than by shutting down
(E) lose less by continuing to produce than by shutting down

20. Suppose that the license paid by each business to operate in a city increases from $400 per year to $500 per year. What effect will this increase have on a firm's short-run costs?

	Marginal Cost	Average Total Cost	Average Variable Cost
(A)	Increase	Increase	Increase
(B)	Increase	Increase	No effect
(C)	No effect	No effect	No effect
(D)	No effect	Increase	Increase
(E)	No effect	Increase	No effect

21. Which of the following statements is true of perfectly competitive firms in long-run equilibrium?

(A) Firm revenues will decrease if production is increased.
(B) Total firm revenues are at a maximum.
(C) Average fixed cost equals marginal cost.
(D) Average total cost is at a minimum.
(E) Average variable cost is greater than marginal cost.

22. If an industry has been dumping its toxic waste free of charge into a river, government action to ensure a more efficient use of resources would have which of the following effects on the industry's output and product price?

	Output	Price
(A)	Decrease	Decrease
(B)	Decrease	Increase
(C)	Increase	Decrease
(D)	Increase	Increase
(E)	Increase	No change

23. Assume that a perfectly competitive industry is in long-run equilibrium. A permanent increase in demand will eventually result in

(A) a decrease in demand because the price will increase and people will buy less of the output
(B) a decrease in supply because the rate of output and the associated cost will both increase
(C) an increase in price but no increase in output
(D) an increase in output
(E) a permanent shortage, since the quantity demanded is now greater than the quantity supplied

24. Economists are critical of monopolies principally because monopolies

    (A) gain too much political influence
    (B) are able to avoid paying their fair share of taxes
    (C) are unfair to low-income consumers
    (D) lead to an inefficient use of scarce productive resources
    (E) cause international political tension by competing with one another overseas for supplies of raw materials

25. Which of the following statements must be true in a perfectly competitive market?

    (A) A firm's marginal revenue equals price.
    (B) A firm's average total cost is above price in the long run.
    (C) A firm's average fixed cost rises in the short run.
    (D) A firm's average variable cost is higher than price in the long run.
    (E) Large firms have lower total costs than small firms.

26. A perfectly competitive firm produces in an industry whose product sells at a market price of $100. At the firm's current rate of production, marginal cost is increasing and is equal to $110. To maximize its profits, the firm should change its output and price in which of the following ways?

	Output	Price
(A)	Decrease	Increase
(B)	Decrease	No change
(C)	No change	Increase
(D)	Increase	No change
(E)	Increase	Decrease

27. The typical firm in a monopolistically competitive industry earns zero economic profit in long-run equilibrium because

    (A) advertising costs make monopolistic competition a high-cost market structure rather than a low-cost market structure
    (B) there are close substitutes for each firm's product
    (C) there are no significant restrictions on entering or exiting the industry
    (D) the firms in the industry are unable to engage in product differentiation
    (E) the firms in the industry do not operate at the minimum point on their long-run average cost curves

28. In the long run, compared with a perfectly competitive firm, a monopolistically competitive firm with the same costs will have

    (A) a higher price and higher output
    (B) a higher price and lower output
    (C) a lower price and higher output
    (D) a lower price and lower output
    (E) the same price and lower output

29. Which of the following describes what will happen to market price and quantity if firms in a perfectly competitive market form a cartel?

	Price	Quantity
(A)	Decrease	Decrease
(B)	Decrease	Increase
(C)	Increase	Increase
(D)	Increase	Decrease
(E)	Increase	No change

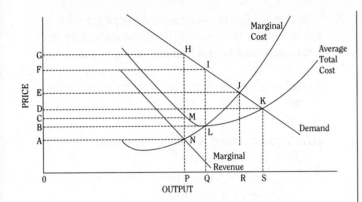

30. The diagram above depicts cost and revenue curves for a firm. What are the firm's profit-maximizing output and price?

Output	Price
(A) 0S	0D
(B) 0R	0E
(C) 0Q	0F
(D) 0Q	0B
(E) 0P	0G

31. Imperfectly competitive firms may be allocatively inefficient because they produce at a level of output such that

(A) average cost is at a minimum

(B) marginal revenue is greater than marginal cost

(C) price equals marginal revenue

(D) price equals marginal cost

(E) price is greater than marginal cost

32. In a market economy, public goods are unlikely to be provided in sufficient quantity by the private sector because

(A) private firms are less efficient at producing public goods than is the government

(B) the use of public goods cannot be withheld from those who do not pay for them

(C) consumers lack information about the benefits of public goods

(D) consumers do not value public goods highly enough for firms to produce them profitably

(E) public goods are inherently too important to be left to private firms to produce

33. Assume that both input and product markets are competitive. If capital is fixed and the product price increases, in the short run firms will increase production by increasing

(A) capital until marginal revenue equals the product price

(B) capital until the average product of capital equals the price of capital

(C) labor until the value of the marginal product of labor equals the wage rate

(D) labor until the marginal product of labor equals the wage rate

(E) labor until the ratio of product price to the marginal product of labor equals the wage rate

34. In which of the following ways does the United States government currently intervene in the working of the market economy?

I. It specifies the amount of goods and services businesses must produce.

II. It regulates the private sector in an effort to achieve a more efficient allocation of resources.

III. It redistributes income through taxation and public expenditures.

(A) I only

(B) II only

(C) III only

(D) II and III only

(E) I, II, and III

35. If hiring an additional worker would increase a firm's total cost by less than it would increase its total revenue, the firm should

(A) not hire that worker

(B) hire that worker

(C) hire that worker only if another worker leaves or is fired

(D) hire that worker only if the worker can raise the firm's productivity

(E) reduce the number of workers employed by that firm

36. If a firm wants to produce a given amount of output at the lowest possible cost, it should use resources in such a manner that

(A) it uses relatively more of the less expensive resource

(B) it uses relatively more of the resource with the highest marginal product

(C) each resource has just reached the point of diminishing marginal returns

(D) the marginal products of each resource are equal

(E) the marginal products per dollar spent on each resource are equal

37. If the firms in an industry pollute the environment and are not charged for the pollution, which of the following is true from the standpoint of the efficient use of resources?

(A) Too much of the industry's product is produced, and the price of the product is higher than the marginal social cost.

(B) Too much of the industry's product is produced, and the price of the product is lower than the marginal social cost.

(C) Too little of the industry's product is produced, and the price of the product is higher than the marginal social cost.

(D) Too little of the industry's product is produced, and the price of the product is lower than the marginal social cost.

(E) The industry is a monopoly.

38. Using equal amounts of resources, Country A can produce either 30 tons of mangoes or 10 tons of bananas, and Country B can produce either 10 tons of mangoes or 6 tons of bananas. Which of the following relationships is consistent with the information above?

(A) Country A Comparative advantage in production of mangoes

Country B Comparative advantage in production of bananas

(B) Country A Comparative advantage in production of bananas

Country B Comparative advantage in production of mangoes

(C) Country A Absolute advantage in production of mangoes

Country B Absolute advantage in production of bananas

(D) Country A Absolute advantage in production of bananas

Country B Absolute advantage in production of mangoes

(E) Country A Comparative disadvantage in production of mangoes

Country B Comparative disadvantage in production of bananas

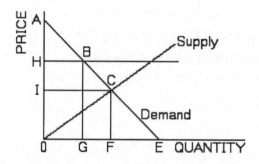

39. The graph above shows the market for chocolates. Suppose that the government imposes a price floor equal to 0H. After the implementation of the price floor, consumer surplus in this market will be equal to

(A) ABH

(B) ACI

(C) AE0

(D) 0CE

(E) 0IC

40. A firm in monopolistic competition CANNOT do which of the following?

   (A) Earn short-run profits
   (B) Advertise its product
   (C) Prevent new firms from entering the market
   (D) Compete by its choice of location
   (E) Set the price for its product

41. Which of the following is a necessary condition for a firm to engage in price discrimination?

   (A) The firm faces a highly elastic demand.
   (B) The firm is able to set its own price.
   (C) The firm is maximizing its revenue.
   (D) Buyers are only concerned about product quality.
   (E) Buyers are not fully informed about price.

42. Which of the following is true if total utility is maximized?

   (A) Marginal utility is equal to zero.
   (B) Marginal utility is positive.
   (C) Marginal utility is negative.
   (D) Average utility is maximized.
   (E) Average utility is minimized.

43. If the cross-price elasticity of demand between good A and good B is negative, then good A and good B are

   (A) substitutes
   (B) complements
   (C) unrelated
   (D) in high demand
   (E) in low demand

44. Assume that a firm in a certain industry hires its workers in a perfectly competitive labor market. As the firm hires additional workers, the marginal factor cost is

   (A) decreasing steadily
   (B) increasing steadily
   (C) constant
   (D) decreasing at first, then increasing
   (E) increasing at first, then decreasing

45. A profit-maximizing monopolist will hire an input up to the point at which

   (A) marginal factor cost equals marginal revenue product
   (B) marginal factor cost equals marginal revenue
   (C) average factor cost equals average revenue product
   (D) average factor cost equals value of the marginal product
   (E) average revenue equals marginal revenue

		Firm B's Choice	
		Restrict Output	Do not Restrict Output
Firm A's Choice	Restrict Output	$50, $50	$10, $80
	Do not Restrict Output	$80, $10	$30, $30

46. The pay-off matrix above gives the profits associated with the strategic choices of two oligopolistic firms. The first entry in each cell is the profit to Firm A and the second to Firm B. Suppose that Firm A and Firm B agree to restrict output but have no power to enforce that agreement. In the long run, each firm will most likely earn which of the following profits?

	Firm A	Firm B
(A)	$10	$80
(B)	$30	$30
(C)	$50	$50
(D)	$80	$10
(E)	$80	$80

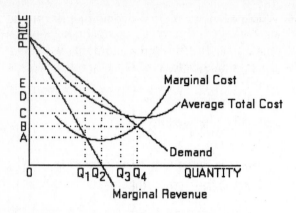

47. Suppose that the natural monopolist whose cost and revenue curves are depicted above is subject to government regulation. If the government's objective is to make this monopoly produce the socially optimal level of output, it should set price equal to

   (A) 0A
   (B) 0B
   (C) 0C
   (D) 0D
   (E) 0E

48. A production possibilities curve can be used to show which of the following?

   (A) Absence of trade-offs in the production of goods
   (B) The limits on production due to scarcity of resources
   (C) The amount of investment spending necessary to reach full employment
   (D) The labor-force participation rate
   (E) The average productivity of resources

49. The total cost of producing 200 mangoes is $2,400, and the total variable cost is $1,400. The average fixed cost of producing 200 mangoes is

   (A) $1,200
   (B) $1,000
   (C) $ 12
   (D) $ 7
   (E) $ 5

50. Which of the following will cause the supply of chocolate to increase?

   (A) An increase in the price of cocoa butter, a product that is jointly produced with chocolate
   (B) An increase in the price of chocolate
   (C) An increase in the price of cocoa beans, a major input in the production of chocolate
   (D) A decrease in the price of butterscotch, a substitute for chocolate
   (E) An effective price ceiling in the market for chocolate

51. In long-run equilibrium, the price charged by a monopolistically competitive firm is

   (A) greater than its average total cost but equal to its marginal cost
   (B) less than its average total cost but equal to its marginal cost
   (C) equal to its average total cost but less than its marginal cost
   (D) equal to its average revenue but less than its average total cost
   (E) equal to its average total cost but greater than its marginal cost

52. Economists call a firm's demand for labor a derived demand because

   (A) the number of workers hired depends mainly on the demand for the product the workers produce
   (B) workers must be at least sixteen years old before they are considered part of the labor force
   (C) workers need the salaries they receive from firms to demand goods and services
   (D) the federal government taxes workers to derive revenues needed to finance its budget
   (E) the firm needs skilled workers to operate its equipment

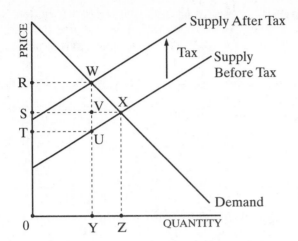

53. The imposition of an excise tax by the government caused the shift of supply curve shown in the diagram above. Which area on the diagram represents the deadweight loss caused by the tax?

    (A) UWX
    (B) VWX
    (C) RSXW
    (D) STUV
    (E) UXZY

54. Which of the following causes an increase in the demand for labor?

    (A) An increase in the wage rate
    (B) An increase in the price of the good that labor is producing
    (C) A decrease in the marginal product of labor
    (D) A decrease in the demand for the good that labor is producing
    (E) A decrease in the price of capital, a substitute for labor

55. According to the law of demand, which of the following increases as the price of a good decreases?

    (A) The quantity demanded of the good
    (B) The demand for the good
    (C) The quantity demanded of a substitute good
    (D) The demand for a substitute good
    (E) The price of a substitute good

56. Which of the following is true of a pure public good?

    (A) The government provides it at zero cost.
    (B) Nonpaying users can be excluded from consuming it.
    (C) People willingly reveal their true preference for it.
    (D) It is difficult to determine a person's marginal valuation of it.
    (E) One person's consumption of it reduces its availability to others.

57. Average total cost is equal to the sum of

    (A) total fixed cost and total variable cost
    (B) marginal cost and average fixed cost
    (C) average fixed cost and average variable cost
    (D) marginal cost and average variable cost
    (E) marginal cost, average fixed cost, and average variable cost

58. Compared to a perfectly competitive industry, a profit-maximizing monopoly with identical costs of production will produce

    (A) a lower quantity of output and charge a higher price
    (B) a higher quantity of output and charge a lower price
    (C) a lower quantity of output and charge a lower price
    (D) a higher quantity of output and charge a higher price
    (E) the same quantity of output and charge a higher price

59. A production possibilities curve is typically bowed outward because of the

   (A) law of demand
   (B) law of increasing opportunity costs
   (C) substitution effect
   (D) income effect
   (E) principle of comparative advantage

60. A firm is currently producing a level of output at which marginal cost is increasing and greater than average variable cost and marginal revenue is greater than marginal cost. To maximize profits, this firm should

   (A) decrease output
   (B) increase output
   (C) maintain its current output level
   (D) shut down
   (E) increase its price

Questions 61 and 62 refer to a firm's production function given in the table below. Assume that the firm uses labor as the only variable input to produce its output.

Number of Workers Hired	Output per Day (units)
0	0
1	15
2	32
3	42
4	50
5	55

61. If the market wage rate is constant no matter how many workers are hired, the marginal cost of the firm is at a minimum after the

   (A) first worker is hired
   (B) second worker is hired
   (C) third worker is hired
   (D) fourth worker is hired
   (E) fifth worker is hired

62. If the total fixed cost is $50 and each worker receives a wage of $100 per day, then the total cost and the average variable cost of producing 50 units of output are which of the following?

	Total Cost	Average Variable Cost
(A)	$550	$10
(B)	$500	$ 8
(C)	$450	$ 8
(D)	$400	$10
(E)	$150	$ 2

Questions 63 and 64 refer to the graph below, which shows the cost and output of a perfectly competitive firm.

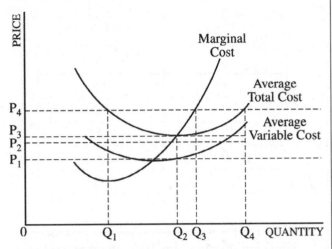

63. If the market price is P_4, the production of which output level will maximize the firm's profit?

(A) Q_1

(B) Q_2

(C) Q_3

(D) Q_4

(E) 0

64. If the market price is P_2, then which of the following is true?

(A) The firm will earn positive economic profits.

(B) The firm will shut down and exit the industry in the short run.

(C) The firm will be in long-run equilibrium.

(D) The firm will operate at a loss and continue to produce in the short run.

(E) The firm will lower its price to increase sales and profit.

65. Suppose that the price elasticity of demand for gasoline is –0.1 in the short run and –0.6 in the long run. If the price of gasoline increases by 60 percent, which of the following shows the percentage change in the quantity demanded of gasoline in the short run and in the long run?

In the Short Run	In the Long Run
(A) Increases by 10%	Increases by 60%
(B) Increases by 6%	Decreases by 36%
(C) Decreases by 6%	Decreases by 6%
(D) Decreases by 6%	Decreases by 36%
(E) Decreases by 10%	Decreases by 60%

Quantity of X	Marginal Utility of X	Quantity of Y	Marginal Utility of Y
1	16	1	40
2	12	2	24
3	10	3	16
4	8	4	12
5	6	5	8
6	4	6	4

66. The table above shows the marginal utilities in utils that Samantha receives from purchasing good X and good Y each week. The price of good X is $2 per unit, and the price of good Y is $4 per unit. Samantha has an income of $26 per week, and she spends it all on the two goods each week.

If Samantha maximizes her utility, what combination of good X and good Y will she purchase?

	Good X	Good Y
(A)	1	6
(B)	2	4
(C)	3	5
(D)	5	4
(E)	6	5

67. If a firm experiences economies of scale in production, its long-run average total cost curve

    (A) rises as output increases
    (B) falls as output increases
    (C) is horizontal
    (D) is the same as its marginal cost curve
    (E) lies above the short-run average total cost curve

68. A perfectly competitive firm's short-run supply curve is

    (A) downward sloping
    (B) horizontal at the market price
    (C) the rising portion of its average variable cost curve above its marginal cost curve
    (D) the rising portion of its average total cost curve above its marginal cost curve
    (E) the rising portion of its marginal cost curve above its average variable cost curve

69. Which of the following is true of a firm's average fixed cost?

    (A) It remains constant as output produced increases.
    (B) It increases as output produced increases.
    (C) It decreases at first, and then it increases as output produced increases.
    (D) It decreases continuously as output produced increases.
    (E) It is zero if the firm shuts down in the short run.

70. The Lorenz curve is a useful device for studying

    (A) the extent of poverty in an economy
    (B) inequality in the distribution of income
    (C) the extent of job losses because of free trade
    (D) the opportunity cost of investing in human capital
    (E) settlement patterns of families in a geographic region

Study Resources

Most textbooks used in college-level introductory microeconomics courses cover the topics in the outline given earlier, but the approaches to certain topics and the emphases given to them may differ. To prepare for the Principles of Microeconomics exam, it is advisable to study one or more college textbooks, which can be found in most college bookstores. When selecting a textbook, check the table of contents against the knowledge and skills required for this test.

There are many introductory economics textbooks that vary greatly in difficulty. Most books are published in one-volume editions, which cover both microeconomics and macroeconomics; some are published in two-volume editions, with one volume covering macroeconomics and the other microeconomics. A companion study guide/workbook is available for most textbooks. The study guides typically include brief reviews, definitions of key concepts, problem sets, and multiple-choice test questions with answers. Many publishers also make available companion Web sites, links to other online resources, or computer-assisted learning packages.

To broaden your knowledge of economic issues, you may read relevant articles published in the economics periodicals that are available in most college libraries—for example, *The Economist*, *The Wall Street Journal*, and the *New York Times*, along with local papers, may also enhance your understanding of economic issues.

Visit www.collegeboard.com/clepprep for additional microeconomics resources. You can also find suggestions for exam preparation in Chapter IV of the *Official Study Guide*. In addition, many college faculty post their course materials on their schools' Web sites.

Answer Key

1.	A	36.	E
2.	E	37.	B
3.	A	38.	A
4.	D	39.	A
5.	C	40.	C
6.	D	41.	B
7.	E	42.	A
8.	B	43.	B
9.	C	44.	C
10.	E	45.	A
11.	A	46.	B
12.	A	47.	B
13.	E	48.	B
14.	D	49.	E
15.	D	50.	A
16.	B	51.	E
17.	C	52.	A
18.	C	53.	A
19.	D	54.	B
20.	E	55.	A
21.	D	56.	D
22.	B	57.	C
23.	D	58.	A
24.	D	59.	B
25.	A	60.	B
26.	B	61.	B
27.	C	62.	C
28.	B	63.	C
29.	D	64.	D
30.	E	65.	D
31.	E	66.	D
32.	B	67.	B
33.	C	68.	E
34.	D	69.	D
35.	B	70.	B

Introductory Psychology

Description of the Examination

The Introductory Psychology examination covers material that is usually taught in a one-semester undergraduate course in introductory psychology. It stresses basic facts, concepts, and generally accepted principles in the thirteen areas listed in the following section.

The examination contains approximately 95 questions to be answered in 90 minutes. Some of these are pretest questions that will not be scored. Any time candidates spend on tutorials and providing personal information is in addition to the actual testing time.

Knowledge and Skills Required

Questions on the Introductory Psychology examination require candidates to demonstrate one or more of the following abilities.

- Knowledge of terminology, principles, and theory
- Ability to comprehend, evaluate, and analyze problem situations
- Ability to apply knowledge to new situations

The subject matter of the Introductory Psychology examination is drawn from the following topics. The percentages next to the main topics indicate the approximate percentage of exam questions on that topic.

8–9% History, Approaches, Methods
History of psychology
Approaches: biological, behavioral, cognitive, humanistic, psychodynamic
Research methods: experimental, clinical, correlational
Ethics in research

8–9% Biological Bases of Behavior
Endocrine system
Etiology
Functional organization of the nervous system
Genetics
Neuroanatomy
Physiological techniques

7–8% Sensation and Perception
Attention
Other senses: somesthesis, olfaction, gustation, vestibular system
Perceptual development
Perceptual processes
Receptor processes: vision, audition
Sensory mechanisms: thresholds, adaptation

5–6% States of Consciousness
Hypnosis and meditation
Psychoactive drug effects
Sleep and dreaming

10–11% Learning
Biological bases
Classical conditioning
Cognitive process in learning
Observational learning
Operant conditioning

8–9% Cognition
Intelligence and creativity
Language
Memory
Thinking and problem solving

7–8% Motivation and Emotion
Biological bases
Hunger, thirst, sex, pain
Social motivation
Theories of emotion
Theories of motivation

8–9% Developmental Psychology

Dimensions of development: physical, cognitive, social, moral

Gender identity and sex roles

Heredity-environment issues

Research methods: longitudinal, cross-sectional

Theories of development

7–8% Personality

Assessment techniques

Growth and adjustment

Personality theories and approaches

Research methods: idiographic, nomothetic

Self-concept, self-esteem

8–9% Psychological Disorders and Health

Affective disorders

Anxiety disorders

Dissociative disorders

Health, stress, and coping

Personality disorders

Psychoses

Somatoform disorders

Theories of psychopathology

7–8% Treatment of Psychological Disorders

Behavioral therapies

Biological and drug therapies

Cognitive therapies

Community and preventive approaches

Insight therapies: psychodynamic and humanistic approaches

7–8% Social Psychology

Aggression/antisocial behavior

Attitudes and attitude change

Attribution processes

Conformity, compliance, obedience

Group dynamics

Interpersonal perception

3–4% Statistics, Tests, and Measurement

Descriptive statistics

Inferential statistics

Measurement of intelligence

Mental handicapping conditions

Reliability and validity

Samples, populations, norms

Types of tests

Sample Test Questions

The following sample questions do not appear on an actual CLEP examination. They are intended to give potential test-takers an indication of the format and difficulty level of the examination and to provide content for practice and review. Knowing the correct answers to all of the sample questions is not a guarantee of satisfactory performance on the exam.

Directions: Each of the questions or incomplete statements below is followed by five suggested answers or completions. Select the one that is best in each case.

1. "The focus of psychological science is the attempt to relate overt responses to observable environmental stimuli."

   This statement is most closely associated with which of the following approaches?

   (A) Cognitive
   (B) Behavioral
   (C) Biological
   (D) Humanistic
   (E) Psychodynamic

2. Which of the following types of research design is most appropriate for establishing a cause-and-effect relationship between two variables?

   (A) Correlational
   (B) Naturalistic observation
   (C) Participant observation
   (D) Experimental
   (E) Case study

3. The science of psychology is typically dated from the establishment of the late-nineteenth-century Leipzig laboratory of

   (A) Hermann Ebbinghaus
   (B) Hermann von Helmholtz
   (C) William James
   (D) Wilhelm Wundt
   (E) John Locke

4. The requirement that prospective participants know the general nature of a study so that they can decide whether to participate is a major part of

   (A) reciprocal determinism
   (B) confidentiality
   (C) informed consent
   (D) duty to inform
   (E) the free-choice paradigm

5. The statement "Response latency is the number of seconds that elapses between the stimulus and the response" is an example of

   (A) introspection
   (B) a description of interaction
   (C) a deduction
   (D) an operational definition
   (E) free association

6. The release of a neurotransmitter into the synaptic cleft is caused by which of the following?

   (A) An extended refractory period
   (B) An action potential
   (C) Reuptake of the neurotransmitter
   (D) Binding of the neurotransmitter to a post-synaptic cell membrane
   (E) Migration of vesicles into the synaptic cleft

7. A neuron is said to be polarized when

   (A) it is in the refractory period
   (B) it is in a resting state
   (C) it is about to undergo an action potential
   (D) the synaptic terminals release chemicals into the synaptic gap
   (E) chemicals outside the cell body cross the cell membrane

8. Down syndrome is caused by

 (A) an extra chromosome

 (B) an imbalance of neurotransmitters

 (C) a tumor in the parietal lobe

 (D) a nutritional deficiency

 (E) a viral infection in the third trimester
    of pregnancy

9. How many pairs of chromosomes are contained
   in most human cells?

 (A) 7

 (B) 10

 (C) 16

 (D) 23

 (E) 31

10. Damage to an individual's parietal lobes would
    most likely result in

 (A) a heightened sense of smell

 (B) reduced sensitivity to touch

 (C) decreased reaction time

 (D) a loss in the ability to understand language

 (E) difficulty with visual discrimination

11. In adults, total sensory deprivation for long periods
    of time produces

 (A) a feeling of well-being similar to that
    achieved through meditation

 (B) no change in emotions or cognition, pro-
    vided the participant was mentally stable
    before the deprivation

 (C) increased efficiency in the senses of sight,
    hearing, and touch

 (D) profound apathy and a subjective sensation
    of powerlessness

 (E) hallucinations and impaired efficiency in all
    areas of intellectual functioning

12. Which of the following statements does NOT
    accurately describe the retina?

 (A) The rods are more dense in the fovea than in
    the periphery.

 (B) The blind spot is closer to the fovea than to
    the edge of the retina.

 (C) The image on the retina is upside down.

 (D) The image is located at the back of the eye.

 (E) The eye contains two kinds of receptors:
    rods and cones.

13. The opponent-process theory in vision best
    explains which of the following?

 (A) Size constancy

 (B) Color afterimages

 (C) Superior visual acuity in the fovea

 (D) Depth perception using monocular cues

 (E) Illusory movement

14. The receptors for hearing are the

 (A) ossicles in the middle ear

 (B) otoliths in the semicircular canals

 (C) hair cells on the basilar membrane

 (D) specialized cells on the tympanic
    membrane

 (E) cells in the lining of the auditory canal

15. The picture above of a road receding in the
    distance represents the depth perception cue
    known as

 (A) accommodation

 (B) retinal disparity

 (C) texture gradient

 (D) relative size

 (E) linear perspective

16. Brain waves during REM sleep generally appear as

    (A) alternating high- and low-amplitude waves
    (B) rapid low-amplitude waves
    (C) irregular medium-amplitude waves
    (D) slow low-amplitude waves
    (E) slow high-amplitude waves

17. Which of the following is a type of sleep pattern that becomes less prevalent as one moves from infancy to adulthood?

    (A) Alpha
    (B) Beta
    (C) Gamma
    (D) Theta
    (E) REM

18. According to current psychological research, hypnosis is most useful for which of the following purposes?

    (A) Pain control
    (B) Age regression
    (C) Treatment of psychotic behavior
    (D) Treatment of a memory disorder
    (E) Treatment of a personality disorder

19. Checking the coin return every time one passes a vending machine is a type of behavior probably being maintained by which of the following schedules of reinforcement?

    (A) Fixed interval only
    (B) Fixed ratio only
    (C) Variable ratio only
    (D) Variable interval and fixed ratio
    (E) Fixed interval and variable ratio

20. Making the amount of time a child can spend playing video games contingent on the amount of time the child spends practicing the piano is an illustration of

    (A) Jeremy Bentham's adaptive hedonism principle
    (B) John Locke's law of association
    (C) aversive conditioning
    (D) classical conditioning
    (E) operant conditioning

21. Which of the following strategies would undermine the effectiveness of punishment?

    (A) Delaying punishment
    (B) Using punishment just severe enough to be effective
    (C) Making punishment consistent
    (D) Explaining punishment
    (E) Minimizing dependence on physical punishment

22. A teacher tells a child to sit down in class. Over the course of several days, the child is standing up more and more frequently, only to be told to sit down each time. It is most likely that the teacher's reprimands are serving as

    (A) a punishment
    (B) approval
    (C) a reinforcer
    (D) an aversive stimulus
    (E) a conditioned stimulus

23. Which of the following is a secondary reinforcer?

    (A) Food
    (B) Warmth
    (C) Water
    (D) Money
    (E) Sex

24. Shortly after learning to associate the word "dog" with certain four-legged furry animals, young children will frequently misidentify a cow or a horse as a dog. This phenomenon is best viewed as an example of

    (A) differentiation
    (B) negative transfer
    (C) imprinting
    (D) stimulus generalization
    (E) linear perspective

25. If on the last day of a psychology class a student is asked to remember what was done in class each day during the term, she will likely be able to remember best the activities of the first and last class meetings. This situation is an example of

    (A) retroactive interference
    (B) positive transfer
    (C) the serial position effect
    (D) proactive interference
    (E) short-term memory

26. "Proactive interference" describes a process by which

    (A) people remember digits better than words
    (B) people remember images better than words
    (C) people remember elements in pairs
    (D) prior learning interferes with subsequent learning
    (E) subsequent learning interferes with prior learning

27. Research has shown that students generally perform better if tested in the same room where they did their learning. This shows the importance of which of the following in memory?

    (A) Insight
    (B) Preparedness
    (C) Context
    (D) Invariance
    (E) Rehearsal

28. Which of the following is true of recall performance on a typical forgetting curve?

    (A) It decreases rapidly at first, and then it levels off.
    (B) It decreases slowly at first, and then it drops off quite sharply.
    (C) It decreases at a steady rate until it reaches a near-zero level.
    (D) It remains steady for about the first week, and then it begins a gradual decline.
    (E) It increases for the first few hours after learning, and then it decreases very slowly over the next few weeks.

29. According to information processing theory, information is progressively processed by

    (A) long-term memory, short-term memory, and then sensory memory
    (B) sensory memory, short-term memory, and then long-term memory
    (C) sensory memory, semantic memory, and then long-term memory
    (D) short-term memory, semantic memory, and then long-term memory
    (E) short-term memory, long-term memory, and then sensory memory

30. In problem solving, which of the following approaches almost always guarantees a solution?

    (A) Insight
    (B) Heuristic
    (C) Algorithm
    (D) Critical thinking
    (E) Convergent thinking

31. One theory of the effects of arousal holds that efficiency of behavior can be described as an inverted U-shaped function of increasing arousal. Which of the following accurately describes this relationship?

    (A) Greater arousal leads to better performance.
    (B) Greater arousal leads to poorer performance.
    (C) Low and high levels of arousal lead to poorest performance.
    (D) Overarousal leads to performance efficiency.
    (E) Underarousal leads to performance efficiency.

32. Which of the following illustrates drive reduction?

    (A) A person wins five dollars in the lottery.
    (B) A dog burned by a hot stove avoids the stove thereafter.
    (C) A child who likes music turns up the volume of the radio.
    (D) A dog salivates at the sound of a tone previously paired with fresh meat.
    (E) A woman who is cold puts on a warm coat.

33. Which of the following presents a pair of needs from Abraham Maslow's hierarchical need structure, in order from lower to higher need?

    (A) Belongingness, safety
    (B) Self-actualization, physiological needs
    (C) Physiological needs, safety
    (D) Esteem, belongingness
    (E) Self-actualization, esteem

34. In an approach-avoidance conflict, as the person nears the goal, the levels of attraction and aversion change in which of the following ways?

    (A) Both increase.
    (B) Both decrease.
    (C) Attraction increases and aversion decreases.
    (D) Attraction decreases and aversion increases.
    (E) Both are extinguished.

35. Which of the following has been identified as correlating most closely with heart disease?

    (A) Anxiety
    (B) Physical overexertion
    (C) Guilt
    (D) Muscle tension
    (E) Hostility

36. In which of the following areas does psychological research show most clearly that girls develop earlier than boys?

    (A) Independence from parents
    (B) Athletic competence
    (C) Intellectual achievement
    (D) Adolescent physical growth spurt
    (E) Self-actualization

37. Developmental psychologists would most likely prefer longitudinal research designs to cross-sectional research designs because longitudinal designs

    (A) usually yield results much more quickly
    (B) offer the advantage of between-subjects comparisons
    (C) are much less likely to be influenced by cultural changes that occur over time
    (D) utilize the subjects as their own experimental controls
    (E) are more valid

38. A young child breaks her cookie into a number of pieces and asserts that "now there is more to eat." In Jean Piaget's analysis, the child's behavior is evidence of

    (A) formal logical operations
    (B) concrete logical operations
    (C) conservation
    (D) preoperational thought
    (E) sensorimotor analysis

39. A school psychologist informs a ninth-grade teacher that Jimmy "identifies" with his twelfth-grade brother. What the psychologist means is that Jimmy tends to

(A) feel inferior to his brother

(B) envy and to be jealous of his brother

(C) influence the way his brother views the world

(D) recognize similarities between his brother and himself

(E) accept his brother's values and to imitate his behavior

40. According to Elisabeth Kübler-Ross, what is the correct order of the stages for confronting impending death?

(A) Anger, denial, bargaining, depression, acceptance

(B) Bargaining, anger, depression, denial, acceptance

(C) Denial, anger, bargaining, depression, acceptance

(D) Depression, anger, denial, bargaining, acceptance

(E) Depression, denial, anger, bargaining, acceptance

41. When preschool children see the world only from their point of view, they are displaying

(A) accommodation

(B) assimilation

(C) egocentric thinking

(D) deductive reasoning

(E) object permanence

42. When insulted by a friend, Sally's first impulse was to strike him. Instead, she yelled loudly and kicked a door several times. This means of reducing aggressive impulses exemplifies which of the following?

(A) Repression

(B) Abreaction

(C) Displacement

(D) Cathexis

(E) Sublimation

43. Carl Jung is associated with which of the following concepts?

(A) Inferiority complex

(B) Need for achievement

(C) Collective unconscious

(D) Self-esteem

(E) Self-actualization

44. Erik Erikson's and Sigmund Freud's theories of personality development are most similar in that both

(A) emphasize the libido

(B) focus on adult development

(C) discount the importance of culture

(D) are based on stages

(E) view behavior as a continuum

45. The use of projective tests is associated with which of the following psychological approaches?

(A) Behaviorism

(B) Psychoanalysis

(C) Cognitive behaviorism

(D) Humanism

(E) Functionalism

46. Lawrence is pessimistic, rigid, and moody. In terms of Hans Eysenck's personality dimensions, Lawrence would be classified as

   (A) independent-dependent
   (B) stable-extraverted
   (C) internal-external
   (D) unstable-introverted
   (E) passive-aggressive

47. The key distinction between a personality trait and an attitude is

   (A) centrality
   (B) salience
   (C) durability
   (D) direction
   (E) valence

48. A diagnosis of schizophrenia typically includes which of the following symptoms?

   (A) Delusions
   (B) Panic attacks
   (C) Hypochondriasis
   (D) Multiple personality
   (E) Psychosexual dysfunction

49. The term "etiology" refers to the study of which of the following aspects of an illness?

   (A) Origins and causes
   (B) Characteristic symptoms
   (C) Expected outcome following treatment
   (D) Frequency of occurrence
   (E) Level of contagiousness

50. An obsession is defined as

   (A) a senseless ritual
   (B) a hallucination
   (C) a delusion
   (D) an unwanted thought
   (E) a panic attack

51. A somatization disorder is characterized chiefly by

   (A) changes in mood
   (B) panic attacks
   (C) agoraphobia
   (D) changes in eating behavior
   (E) physical complaints

52. Personality disorders are characterized by which of the following?

   (A) A fear of public places, frequently accompanied by panic attacks
   (B) Problematic social relationships and inflexible and maladaptive responses to stress
   (C) A successful response to neuroleptic drugs
   (D) A deficiency of acetylcholine in the brain
   (E) An increased level of serotonin in the brain

53. Research on the effectiveness of psychotherapy has indicated that

   (A) certain therapeutic methods have been shown to be especially effective for particular psychological disorders
   (B) nondirective techniques are generally superior to directive ones
   (C) the effectiveness of a method depends on the length of time a therapist was trained in the method
   (D) psychoanalysis is the most effective technique for eliminating behavior disorders
   (E) psychoanalysis is the most effective technique for curing anxiety disorders

54. Which of the following kinds of therapy attempts to correct irrational beliefs that lead to psychological distress?

   (A) Behavioral
   (B) Cognitive
   (C) Existential
   (D) Gestalt
   (E) Psychoanalytic

55. An individual undergoing psychotherapy shows improvement due only to that person's belief in the therapy and not because of the therapy itself. This result illustrates a

(A) transference effect
(B) placebo effect
(C) cathectic effect
(D) primary gain
(E) conditioned response

56. Which of the following can be a significant side effect of electroconvulsive therapy?

(A) Aphasia
(B) Sustained convulsions
(C) Muscle tremors
(D) Loss of muscle control
(E) Temporary loss of memory

57. Selective serotonin reuptake inhibitors (SSRIs) are used primarily in the treatment of which of the following?

(A) Anxiety
(B) Schizophrenia
(C) Depression
(D) Mania
(E) Sleep disorders

58. Similarity, proximity, and familiarity are important determinants of

(A) observational learning
(B) friendship formation
(C) sexual orientation
(D) aggression
(E) imprinting

59. All of the following are true about altruism EXCEPT

(A) It is more common in small towns and rural areas than in cities.
(B) It is more likely to be inherited than is aggressive behavior.
(C) A person is more likely to perform an altruistic act when another person has modeled altruistic behavior.
(D) A person is more likely to perform an altruistic act when another person has pointed out the need.
(E) A person is more likely to be altruistic when not in a hurry.

60. The bystander effect has been explained by which of the following?

(A) Empathy
(B) Diffusion of responsibility
(C) Social facilitation
(D) Reactive devaluation
(E) Defective schemas

61. According to Robert Sternberg, love is composed of which of the following?

(A) Maturity, romance, liking
(B) Assimilation, accommodation, altruism
(C) Intimacy, passion, commitment
(D) Selflessness, agape, companionship
(E) Tolerance, humility, trust

62. Job satisfaction has an inverse relationship with

(A) productivity
(B) career interest
(C) turnover
(D) age
(E) skill level

63. An attribution that focuses on an individual's ability or personality characteristics is described as

   (A) situational
   (B) collectivist
   (C) dispositional
   (D) stereotypic
   (E) homogeneous

64. Which of the following terms refers to the strategy of making a small request to gain listeners' compliance, then making a larger request?

   (A) Door-in-the-face
   (B) Foot-in-the-door
   (C) Social facilitation
   (D) Matching
   (E) Overjustification

65. Which of the following is a true statement about the relationship between test validity and test reliability?

   (A) A test can be reliable without being valid.
   (B) A test that has high content validity will have high reliability.
   (C) A test that has low content validity will have low reliability.
   (D) The higher the test's validity, the lower its reliability will be.
   (E) The validity of a test always exceeds its reliability.

66. Which of the following statistics indicates the distribution with the greatest variability?

   (A) A variance of 30.6
   (B) A standard deviation of 11.2
   (C) A range of 6
   (D) A mean of 61.5
   (E) A median of 38

67. Which of the following techniques would be most useful in studying focal brain activity as a participant generates words?

   (A) Computerized axial tomography (CAT)
   (B) Positron-emission tomography (PET)
   (C) Magnetic resonance imaging (MRI)
   (D) Electrooculography (EOG)
   (E) Electroencephalography (EEG)

68. The case study method of conducting research is justifiably criticized because

   (A) the researcher cannot focus on a specific individual
   (B) the researcher cannot collect detailed observations
   (C) the results are difficult to generalize to a larger population
   (D) it does not allow for the generation of hypotheses that can be tested in future experiments
   (E) it does not allow for the examination of unusual cases

69. A person who wants to see an object in low light conditions should focus the object on

   (A) the fovea because that is where the cones are more densely packed
   (B) the fovea because that is where the rods are more densely packed
   (C) the periphery of the retina because that is where the cones are more densely packed
   (D) the periphery of the retina because that is where the rods are more densely packed
   (E) both the fovea and the periphery of the retina to optimize the use of both rods and cones

70. Cara frequently sees a television commercial that features her favorite celebrity and a new cola. While shopping, she sees the new cola on the shelf, feels positively about it, and wants to buy it. She most likely wants to buy the cola for which of the following reasons?

(A) She felt negatively reinforced for wanting the cola.

(B) She felt positively reinforced for wanting the cola.

(C) The good feelings she had toward the celebrity were paired with the cola, and later, the cola by itself elicited positive feelings.

(D) The good feelings she has toward the cola made her feel even more positively about the celebrity.

(E) She felt positively about a bag of chips that was on the same aisle as the cola.

71. A father uses operant conditioning to encourage his child to share. He praises his child whenever she shares her favorite teddy bear with a friend. Now, she is sharing the bear more and more often. She also increases her sharing of her stuffed frog and her stuffed pig. The child's increase in her sharing her frog and pig is most likely attributable to

(A) discrimination

(B) generalization

(C) the partial-reinforcement effect

(D) extinction

(E) spontaneous recovery

72. Which of the following is a measure of central tendency that can be easily distorted by unusually high or low scores?

(A) Mean

(B) Mode

(C) Median

(D) Range

(E) Standard deviation

73. Stimulation of the lateral hypothalamus will result in which of the following behaviors in laboratory rats?

(A) An increase in sexual behavior

(B) An increase in eating behavior

(C) An increase in aggression

(D) A decrease in auditory perception

(E) A decrease in memory functioning

74. Stella Chess and Alexander Thomas have classified temperament into which of the following clusters?

(A) Sensorimotor, preoperational, concrete operational

(B) Easy, difficult, slow to warm up

(C) Secure, insecure, resilient

(D) Authoritarian, authoritative, indulgent

(E) Preconventional, conventional, postconventional

75. Every day when Carlos leaves his apartment, he locks the door, walks to the corner, turns around, and returns to his apartment in order to check that the door is locked. He returns to check the door several times before finally crossing the street and going about his day. Carlos is most likely suffering from which of the following conditions?

(A) Narcissistic personality disorder

(B) Panic disorder

(C) Generalized anxiety disorder

(D) Bipolar disorder

(E) Obsessive-compulsive disorder

76. A treatment technique, often used to treat phobias, that builds upon the principles of classical conditioning is

(A) token economy

(B) rational-emotive behavior therapy

(C) systematic desensitization

(D) the placebo effect

(E) dream analysis

Study Resources

Most textbooks used in college-level introductory psychology courses cover the topics in the outline given earlier, but the approaches to certain topics and the emphases given to them may differ. To prepare for the Introductory Psychology exam, it is advisable to study one or more college textbooks, which can be found in most college bookstores. When selecting a textbook, check the table of contents against the knowledge and skills required for this test.

You may also find it helpful to supplement your reading with books listed in the bibliographies that can be found in most psychology textbooks.

Visit www.collegeboard.com/clepprep for additional psychology resources. You can also find suggestions for exam preparation in Chapter IV of the *Official Study Guide*. In addition, many college faculty post their course materials on their schools' Web sites.

Answer Key

#	Ans	#	Ans
1.	B	39.	E
2.	D	40.	C
3.	D	41.	C
4.	C	42.	C
5.	D	43.	C
6.	B	44.	D
7.	B	45.	B
8.	A	46.	D
9.	D	47.	C
10.	B	48.	A
11.	E	49.	A
12.	A	50.	D
13.	B	51.	E
14.	C	52.	B
15.	E	53.	A
16.	B	54.	B
17.	E	55.	B
18.	A	56.	E
19.	C	57.	C
20.	E	58.	B
21.	A	59.	B
22.	C	60.	B
23.	D	61.	C
24.	D	62.	C
25.	C	63.	C
26.	D	64.	B
27.	C	65.	A
28.	A	66.	B
29.	B	67.	B
30.	C	68.	C
31.	C	69.	D
32.	E	70.	C
33.	C	71.	B
34.	A	72.	A
35.	E	73.	B
36.	D	74.	B
37.	D	75.	E
38.	D	76.	C

Introductory Sociology

Description of the Examination

The Introductory Sociology examination is designed to assess an individual's knowledge of the material typically presented in a one-semester introductory sociology course at most colleges and universities. The examination emphasizes basic facts and concepts as well as general theoretical approaches used by sociologists. Highly specialized knowledge of the subject and the methodology of the discipline is not required or measured by the test content.

The examination contains approximately 100 questions to be answered in 90 minutes. Some of these are pretest questions that will not be scored. Any time candidates spend on tutorials and providing personal information is in addition to the actual testing time.

Knowledge and Skills Required

Questions on the Introductory Sociology examination require candidates to demonstrate one or more of the following abilities. Some questions may require more than one of these abilities.

- Identification of specific names, facts, and concepts from sociological literature
- Understanding of relationships between concepts, empirical generalizations, and theoretical propositions of sociology
- Understanding of the methods by which sociological relationships are established
- Application of concepts, propositions, and methods to hypothetical situations
- Interpretation of tables and charts

The subject matter of the Introductory Sociology examination is drawn from the following topics. The percentages next to the main topics indicate the approximate percentage of exam questions on that topic.

20% Institutions
  Economic
  Educational
  Family
  Medical
  Political
  Religious

15% Social Patterns
  Community
  Demography
  Human ecology
  Rural/urban patterns

20% Social Processes
  Collective behavior and social movements
  Culture
  Deviance and social control
  Groups and organizations
  Social change
  Social interaction
  Socialization

30% Social Stratification (Process and Structure)
  Aging
  Power and social inequality
  Professions and occupations
  Race and ethnic relations
  Sex and gender roles
  Social class
  Social mobility

15% The Sociological Perspective
  History of sociology
  Methods
  Sociological theory

Sample Test Questions

The following sample questions do not appear on an actual CLEP examination. They are intended to give potential test-takers an indication of the format and difficulty level of the examination and to provide content for practice and review. Knowing the correct answers to all of the sample questions is not a guarantee of satisfactory performance on the exam.

Directions: Each of the questions or incomplete statements below is followed by five suggested answers or completions. Select the one that is best in each case.

1. All of the following are examples of voluntary associations EXCEPT the

   (A) Republican Party
   (B) League of Women Voters
   (C) Federal Bureau of Investigation
   (D) First Baptist Church of Atlanta
   (E) Little League Baseball Association

2. A sex ratio of 120 means that in a population there are

   (A) 120 more males than females
   (B) 120 more females than males
   (C) 120 males for every 100 females
   (D) 120 females for every 100 males
   (E) 12% more men than women

3. Industrialization is most likely to reduce the importance of which of the following functions of the family?

   (A) Economic production
   (B) Care of young children
   (C) Regulation of sexual behavior
   (D) Socialization of the individual
   (E) Social control

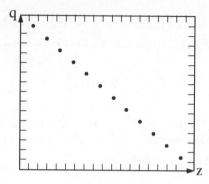

4. Which of the following best describes the relationship between q and z on the scattergram above?

   (A) A perfect positive correlation
   (B) A perfect negative correlation
   (C) A perfect curvilinear correlation
   (D) A low negative correlation
   (E) A correlation of zero

5. The process by which an individual learns how to live in his or her social surroundings is known as

   (A) amalgamation
   (B) association
   (C) collective behavior
   (D) socialization
   (E) innovation

6. Which of the following can properly be considered norms?

   I. Laws
   II. Folkways
   III. Mores

   (A) I only
   (B) III only
   (C) I and II only
   (D) II and III only
   (E) I, II, and III

7. Which of the following theorists argued that class conflict was inevitable in a capitalistic society and would result in revolution?

(A) C. Wright Mills
(B) Karl Marx
(C) Robert Park
(D) Max Weber
(E) Karl Mannheim

8. Which of the following relies most heavily on sampling methods?

(A) Small group experiment
(B) Laboratory experiment
(C) Participant observation
(D) Survey research
(E) Case study

9. Which of the following is NOT characteristic of the Chicago School of Sociology?

(A) They studied urban neighborhoods in the city of Chicago.
(B) They were influenced by Herbert Spencer and Frederic Clements.
(C) They used ethnography and field methods in their research.
(D) Talcott Parsons was a proponent of the school.
(E) They were most influential during the twentieth century.

10. Which of the following allows human beings to adapt to diverse physical environments?

(A) Instinct
(B) Heredity
(C) Culture
(D) Stratification
(E) Ethnocentrism

11. All of the following are properties of primary groups EXCEPT

(A) They are important sources of social support.
(B) They tend to be ethnocentric.
(C) They significantly influence personality development.
(D) They tend to be large in number.
(E) They are frequently characterized by face-to-face relationships.

12. According to Émile Durkheim, a society that lacks clear-cut norms to govern aspirations and moral conduct is characterized by

(A) rationalism
(B) altruism
(C) egoism
(D) secularism
(E) anomie

13. The process by which an immigrant or an ethnic minority is absorbed socially into a receiving society is called

(A) assimilation
(B) accommodation
(C) cooperation
(D) interaction
(E) equilibrium

14. The term "sociology" was coined by its founder, the nineteenth-century positivist

(A) Émile Durkheim
(B) Auguste Comte
(C) Max Weber
(D) Harriet Martineau
(E) George Herbert Mead

15. According to Émile Durkheim, the more homogeneous a group the greater its

(A) organic solidarity
(B) mechanical solidarity
(C) functional differentiation
(D) co-optation
(E) stratification

16. Demographic patterns have clearly demonstrated that more males than females are born in

(A) technologically developing countries only
(B) technologically developed countries only
(C) virtually every known human society
(D) highly urbanized countries only
(E) countries with high nutritional standards only

17. Max Weber's three dimensions of social stratification are which of the following?

(A) Class, politics, education
(B) Prestige, politics, occupation
(C) Residence, occupation, religion
(D) Status, class, power
(E) Status, religion, prestige

18. The term "SMSA" used in the United States census refers to a

(A) summary of many small areas
(B) statistical mean of sampling error
(C) summary of metropolitan shopping areas
(D) standard measure of suburban areas
(E) standard metropolitan statistical area

19. In order for an occupation to be considered a profession by a sociologist, it must be an occupation that

(A) is based on abstract knowledge and a body of specialized information
(B) has high public visibility in the community
(C) requires training from a specialized school rather than from a university
(D) serves government and industry as well as individuals
(E) is a full-time position with a regular salary

20. In the study of social class, a sociologist would be LEAST likely to focus on

(A) power
(B) social mobility
(C) style of life
(D) motivation
(E) occupational status

21. An example of a folkway in American society is

(A) joining a religious cult
(B) eating a sandwich for lunch
(C) not paying income taxes on time
(D) stopping for a red light
(E) being fined for jaywalking

22. Socialization takes place

(A) only in childhood
(B) mainly in adolescence
(C) mainly in early adulthood
(D) mainly through the reproductive years
(E) throughout the life cycle

23. A school system that teaches children of different ethnic groups in the children's own language and about their own particular ethnic heritage illustrates a policy of

(A) structural assimilation
(B) cultural assimilation
(C) accommodation
(D) rationalization
(E) ethnocentrism

24. Max Weber linked the emergence of capitalism to the

(A) Calvinist doctrine of predestination
(B) Catholic monks' belief in asceticism
(C) Protestants' desire for material luxuries
(D) increasing power of the nobility in medieval Europe
(E) Hindu belief in reincarnation

25. The economy of the postindustrial United States is characterized by all of the following EXCEPT

(A) computer-facilitated automation
(B) relocation of manufacturing plants to less-developed countries
(C) international competition in the manufacturing sector of the economy
(D) increasing numbers of service compared to manufacturing jobs
(E) increased job security due to globalization

26. Which statement about political participation in the United States is true?

(A) Almost everyone of voting age in the United States is registered to vote.
(B) Voter turnout in the United States is lower than in most European nations.
(C) Voter turnout has increased substantially in the last twenty years.
(D) People of higher social class tend to participate less in voting than lower social classes.
(E) Younger adults are more likely to vote than those over 65.

27. Which of the following is defined as an organized sphere of social life, or societal subsystem, designed to support important values and to meet human needs?

(A) Social structure
(B) Social organization
(C) Social institution
(D) Social culture
(E) Economic corporation

28. Most of the funding for public schools in the United States comes from

(A) lottery revenues
(B) state income taxes
(C) local sales taxes
(D) local income taxes
(E) local property taxes

29. According to Max Weber, authority derived from the understanding that individuals have clearly defined rights and duties to uphold and that they implement rules and procedures impersonally is

(A) traditional authority
(B) charismatic authority
(C) legal-rational authority
(D) coercion
(E) persuasion

30. Raw materials are processed and converted into finished goods in which sector of the economy?

(A) Agricultural
(B) Industrial
(C) Public
(D) Service
(E) Information

31. In the United States, the economic growth of the 1980s and 1990s resulted in

    (A) a growth in the gap between the rich and poor
    (B) a narrowing of the gap between the rich and poor
    (C) no change in the gap between the rich and poor
    (D) a growth in the economic gap between men and women
    (E) no change in the economic gap between men and women

32. Within the scientific perspective, which of the following are the most important sources of knowledge?

    (A) Common sense and tradition
    (B) Empiricism and reason
    (C) Authority and structure
    (D) Paradigms and intuition
    (E) Existentialism and reference groups

33. Which of the following statements is true about those living below the poverty line in the United States?

    (A) Approximately 40 percent are young adult householders.
    (B) The majority are African American.
    (C) Most have an illness that prevents them from working.
    (D) The families are more likely to live in the northeast than in other regions of the country.
    (E) The majority of the householders are single mothers with children.

34. Which of the following made up the largest number of immigrants to the United States in the 1990s?

    (A) Mexicans
    (B) Chinese
    (C) Italians
    (D) Canadians
    (E) Russians

35. Compared to the United States population in general, Asian Americans have

    (A) larger proportions of their populations in poverty
    (B) lower median family incomes
    (C) a higher level of formal educational achievement
    (D) fewer ties to their family's country of origin
    (E) a lower proportion of first-generation immigrants

36. In the world's economic system, which of the following is true about the relationship between high-income countries and low-income countries?

    (A) High-income countries depend on low-income countries to purchase natural resources from them.
    (B) High-income countries build manufacturing plants in low-income countries to obtain cheap labor.
    (C) High-income countries encourage the development of state-owned economic enterprises in low-income countries.
    (D) High-income countries are more likely than low-income countries to have an agriculturally based economy.
    (E) High-income countries have less-diversified sources of income.

37. Sociological studies of gender socialization show that

   (A) girls' games are more likely than boys' games to encourage assertive behaviors
   (B) girls' games are more likely than boys' games to emphasize strict observance of rules
   (C) girls are more likely than boys to learn to suppress emotions of sadness
   (D) girls are more likely to engage in competitive play and boys in cooperative play
   (E) girls are less likely than boys to receive attention from teachers

38. The increase in prejudice that sometimes resulted from court-ordered desegregation in public schools is a

   (A) manifest function of desegregation
   (B) latent dysfunction of desegregation
   (C) functional alternative to desegregation
   (D) secondary function of desegregation
   (E) rational exchange for desegregation

39. The practice of judging another culture by the standards of one's own culture is called

   (A) ethnocentrism
   (B) cultural relativism
   (C) cultural integration
   (D) transference
   (E) multiculturalism

40. In *Gesellschaft,* people are more likely than in *Gemeinschaft* to

   (A) have frequent face-to-face contact with those they know
   (B) see others as a means of advancing their own individual goals
   (C) be united by primary group bonds
   (D) have altruistic concerns for others
   (E) be tradition-directed

41. Demographic transition theory explains population changes by

   (A) connecting them exclusively to changes in the food supply
   (B) linking population changes to technological development
   (C) focusing on the migration of people in and out of specified territories
   (D) tying population growth to changes in the sex ratio
   (E) referring to a culture's religious attitudes

42. Which theory assumes that deviance occurs among individuals who are blocked from achieving socially approved goals by legitimate means?

   (A) Hirschi's social control theory
   (B) Labeling theory
   (C) Merton's anomie theory
   (D) Differential association theory
   (E) Cultural transmission theory

43. Sandra is female, she is African American, and she is sixteen years of age. These three characteristics are examples of Sandra's

   (A) role sets
   (B) cultural roles
   (C) achieved status
   (D) ascribed status
   (E) mobility aspirations

44. Cooley called a person's self-conception based on the responses of others

   (A) the divided self
   (B) self-esteem
   (C) the concrete operational stage
   (D) the looking-glass self
   (E) the "I" and "me"

45. The philosopher Thomas Hobbes believed that social order developed out of the

    (A) recognition of the transcendent power of God
    (B) biological need for humans to reproduce
    (C) desire to escape a state of continuous social conflict
    (D) discovery of agriculture
    (E) reaction to the industrial revolution

46. Max Weber's principle of *verstehen* was meant to

    (A) explain the subjective beliefs that motivate people to act
    (B) determine how society is dysfunctionally organized
    (C) focus on the inequality in society
    (D) search for the social structures that fulfill people's needs
    (E) identify the patterns of exchange among individuals or groups

47. According to sociological terminology, an analysis of the amount of violence in mass media, such as television shows, would be which of the following?

    (A) Content analysis
    (B) Secondary analysis
    (C) Quasi-experiment
    (D) Participant observation
    (E) Ethnographic interview

48. Which of the following is true of social norms for the structure of marriage?

    (A) They have consistently required monogamy across all periods of history and cross-culturally around the globe.
    (B) They have favored polyandry in those societies wanting to increase their birth rate.
    (C) They have frequently held polygyny as the societal ideal, although this pattern was functionally available to and practiced primarily by the most wealthy and powerful.
    (D) They have no impact in democratic societies, since democracies allow individuals to choose their own form of marriage.
    (E) They are based on the ideal of gender equality.

49. In the past 30 years, the infant mortality rate in the United States has

    (A) remained about the same as in other industrialized countries
    (B) declined for African American people but not for Caucasian people
    (C) declined among Caucasian people, while increasing among African American people
    (D) declined among Caucasian people, while remaining stable among African American people
    (E) declined among both African American people and Caucasian people, while remaining twice as high among African American people

50. In the United States, semiskilled positions held primarily by women, such as waitperson, cashier, and receptionist, are known as which type of occupation?

    (A) Blue-collar
    (B) Pink-collar
    (C) White-collar
    (D) Nonpatriarchal
    (E) Matriarchal

51. Tamara worked as a waitress for five years after high school before she went to college. After college, Tamara got a job as a sales representative for a pharmaceutical company. This best exemplifies which of the following types of mobility?

(A) Intergenerational

(B) Intragenerational

(C) Unilateral

(D) Horizontal

(E) Structural

52. The concept of "glass ceiling" affecting women in the workforce is best illustrated by which of the following?

(A) The instability of female-dominated jobs

(B) The pay inequity between men and women for comparable jobs

(C) The breakdown of gender stereotypes in the job market

(D) The instability of marriages for women who are successful in the workforce

(E) The barriers that limit career advancement for women

53. Which of the following statements is most accurate regarding patriarchy?

(A) It is a form of political organization where the state assumes paternal responsibility for citizens.

(B) It is a form of social organization in which one's kinship lineage is traced through the family of the mother.

(C) It is a form of social organization in which males control most formal and informal power.

(D) It is found only in those societies that practice polyandry.

(E) It is not found in those societies that practice polygyny.

54. Which of the following distinguishes a crime from a deviant act?

(A) The degree of harm caused by the act

(B) The number of people who disapprove of the act

(C) The definition of the act as criminal by a political entity

(D) The social status of the person who committed the act

(E) The social status of the person who is harmed by the act

55. A collection of people who happen to be walking down the street at the same time but who have nothing else in common is known as

(A) a social movement

(B) a social category

(C) an aggregate

(D) a primary group

(E) a secondary group

56. "This may sound really strange, but ..."

The statement above is an example of

(A) a disclaimer

(B) an account

(C) an excuse

(D) a justification

(E) a concession

57. Nathan wants to study the behavior of city residents as they travel on the subway to work every day. What type of research would be most appropriate for Nathan's research project?

(A) Experimental research

(B) Field research

(C) Content analysis

(D) Secondary analysis

(E) Survey method

58. Which of the following is true of a dependent variable?

(A) It is spurious.

(B) It is influenced by another variable.

(C) It is manipulated.

(D) It causes other variables to increase.

(E) It is used to draw a sample from a population.

59. Which of the following is an example of an informal positive sanction?

(A) Marguerite receives a bronze medal for gymnastics at the Olympics.

(B) Hank is awarded a high school diploma by the school board.

(C) Halle receives a million dollars for her performance in a movie.

(D) Danisha receives a new car from her parents when she scores 2300 on the SAT®.

(E) William is sentenced to one year of community service and a $5,000 fine for shoplifting.

60. In general, females perform better than males do on tests of

(A) general intelligence

(B) verbal ability

(C) visual-spatial ability

(D) scientific information

(E) mathematics

61. Ken works on an assembly line in a paper factory in the midwestern United States. He believes that if he works hard enough, he will become very wealthy. According to Karl Marx, Ken's belief reflects which of the following?

(A) False consciousness

(B) Class consciousness

(C) Collective consciousness

(D) The caste system

(E) Rational choice

62. In structural functionalism, which of the following terms refers to something that has a detrimental effect on social institutions or society?

(A) Secret function

(B) Dysfunction

(C) Manifest function

(D) Latent function

(E) Mutative function

63. Which of the following terms refers to a philosophical system under which knowledge of the world and human behavior is derived from scientific observation?

(A) Theology

(B) Determinism

(C) Positivism

(D) Phenomenology

(E) Metaphysics

64. Mrs. Jones has a parent-teacher meeting scheduled at the school where she teaches. The meeting is scheduled at the same time as her daughter's piano recital. Mrs. Jones will have to decide how to juggle the contradictory expectations of teacher and parent. This situation is referred to as

(A) role strain

(B) role conflict

(C) status conflict

(D) status set

(E) role set

65. Which of the following would most likely be an agent of involuntary resocialization?

(A) Mass media

(B) An institution of higher learning

(C) A peer group

(D) A total institution

(E) The family

66. All of the following characteristics are commonly attributed to postmodern culture EXCEPT

   (A) moral relativism
   (B) skepticism toward traditional authority
   (C) growing tolerance of diversity
   (D) loss of faith in absolutes
   (E) adherence to traditional gender roles

67. Joe is on trial for selling drugs. He looks very different from when he was arrested. He has washed, cut, and combed his hair, and is wearing a clean, conservative suit and tie at the trial. Joe is engaged in

   (A) dysfunctional behavior
   (B) altruism
   (C) impression management
   (D) exchange
   (E) anticipatory socialization

68. A characteristic of a triad is that it

   (A) is prone to coalition formation
   (B) allows more power per member than a dyad
   (C) is the smallest type of group
   (D) can develop the strongest relationships
   (E) has little impact on human behavior

69. Laura is conducting an experiment to determine the effect of caffeine on wakefulness. She gives half of her subjects a caffeinated beverage to drink. These subjects are the

   (A) control group
   (B) experimental group
   (C) independent variable
   (D) dependent variable
   (E) study population

Study Resources

Most textbooks used in college-level introductory sociology courses cover the topics in the outline given earlier, but the approaches to certain topics and the emphases given to them may differ. To prepare for the Introductory Sociology exam, it is advisable to study one or more college textbooks, which can be found in most college bookstores. When selecting a textbook, check the table of contents against the knowledge and skills required for this test.

As you read, take notes that address the following issues, which are fundamental to most questions that appear on the test:

- What is society? What is culture? What is common to all societies, and what is characteristic of American society?

- What are other basic concepts in sociology that help to describe human nature, human interaction, and the collective behavior of groups, organizations, institutions, and societies?

- What methods do sociologists use to study, describe, analyze, and observe human behavior?

Visit www.collegeboard.com/clepprep for additional sociology resources. You can also find suggestions for exam preparation in Chapter IV of the *Official Study Guide*. In addition, many college faculty post their course materials on their schools' Web sites.

Answer Key

1.	C	36.	B
2.	C	37.	E
3.	A	38.	B
4.	B	39.	A
5.	D	40.	B
6.	E	41.	B
7.	B	42.	C
8.	D	43.	D
9.	D	44.	D
10.	C	45.	C
11.	D	46.	A
12.	E	47.	A
13.	A	48.	C
14.	B	49.	E
15.	B	50.	B
16.	C	51.	B
17.	D	52.	E
18.	E	53.	C
19.	A	54.	C
20.	D	55.	C
21.	B	56.	A
22.	E	57.	B
23.	C	58.	B
24.	A	59.	D
25.	E	60.	B
26.	B	61.	A
27.	C	62.	B
28.	E	63.	C
29.	C	64.	B
30.	B	65.	D
31.	A	66.	E
32.	B	67.	C
33.	E	68.	A
34.	A	69.	B
35.	C		

Social Sciences and History

Description of the Examination

The Social Sciences and History examination covers a wide range of topics from the social sciences and history disciplines. While the exam is based on no specific course, its content is drawn from introductory college courses that cover United States history, Western civilization, world history, government/political science, geography, sociology, economics, psychology, and anthropology.

The primary objective of the exam is to give candidates the opportunity to demonstrate that they possess the level of knowledge and understanding expected of college students who meet a distribution or general education requirement in the social sciences/history areas.

The Social Sciences and History examination contains approximately 120 questions to be answered in 90 minutes. Some of them are pretest questions that will not be scored. Any time candidates spend on tutorials and providing personal information is in addition to the actual testing time.

Note: This examination uses the chronological designations B.C.E. (before the common era) and C.E. (common era). These labels correspond to B.C. (before Christ) and A.D. (anno Domini), which are used in some textbooks.

Knowledge and Skills Required

The Social Sciences and History examination requires candidates to demonstrate one or more of the following abilities.

- Familiarity with terminology, facts, conventions, methodology, concepts, principles, generalizations, and theories
- Ability to understand, interpret, and analyze graphic, pictorial, and written material
- Ability to apply abstractions to particulars and to apply hypotheses, concepts, theories, and principles to given data

The content of the exam is drawn from the following disciplines. The percentages next to the main disciplines indicate the approximate percentage of exam questions on that topic.

40% History

Requires general knowledge and understanding of time- and place-specific human experiences. Topics covered include political, diplomatic, social, economic, intellectual, and cultural material.

17% United States History

Covers the colonial period, the American Revolution, the early republic, the Civil War and Reconstruction, industrialization, the Progressive Era, the First World War, the 1920s, the Great Depression and the New Deal, the Second World War, the 1950s, the Cold War, social conflict—the 1960s and 1970s, the late twentieth century

15% Western Civilization

Covers ancient Western Asia, Egypt, Greece, and Rome as well as medieval Europe and modern Europe, including its expansion and outposts in other parts of the world

8% World History

Covers Africa, Asia, Australia, Europe, North America, and South America from prehistory to the present, including global themes and interactions

13% Government/Political Science, including

Comparative politics
International relations
Methods
United States institutions
Voting and political behavior

11%   **Geography, including**

Cartographic methods
Cultural geography
Physical geography
Population
Regional geography
Spatial interaction

10%   **Economics, including**

Economic measurements
International trade
Major theorists and schools
Monetary and fiscal policy
Product markets
Resource markets
Scarcity, choice, and cost

10%   **Psychology, including**

Aggression
Biopsychology
Conformity
Group process
Major theorists and schools
Methods
Performance
Personality
Socialization

10%   **Sociology, including**

Demography
Deviance
Family
Interaction
Major theorists and schools
Methods
Social change
Social organization
Social stratification
Social theory

6%   **Anthropology, including**

Cultural anthropology
Ethnography
Major theorists and schools
Methods
Paleoanthropology

Sample Test Questions

The following sample questions do not appear on an actual CLEP examination. They are intended to give potential test-takers an indication of the format and difficulty level of the examination and to provide content for practice and review. Knowing the correct answers to all of the sample questions is not a guarantee of satisfactory performance on the exam.

Directions: Each of the questions or incomplete statements below is followed by five suggested answers or completions. Select the one that is best in each case.

1. Prior to the campaign of 1828, most candidates for president of the United States were nominated by

    (A) state legislatures
    (B) the electoral college
    (C) national party conventions
    (D) state primary elections
    (E) party leaders in Congress

2. Which of the following best describes the impact of Spanish colonization on the indigenous peoples of Central and South America in the sixteenth and early seventeenth centuries?

    (A) Their economic well-being was improved by the wealth they produced at the direction of the Spanish ruler.
    (B) They kept their own political system and culture, which coexisted with that of the Spanish colonial system.
    (C) They migrated in large numbers to Spain.
    (D) Their system of religious beliefs and practices was unaffected.
    (E) Their populations decreased dramatically as a result of contact with the Spanish.

3. An individual who believes that "government is best which governs not at all" favors

    (A) anarchy
    (B) tyranny
    (C) monarchy
    (D) oligarchy
    (E) democracy

4. Which of the following statements concerning the process of socialization is true?

    (A) In the upbringing of a child, the agencies of socialization tend to function together harmoniously.
    (B) In a modern society, the individual is subjected to many diverse socializing influences.
    (C) In a modern society, the media have little impact on the socialization of children.
    (D) In a traditional society, there are no socializing agencies.
    (E) In a traditional society, socializing influences are likely to be in conflict.

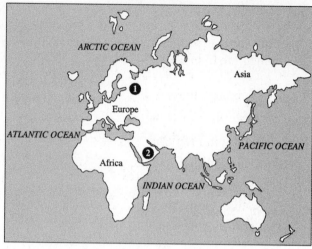

5. As depicted above, the Kurds could be described as which of the following?

   (A) Nation-state
   (B) Perforated state
   (C) Multinational state
   (D) Stateless nation
   (E) Fragmented state

6. Which of the following statements about the concept of charisma is correct?

   (A) It is possible only in the absence of legitimate authority.
   (B) It involves a basically political appeal.
   (C) It rests on the devotion of followers to an individual with exceptional qualities.
   (D) It is an inherited personality trait.
   (E) It is a prerequisite for high office in traditional societies.

7. A traveler going from point 1 to point 2 on the map above would experience a climatic change from

   (A) humid continental to desert
   (B) humid subtropical to Mediterranean
   (C) desert to tropical rain forest
   (D) tropical wet to Mediterranean
   (E) Mediterranean to humid continental

8. In general, cultures in which a belief in ancestral spirits exists regard such beings as

   (A) residing in heaven
   (B) responsible for natural disasters
   (C) unable to communicate directly with the living
   (D) beyond the spiritual reach of the living
   (E) retaining an active membership in the society

9. "To industry and frugality I owe the early easiness of my circumstances and the acquisition of my fortune with all that knowledge that has enabled me to be a useful citizen."

The statement above is most characteristic of which of the following?

(A) Benjamin Franklin
(B) Ralph Waldo Emerson
(C) Henry David Thoreau
(D) Samuel Gompers
(E) Thomas Jefferson

10. One of the fundamental changes that took place in the twentieth century was a gradual

(A) increase in manufacturing, as opposed to services, in developed nations
(B) increase in economic interdependence
(C) decrease in the pressure of world population on economic resources
(D) decline in world trade
(E) decline in nationalistic feelings among peoples of the Eastern Hemisphere

11. A person who lived in the 1790s in the United States and who believed in a strong central government, broad construction of the Constitution, and funding of the public debt would most probably have been

(A) a socialist
(B) an Anti-Federalist
(C) a Federalist
(D) a believer in monarchy
(E) a Jeffersonian Republican

12. Public opinion polls in the United States commonly make use of

(A) sampling theory
(B) case studies
(C) intelligence tests
(D) Rorschach tests
(E) clinical interviews

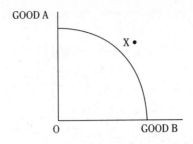

13. For the economy described by the production possibilities curve above, which of the following is true?

(A) Intended investment is greater than intended saving at point X.
(B) The economy cannot produce at point X using currently available resources and technology.
(C) The economy is more efficient in producing good A than good B.
(D) To produce additional units of good B, the economy must forgo fewer and fewer units of good A.
(E) Income is unequally distributed to the factors of production.

14. Which of the following statements about the control group in a well-designed experiment is correct?

(A) It differs from the experimental group in the way in which participants are sampled.
(B) It is like the experimental group and receives the same experimental treatment.
(C) It is like the experimental group except for differences in exposure to the dependent variable.
(D) It is like the experimental group except for differences in exposure to the independent variable.
(E) It must contain exactly the same number of individuals as does the experimental group.

15. The area of the African continent is approximately

    (A) half the area of western Europe
    (B) the same as the area of the United States east of the Mississippi River
    (C) two times the area of California
    (D) four times the area of the continental United States
    (E) five times the area of South America

16. Chinese culture and influence were most significant in shaping the institutions of which of the following countries?

    (A) Bangladesh, Pakistan, and Sri Lanka
    (B) India, Japan, and Korea
    (C) Indonesia, the Philippines, and Thailand
    (D) Japan, Korea, and Vietnam
    (E) Korea, Nepal, and the Philippines

17. The most immediate consequence of abolitionism in the United States in the 1830s and 1840s was

    (A) widespread support for the abolition of slavery
    (B) intensified slaveholders' resentment toward the movement
    (C) better treatment of freed African Americans in the North
    (D) greater sympathy for popular sovereignty
    (E) increased interest in African colonization

18. "We know so little about how to live in this life that there is no point in worrying about what may happen to us after death. First let us learn to live in the right way with other people and then let whatever happens next take care of itself."

    The quotation above best expresses the philosophy of

    (A) Jesus
    (B) Muhammad
    (C) Confucius
    (D) Karl Marx
    (E) Thomas Aquinas

19. Major political revolutions in the twentieth century most often occurred in countries with

    (A) comparatively low unemployment
    (B) high levels of industrialization
    (C) small industrial and large agricultural sectors
    (D) representative governments
    (E) small populations

20. The tendency for an individual's rank on one dimension of status to be positively correlated with that individual's rank on other dimensions of status is called

    (A) structural balance
    (B) rank ordering
    (C) status polarization
    (D) status congruence
    (E) status stability

21. To reduce inflationary pressure in the economy of the United States, the Federal Reserve would most likely

    (A) sell government securities on the open market
    (B) reduce margin requirements
    (C) lower legal reserve requirements
    (D) decrease the discount rate
    (E) encourage member banks to increase their loans

22. Participant satisfaction increases in those groups that

    (A) have competing subgroup interaction
    (B) are low in cohesion among group members
    (C) identify clear goals and supportive roles
    (D) have incompatible directions
    (E) fail to coordinate member interaction

23. Construction of the Panama Canal shortened the sailing time between New York and

    (A) London
    (B) Port-au-Prince
    (C) Rio de Janeiro
    (D) New Orleans
    (E) San Francisco

24. Of the following, which is the earliest human innovation?

    (A) Development of urban centers
    (B) Use of written language
    (C) Use and control of fire
    (D) Dependence on agriculture as the major source of food
    (E) Domestication of animals

25. Which of the following prompted African Americans to move to cities in the North during the first quarter of the twentieth century?

    I. The impact of the boll weevil
    II. The availability of industrial jobs in the North
    III. The impact of segregation legislation in the South

    (A) II only
    (B) I and II only
    (C) I and III only
    (D) II and III only
    (E) I, II, and III

26. Abolition of the transatlantic slave trade was difficult to achieve in the early 1800s because

    (A) the British were strongly in favor of slavery
    (B) slave labor was needed in Europe
    (C) profits from the slave trade were high
    (D) most countries in Europe had extensive African colonies
    (E) slavery was widespread in all parts of the Americas

27. Among the several social science methods of research, the one used for conducting public opinion polls can best be described as

    (A) laboratory experimentation
    (B) participant observation
    (C) field experimentation
    (D) survey research
    (E) computer simulation

28. An aging population necessarily has

    (A) a population pyramid with a large base
    (B) more males than females
    (C) a decreasing death rate
    (D) an increasing median age
    (E) an increasing birth rate

UNITED STATES MARKET FOR APPLES

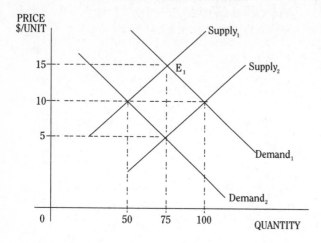

29. The United States market for apples is in equilibrium at E_1, where 75 units are sold at a price of $15 per unit. If consumers' per capita disposable income decreases, the equilibrium price and quantity of apples sold can be which of the following?

	Unit Price	Quantity
(A)	$15	75
(B)	$10	50
(C)	$10	100
(D)	$ 5	75
(E)	$ 5	100

30. In psychology, the biosocial approach seeks to explain behavior in terms of

(A) environmental influences

(B) genetic factors

(C) unconscious motivations

(D) an integration of cultural and biological factors

(E) genetic drifts within population groups

31. In the late twentieth century, Islamic fundamentalism had the LEAST influence in which of the following countries?

(A) Algeria

(B) China

(C) Egypt

(D) India

(E) Indonesia

32. Which of the following is true of the First Amendment to the United States Constitution?

(A) It established presidential control over the budget.

(B) It created the Supreme Court.

(C) It declared all people to be equal.

(D) It established the foundations for church-state relations.

(E) It guaranteed citizens the right to bear arms.

33. The Peloponnesian Wars were primarily the result of

(A) Athenian imperialism

(B) Spartan militarism

(C) the invasion of Greece by Rome

(D) the conquests of Alexander the Great

(E) the spread of Athenian democracy

34. Which of the following economic policies is likely to result in the greatest reduction in aggregate demand?

(A) A $5-billion increase in personal income taxes only

(B) A $5-billion decrease in government transfer payments only

(C) A $5-billion decrease in government purchases of goods and services only

(D) A $5-billion decrease in government purchases accompanied by a $5-billion increase in personal income taxes

(E) A $5-billion decrease in government purchases accompanied by a $5-billion decrease in personal income taxes

35. Which of the following philosophers asserted that all human beings possess the natural rights to life, liberty, and property?

(A) Thomas Hobbes

(B) John Locke

(C) Augustine of Hippo

(D) Aristotle

(E) Socrates

36. Which of the following is NOT compatible with the traditional conception of bureaucracy?

(A) Salaried remuneration

(B) Recruitment of personnel by examination

(C) A hierarchical structure

(D) Decentralization of authority

(E) Formal allocation of obligation and duties

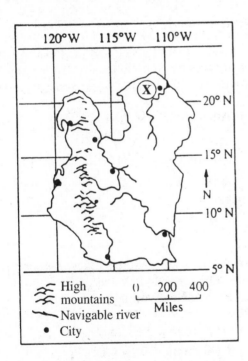

37. According to the map above, which of the following land formations would most likely be found near City X?

(A) A plateau

(B) A volcano

(C) A delta

(D) A peninsula

(E) A mountain

38. On the basis of empirical evidence gathered during the Second World War, which of the following was most successful in motivating United States soldiers to perform well under overseas combat conditions?

(A) Emphasizing to them that the civilian population was dependent on them

(B) Developing their dedication to dominant political and ethical values

(C) Instilling in the soldiers a loyalty to national leaders

(D) Developing in the soldiers a satisfactory self-image of their individual abilities

(E) Emphasizing positive relationships among members of small combat units

39. Of the following, which group was the first to establish trade links with both East Africa and the upper Niger Valley?

(A) The Portuguese

(B) The English

(C) The Arabs

(D) The Spanish

(E) The French

40. John Steinbeck's novel *The Grapes of Wrath* depicts the period of United States history known as the

(A) Gilded Age

(B) Roaring Twenties

(C) Great Depression

(D) Cold War

(E) Vietnam era

41. The Green Revolution of the twentieth century refers to

    (A) the unparalleled strength of the United States dollar
    (B) increased agricultural productivity due to the introduction of new crops and technologies
    (C) the rise of a social and political movement expressing strong environmental concerns
    (D) the destruction of Brazilian rain forests
    (E) the political development of tropical countries previously under colonial rule

42. Which of the following is the most significant effect of mass media on national elections in the United States?

    (A) Helping shape the agenda for political debate
    (B) Improving the exposure of little-known candidates
    (C) Defining party platforms
    (D) Reducing the influence of money in politics
    (E) Decreasing the accountability of incumbent officials

43. Which of the following methods of data collection provides the most comprehensive information?

    (A) Face-to-face interviews
    (B) Telephone surveys
    (C) Mail surveys
    (D) Interest inventories
    (E) Opinion polls

44. Which of the following would increase the demand for workers in the short run?

    (A) A decrease in the demand for machinery
    (B) An increase in the cost of production
    (C) An increase in the price of the product
    (D) A decrease in the demand for the product
    (E) A decrease in available natural resources

45. Which of the following areas of the brain is involved in control of aggression and fear?

    (A) Hypothalamus
    (B) Cerebellum
    (C) Amygdala
    (D) Cortex
    (E) Pituitary

46. The cartoonist for *Harper's Weekly* who played a major role in turning public sentiment against New York City's Boss Tweed was

    (A) Grant Wood
    (B) Winslow Homer
    (C) Matt Morgan
    (D) Thomas Nast
    (E) Norman Rockwell

47. Which of the following cultures provided a link between ancient Greece and medieval western Europe, designed methods for making steel and leather, and contributed to scientific knowledge of mathematics?

    (A) Celtic
    (B) Carolingian
    (C) Gothic
    (D) Islamic
    (E) Norman

48. After their defeat by the Chinese Communists in 1949, Chiang Kai-shek and many supporters of his Nationalist government chose to

    (A) emigrate to the United States
    (B) ally with the Soviet Union
    (C) flee to Tibet
    (D) accept Chinese Communist rule
    (E) flee to the island of Taiwan (Formosa)

49. In sociology and anthropology, a cultural lag occurs when

    (A) cultural norms have not adapted to new material conditions

    (B) wealth and income are distributed unequally

    (C) individuals who are labeled deviate fail to live up to their potential

    (D) people from one culture are immersed in a wholly different culture

    (E) the younger generation of a society rejects the ideas of the older generation

50. According to international relations (IR) theory, nation-states that join international organizations are usually motivated by

    (A) the desire to move toward world government

    (B) respect for legal norms

    (C) popular pressure to join such organizations

    (D) self-interest

    (E) religious belief

51. The Russo-Japanese War (1904–1905) resulted in

    (A) expanded export trade for Russia

    (B) predominance of the Russian navy in East Asia

    (C) Japan's acquisition of Taiwan

    (D) the opening of Japanese ports to foreign trade

    (E) a significant weakening of the tsarist government

52. The Dawes Severalty Act, which was passed by the United States Congress in 1887, did which of the following?

    (A) Stopped all homesteading west of the Mississippi River.

    (B) Extended voting rights to Native Americans.

    (C) Resulted in the notorious Trail of Tears.

    (D) Divided tribally held lands among individual Native Americans.

    (E) Extended welfare assistance to Native Americans.

53. European imperialism in Africa in the last quarter of the nineteenth century differed from European imperialism in Africa of earlier periods in which of the following ways?

    (A) It encouraged the African colonization movement in the United States.

    (B) It promoted the integration of indigenous peoples into all sectors of colonial society.

    (C) It combined commerce with extensive territorial acquisitions.

    (D) Its aim was to prepare colonies for independence and democracy.

    (E) Its central goal was the abolition of the slave trade.

54. For African Americans, the reduction of European immigration during the First World War resulted in which of the following?

    (A) Government encouragement of African immigration to the United States

    (B) The endorsement of the racial policies of Woodrow Wilson by the National Association for the Advancement of Colored People (NAACP)

    (C) The rise of African Americans to positions of power in Southern politics

    (D) The establishment of Marcus Garvey's Back to Africa movement

    (E) The opening of industrial jobs to African American workers

55. Which of the following would be an example of the Columbian Exchange?

   (A) The exchange rate between the Colombian peso and the United States dollar
   (B) The introduction of horses and cattle into the Western Hemisphere
   (C) The expansion of cocoa bean production to Bolivia and Peru
   (D) The introduction of rice to Europe
   (E) The introduction of coffee to Europe

56. Puerto Rico became part of the territorial holdings of the United States as a result of the

   (A) Monroe Doctrine
   (B) Gadsden Purchase
   (C) Treaty of Guadalupe Hidalgo
   (D) Spanish-American War
   (E) Adams-Onís Treaty

57. Which of the following is an example of a tertiary economic activity?

   (A) Cultivation of wheat in the Midwest
   (B) Manufacture of automobiles in Detroit
   (C) Offshore oil drilling in the Gulf of Mexico
   (D) Development of ecotourism in Costa Rica
   (E) Clothing assembly in Malaysia

58. An isogloss delineates a region of common

   (A) temperature
   (B) barometric pressure
   (C) altitude
   (D) dialect
   (E) religion

59. Which of the following Latin American countries was one of the original members of the Organization of the Petroleum Exporting Countries (OPEC)?

   (A) Mexico
   (B) Brazil
   (C) Venezuela
   (D) Colombia
   (E) Peru

60. Which of the following has been a sacred site for both Christians and Muslims?

   (A) The Kaaba in Mecca
   (B) Taj Mahal in Agra
   (C) Hagia Sophia in Istanbul
   (D) Pyramids in Egypt
   (E) Angkor Wat in Cambodia

61. In the United States and European countries, mobilization for the Second World War differed from mobilization for the First World War for which of the following reasons?

   (A) During the First World War, governments rationed supplies.
   (B) During the First World War, governments banned immigration.
   (C) During the First World War, governments banned labor unions.
   (D) During the Second World War, governments recruited women to work in weapons industries.
   (E) During the Second World War, governments established agencies to regulate industrial production.

62. The United States Immigration Act of 1965 was significant because it

(A) led to increased immigration of scientists from Western Europe

(B) led to increased immigration of professionals from Asia

(C) led to increased immigration of agricultural laborers from Mexico

(D) prohibited immigration from Communist countries

(E) prohibited immigration of unskilled laborers

63. Phillis Wheatley, a slave during the revolutionary era in the United States, was

(A) a seamstress who bought her freedom from slavery

(B) a domestic servant who shielded patriots

(C) a published author who wrote many poems

(D) an artist who painted revolutionary scenes

(E) a spy who provided information on British troop movements

64. Which of the following would shift the supply curve for gasoline rightward?

(A) An increase in the demand for sport-utility vehicles, which use more gas

(B) A situation where the quantity demanded exceeds the quantity supplied

(C) A decrease in the price of a resource used to produce gasoline, such as crude oil

(D) An increase in the price of gasoline

(E) An increase in the price of a resource used to produce gasoline, such as crude oil

65. A map 2 feet by 3 feet at a scale of 1:100,000 would display the appropriate amount of detail for doing which of the following?

(A) Providing block-level directions from a residence to a local elementary school

(B) Displaying national weather patterns

(C) Determining the best location for a new shopping center

(D) Planning a cross-country road trip

(E) Identifying highway directions to a city 25 miles away

66. The United States Constitution denies some powers to both national and state governments in order to

(A) prevent the deployment of the National Guard

(B) allow citizens to hold federal officers accountable

(C) safeguard individual rights

(D) deny unfair welfare practices

(E) provide protection of labor rights

67. The greatest crisis of the United States federal system occurred during the

(A) American Revolution

(B) Civil War

(C) First World War

(D) Cold War

(E) Vietnam War

68. To maximize total utility, a consumer will consume a product at the point where

(A) marginal utility per dollar spent on each good is equal

(B) total utility per dollar spent on each good is equal

(C) total utility from each good is equal to zero

(D) marginal utility from each good is equal to zero

(E) marginal utility is equal to zero

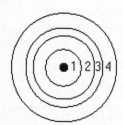
- City
1. Dairying and market gardening
2. Cash grain and livestock
3. Mixed farming
4. Extensive grain farming or stock raising

69. According to von Thünen's model, shown above, key factors in determining the relative locations of agricultural activities near a city include which of the following?

I. Distance to market for perishable goods

II. Land costs versus land needs for different forms of agriculture

III. Population size of the market area

IV. Modes of transportation

(A) I only

(B) I and II only

(C) II and III only

(D) II, III, and IV only

(E) I, II, III, and IV

Study Resources

Most of the textbooks used in college-level social sciences and history courses cover the topics in the outline given earlier, but the approaches to certain topics and the emphases given to them may differ. To prepare for the Social Sciences and History exam, it is advisable to study one or more college textbooks for United States and world history, sociology, Western civilization, and other related courses, which can be found in most college bookstores. When selecting a textbook, check the table of contents against the knowledge and skills required for this test.

The materials suggested for preparing for other CLEP exams may also be helpful. Study resources for the American Government, History of the United States I and II, Principles of Macroeconomics and Principles of Microeconomics, Introductory Psychology, Introductory Sociology, and Western Civilization I and II exams are particularly relevant and can be found in the Study Resources section of the *Official Study Guide* for these exams.

Visit www.collegeboard.com/clepprep for additional social sciences and history resources. You can also find suggestions for exam preparation in Chapter IV of the *Official Study Guide*. In addition, many college faculty post their course materials on their schools' Web sites.

Answer Key

1.	E	36.	D
2.	E	37.	C
3.	A	38.	E
4.	B	39.	C
5.	D	40.	C
6.	C	41.	B
7.	A	42.	A
8.	E	43.	A
9.	A	44.	C
10.	B	45.	C
11.	C	46.	D
12.	A	47.	D
13.	B	48.	E
14.	D	49.	A
15.	D	50.	D
16.	D	51.	E
17.	B	52.	D
18.	C	53.	C
19.	C	54.	E
20.	D	55.	B
21.	A	56.	D
22.	C	57.	D
23.	E	58.	D
24.	C	59.	C
25.	E	60.	C
26.	C	61.	D
27.	D	62.	B
28.	D	63.	C
29.	B	64.	C
30.	D	65.	E
31.	B	66.	C
32.	D	67.	B
33.	A	68.	A
34.	D	69.	B
35.	B		

Western Civilization I

Description of the Examination

The Western Civilization I: Ancient Near East to 1648 examination covers material that is usually taught in the first semester of a two-semester course in Western Civilization. Questions deal with the civilizations of Ancient Greece, Rome, and the Near East; the Middle Ages; the Renaissance and Reformation; and early modern Europe. Candidates may be asked to choose the correct definition of a historical term, select the historical figure whose political viewpoint is described, identify the correct relationship between two historical factors, or detect the inaccurate pairing of an individual with a historical event. Groups of questions may require candidates to interpret, evaluate, or relate the contents of a passage, a map, or a picture to other information, or to analyze and utilize the data contained in a graph or table.

The examination contains approximately 120 questions to be answered in 90 minutes. Some of these are pretest questions that will not be scored. Any time candidates spend on tutorials and providing personal information is in addition to the actual testing time. This examination uses the chronological designations B.C.E. (before the common era) and C.E. (common era). The labels correspond to B.C. (before Christ) and A.D. (anno Domini), which are used in some textbooks.

Knowledge and Skills Required

Questions on the Western Civilization I examination require candidates to demonstrate one or more of the following abilities.

- Understanding important factual knowledge of developments in Western Civilization
- Ability to identify the causes and effects of major historical events
- Ability to analyze, interpret, and evaluate textual and graphic historical materials
- Ability to distinguish the relevant from the irrelevant
- Ability to reach conclusions on the basis of facts

The subject matter of the Western Civilization I examination is drawn from the following topics. The percentages next to the main topics indicate the approximate percentage of exam questions on that topic.

8–10% Ancient Near East

Political evolution

Religion, culture, and technical developments in and near the Fertile Crescent

15–17% Ancient Greece and Hellenistic Civilization

Political evolution to Periclean Athens

Periclean Athens through the Peloponnesian Wars

Culture, religion, and thought of Ancient Greece

The Hellenistic political structure

The culture, religion, and thought of Hellenistic Greece

15–17% Ancient Rome

Political evolution of the Republic and of the Empire (economic and geographical context)

Roman thought and culture

Early Christianity

The Germanic invasions

The late empire

23–27% Medieval History

Byzantium and Islam

Early medieval politics and culture through Charlemagne

Feudal and manorial institutions

The medieval Church

Medieval thought and culture

Rise of the towns and changing economic forms

Feudal monarchies

The late medieval church

13–17% Renaissance and Reformation

The Renaissance in Italy

The Renaissance outside Italy

The New Monarchies

Protestantism and Catholicism reformed and reorganized

10–15% Early Modern Europe, 1560–1648

The opening of the Atlantic

The Commercial Revolution

Dynastic and religious conflicts

Thought and culture

Sample Test Questions

The following sample questions do not appear on an actual CLEP examination. They are intended to give potential test-takers an indication of the format and difficulty level of the examination and to provide content for practice and review. Knowing the correct answers to all of the sample questions is not a guarantee of satisfactory performance on the exam.

Directions: Each of the questions or incomplete statements below is followed by five suggested answers or completions. Select the one that is best in each case.

1. The earliest urban settlements arose in which of the following types of areas?

   (A) Coastal plains

   (B) Inland deforested plains

   (C) Desert oases

   (D) Fertile river valleys

   (E) Narrow valleys well protected by mountains

© Bettman/CORBIS

2. The panel above from ancient Ur supports which of the following conclusions about Mesopotamian society?

   (A) It was primarily composed of hunter-gatherers.

   (B) It had distinct class divisions.

   (C) Religion pervaded daily life.

   (D) Soldiers were drawn primarily from the nobility.

   (E) Most commoners were slaves.

3. "The great wealth of the palaces and the widespread prosperity of the land were due to the profits of trade, protected or exploited by naval vessels equipped with rams. The palaces and towns were unfortified, and peaceful scenes predominated in the frescoes, which revealed a love of dancing, boxing, and a sport in which boys and girls somersaulted over the backs of charging bulls."

   The culture described above was that of the ancient

   (A) Minoans

   (B) Hittites

   (C) Macedonians

   (D) Assyrians

   (E) Persians

4. "These people maintained their skill as seafarers, traders, and artists. They planted Carthage and other colonies in the western Mediterranean. They developed a new script in which a separate sign stood not for a syllable, but for a consonant or vowel sound."

   The people described above were the

   (A) Phoenicians

   (B) Hittites

   (C) Assyrians

   (D) Mycenaeans

   (E) Philistines

5. Pharaoh Akhenaton of Egypt (c. 1375–1358 B.C.E.) is best known today for

   (A) building the largest pyramid in the Valley of the Kings

   (B) conquering large expanses of territory outside of the Nile Valley

   (C) developing a monotheistic religion

   (D) uniting upper and lower Egypt under a single administrative system

   (E) writing down the first code of Egyptian law

6. Among the ancient Hebrews, a prophet was

    (A) a teacher who expounded the Scriptures
    (B) a king with hereditary but limited powers
    (C) a judge who administered traditional law
    (D) a priest with exclusive rights to perform functions at the temple
    (E) an individual who was inspired by God to speak to the people

7. The outstanding achievement of King Hammurabi of Mesopotamia was that he

    (A) issued a more comprehensive law code than had any known predecessor
    (B) conquered and established dominion over all of Egypt
    (C) built the Hanging Gardens of Babylon
    (D) established the first democratic government
    (E) successfully defended his kingdom against the Assyrians

8. Of the following, which helps explain why the Roman Republic gave way to dictatorship during the first century B.C.E.?

    (A) The government that was suitable for a small city-state failed to meet the needs of an empire.
    (B) A strong leader was needed because the upper classes feared a rebellion on the part of the slave population.
    (C) Outside pressures on boundaries could not be resisted by republican armies.
    (D) Rome's period of expansion was over.
    (E) The Roman senatorial class was declining in number.

9. All of the following were emphasized by the early Christian church EXCEPT a

    (A) ritual fellowship meal in memory of Christ
    (B) toleration of other religious sects
    (C) belief in the value of the souls of women and slaves as well as those of free men
    (D) belief in life after death for all believers in Christ
    (E) belief in the value of martyrdom, defined as dying for the faith

10. The Roman emperor whose policies rescued Rome from its crisis in the third century C.E. was

    (A) Augustus
    (B) Marcus Aurelius
    (C) Constantine
    (D) Diocletian
    (E) Theodosius

11. Which of the following established Christianity as a legal religion in the Roman Empire?

    (A) The defeat of the Huns, 451 C.E.
    (B) The accession of Justinian I
    (C) The Council of Nicaea
    (D) The accession of Diocletian
    (E) The Edict of Milan

12. All of the following invaded the Roman Empire EXCEPT the

    (A) Vikings
    (B) Ostrogoths
    (C) Visigoths
    (D) Vandals
    (E) Huns

13. The craft guilds of the Middle Ages had as their primary purpose the

    (A) promotion of trade and the protection of merchants
    (B) control of town government
    (C) regulation of production and quality
    (D) guardianship of the social and financial affairs of their members
    (E) accumulation of capital and the lending of money

14. Between the ninth and the thirteenth centuries, all of the following technological elements contributed to improved agricultural production in Europe EXCEPT the

    (A) heavy plow
    (B) horse collar
    (C) horseshoe
    (D) water mill
    (E) seed drill

15. The orders of Franciscan and Dominican friars founded in the thirteenth century differed from earlier monastic orders principally in that the friars

    (A) took vows of poverty, chastity, and obedience
    (B) broke away from the control of the pope
    (C) introduced the ideas of Plato and other early Greek philosophers into their teaching
    (D) devoted themselves mainly to copying ancient manuscripts
    (E) traveled among the people instead of living in monasteries

16. All of the following factors played a part in bringing about the Hundred Years' War EXCEPT

    (A) The English king had lands in Gascony.
    (B) A French princess was the mother of an English king.
    (C) Flemish towns were dependent on England for raw wool.
    (D) The Holy Roman Emperor wanted to bring pressure on the Swiss cantons.
    (E) The Capetian dynasty had come to an end.

17. Civil peace and personal security were enjoyed to a greater degree in Norman England than in continental Europe principally because the Norman kings

    (A) maintained a large standing army
    (B) claimed the direct allegiance of the mass of the peasantry
    (C) avoided conflicts with the Church
    (D) kept their vassals occupied with continental conflicts
    (E) developed a centralized and efficient type of feudalism

18. Which of the following could have been made immediately available to the reading public in large quantities as soon as it was written?

    (A) *On Christian Liberty*, Martin Luther
    (B) *Travels*, Marco Polo
    (C) *The Divine Comedy*, Dante Alighieri
    (D) *Canterbury Tales*, Geoffrey Chaucer
    (E) English translation of the Bible, John Wycliffe

19. A central feature of the Catholic Reformation was the

    (A) Roman Catholic church's inability to correct abuses
    (B) establishment of new religious orders such as the Jesuits
    (C) transfer of authority from Rome to the bishoprics
    (D) rejection of Baroque art
    (E) toleration of Protestants in Roman Catholic countries

© Bettman/CORBIS

20. The building in Córdoba, Spain, shown above, illustrates the influence of

(A) Islam
(B) Buddhism
(C) Hinduism
(D) Shinto
(E) Animism

21. The major consequence of the rise of towns in the eleventh and twelfth centuries was

(A) a lessening of the distinction among social classes
(B) the practice of caring for the indigent
(C) the decline of royal authority
(D) the decline in the social status of the lesser clergy
(E) a new social class enriched by manufacturing and trade

22. In *The Prince*, Machiavelli asserted that

(A) historical examples are useless for understanding political behavior
(B) the intelligent prince should keep his state neutral in the event of war
(C) people are not trustworthy and cannot be relied on in time of need
(D) the prince should be guided by the ethical principles of Christianity
(E) luck is of no consequence in the success or failure of princes

23. On which of the following issues did Luther and Calvin DISAGREE?

(A) The toleration for minority viewpoints
(B) The relationship of the church to civil authority
(C) The authority of the Scriptures
(D) The existence of the Trinity
(E) The retention of the sacrament of baptism

24. The principle that the religion of the ruler of a state determines the established church in that state was central to the

(A) Peace of Augsburg
(B) Peace of the Pyrenees
(C) Congress of Vienna
(D) Edict of Restitution
(E) Peace of Westphalia

25. Between 1629 and 1639, Charles I of England tried to obtain revenues by all of the following means EXCEPT

(A) the levying of ship money
(B) income from crown lands
(C) forced loans
(D) the sale of monopolies
(E) grants from Parliament

26. All of the following are associated with the commercial revolution in early modern Europe EXCEPT

(A) an increase in the number of entrepreneurial capitalists
(B) the appearance of state-run trading companies
(C) a large influx of precious metals into Europe
(D) an expansion of the guild system
(E) a "golden age" for the Netherlands

27. Castiglione's *Book of the Courtier* (1528) was intended as

(A) a collection of entertaining travel stories

(B) a guide to the military affairs of the Italian peninsula

(C) a collection of meditations and spiritual reflections

(D) a guide to refined behavior and etiquette

(E) an allegory of courtly love

28. Which of the following resulted from the defeat of the Spanish Armada in 1588?

(A) Spanish domination of the Mediterranean was ended.

(B) The invasion of England was prevented.

(C) Dutch sympathies for the Spanish cause increased.

(D) War broke out between England and France.

(E) There was a series of uprisings in the Spanish colonies of Central and South America.

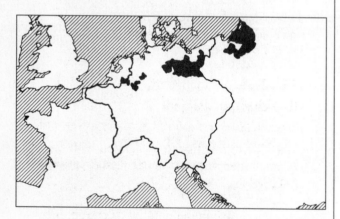

29. In the mid-seventeenth century, the area shaded black on the map above belonged to

(A) Russia

(B) Poland

(C) Sweden

(D) Austria

(E) Brandenburg-Prussia

30. The theory concerning the solar system that was published by Copernicus in 1543 REJECTED the popular belief that

(A) Earth revolves around the Sun

(B) Earth revolves around the Moon

(C) Earth is the center of the universe

(D) the Sun is the center of the universe

(E) the stars revolve around the Sun

31. During their next war with the Persians following the battle of Marathon, the Athenians won a decisive victory through their use of

(A) horse-drawn chariots

(B) new kinds of iron weapons

(C) mounted archers

(D) incendiary weapons

(E) sea power

32. "Almost every kind of human activity was accepted as worthy of offering to the gods—athletic contests, poetry reading, song, dance, drama, prayer, giftbearing . . . There were no elaborate priesthoods; fathers conducted rituals in the household and elected officials served as priests in the civic ceremonies."

The religion described above is probably that of the ancient

(A) Egyptians

(B) Sumerians

(C) Greeks

(D) Hebrews

(E) Persians

33. All of the following peoples settled Roman lands bordering on the Mediterranean EXCEPT the

(A) Franks

(B) Visigoths

(C) Jutes

(D) Ostrogoths

(E) Vandals

34. "I found Rome a city of brick and left it a city of marble."

The claim above was made by

(A) Pompey

(B) Julius Caesar

(C) Augustus

(D) Tiberius

(E) Hadrian

35. Which of the following did St. Francis of Assisi and Dante Alighieri have in common?

(A) They were heretics.

(B) They were university teachers.

(C) They were religious mystics.

(D) They were products of commercial towns.

(E) They favored the supremacy of the state over the Church.

36. Henry II (1154–1189) increased royal authority in England chiefly by his

(A) confiscation of Church lands

(B) usurpation of the legislative authority of Parliament

(C) proclamation of the divine right of kings

(D) formation of an alliance with the papacy

(E) enlargement of the jurisdiction and powers of royal courts

37. Which of the following was a primary goal of Cardinal Richelieu's foreign policy?

(A) The weakening of the Hapsburgs diplomatically and militarily

(B) The reestablishment of religious unity in Europe

(C) The consolidation of French holdings in North America

(D) The strengthening of papal influence within the French government

(E) The founding of commercial companies on the Anglo-Dutch model

38. Which of the following was the most effective leader of the Protestant forces in the Thirty Years' War?

(A) Albert of Wallenstein

(B) Emperor Ferdinand II

(C) The Elector Palatine Frederick V

(D) Gustavus Adolphus of Sweden

(E) Christian IV of Denmark

39. The reluctance of Elizabeth I of England to open "windows into men's souls" was an indication of her

(A) atheism

(B) withdrawal from public pageantry

(C) reluctance to inquire closely into personal religious views

(D) reluctance to prosecute political opponents

(E) insistence on personal rule

The Metropolitan Museum of Art, Rogers Fund, 1930 (30.4.44)
Image © The Metropolitan Museum of Art

40. The wall painting shown above depicts which of the following?

   (A) The division of labor by gender in rural Etruscan society

   (B) The poor treatment of slaves in ancient Greece

   (C) Activities of children in Sumerian society

   (D) Men and women working in the fields in ancient Egypt

   (E) Roman soldiers celebrating a victory

41. Which of the following was a major innovation of the Renaissance period?

   (A) The use of linear perspective in painting

   (B) The use of marble as a medium for statuary

   (C) The dome

   (D) The portico

   (E) Fresco painting

Bridgeman Art Library

42. The equestrian statue shown depicts a warrior active in

(A) Rome under Augustus
(B) Asia under the Mongol Empire
(C) Italy during the Renaissance
(D) France during the Protestant Reformation
(E) Bohemia at the time of the Thirty Years' War

43. Which of the following describes Luther's reaction to the Peasants' Revolt of 1525?

(A) He first sought what he considered a balanced solution and then strongly supported the lords.
(B) He abandoned his initial support of the lords in favor of the peasants.
(C) He sought throughout to act as a mediator between the lords and peasants.
(D) He declined to act on the grounds that his ministry did not concern itself with politics.
(E) He called on the Holy Roman Emperor to intervene.

44. "The height of the medieval papacy came with his pontificate . . . In the year before his death he called the greatest church council since antiquity, attended by five hundred bishops and even by the patriarchs of Constantinople and Jerusalem."

The pope referred to in the passage above is

(A) Julius II
(B) Urban II
(C) Innocent III
(D) Nicholas V
(E) Pius II

45. Which of the following was true of medieval universities?

(A) They taught only philosophy.
(B) They were open only to men of noble birth.
(C) They were considered subversive of the feudal system by many kings.
(D) They were corporations of teachers and students.
(E) They emphasized instruction in the vernacular.

46. Which of the following is a major tenet of scholasticism?

(A) An insistence on the freedom of the individual
(B) The use of logic as a tool of analysis and inquiry
(C) The belief in benevolence as the greatest human virtue
(D) A dedication to the ideals of classical art
(E) A devotion to the spirit of Roman poetry and literature

47. Which of the following contributed to Portugal's lead in overseas expansion in the fifteenth century?

   I. The creation of accurate maps

   II. The development of better navigational instruments

   III. Improvement in the design of ships

   IV. Availability of large numbers of galley slaves

    (A) I only

    (B) II and III only

    (C) I, II, and III only

    (D) I, II, and IV only

    (E) II, III, and IV only

48. Which of the following explains why mercantilism was adopted by most absolute monarchs?

    (A) Many merchants became advisers to the kings.

    (B) Mercantilists favored railroad development, which increased the mobility of the royal armies.

    (C) Mercantilists proposed the enrichment of the state as their chief objective.

    (D) Mercantilists were invariably opposed to parliamentary government.

    (E) Mercantilism encouraged local autonomy, weakening the power of the aristocracy.

The Metropolitan Museum of Art, Bequest of Walter C. Baker, 1971 (1972.118.95)
Image © The Metropolitan Museum of Art.

49. The picture above shows a bronze statue created in which of the following cultures?

    (A) Mycenaean

    (B) Etruscan

    (C) Hellenistic

    (D) Egyptian

    (E) Byzantine

50. "O supreme generosity of God the Father, O highest and most marvelous felicity of man! To him it is granted to have whatever he chooses, to be whatever he wills."

The quotation above is taken from

    (A) Petrarch, *Lives of Illustrious Men*

    (B) Dante Alighieri, *The New Life*

    (C) Machiavelli, *The Prince*

    (D) Pico della Mirandola, *Oration on the Dignity of Man*

    (E) Chaucer, *The Canterbury Tales*

51. "You must realize this: that a prince, and especially a new prince, cannot observe all those things which give men a reputation for virtue, because in order to maintain his state he is often forced to act in defiance of good faith, of charity, of kindness, of religion."

The quote above addresses which of the following in Renaissance Italy?

(A) The transitory nature of political power

(B) The threat of papal power

(C) The dangers of political liberty

(D) The threat of French Invasion

(E) The bad reputation of certain Renaissance artists

52. The Treaty of Westphalia, which ended the Thirty Years' War in 1648, resulted in

(A) a defeat for Swedish imperialism in northern Europe

(B) the consolidation of Bourbon control over Germany

(C) ratification of the territorial fragmentation of Germany

(D) a step toward restoring religious unity in Europe

(E) the restoration of an independent kingdom of Bohemia

53. Which of the following did ancient Grecian Homeric society value most?

(A) Education for all children

(B) An aristocratic warrior class

(C) A patron-client relationship

(D) Peace and pacifism

(E) Women as entrepreneurs

54. Which of the following statements best illustrates the status of women in the High Middle Ages?

(A) Courtly literature portrayed women as objects of devotion.

(B) Formal education was available to middle-class women.

(C) Religious orders offered a protective haven for abused women.

(D) Only propertied widows were allowed to remarry.

(E) Women artisans often joined guilds.

55. Which of the following was a major feature of the Hebrew religion?

(A) It promoted the feeling that the Hebrews were God's chosen people.

(B) It allowed the worship of different gods and goddesses.

(C) It owed much of its theology to ancient Mesopotamian religious cults.

(D) It did not apply to the social, political, or economic areas of life.

(E) It made its greatest impact in the arts and architecture.

56. A major effect of the flying buttress used in the construction of Gothic buildings was to

(A) eliminate the use of mortar

(B) reduce the size of the clerestory

(C) allow more light into the buildings

(D) provide more exterior space for decoration

(E) create the optical illusion that cathedrals were wider at their bases

57. The success of the First Crusade in gaining control of Muslim territory was primarily attributed to the

    (A) participation of women
    (B) superior firepower of the papal armies
    (C) neutrality maintained by the papacy
    (D) disunity of the Muslim world
    (E) desire for a Jewish state

58. Which of the following rightfully could be called the Empire of the Steppe?

    (A) The Ottoman Empire
    (B) The Mongol Empire
    (C) The Parthian Empire
    (D) The Byzantine Empire
    (E) The T'ang Empire

59. Russia's Time of Troubles (1604–1613) ended with which of the following?

    (A) Expulsion of a Polish occupying army and election of a new ruling family
    (B) Ejection of the Mongol/Tatar occupiers from Russia
    (C) A successful war against the Turks
    (D) Annexation of Ukraine
    (E) Massive serf revolts

60. Which of the following individuals did the most to spread Greek culture?

    (A) Aristotle
    (B) Xerxes
    (C) Ptolemy
    (D) Euclid
    (E) Alexander the Great

61. The Reformation in Germany and the Reformation in England had which of the following in common?

    (A) The King of England and the Holy Roman Emperor led the Reformation.
    (B) Both permitted believers to freely choose among doctrines.
    (C) Both preserved monastic orders.
    (D) They modified Roman Catholic teaching on divorce.
    (E) They spread their doctrines by military conquest.

62. Which of the following most accurately defines feudalism?

    (A) A system of strong central government
    (B) An economic agreement between social unequals
    (C) An agreement to substitute money payments for military service
    (D) A political and military relationship between social equals
    (E) A religious movement

63. The bubonic plague led to improvements in which of the following?

    (A) Workers' wages
    (B) Church reform
    (C) Prison conditions
    (D) Transportation
    (E) Bookbinding

64. Augustine (354–430) asserted in his *City of God*, written between 413 and 426, that

(A) laws and government are unnecessary in a Christian society

(B) humans must strive for spiritual purity, not earthly pleasures

(C) sexual abstinence is unnatural

(D) God rarely intervenes in the events of human history

(E) Jesus Christ is not divine

65. The Age of Pericles was characterized by all of the following EXCEPT

(A) the political domination of Greece by Athens

(B) the historical writings of Herodotus

(C) an ambitious building program

(D) the formation of the Delian League

(E) reforms of Athenian democracy

66. Which ancient culture produced the "Epic of Gilgamesh"?

(A) Egyptian

(B) Hittite

(C) Assyrian

(D) Hebrew

(E) Sumerian

67. An important contribution of Thomas Aquinas was his effort to

(A) reconcile reason and the teachings of Aristotle with Christian faith

(B) reestablish the supremacy of the Pope

(C) defeat the Franks

(D) win northern Africa back from Islam

(E) halt the progress of the Reformation in Spain

68. Which of the following is a true statement regarding John Calvin?

(A) He agreed with both Luther and Zwingli on the Eucharist.

(B) He opposed the doctrine of predestination.

(C) He emphasized the omnipotence and omnipresence of God.

(D) He believed in the separation of church and state.

(E) He practiced religious tolerance when he governed Geneva.

69. The Investiture Controversy pitted Pope Gregory VII against which of the following?

(A) Henry III

(B) Henry IV

(C) Frederick Barbarossa

(D) Maximilian

(E) Charles V

70. The constitution of the Roman Republic was comparable to the constitution of England in that it was

(A) appended with a bill of rights

(B) written in Latin

(C) never a written document

(D) intended to provide limits on the ruler and the nobility

(E) flexible enough to not require amendments

Study Resources

Most textbooks used in college-level Western civilization courses cover the topics in the outline given earlier, but the approaches to certain topics and the emphases given to them may differ. To prepare for the Western Civilization I exam, it is advisable to study one or more college textbooks, which can be found in most college bookstores. When selecting a textbook, check the table of contents against the knowledge and skills required for this test.

You may also find it helpful to supplement your reading with books listed in the bibliographies found in most history textbooks. In addition, contemporary historical novels, plays, and films provide rich sources of information. Actual works of art in museums can bring to life not only the reproductions found in books but history itself.

Visit www.collegeboard.com/clepprep for additional Western civilization resources. You can also find suggestions for exam preparation in Chapter IV of the *Official Study Guide*. In addition, many college faculty post their course materials on their schools' Web sites.

Answer Key

No.	Ans	No.	Ans
1.	D	36.	E
2.	B	37.	A
3.	A	38.	D
4.	A	39.	C
5.	C	40.	D
6.	E	41.	A
7.	A	42.	C
8.	A	43.	A
9.	B	44.	C
10.	D	45.	D
11.	E	46.	B
12.	A	47.	C
13.	C	48.	C
14.	E	49.	C
15.	E	50.	D
16.	D	51.	A
17.	E	52.	C
18.	A	53.	B
19.	B	54.	A
20.	A	55.	A
21.	E	56.	C
22.	C	57.	D
23.	B	58.	B
24.	A	59.	A
25.	E	60.	E
26.	D	61.	D
27.	D	62.	D
28.	B	63.	A
29.	E	64.	B
30.	C	65.	A
31.	E	66.	E
32.	C	67.	A
33.	C	68.	C
34.	C	69.	B
35.	D	70.	C

Western Civilization II

Description of the Examination

The Western Civilization II: 1648 to the Present examination covers material that is usually taught in the second semester of a two-semester course in Western Civilization. Questions cover European history from the mid-seventeenth century through the post-Second World War period including political, economic, and cultural developments such as Scientific Thought, the Enlightenment, the French and Industrial Revolutions, and the First and Second World Wars. Candidates may be asked to choose the correct definition of a historical term, select the historical figure whose political viewpoint is described, identify the correct relationship between two historical factors, or detect the inaccurate pairing of an individual with a historical event. Groups of questions may require candidates to interpret, evaluate, or relate the contents of a passage, a map, a picture, or a cartoon to the other information or to analyze and use the data contained in a graph or table.

The examination contains approximately 120 questions to be answered in 90 minutes. Some of these are pretest questions that will not be scored. Any time candidates spend on tutorials and providing personal information is in addition to the actual testing time.

Knowledge and Skills Required

Questions on the Western Civilization II examination require candidates to demonstrate one or more of the following abilities.

- Ability to understand important factual knowledge of developments in Western Civilization
- Ability to identify the causes and effects of major events in history
- Ability to analyze, interpret, and evaluate textual and graphic historical materials
- Ability to distinguish the relevant from the irrelevant
- Ability to reach conclusions on the basis of facts

The subject matter of the Western Civilization II examination is drawn from the following topics. The percentages next to the main topics indicate the approximate percentage of exam questions on that topic.

7–9% Absolutism and Constitutionalism, 1648–1715
The Dutch Republic
The English Revolution
France under Louis XIV
Formation of Austria and Prussia
The "westernization" of Russia

4–6% Competition for Empire and Economic Expansion
Global economy of the
  eighteenth century
Europe after Utrecht, 1713–1740
Demographic change in the
  eighteenth century

5–7% The Scientific View of the World
Major figures of the scientific revolution
New knowledge of man and society
Political theory

7–9% Period of Enlightenment
Enlightenment thought
Enlightened despotism
Partition of Poland

10–13% Revolution and Napoleonic Europe
The Revolution in France
The Revolution and Europe
The French Empire
Congress of Vienna

7–9% The Industrial Revolution
Agricultural and industrial revolution
Causes of revolution
Economic and social impact on working
  and middle class
British reform movement

6–8% Political and Cultural Developments, 1815–1848
Conservatism
Liberalism
Nationalism
Socialism
The Revolutions of 1830 and 1848

8–10% Politics and Diplomacy in the Age of Nationalism, 1850–1914

The unification of Italy and Germany
Austria-Hungary
Russia
France
Socialism and labor unions
European diplomacy, 1871–1900

7–9% Economy, Culture, and Imperialism, 1850–1914

Demography
World economy of the nineteenth century
Technological developments
Science, philosophy, and the arts
Imperialism in Africa and Asia

10–12% The First World War and the Russian Revolution

The causes of the First World War
The economic and social impact of the war
The peace settlements
The Revolution of 1917 and its effects

**7–9% Europe Between the Wars
The Great Depression**

International politics, 1919–1939
Stalin's five-year plans and purges
Italy and Germany between the wars
Interwar cultural developments

8–10% The Second World War and Contemporary Europe

The causes and course of the Second
    World War
Postwar Europe
Science, philosophy, the arts, and religion
Social and political developments

Sample Test Questions

The following sample questions do not appear on an actual CLEP examination. They are intended to give potential test-takers an indication of the format and difficulty level of the examination and to provide content for practice and review. Knowing the correct answers to all of the sample questions is not a guarantee of satisfactory performance on the exam.

Directions: Each of the questions or incomplete statements below is followed by five suggested answers or completions. Select the one that is best in each case.

1. Colbert's economic policies ran into difficulties chiefly because of the

    (A) relative poverty of France

    (B) loss of France's colonial empire

    (C) wars of Louis XIV

    (D) abandonment of the salt tax

    (E) reckless spending by the nobility

2. Which of the following best describes the use of the inductive method, as described by Francis Bacon?

    (A) Consult established scientific opinion and formulate a philosophical system based on it.

    (B) Begin with a mathematical principle and draw inferences from it.

    (C) Begin by making observations and then draw conclusions from them.

    (D) Begin with self-evident truths and draw inferences from them.

    (E) Advance learning by comparisons, analogies, and insights.

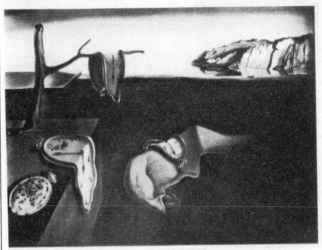

Digital Image © The Museum of Modern Art/Licensed by SCALA/ Art Resource, NY

3. Which of the following is a major theme depicted in the painting above?

    (A) A scientific view of the world

    (B) Enlightened rationalism

    (C) Romantic concern with nature

    (D) Realistic appraisal of industrial progress

    (E) The world of the unconscious mind

4. Which of the following occurred as a result of the War of the Austrian Succession (1740–1748) and the Seven Years' War (1756–1763)?

    (A) Prussia emerged as an important economic and military power.

    (B) Sweden ceased to be a great power.

    (C) Russia extended its territory to the shores of the Baltic Sea.

    (D) Hapsburg claims to Polish territory were dropped.

    (E) France acquired the provinces of Alsace and Lorraine.

5. Which of the following describes Joseph II of Austria?

(A) An absolute monarch who consolidated his authority through military force

(B) An absolute monarch whose policies were considered reactionary by the intelligentsia

(C) An adroit politician who coined the expression "Politics is the art of the possible"

(D) A monarch who tried to impose religious uniformity throughout his domains

(E) A monarch who sought to translate Enlightenment principles into government policies and objectives

6. Which of the following statements best describes the term "romanticism?"

(A) A belief that the rules of art are eternal and unchanging

(B) Interest in expressing general and universal truths rather than particular and concrete ones

(C) Emphasis on logical reasoning and exact factual knowledge

(D) Emphasis on a high degree of emotional subjectivity

(E) A value system that rejects idealism

7. All of the following were related to the Eastern Question EXCEPT

(A) Pan-Slavism

(B) the Congress of Berlin of 1878

(C) the Crimean War

(D) the Kruger Telegram

(E) the Treaty of San Stefano

8. The cartoon above refers to the

(A) Napoleonic Wars

(B) Crimean War

(C) Boer War

(D) Russo-Japanese War

(E) First World War

9. All of the following were instrumental in the emergence of Italy as a modern nation-state EXCEPT

(A) Mazzini

(B) Napoleon III

(C) Cavour

(D) Francis II

(E) Garibaldi

10. "Men being by nature all free, equal, and independent, no one can be put out of this estate and subjected to the political power of another without his own consent, which is done by agreeing with other men, to join and unite into a community for their comfortable, safe, and peaceable living in a secure enjoyment of their properties."

The quotation above is from a work by

(A) John Locke

(B) Karl Marx

(C) Edmund Burke

(D) Voltaire

(E) Adam Smith

11. Which of the following characterizes the size of the population of Europe during the eighteenth century?

   (A) It increased rapidly.

   (B) It stayed about the same.

   (C) It declined.

   (D) It dropped drastically in Western Europe but rose in Eastern Europe.

   (E) It dropped drastically in Eastern Europe but rose in Western Europe.

12. The term "collective security" would most likely be discussed in which of the following studies?

   (A) A book on the twentieth-century welfare state

   (B) A monograph on Soviet agricultural policy during the 1920s

   (C) A book on Bismarckian imperialism

   (D) A treatise on Social Darwinism

   (E) A work on European diplomacy during the 1930s

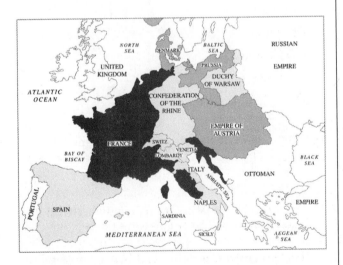

13. The map above shows national boundaries in which of the following years?

   (A) 1789

   (B) 1812

   (C) 1815

   (D) 1870

   (E) 1914

14. "The three classes, being associated and united in interest, would forget their hatred. . . . Labor would put an end to the drudgery of the people and the disdain of the rich for their inferiors, whose labors . . . they would share. . . . There would no longer be any . . . poor, and social antipathies would disappear with the causes which produced them."

The quotation above typifies which of the following schools of thought?

   (A) Utopian socialism

   (B) Marxism

   (C) Utilitarianism

   (D) Social Darwinism

   (E) Stalinism

15. The British economist John Maynard Keynes did which of the following?

   (A) He urged governments to increase mass purchasing power in times of deflation.

   (B) He defended the principles of the Versailles Treaty.

   (C) He helped to establish the British Labour party.

   (D) He prophesied the inevitable economic decline of capitalism.

   (E) He defined the concept of marginal utility to replace the labor theory of value.

16. The vast increase in German military expenditures in the two decades preceding the First World War occurred primarily because Germany

   (A) had extended its imperialistic activities to the Far East

   (B) was planning to militarize the provinces of Alsace and Lorraine

   (C) was extending military aid to Russia

   (D) feared an attack from France

   (E) was rapidly expanding its navy

17. In comparison to a preindustrial economy, the most distinctive feature of a modern economy is its

   (A) greater capacity to sustain growth over time
   (B) increased democratization of the workplace
   (C) lower wages for the literate middle class
   (D) lack of economic cycles
   (E) elimination of hunger and poverty

18. Which of the following was NOT an issue disturbing Europe on the eve of the Revolutions of 1848?

   (A) Socialism *versus* capitalism
   (B) Hungarian independence
   (C) The unification of France
   (D) The power of the papacy
   (E) The condition of serfs

19. The primary goal of Marxist socialists in the latter half of the nineteenth century was to

   (A) establish constitutional government
   (B) ensure equal rights for women
   (C) end government regulation of business
   (D) institute trial by jury in all criminal cases
   (E) abolish private ownership of the means of production

20. "Each individual, bestowing more time and attention upon the means of preserving and increasing his portion of wealth than is or can be bestowed by government, is likely to take a more effectual course than what, in this instance and on his behalf, would be taken by government."

   The quotation above best illustrates which of the following?

   (A) Fascism
   (B) Mercantilism
   (C) Syndicalism
   (D) Classical liberalism
   (E) Utopian socialism

21. The aim of the Soviet Union's First Five-Year Plan was to

   (A) acquire foreign capital
   (B) produce an abundance of consumer goods
   (C) encourage agricultural production by subsidizing the kulaks
   (D) build up heavy industry
   (E) put industrial policy in the hands of the proletariat

POPULATION DENSITY IN FRANCE PER SQUARE KILOMETER

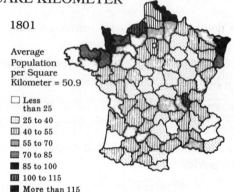

1801

Average Population per Square Kilometer = 50.9

☐ Less than 25
▦ 25 to 40
▥ 40 to 55
▤ 55 to 70
▦ 70 to 85
■ 85 to 100
▦ 100 to 115
■ More than 115

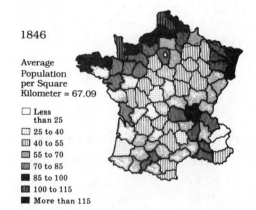

1846

Average Population per Square Kilometer = 67.09

☐ Less than 25
▦ 25 to 40
▥ 40 to 55
▤ 55 to 70
▦ 70 to 85
■ 85 to 100
▦ 100 to 115
■ More than 115

22. The increase in population density between 1801 and 1846 shown above indicates that

   (A) the growth of Paris absorbed any natural population increase
   (B) there was a reversing trend in which industry moved to the center of France while agriculture moved to the north
   (C) the population distribution in existence in 1801 was almost unchanged in 1846
   (D) by 1846 southern France was declining in population
   (E) by 1846 central France was declining in population

23. The National Assembly in France (1789–1791) did all of the following EXCEPT

   (A) issue assignats
   (B) ban strikes
   (C) pass the Civil Constitution of the Clergy
   (D) abolish guilds
   (E) abolish private property

24. Historical explanations for nineteenth-century European imperialism include all of the following EXCEPT

   (A) a need to discover new sources of raw materials
   (B) a need to find new markets for manufactured goods
   (C) a need to invest excess financial resources
   (D) a desire to establish world government
   (E) a desire to maintain the European balance of power

25. All of the following factors contributed to the rise of the National Socialist German Workers' party (Nazis) EXCEPT

   (A) the weakness of the Weimar Republic
   (B) the dissatisfaction with the Versailles Treaty
   (C) the impact of the Great Depression
   (D) the support of German conservatives
   (E) the support of Socialist trade unions

26. "He used extreme methods and mass repressions at a time when the Revolution was already victorious, when the Soviet state was strengthened, when the exploiting classes were already liquidated and Socialist relations were rooted solidly in all phases of the national economy, when our party was politically consolidated and had strengthened itself both numerically and ideologically."

In the quotation above, which of the following spoke and about whom?

   (A) Khrushchev about Stalin
   (B) Khrushchev about Trotsky
   (C) Stalin about Trotsky
   (D) Trotsky about Lenin
   (E) Brezhnev about Lenin

27. Albert Einstein's theory of relativity proposed

   (A) a new structure for the atom
   (B) a new conception of space and time
   (C) the fundamental concepts for developing the computer
   (D) the origin of the universe from the explosion of a single mass
   (E) the particulate nature of light

28. Which of the following is a central and essential component of the European welfare state?

   (A) Nationalization of all major sectors of the economy
   (B) Decentralization of the state
   (C) State responsibility for assuring access to medical care for all citizens
   (D) Elimination of large private fortunes through taxation
   (E) Elimination of independent trade unions

29. In the mid-eighteenth century, European population increased sharply for all of the following reasons EXCEPT

(A) improved agricultural techniques

(B) improvements in medical care

(C) fewer famines

(D) a decline in the death rate

(E) a decline of the plague

30. One of the goals of the physiocrats was to

(A) reform the French monarchy along Dutch lines

(B) implement more stringent mercantilist economic policies

(C) implement free-trade policies

(D) repudiate the national debt

(E) effect a complete redistribution of arable land in France

31. During the reign of Catherine the Great (1762–1796), all of the following occurred EXCEPT

(A) Russia increased its commercial and cultural contacts with the West.

(B) In the wake of peasant uprisings, manorial controls over the serfs were increased.

(C) A new class of powerful merchants appeared in Russia's major cities.

(D) The Russian population increased in size.

(E) Increasingly, the upper classes were educated in and spoke French.

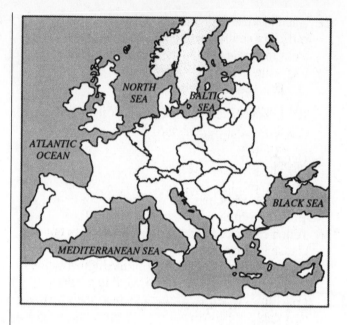

32. The map of Europe shown portrays national boundaries as they existed in

(A) 1871

(B) 1913

(C) 1925

(D) 1948

(E) 1950

33. The dictum "form follows function" is associated with which of the following trends in the arts?

(A) Neoclassicism

(B) Modernism

(C) Humanism

(D) Romanticism

(E) Realism

34. The *Ostpolitik* of West German Chancellor Willy Brandt was designed to

(A) nationalize German banks

(B) win Soviet diplomatic recognition for West Germany

(C) deepen West Germany's commitment to the North Atlantic Treaty Organization (NATO)

(D) normalize West German relations with the communist states of Eastern Europe

(E) promote free trade in Europe

35. Which of the following largely resolved the battle for sovereignty between crown and Parliament in England?

(A) The Test Act of 1673
(B) The acceptance of the divine right of kings
(C) John Locke's *Second Treatise of Civil Government*
(D) The Glorious Revolution
(E) The English Civil War

36. "Each contract of each particular state is but a clause in the great primeval contract of eternal society, linking the lower with the higher natures, connecting the visible and invisible world, according to a fixed compact sanctioned by the inviolable oath which holds all physical and all moral natures, each in their appointed place."

The quotation above reflects the ideas of

(A) Charles Fourier
(B) Voltaire
(C) Rousseau
(D) Adam Smith
(E) Edmund Burke

37. Which of the following is true of the French Revolution of 1830?

(A) It strengthened the power of the working class.
(B) It overthrew the Bourbon Monarch Charles X.
(C) It produced a constitutional monarchy based on universal adult male suffrage.
(D) It was suppressed by Charles X with the aid of Austria and Russia.
(E) It strengthened the power of the Roman Catholic Church in France.

38. Which of the following countries remained most closely aligned, ideologically and economically, with the Soviet Union from 1945 to 1989?

(A) The People's Republic of China
(B) Bulgaria
(C) Czechoslovakia
(D) Hungary
(E) Poland

39. "We are fifty or a hundred years behind the advanced countries. We must make good this distance in ten years. Either we do it or they crush us."

The quotation above is attributed to

(A) Charles de Gaulle calling for France to prepare for tank warfare
(B) Winston Churchill demanding that Britain expand its air force and navy
(C) Joseph Stalin explaining the need for continued industrial development in the Soviet Union
(D) Mao Zedong (Mao Tse-tung) introducing the Cultural Revolution in China
(E) Adolf Hitler inaugurating German rearmament

40. By the end of the seventeenth century, which of the following was a social or political consequence of the policies pursued by Spain in its colonial possessions in the New World?

(A) Economic and social mobility were greatly inhibited by a rigid ethnic and class structure.
(B) The native inhabitants had secured a degree of political independence.
(C) The Roman Catholic Church had been forced to tolerate Protestant missionary activities.
(D) Most colonists had come to view themselves as fundamentally opposed to their compatriots remaining in Spain.
(E) There had been virtually no intermarriage among various racial groups.

The Granger Collection, New York

41. The eighteenth-century political cartoon reproduction shown above relates most closely to which of the following events of the French Revolution?

(A) The emergence of the power of the Third Estate
(B) The tensions between the nobility and clergy
(C) The mistreatment of political prisoners
(D) The death of Marat
(E) The Thermidorean Reaction

42. Which of the following joined Nazi Germany in its attack on the Soviet Union?

(A) Vichy France
(B) Finland
(C) Sweden
(D) Turkey
(E) Japan

43. Churchill's famous phrase "Never—was so much owed by so many to so few" referred to

(A) those who evacuated the Allied army from Dunkirk
(B) those who convoyed food and materiel across the Atlantic in the early 1940s
(C) the scientists who developed radar and other early warning technologies
(D) the fighter pilots of the Royal Air Force who won the Battle of Britain
(E) the cryptographers who broke the German and Japanese military and diplomatic codes

44. The Soviet foreign policy of "peaceful coexistence" was most closely associated with which of the following Soviet domestic policies?

(A) Lenin's New Economic Policy (NEP)
(B) Stalin's program of collectivization
(C) Khrushchev's policy of de-Stalinization
(D) Brezhnev's policy toward dissidents
(E) Andropov's program of increased industrial output

45. "This is what I see and what troubles me. I look on all sides and I see only darkness everywhere. Nature presents to me nothing which is not a matter of doubt and concern. It is incomprehensible that God should exist and that God should not exist."

The quotation above expresses the view of

(A) Pascal
(B) Newton
(C) Bacon
(D) Galileo
(E) Hobbes

46. Which of the following countries intervened militarily in Mexico in the 1860s in an attempt to establish colonial control?

(A) Germany
(B) Sweden
(C) Portugal
(D) Italy
(E) France

47. The theories of which of the following had the most influence on the American and French Revolutions?

    (A) Condorcet, Voltaire, Jefferson
    (B) Pitt, Hobbes, Raynal
    (C) Diderot, Burke, Fox
    (D) Montesquieu, Locke, Rousseau
    (E) Wilkes, Turgot, Helvetius

48. The country that pioneered social insurance legislation in the late nineteenth century was

    (A) Great Britain
    (B) France
    (C) Germany
    (D) Austria
    (E) Russia

49. One accomplishment of the British Reform Bill of 1832 was the

    (A) reduction in the parliamentary power of the House of Lords
    (B) reduction in the constitutional powers of the Crown
    (C) extension of parliamentary representation to the new industrial centers
    (D) extension of the right to vote to all males over the age of 21
    (E) increase in the representation of the colonies in Parliament

50. Which of the following was an outcome of the First World War?

    (A) The downfall of the German, Ottoman, Italian, and British Empires
    (B) Territorial gains for Italy, Romania, Austria, and Hungary
    (C) National independence for Poland, Czechoslovakia, Yugoslavia, and Finland
    (D) Technological changes but a decrease in the number of parliamentary democracies
    (E) Successful Communist revolutions in Russia and Germany

51. Women did not gain the right to vote until after the Second World War in which of the following groups of countries?

    (A) Great Britain, the United States, and France
    (B) France, Italy, and Switzerland
    (C) Germany, Austria, and Russia
    (D) Poland, Czechoslovakia, and Hungary
    (E) Norway, the Netherlands, and Sweden

52. Pablo Picasso is credited with founding the twentieth-century art movement called

    (A) fauvism
    (B) expressionism
    (C) cubism
    (D) futurism
    (E) baroque

53. The importance of Sigmund Freud in the development of Western thought is that

    (A) he proved the Enlightenment belief that the mind responded to conscious motives in a rational manner
    (B) his ideas on the id, ego, and superego have gone unchallenged since the late-nineteenth century
    (C) he paved the way for the sexual revolution in the late-twentieth century
    (D) his theories have had a great impact on twentieth-century thought, culture, and science
    (E) his method of psychoanalysis has proved to cure all kinds of mental illnesses

54. Film director Leni Riefenstahl depicts the birth of the new Germany in her 1934 film "Triumph of the Will" through

    (A) Wagnerian music and smiling German youths
    (B) Olympic games
    (C) military armaments
    (D) the defeat of France
    (E) the Luftwaffe

55. The National Workshops were established in France in order to

(A) compete with cheap goods being produced in America

(B) mass produce military weapons

(C) produce quality wines for the European market

(D) reduce high urban, especially Parisian, unemployment

(E) promote Protestant social reforms

56. The Agricultural Revolution included all of the following features EXCEPT

(A) France and Prussia pioneered in agricultural innovations

(B) new crops, such as turnips, clover, and legumes replenished the soil

(C) enclosures of land made food production more efficient

(D) seed drills often replaced the broadcast method of sowing

(E) crossbreeding practices improved livestock production

57. All of the following were among the Great Reforms implemented in Russia during the reign of Alexander II (1855–1881) EXCEPT

(A) the establishment of the *Duma*

(B) the creation of regional councils known as *zemstvos*

(C) the emancipation of the serfs

(D) judicial reforms that granted all Russians access to civil courts

(E) military reforms that reduced the length of the term of service for conscripts

58. The Second International, formed in 1889, lost its reason for existence primarily because of the

(A) disintegration of socialist international solidarity in the face of wartime nationalism

(B) disintegration of the German social Democratic party

(C) Russian Bolshevik Revolution, which was repudiated by western European socialists

(D) militarism of the French socialist leader, Jean Jaurès

(E) disputes between French and German socialists over the question of Alsace-Lorraine

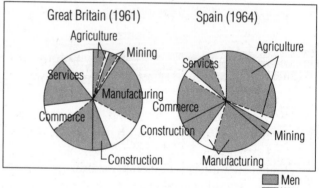

ACTIVE WORKFORCE

59. The chart shown above supports which of the following conclusions about employment during the 1960s?

(A) A large proportion of the working population in Spain was engaged in agriculture.

(B) Over half the working population in both countries was employed in mining and manufacturing.

(C) There was very little unemployment in Great Britain.

(D) A majority of women in both countries were employed in commerce.

(E) Women in both countries earned higher wages than their male counterparts.

60. All of the following were results of the Treaty of Paris (1763) EXCEPT

(A) Britain controlled much of India.

(B) France retained its sugar colonies in the West Indies.

(C) France suffered no decline in its overseas trade.

(D) Britain emerged as the predominant sea power.

(E) France had to give up its North American mainland colonies.

61. In the mid-nineteenth century, women were LEAST likely to be employed in which of the following occupations?

(A) Factory work

(B) Domestic service

(C) Shopkeeping

(D) Teaching

(E) Legal services

62. The Great Elector, Frederick William of Brandenburg-Prussia (1640–1688), advocated all of the following policies EXCEPT

(A) a uniform currency system

(B) profitable dynastic marriages

(C) Jewish immigration

(D) a citizen army rather than a standing army

(E) consolidation of Hohenzollern lands

63. In 1936 it was widely assumed that France would come to the aid of the Republicans in Spain because France

(A) had been a consistent supporter of Franco

(B) opposed the Moscow-dominated government in Madrid

(C) wanted to seize Gibraltar

(D) was mandated by the League of Nations to defend Spain

(E) had a Popular Front government, as did Spain

64. Disraeli led the Conservatives in taking "a leap in the dark" in 1867. This phrase refers to the

(A) extension of the franchise to male working-class householders

(B) establishment of a more vigorous foreign policy vis-à-vis continental Europe

(C) plan proposed for establishing home rule in Ireland

(D) attempt to stimulate the economy through the use of deficit spending

(E) decision to grant dominion status to Canada

65. Which of the following statements about female industrial workers in eighteenth-century England is correct?

(A) They outnumbered male workers.

(B) Most left employment when they married.

(C) Most left the mills soon after employment to return to the countryside.

(D) They generally received lower pay than male workers.

(E) They were protected by law from hazardous occupations such as mining.

66. The enormous business success of the eighteenth-century English potter Josiah Wedgwood can be attributed primarily to

(A) the wealth of the aristocracy and their desire for elaborate china

(B) the rising prominence of the middle class, who sought to emulate the upper class

(C) the development of a huge overseas market for English china

(D) the prominence of coffee and tea drinking in the eighteenth century

(E) royal patronage for potters and weavers

67. "Separate spheres" refers to which of the following in nineteenth-century Europe?

(A) The post-1789 legal relationship between the Catholic Church and the civil authority

(B) The division of domestic and foreign policy making in modern constitutional states

(C) Different roles of men and women in Victorian society

(D) Parts of the human psyche as defined by Sigmund Freud

(E) Gregor Mendel's techniques for determining heredity

68. The "Velvet Revolution" refers to the collapse of communism in which of the following Eastern European countries?

(A) Poland

(B) Hungary

(C) Yugoslavia

(D) Czechoslovakia

(E) Romania

69. Which of the following political philosophers believed that liberty could be preserved through separation of powers and checks and balances?

(A) Jean-Jacques Rousseau

(B) Adam Smith

(C) Baron de La Brède et de Montesquieu

(D) Thomas Hobbes

(E) Voltaire

70. Which of the following attempted to establish an empire in Mexico during the mid-nineteenth century?

(A) Great Britain

(B) Germany

(C) France

(D) Spain

(E) Italy

Study Resources

Most textbooks used in college-level Western civilization courses cover the topics in the outline given earlier, but the approaches to certain topics and the emphases given to them may differ. To prepare for the Western Civilization II exam, it is advisable to study one or more college textbooks, which can be found in most college bookstores. When selecting a textbook, check the table of contents against the knowledge and skills required for this test.

You may also find it helpful to supplement your reading with books listed in the bibliographies found in most history textbooks. In addition, contemporary historical novels, plays, and films provide rich sources of information. Actual works of art in museums can bring to life not only the reproductions found in books but history itself.

Visit www.collegeboard.com/clepprep for additional Western civilization resources. You can also find suggestions for exam preparation in Chapter IV of the *Official Study Guide*. In addition, many college faculty post their course materials on their schools' Web sites.

Answer Key

1.	C	36.	E
2.	C	37.	B
3.	E	38.	B
4.	A	39.	C
5.	E	40.	A
6.	D	41.	A
7.	D	42.	B
8.	E	43.	D
9.	D	44.	C
10.	A	45.	A
11.	A	46.	E
12.	E	47.	D
13.	B	48.	C
14.	A	49.	C
15.	A	50.	C
16.	E	51.	B
17.	A	52.	C
18.	C	53.	D
19.	E	54.	A
20.	D	55.	D
21.	D	56.	A
22.	C	57.	A
23.	E	58.	A
24.	D	59.	A
25.	E	60.	C
26.	A	61.	E
27.	B	62.	D
28.	C	63.	E
29.	B	64.	A
30.	C	65.	D
31.	C	66.	B
32.	C	67.	C
33.	B	68.	D
34.	D	69.	C
35.	D	70.	C

Biology

Description of the Examination

The Biology examination covers material that is usually taught in a one-year college general biology course. The subject matter tested covers the broad field of the biological sciences, organized into three major areas: molecular and cellular biology, organismal biology, and population biology. The examination gives approximately equal weight to these three areas.

The examination contains approximately 115 questions to be answered in 90 minutes. Some of these are pretest questions that will not be scored. Any time candidates spend on tutorials and providing personal information is in addition to the actual testing time.

Knowledge and Skills Required

Questions on the Biology examination require candidates to demonstrate one or more of the following abilities.

- Knowledge of facts, principles, and processes of biology
- Understanding the means by which information is collected, how it is interpreted, how one hypothesizes from available information, how one draws conclusions and makes further predictions
- Understanding that science is a human endeavor with social consequences

The subject matter of the Biology examination is drawn from the following topics. The percentages next to the main topics indicate the approximate percentage of exam questions on that topic.

33% Molecular and Cellular Biology

Chemical composition of organisms
- Simple chemical reactions and bonds
- Properties of water
- Chemical structure of carbohydrates, lipids, proteins, nucleic acids
- Origin of life

Cells
- Structure and function of cell organelles
- Properties of cell membranes
- Comparison of prokaryotic and eukaryotic cells

Enzymes
- Enzyme-substrate complex
- Roles of coenzymes
- Inorganic cofactors
- Inhibition and regulation

Energy transformations
- Glycolysis, respiration, anaerobic pathways
- Photosynthesis

Cell division
- Structure of chromosomes
- Mitosis, meiosis, and cytokinesis in plants and animals

Chemical nature of the gene
- Watson-Crick model of nucleic acids
- DNA replication
- Mutations
- Control of protein synthesis: transcription, translation, post-transcriptional processing
- Structural and regulatory genes
- Transformation
- Viruses

34% Organismal Biology

Structure and function in plants with emphasis on angiosperms

- Root, stem, leaf, flower, seed, fruit
- Water and mineral absorption and transport
- Food translocation and storage

Plant reproduction and development

- Alternation of generations in ferns, conifers, and flowering plants
- Gamete formation and fertilization
- Growth and development: hormonal control
- Tropisms and photoperiodicity

Structure and function in animals with emphasis on vertebrates

- Major systems (e.g., digestive, gas exchange, skeletal, nervous, circulatory, excretory, immune)
- Homeostatic mechanisms
- Hormonal control in homeostasis and reproduction

Animal reproduction and development

- Gamete formation, fertilization
- Cleavage, gastrulation, germ layer formation, differentiation of organ systems
- Experimental analysis of vertebrate development
- Extraembryonic membranes of vertebrates
- Formation and function of the mammalian placenta
- Blood circulation in the human embryo

Principles of heredity

- Mendelian inheritance (dominance, segregation, independent assortment)
- Chromosomal basis of inheritance
- Linkage, including sex-linked
- Polygenic inheritance (height, skin color)
- Multiple alleles (human blood groups)

33% Population Biology

Principles of ecology

- Energy flow and productivity in ecosystems
- Biogeochemical cycles
- Population growth and regulation (natality, mortality, competition, migration, density, r- and K-selection)
- Community structure, growth, regulation (major biomes and succession)
- Habitat (biotic and abiotic factors)
- Concept of niche
- Island biogeography
- Evolutionary ecology (life history strategies, altruism, kin selection)

Principles of evolution

- History of evolutionary concepts
- Concepts of natural selection (differential reproduction, mutation, Hardy-Weinberg equilibrium, speciation, punctuated equilibrium)
- Adaptive radiation
- Major features of plant and animal evolution
- Concepts of homology and analogy
- Convergence, extinction, balanced polymorphism, genetic drift
- Classification of living organisms
- Evolutionary history of humans

Principles of behavior

- Stereotyped, learned social behavior
- Societies (insects, birds, primates)

Social biology

- Human population growth (age composition, birth and fertility rates, theory of demographic transition)
- Human intervention in the natural world (management of resources, environmental pollution)
- Biomedical progress (control of human reproduction, genetic engineering)

Sample Test Questions

The following sample questions do not appear on an actual CLEP examination. They are intended to give potential test-takers an indication of the format and difficulty level of the examination and to provide content for practice and review. Knowing the correct answers to all of the sample questions is not a guarantee of satisfactory performance on the exam.

Directions: Each of the questions or incomplete statements below is followed by five suggested answers or completions. Select the one that is best in each case.

1. In which of the following ways do social insects benefit most from having several types or castes within the species?

    (A) Each colony is able to include a large number of individuals.

    (B) The secretions or odors produced by the protective caste are an effective defense.

    (C) The division of the species into castes ensures the survival of the fittest.

    (D) Large numbers of the worker caste can migrate to start new colonies.

    (E) The specialized structure of each caste permits division of labor and greater efficiency.

2. The greatest diversity of structure and of methods of locomotion is exhibited in the individuals of

    (A) a class
    (B) a family
    (C) an order
    (D) a species
    (E) a phylum

3. Of the following, which is an example of a mutualistic relationship?

    (A) The protozoan *Trichonympha* digesting wood in the gut of a termite

    (B) The sporozoan *Plasmodium* reproducing in human blood cells and liberating toxins into the human body

    (C) Two species of *Paramecium* deriving food from a common laboratory culture

    (D) Rabbits being eaten by foxes

    (E) Humans inadvertently providing food for cockroaches

4. Evidence that multicellular green plants may have evolved from green algae is best supplied by the fact that in both

    (A) the gametophyte generation is dominant

    (B) the sporophyte generation is dominant

    (C) chlorophylls *a* and *b* are photosynthetic pigments

    (D) xylem vessels are pitted and spiraled

    (E) male gametes are nonflagellated

5. All of the following statements concerning the light-dependent reactions of photosynthesis are true EXCEPT

    (A) An initial event is the excitation of electrons from chlorophyll by light energy.

    (B) The excited electrons are raised to a higher energy level.

    (C) If not captured, the excited electrons drop back to their initial energy levels.

    (D) If captured, some of the energy of the excited electrons is used to split carbon dioxide into carbon and oxygen.

    (E) Light is absorbed by pigments that are embedded in membranes.

6. Which of the following statements best explains the hypothesis that the development of sexual reproduction has resulted in acceleration of the rate of evolution?

(A) Mutations are more likely to occur in spermatogenesis and oogenesis than in mitotically dividing cells.

(B) Sexual reproduction results in more offspring than does asexual reproduction.

(C) Those members of a species that are best adapted to their environment are most likely to be successful in sexual reproduction.

(D) Mutations usually do not occur in the production of spores or in cells dividing by fission.

(E) Sexual reproduction is more likely to result in genetic recombination than is asexual reproduction.

7. A frog gastrocnemius muscle gives a smooth tetanic contraction at any rate of stimulation above 20 per second. At threshold stimulus intensity, a response of some specific strength will be obtained. Increase of the stimulus intensity by 50 percent will increase the strength of response nearly 50 percent. If the intensity is again increased 50 percent, the response will increase only about another 25 percent. Further increase in the stimulus intensity produces no further increase in response.

The observations above are best explained by which of the following?

(A) A muscle functions with an all-or-none mechanism.

(B) Muscle-fiber sarcolemma is electrically resistant.

(C) The fibers of a muscle do not all contract at the same rate.

(D) The fibers of a muscle fatigue at varying rates.

(E) The fibers of a muscle have varying thresholds for response.

8. In an amphibian gastrula, transplantation experiments that involve the dorsal lip of the blastopore indicate that this tissue

(A) is destined to be ectoderm

(B) does not differ from other tissues of the blastula in any significant manner

(C) will cause a concentration of yolk in adjacent cells

(D) has the ability to initiate differentiation of the embryonic neural tube

(E) is so sensitive that it will develop into any embryonic structure, depending on its surroundings

9. Deposits of coal in Greenland and the Antarctic indicate that

(A) these regions once contained numerous mollusks that deposited carbohydrates in their shells

(B) the Earth's crust in these regions contains vast amounts of limestone

(C) these regions were once thickly vegetated

(D) there is a rich store of dissolved carbon dioxide in the seas surrounding these regions

(E) a geologic uplift of coral rock and ocean bed has recently occurred in these regions

10. Thirst, loss of weight, and sugar in the urine result from the undersecretion of a hormone by which of the following glands?

(A) Thyroid

(B) Parathyroid

(C) Pancreas

(D) Adrenal

(E) Thymus

11. Considering the role of mitochondria in cells, mitochondria would likely be most abundant in which of the following?

   (A) Mature red blood cells
   (B) Callous cells of the skin
   (C) Cells of the heart muscle
   (D) Epithelial cells of the cheek lining
   (E) Fat cells

12. All of the following statements about enzymes are true EXCEPT

   (A) A single enzyme molecule can be used over and over again.
   (B) Most enzymes are highly specific with regard to the reactions they catalyze.
   (C) Some enzymes contain an essential nonprotein component.
   (D) Enzymes can function only within living cells.
   (E) Most enzymes are denatured by high temperatures.

13. Which of the following is most significant in limiting the size to which an animal cell may grow?

   (A) The ratio of cell surface to cell volume
   (B) The abundance of mitochondria in the cytoplasm
   (C) The chemical composition of the cell membrane
   (D) The presence of an inelastic cell wall
   (E) The relative number of nucleoli

14. Which of the following best describes the effect on heart action of the stimulation of the parasympathetic nerve fibers of the vagus nerve?

   (A) There is a decrease in the volume of blood pumped and an increase in the heartbeat rate.
   (B) There is an increase in the volume of blood pumped without a decrease in the heartbeat rate.
   (C) There is a prolonged acceleration in the heartbeat rate.
   (D) There is a decrease in the heartbeat rate.
   (E) There is an increase in the blood pressure.

15. If poorly drained soils encourage the growth of bacteria that convert nitrate to nitrogen, the effect on higher plants will be to

   (A) increase lipid production
   (B) decrease protein production
   (C) increase carbohydrate production
   (D) produce unusually large fruits
   (E) stimulate chlorophyll production

16. A patient is placed on a restricted diet of water, pure cooked starch, olive oil, adequate minerals, and vitamins. If a urinalysis several weeks later reveals the presence of relatively normal amounts of urea, the urea probably came from the

   (A) food eaten during the restricted diet
   (B) withdrawal of reserve urea stored in the liver
   (C) chemical combination of water, carbon dioxide, and free nitrogen
   (D) deamination of cellular proteins
   (E) urea synthesized by kidney tubule cells

17.

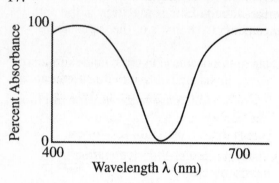

Shown above is the absorption spectrum of a compound of biological importance. If a person with normal human color vision viewed this compound under ordinary white light, what color would it appear to be?

(A) Red

(B) Blue

(C) Green

(D) Black

(E) White

18. The codon for a particular amino acid is 5'CAU3'. The DNA sequence that complements this codon is

(A) 3'CAU5'

(B) 3'GTA5'

(C) 3'GTT5'

(D) 3'GUA5'

(E) 3'GUT5'

19. Viral DNA would be most likely to contain genes that code for

(A) regulatory hormones

(B) viral-coat protein

(C) viral-ribosome proteins

(D) glycolytic enzymes

(E) restriction enzymes

20. Which of the following statements about imprinting is NOT true?

(A) The capacity for imprinting may be limited to a specific and brief period in the early life of the organism.

(B) The behavior pattern associated with imprinting is the result of reward or punishment.

(C) The learned behavior resulting from imprinting is difficult to reverse in later life.

(D) A gosling imprinted by a moving wooden decoy may exhibit courting behavior to the decoy in later life.

(E) Odors and sounds may serve as stimuli for imprinting.

21. Which of the graphs below illustrates the effect of substrate concentration on the initial rate of reaction when a limited amount of enzyme is present?

(A)
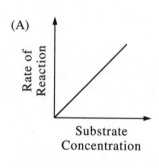

(B)
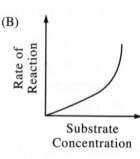

(C)
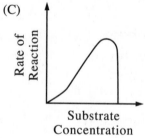

(D)
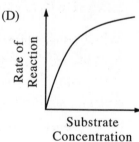

(E)
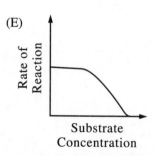

22. Which of the following is the final electron acceptor in the mitochondrial electron transport system?

   (A) ADP + Pi
   (B) ATP
   (C) NAD or FAD
   (D) H_2O
   (E) O_2

23. In a eukaryotic cell, glycolysis occurs in which of the following parts of the cell?

   (A) Chloroplast
   (B) Cytosol
   (C) Nucleolus
   (D) Mitochondrion
   (E) Ribosome

24. The clotting process in blood is initiated by

   (A) erythrocytes
   (B) lymphocytes
   (C) hemoglobins
   (D) platelets
   (E) neutrophils

25. Which of the following membranes is correctly matched to its function?

   (A) Allantois .. food absorption
   (B) Yolk sac .. embryonic bladder
   (C) Amnion .. gas exchange
   (D) Dura mater .. brain protection
   (E) Peritoneum .. heart protection

26. Which of the following statements best describes the movement of energy in an ecosystem?

   (A) Radiant energy is converted into chemical energy in plant photosynthesis and then released as heat energy during cellular respiration.
   (B) Energy cycles within an ecosystem.
   (C) Plants get energy from the nutrients in the soil.
   (D) The animals in an ecosystem absorb the radiant energy of the Sun and use it to make organic molecules such as proteins.
   (E) Some chemoautotrophic bacteria release energy that can then be used by soil animals to make food.

27. Which of the following elements is correctly linked to its role in a living organism?

   (A) Calcium .. component of proteins
   (B) Carbon .. component of lipids
   (C) Magnesium .. neuron action potential
   (D) Potassium .. component of ATP
   (E) Zinc .. component of carbohydrates

28. Mistletoe is attached to the branches of trees such as sweet gum, from which it obtains water and some nutrients. The trees do not benefit from this association. Which of the following terms describes the relationship between the two plants?

   (A) Commensalism
   (B) Competition
   (C) Mutualism
   (D) Parasitism
   (E) Predation

29. ATP is which type of molecule?

(A) A nucleotide

(B) A peptide

(C) A phospholipid

(D) A disaccharide

(E) A tripeptide

30. Which of the following is generally true about bacterial viruses?

(A) They infect animal cells only.

(B) They have a protective capsid made of chitin.

(C) They inject their nucleic acids into the cells that they infect.

(D) They produce haploid gametes in meiosis.

(E) They carry out glycolysis but not the Krebs cycle.

31. A typical photosynthetic eukaryotic cell contains which of the following?

I. Ribosomes

II. Chloroplasts

III. Mitochondria

(A) II only

(B) I and II only

(C) II and III only

(D) I and III only

(E) I, II, and III

32. Which of the following pairs of organisms are most closely related?

(A) *Mus bufo* and *Bufo americanus*

(B) *Lynx lynx* and *Alces alces*

(C) *Panthera leo* and *Felis concolor*

(D) *Odocoileus virginianus* and *Colinus virginianus*

(E) *Canis latrans* and *Canis lupus*

33. Which of the following is an example of a testcross?

(A) *AA* x *Aa*

(B) *A?* x *AA*

(C) *A?* x *Aa*

(D) *A?* x *aa*

(E) *a?* x *aa*

Directions: The following group of questions consists of five lettered headings followed by a list of numbered phrases. For each numbered phrase select the one heading that is most closely related to it. A heading may be used once, more than once, or not at all.

Questions 34–36 refer to the following.

(A) Fertilization

(B) Meiosis

(C) Mitosis

(D) Pollination

(E) Nondisjunction

34. The process by which a zygote is formed

35. The process by which the nuclei of somatic (body) cells divide

36. The process by which monoploid (haploid) cells are formed from diploid cells

Questions 37–41 refer to the following classes of vertebrates.

    (A) Amphibians

    (B) Bony fish

    (C) Cartilaginous fish

    (D) Mammals

    (E) Reptiles

37. Birds are most closely related to which class?

38. Which class includes animals that have a moist skin as the primary organ for gas exchange?

39. Which class includes whales?

40. Members of which class produce milk for their young in specialized skin glands?

41. Which class includes snakes?

Directions: Each group of questions below concerns an experimental situation. In each case, first study the description of the situation. Then choose the best answer to each question following it.

Questions 42–44

Expenditures of solar energy, calculated by C. Juday for Lake Mendota in southern Wisconsin, appear in the table below.

Reflected or otherwise lost. 49.5%

Absorbed in evaporation of water . . 25.0%

Raised temperatures in the lake 21.7%

Melted ice in the spring 3.0%

Used directly by organisms 0.8%

The pyramid of biomass for this same lake is represented by the following diagram.

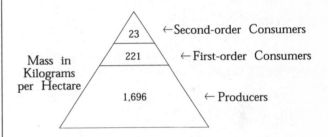

42. The most probable explanation for the relative masses of the first- and second-order consumers is that

    (A) each link in the food chain of an ecosystem has less available energy than the previous link has

    (B) only a small fraction of sunlight that reaches the Earth is transformed into chemical energy by photosynthesis

    (C) the total energy of the decomposers is greater than that of the rest of the organisms put together

    (D) seasonal fluctuations in weather limit the number of consumers

    (E) second-order consumers require more total energy than first-order consumers do

43. The energy incorporated into this ecosystem is most dependent on the

    (A) photoperiod
    (B) total amount of photosynthesis
    (C) predator-prey relationships
    (D) length of the food chains
    (E) total amount of respiration

44. If the lake is assumed to be a typical ecosystem, the percent of radiant energy from the Sun that is trapped in photosynthesis is about

    (A) 100%
    (B) 10%
    (C) 1%
    (D) 0.1%
    (E) 0.01%

Questions 45–47

Inheritance of certain characteristics of the fruit fly, *Drosophila*, is as indicated by the table below.

Characteristic	Dominant	Recessive
Body color	Gray	Black
Eye color	Red	White

A female fruit fly had a gray body and white eyes. After being mated with a male fruit fly, she laid 112 eggs that developed into the following kinds of offspring.

Number	Body	Eyes
28	Gray	Red
29	Gray	White
28	Black	Red
27	Black	White

45. With respect to body color, the male parent of the 112 offspring was most probably

    (A) homozygous gray
    (B) heterozygous gray
    (C) homozygous black
    (D) heterozygous black
    (E) hemizygous gray

46. Examination revealed that all of the 56 red-eyed offspring were females and all of the 56 white-eyed offspring were males. This observation indicates that

    (A) red and white eye colors segregate independently of sex
    (B) all of the red-eyed offspring inherited their eye color from their female parent
    (C) all of the red-eyed offspring were homozygous
    (D) the gene for eye color is linked to the gene for body color
    (E) the gene for red or for white eye color is carried on the X chromosome

47. In this experiment, the number of offspring that exhibit both recessive characters is

    (A) 1
    (B) 27
    (C) 28
    (D) 55
    (E) 56

48. Carbon dioxide is produced by which of the following?

 I. A mesophyll cell in a flowering plant during the night
 II. A muscle cell in a mammalian heart during contraction
 III. A yeast cell growing under anaerobic conditions

(A) I only
(B) II only
(C) III only
(D) I and II only
(E) I, II, and III

49. Which of the following is a function of ATP?

(A) It creates energy.
(B) It transports energy.
(C) It is a building block of proteins.
(D) It stores amino acids.
(E) It gives the cells shape.

50. Protein synthesis is the main function of which of the following structures?

(A) Nucleus
(B) Ribosome
(C) Chromosome
(D) Mitochondrion
(E) Vacuole

Questions 51–55

Several different samples of DNA were digested with different restriction enzymes (endonucleases) and separated by gel electrophoresis, as shown below.

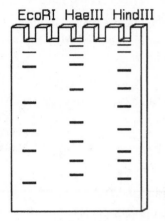

51. The terms "EcoRI," "HaeIII," and "HindIII" refer to which of the following?

(A) The voltage intensity used to prepare the electrophoresis medium
(B) The restriction enzymes used
(C) The organisms from which the original DNA sample was obtained
(D) The types of buffers used to maintain a constant pH in the preparation as the sample was processed
(E) The types of proteins encoded by each fragment

52. The patterns of bands in the different lanes result from which of the following?

(A) Different voltages applied to different lanes
(B) Different buffers applied to different lanes
(C) Different sizes of fragments in the samples in different lanes
(D) Different terminal configurations of the fragments, with some having blunt ends while others have sticky ends
(E) Mutations produced by the electrophoresis

53. In this gel, the smallest fragments are

(A) at the top of the gel, near the wells

(B) at the bottom of the gel, furthest from the wells

(C) at the left side of the gel

(D) at the right side of the gel

(E) randomly scattered from top to bottom in each lane

54. Restriction enzymes cut samples of DNA into fragments by

(A) binding to specific sequences of nucleotides

(B) oxidizing the DNA

(C) heating the DNA to its denaturation point

(D) breaking peptide bonds

(E) unwinding the DNA

55. Which of the following is the most probable explanation for the different numbers of fragments in the different lanes?

(A) There were more EcoRI cut sites than HaeIII or HindIII cut sites.

(B) There were more HaeIII cut sites than EcoRI or HindIII cut sites.

(C) There were more HindIII cut sites than HaeIII or EcoRI cut sites.

(D) A stronger voltage was applied to the first lane.

(E) Different buffers were used in the different lanes.

56. Which of the following best explains why a pictorial presentation of the biomass at each trophic level of an ecosystem is a pyramid?

(A) The loss of iron from an ecosystem

(B) The amount of energy passed from one trophic level to the next

(C) The number of predators in the ecosystem

(D) The chemical compounds in an ecosystem are recycled

(E) The average size of the individuals in each species

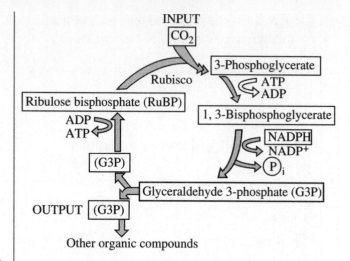

57. The original description of the pathway shown above is attributed to

(A) Louis Pasteur

(B) James Watson and Francis Crick

(C) Hans Krebs

(D) Robert Hooke

(E) Melvin Calvin and Andrew Benson

58. A diet with insufficient iodine will most likely lead to which of the following symptoms in an individual?

(A) Bleeding gums

(B) Decreased metabolic rate

(C) Increased body temperature

(D) Increased respiratory rate

(E) Weight loss

59. Which of the following structures is correctly paired with its function?

(A) Alveolus . . locomotion

(B) Cilium . . impulse transmission

(C) Sarcomere . . nutrient uptake

(D) Neuron . . gas exchange

(E) Nephron . . filtration

60. Based on the information in the table, which of the following substitutions is synonymous?

		SECOND BASE			
	U	C	A	G	
U	UUU Phe, UUC Phe, UUA Leu, UUG Leu	UCU, UCC, UCA, UCG Ser	UAU Tyr, UAC Tyr, UAA Stop, UAG Stop	UGU Cys, UGC Cys, UGA Stop, UGG Trp	U C A G
C	CUU, CUC, CUA, CUG Leu	CCU, CCC, CCA, CCG Pro	CAU His, CAC His, CAA Gln, CAG Gln	CGU, CGC, CGA, CGG Arg	U C A G
A	AUU Ile, AUC Ile, AUA Ile, AUG Met or Start	ACU, ACC, ACA, ACG Thr	AAU Asn, AAC Asn, AAA Lys, AAG Lys	AGU Ser, AGC Ser, AGA Arg, AGG Arg	U C A G
G	GUU, GUC, GUA, GUG Val	GCU, GCC, GCA, GCG Ala	GAU Asp, GAC Asp, GAA Lys, GAG Lys	GGU, GGC, GGA, GGG Gly	U C A G

FIRST BASE (left), THIRD BASE (right)

(A) AGU to AGA

(B) GUU to GCU

(C) UUG to CUG

(D) UGA to GGA

(E) CAA to CCA

61. Excess sewage can lead to the death of aquatic animals in a lake because sewage pollution promotes

(A) mineral starvation

(B) erosion

(C) thermal stratification

(D) oxygen depletion

(E) a temperature decrease

62. The aerobic cellular respiration of glucose is different from the simple burning of glucose in that the aerobic respiration of glucose

(A) releases no heat

(B) requires no oxygen

(C) releases more energy

(D) releases hydrocarbons

(E) occurs at a lower temperature

63. A given trait occurs in two alternative types, M and m, in a population at Hardy-Weinberg equilibrium. If 49 percent of the population has only type M alleles, what percentage of the population is expected to be heterozygous for the trait?

(A) 9%

(B) 14%

(C) 21%

(D) 42%

(E) 51%

64. The forelimbs of horses and frogs are considered to be homologous structures. The best evidence for this homology is that the forelimbs have

(A) a similar appearance in both species

(B) a similar function in both species

(C) a common embryological origin

(D) the same chemical composition

(E) the same number of bones

65. Which of the following types of plant cells is dead at functional maturity?

(A) Phloem companion cell

(B) Xylem vessel element

(C) Root endodermal cell

(D) Stem cortex cell

(E) Mesophyll cell

66. In a particular plant species, the allele for tall plants is dominant and the allele for dwarfing is recessive. Which of the following is the expected phenotypic ratio of the offspring from a cross between a heterozygous plant and a dwarf plant?

 (A) 1 tall plant : 3 dwarf plants
 (B) 1 tall plant : 9 dwarf plants
 (C) 1 tall plant : 1 dwarf plant
 (D) 3 tall plants : 1 dwarf plant
 (E) 9 tall plants : 3 dwarf plants

67. Which of the following best describes the decomposers in an ecological community?

 (A) They are the top predators.
 (B) They do not occur in early successional stages.
 (C) They are the main contributors to the gross primary productivity.
 (D) They fix carbon for plant respiration.
 (E) They are heterotrophic.

68. The nearly universal nature of the genetic code supports the view that

 (A) all living organisms on Earth share a common ancestor
 (B) nucleic acids were the first living things
 (C) proteins are of secondary importance to living systems
 (D) the protein composition of all living organisms is the same
 (E) there is redundancy in the genetic code

Questions 69–70

The pedigree below shows the occurrence of a rare, sex-linked genetic condition in a family. Shaded symbols indicate the presence of the condition. Circles indicate females, and squares indicate males.

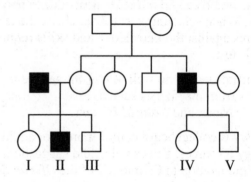

69. Individual I most likely has the same genotype as

 (A) her father
 (B) her grandfather
 (C) Individual III
 (D) Individual IV
 (E) Individual V

70. If the parents of Individuals I, II, and III have a second daughter, what is the probability that the daughter will exhibit the condition?

 (A) 0%
 (B) 25%
 (C) 33%
 (D) 50%
 (E) 100%

Study Resources

Most textbooks used in college-level biology courses cover the topics in the outline given earlier, but the approaches to certain topics and the emphases given to them may differ. To prepare for the Biology exam, it is advisable to study one or more college textbooks, which can be found in most college bookstores. When selecting a textbook, check the table of contents against the knowledge and skills required for this test.

Candidates would do well to consult pertinent articles from magazines such as *Scientific American*, *Science News*, and *Natural History*.

Visit www.collegeboard.com/clepprep for additional biology resources. You can also find suggestions for exam preparation in Chapter IV of the *Official Study Guide*. In addition, many college faculty post their course materials on their schools' Web sites.

Answer Key

1.	E	36.	B
2.	E	37.	E
3.	A	38.	A
4.	C	39.	D
5.	D	40.	D
6.	E	41.	E
7.	E	42.	A
8.	D	43.	B
9.	C	44.	C
10.	C	45.	C
11.	C	46.	E
12.	D	47.	B
13.	A	48.	E
14.	D	49.	B
15.	B	50.	B
16.	D	51.	B
17.	C	52.	C
18.	B	53.	B
19.	B	54.	A
20.	B	55.	C
21.	D	56.	B
22.	E	57.	E
23.	B	58.	B
24.	D	59.	E
25.	D	60.	C
26.	A	61.	D
27.	B	62.	E
28.	D	63.	D
29.	A	64.	C
30.	C	65.	B
31.	E	66.	C
32.	E	67.	E
33.	D	68.	A
34.	A	69.	D
35.	C	70.	D

Calculus

Description of the Examination

The Calculus examination covers skills and concepts that are usually taught in a one-semester college course in calculus. The content of each examination is approximately 60% limits and differential calculus and 40% integral calculus. Algebraic, trigonometric, exponential, logarithmic, and general functions are included. The exam is primarily concerned with an intuitive understanding of calculus and experience with its methods and applications. Knowledge of preparatory mathematics, including algebra, geometry, trigonometry, and analytic geometry is assumed.

The examination contains 44 questions, in two sections, to be answered in approximately 90 minutes. Any time candidates spend on tutorials and providing personal information is in addition to the actual testing time.

- Section 1: 27 questions, approximately 50 minutes. No calculator is allowed for this section.
- Section 2: 17 questions, approximately 40 minutes. The use of an **online graphing calculator (non-CAS)** is allowed for this section. Only some of the questions will require the use of the calculator.

Graphing Calculator

A graphing calculator is integrated into the exam software, and it is available to students during Section 2 of the exam. Since only some of the questions in Section 2 actually require the calculator, students are expected to know how and when to make appropriate use of it. The graphing calculator, together with a brief tutorial, is available to students as a free download for a 30-day trial period. **Students are expected to download the calculator and become familiar with its functionality prior to taking the exam.**

For more information about downloading the practice version of the graphing calculator, please visit the Calculus exam description on the CLEP Web site, www.collegeboard.com/clep.

In order to answer some of the questions in Section 2 of the exam, students may be required to use the online graphing calculator in the following ways:

- Perform calculations (e.g., exponents, roots, trigonometric values, logarithms).
- Graph functions and analyze the graphs.
- Find zeros of functions.
- Find points of intersection of graphs of functions.
- Find minima/maxima of functions.
- Find numerical solutions to equations.
- Generate a table of values for a function.

Knowledge and Skills Required

Questions on the exam require candidates to demonstrate the following abilities:

- Solving routine problems involving the techniques of calculus (approximately 50% of the exam)
- Solving nonroutine problems involving an understanding of the concepts and applications of calculus (approximately 50% of the exam)

The subject matter of the Calculus exam is drawn from the following topics. The percentages next to the main topics indicate the approximate percentage of exam questions on that topic.

10% Limits

- Statement of properties, e.g., limit of a constant, sum, product, or quotient
- Limit calculations, including limits involving infinity, e.g., $\lim\limits_{x \to 0} \dfrac{\sin x}{x} = 1$, $\lim\limits_{x \to 0} \dfrac{1}{x}$ is nonexistent, and $\lim\limits_{x \to \infty} \dfrac{\sin x}{x} = 0$
- Continuity

50% Differential Calculus

The Derivative

- Definitions of the derivative e.g., $f'(a) = \lim\limits_{x \to a} \dfrac{f(x) - f(a)}{x - a}$ and $f'(x) = \lim\limits_{h \to 0} \dfrac{f(x + h) - f(x)}{h}$
- Derivatives of elementary functions
- Derivatives of sums, products, and quotients (including $\tan x$ and $\cot x$)
- Derivative of a composite function (chain rule), e.g., $\sin(ax + b)$, ae^{kx}, $\ln(kx)$
- Implicit differentiation
- Derivative of the inverse of a function (including $\arcsin x$ and $\arctan x$)
- Higher order derivatives
- Corresponding characteristics of graphs of f, f', and f''
- Statement of the Mean Value Theorem; applications and graphical illustrations
- Relation between differentiability and continuity
- Use of L'Hospital's Rule (quotient and indeterminate forms)

Applications of the Derivative

- Slope of a curve at a point
- Tangent lines and linear approximation
- Curve sketching: increasing and decreasing functions; relative and absolute maximum and minimum points; concavity; points of inflection
- Extreme value problems
- Velocity and acceleration of a particle moving along a line
- Average and instantaneous rates of change
- Related rates of change

40% Integral Calculus

Antiderivatives and Techniques of Integration

- Concept of antiderivatives
- Basic integration formulas
- Integration by substitution (use of identities, change of variable)

Applications of Antiderivatives

- Distance and velocity from acceleration with initial conditions
- Solutions of $y' = ky$ and applications to growth and decay

The Definite Integral

- Definition of the definite integral as the limit of a sequence of Riemann sums and approximations of the definite integral using areas of rectangles
- Properties of the definite integral
- The Fundamental Theorem: $\dfrac{d}{dx} \int_a^x f(t)\, dt = f(x)$ and $\int_a^b F'(x)\, dx = F(b) - F(a)$

Applications of the Definite Integral

- Average value of a function on an interval
- Area, including area between curves
- Other (e.g., accumulated change from a rate of change)

Notes and Reference Information

(1) Figures that accompany questions are intended to provide information useful in answering the questions. All figures lie in a plane unless otherwise indicated. The figures are drawn as accurately as possible EXCEPT when it is stated in a specific question that the figure is not drawn to scale. Straight lines and smooth curves may appear slightly jagged.

(2) Unless otherwise specified, all angles are measured in radians, and all numbers used are real numbers.

(3) Unless otherwise specified, the domain of any function f is assumed to be the set of all real numbers x for which $f(x)$ is a real number. The range of f is assumed to be the set of all real numbers $f(x)$, where x is in the domain of f.

(4) In this test, $\ln x$ denotes the natural logarithm of x (that is, the logarithm to the base e).

(5) The inverse of a trigonometric function f may be indicated using the inverse function notation f^{-1} or with the prefix "arc" (e.g., $\sin^{-1} x = \arcsin x$).

Sample Test Questions

The following sample questions do not appear on an actual CLEP Examination. They are intended to give potential test-takers an indication of the format and difficulty level of the examination, and to provide content for practice and review. Knowing the correct answers to all of the sample questions is not a guarantee of satisfactory performance on the exam.

Section I

Directions: A calculator will <u>not</u> be available for questions in this section. Some questions will require you to select from among five choices. For these questions, select the BEST of the choices given. Some questions will require you to enter a numerical answer in the box provided.

1. If $f(x) = -2x^{-3}$, then $f'(x) =$

   (A) $6x^2$
   (B) $6x^{-2}$
   (C) $6x^{-4}$
   (D) $-6x^{-2}$
   (E) $-6x^{-4}$

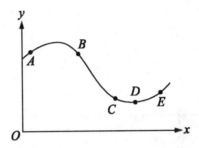

2. At which of the five points on the graph in the figure above are $\dfrac{dy}{dx}$ and $\dfrac{d^2y}{dx^2}$ both negative?

   (A) A (B) B (C) C (D) D (E) E

3. Which of the following is an equation of the line tangent to the graph of $f(x) = x^3 - x$ at the point where $x = 2$?

   (A) $y - 6 = 4(x - 2)$
   (B) $y - 6 = 5(x - 2)$
   (C) $y - 6 = 6(x - 2)$
   (D) $y - 6 = 11(x - 2)$
   (E) $y - 6 = 12(x - 2)$

4. $\displaystyle\int \left(e^x + e\right) dx =$

   (A) $e^x + C$
   (B) $e^x + e + C$
   (C) $e^x + ex + C$
   (D) $\dfrac{e^{x+1}}{x+1} + ex + C$
   (E) $\dfrac{e^{x+1}}{x+1} + \dfrac{e^2}{2} + C$

5. What is $\displaystyle\lim_{x\to\infty} \frac{x^2 - 4}{2 + x - 4x^2}$?

(A) -2

(B) $-\dfrac{1}{4}$

(C) $\dfrac{1}{2}$

(D) 1

(E) The limit does not exist.

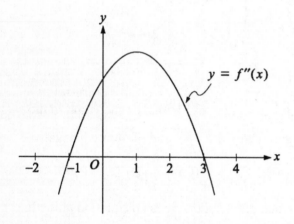

6. The graph of f'', the second derivative of the function f, is shown in the figure above. On what intervals is the graph of f concave up?

(A) $(-\infty, \infty)$

(B) $(-\infty, -1)$ and $(3, \infty)$

(C) $(-\infty, 1)$

(D) $(-1, 3)$

(E) $(1, \infty)$

7. $\displaystyle\int (x-1)\sqrt{x}\ dx =$

(A) $\dfrac{2}{5}x^{\frac{5}{2}} - \dfrac{2}{3}x^{\frac{3}{2}} + C$

(B) $\dfrac{1}{2}x^2 + 2x^{\frac{2}{3}} - x + C$

(C) $\dfrac{1}{2}x^2 - x + C$

(D) $\dfrac{2}{3}x^{\frac{3}{2}} + 2x^{\frac{1}{2}} + C$

(E) $\dfrac{3}{2}x^{\frac{1}{2}} - x^{-\frac{1}{2}} + C$

8. Let f and g be the functions defined by $f(x) = \sin x$ and $g(x) = \cos x$. For which of the following values of a is the line tangent to the graph of f at $x = a$ parallel to the line tangent to the graph of g at $x = a$?

(A) 0 (B) $\dfrac{\pi}{4}$ (C) $\dfrac{\pi}{2}$ (D) $\dfrac{3\pi}{4}$ (E) π

9. The acceleration, at time t, of a particle moving along the x-axis is given by $a(t) = 20t^3 + 6$. At time $t = 0$, the velocity of the particle is 0 and the position of the particle is 7. What is the position of the particle at time t ?

(A) $120t + 7$

(B) $60t^2 + 7t$

(C) $5t^4 + 6t + 7$

(D) $t^5 + 3t^2 + 7$

(E) $t^5 + 3t^2 + 7t$

10. If $f(x) = \dfrac{\sin x}{2x}$, then $f'(x) =$

(A) $\dfrac{\cos x}{2}$

(B) $\dfrac{x\cos x - \sin x}{2x^2}$

(C) $\dfrac{x\cos x - \sin x}{4x^2}$

(D) $\dfrac{\sin x - x\cos x}{2x^2}$

(E) $\dfrac{\sin x - x\cos x}{4x^2}$

x	$f(x)$	$f'(x)$	$g(x)$	$g'(x)$
10	35	15	6	4
20	8	5	12	10
30	24	25	20	10

11. Selected values of the functions f and g and their derivatives, f' and g', are given in the table above. If $h(x) = f(g(x))$, what is the value of $h'(30)$?

(A) 5   (B) 15   (C) 35   (D) 50   (E) 250

12. What is $\displaystyle\lim_{h\to 0} \dfrac{\cos\left(\dfrac{\pi}{2} + h\right) - \cos\dfrac{\pi}{2}}{h}$?

(A) $-\infty$ (B) -1 (C) 0   (D) 1   (E) ∞

13. If $x^2 + y^3 = x^3 y^2$, then $\dfrac{dy}{dx} =$

(A) $\dfrac{2x + 3y^2 - 3x^2 y^2}{2x^3 y}$

(B) $\dfrac{2x^3 y + 3x^2 y^2 - 2x}{3y^2}$

(C) $\dfrac{3x^2 y^2 - 2x}{3y^2 - 2x^3 y}$

(D) $\dfrac{3y^2 - 2x^3 y}{3x^2 y^2 - 2x}$

(E) $\dfrac{6x^2 y - 2x}{3y^2}$

14. For which of the following functions does $\dfrac{d^3 y}{dx^3} = \dfrac{dy}{dx}$?

   I. $y = e^x$

   II. $y = e^{-x}$

   III. $y = \sin x$

(A) I only

(B) II only

(C) III only

(D) I and II

(E) II and III

15. The vertical height, in feet, of a ball thrown upward from a cliff is given by $s(t) = -16t^2 + 64t + 200$, where t is measured in seconds. What is the height of the ball, in feet, when its velocity is zero?

16. Which of the following statements about the curve $y = x^4 - 2x^3$ is true?

(A) The curve has no relative extremum.

(B) The curve has one point of inflection and two relative extrema.

(C) The curve has two points of inflection and one relative extremum.

(D) The curve has two points of inflection and two relative extrema.

(E) The curve has two points of inflection and three relative extrema.

17. $\dfrac{d}{dx}(\sin(\cos x)) =$

(A) $\cos(\cos x)$

(B) $\sin(-\sin x)$

(C) $(\sin(-\sin x))\cos x$

(D) $-(\cos(\cos x))\sin x$

(E) $-(\sin(\cos x))\sin x$

18. Let f be the function defined by

$$f(x) = \begin{cases} \dfrac{x^2 - 25}{x - 5} & \text{for } x \neq 5 \\ 0 & \text{for } x = 5 \end{cases}.$$

Which of the following statements about f are true?

I. $\lim\limits_{x \to 5} f(x)$ exists.

II. $f(5)$ exists.

III. $f(x)$ is continuous at $x = 5$.

(A) None

(B) I only

(C) II only

(D) I and II only

(E) I, II, and III

19. What is the average rate of change of the function f defined by $f(x) = 100 \cdot 2^x$ on the interval $[0, 4]$?

(A) 100

(B) 375

(C) 400

(D) 1,500

(E) 1,600

20. If the functions f and g are defined for all real numbers and f is an antiderivative of g, which of the following statements is NOT necessarily true?

(A) If $g(x) > 0$ for all x, then f is increasing.

(B) If $g(a) = 0$, then the graph of f has a horizontal tangent at $x = a$.

(C) If $f(x) = 0$ for all x, then $g(x) = 0$ for all x.

(D) If $g(x) = 0$ for all x, then $f(x) = 0$ for all x.

(E) f is continuous for all x.

21. If $f(x) = \arctan(\pi x)$, then $f'(0) =$

(A) $-\pi$ (B) -1 (C) 0   (D) 1   (E) π

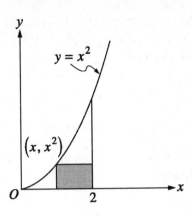

y = x²

(x, x²)

O   2

22. A rectangle with one side on the x-axis and one side on the line $x = 2$ has its upper left vertex on the graph of $y = x^2$, as indicated in the figure above. For what value of x does the area of the rectangle attain its maximum value?

(A) 2   (B) $\frac{4}{3}$ (C) 1   (D) $\frac{3}{4}$ (E) $\frac{2}{3}$

23. Let $f(x) = x^3 + x$. If h is the inverse function of f, then $h'(2) =$

(A) $\frac{1}{13}$ (B) $\frac{1}{4}$ (C) 1   (D) 4   (E) 13

24. Let F be the number of trees in a forest at time t, in years. If F is decreasing at a rate given by the equation $\frac{dF}{dt} = -2F$ and if $F(0) = 5000$, then $F(t) =$

(A) $5000t^{-2}$

(B) $5000e^{-2t}$

(C) $5000 - 2t$

(D) $5000 + t^{-2}$

(E) $5000 + e^{-2t}$

25. The function f is given by $f(x) = \sin(12x)$. Which of the following is the local linear approximation for f at $x = 0$?

(A) $y = 12x$

(B) $y = -12x$

(C) $y = 1 + 12x$

(D) $y = 1 - 12x$

(E) $y = -1 + 12x$

26. What is the area of the region in the first quadrant that is bounded by the line $y = 6x$ and the parabola $y = 3x^2$?

27. Let f be a differentiable function defined on the closed interval $[a, b]$ and let c be a point in the open interval (a, b) such that

- $f'(c) = 0$,
- $f'(x) > 0$ when $a \le x < c$, and
- $f'(x) < 0$ when $c < x \le b$.

Which of the following statements must be true?

(A) $f(c) = 0$

(B) $f''(c) = 0$

(C) $f(c)$ is an absolute maximum value of f on $[a, b]$.

(D) $f(c)$ is an absolute minimum value of f on $[a, b]$.

(E) The graph of f has a point of inflection at $x = c$.

28. The function f is continuous on the open interval $(-\pi, \pi)$. If $f(x) = \dfrac{\cos x - 1}{x \sin x}$ for $x \neq 0$, what is the value of $f(0)$?

   (A) -1 (B) $-\dfrac{1}{2}$ (C) 0 (D) $\dfrac{1}{2}$ (E) 1

$$g(20) = 0$$
$$g'(t) > 0 \text{ for all values of } t$$

29. The function g is differentiable and satisfies the conditions above. Let F be the function given by $F(x) = \displaystyle\int_0^x g(t)\, dt$. Which of the following must be true?

   (A) F has a local minimum at $x = 20$.

   (B) F has a local maximum at $x = 20$.

   (C) The graph of F has a point of inflection at $x = 20$.

   (D) F has no local minima or local maxima on the interval $0 \leq x < \infty$.

   (E) $F'(20)$ does not exist.

30. The Riemann sum $\displaystyle\sum_{i=1}^{50} \left(\dfrac{i}{50}\right)^2 \dfrac{1}{50}$ on the closed interval $[0, 1]$ is an approximation for which of the following definite integrals?

   (A) $\displaystyle\int_0^1 x^2\, dx$

   (B) $\displaystyle\int_0^{50} x^2\, dx$

   (C) $\displaystyle\int_0^1 \left(\dfrac{x}{50}\right)^2 dx$

   (D) $\displaystyle\int_0^{50} \left(\dfrac{x}{50}\right)^2 dx$

   (E) $\displaystyle\int_0^1 \dfrac{x^2}{50^3}\, dx$

Section II

Directions: A graphing calculator will be available for the questions in this section. Some questions will require you to select from among five choices. For these questions, select the BEST of the choices given. If the exact numerical value of your answer is not one of the choices, select the choice that best approximates this value. Some questions will require you to enter a numerical answer in the box provided.

31. $\displaystyle\int_5^{10} \dfrac{\ln(10x)}{x}\, dx =$

   (A)   1.282

   (B)   2.952

   (C)   5.904

   (D)   6.797

   (E)   37.500

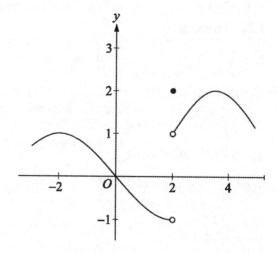

32. The graph of the function f is shown in the figure above. What is $\displaystyle\lim_{x \to 2} f(x)$?

   (A) -1

   (B) 0

   (C) 1

   (D) 2

   (E)   The limit does not exist.

33. If the function f is continuous for all real numbers and $\lim\limits_{h \to 0} \dfrac{f(a+h) - f(a)}{h} = 7$, then which of the following statements must be true?

(A) $f(a) = 7$
(B) f is differentiable at $x = a$.
(C) f is differentiable for all real numbers.
(D) f is increasing for $x > 0$.
(E) f is increasing for all real numbers.

34. Let f be a function with second derivative given by $f''(x) = \sin(2x) - \cos(4x)$. How many points of inflection does the graph of f have on the interval $[0, 10]$?

(A) Six
(B) Seven
(C) Eight
(D) Ten
(E) Thirteen

35. The area of the region in the first quadrant between the graph of $y = x\sqrt{4 - x^2}$ and the x-axis is

(A) $\dfrac{2}{3}\sqrt{2}$
(B) $\dfrac{8}{3}$
(C) $2\sqrt{2}$
(D) $2\sqrt{3}$
(E) $\dfrac{16}{3}$

36. The function f is given by $f(x) = 3x^2 + 1$. What is the average value of f over the closed interval $[1, 3]$?

37. Starting at $t = 0$, a particle moves along the x-axis so that its position at time t is given by $x(t) = t^4 - 5t^2 + 2t$. What are all values of t for which the particle is moving to the left?

(A) $0 < t < 0.913$
(B) $0.203 < t < 1.470$
(C) $0.414 < t < 0.913$
(D) $0.414 < t < 2.000$
(E) There are no values of t for which the particle is moving to the left.

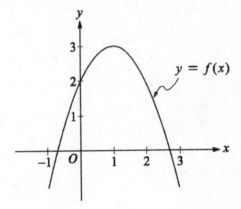

38. The function f has a relative maximum value of 3 at $x = 1$, as shown in the figure above. If $h(x) = x^2 f(x)$, then $h'(1) =$

(A) -6 (B) -3 (C) 0 (D) 3 (E) 6

39. $\int \cos^2 x \sin x \, dx =$

(A) $-\dfrac{\cos^3 x}{3} + C$

(B) $-\dfrac{\cos^3 x \sin^2 x}{6} + C$

(C) $\dfrac{\sin^2 x}{2} + C$

(D) $\dfrac{\cos^3 x}{3} + C$

(E) $\dfrac{\cos^3 x \sin^2 x}{6} + C$

$$f'(x) = 1 - \left(x^2 + x\right)e^{-x}$$

40. The first derivative of the function f is given above. At what value of x does the function f attain its minimum value on the closed interval $[-5, 5]$?

(A) -5.000

(B) -1.235

(C) -0.618

(D) 0.160

(E) 1.618

41. The function f is differentiable on $[a, b]$ and $a < c < b$. Which of the following is NOT necessarily true?

(A) $\displaystyle\int_a^b f(x) \, dx = \int_a^c f(x) \, dx + \int_c^b f(x) \, dx$

(B) There exists a point d in the open interval (a, b) such that $f'(d) = \dfrac{f(b) - f(a)}{b - a}$.

(C) $\displaystyle\int_a^b f(x) \, dx \geq 0$

(D) $\displaystyle\lim_{x \to c} f(x) = f(c)$

(E) If k is a real number, then $\displaystyle\int_a^b k f(x) \, dx = k \int_a^b f(x) \, dx$.

$$g'(x) = \tan\left(\frac{2}{1 + x^2}\right)$$

42. Let g be the function with first derivative given above and $g(1) = 5$. If f is the function defined by $f(x) = \ln(g(x))$, what is the value of $f'(1)$?

(A) 0.311

(B) 0.443

(C) 0.642

(D) 0.968

(E) 3.210

43. Let $r(t)$ be a differentiable function that is positive and increasing. The rate of increase of r^3 is equal to 12 times the rate of increase of r when $r(t) =$

(A) $\sqrt[3]{4}$

(B) 2

(C) $\sqrt[3]{12}$

(D) $2\sqrt{3}$

(E) 6

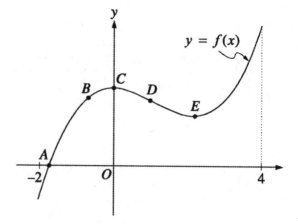

44. The function f is shown in the figure above. At which of the following points could the derivative of f be equal to the average rate of change of f over the closed interval $[-2, 4]$?

(A) A (B) B (C) C (D) D (E) E

45. $\dfrac{d}{dx}\displaystyle\int_1^x t^2\, dt =$

(A) $2x$

(B) $x^2 - 1$

(C) x^2

(D) $\dfrac{x^3}{3} - \dfrac{1}{3}$

(E) $\dfrac{x^3}{3} + C$

46. A college is planning to construct a new parking lot. The parking lot must be rectangular and enclose 6,000 square meters of land. A fence will surround the parking lot, and another fence parallel to one of the sides will divide the parking lot into two sections. What are the dimensions, in meters, of the rectangular lot that will use the least amount of fencing?

(A) 1,000 by 1,500

(B) $20\sqrt{5}$ by $60\sqrt{5}$

(C) $20\sqrt{10}$ by $30\sqrt{10}$

(D) $20\sqrt{15}$ by $20\sqrt{15}$

(E) $20\sqrt{15}$ by $40\sqrt{15}$

x	1	2	3	4	5
$f(x)$	15	10	9	6	5

47. The function f is continuous on the closed interval $[1, 5]$ and has values that are given in the table above. If two subintervals of equal length are used, what is the <u>midpoint</u> Riemann sum approximation of $\displaystyle\int_1^5 f(x)\, dx$?

(A) –3　(B) 9　(C) 14　(D) 32　(E) 35

48. If f is continuous for all x, which of the following integrals necessarily have the same value?

I. $\displaystyle\int_a^b f(x)\, dx$

II. $\displaystyle\int_0^{b-a} f(x + a)\, dx$

III. $\displaystyle\int_{a+c}^{b+c} f(x + c)\, dx$

(A) I and II only

(B) I and III only

(C) II and III only

(D) I, II, and III

(E) No two necessarily have the same value.

49. A spherical balloon is being inflated at a constant rate of 25 cm³/sec. At what rate, in cm/sec, is the radius of the balloon changing when the radius is 2 cm? (The volume of a sphere with radius r is $V = \dfrac{4}{3}\pi r^3$.)

(A) $\dfrac{25}{16\pi}$

(B) $\dfrac{25}{8\pi}$

(C) $\dfrac{75}{16\pi}$

(D) $\dfrac{32\pi}{25}$

(E) $\dfrac{32\pi}{3}$

50. *R* is the region below the curve $y = x$ and above the *x*-axis from $x = 0$ to $x = b$, where *b* is a positive constant. *S* is the region below the curve $y = \cos x$ and above the *x*-axis from $x = 0$ to $x = b$. For what value of *b* is the area of *R* equal to the area of *S* ?

(A) 0.739

(B) 0.877

(C) 0.986

(D) 1.404

(E) 4.712

Study Resources

To prepare for the Calculus exam, you should study the contents of at least one introductory college-level calculus textbook, which you can find in most college bookstores. You would do well to consult several textbooks, because the approaches to certain topics may vary. When selecting a textbook, check the table of contents against the knowledge and skills required for this exam.

Visit www.collegeboard.com/clepprep for additional calculus resources. You can also find suggestions for exam preparation in Chapter IV of the *Official Study Guide*. In addition, many college faculty post their course materials on their schools' Web sites.

Answer Key

Section 1		Section 2	
1.	C	31.	B
2.	B	32.	E
3.	D	33.	B
4.	C	34.	B
5.	B	35.	B
6.	D	36.	14
7.	A	37.	B
8.	D	38.	E
9.	D	39.	A
10.	B	40.	B
11.	D	41.	C
12.	B	42.	A
13.	C	43.	B
14.	D	44.	B
15.	264	45.	C
16.	C	46.	C
17.	D	47.	D
18.	D	48.	A
19.	B	49.	A
20.	D	50.	D
21.	E		
22.	B		
23.	B		
24.	B		
25.	A		
26.	4		
27.	C		
28.	B		
29.	A		
30.	A		

Chemistry

Description of the Examination

The Chemistry examination covers material that is usually taught in a one-year college course in general chemistry. Understanding of the structure and states of matter, reaction types, equations and stoichiometry, equilibrium, kinetics, thermodynamics, and descriptive and experimental chemistry is required, as is the ability to interpret and apply this material to new and unfamiliar problems. During this examination, an online scientific calculator function and a periodic table are available as part of the testing software.

The examination contains approximately 75 questions to be answered in 90 minutes. Some of these are pretest questions that will not be scored. Any time spent on tutorials and providing personal information is in addition to the actual testing time.

Knowledge and Skills Required

Questions on the Chemistry examination require candidates to demonstrate one or more of the following abilities.

- **Recall**—remember specific facts; demonstrate straightforward knowledge of information and familiarity with terminology

- **Application**—understand concepts and reformulate information into other equivalent terms; apply knowledge to unfamiliar and/or practical situations; use mathematics to solve chemistry problems

- **Interpretation**—infer and deduce from data available and integrate information to form conclusions; recognize unstated assumptions

The subject matter of the Chemistry examination is drawn from the following topics. The percentages next to the main topics indicate the approximate percentage of exam questions on that topic.

20% Structure of Matter

Atomic theory and atomic structure
- Evidence for the atomic theory
- Atomic masses; determination by chemical and physical means
- Atomic number and mass number; isotopes and mass spectroscopy
- Electron energy levels: atomic spectra, quantum numbers, atomic orbitals
- Periodic relationships, including, for example, atomic radii, ionization energies, electron affinities, oxidation states

Chemical bonding
- Binding forces
  - Types: covalent, ionic, metallic, macromolecular (or network), dispersion, hydrogen bonding
  - Relationships to structure and to properties
  - Polarity of bonds, electronegativities
- Geometry of molecules, ions, and coordination complexes: structural isomerism, dipole moments of molecules, relation of properties to structure
- Molecular models
  - Valence bond theory; hybridization of orbitals, resonance, sigma and pi bonds
  - Other models, for example, molecular orbital

Nuclear chemistry: nuclear equations, half-lives, and radioactivity; chemical applications

19%   States of Matter

Gases

- Laws of ideal gases; equations of state for an ideal gas
- Kinetic-molecular theory
  - Interpretation of ideal gas laws on the basis of this theory
  - The mole concept; Avogadro's number
  - Dependence of kinetic energy of molecules on temperature: Boltzmann distribution
  - Deviations from ideal gas laws

Liquids and solids

- Liquids and solids from the kinetic-molecular viewpoint
- Phase diagrams of one-component systems
- Changes of state, critical phenomena
- Crystal structure

Solutions

- Types of solutions and factors affecting solubility
- Methods of expressing concentration
- Colligative properties; for example, Raoult's law
- Effect of interionic attraction on colligative properties and solubility

12%   Reaction Types

Formation and cleavage of covalent bonds

- Acid-base reactions; concepts of Arrhenius, Brønsted-Lowry, and Lewis; amphoterism
- Reactions involving coordination complexes

Precipitation reactions

Oxidation-reduction reactions

- Oxidation number
- The role of the electron in oxidation-reduction
- Electrochemistry; electrolytic cells, standard half-cell potentials, prediction of the direction of redox reactions, effect of concentration changes

10%   Equations and Stoichiometry

Ionic and molecular species present in chemical systems; net-ionic equations

Stoichiometry: mass and volume relations with emphasis on the mole concept

Balancing of equations, including those for redox reactions

7%   Equilibrium

Concept of dynamic equilibrium, physical and chemical; LeChâtelier's principle; equilibrium constants

Quantitative treatment

- Equilibrium constants for gaseous reactions in terms of both molar concentrations and partial pressure (K_c, K_p)
- Equilibrium constants for reactions in solutions
  - Constants for acids and bases; pK; pH
  - Solubility-product constants and their application to precipitation and the dissolution of slightly soluble compounds
  - Constants for complex ions
  - Common ion effect; buffers

4%   Kinetics

Concept of rate of reaction

Order of reaction and rate constant: their determination from experimental data

Effect of temperature change on rates

Energy of activation; the role of catalysts

The relationship between the rate-determining step and a mechanism

5% **Thermodynamics**

State functions

First law: heat of formation; heat of reaction; change in enthalpy, Hess's law; heat capacity; heats of vaporization and fusion

Second law: free energy of formation; free energy of reaction; dependence of change in free energy on enthalpy and entropy changes

Relationship of change in free energy to equilibrium constants and electrode potentials

14% **Descriptive Chemistry**

The accumulation of certain specific facts of chemistry is essential to enable students to comprehend the development of principles and concepts, to demonstrate applications of principles, to relate fact to theory and properties to structure, and to develop an understanding of systematic nomenclature that facilitates communication. The following areas are normally included on the examination:

- Chemical reactivity and products of chemical reactions
- Relationships in the periodic table: horizontal, vertical, and diagonal
- Chemistry of the main groups and transition elements, including typical examples of each
- Organic chemistry, including such topics as functional groups and isomerism (may be treated as a separate unit or as exemplary material in other areas, such as bonding)

9% **Experimental Chemistry**

Some questions are based on laboratory experiments widely performed in general chemistry and ask about the equipment used, observations made, calculations performed, and interpretation of the results. The questions are designed to provide a measure of understanding of the basic tools of chemistry and their applications to simple chemical systems.

Sample Test Questions

The following sample questions do not appear on an actual CLEP examination. They are intended to give potential test-takers an indication of the format and difficulty level of the examination and to provide content for practice and review. Knowing the correct answers to all of the sample questions is not a guarantee of satisfactory performance on the exam.

Note: For all questions involving solutions and/or chemical equations, assume that the system is in pure water and at room temperature unless otherwise stated.

Part A

Directions: Each set of lettered choices below refers to the numbered questions or statements immediately following it. Select the one lettered choice that best answers each question or best fits each statement. A choice may be used once, more than once, or not at all in each set.

Questions 1–3

(A) F
(B) S
(C) Mg
(D) Ar
(E) Mn

1. Forms monatomic ions with –2 charge in solutions

2. Forms a compound having the formula KXO_4

3. Forms oxides that are common air pollutants and that yield acidic solutions in water

Questions 4–6

(A) Hydrofluoric acid
(B) Carbon dioxide
(C) Aluminum hydroxide
(D) Ammonia
(E) Hydrogen peroxide

4. Is a good oxidizing agent

5. Is used extensively for the production of fertilizers

6. Has amphoteric properties

Questions 7–8

(A) A network solid with covalent bonding
(B) A molecular solid with London (dispersion) forces only
(C) A molecular solid with hydrogen bonding
(D) An ionic solid
(E) A metallic solid

7. Solid ethyl alcohol, C_2H_5OH

8. Silicon dioxide, SiO_2

Questions 9–11

(A) CO_3^{2-}
(B) MnO_4^-
(C) NH_4^+
(D) Ba^{2+}
(E) Al^{3+}

Assume that you have several "unknowns," each consisting of an aqueous solution of a salt that contains one of the ions listed above. Which ion <u>must</u> be present if the following observations are made of that unknown?

9. The solution is colored.

10. An odor can be detected when a sample of the solution is added drop by drop to a warm solution of sodium hydroxide.

11. A precipitate is formed when a dilute solution of H_2SO_4 is added to a sample of the solution.

Questions 12–13

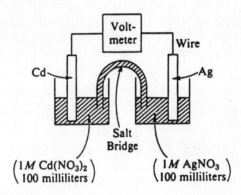

The spontaneous reaction that occurs when the cell above operates is

$$2\,Ag^+ + Cd(s) \rightarrow 2\,Ag(s) + Cd^{2+}.$$

(A) Voltage increases.
(B) Voltage decreases but remains above zero.
(C) Voltage becomes zero and remains at zero.
(D) No change in voltage occurs.
(E) Direction of voltage change cannot be predicted without additional information.

Which of the above occurs for each of the following circumstances?

12. The silver electrode is made larger.

13. The salt bridge is replaced by a platinum wire.

Part B

Directions: Each of the questions or incomplete statements below is followed by five suggested answers or completions. Select the one that is best in each case.

14.
Hydrogen Halide	Normal Boiling Point, °C
HF	+19
HCl	−85
HBr	−67
HI	−35

The liquefied hydrogen halides have the normal boiling points given above. The relatively high boiling point of HF can be correctly explained by which of the following?

(A) HF gas is more ideal.

(B) HF is the strongest acid.

(C) HF molecules have a smaller dipole moment.

(D) HF is much less soluble in water.

(E) HF molecules tend to form hydrogen bonds.

15.
$$1s^2 \, 2s^2 \, 2p^6 \, 3s^2 \, 3p^3$$

Atoms of an element, X, have the electronic configuration shown above. The compound most likely formed with magnesium, Mg, is

(A) MgX

(B) Mg_2X

(C) MgX_2

(D) Mg_2X_3

(E) Mg_3X_2

16. The density of an unknown gas is 4.20 grams per liter at 3.00 atmospheres pressure and 127°C. What is the molar mass of this gas? ($R = 0.0821$ liter·atm/mole·K)

(A) 14.6 g

(B) 46.0 g

(C) 88.0 g

(D) 94.1 g

(E) 138.0 g

Questions 17–18

$$H_3AsO_4 + 3\,I^- + 2\,H_3O^+ \rightarrow H_3AsO_3 + I_3^- + 3\,H_2O$$

The oxidation of iodide ions by arsenic acid in acidic aqueous solution occurs according to the balanced equation shown above. The experimental rate law for the reaction at 25°C is

$$\text{Rate} = k\,[H_3AsO_4]\,[I^-]\,[H_3O^+].$$

17. What is the order of the reaction with respect to I^- ?

(A) 1

(B) 2

(C) 3

(D) 5

(E) 6

18. According to the rate law for the reaction, an increase in the concentration of the hydronium ion has what effect on the reaction at 25°C?

(A) The rate of reaction increases.

(B) The rate of reaction decreases.

(C) The value of the equilibrium constant increases.

(D) The value of the equilibrium constant decreases.

(E) Neither the rate nor the value of the equilibrium constant is changed.

19. The critical temperature of a substance is the

(A) temperature at which the vapor pressure of the liquid is equal to the external pressure

(B) temperature at which the vapor pressure of the liquid is equal to 760 mm Hg

(C) temperature at which the solid, liquid, and vapor phases are all in equilibrium

(D) temperature at which the liquid and vapor phases are in equilibrium at 1 atmosphere

(E) lowest temperature above which a substance cannot be liquefied at any applied pressure

20. $$Cu(s) + 2\,Ag^+ \rightarrow Cu^{2+} + 2\,Ag(s)$$

If the equilibrium constant for the reaction above is 3.7×10^{15}, which of the following correctly describes the standard voltage, $E°$, and the standard free energy change, $\Delta G°$, for this reaction?

(A) $E°$ is positive and $\Delta G°$ is negative.

(B) $E°$ is negative and $\Delta G°$ is positive.

(C) $E°$ and $\Delta G°$ are both positive.

(D) $E°$ and $\Delta G°$ are both negative.

(E) $E°$ and $\Delta G°$ are both zero.

21. When $^{214}_{84}Po$ decays, the emission consists consecutively of an α particle, then two β particles, and finally another α particle. The resulting stable nucleus is

(A) $^{206}_{83}Bi$

(B) $^{210}_{83}Bi$

(C) $^{206}_{82}Pb$

(D) $^{208}_{82}Pb$

(E) $^{210}_{81}Tl$

22. The pH of $0.1\,M$ ammonia is approximately

(A) 1

(B) 4

(C) 7

(D) 11

(E) 14

23. $$\dots CrO_2^- + \dots OH^- \rightarrow$$
$$\dots CrO_4^{2-} + \dots H_2O + \dots e^-$$

When the equation for the half reaction above is balanced, what is the ratio of the coefficients $OH^- : CrO_2^-$?

(A) $1 : 1$

(B) $2 : 1$

(C) $3 : 1$

(D) $4 : 1$

(E) $5 : 1$

24. $$CuO(s) + H_2(g) \leftrightarrows Cu(s) + H_2O(g) \quad \Delta H = -2.0\ kJ$$

The substances in the equation above are at equilibrium at pressure P and temperature T. The equilibrium can be shifted to favor the products by

(A) increasing the pressure by means of a moving piston at constant T

(B) increasing the pressure by adding an inert gas such as nitrogen

(C) decreasing the temperature

(D) allowing some gases to escape at constant P and T

(E) adding a catalyst

25. The molality of the glucose in a $1.0\,M$ glucose solution can be obtained by using which of the following?

(A) Solubility of glucose in water

(B) Degree of dissociation of glucose

(C) Volume of the solution

(D) Temperature of the solution

(E) Density of the solution

26. The geometry of the SO_3 molecule is best described as

(A) trigonal planar

(B) trigonal pyramidal

(C) square pyramidal

(D) bent

(E) tetrahedral

27. Which of the following molecules has the shortest bond length?

(A) N_2

(B) O_2

(C) Cl_2

(D) Br_2

(E) I_2

28. What number of moles of O_2 is needed to produce 14.2 grams of P_4O_{10} (molar mass 284 g) from P?

(A) 0.0500 mole

(B) 0.0625 mole

(C) 0.125 mole

(D) 0.250 mole

(E) 0.500 mole

29. If 0.060 faraday is passed through an electrolytic cell containing a solution of In^{3+} ions, the maximum number of moles of In that could be deposited at the cathode is

(A) 0.010 mole

(B) 0.020 mole

(C) 0.030 mole

(D) 0.060 mole

(E) 0.18 mole

30. $CH_4(g) + 2\,O_2(g) \rightarrow CO_2(g) + 2\,H_2O(l)$
$$\Delta H^\circ_{rxn} = -889.1 \text{ kJ mol}^{-1}$$

$\Delta H^\circ_f\, H_2O(l) = -285.8 \text{ kJ mol}^{-1}$
$\Delta H^\circ_f\, CO_2(g) = -393.3 \text{ kJ mol}^{-1}$

What is the standard heat of formation, ΔH°_f, of methane, $CH_4(g)$, as calculated from the data above?

(A) −210.0 kJ mol^{-1}

(B) −107.5 kJ mol^{-1}

(C) −75.8 kJ mol^{-1}

(D) 75.8 kJ mol^{-1}

(E) 210.0 kJ mol^{-1}

31. Each of the following can act as both a Brønsted acid and a Brønsted base EXCEPT

(A) HCO_3^-

(B) $H_2PO_4^-$

(C) NH_4^+

(D) H_2O

(E) HS^-

32. Two flexible containers for gases are at the same temperature and pressure. One holds 0.50 gram of hydrogen and the other holds 8.0 grams of oxygen. Which of the following statements regarding these gas samples is FALSE?

(A) The volume of the hydrogen container is the same as the volume of the oxygen container.

(B) The number of molecules in the hydrogen container is the same as the number of molecules in the oxygen container.

(C) The density of the hydrogen sample is less than that of the oxygen sample.

(D) The average kinetic energy of the hydrogen molecules is the same as the average kinetic energy of the oxygen molecules.

(E) The average speed of the hydrogen molecules is the same as the average speed of the oxygen molecules.

33. Pi (π) bonding occurs in each of the following species EXCEPT

(A) CO_2

(B) C_2H_4

(C) CN^-

(D) C_6H_6

(E) CH_4

34. $3\,Ag(s) + 4\,HNO_3 \rightarrow 3\,AgNO_3 + NO(g) + 2\,H_2O$

The reaction of silver metal and dilute nitric acid proceeds according to the equation above. If 0.10 mole of powdered silver is added to 10. milliliters of 6.0-molar nitric acid, the number of moles of NO gas that can be formed is

(A) 0.015 mole

(B) 0.020 mole

(C) 0.030 mole

(D) 0.045 mole

(E) 0.090 mole

35. Which, if any, of the following species are in the greatest concentration in a 0.100 M solution of H_2SO_4 in water?

(A) H_2SO_4 molecules
(B) H_3O^+ ions
(C) HSO_4^- ions
(D) SO_4^{2-} ions
(E) All species are in equilibrium and therefore have the same concentrations.

36. At 20.°C, the vapor pressure of toluene is 22 mm Hg and that of benzene is 75 mm Hg. An ideal solution, equimolar in toluene and benzene, is prepared. At 20.°C, what is the mole fraction of benzene in the vapor in equilibrium with this solution?

(A) 0.23
(B) 0.29
(C) 0.50
(D) 0.77
(E) 0.83

37. Which of the following aqueous solutions has the highest boiling point?

(A) 0.10 M potassium sulfate, K_2SO_4
(B) 0.10 M hydrochloric acid, HCl
(C) 0.10 M ammonium nitrate, NH_4NO_3
(D) 0.10 M magnesium sulfate, $MgSO_4$
(E) 0.20 M sucrose, $C_{12}H_{22}O_{11}$

38. When 70 milliliters of 3.0 M Na_2CO_3 is added to 30 milliliters of 1.0 M $NaHCO_3$, the resulting concentration of Na^+ is

(A) 2.0 M
(B) 2.4 M
(C) 4.0 M
(D) 4.5 M
(E) 7.0 M

39. Which of the following species CANNOT function as an oxidizing agent?

(A) $Cr_2O_7^{2-}$
(B) MnO_4^-
(C) NO_3^-
(D) S
(E) I^-

40. A student wishes to prepare 2.00 liters of 0.100 M KIO_3 (molar mass 214 g). The proper procedure is to weigh out

(A) 42.8 grams of KIO_3 and add 2.00 kilograms of H_2O
(B) 42.8 grams of KIO_3 and add H_2O until the final homogeneous solution has a volume of 2.00 liters
(C) 21.4 grams of KIO_3 and add H_2O until the final homogeneous solution has a volume of 2.00 liters
(D) 42.8 grams of KIO_3 and add 2.00 liters of H_2O
(E) 21.4 grams of KIO_3 and add 2.00 liters of H_2O

41. A 20.0-milliliter sample of 0.200 M K_2CO_3 solution is added to 30.0 milliliters of 0.400 M $Ba(NO_3)_2$ solution. Barium carbonate precipitates. The concentration of barium ion, Ba^{2+}, in solution after reaction is

(A) 0.150 M
(B) 0.160 M
(C) 0.200 M
(D) 0.240 M
(E) 0.267 M

42. One of the outermost electrons in a strontium atom in the ground state can be described by which of the following sets of four quantum numbers?

    (A) 5, 2, 0, $\frac{1}{2}$

    (B) 5, 1, 1, $\frac{1}{2}$

    (C) 5, 1, 0, $\frac{1}{2}$

    (D) 5, 0, 1, $\frac{1}{2}$

    (E) 5, 0, 0, $\frac{1}{2}$

43. Which of the following reactions does NOT proceed significantly to the right in aqueous solutions?

    (A) $H_3O^+ + OH^- \rightarrow 2\ H_2O$

    (B) $HCN + OH^- \rightarrow H_2O + CN^-$

    (C) $Cu(H_2O)_4^{2+} + 4\ NH_3 \rightarrow Cu(NH_3)_4^{2+} + 4\ H_2O$

    (D) $H_2SO_4 + H_2O \rightarrow H_3O^+ + HSO_4^-$

    (E) $H_2O + HSO_4^- \rightarrow H_2SO_4 + OH^-$

44. A compound is heated to produce a gas whose molar mass is to be determined. The gas is collected by displacing water in a water-filled flask inverted in a trough of water. Which of the following is necessary to calculate the molar mass of the gas but does <u>not</u> need to be measured during the experiment?

    (A) Mass of the compound used in the experiment

    (B) Temperature of the water in the trough

    (C) Vapor pressure of the water

    (D) Barometric pressure

    (E) Volume of water displaced from the flask

45. A 27.0 gram sample of an unknown hydrocarbon was burned in excess oxygen to form 88.0 grams of carbon dioxide and 27.0 grams of water. What is a possible molecular formula of the hydrocarbon?

    (A) CH_4

    (B) C_2H_2

    (C) C_4H_3

    (D) C_4H_6

    (E) C_4H_{10}

46. If the acid dissociation constant, K_a, for an acid HA is 8×10^{-4} at 25°C, what percent of the acid is dissociated in a 0.50 M solution of HA at 25°C?

    (A) 0.08%

    (B) 0.2%

    (C) 1%

    (D) 2%

    (E) 4%

$$CH_3 - \overset{\displaystyle\overset{O}{\|}}{C} - CH_2 - CH_3$$

47. The organic compound represented above is an example of

    (A) an alcohol

    (B) an aldehyde

    (C) an ether

    (D) an organic acid

    (E) a ketone

48. Equal numbers of moles of $H_2(g)$, $Ar(g)$, and $N_2(g)$ are placed in a glass vessel at room temperature. If the vessel has a pinhole-sized leak, which of the following will be true regarding the relative values of the partial pressures of the gases remaining in the vessel after some of the gas mixture has effused?

(A) $P_{H_2} < P_{N_2} < P_{Ar}$
(B) $P_{H_2} < P_{Ar} < P_{N_2}$
(C) $P_{N_2} < P_{Ar} < P_{H_2}$
(D) $P_{Ar} < P_{H_2} < P_{N_2}$
(E) $P_{H_2} = P_{Ar} = P_{N_2}$

49. Which of the following is a correct interpretation of the results of Rutherford's experiments in which gold atoms were bombarded with alpha particles?

(A) Atoms have equal numbers of positive and negative charges.

(B) Electrons in atoms are arranged in shells.

(C) Neutrons are at the center of an atom.

(D) Neutrons and protons in atoms have nearly equal mass.

(E) The positive charge of an atom is concentrated in a small region.

50. A 0.1 M solution of which of the following ions is orange?

(A) $Fe(H_2O)_4^{2+}$
(B) $Cu(NH_3)_4^{2+}$
(C) $Zn(OH)_4^{2-}$
(D) $Zn(NH_3)_4^{2+}$
(E) $Cr_2O_7^{2-}$

51. In the formation of 1.0 mole of the following crystalline solids from the gaseous ions, the most energy is released by

(A) NaF
(B) MgF_2
(C) $MgBr_2$
(D) AlF_3
(E) $AlBr_3$

52. If 1 mole of a nonvolatile nonelectrolyte dissolves in 9 moles of water to form an ideal solution, what is the vapor pressure of this solution at 25°C? (The vapor pressure of pure water at 25°C is 23.8 mm Hg.)

(A) 23.8 mm Hg

(B) $\frac{9}{10}$ 23.8 mm Hg

(C) $\frac{10}{9}$ 23.8 mm Hg

(D) $\frac{1}{10}$ 23.8 mm Hg

(E) It cannot be determined from the information given.

53. ... $MnO_4^-(aq) + ... NO_2^-(aq) + ... H_2O(l) \rightarrow$ ... $MnO_2(s) + ... NO_3^-(aq) + ... OH^-(aq)$

When the redox equation shown above is balanced by using coefficients reduced to lowest whole numbers, the coefficient for MnO_4^- is

(A) 1
(B) 2
(C) 3
(D) 4
(E) 6

54. If a certain solid solute dissolves in water with the evolution of heat, which of the following is most likely to be true?

(A) The temperature of the solution decreases as the solute dissolves.

(B) The resulting solution is ideal.

(C) The solid has a large lattice energy.

(D) The solid has a large heat of fusion.

(E) The solid has a large energy of hydration.

55. A 0.1-molar aqueous solution of which of the following is neutral?

(A) $NaNO_3$
(B) Na_2CO_3
(C) NH_4Br
(D) KCN
(E) $AlCl_3$

56. Which of the following is a true statement about the halogens?

(A) Fluorine is the weakest oxidizing agent.

(B) Bromine is more electronegative than chlorine.

(C) The halide ions are larger than their respective halogen atoms.

(D) Adding $I_2(s)$ to a solution containing $Br^-(aq)$ will produce $Br_2(l)$.

(E) The first ionization energies increase as the atomic number increases.

$$CH_3CHOHCH_2OH \quad CH_3CH_2CH_2CH_3 \quad CH_3CH_2CHOHCH_3$$
$$X \qquad\qquad Y \qquad\qquad Z$$

57. Considering the structures of the three compounds, X, Y, and Z, shown above, the ranking of their solubility in water from least to greatest is which of the following?

(A) $X < Y < Z$

(B) $X < Z < Y$

(C) $Z < Y < X$

(D) $Y < Z < X$

(E) $Y < X < Z$

58. Of the following compounds, which is involved in the environmental problem known as acid rain?

(A) CO_2

(B) CF_2Cl_2

(C) SO_2

(D) H_2S

(E) SiO_2

$$\ldots P_4O_{10} + \ldots Ca(OH)_2 \rightarrow \ldots Ca_3(PO_4)_2 + \ldots H_2O$$

59. When the chemical equation above is balanced in terms of lowest whole-number coefficients, the coefficient for H_2O is

(A) 1

(B) 2

(C) 3

(D) 6

(E) 8

60. Which of the following best describes the role of a catalyst in a chemical reaction?

(A) The catalyst lowers the activation energy by changing the mechanism of the reaction.

(B) The catalyst increases the strength of the chemical bonds in the reactant molecules.

(C) The catalyst increases the value of the equilibrium constant.

(D) The catalyst provides kinetic energy to reactant molecules to increase the reaction rate.

(E) The catalyst bonds to the reaction products and drives the equilibrium toward the products.

61. On the basis of trends in the periodic table, an atom of which of the following elements is predicted to have the lowest first ionization energy?

(A) Ar

(B) Cl

(C) K

(D) Rb

(E) I

$$X(g) + Y(g) \rightleftarrows Z(g)$$

62. Which of the following statements is true for the chemical system represented above when the system has reached a state of equilibrium at a constant temperature and pressure?

(A) The forward and reverse reactions have stopped.

(B) The forward and reverse reactions occur at the same rate.

(C) The rate of formation of $Z(g)$ is equal to half the rate of consumption of $X(g)$.

(D) Introducing a catalyst will result in an increased amount of $Z(g)$ at equilibrium.

(E) Introducing more $Y(g)$ to the system will cause more $X(g)$ to form.

63. If a 1.0 M solution of HA, a weak acid, has a pH of 2.0, then the value of K_a, the acid-dissociation constant, for HA is closest to

(A) 1.0×10^{-4}

(B) 1.4×10^{-4}

(C) 1.0×10^{-2}

(D) 1.4×10^{-2}

(E) 1.4×10^{-1}

64. Which of the following elements is <u>never</u> found pure (i.e., chemically uncombined with one or more other elements) in Earth's crust?

(A) S

(B) K

(C) Cu

(D) Pt

(E) Au

65. If an endothermic reaction occurs spontaneously, then it can be correctly inferred that

(A) a catalyst must be present

(B) the reaction occurs at a slow rate

(C) $\Delta G_{rxn} > 0$

(D) $\Delta H_{rxn} < 0$

(E) $\Delta S_{rxn} > 0$

Study Resources

Most textbooks used in college-level chemistry courses cover the topics in the outline given earlier, but the approaches to certain topics and the emphases given to them may differ. To prepare for the Chemistry exam, it is advisable to study one or more college textbooks, which can be found in most college bookstores. When selecting a textbook, check the table of contents against the knowledge and skills required for this test.

Visit www.collegeboard.com/clepprep for additional chemistry resources. You can also find suggestions for exam preparation in Chapter IV of the *Official Study Guide*. In addition, many college faculty post their course materials on their schools' Web sites.

Answer Key

1.	B	34.	A
2.	E	35.	B
3.	B	36.	D
4.	E	37.	A
5.	D	38.	D
6.	C	39.	E
7.	C	40.	B
8.	A	41.	B
9.	B	42.	E
10.	C	43.	E
11.	D	44.	C
12.	D	45.	D
13.	C	46.	E
14.	E	47.	E
15.	E	48.	A
16.	B	49.	E
17.	A	50.	E
18.	A	51.	D
19.	E	52.	B
20.	A	53.	B
21.	C	54.	E
22.	D	55.	A
23.	D	56.	C
24.	C	57.	D
25.	E	58.	C
26.	A	59.	D
27.	A	60.	A
28.	D	61.	D
29.	B	62.	B
30.	C	63.	A
31.	C	64.	B
32.	E	65.	E
33.	E		

College Algebra

Description of the Examination

The College Algebra examination covers material that is usually taught in a one-semester college course in algebra. Nearly half of the test is made up of routine problems requiring basic algebraic skills; the remainder involves solving nonroutine problems in which candidates must demonstrate their understanding of concepts. The test includes questions on basic algebraic operations; linear and quadratic equations, inequalities, and graphs; algebraic, exponential, and logarithmic functions; and miscellaneous other topics. It is assumed that candidates are familiar with currently taught algebraic vocabulary, symbols, and notation. The test places little emphasis on arithmetic calculations. However, an online scientific calculator (nongraphing) will be available during the examination.

The examination contains approximately 60 questions to be answered in 90 minutes. Some of these are pretest questions that will not be scored. Any time candidates spend on tutorials and providing personal information is in addition to the actual testing time.

Knowledge and Skills Required

Questions on the College Algebra examination require candidates to demonstrate the following abilities in the approximate proportions indicated.

- Solving routine, straightforward problems (about 50 percent of the examination)
- Solving nonroutine problems requiring an understanding of concepts and the application of skills and concepts (about 50 percent of the examination)

The subject matter of the College Algebra examination is drawn from the following topics. The percentages next to the main topics indicate the approximate percentage of exam questions on that topic.

25% Algebraic Operations

Factoring and expanding polynomials
Operations with algebraic expressions
Operations with exponents
Properties of logarithms

25% Equations and Inequalities

Linear equations and inequalities
Quadratic equations and inequalities
Absolute value equations and inequalities
Systems of equations and inequalities
Exponential and logarithmic equations

30% Functions and Their Properties*

Definition and interpretation
Representation/modeling (graphical, numerical, symbolic, and verbal representations of functions)
Domain and range
Algebra of functions
Graphs and their properties (including intercepts, symmetry, and transformations)
Inverse functions

20% Number Systems and Operations

Real numbers
Complex numbers
Sequences and series
Factorials and Binomial Theorem
Determinants of 2-by-2 matrices

---

*Each test may contain a variety of functions, including linear, polynomial (degree ≤ 5), rational, absolute value, power, exponential, logarithmic, and piecewise-defined.

Sample Test Questions

The following sample questions do not appear on an actual CLEP examination. They are intended to give potential test-takers an indication of the format and difficulty level of the examination and to provide content for practice and review. Knowing the correct answers to all of the sample questions is not a guarantee of satisfactory performance on the exam.

Directions: An online scientific calculator will be available for the questions in this test.

Some questions will require you to select from among five choices. For these questions, select the BEST of the choices given.

Some question will require you to type a numerical answer in the box provided.

Notes: (1) Unless otherwise specified, the domain of any function f is assumed to be the set of all real numbers x for which $f(x)$ is a real number.

(2) i will be used to denote $\sqrt{-1}$.

(3) Figures that accompany questions are intended to provide information useful in answering the questions. All figures lie in a plane unless otherwise indicated. The figures are drawn as accurately as possible EXCEPT when it is stated in a specific question that the figure is not drawn to scale. Straight lines and smooth curves may appear slightly jagged on the screen.

1. $(2x-1)^2 =$

(A) $2x^2 + 1$

(B) $4x^2 - 1$

(C) $4x^2 + 1$

(D) $4x^2 - 2x + 1$

(E) $4x^2 - 4x + 1$

2. Which of the following is a factor of $4 - (x + y)^2$?

(A) $-(x+y)^2$
(B) $x+y$
(C) $2-x+y$
(D) $2+x+y$
(E) $4+x+y$

3. $2v(3v^2 - 1) - (6 - 8v^3 + 14v) + 3 =$

(A) $-2v^3 + 12v - 3$

(B) $14v^3 + 12v - 3$

(C) $14v^3 - 14v - 4$

(D) $14v^3 - 16v - 3$

(E) $14v^3 - 16v - 6$

4. If $x + 2 = y$, what is the value of $|x - y| + |y - x|$?

(A) -4
(B) 0
(C) 2
(D) 4
(E) It cannot be determined from the information given.

5. Where defined, $\dfrac{\dfrac{x^2-9}{x+2}}{\dfrac{x-3}{x-2}} =$

(A) $\dfrac{x-2}{x+2}$

(B) $\dfrac{(x-2)(x+3)}{x+2}$

(C) $\dfrac{x^2 - x + 6}{x+2}$

(D) $\dfrac{1}{(x-2)(x+2)}$

(E) $\dfrac{x+3}{(x-2)(x+2)}$

6. Which of the following are the solutions of the equation $2x(1 - 3x) - 1 + 3x = 0$?

(A) $x = \dfrac{1}{2}$ and $x = \dfrac{1}{3}$

(B) $x = \dfrac{1}{2}$ and $x = -\dfrac{1}{3}$

(C) $x = -\dfrac{1}{2}$ and $x = \dfrac{1}{3}$

(D) $x = -\dfrac{1}{2}$ and $x = -\dfrac{1}{3}$

(E) $x = 0$ and $x = 1$

7. Of the following, which is greatest?

(A) $2^{\left(3^5\right)}$

(B) $\left(2^3\right)^5$

(C) $3^{\left(2^5\right)}$

(D) $\left(3^2\right)^5$

(E) $5^{\left(3^2\right)}$

8. For any positive integer n, $\dfrac{(n+1)!}{n!} - n =$

(A) 0   (B) 1   (C) n (D) $n+1$ (E) $n!$

9. Which of the following is equal to $r^2 t^{1/2} r^{2/3} t^{-3/2}$?

(A) $-r^{8/3} t$

(B) $\dfrac{r^{4/3}}{t^{3/4}}$

(C) $\dfrac{r^{4/3}}{t}$

(D) $\dfrac{r^{5/2}}{t^{5/6}}$

(E) $\dfrac{r^{8/3}}{t}$

10. A ball is dropped from a height of h feet and repeatedly bounces off the floor. After each bounce, the ball reaches a height that is $\dfrac{2}{3}$ of the height from which it previously fell. For example, after the first bounce, the ball reaches a height of $\dfrac{2}{3}h$ feet. Which of the following represents the total number of feet the ball travels between the first and the sixth bounce?

(A) $\displaystyle\sum_{i=1}^{5} (2h)\left(\dfrac{2}{3}\right)^{i}$

(B) $\displaystyle\sum_{i=1}^{5} h\left(\dfrac{2}{3}\right)^{i}$

(C) $\displaystyle\sum_{i=1}^{5} \left(\dfrac{2}{3}h\right)^{i}$

(D) $\displaystyle\sum_{i=1}^{6} (2h)\left(\dfrac{2}{3}\right)^{i-1}$

(E) $\displaystyle\sum_{i=1}^{\infty} h\left(\dfrac{2}{3}\right)^{i}$

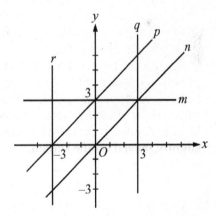

11. Which of the lines in the figure above is the graph of $x = 3$?

(A) m (B) n (C) p (D) q (E) r

12. Which of the following gives all values of x for which $|x - 2| \le 5$?

   (A) $\{x \mid -7 \le x \le 3\}$
   (B) $\{x \mid -5 \le x \le 5\}$
   (C) $\{x \mid -3 \le x \le 7\}$
   (D) $\{x \mid x < -5\}$
   (E) $\{x \mid x < -7 \text{ or } x > 3\}$

13. Which of the following are the solutions of the equation $2x^2 + 2x = 4 - x$?

   (A) $x = 4$ and $x = 1$

   (B) $x = 4$ and $x = -\dfrac{1}{2}$

   (C) $x = \dfrac{3 + \sqrt{35}}{4}$ and $x = \dfrac{3 - \sqrt{35}}{4}$

   (D) $x = \dfrac{-3 + \sqrt{41}}{4}$ and $x = \dfrac{-3 - \sqrt{41}}{4}$

   (E) $x = \dfrac{-3 + i\sqrt{23}}{2}$ and $x = \dfrac{-3 - i\sqrt{23}}{2}$

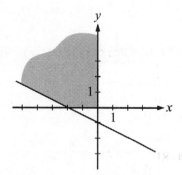

14. The shaded region in the figure above represents the intersection of the graphs of $x \le 0$, $y \ge 0$, and which of the following inequalities?

   (A) $y \le -2x - 1$

   (B) $y \le -\dfrac{1}{2}x + 1$

   (C) $y \ge -2x - 1$

   (D) $y \ge -\dfrac{1}{2}x - 1$

   (E) $y \ge \dfrac{1}{2}x - 1$

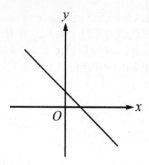

15. The graph of the line with equation $ax + by = 1$ is shown above. Which of the following must be true?

   (A) $a > 0$ and $b < 0$
   (B) $a > 0$ and $b > 0$
   (C) $a < 0$ and $b < 0$
   (D) $a < 0$ and $b > 0$
   (E) $a = 0$ and $b > 0$

16. The set of all values of b for which the equation $4x^2 + bx + 1 = 0$ has either one real root or two real roots is defined by

   (A) $b > 4$
   (B) $b < 4$
   (C) $b \ge 1$ or $b \le -1$
   (D) $b > 4$ or $b < -4$
   (E) $b \ge 4$ or $b \le -4$

17. Which quadrants of the xy-plane contain points of the graph of $2x - y > 4$?

   (A) I, II, and III only
   (B) I, II, and IV only
   (C) I, III, and IV only
   (D) II, III, and IV only
   (E) I, II, III, and IV

18. Joe invests $40,000 and, at the same time, Tom invests $10,000. The value of Joe's investment decreases by $4,000 per year, while the value of Tom's investment increases by $1,000 per year. Which of the following systems of equations could be used to find the number of years, t, that it will take for the values, v, of the two investments to be equal?

    (A) $v = 40,000 - t$ and $v = 10,000 + t$
    (B) $v = 40,000 - 4t$ and $v = 10,000 + t$
    (C) $v = 40,000 + 1,000t$ and
        $v = 10,000 - 4,000t$
    (D) $v = 40,000 + 4,000t$ and
        $v = 10,000 - 1,000t$
    (E) $v = 40,000 - 4,000t$ and
        $v = 10,000 + 1,000t$

19. Which of the following is the equation of the line that passes through the points with coordinates $(-2, 1)$ and $(1, 2)$?

    (A) $2x + y = -3$
    (B) $x + 3y = 7$
    (C) $x + 2y = 0$
    (D) $x - 3y = -5$
    (E) $-x + 2y = 0$

20. Which of the following numbers are irrational?

    I. $5.\overline{25}$
    II. $-\sqrt{6}$
    III. π

    (A) II only
    (B) III only
    (C) I and III only
    (D) II and III only
    (E) I, II, and III

21. When $\dfrac{3 + 4i}{2 + i}$ is expressed in the form $a + bi$, what is the value of a ?

    [ ]

22. If $a < 0 < b < c$, then each of the following must be true EXCEPT

    (A) $ac < ab$
    (B) $a^2 < b^2 < c^2$
    (C) $a^3 < b^3 < c^3$
    (D) $ab < b^2 < bc$
    (E) $a^2 b < a^2 c$

23. What is the determinant of the matrix $\begin{bmatrix} -1 & 2 \\ 1 & 3 \end{bmatrix}$?

    (A) -5
    (B) -3
    (C) -1
    (D) 1
    (E) 5

24. What are all real values of x for which
    $\dfrac{2}{3 - x} = \dfrac{1}{3} - \dfrac{1}{x}$?

    (A) $x = -3$ only
    (B) $x = 3$ only
    (C) $x = -3$ and $x = 0$
    (D) $x = -3$ and $x = 3$
    (E) There are no real solutions.

25. Which of the following is the solution set of the inequality $4 - 7\left| \dfrac{x}{2} - 3 \right| \geq -3$?

    (A) $(-\infty, 4]$
    (B) $[8, \infty)$
    (C) $[4, 8]$
    (D) $(-\infty, 4] \cup [8, \infty)$
    (E) $(-\infty, -4]$

x	0	1	2	3	4	5	6	7
$p(x)$	-30	22	110	150	34	-130	222	2,350

26. The table above gives some of the values of a 5th degree polynomial $p(x)$. Based on the values shown, what is the minimum number of real roots of the equation $p(x) = 0$?

    (A) One
    (B) Two
    (C) Three
    (D) Four
    (E) Five

27. The number of bricks in the bottom row of a brick wall is 49. The next row up from the bottom contains 47 bricks, and each subsequent row contains 2 fewer bricks than the row immediately below it. The number of bricks in the top row is 3. If the wall is one brick thick, what is the total number of bricks in the wall?

28. What is the middle term in the expansion of $\left(x - \dfrac{1}{x}\right)^6$?

(A) $20x^3$

(B) $\dfrac{20}{x^3}$

(C) $-15x^2$

(D) -15

(E) -20

29. If $x = -3$ is a root of the equation $x^3 + 3x^2 - ax - 12 = 0$, what is the value of a ?

30. If the first term of a geometric sequence is $\dfrac{3}{2}$ and the second and third terms are $-\dfrac{3}{4}$ and $\dfrac{3}{8}$, respectively, which of the following represents the nth term of the sequence?

(A) $\dfrac{3(-1)^{n-1}}{2n}$

(B) $\dfrac{3(-1)^n}{2n}$

(C) $\dfrac{3(-1)^{n-1}}{2^n}$

(D) $\dfrac{3(-1)^n}{2^n}$

(E) $\dfrac{3(-1)^{n-1}}{2^{n+1}}$

31. A clothing company has budgeted $58,000 for the purchase of 7 sewing machines. The 7 sewing machines are to be chosen from two models, model X and model Y. If a model X sewing machine costs $8,000 and a model Y sewing machine costs $9,000, how many model X sewing machines should the company purchase to use exactly the budgeted money?

(A) 2   (B) 3   (C) 4   (D) 5   (E) 6

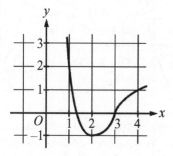

32. The graph of the function f is shown above. What is the value of $f(f(1))$?

(A) -1 (B) 0   (C) 1   (D) 2   (E) 4

33. In the xy-plane, what is the x-intercept of the graph of $y = -\dfrac{2}{3}x - 4$?

34. Which of the following define y as a function of x ?

   I. $2x^2 + y = 7$

   II.

x	1	2	3	4
y	2	5	-1	2

   III.

(A) None
(B) I and II only
(C) I and III only
(D) II and III only
(E) I, II, and III

35. If $3^{x+1} = 9^{2x-1}$, then $x =$

[ ]

36. Which of the following could be the graph of $y = 3^x$?

(A)

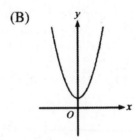

(B)

(C)

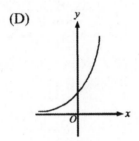

(D)

(E)

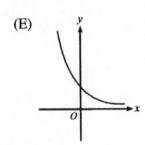

37. If $f(x) = 2x+1$ and $g(x) = 3x-1$, then $f(g(x)) =$

(A) $5x$
(B) $x-2$
(C) $6x-1$
(D) $6x+2$
(E) $6x^2 + x - 1$

38. If $\log_4(y+2) = 3$, what is the value of y ?

(A) 10 (B) 62 (C) 64 (D) 79 (E) 83

39. A colony of bacteria starts with 2 bacteria at noon. If the number of bacteria triples every 30 minutes, how many bacteria will be present at 3:00 P.M. on the same day?

(A)   486
(B)   729
(C)   1,458
(D)   46,656
(E) 118,098

40. Which of the following must be true?

I. $\log_3 3^t = t$

II. $\ln 10^{4.3} = 4.3 \ln 10$

III. $\log_{10}(xy^n) = \log_{10} x + n \log_{10} y$

(A) I only
(B) II only
(C) I and II only
(D) II and III only
(E) I, II, and III

41. If $f(x) = 5 - 2x^3$ and f^{-1} denotes the inverse function of f, then $f^{-1}(x) =$

(A) $\sqrt[3]{\dfrac{5-x}{2}}$

(B) $\dfrac{\sqrt[3]{5-x}}{2}$

(C) $\sqrt[3]{\dfrac{x-5}{2}}$

(D) $\dfrac{1}{5-2x^3}$

(E) $5x^3 + 2$

415

42. $\dfrac{2x-1}{x+3}-\dfrac{x-2}{2x+1}=$

(A) $\dfrac{x+1}{3x+4}$

(B) $\dfrac{x-3}{(x+3)(2x+1)}$

(C) $\dfrac{3x-3}{(x+3)(2x+1)}$

(D) $\dfrac{3x^2-x+5}{(x+3)(2x+1)}$

(E) $\dfrac{3x^2+x-7}{(x+3)(2x+1)}$

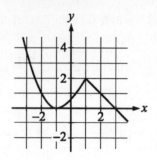

43. The graph of the function $y=f(x)$ is shown above. Which of the following is the graph of $y=f(x-1)+1$?

(A)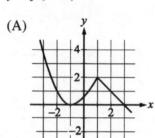

(B)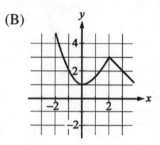

(C)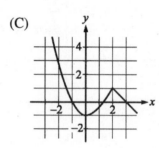

(D)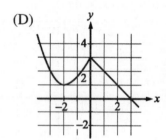

(E)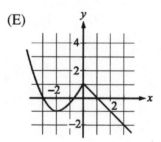

44. $(i+1)(3-i)+(2i-1)=$

(A) -6
(B) $1+4i$
(C) $2+4i$
(D) $3+4i$
(E) $4+2i$

45. f is an exponential function defined by $f(x) = ab^x$, where a and b are positive constants. If $f(5) = 96$ and $f(7) = 384$, what is the value of a?

[　　　　　　]

46. Which of the following, when added to $4a^2 + 9$, will result in a perfect square for all integer values of a?

(A) 0 (B) $3a$ (C) $6a$ (D) $9a$ (E) $12a$

$$x^2 + y^2 = 25$$
$$x + y = 1$$

47. For what values of x will (x, y) be a solution of the system of equations above?

(A) $x = -4$ and $x = 3$
(B) $x = -4$ and $x = 5$
(C) $x = -3$ and $x = 4$
(D) $x = 1$ and $x = 5$
(E) The system has no solutions.

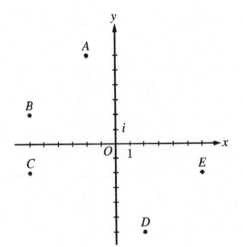

48. Which of the points in the figure above represents the complex number $6 - 2i$?

(A) A (B) B (C) C (D) D (E) E

$$f(x) = \begin{cases} x^2 & \text{for } x \le 0 \\ ax+b & \text{for } x > 0 \end{cases}$$

49. The function f above has an inverse function for which of the following values of a and b?

(A) $a = -1$, $b = -2$
(B) $a = -1$, $b = 2$
(C) $a = 0$, $b = -1$
(D) $a = 1$, $b = -2$
(E) $a = 1$, $b = 2$

50. For the function $g(x) = \log_2 x$, which of the following must be true?

I. The domain is $[0, \infty)$.
II. The range is $(-\infty, \infty)$.
III. $g(x)$ increases with increasing values of x.

(A) III only
(B) I and II only
(C) I and III only
(D) II and III only
(E) I, II, and III

51. A rectangular box has volume $x^3 - 8$ cubic inches. If the height of the box is $x - 2$ inches, what is the area of the base of the box, in square inches? (The volume of a box equals the area of the base times the height.)

(A) $x^2 + 4$
(B) $x^2 - 2x - 4$
(C) $x^2 - 2x + 4$
(D) $x^2 + 2x + 4$
(E) $x^2 + 4x + 4$

52. If $y = 8x^2 + 4x - 1$ is expressed in the form $y = a(x - h)^2 + k$, where a, h, and k are constants, what is the value of k ?

(A) −3

(B) −2

(C) $-\dfrac{3}{2}$

(D) $-\dfrac{17}{16}$

(E) $-\dfrac{1}{2}$

53. If b and c are integers such that the equation $3x^2 + bx + c = 0$ has only one real root, which of the following statements must be true?

  I. b is even.

  II. c is odd.

  III. b^2 is a multiple of 3.

(A) I only

(B) III only

(C) I and II only

(D) I and III only

(E) I, II, and III

54. A rock is thrown straight up into the air from a height of 4 feet. The height of the rock above the ground, in feet, t seconds after it is thrown is given by $-16t^2 + 56t + 4$. For how many seconds will the height of the rock be at least 28 feet above the ground?

(A) 0.5

(B) 1.5

(C) 2.5

(D) 3.0

(E) 3.5

55. $\log_5 \sqrt{125} - \log_2 \sqrt{2} =$

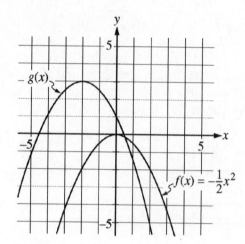

56. In the figure shown above, the graph of the function g is a transformation of the graph of the function f. Which of the following is the equation of g ?

(A) $g(x) = -\dfrac{1}{2}x^2 + 3$

(B) $g(x) = -\dfrac{1}{2}(x - 2)^2 + 3$

(C) $g(x) = -\dfrac{1}{2}(x - 2)^2 - 3$

(D) $g(x) = -\dfrac{1}{2}(x + 2)^2 + 3$

(E) $g(x) = -\dfrac{1}{2}(x + 2)^2 - 3$

57. The polynomial $p(x) = x^3 + 2x - 11$ has a real zero between which two consecutive integers?

(A) 0 and 1

(B) 1 and 2

(C) 2 and 3

(D) 3 and 4

(E) 4 and 5

58. Which of the following could be the graph of $y = ax^2 + bx + c$, where $b^2 - 4ac = 0$?

(A)
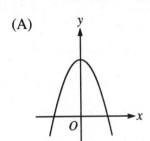

(B)
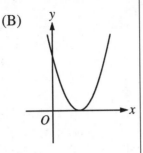

(C)
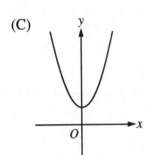

(D)
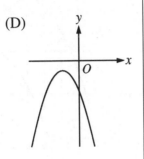

(E)
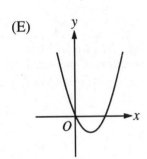

59. Consider each function below. Is the domain of the function the set of all real numbers?

Function	Yes	No
$f(x) = \dfrac{x-1}{x^2+2}$		
$g(x) = \dfrac{x^2}{x+1}$		
$h(x) = \dfrac{\sqrt{x}}{x^2+3}$		

60. The sum of the first n terms of an arithmetic sequence $a_1, a_2, a_3, \ldots, a_n$ is $\dfrac{1}{2}n(a_1 + a_n)$, where a_1 and a_n are the first and the nth terms of the sequence, respectively. What is the sum of the odd integers from 1 to 99, inclusive?

(A) 2,400
(B) 2,450
(C) 2,475
(D) 2,500
(E) 2,550

61. The function f is defined for all real numbers x by $f(x) = ax^2 + bx + c$, where a, b, and c are constants and a is negative. In the xy-plane, the x-coordinate of the vertex of the parabola $y = f(x)$ is -1. If t is a number for which $f(t) > f(0)$, which of the following must be true?

I. $-2 < t < 0$
II. $f(t) < f(-2)$
III. $f(t) > f(1)$

(A) I only
(B) II only
(C) I and III only
(D) II and III only
(E) I, II, and III

x	$h(x)$
-3	5
-2	-4
2	c

62. The table above shows some values of the function h, which is defined for all real numbers x. If h is an odd function, what is the value of c ?

(A) -5
(B) -4
(C) -2
(D) 2
(E) 4

63. If $\displaystyle\sum_{n=1}^{10} a_n = 50$, what is the value of $\displaystyle\sum_{n=1}^{10}\left(4a_n + 3\right)$?

(A) 53
(B) 80
(C) 203
(D) 223
(E) 230

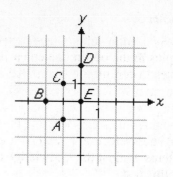

64. If $z = -1 + i$ and $\overline{z}$ denotes the complex conjugate of z, which of the following points in the complex plane above represents $z + \overline{z}$?

(A) A
(B) B
(C) C
(D) D
(E) E

65. What is the remainder when the polynomial $9x^{23} - 7x^{12} - 2x^5 + 1$ is divided by $x + 1$?

(A) -19
(B) -13
(C) -7
(D) 1
(E) 11

Study Resources

Most textbooks used in college-level algebra courses cover the topics in the outline given earlier, but the approaches to certain topics and the emphases given to them may differ. To prepare for the College Algebra exam, it is advisable to study one or more college textbooks, which can be found in most college bookstores. When selecting a textbook, check the table of contents against the knowledge and skills required for this test.

Visit www.collegeboard.com/clepprep for additional college algebra resources. You can also find suggestions for exam preparation in Chapter IV of the *Official Study Guide*. In addition, many college faculty post their course materials on their schools' Web sites.

Answer Key

1. E		33. –6	
2. D		34. E	
3. D		35. 1	
4. D		36. D	
5. B		37. C	
6. A		38. B	
7. A		39. C	
8. B		40. E	
9. E		41. A	
10. A		42. D	
11. D		43. B	
12. C		44. D	
13. D		45. 3	
14. D		46. E	
15. B		47. C	
16. E		48. E	
17. C		49. A	
18. E		50. D	
19. D		51. D	
20. D		52. C	
21. 2		53. D	
22. B		54. C	
23. A		55. 1	
24. E		56. D	
25. C		57. B	
26. C		58. B	
27. 624		59. See below	
28. E		60. D	
29. 4		61. C	
30. C		62. E	
31. D		63. E	
32. A		64. B	
		65. B	

59.

Function	Yes	No
$f(x) = \dfrac{x-1}{x^2+2}$	√	
$g(x) = \dfrac{x^2}{x+1}$		√
$h(x) = \dfrac{\sqrt{x}}{x^2+3}$		√

College Mathematics

Description of the Examination

The College Mathematics examination covers material generally taught in a college course for nonmathematics majors and majors in fields not requiring knowledge of advanced mathematics.

The examination contains approximately 60 questions to be answered in 90 minutes. Some of these are pretest questions that will not be scored. Any time candidates spend on tutorials and providing personal information is in addition to the actual testing time.

The examination places little emphasis on arithmetic calculations, and it does not contain any questions that require the use of a calculator. However, an online scientific calculator (nongraphing) is available to candidates during the examination as part of the testing software.

It is assumed that candidates are familiar with currently taught mathematics vocabulary, symbols, and notation.

Knowledge and Skills Required

Questions on the College Mathematics examination require candidates to demonstrate the following abilities in the approximate proportions indicated.

- Solving routine, straightforward problems (about 50 percent of the examination)
- Solving nonroutine problems requiring an understanding of concepts and the application of skills and concepts (about 50 percent of the examination)

The subject matter of the College Mathematics examination is drawn from the following topics. The percentages next to the main topics indicate the approximate percentage of exam questions on that topic.

10% Sets
Union and intersection
Subsets, disjoint sets, equivalent sets
Venn diagrams
Cartesian product

10% Logic
Truth tables
Conjunctions, disjunctions, implications, and negations
Conditional statements
Necessary and sufficient conditions
Converse, inverse, and contrapositive
Hypotheses, conclusions, and counterexamples

20% Real Number System
Prime and composite numbers
Odd and even numbers
Factors and divisibility
Rational and irrational numbers
Absolute value and order
Open and closed intervals

20% Functions and Their Graphs
Properties and graphs of functions
Domain and range
Composition of functions and inverse functions
Simple transformations of functions: translations, reflections, symmetry

25% Probability and Statistics
Counting problems, including permutations and combinations
Computation of probabilities of simple and compound events
Simple conditional probability
Mean, median, mode, and range
Concept of standard deviation
Data interpretation and representation: tables, bar graphs, line graphs, circle graphs, pie charts, scatterplots, histograms

15% Additional Topics from Algebra and Geometry
Complex numbers
Logarithms and exponents
Applications from algebra and geometry
Perimeter and area of plane figures
Properties of triangles, circles, and rectangles
The Pythagorean theorem
Parallel and perpendicular lines
Algebraic equations, systems of linear equations, and inequalities
Fundamental Theorem of Algebra, Remainder Theorem, Factor Theorem

Sample Test Questions

The following sample questions do not appear on an actual CLEP examination. They are intended to give potential test-takers an indication of the format and difficulty level of the examination and to provide content for practice and review. Knowing the correct answers to all of the sample questions is not a guarantee of satisfactory performance on the exam.

Directions: An online scientific calculator will be available for the questions in this test.

Some questions will require you to select from among four choices. For these questions, select the BEST of the choices given.

Some questions will require you to type a numerical answer in the box provided.

Some questions refer to a table in which statements appear in the first column. For each statement, select the correct properties by check-marking the appropriate cell(s) in the table.

Notes: (1) Unless otherwise specified, the domain of any function f is assumed to be the set of all real numbers x for which $f(x)$ is a real number.

      (2) i will be used to denote $\sqrt{-1}$.

      (3) Figures that accompany questions are intended to provide information useful in answering the questions. All figures lie in a plane unless otherwise indicated. The figures are drawn as accurately as possible EXCEPT when it is stated in a specific question that the figure is not drawn to scale.

1. Which of the following is an irrational number?

   (A) $\sqrt{36}$ (B) $\sqrt{14}$ (C) $\dfrac{2}{\sqrt{9}}$ (D) $\sqrt[3]{-8}$

2. Which of the following represents the graph of all x such that $x < -3$ or $x \geq 4$?

(A)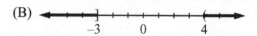

(B)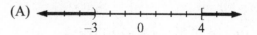

(C)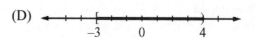

(D)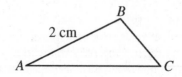

3. Triangle DEF (not shown) is similar to $\triangle ABC$ shown, and the length of side DE is 6 cm. If the area of $\triangle ABC$ is 5 square centimeters, what is the area of $\triangle DEF$?

   (A) 10 cm²

   (B) 12 cm²

   (C) 18 cm²

   (D) 45 cm²

4. m is an odd integer. For each of the following numbers, indicate whether the number is odd or even.

Number	Odd	Even
$2m - 1$		
$2m + 1$		
$m^2 - m$		
$m^2 + m + 1$		

Click on your choices.

5. If $0 < a < b$ and $c < d < 0$, which of the following must be true?

   (A) $ab < cd$

   (B) $ac < bc$

   (C) $bc < ad$

   (D) $bd < ac$

6. If a and b are prime numbers, what is the greatest common divisor of a^4b^2 and a^3b^3?

    (A) ab (B) a^3b^2 (C) a^4b^3 (D) a^7b^5

7. Based on the number line above, which of the following inequalities is correct?

    (A) $|a|-|b|<0$
    (B) $|b|-a<0$
    (C) $|a|-|b|>0$
    (D) $b-|a|>0$

8. x is the standard deviation of the set of numbers $\{a,b,c,d,e\}$. For each of the following sets, indicate which sets must have a standard deviation equal to x.

Set	Must Have Standard Deviation Equal to x
$\{a+2,\ b+2,\ c+2,\ d+2,\ e+2\}$	
$\{a-2,\ b-2,\ c-2,\ d-2,\ e-2\}$	
$\{2a,\ 2b,\ 2c,\ 2d,\ 2e\}$	
$\left\{\frac{a}{2},\frac{b}{2},\frac{c}{2},\frac{d}{2},\frac{e}{2}\right\}$	

Click on your choices.

9. When Bill makes a sandwich, he may choose from among 3 kinds of rolls, 4 varieties of meat, and 2 types of sliced cheese. If he chooses one roll, one meat, and one type of cheese, how many different kinds of sandwiches can he make?

    (A) 9 (B) 14 (C) 24 (D) 288

10. If the mean of the numbers a, b, c, d, and e is m and $m \neq 0$, then $\dfrac{a + b + c + d + e}{m} =$

    (A) $\dfrac{1}{5}$ (B) 5 (C) $\dfrac{m}{5}$ (D) $5m$

11. Which of the following statements about an event A are true?

    I. The probability that the event A will occur can be less than 0.

    II. The probability that the event A will occur can be equal to 1.

    III. The sum of the probability that event A will occur and the probability that event A will not occur is equal to 1.

    (A) II only
    (B) I and III only
    (C) II and III only
    (D) I, II, and III

12. The difference between the mean and the median of the numbers 27, 27, 29, 32, and 35 is

    (A) 0 (B) 1 (C) 3 (D) 8

13. In a class with 50 students, 25 of the students are female, 15 of the students are mathematics majors, and 10 of the mathematics majors are female. If a student in the class is to be selected at random, what is the probability that the student selected will be female or a mathematics major or both?

    (A) 0.4 (B) 0.5 (C) 0.6 (D) 0.8

14. On an exam for a class with 32 students, the mean score was 67.2 points. The instructor rescored the exam by adding 8 points to the exam score for every student. What is the mean of the scores on the rescored exam?

    [   ]

15. In the truth table below, T and F are used to indicate that statements are true and false, respectively. In the fourth column, click on each box for which the statement is <u>true</u>. (Note: $\sim p$ means not p)

p	q	$\sim p$	$\sim p \wedge q$
T	T	F	
T	F	F	
F	T	T	
F	F	T	

    Click on your choices.

16. A new computer graphics company employs 10 programmers. The company decides to expand into digital animation and needs to transfer 3 of the programmers into the new department. How many different combinations of 3 programmers can be chosen to transfer to the new department?

    (A) 3   (B) 30   (C) 120   (D) 840

17. The faces of a fair cube are numbered 1 through 6; the probability of rolling any number from 1 through 6 is equally likely. If the cube is rolled twice, what is the probability that an even number will appear on the top face in the first roll or that the number 1 will appear on the top face in the second roll?

    (A) $\dfrac{1}{12}$ (B) $\dfrac{7}{12}$ (C) $\dfrac{2}{3}$ (D) $\dfrac{3}{4}$

18. If $R = \{x \mid x > 0\}$ and $S = \{x \mid x < 3\}$, what is the number of integers in $R \cap S$?

    (A) None (B) Two (C) Three (D) Four

19. The sum of eight times a number n and the reciprocal of n is equal to 6.

    Which of the following is an algebraic representation of the statement above?

    (A) $8n + \dfrac{1}{n} = 6$

    (B) $(8n)\left(\dfrac{1}{n}\right) = 6$

    (C) $8\left(n + \dfrac{1}{n}\right) = 6$

    (D) $(8+n)\left(\dfrac{1}{n}\right) = 6$

20. Which of the following is the negation of the statement "If R, then S" ?

    (A) R and not S
    (B) S and not R
    (C) If not R, then not S
    (D) If not S, then not R

21. The width of a rectangular yard is x feet. If 300 feet of fencing is needed to enclose the yard, which of the following represents the length of the yard, in feet?

    (A) $300 - x$
    (B) $300 - 2x$
    (C) $150 - x$
    (D) $150 - 2x$

22. In the Venn diagram below, A, B, and C represent sets. Shade the regions representing $A \cap (B \cup C)$.

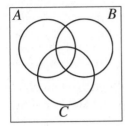

Click on a region to shade it.

23. $m = 4$ and $n = 2$

For each of the following expressions, indicate whether the value will be a rational or irrational number.

Expression	Rational	Irrational
$\sqrt[3]{m - n}$		
$\sqrt{m^3}$		
$\sqrt[3]{\dfrac{m}{n}}$		
$\sqrt{m + n^2}$		

Click on your choices.

24. A student asserted that n^2 is greater than or equal to n for all real numbers n. Of the following, which is a value of n that provides a counterexample to the student's claim?

    (A) $-\dfrac{1}{2}$ (B) 0 (C) $\dfrac{1}{2}$ (D) 2

25. What is the remainder when $x^3 + 5x^2 - 6x + 10$ is divided by $x + 3$?

    (A) 7 (B) 10 (C) 46 (D) 64

26. Which of the following are infinite sets?

    I. The set of all rational numbers between 0 and 1
    II. The set of all irrational numbers between 0 and 1
    III. The set of all real numbers between 0 and 1

    (A) I and II only
    (B) I and III only
    (C) II and III only
    (D) I, II, and III

27. The area of a rectangular field is the product of its length and width. If each dimension of a certain field is multiplied by 3, then the area of the new field is how many times the area of the original field?

    [   ]

    If it snows, then school is closed.

28. Which of the following is logically equivalent to the statement above?

    (A) If it snows, then school is not closed.
    (B) If school is closed, then it snows.
    (C) If it does not snow, then school is not closed.
    (D) If school is not closed, then it does not snow.

29. Which of the following is a root of $x^2 + x + 1 = 0$?

    (A) $-\dfrac{1}{2}$

    (B) $\dfrac{i\sqrt{3}}{2}$

    (C) $\dfrac{1}{2} - \dfrac{i\sqrt{3}}{2}$

    (D) $-\dfrac{1}{2} + \dfrac{i\sqrt{3}}{2}$

30. A bookstore has 900 books in stock, of which 600 are paperback and 300 are hardcover. All of the books are either fiction or nonfiction. If 525 of the books are nonfiction and 375 of the nonfiction books are paperback, how many of the books are fiction and hardcover?

(A) 150   (B) 225   (C) 300   (D) 375

31. If $\ln x = 6$ and $\ln y = 2$, then $\ln\left(\dfrac{x^2}{y}\right) =$

(A) 4   (B) 8   (C) 10   (D) 18

32. The results of a survey of 200 college students showed that some students who were business majors were women and all students who were business majors took calculus. Which of the following is a valid conclusion from the survey?

(A) All students who were women took calculus.

(B) Some students who were women took calculus.

(C) Some students who were women did not take calculus.

(D) Some students who were women were not business majors.

33. If $g(x) = x^3 - 2x - 1$, then $g(-2) =$

[　　　　　　]

$$f(x) = \begin{cases} 3x & \text{if } 0 < x \le 2 \\ 3 & \text{if } 2 < x < 4 \end{cases}$$

34. What is the domain of the function shown?

(A) All real numbers
(B) All real numbers except 2
(C) All real numbers greater than 0 and less than 4
(D) All real numbers greater than 0 and less than 6

35. In the xy-plane, the graph of which of the following linear equations is perpendicular to the graph of the linear equation $3x - 4y = 0$?

(A) $y = -\dfrac{4}{3}x + 12$

(B) $y = -\dfrac{3}{4}x + 12$

(C) $y = \dfrac{3}{4}x + 12$

(D) $y = \dfrac{4}{3}x + 12$

36. On Friday afternoon, Gloria left work, which is 1 mile from home, and drove to the bank, which is 4 miles from home. She spent 20 minutes at the bank and then drove home. Which of the following graphs could represent Gloria's distance from home as a function of the time from when she left work on Friday afternoon?

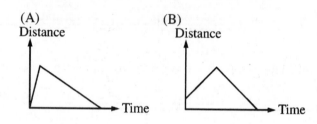

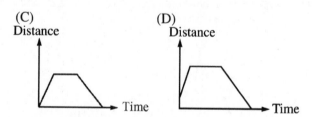

37. Which of the following functions has two zeros?

(A) $f(x) = |x + 1|$
(B) $f(x) = |x| + 1$
(C) $f(x) = -|x| - 1$
(D) $f(x) = -|x| + 1$

x	3	4	5
$f(x)$	2	3	4

x	2	3	4
$g(x)$	3	5	7

38. Values for the functions f and g are given in the tables above. What is the value of $f(g(3))$?

[　　　　　　]

39. A house was purchased for $140,000. Three years later, the value of the house was $155,000. If the value V of the house increased linearly from the date it was purchased, which of the following represents the value, in dollars, of the house t years after the date it was purchased?

(A) $V = 140,000 + 15,000t$
(B) $V = 140,000 + 5,000t$
(C) $V = 140,000 + 15,000(t-3)$
(D) $V = 140,000 + 5,000(t-3)$

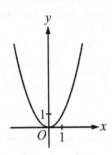

40. The graph of $y = f(x)$ is shown above. Which of the following could be the graph of $y = -3f(x)$?

(A) 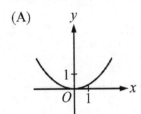   (B)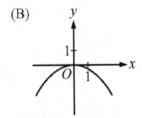

(C) 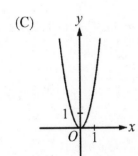   (D)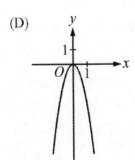

41. If $f(g(x)) = \dfrac{x+5}{x}$ and $g(x) = x+5$, then $f(x) =$

(A) $\dfrac{1}{x}$ (B) $\dfrac{1}{x-5}$ (C) $\dfrac{x}{x-5}$ (D) $\dfrac{x-5}{x}$

42. If x and y are nonzero integers, which of the following must be an integer?

(A) $x + \dfrac{y}{x}$

(B) $\dfrac{x+y^2}{x}$

(C) $\dfrac{x^2+xy}{x}$

(D) $\dfrac{x^2+y^2}{x}$

$$A = \{a,b\} \text{ and } B = \{b,c\},$$
where $a, b,$ and c are distinct numbers.

43. Which of the following ordered pairs is NOT in the Cartesian product $A \times B$?

(A) (a,b) (B) (b,a) (C) (b,b) (D) (b,c)

44. Each number in data set A is increased by 3 to form data set B. Which of the following is the same for sets A and B ?

(A) Mean
(B) Median
(C) Mode
(D) Range

45. If f is a linear function such that $f(-1) = 3$ and $f(5) = 15,$ then $f(2) =$

(A) 6   (B) 8   (C) 9   (D) 12

46. Which of the following conditions is necessary but not sufficient for an integer n to be a prime number?

(A) n is equal to 17.
(B) n is an odd number.
(C) n is not divisible by 3.
(D) n is not a perfect square.

429

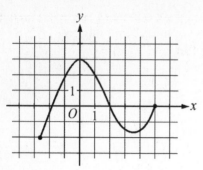

47. What is the range of the function $y = f(x)$ shown above?

(A) $-2.5 \le y \le 0$
(B) $-2 \le y \le 2$
(C) $-2 \le y \le 3$
(D) $0 \le y \le 5$

48. A drawer contains exactly 5 red, 4 blue, and 3 green pencils. If two pencils are selected at random one after the other without replacing the first, what is the probability that the first one is red and the second one is green?

(A) $\dfrac{5}{44}$ (B) $\dfrac{5}{48}$ (C) $\dfrac{91}{132}$ (D) $\dfrac{2}{3}$

49. If $8^x = 15$ and $8^y = 25$, then $8^{(2x+y)} =$

(A) 55 (B) 80 (C) 250 (D) 5,625

50. If $x - 3$ is a factor of $x^4 - 3x^3 + kx + 3$, what is the value of k ?

(A) -1
(B) 0
(C) $\dfrac{1}{3}$
(D) 1

51. Which of the following is NOT a subset of the set $\{2, 4, 6, 8\}$?

(A) The empty set
(B) $\{2\}$
(C) $\{2, 8\}$
(D) $\{2, \{4, 6\}\}$

52. If $f(x) = \dfrac{1}{x-2}$, where $x \ne 2$, and $g(x) = 2^x$ for all values of x, then $f(g(0))$ is

(A) -1
(B) $-\dfrac{1}{2}$
(C) 0
(D) undefined

53. The six students, $P, Q, R, S, T,$ and U in a class took four exams, and the scores for the four exams were recorded in the following graphs. In which graph do the scores shown have the least standard deviation?

(A)

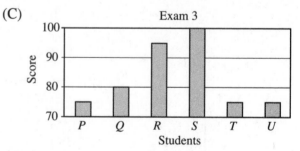

(B)

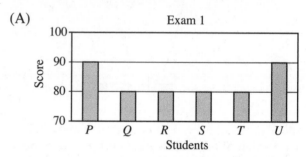

(C)

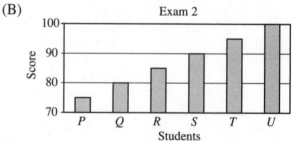

(D)

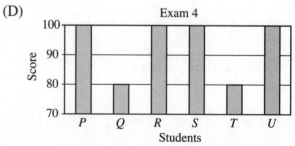

54. For all nonzero numbers, if $f(x) = \dfrac{x^2 - 1}{x^2 + 1}$

and $g(x) = \dfrac{1}{x^2}$, then $g(f(x)) =$

(A) $\dfrac{\left(x^2 + 1\right)^2}{\left(x^2 - 1\right)^2}$

(B) $\dfrac{\left(x^2 - 1\right)^2}{\left(x^2 + 1\right)^2}$

(C) $\dfrac{x^4 + 1}{x^4 - 1}$

(D) $\dfrac{x^4 - 1}{x^4 + 1}$

55. Which of the following best represents the graph of the function $f(x) = \begin{cases} x^2 & \text{for } x < 1 \\ 2 & \text{for } x \geq 1 \end{cases}$ in the xy-plane?

(A)

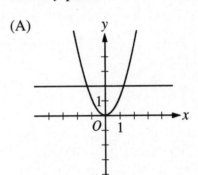

(B)

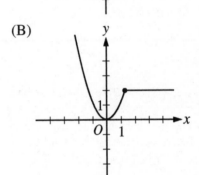

(C)

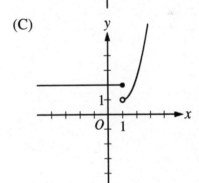

(D)

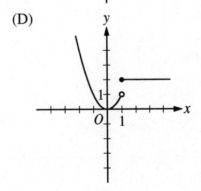

56. A rectangular flat-screen computer monitor has a diagonal that measures 20 inches. The ratio of the length of the screen to the width of the screen is 4 to 3. What is the perimeter of the screen, in inches?

(A) 48

(B) 56

(C) 64

(D) 192

57. Which of the following is an equation of the line in the xy-plane that passes through the point $(2,-1)$ and that is parallel to the line with equation $2x-3y=5$?

(A) $y=-2x-\dfrac{3}{2}$

(B) $y=-\dfrac{3}{2}x+2$

(C) $y=\dfrac{2}{3}x-\dfrac{7}{3}$

(D) $y=\dfrac{2}{3}x-1$

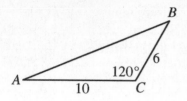

58. In triangle ABC shown above, what is the length of line segment AB ?

(A) $17\sqrt{3}$

(B) 16

(C) 14

(D) $2\sqrt{34}$

59. A circular pizza with a 16-inch diameter is cut into 12 equal slices. What is the area, in square inches, of each slice?

(A) $\dfrac{16}{3}\pi$

(B) $\dfrac{8}{3}\pi$

(C) $\dfrac{4}{3}\pi$

(D) $\dfrac{2}{3}\pi$

60. A square tablecloth lies flat on top of a circular table with area π square feet. If the four corners of the tablecloth just touch the edge of the circular table, what is the area of the tablecloth, in square feet?

[   ] square feet

Study Resources

Most textbooks used in college-level mathematics courses cover the topics in the outline given earlier, but the approaches to certain topics and the emphases given to them may differ. To prepare for the College Mathematics exam, it is advisable to study one or more introductory college-level mathematics textbooks, which can be found in most college bookstores. Elementary algebra textbooks also cover many of the topics on the College Mathematics exam. When selecting a textbook, check the table of contents against the knowledge and skills required for this test.

Visit www.collegeboard.com/clepprep for additional math resources. You can also find suggestions for exam preparation in Chapter IV of the *Official Study Guide*. In addition, many college faculty post their course materials on their schools' Web sites.

4.

Number	Odd	Even
$2m - 1$	√	
$2m + 1$	√	
$m^2 - m$		√
$m^2 + m + 1$	√	

8.

Set	Must Have Standard Deviation Equal to x
$\{a+2,\ b+2,\ c+2,\ d+2,\ e+2\}$	√
$\{a-2,\ b-2,\ c-2,\ d-2,\ e-2\}$	√
$\{2a,\ 2b,\ 2c,\ 2d,\ 2e\}$	
$\left\{\dfrac{a}{2},\ \dfrac{b}{2},\ \dfrac{c}{2},\ \dfrac{d}{2},\ \dfrac{e}{2}\right\}$	

15.

p	q	$\sim p$	$\sim p \wedge q$
T	T	F	
T	F	F	
F	T	T	√
F	F	T	

22.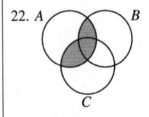

23.

Expression	Rational	Irrational
$\sqrt[3]{m - n}$		√
$\sqrt{m^3}$	√	
$\sqrt[3]{\dfrac{m}{n}}$		√
$\sqrt{m + n^2}$		√

Answer Key

1.	B	31.	C
2.	A	32.	B
3.	D	33.	−5
4.	to the right	34.	C
5.	C	35.	A
6.	B	36.	D
7.	A	37.	D
8.	to the right	38.	4
9.	C	39.	B
10.	B	40.	D
11.	C	41.	C
12.	B	42.	C
13.	C	43.	B
14.	75.2	44.	D
15.	to the right	45.	C
16.	C	46.	D
17.	B	47.	C
18.	B	48.	A
19.	A	49.	D
20.	A	50.	A
21.	C	51.	D
22.	to the right	52.	A
23.	to the right	53.	A
24.	C	54.	A
25.	C	55.	D
26.	D	56.	B
27.	9	57.	C
28.	D	58.	C
29.	D	59.	A
30.	A	60.	2

Natural Sciences

Description of the Examination

The Natural Sciences examination covers a wide range of topics frequently taught in introductory courses surveying both biological and physical sciences at the freshman or sophomore level. Such courses generally satisfy distribution or general education requirements in science that usually are not required of nor taken by science majors. The Natural Sciences exam is not intended for those specializing in science; it is intended to test the understanding of scientific concepts that an adult with a liberal arts education should have. It does not stress the retention of factual details; rather, it emphasizes the knowledge and application of the basic principles and concepts of science, the comprehension of scientific information, and the understanding of issues of science in contemporary society.

The primary objective of the examination is to give candidates the opportunity to demonstrate a level of knowledge and understanding expected of college students meeting a distribution or general education requirement in the natural sciences. An institution may grant up to six semester hours (or the equivalent) of credit toward fulfillment of such a requirement for satisfactory scores on the examination. Some may grant specific course credit, on the basis of the total score for a two-semester survey course covering both biological and physical sciences.

The examination contains approximately 120 questions to be answered in 90 minutes. Some of these are pretest questions that will not be scored. Any time candidates spend on tutorials and providing personal information is in addition to the actual testing time.

Knowledge and Skills Required

The Natural Sciences examination requires candidates to demonstrate one or more of the following abilities in the approximate proportions indicated.

- Knowledge of fundamental facts, concepts, and principles (about 40 percent of the examination)
- Interpretation and comprehension of information (about 20 percent of the examination) presented in the form of graphs, diagrams, tables, equations, or verbal passages
- Qualitative and quantitative application of scientific principles (about 40 percent of the examination), including applications based on material presented in the form of graphs, diagrams, tables, equations, or verbal passages; more emphasis is given to qualitative than quantitative applications

The subject matter of the Natural Sciences examination is drawn from the following topics. The percentages next to the main topics indicate the approximate percentage of exam questions on that topic.

Biological Science (50%)

10%	Origin and evolution of life, classification of organisms
10%	Cell organization, cell division, chemical nature of the gene, bioenergetics, biosynthesis
20%	Structure, function, and development in organisms; patterns of heredity
10%	Concepts of population biology with emphasis on ecology

Physical Science (50%)

7%	Atomic and nuclear structure and properties, elementary particles, nuclear reactions
10%	Chemical elements, compounds and reactions, molecular structure and bonding
12%	Heat, thermodynamics, and states of matter; classical mechanics; relativity
4%	Electricity and magnetism, waves, light, and sound
7%	The universe: galaxies, stars, the solar system
10%	The Earth: atmosphere, hydrosphere, structure features, geologic processes, and history

The examination includes some questions that are interdisciplinary and cannot be classified in one of the listed categories. Some of the questions cover topics that overlap with those listed previously, drawing on areas such as history and philosophy of science, scientific methods, science applications and technology, and the relationship of science to contemporary problems of society, such as environmental pollution and depletion of natural resources. Some questions are laboratory oriented.

Sample Test Questions

The following sample questions do not appear on an actual CLEP examination. They are intended to give potential test-takers an indication of the format and difficulty level of the examination and to provide content for practice and review. Knowing the correct answers to all of the sample questions is not a guarantee of satisfactory performance on the exam.

Directions: Each group of questions that follow consists of five lettered choices followed by a list of numbered phrases or sentences. For each numbered phrase or sentence, select the one choice that is most clearly related to it. Each choice may be used once, more than once, or not at all in each group.

Questions 1–2

   (A) Cell wall

   (B) Cell membrane

   (C) Nucleus

   (D) Mitochondrion

   (E) Ribosome

1. The chief site of energy production in the cell

2. The site of protein synthesis in the cell

Questions 3–5

(A) 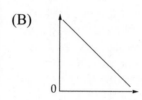   (D)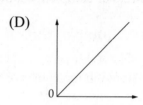

(B) 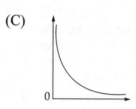   (E)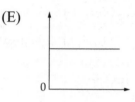

(C)

3. A sample of gas remains at constant temperature.
   Vertical axis: Volume of the sample
   Horizontal axis: Pressure on the sample

4. An object moves at constant speed.
   Vertical axis: Distance traveled since time $t = 0$
   Horizontal axis: Time

5. A constant unbalanced force acts on an object.
   Vertical axis: Acceleration of the object
   Horizontal axis: Time

Questions 6–7

   (A) Tuberculosis

   (B) Phenylketonuria

   (C) Huntington chorea

   (D) Cystic fibrosis

   (E) Tay-Sachs disease

6. The disease that is NOT genetically inherited

7. The disease that can be controlled merely through regulation of diet

Directions: Each of the questions or incomplete statements below is followed by five suggested answers or completions. Select the one that is best in each case.

8. As a direct result of photosynthesis, energy is stored in molecules of which of the following?

(A) RNA
(B) DNA
(C) $C_6H_{12}O_6$ (glucose)
(D) H_2O
(E) CO_2

9. A person whose gallbladder has been removed has a decreased ability to store bile and therefore to digest

(A) fats
(B) starches
(C) sugars
(D) proteins
(E) vitamins

Questions 10–11

In fruit flies, "straight wings" (S) is dominant over "curly wings" (s), and gray body color (G) is dominant over black body color (g). A straight-winged female with gray body color was mated with a straight-winged male with black body color and the following ratios of offspring resulted. The experiment was conducted at 25°C.

Ratio	Phenotype
3/8	straight-winged; gray body color
3/8	straight-winged; black body color
1/8	curly-winged; gray body color
1/8	curly-winged; black body color

10. The data above suggest that the genotype of the male parent is

(A) SsGg
(B) SSGg
(C) ssgg
(D) Ssgg
(E) ssGg

11. The data above suggest that the genotype of the offspring with curly wings and black body color is

(A) SsGg
(B) SSGg
(C) ssgg
(D) Ssgg
(E) ssGg

12. The classification characteristics that define the genus of an animal or a plant are usually more general than those defining

(A) a class
(B) an order
(C) a species
(D) a family
(E) a phylum

13. Hard water is undesirable and is often softened because hard water

(A) is too viscous for regular uses

(B) contains trace amounts of toxic substances

(C) forms insoluble precipitates when boiled or when used with soap

(D) cannot be used efficiently by the body due to dissolved impurities

(E) evaporates more rapidly than soft water

14. Which of the following adaptations is more likely to be found in the leaves of desert plants than in those of plants that grow in moist regions?

(A) Stomata mostly on upper leaf surface

(B) A thin, transparent cuticle

(C) A smooth leaf surface free of hairs

(D) A thickened epidermis and cuticle

(E) A loosely packed mesophyll layer

15. If all the xylem from a section of tree trunk could be removed, which of the following would most likely happen first?

(A) Food could not pass from the leaves to the roots.

(B) The roots would be unable to transfer any stored food to the spring buds.

(C) The leaves would be unable to get any carbon dioxide.

(D) The roots would be unable to store food.

(E) The leaves would be unable to get sufficient water.

16. Whereas the ultimate source of energy for most organisms is sunlight, the immediate source is

(A) chemical

(B) electrical

(C) thermal

(D) gravitational

(E) radiant

17. In embryonic origin, nerve cells are most similar to

(A) epidermal cells

(B) bone cells

(C) red blood cells

(D) liver cells

(E) reproductive cells

18. In the name *Homo sapiens*, the word *sapiens* refers to the

(A) species

(B) family

(C) class

(D) genus

(E) order

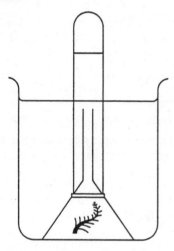

19. A student placed a sprig of green water plant under a funnel in a glass vessel full of water and then placed a test tube full of water mouth-downward over the stem of the funnel. After the setup had been exposed to sunlight for several hours, the student tested a gas that had collected in the test tube and concluded that the plant had produced oxygen. The results of this experiment could have been interpreted more satisfactorily if

(A) the water had been tested for carbon dioxide

(B) only the leaves of the plant had been used

(C) air had been forced through the water

(D) the plant had not been exposed to sunlight

(E) a similar experiment had been set up without sunlight

20. Which of the following best completes the statement below?

    Among multicellular animals, the insects exhibit the greatest diversity of life-forms; therefore _____.

    (A) the total number of insect species is limited
    (B) the presence of wings on an insect is probably an evolutionary error
    (C) insects probably occupy the greatest number of niches
    (D) insect control by human beings is simplified
    (E) any genetic mutation in fruit flies is likely to escape detection

21. The percentage of phosphates in commercial detergents was reduced primarily because phosphates were shown to

    (A) be less effective cleaning agents than most other compounds
    (B) build up in animal tissues and cause sterility
    (C) cause cancer in animals
    (D) cause birth defects in animals
    (E) increase the growth rates of algae in lakes and rivers

22. Carbohydrates are most commonly stored in plants in the form of

    (A) starch
    (B) cellulose
    (C) lactose
    (D) ribose
    (E) sucrose

23. A father will transmit the genes of his Y chromosome to

    (A) one-half of his sons only
    (B) one-half of his daughters only
    (C) all of his sons only
    (D) all of his daughters only
    (E) none of his sons

24. In many cultivated plants (such as oranges, bananas, and potatoes), favorable characteristics often are created by careful genetic crosses. Of the following, which would be the best way to maintain the traits of a new variety with favorable characteristics?

    (A) Selfing individuals of this new variety (i.e., crossing the offspring of one parental plant)
    (B) Artificially pollinating wild varieties with pollen from the new variety
    (C) Artificially pollinating the new variety with pollen from wild varieties
    (D) Crossing the new variety with a variety that was homozygous recessive for all traits of concern
    (E) Vegetative reproduction of the new variety

25. In mammals, insulin is produced in which of the following structures?

    (A) Pancreas
    (B) Liver
    (C) Salivary glands
    (D) Hypothalamus
    (E) Pituitary gland

26. Which of the following occurs during anaphase I of meiosis?

    (A) The sister chromatids are pulled to opposite poles of the spindle.
    (B) The spindle apparatus forms.
    (C) The nuclear envelope disintegrates.
    (D) The centromeres replicate.
    (E) The homologous pairs of chromosomes separate.

27. All living cells have which of the following structures?

    (A) Endoplasmic reticulum
    (B) Nucleus
    (C) Plasma membrane
    (D) Cilia
    (E) Vacuole

28. Digestion of proteins in mammals begins in which of the following organs?

    (A) Mouth
    (B) Stomach
    (C) Small intestine
    (D) Colon
    (E) Gallbladder

29. Which of the following terrestrial biomes typically has the greatest species diversity?

    (A) Tundra
    (B) Taiga
    (C) Deciduous forest
    (D) Chaparral
    (E) Tropical rain forest

30. Which of the following instruments would be most useful for studying the internal structure of a chloroplast?

    (A) Transmission electron microscope
    (B) Scanning electron microscope
    (C) Compound light microscope
    (D) Dissecting microscope
    (E) Phase-contrast microscope

31. A hawk can have which of the following ecological roles?

     I. Primary consumer
    II. Secondary consumer
    III. Tertiary consumer

    (A) I only
    (B) II only
    (C) III only
    (D) I and II only
    (E) II and III only

32. Which of the following most directly leads to changes in cellular specialization during embryonic development?

    (A) Meiosis in the embryo's cells
    (B) Changes in the environmental stimuli the embryo experiences in the uterus
    (C) Formation of the placenta
    (D) An increase in the amount of DNA in the embryo due to replication
    (E) Changes in gene expression

33. Which of the following animals is most closely related to the cheetah?

    (A) Chicken
    (B) Alligator
    (C) Frog
    (D) Squirrel
    (E) Eagle

34. Which of the following organisms transmits the West Nile virus to humans?

    (A) Housefly
    (B) Tsetse fly
    (C) Mosquito
    (D) Tick
    (E) Mouse

35. A photosynthetic eukaryotic cell typically contains

    (A) chloroplasts only
    (B) mitochondria only
    (C) both chloroplasts and mitochondria
    (D) either chloroplasts or mitochondria, but never both at once
    (E) neither chloroplasts nor mitochondria

36. A theory fails to meet the criteria of scientific methodology if

(A) it is unpopular
(B) it contradicts other theories
(C) it has not been conclusively proved
(D) it has not been stated in mathematical terms
(E) no experiments can be designed to test it

37. Dark lines in the Sun's spectrum are explained as resulting from

(A) emission of radiation of certain frequencies from the Sun's atmosphere
(B) absorption of energy by atoms in the outer layers of the Sun
(C) radiation of ultraviolet light from sunspots
(D) continuous radiation from the corona
(E) x-rays emanating from the Sun's atmosphere

38. Scientists estimate the age of the Sun to be about

(A) 100 billion years
(B) 25 billion years
(C) 14 billion years
(D) 4.6 billion years
(E) 3.8 billion years

39. Sunspots on the surface of the Sun are correlated with which of the following?

(A) Relatively low temperatures compared with the surrounding surface
(B) Relatively high temperatures compared with the surrounding surface
(C) Periods of low solar activity
(D) Fusion of helium nuclei rather than hydrogen nuclei
(E) The warming of ocean surface waters in the eastern Pacific (El Niño)

40. Which of the following best describes the principal way in which Earth's atmosphere is heated?

(A) Heat flows from the center of Earth and is conducted through the ground to the air.
(B) The atmosphere absorbs short-wave radiation from the Sun as the Sun's rays pass through it.
(C) Earth absorbs short-wave radiation from the Sun and reradiates long-wave radiation, which is absorbed by the atmosphere.
(D) The air absorbs short-wave radiation from the Sun after the radiation has been reflected by the clouds.
(E) Warm air rises and cold air sinks and, as it sinks, is warmed by compression.

41. Most of Earth's water exists in

(A) the oceans
(B) the atmosphere
(C) groundwater
(D) lakes and rivers
(E) polar ice caps

42. If the present electric power needs of the United States are to be provided by solar power only, all the sunlight incident on which of the following areas must be collected? (Assume 100 percent efficiency.)

(A) A small percent of the area in the United States
(B) All of the area in the United States
(C) All of the area in the Western Hemisphere
(D) All of the area of Earth
(E) All of the area of Earth plus some in outer space

43. Which of the following natural resources is NOT a fossil fuel?

(A) Uranium

(B) Natural gas

(C) Petroleum

(D) Anthracite coal

(E) Bituminous coal

44. All of the following geologic time intervals are characterized correctly EXCEPT

(A) Cambrian period . . . age of birds

(B) Carboniferous period . . . age of amphibians

(C) Devonian period . . . age of fishes

(D) Cenozoic era . . . age of mammals

(E) Mesozoic era . . . age of dinosaurs

45. Which of the following is the farthest, on average, from Earth?

(A) Andromeda galaxy

(B) Halley's comet

(C) Jupiter

(D) Sirius

(E) Uranus

$$CaO + CO_2 \rightarrow CaCO_3$$

46. What mass of CaO is needed to absorb 22 grams of CO_2 according to the balanced chemical equation above? (Molar masses: CaO = 56 g/mol, CO_2 = 44 g/mol)

(A) 112 g

(B) 100 g

(C) 56 g

(D) 28 g

(E) 22 g

47. The half-life of $^{14}_6C$ is 5,600 years. Which of the following statements about a 10-gram sample of $^{14}_6C$ is correct?

(A) The radioactive decay of the sample will be complete after 5,600 years.

(B) The $^{14}_6C$ sample will start radioactive decay after 5,600 years.

(C) A time of 5,600 years has been required to produce this sample of $^{14}_6C$ in nature.

(D) After 5,600 years the sample will contain only 5 grams of $^{14}_6C$.

(E) After 11,200 years the sample will not contain any $^{14}_6C$.

48. Impact craters dominate the Moon's surface, yet are rare on Earth's surface. Reasons for this difference include which of the following?

  I. The Moon has no atmosphere.

 II. The Moon is geologically inactive.

III. The Moon is much older.

(A) I only

(B) II only

(C) I and II only

(D) II and III only

(E) I, II, and III

49. At a fixed pressure, when the temperature of a gas sample increases, its volume increases. This relationship between the temperature and the volume of a gas is best described as which of the following?

(A) Direct proportion

(B) Inverse proportion

(C) Limiting ratio

(D) Hyperbolic function

(E) Logarithmic function

50. The notation $1s^2 2s^2 2p^4$ represents

   (A) a noble gas
   (B) an atomic nucleus
   (C) an element with atomic mass 8
   (D) an element with atomic number 8
   (E) an element with an oxidation state of 4

51. Which of the following molecules can have more than one equivalent Lewis structure?

   (A) H–O–H (bent structure with O lone pairs)

   (B) H–C ≡ C–H

   (C) O–O–O (with central O)

   (D) H–N–H with H below

   (E) H–C–O–H with H above and below C

52. In old-fashioned flashbulbs, light was produced by the reaction of magnesium metal, Mg, sealed in the bulb with oxygen gas, O_2. After the flash, the mass of the sealed bulb was

   (A) definitely greater than it was before use
   (B) definitely smaller than it was before use
   (C) essentially the same as it was before use
   (D) greater or smaller depending on the amount of O_2 consumed
   (E) greater or smaller depending on the amount of light produced

53. Of the following planets that are visible with the naked eye—Venus, Mars, Jupiter, and Saturn—only Venus has an orbit smaller than that of Earth. This means that Venus

   (A) is seen only in the morning or the evening sky
   (B) can be seen in the sky near midnight more often than at other times
   (C) can rarely be seen at all
   (D) has an orbit that is more elliptical than that of Earth
   (E) has a longer year than Earth

54. Which of the following is NOT generally true of metals?

   (A) They are usually solid at room temperature.
   (B) They are good conductors of heat and electricity.
   (C) They easily form negative ions.
   (D) They have luster.
   (E) They can be hammered into sheets or rolled into wires.

55. Within molecules of a compound, atoms are held together by chemical bonds that are primarily

   (A) thermal
   (B) frictional
   (C) gravitational
   (D) electrostatic
   (E) magnetic

56. An unsorted mixture of clay, boulders, sand, and silt would most likely be deposited from which of the following?

   (A) Glacial ice
   (B) Subsurface water
   (C) Streams
   (D) Waves
   (E) Wind

57. Valleys with U-shaped cross sections are the result of erosion by which of the following?

    (A) Glaciers
    (B) Perennial streams
    (C) Intermittent streams
    (D) Mudflows
    (E) Wind

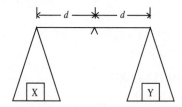

58. The balance shown above is in equilibrium at Earth's surface, and the two arms have the same length d. Thus the two objects, X and Y (not necessarily drawn to scale), must have identical

    (A) densities
    (B) masses
    (C) shapes
    (D) specific gravities
    (E) volumes

59. On a global basis, for which of the following activities is the most water used each day?

    (A) Crop irrigation
    (B) Cooling in power plants
    (C) Commercial laundering
    (D) Manufacturing of textiles
    (E) Production of steel

60. Which of the following correctly identifies the constituents of an atom of the isotope $^{131}_{53}$I ?

	Protons	Neutrons	Electrons
(A)	53	78	78
(B)	78	53	78
(C)	53	78	53
(D)	78	131	78
(E)	131	53	53

61. Which of the following types of electromagnetic radiation has photons of the LEAST energy?

    (A) Visible light
    (B) Ultraviolet light
    (C) Microwaves
    (D) Gamma radiation
    (E) Radio waves

62. The atomic mass of carbon is 12 and the atomic mass of hydrogen is 1. What is the percent by mass of carbon in methane gas, CH_4?

    (A) 20%
    (B) 25%
    (C) 50%
    (D) 75%
    (E) 80%

63. Southern California experienced an earthquake that registered magnitude 3.5 on the Richter scale. One month later the same area experienced an earthquake that registered 5.5. About how many times as much energy was released by the magnitude 5.5 earthquake than by the magnitude 3.5 earthquake?

    (A)   2
    (B)   10
    (C)   200
    (D) 1,000
    (E) 2,000

64. The study of which of the following would likely be the most helpful in providing information about the composition of Earth's upper mantle?

   (A) Temperatures of hot springs

   (B) Size of vesicles in basalt flows

   (C) Xenolith inclusions in igneous rocks

   (D) Carbonate sediments from the ocean floor

   (E) Minerals formed through contact metamorphism

65. Which of the following are found in greater number in the nuclei of carbon-14 atoms than in the nuclei of carbon-12 atoms?

   (A) Alpha particles

   (B) Positrons

   (C) Neutrons

   (D) Protons

   (E) Electrons

66. Which of the following best describes the motion of winds within large storm systems in the Northern Hemisphere?

   (A) North to south

   (B) West to east

   (C) Southwest to northeast

   (D) Clockwise

   (E) Counterclockwise

67. The amount of heat energy released when a certain type of candle is burned is 48,000 joules per gram of wax consumed. Which of the following expressions is equal to the number of grams of wax that need to be burned in order to raise the temperature of 500 grams of water from 20°C to 30°C, assuming all the heat released goes into heating the water? (The specific heat of water is 4.19 J/g°C.)

   (A) $\dfrac{(48,000)(10)(4.19)}{500}$

   (B) $\dfrac{(48,000)(4.19)}{(500)(10)}$

   (C) $\dfrac{(4.19)(10)(500)}{48,000}$

   (D) $\dfrac{(4.19)(500)}{(10)(48,000)}$

   (E) $\dfrac{(30)(4.19)(500)}{(20)(48,000)}$

68. Which of the following types of radiation is typically produced in the laboratory by a high-voltage electron beam impacting a metallic target?

   (A) Primary cosmic radiation

   (B) X-ray radiation

   (C) Neutron radiation

   (D) Ultraviolet radiation

   (E) Beta radiation

Questions 69–71

$$CuO + H_2 \rightarrow Cu + H_2O$$

The drawing below depicts an apparatus for reducing copper(II) oxide to the metal by the reaction above.

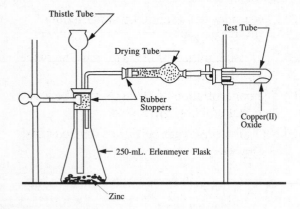

69. In order to produce a stream of hydrogen gas for this reaction, one should add which of the following through the thistle tube?

   (A) Water
   (B) Dilute hydrochloric acid
   (C) Dilute copper(II) sulfate solution
   (D) Hydrogen peroxide
   (E) Dilute ammonia solution

70. After the production of hydrogen gas starts, withdrawing the thistle tube would result in which of the following?

   (A) Moisture would collect in the flask.
   (B) The evolution of hydrogen gas would stop.
   (C) Much hydrogen gas would escape without coming in contact with the copper oxide.
   (D) Air would enter the flask faster than hydrogen gas would be evolved.
   (E) The rate of production of hydrogen gas would increase.

71. Which of the following would most likely increase the effectiveness of the hydrogen gas reducing the copper(II) oxide?

   (A) Heating the test tube
   (B) Cooling the test tube
   (C) Putting the test tube under reduced pressure
   (D) Filling the test tube with dilute HCl solution
   (E) Filling the test tube with dilute NaOH solution

72. Which of the following typically occurs when a forested watershed is clear-cut?

   (A) Annual rainfall increases.
   (B) Soil erosion increases.
   (C) The water temperature in streams decreases.
   (D) The sediment load in streams decreases.
   (E) Atmospheric concentration of O_2 increases.

73. Which characteristic of a star most directly relates to the likelihood of that star's eventually becoming a black hole?

   (A) Apparent magnitude
   (B) Absolute magnitude
   (C) Surface temperature
   (D) Diameter
   (E) Mass

74. How many joules of energy are absorbed by a 20.0 g sample of water as the temperature of the sample is raised from 273 K to 283 K? (The specific heat capacity of water is 4.2 J g^{-1}K^{-1}.)

(A)   42 J

(B)   84 J

(C)   200 J

(D)   840 J

(E) 4,200 J

$$2 NO_2(g) \leftrightharpoons N_2O_4(g)$$

75. The equation above represents a system that has reached a state of chemical equilibrium. Which of the following is a true statement about the system?

(A) All chemical reaction rates have dropped to zero.

(B) The system will eventually contain only N_2O_4 molecules.

(C) The concentration of $NO_2(g)$ must be twice that of $N_2O_4(g)$.

(D) The concentration of $NO_2(g)$ must be less than that of $N_2O_4(g)$.

(E) N_2O_4 molecules are being consumed as fast as they are produced.

Study Resources

Most textbooks used in college-level natural sciences courses cover the topics in the outline given earlier, but the approaches to certain topics and the emphases given to them may differ. To prepare for the Natural Sciences exam, it is advisable to study one or more college textbooks (selecting at least one biological science and one physical science textbook), which can be found in most college bookstores. When selecting a textbook, check the table of contents against the knowledge and skills required for this test.

If candidates maintain an interest in scientific issues; read science articles in newspapers and magazines; watch educational television programs on scientific topics; or work in fields that require a knowledge of certain areas of science, such as nursing and laboratory work, they will probably be knowledgeable about many of the topics included on the Natural Sciences exam.

Visit www.collegeboard.com/clepprep for additional science resources. You can also find suggestions for exam preparation in Chapter IV of the *Official Study Guide*. In addition, many college faculty post their course materials on their schools' Web sites.

Answer Key

#	Ans	#	Ans
1.	D	38.	D
2.	E	39.	A
3.	C	40.	C
4.	D	41.	A
5.	E	42.	A
6.	A	43.	A
7.	B	44.	A
8.	C	45.	A
9.	A	46.	D
10.	D	47.	D
11.	C	48.	C
12.	C	49.	A
13.	C	50.	D
14.	D	51.	C
15.	E	52.	C
16.	A	53.	A
17.	A	54.	C
18.	A	55.	D
19.	E	56.	A
20.	C	57.	A
21.	E	58.	B
22.	A	59.	A
23.	C	60.	C
24.	E	61.	E
25.	A	62.	D
26.	E	63.	D
27.	C	64.	C
28.	B	65.	C
29.	E	66.	E
30.	A	67.	C
31.	E	68.	B
32.	E	69.	B
33.	D	70.	C
34.	C	71.	A
35.	C	72.	B
36.	E	73.	E
37.	B	74.	D
		75.	E

Precalculus

Description of the Examination

The Precalculus examination assesses student mastery of skills and concepts required for success in a first-semester calculus course. A large portion of the exam is devoted to testing a student's understanding of functions and their properties. Many of the questions test a student's knowledge of specific properties of the following types of functions: linear, quadratic, absolute value, square root, polynomial, rational, exponential, logarithmic, trigonometric, inverse trigonometric, and piecewise-defined. Questions on the exam will present these types of functions symbolically, graphically, verbally, or in tabular form. A solid understanding of these types of functions is at the core of all precalculus courses, and it is a prerequisite for enrolling in calculus and other college-level mathematics courses.

The examination contains approximately 48 questions, in two sections, to be answered in 90 minutes. Any time candidates spend on tutorials and providing personal information is in addition to the actual testing time.

- Section 1: 25 questions, 50 minutes.
  The use of an **online graphing calculator (non-CAS)** is allowed for this section. Only some of the questions will require the use of the calculator.

- Section 2: 23 questions, 40 minutes.
  No calculator is allowed for this section.

Although most of the questions on the exam are multiple-choice, there are some questions that require students to enter a numerical answer.

Graphing Calculator

A graphing calculator, which is integrated into the exam software, is available to students only during Section 1 of the exam. Students are expected to know how and when to make use of it. The graphing calculator, together with a brief tutorial, is available to students as a free download for a 30-day trial period. **Students are expected to become familiar with its functionality prior to taking the exam.**

> **For more information about downloading the practice version of the graphing calculator, please visit the Precalculus exam description on the CLEP Web site, www.collegeboard.com/clep.**

In order to answer some of the questions in Section 1 of the exam, students may be required to use the online graphing calculator in the following ways:

- Perform calculations (e.g., exponents, roots, trigonometric values, logarithms).

- Graph functions and analyze the graphs.

- Find zeros of functions.

- Find points of intersection of graphs of functions.

- Find minima/maxima of functions.

- Find numerical solutions to equations.

- Generate a table of values for a function.

Knowledge and Skills Required

Questions on the examination require candidates to demonstrate the following abilities in the approximate proportions indicated.

- Recalling factual knowledge and/or performing routine mathematical manipulation.

- Solving problems that demonstrate comprehension of mathematical ideas and/or concepts.

- Solving nonroutine problems or problems that require insight, ingenuity, or higher mental processes.

The subject matter of the Precalculus examination is drawn from the following topics. The percentages next to the topics indicate the approximate percentage of exam questions on that topic.

20% Algebraic Expressions, Equations, and Inequalities

Ability to perform operations on algebraic expressions

Ability to solve equations and inequalities, including linear, quadratic, absolute value, polynomial, rational, radical, exponential, logarithmic, and trigonometric

Ability to solve systems of equations, including linear and nonlinear

15% Functions: Concept, Properties, and Operations

Ability to demonstrate an understanding of the concept of a function, the general properties of functions (e.g., domain, range), function notation, and to perform symbolic operations with functions (e.g., evaluation, inverse functions)

30% Representations of Functions: Symbolic, Graphical, and Tabular

Ability to recognize and perform operations and transformations on functions presented symbolically, graphically, or in tabular form

Ability to demonstrate an understanding of basic properties of functions and to recognize elementary functions (linear, quadratic, absolute value, square root, polynomial, rational, exponential, logarithmic, trigonometric, inverse trigonometric, and piecewise-defined functions) that are presented symbolically, graphically, or in tabular form

10% Analytic Geometry

Ability to demonstrate an understanding of the analytic geometry of lines, circles, parabolas, ellipses, and hyperbolas

15% Trigonometry and its Applications*

Ability to demonstrate an understanding of the basic trigonometric functions and their inverses and to apply the basic trigonometric ratios and identities (in right triangles and on the unit circle)

Ability to apply trigonometry in various problem-solving contexts

10% Functions as Models

Ability to interpret and construct functions as models and to translate ideas among symbolic, graphical, tabular, and verbal representations of functions

*Note that trigonometry permeates most of the major topics and accounts for more than 15 percent of the exam. The actual proportion of exam questions that requires knowledge of either right triangle trigonometry or the properties of the trigonometric functions is approximately 30–40 percent.

Notes and Reference Information

The following information will be available for reference during the exam.

(1) Figures that accompany questions are intended to provide information useful in answering the questions. All figures lie in a plane unless otherwise indicated. The figures are drawn as accurately as possible EXCEPT when it is stated in a specific question that the figure is not drawn to scale. Straight lines and smooth curves may appear slightly jagged on the screen.

(2) Unless otherwise specified, all angles are measured in radians, and all numbers used are real numbers. For some questions in this test, you may have to decide whether the calculator should be in radian mode or degree mode.

(3) Unless otherwise specified, the domain of any function f is assumed to be the set of all real numbers x for which $f(x)$ is a real number. The range of f is assumed to be the set of all real numbers $f(x)$, where x is in the domain of f.

(4) In this test, log x denotes the common logarithm of x (that is, the logarithm to the base 10) and ln x denotes the natural logarithm of x (that is, the logarithm to the base e).

(5) The inverse of a trigonometric function f may be indicated using the inverse function notation f^{-1} or with the prefix "arc" (e.g., $\sin^{-1} x = \arcsin x$).

(6) The range of $\sin^{-1} x$ is $\left[-\dfrac{\pi}{2}, \dfrac{\pi}{2}\right]$.

The range of $\cos^{-1} x$ is $[0, \pi]$.

The range of $\tan^{-1} x$ is $\left(-\dfrac{\pi}{2}, \dfrac{\pi}{2}\right)$.

(7) Law of Sines: $\dfrac{a}{\sin A} = \dfrac{b}{\sin B} = \dfrac{c}{\sin C}$

Law of Cosines: $c^2 = a^2 + b^2 - 2ab\cos C$

(8) Sum and Difference Formulas:

$\sin(\alpha + \beta) = \sin\alpha\cos\beta + \cos\alpha\sin\beta$

$\sin(\alpha - \beta) = \sin\alpha\cos\beta - \cos\alpha\sin\beta$

$\cos(\alpha + \beta) = \cos\alpha\cos\beta - \sin\alpha\sin\beta$

$\cos(\alpha - \beta) = \cos\alpha\cos\beta + \sin\alpha\sin\beta$

Sample Test Questions

The following sample questions do not appear on an actual CLEP examination. They are intended to give potential test-takers an indication of the format and difficulty level of the examination and to provide content for practice and review. Knowing the correct answers to all of the sample questions is not a guarantee of satisfactory performance on the exam.

Section 1

Directions: A graphing calculator will be available for the questions in this section. Some questions will require you to select from among five choices. For these questions, select the BEST of the choices given. If the exact numerical value of your answer is not one of the choices, select the choice that best approximates this value. Some questions will require you to enter a numerical answer in the box provided.

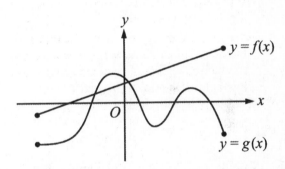

1. The figure above shows the complete graphs of the functions f and g. Based on the graphs, the equation $f(x) - g(x) = 0$ has how many roots?

(A) One

(B) Two

(C) Four

(D) Five

(E) Seven

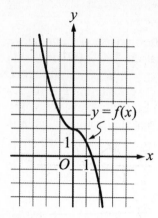

x	$g(x)$
-2	-4
-1	0
0	2
1	2
2	4

2. The graph of the function f and a table of values for the function g are shown above. What is the value of $f(g(0))$?

    (A) -4
    (B) -2
    (C) $\ \ 0$
    (D) $\ \ 2$
    (E) $\ \ 4$

3. The domain of the function f is $\{x : -1 \le x \le 5\}$. If $g(x) = 2f(-x)$, what is the domain of the function g ?

    (A) $\{x : -10 \le x \le 2\}$
    (B) $\{x : -5 \le x \le 1\}$
    (C) $\{x : -2 \le x \le 10\}$
    (D) $\{x : -1 \le x \le 5\}$
    (E) $\{x : 1 \le x \le 5\}$

4. $(\sin t + \cos t)^2 =$

    (A) 1
    (B) $1 + 2\sin t$
    (C) $1 + \sin 2t$
    (D) $\sin(t^2) + \cos(t^2)$
    (E) $\sin(t^2) + 2\sin t \cos t + \cos(t^2)$

$$f(x) = x(x - 1)$$
$$g(x) = x$$

5. The functions f and g are defined above. What are all values of x for which $f(x) < g(x)$?

    (A) $x < 0$ or $x > 1$
    (B) $x < 0$ or $x > 2$
    (C) $0 < x < 1$
    (D) $0 < x < 2$
    (E) $1 < x < 2$

6. If $\pi \le \theta \le 2\pi$ and $\cos \theta = \cos 1$, what is the value of θ ? Round your answer to the nearest hundredth.

$$h(x) = \frac{x^2 e^x}{x}$$

7. The function h is defined above. Which of the following are true about the graph of $y = h(x)$?

    I.   The graph has a vertical asymptote at $x = 0$.
    II. The graph has a horizontal asymptote at $y = 0$.
    III. The graph has a minimum point.

    (A) None
    (B) I and II only
    (C) I and III only
    (D) II and III only
    (E) I, II, and III

8. An antenna that is 90 feet high is on top of a hill. From a point at the base of the hill, the angles of elevation to the top and bottom of the antenna are 28.5° and 25°, respectively. To the nearest whole number of feet, how high is the hill?

(A) 189 ft

(B) 213 ft

(C) 548 ft

(D) 623 ft

(E) 697 ft

9. Let g be the function defined by $g(x) = 10\sin(20x) + 30$. The maximum value of g is attained at which of the following values of x ?

(A) $\dfrac{\pi}{2}$

(B) $\dfrac{\pi}{10}$

(C) $\dfrac{\pi}{20}$

(D) $\dfrac{\pi}{30}$

(E) $\dfrac{\pi}{40}$

10. In the xy-plane, the equation of line ℓ is $y = 6x - 3$. What is the measure, in degrees, of the acute angle formed between ℓ and the x-axis?

(A) 26.6°

(B) 60.0°

(C) 63.4°

(D) 71.6°

(E) 80.5°

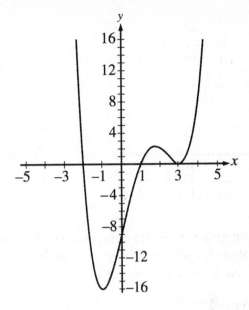

11. The figure above shows the graph of $y = 0.5x^4 - 2.5x^3 + 0.5x^2 + 10.5x + k$, where k is a constant. Which of the following could be the value of k ?

(A) −18

(B) −16

(C) −9

(D) 9

(E) 16

12. Let f be the function defined by $f(x) = -|x|$. The graph of the function g in the xy-plane is obtained by first translating the graph of f horizontally 3 units to the left and then vertically translating this result 2 units up. What is the value of $g(-2)$?

(A) −7

(B) −3

(C) 0

(D) 1

(E) 3

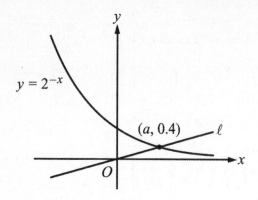

$y = 2^{-x}$

$(a, 0.4)$

ℓ

O

13. In the figure above, line ℓ passes through the origin and intersects the graph of $y = 2^{-x}$ at the point $(a, 0.4)$. What is the slope of line ℓ ?

(A) 0.200
(B) 0.303
(C) 0.528
(D) 1.322
(E) 3.305

14. In the xy-plane, the graph of $y = x^2 + bx + c$ is symmetric about the line $x = 3$ and passes through the point $(5, 2)$. What is the value of c ?

$A(t) = ke^{-0.001t}$, where k is a constant.

15. When a certain radioactive element decays, the amount, in milligrams, that remains after t years can be approximated by the function A above. Approximately how many years would it take for an initial amount of 800 milligrams of this element to decay to 400 milligrams?

(A)   173
(B)   347
(C)   693
(D) 1,386
(E) 2,772

$$f(x) = \begin{cases} 3\sin x & \text{for } x < 0 \\ \sqrt{x} & \text{for } x \geq 0 \end{cases}$$

16. What is the range of the function f defined above?

(A) All real numbers greater than or equal to -3

(B) All real numbers greater than or equal to 0

(C) All real numbers greater than or equal to -3 and less than or equal to 0

(D) All real numbers greater than or equal to -3 and less than or equal to 3

(E) All real numbers

$h(t) = 64 - 46\cos\left(\frac{\pi}{5}t\right)$, where $0 \leq t \leq 10$

17. The function h above gives the height above the ground, in feet, of a passenger on a Ferris wheel t minutes after the ride begins. During one revolution of the Ferris wheel, for how many minutes is the passenger at least 100 feet above the ground? Round your answer to the nearest <u>hundredth</u> of a minute.

18. How many different values of x satisfy the equation $\sin x + 2\sin(2x) = \sqrt{x}$?

(A) One
(B) Two
(C) Three
(D) Five
(E) Infinitely many

19. A ball is dropped from an initial height of d feet above the floor and repeatedly bounces off the floor. Each time the ball hits the floor, it rebounds to a maximum height that is $\frac{3}{4}$ of the height from which it previously fell. The function h models the maximum height, in feet, to which the ball rebounds on the nth bounce. Which of the following is an expression for $h(n)$?

(A) $h(n) = \left(\frac{3}{4}\right)^n d$

(B) $h(n) = \left(\frac{3}{4}d\right)^n$

(C) $h(n) = \frac{3}{4}d^n$

(D) $h(n) = d^{\frac{3}{4}n}$

(E) $h(n) = n^{\frac{3}{4}d}$

Section 2

Directions: A calculator will <u>not</u> be available for the questions in this section. Some questions will require you to select from among five choices. For these questions, select the BEST of the choices given. Some questions will require you to enter a numerical answer in the box provided.

20. If $\left(x - \sqrt{5}\right)\left(x + \sqrt{5}\right) = 5$, what is the value of x ?

(A) $5 \pm \sqrt{5}$

(B) $-5 \pm \sqrt{5}$

(C) ± 5

(D) $\pm\sqrt{10}$

(E) $\pm\sqrt{30}$

21. If $f(x) = 2x + 1$ and $g(x) = 3x - 1$, then $f(g(x)) =$

(A) $5x$

(B) $x - 2$

(C) $6x - 1$

(D) $6x + 2$

(E) $6x^2 + x - 1$

22. The graph in the xy-plane of which of the following equations is a parabola?

(A) $2xy = 1$

(B) $x^2 - 2x + 3y = 1$

(C) $x^2 - 4x + y^2 - y = 1$

(D) $x^2 - y^2 + 6y = 1$

(E) $(x - 2)^2 = y^2$

23. An experiment designed to measure the growth of bacteria began at 2:00 P.M. and ended at 8:00 P.M. on the same day. The number of bacteria is given by the function N, where $N(t) = 1000 \cdot 3^{2t/3}$ and t represents the number of hours that have elapsed since the experiment began. How many more bacteria were there at the end of the experiment than at the beginning of the experiment?

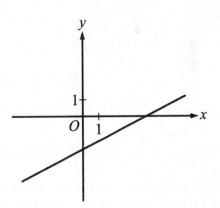

24. The equation of the line shown in the graph above is $y = ax + b$. Which of the following is always true for this line?

(A) $ab < 0$

(B) $ab > 0$

(C) $ab = 0$

(D) $a = b$

(E) $a = -b$

25. What is the x-intercept of the graph of
$y = \frac{1}{8}x^{3/2} - 8$?

(A) −16

(B) −8

(C) $\frac{1}{16}$

(D) 16

(E) 512

26. The function h is given by $h(x) = \log_2\left(x^2 + 2\right)$. For what positive value of x does $h(x) = 3$?

(A) 1

(B) 2

(C) 8

(D) $\sqrt{6}$

(E) $\sqrt{7}$

27. Which of the following relations define y as a function of x ?

I. $x^2 + (y - 3)^2 = 4$

II.

x	0	1	2	3	4
y	10	20	30	20	10

III.

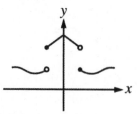

(A) II only

(B) III only

(C) I and II

(D) I and III

(E) II and III

28. In the xy-plane, the lines with equations $2x + 2y = 1$ and $4x - y = 4$ intersect at the point with coordinates (a, b). What is the value of b ?

29. Which of the following is the graph in the xy-plane of $y = 3\sin(2x - \pi)$?

(A)

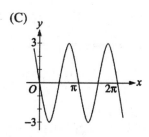

(B)

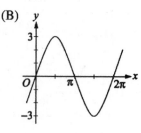

(C)

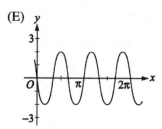

(D)

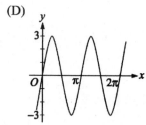

(E)

30. The function f is given by $f(x) = x + |x - 10|$. Which of the following defines $f(x)$ for all $x \leq 10$?

(A) $f(x) = 10$

(B) $f(x) = -10$

(C) $f(x) = 10 - 2x$

(D) $f(x) = -10 + 2x$

(E) $f(x) = -10 - 2x$

x	$f(x)$
5	a
10	32
15	b

31. The table above shows some values for the function f. If f is a linear function, what is the value of $a + b$?

(A) 32

(B) 42

(C) 48

(D) 64

(E) It cannot be determined from the information given.

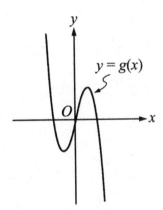

32. The figure above shows the graph of a polynomial function g. Which of the following could define $g(x)$?

(A) $g(x) = x^3 - 4$

(B) $g(x) = x^3 - 4x$

(C) $g(x) = -x^3 + 4x$

(D) $g(x) = x^4 - 4x^2$

(E) $g(x) = -x^4 + 4x^2$

33. If a and b are numbers such that $\ln a = 2.1$ and $\ln b = 1.4$, what is the value of $\ln\left(\dfrac{a^2}{b}\right)$?

[   ]

34. If $0 < \theta < \dfrac{\pi}{2}$ and $10\sin\theta = z$, what is $\tan\theta$ in terms of z ?

(A) $\dfrac{z}{\sqrt{100 - z^2}}$

(B) $\dfrac{10}{\sqrt{z^2 - 100}}$

(C) $\dfrac{\sqrt{100 - z^2}}{10}$

(D) $\dfrac{\sqrt{z^2 - 100}}{10}$

(E) $\dfrac{\sqrt{100 - z^2}}{z}$

WEEKLY SALES OF PRODUCT X

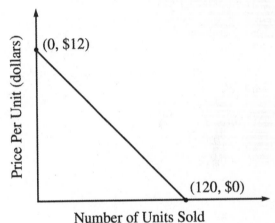

35. Based on past sales, a convenience store has observed a linear relationship between the number of units of Product X that will be sold to customers each week and the price per unit. The figure above models this linear relationship. Based on the model, how many dollars would the convenience store expect to earn from its sales of Product X in a week when the price per unit is $5 ?

(A) $125

(B) $250

(C) $350

(D) $600

(E) $720

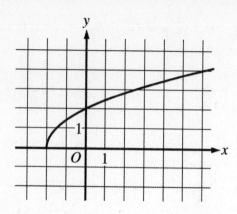

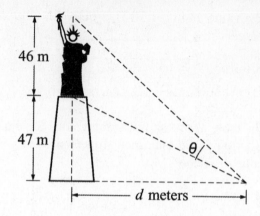

36. The figure above shows the graph of the function f defined by $f(x) = \sqrt{2x + 4}$. If f^{-1} is the inverse function of f, what is the value of $f^{-1}(2)$?

(A) $-\sqrt{8}$

(B) -2

(C) 0

(D) $\dfrac{1}{\sqrt{8}}$

(E) $\sqrt{8}$

37. The Statue of Liberty is 46 meters tall and stands on a pedestal that is 47 meters above the ground. An observer is located d meters from the pedestal and is standing level with the base, as shown in the figure above. Which of the following best expresses the angle θ in terms of d ?

(A) $\theta = \arcsin\left(\dfrac{47}{d}\right) - \arcsin\left(\dfrac{46}{d}\right)$

(B) $\theta = \arcsin\left(\dfrac{93}{d}\right) - \arcsin\left(\dfrac{47}{d}\right)$

(C) $\theta = \arctan\left(\dfrac{47}{d}\right) - \arctan\left(\dfrac{46}{d}\right)$

(D) $\theta = \arctan\left(\dfrac{d}{93}\right) - \arctan\left(\dfrac{d}{47}\right)$

(E) $\theta = \arctan\left(\dfrac{93}{d}\right) - \arctan\left(\dfrac{47}{d}\right)$

38. The value of $\log(1,732)$ is between what two integers?

   (A) 2 and 3
   (B) 3 and 4
   (C) 4 and 5
   (D) 17 and 18
   (E) 173 and 174

39. In the xy-plane, which of the following is an equation of a vertical asymptote to the graph of $y = \sec(6x - \pi)$?

   (A) $x = \dfrac{\pi}{6}$

   (B) $x = \dfrac{\pi}{4}$

   (C) $x = \dfrac{\pi}{3}$

   (D) $x = \dfrac{\pi}{2}$

   (E) $x = \pi$

$$f(x) = \frac{x^2 - 5x + 6}{x - 2}$$

40. The function f is defined above. Which of the following statements are true?

   I. The graph of f in the xy-plane has two x-intercepts.
   II. The graph of f in the xy-plane is the same as the graph of $y = x - 3$.
   III. The range of f is the set of all real numbers.

   (A) None
   (B) II only
   (C) I and III only
   (D) II and III only
   (E) I, II, and III

Study Resources

Most textbooks used in college-level precalculus courses cover the topics in the outline given earlier, but the approaches to certain topics and the emphases given to them may differ. To prepare for the Precalculus exam, it is advisable to study one or more college textbooks, which can be found in most college bookstores. When selecting a textbook, check the table of contents against the knowledge and skills required for this test.

Visit www.collegeboard.com/clepprep for additional precalculus resources. You can also find suggestions for exam preparation in Chapter IV of the *Official Study Guide*. In addition, many college faculty post their course materials on their schools' Web sites.

Answer Key

Section 1		Section 2	
1.	B	20.	D
2.	B	21.	C
3.	B	22.	B
4.	C	23.	80000
5.	D	24.	A
6.	5.28	25.	D
7.	D	26.	D
8.	C	27.	E
9.	E	28.	−0.4
10.	E	29.	C
11.	C	30.	A
12.	D	31.	D
13.	B	32.	C
14.	7	33.	2.8
15.	C	34.	A
16.	A	35.	C
17.	2.14	36.	C
18.	D	37.	E
19.	A	38.	B
		39.	B
		40.	A

Financial Accounting

Description of the Examination

The Financial Accounting examination covers skills and concepts that are generally taught in a first-semester undergraduate financial accounting course. Colleges may award credit for a one-semester course in financial accounting.

The exam contains approximately 75 questions to be answered in 90 minutes. Some of these are pretest questions that will not be scored. Any time candidates spend on tutorials or providing personal information is in addition to the actual testing time.

Knowledge and Skills Required

Questions on the Financial Accounting examination require candidates to demonstrate one or more of the following abilities.

- Familiarity with accounting concepts and terminology
- Preparation, use, and analysis of accounting data and financial reports issued for both internal and external purposes
- Application of accounting techniques to simple problem situations involving computations
- Understanding the rationale for generally accepted accounting principles and procedures

The subject matter of the Financial Accounting examination is drawn from the following topics. The percentages next to the main topics indicate the approximate percentage of exam questions on that topic.

20–30% **General Topics**
- Generally accepted accounting principles
- Rules of double-entry accounting/ transaction analysis/accounting equation
- The accounting cycle
- Business ethics
- Purpose of, presentation of, and relationships between financial statements
- Forms of business

20–30% **The Income Statement**
- Presentation format issues
- Recognition of revenue and expenses
- Cost of goods sold
- Irregular items (e.g., discontinued operations, extraordinary items, etc.)
- Profitability analysis

30–40% **The Balance Sheet**
- Cash and internal controls
- Valuation of accounts and notes receivable (including bad debts)
- Valuation of inventories
- Acquisition and disposal of long-term asset
- Depreciation/amortization/ depletion
- Intangible assets (e.g., patents, goodwill, etc.)
- Accounts and notes payable
- Long-term liabilities (e.g., bonds payable)
- Owner's equity
- Preferred and common stock
- Retained earnings
- Liquidity, solvency, and activity analysis

5–10% **Statement of Cash Flows**
- Indirect method
- Cash flow analysis
- Operating, financing, and investing activities

Less than 5% **Miscellaneous**
- Investments
- Contingent liabilities

Sample Test Questions

The following sample questions do not appear on an actual CLEP examination. They are intended to give potential test-takers an indication of the format and difficulty level of the examination and to provide content for practice and review. Knowing the correct answers to all of the sample questions is not a guarantee of satisfactory performance on the exam.

Directions: Each of the questions or incomplete statements below is followed by five suggested answers or completions. Select the one that is best in each case.

1. Which of the following always increases as a result of net income?

   (A) Liabilities
   (B) Cash
   (C) Merchandise
   (D) Sales
   (E) Capital

2. What is the number of days' inventory on hand for a firm with cost of goods sold of $750,000 and average ending inventory of $150,000?

   (A) 5
   (B) 10
   (C) 20
   (D) 50
   (E) 73

3. During the current year, accounts receivable increased from $27,000 to $41,000, and sales were $225,000. Based on this information, how much cash did the company collect from its customers during the year?

   (A) $225,000
   (B) $239,000
   (C) $211,000
   (D) $252,000
   (E) $266,000

4. Accounts receivable turnover helps determine

   (A) the balance of accounts payable
   (B) the customers who have recently paid their bills
   (C) how quickly a firm collects cash on its credit sales
   (D) when to write off delinquent accounts
   (E) credit sales

5. The income statement is designed to measure

   (A) whether a firm is able to pay its bills
   (B) how solvent a company has been
   (C) how much cash flow a firm is likely to generate
   (D) the financial position of a firm
   (E) the results of business operations

6. A company prepares a bank reconciliation in order to

   (A) determine the correct amount of the cash balance
   (B) satisfy banking regulations
   (C) determine deposits not yet recorded by the bank
   (D) double-check the amount of petty cash
   (E) record all check disbursements

7. An inventory valuation method affects

   (A) the cost of goods sold but not the balance sheet
   (B) the balance sheet but not the cost of goods sold
   (C) both the income statement and the balance sheet
   (D) neither the income statement nor the balance sheet
   (E) the cost of goods sold but not the income statement

8. A liability for dividends is recorded on which of the following?

   (A) The declaration date

   (B) The record date

   (C) The payment date

   (D) The collection date

   (E) The statement date

9. Assets are classified as intangible under which of the following conditions?

   (A) They are converted into cash within one year.

   (B) They have no physical substance.

   (C) They are acquired in a merger.

   (D) They are held for resale.

   (E) They are short term and used in operations.

10. Return on assets helps users of financial statements evaluate which of the following?

   (A) Profitability

   (B) Liquidity

   (C) Solvency

   (D) Cash flow

   (E) Reliability

11. The accounting concept that emphasizes the existence of a business firm separate and apart from its owners is ordinarily termed the

   (A) business separation concept

   (B) consistency concept

   (C) going-concern concept

   (D) business materiality concept

   (E) business entity concept

12. The financial statement that includes classifications for operating, financing, and investing activities of a business entity for a period of time is called the

   (A) Income Statement

   (B) Statement of Retained Earnings

   (C) Balance Sheet

   (D) Statement of Changes in Owners' Equity

   (E) Statement of Cash Flows

13. In a period of rising prices, which of the following inventory methods results in the highest cost of goods sold?

   (A) FIFO

   (B) LIFO

   (C) Average cost

   (D) Periodic inventory

   (E) Perpetual inventory

14. Treasury stock may be correctly defined as

   (A) a corporation's own stock that has been issued and then reacquired

   (B) new issues of a corporation's stock before they are sold on the open market

   (C) stock issued by the United States Office of the Treasury

   (D) any stock that a corporation acquires and holds for more than 90 days

   (E) any stock held by a corporation that receives dividends in excess of 5 percent of the initial cost of the stock

15. Equity investors are most interested in which aspect(s) of a company?

   I. Book value
   II. Profitability
   III. Cash flow

   (A) I only
   (B) II only
   (C) III only
   (D) I and II only
   (E) II and III only

16. Entries made on the books at the end of a period to take care of changes occurring in accounts are called

   (A) fiscal entries
   (B) balancing entries
   (C) reversing entries
   (D) correcting entries
   (E) adjusting entries

17. One disadvantage of the corporation as compared to other types of business organizations is that

   (A) greater legal liability is assigned to stockholders
   (B) greater ethical responsibility is expected of officers and employees
   (C) greater profit is required by owners
   (D) shares of stock can be sold and transferred to new owners
   (E) greater tax burden is levied on the entity

18. Green Corporation with assets of $5,000,000 and liabilities of $2,000,000 has 6,000 shares of capital stock outstanding (par value $300). What is the book value per share?

   (A) $ 200
   (B) $ 300
   (C) $ 500
   (D) $ 833
   (E) $1,167

19. Cost of goods sold is determined by which of the following?

   (A) Beginning inventory plus net purchases minus ending inventory
   (B) Beginning inventory plus purchases plus purchase returns minus ending inventory
   (C) Beginning inventory minus net purchases plus ending inventory
   (D) Purchases minus transportation-in plus beginning inventory minus ending inventory
   (E) Net sales minus ending inventory

20. The owner's equity in a business increases from which of the following?

   I. Excess of revenue over expenses
   II. Investments by the owner
   III. Accounts payable

   (A) I only
   (B) II only
   (C) III only
   (D) I and II only
   (E) I, II, and III

21. The Accumulated Depreciation account should be shown in the financial statements as

   (A) an operating expense
   (B) an extraordinary loss
   (C) a liability
   (D) stockholders' equity
   (E) a contra (deduction) to an asset account

22. If an individual borrows $95,000 on July 1, 2000, from Community Bank by signing a $95,000, 9 percent, one-year note, what is the accrued interest as of December 31, 2000?

    (A) $ 0
    (B) $2,138
    (C) $4,275
    (D) $6,413
    (E) $8,550

23. Net purchases for the year amounted to $80,000. The merchandise inventory at the beginning of the year was $19,000. On sales of $120,000, a 30 percent gross profit on the selling price was realized. The inventory at the end of the year was

    (A) $13,000
    (B) $15,000
    (C) $17,000
    (D) $25,000
    (E) $63,000

24. X Corporation declares and issues a 5 percent stock dividend on common stock, payable in common stock, shortly after the close of the year. Which of the following statements about the nature and effect of the dividend is FALSE?

    (A) The total stockholders' equity in the corporation is not changed.
    (B) The dividend does not constitute income to the stockholders.
    (C) The book value per share of common stock is not changed.
    (D) The amount of retained earnings is reduced.
    (E) The amount of total assets is not changed.

25. "In determining net income from business operations, the costs involved in generating revenue should be charged against that revenue."

    The statement above best describes which of the following?

    (A) The cost principle
    (B) The going-concern principle
    (C) The profit principle
    (D) The matching principle
    (E) The business entity principle

26. All of the following expenditures should be charged to an asset account rather than to an expense account of the current period EXCEPT the cost of

    (A) overhauling a delivery truck, which extends its useful life by two years
    (B) purchasing a new component for a machine, which serves to increase the productive capacity of the machine
    (C) constructing a parking lot for a leased building
    (D) installing a new equipment item
    (E) replacing worn-out tires on a delivery truck

27. The balance sheet of Harold Company shows current assets of $200,000 and current liabilities of $100,000. The company uses cash to acquire merchandise inventory. As a result of this transaction, which of the following is true of working capital and the current ratio?

    (A) Both are unchanged.
    (B) Working capital is unchanged; the current ratio increases.
    (C) Both decrease.
    (D) Working capital decreases; the current ratio increases.
    (E) Working capital decreases; the current ratio is unchanged.

28. In the preparation of the Statement of Cash Flows, which of the following transactions will NOT be reported as a financing activity?

(A) Sale of common stock

(B) Sale of bonds

(C) Issuance of long-term note to bank

(D) Issuance of 30-day note to trade creditor

(E) Purchase of treasury stock

29. On December 31, before making year-end adjusting entries, Accounts Receivable had a debit balance of $80,000, and the Allowance for Uncollectible Accounts had a credit balance of $3,500. Credit sales for the year were $600,000. If credit losses are estimated at 1/2 percent of credit sales, which of the following is true?

(A) The balance of the Allowance for Uncollectible Accounts will be $500 after adjustment.

(B) The balance of the Allowance for Uncollectible Accounts will be $3,500 after adjustment.

(C) The balance of the Allowance for Uncollectible Accounts will be $6,500 after adjustment.

(D) The Uncollectible Accounts Expense for the year will be $500.

(E) The Uncollectible Accounts Expense for the year will be $6,500.

30. A company bought a patent at a cost of $180,000. The patent had an original legal life of 17 years. The remaining legal life is 10 years, but the company expects its useful life will only be 6 years. When should the cost of the patent be charged to expenses?

(A) Immediately

(B) Over the next 6 years

(C) Over the next 10 years

(D) Over the next 17 years

(E) Over the next 40 years

31. How is treasury stock reported on the balance sheet?

(A) As an increase in liabilities

(B) As an increase in assets

(C) As a decrease in assets

(D) As an increase in stockholders' equity

(E) As a decrease in stockholders' equity

32.
Cash:	$ 40,000
Accounts receivable:	$120,000
Inventory:	$300,000
Prepaid rent:	$ 2,000
Accounts payable:	$150,000
Salaries payable:	$ 7,000
Long-term bonds payable:	$200,000

The selected accounts above are from TJ Supply's balance sheet. What is TJ Supply's working capital?

(A) $ 40,000

(B) $105,000

(C) $160,000

(D) $305,000

(E) $462,000

33. A machine with a useful life of eight years was purchased for $600,000 on January 1. The estimated salvage value is $50,000. What is the first year's depreciation by using the double-declining-balance method?

(A) $ 50,000

(B) $ 68,000

(C) $ 75,000

(D) $137,500

(E) $150,000

34. Newman Corporation uses the allowance method of accounting for its accounts receivable. The company currently has a $100,000 balance in accounts receivable and a $5,000 balance in its allowance for uncollectible accounts. The company decides to write off $4,000 of its accounts receivable. What would be the balance in its net accounts receivable before and after the write-off?

	Before	After
(A)	$ 95,000	$ 91,000
(B)	$ 95,000	$ 95,000
(C)	$100,000	$ 96,000
(D)	$105,000	$101,000
(E)	$105,000	$105,000

35. Trading securities must be reported on the balance sheet at

(A) historical cost

(B) cost plus earnings minus dividends

(C) book value

(D) fair market value

(E) net present value

36. An accrued expense results in

(A) a liability

(B) a revenue

(C) a prepaid expense

(D) an unearned revenue

(E) a contra owner's equity account

37. The L Company purchased new machinery and incurred the following costs:

Invoice price	$30,000
Freight (F.O.B. shipping point)	$ 2,000
Foundation for machinery	$ 1,000
Installation costs	$ 900
Annual maintenance of machinery	$ 600

The total cost of the machinery is

(A) $30,000

(B) $31,900

(C) $32,000

(D) $33,900

(E) $34,500

38. ABC Company issued $5,000,000 of bonds on January 1, the date of record, receiving cash of $5,300,000. Which of the following is true about the bonds?

(A) The bonds were issued at a discount.

(B) The bonds are not interest bearing.

(C) The market value of the bonds on the date of issue was $5,100,000.

(D) The market quote for the bonds was 108.

(E) The amount of annual interest expense will be less than the amount of interest paid annually in cash.

39. Brock Company purchased a patent for $72,000 from Carter Company. The patent has a remaining legal life of 6 years, with an expected useful life of 4 years. The first year's amortization is

(A) $ 0

(B) $ 6,000

(C) $12,000

(D) $18,000

(E) $24,000

40. Which of the following is true of annual depreciation expense?

(A) It represents the amount required for annual maintenance of a long-term asset.

(B) It represents the annual revenue earned by an asset.

(C) It allocates the cost of use of a long-term asset to the revenue that it generates.

(D) It is required to fulfill the economic entity assumption.

(E) It reduces cash.

41. Information in Covington Corporation's accounting records concerning its common stock shows that there are 100,000 shares authorized, 80,000 shares issued, and 5,000 shares held as treasury stock. If a $3.00-per-share dividend is declared by the board of directors, the total amount of the cash dividend would be

(A) $ 15,000

(B) $225,000

(C) $240,000

(D) $300,000

(E) $315,000

42. The matching concept matches

(A) customers with businesses

(B) expenses with revenues

(C) assets with liabilities

(D) creditors with businesses

(E) debits with credits

43. Cindy Company is preparing a bank reconciliation. Which of the following should be subtracted from the balance per bank statement to arrive at the adjusted cash balance?

(A) Deposits in transit

(B) Bank service charge

(C) Interest credited to the account

(D) Outstanding checks

(E) Customer check returned for insufficient funds

44. Which of the following equals the net assets of a company?

(A) Current assets minus current liabilities

(B) Total assets minus current liabilities

(C) Total assets minus current assets

(D) Long-term assets minus accumulated depreciation

(E) Stockholders' equity

45. New World, Inc., purchased $30,000 in goods on account that in turn were sold on account for $35,000. If New World uses accrual accounting, how much should they record in expenses and revenue?

(A) $35,000 in revenue but no expenses

(B) $30,000 in expenses but no revenue

(C) $35,000 in revenue and $30,000 in expenses

(D) $30,000 in revenue and $30,000 in expenses

(E) $5,000 in revenue but no expenses

46. Sonny Corporation has a simple capital structure of 100,000 shares of $1 par common stock and 20,000 shares of 5 percent preferred stock, $50 par. Both classes of stock were outstanding for the entire year. During the year, the company reported net income of $550,000 and declared dividends of $75,000 and $50,000 on the common stock and the preferred stock, respectively. Sonny's earnings per share for the year were

(A) $4.25

(B) $4.58

(C) $4.75

(D) $5.00

(E) $5.50

47. A machine that cost $25,000 three years ago is sold in the current year for $6,000. The accumulated depreciation taken on the machine was $20,000. This sale would be reported in the current year's statement of cash flows as

   (A) $25,000 outflow in the cash from investing activities section
   (B) $6,000 inflow in the cash from investing activities section
   (C) $1,000 inflow in the cash from investing activities section
   (D) $1,000 inflow in the cash from operations section
   (E) $1,000 inflow in the cash from financing activities section

48. On a classified balance sheet, which of the following should be considered part of the asset category "Investments"?

   (A) Land held for possible future expansion
   (B) Treasury stock
   (C) Machinery used in the business
   (D) Short-term notes receivable
   (E) Patents

49. During the past year, a company reported net income of $230,000. Depreciation expense was $22,000. In December the company received $7,000 representing rent for the next year on a vacant warehouse. What is the amount of cash provided by operating activities that should appear on a statement of cash flows?

   (A) $215,000
   (B) $237,000
   (C) $245,000
   (D) $252,000
   (E) $259,000

50. Ling is an accountant at a publicly traded corporation. She recently discovered in the accounting records a material error that affected last year's financial statements and will affect this year's statements. If the error is not corrected, it will reverse itself this year and probably no one else will discover it. Even though last year's net income was materially overstated and this year's net income will be materially understated, the overall effect on the two years combined net incomes is that the overstatement and the understatement will completely offset each other. Which of the following is the best action that Ling should take?

   (A) Do nothing, since no one will be harmed because of the offset
   (B) Immediately inform the local law enforcement agency
   (C) Place a phone call to the local newspaper to inform the public about the error
   (D) Immediately contact the Securities and Exchange Commission, since she is not sure what action her supervisor will take
   (E) Inform her immediate supervisor and help correct last year's statements

51. Which of the following identifies the income statement items in their proper order as found in a correctly prepared income statement?

   (A) Gross profit, net income, cost of goods sold, operating expenses, sales
   (B) Sales, operating expenses, cost of goods sold, gross profit, net income
   (C) Sales, cost of goods sold, operating expenses, gross profit, net income
   (D) Sales, cost of goods sold, gross profit, operating expenses, net income
   (E) Gross profit, cost of goods sold, sales, operating expenses, net income

52. Magoo Wholesaler finds that 30 percent of its customers pay cash for their purchases. The rest buy on credit, 60 percent of which is collected in the month of purchase, and the rest in the month after purchase. If sales in January are $120,000, what is the balance of accounts receivable on January 31?

(A) $0

(B) $12,000

(C) $33,600

(D) $48,000

(E) $50,400

53. If $10,000,000 of 6 percent bonds is issued at 105½, the amount of cash received from the sale is

(A) $10,000,000

(B) $10,105,500

(C) $10,512,000

(D) $10,550,000

(E) $10,600,000

54. On August 1 Carlos Company pays $3,600 for a two-year insurance policy covering the period beginning September 1. How much insurance expense should be recognized by Carlos this year if the company reports on a calendar-year basis?

(A) $600

(B) $750

(C) $1,050

(D) $1,800

(E) $3,600

55. If a corporation has total assets of $1,568,000, current liabilities of $60,000, and long-term liabilities of $388,000, what is its approximate debt-to-equity ratio?

(A) 0.15

(B) 0.25

(C) 0.29

(D) 0.40

(E) 0.43

Directions: Choose among the corresponding properties in each column for each entry by clicking on your choice. When you click on a blank cell, a check mark will appear. No credit is given unless the correct cell is marked for each entry.

56. At the end of Dugan Retail Corporation's first year of operation, it was determined that the company had overstated its merchandise inventory.

Indicate the effect that the overstatement will have on the current year's cost of goods sold and net income.

	Overstated	Understated	No Effect
Cost of goods sold			
Net income			

Directions: Select a choice and click on the blank in which you want the choice to appear. Repeat until all of the blanks have been filled. A correct answer must have a different choice in each blank.

57. Match each of the following terms with the corresponding asset category.

| Depreciation |
| Depletion |
| Amortization |

Intangible assets _____

Tangible assets _____

Natural resources _____

Study Resources

Most textbooks used in the first semester of college-level financial accounting courses cover the topics in the outline given earlier, but the approaches to certain topics and the emphases given to them may differ. To prepare for the Financial Accounting exam, it is advisable to study one or more college textbooks, which can be found in most college bookstores. When selecting a textbook, check the table of contents against the knowledge and skills required for this test.

Visit www.collegeboard.com/clepprep for additional financial accounting resources. You can also find suggestions for exam preparation in Chapter IV of the *Official Study Guide*. In addition, many college faculty post their course materials on their schools' Web sites.

Answer Key

1.	E	30.	B
2.	E	31.	E
3.	C	32.	D
4.	C	33.	E
5.	E	34.	B
6.	A	35.	D
7.	C	36.	A
8.	A	37.	D
9.	B	38.	E
10.	A	39.	D
11.	E	40.	C
12.	E	41.	B
13.	B	42.	B
14.	A	43.	D
15.	E	44.	E
16.	E	45.	C
17.	E	46.	D
18.	C	47.	B
19.	A	48.	A
20.	D	49.	E
21.	E	50.	E
22.	C	51.	D
23.	B	52.	C
24.	C	53.	D
25.	D	54.	A
26.	E	55.	D
27.	A	56.	See below
28.	D	57.	See below
29.	C		

56. Cost of goods sold–Understated
Net income–Overstated

57. Intangible assets–Amortization
Tangible assets–Depreciation
Natural resources–Depletion

Information Systems and Computer Applications

Description of the Examination

The Information Systems and Computer Applications examination covers material that is usually taught in an introductory college-level business information systems course. Questions test knowledge, terminology, and basic concepts about information systems as well as the application of that knowledge. The examination does not emphasize the details of hardware design and language-specific programming techniques. References to applications such as word processing or spreadsheets do not require knowledge of a specific product. The focus is on concepts and techniques applicable to a variety of products and environments. Knowledge of arithmetic and mathematics equivalent to that of a student who has successfully completed a traditional first-year high school algebra course is assumed.

The examination contains approximately 100 questions to be answered in 90 minutes. Some of these are pretest questions and will not be scored. The time candidates spend on tutorials and providing personal information is in addition to the actual testing time.

Knowledge and Skills Required

Questions on the Information Systems and Computer Applications examination require candidates to demonstrate knowledge of the following content. The percentages next to each main topic indicates the approximate percentage of exam questions on that topic.

25% Information Systems and Office Application Software in Organizations
- Standard office suite tools (word processors, spreadsheets, presentation packages, end-user database packages)
- Basic user functions of a desktop operating system
- Office systems (electronic mail, conferencing, cooperative work environments)
- Web browsers
- Internet and other online services and methods (World Wide Web, FTP, Web search engines, Web bots)
- Specialized systems (statistical analysis, expert systems, DSS, GIS, BI)

- Electronic Data Interchange
- Enterprise-wide systems (ERP, CRM, SCM)

20% Hardware and Systems Technology
- Devices for processing, storage, input and output, telecommunications, and networking
- Functions performed by computer, telecommunications, and network hardware
- Digital representation of data for storage and processing (numeric, text, images, audio, video)
- Concepts of local, wide-area, and enterprise network architectures
- Concept of mainframe versus client/server architectures
- Operating system and network operating system functions and architectures
- Wireless computing/communication devices (cellular, satellite devices, PDA, GPS)

15% Information Systems Software Development
- Software development methods and tools
- Systems development life cycle concepts
- Project management functions and roles
- Types of information processing methods (batch, real-time, transaction)
- User interface design
- Development and purpose of standards

25% Programming Concepts and Data Management
- Programming language syntax and structures (pseudocode)
- Programming logic
- Object-oriented methods
- Data concepts, types, and structures
- File types and structures
- Database management systems
- SQL coding and structures
- Web technologies (HTML, XML)
- Web page development (analysis and design)
- Data warehousing and data mining

15%   Business, Social, and Ethical Implications and Issues

- Economic effects
- Privacy concerns
- Intellectual property rights and legal issues, including open source initiatives
- Effects of information technology on careers (ergonomics, virtual teams, telecommuting, job design)
- Impact of technology on careers (globalization, outsourcing, insourcing)
- Careers in information systems and information technology
- Knowledge management
- System, application, and personal computer security and controls
- Business strategies (competition, reengineering, process modeling, e-commerce, TQM)

Sample Test Questions

The following sample questions do not appear on an actual CLEP examination. They are intended to give potential test-takers an indication of the format and difficulty level of the examination and to provide content for practice and review. Knowing the correct answers to all of the sample questions is not a guarantee of satisfactory performance on the exam.

Directions: Each of the questions or incomplete statements below is followed by five suggested answers or completions. Select the one that is best in each case.

1. Which of the following support tools is NOT provided with most word processing software?

   (A) A spelling checker
   (B) A thesaurus
   (C) An encyclopedia
   (D) Mail-merge capability
   (E) A grammar checker

2. Which of the following is designed for the purpose of having a team discuss a topic over an extended period of time while keeping the responses organized by topic?

   (A) Data library
   (B) File sharing
   (C) Push technology
   (D) Internet telephony
   (E) Threaded discussion group

3. Which of the following would NOT be used as an input device for a computer system?

   (A) Image scanner
   (B) CD-ROM drive
   (C) Keyboard
   (D) Mouse
   (E) PC speaker

4. Which of the following capabilities permits the simultaneous usage of multiple CPUs in a single computer system?

   (A) Multimedia
   (B) Multiplexing
   (C) Multiprocessing
   (D) Multiprogramming
   (E) Multitasking

5. One responsibility that is NOT traditionally given to a beginning programmer is

   (A) coding
   (B) debugging
   (C) program testing
   (D) documentation
   (E) systems design

6. In most computer languages, the absence of parentheses implies that the order of mathematical operation, from highest to lowest precedence, is

(A) exponentiation; addition and subtraction; multiplication and division

(B) addition and subtraction; multiplication and division; exponentiation

(C) multiplication and division; exponentiation; addition and subtraction

(D) exponentiation; multiplication and division; addition and subtraction

(E) exponentiation; multiplication; division; addition; subtraction

7. Input data controls related to information processing include each of the following EXCEPT

(A) reasonableness checks

(B) check digit verification

(C) program debugging

(D) syntax checks

(E) batch totals

8. Applications software is designed to be compatible with the

(A) Internet browser

(B) LAN configuration

(C) operating system

(D) programming language

(E) hardware interface

9. Which of the following types of systems development methods would be appropriate when a company does not have an expert IS department?

  I. Outsourcing

 II. Traditional SDLC

III. Prototyping

(A) I only

(B) II only

(C) III only

(D) I and III only

(E) I, II, and III

10. In the case of a power failure, the contents of RAM will be

(A) automatically printed out

(B) automatically saved on disk

(C) displayed on the screen

(D) lost

(E) refreshed

11. Which of the following has as its primary function locating Web sites that deal with particular subjects?

(A) Uniform resource locator

(B) Search engine

(C) Hypertext

(D) Outsourcer

(E) Browser

12. Conversion of data files is part of which of the following phases of the system development process?

(A) Analysis

(B) Design

(C) Implementation

(D) Development

(E) Maintenance

13. Which of the following is a database whose data are scattered across several physical servers?

(A) Data mine

(B) Data warehouse

(C) Relational database

(D) Distributed database

(E) Integrated database

14. Each of the following applications is typically available for a personal digital assistant EXCEPT

(A) statistical analysis software

(B) two-way wireless messaging

(C) appointment calendar

(D) address book

(E) memo pad

15. During preparation of a document using word processing software, a SAVE operation copies the document from

(A) a disk to main memory

(B) main memory to a printer

(C) main memory to a disk

(D) a hard disk to a floppy disk

(E) one floppy disk to another

16. Which of the following best describes how GPS units function?

(A) The receiver sends out regular query pulses and waits to receive responses from a GPS satellite.

(B) The receiver is passive and listens for the regular signals from GPS satellites, which are then processed to find the distance from the satellites.

(C) The receiver sends out radio signals that are reflected back by satellites and detected by the unit.

(D) The receiver acts as a homing beacon that is tracked by the GPS satellites, which periodically send out position updates for each tracked receiver.

(E) The receiver can detect an invisible electronic grid projected onto Earth's surface and compares the location on this grid to a stored map of Earth.

17. A plan to safeguard a company's computer system against damage caused by earthquakes, floods, or fires is called

(A) a disaster recovery plan

(B) a safeguard system plan

(C) a system recovery plan

(D) an emergency recovery plan

(E) a personnel and facility control plan

18. Using an enterprise resource planning system has which of the following advantages?

  I. It is easier to install than a typical transaction processing system.

 II. It provides a centralized database for organizational data.

III. It integrates processes over the organization.

(A) I only

(B) II only

(C) I and II only

(D) II and III only

(E) I, II, and III

19. In a relational database, each column represents

(A) a record
(B) an attribute
(C) a key
(D) an entity
(E) a file

20. Which of the following is required to access the Internet from a home location?

(A) Access to an Internet node or a service provider
(B) Access to a LAN
(C) Access to a mainframe
(D) An e-mail address
(E) One's own home page

21. Which of the following is NOT a correct characterization of batch processing?

(A) It allows immediate updating of master files.
(B) It provides physical batch totals to be used in control procedures.
(C) It provides efficient updating of master files.
(D) It is most applicable for processing routine periodic activities.
(E) It allows efficient scheduling of processing.

22. Which of the following pseudocode commands would most likely require a calculation step in an algorithm?

(A) GET
(B) SHOW
(C) PRINT
(D) SET
(E) INCREMENT

23. Which of the following describes a Web site that provides access to multiple services such as news, weather, sports, and stock indexes?

(A) Host
(B) Portal
(C) Domain
(D) Hyperlink
(E) Home page

24. Which of the following is the minimum distance range of a class 2 Bluetooth device such as a hands-free cell phone headset?

(A)   3 feet
(B)   30 feet
(C)   300 feet
(D) 1,000 feet
(E) 3,000 feet

25. The special formatting language used to create Web pages is called

(A) HTML
(B) XML
(C) Perl
(D) Java
(E) Script

26. Goals of a supply-chain management system include which of the following?

I. Facilitate up-selling of the product.
II. Deliver the product to the customer more rapidly.
III. Reduce the cost of the product.

(A) I only
(B) I and II only
(C) I and III only
(D) II and III only
(E) I, II, and III

27. The process through which a user is verified and validated to access a computer network/system is referred to as

    (A) encryption
    (B) password protection
    (C) authentication
    (D) account validation
    (E) certification

28. A program written to access and update a master database that maintains sales of tickets to an upcoming concert is called

    (A) system software
    (B) networking software
    (C) a transaction processing system
    (D) an operating system
    (E) a knowledge management system

29. In a spreadsheet formula, what type of cell address is fixed and does not change when the formula is copied?

    (A) Relative address
    (B) Constant address
    (C) Fixed address
    (D) Static address
    (E) Absolute address

30. Which of the following is the term used when a Web site automatically downloads data or files to a computer whenever new data are available or at scheduled intervals?

    (A) Web streaming
    (B) Push technology
    (C) Pipelining
    (D) Spamming
    (E) Web crawling

31. When applied to the development of computer systems, the term "ergonomics" means

    (A) designing computer systems to maximize the cost-benefit ratio
    (B) incorporating human comfort, efficiency, and safety into the design of the human-machine interface
    (C) following the systems development life cycle
    (D) fostering development team interaction through the use of computer-aided software engineering tools
    (E) optimizing the throughput rate by adjusting the operating system interrupts

32. All of the following can be used to secure data against inappropriate access EXCEPT

    (A) data redundancy
    (B) data encryption
    (C) database passwords
    (D) segregation of functions
    (E) user profiles

33. A set of 8 bits can represent, at most, how many different characters?

    (A)   8
    (B)   16
    (C)   64
    (D) 128
    (E) 256

34. Which of the following is NOT a characteristic of a decision support system, as it is usually defined?

    (A) It can be used as an aid in solving ad hoc problems.
    (B) It is useful for what-if analysis.
    (C) It is intended to help managers make decisions.
    (D) It makes the one best or optimal decision.
    (E) It uses appropriate statistical and mathematical models.

35. Meta data is best described as which of the following?

(A) End-user data

(B) Data about data

(C) Data stored in a Web file format

(D) Data gathered by spyware

(E) Data returned by an Internet search engine

36. Which of the following is NOT true about computer software documentation?

(A) End-user documentation may be provided online through access to a help file or subsystem.

(B) End-user documentation may be provided by means of a hard copy reference manual.

(C) End-user documentation may be embedded in the programming code by the use of comment statements.

(D) Documentation should be an activity that takes place throughout the system development process.

(E) Documentation that is designed for end-users will generally be less technical than documentation prepared for programmers.

37. For which of the following programming languages is there always a one-to-one correspondence between a line of code in that language and a line of code in machine language?

(A) COBOL

(B) Java

(C) C++

(D) Assembler

(E) Visual BASIC

38. For which of the following conditions is it NEVER possible to recover a file from the disk to which it was written?

(A) A different file with the same name is copied to the same location on the disk.

(B) The file has been deleted.

(C) The file becomes fragmented.

(D) The disk drive malfunctions after the file is written.

(E) The disk with the file on it contains some bad sectors.

39. The American Charity Association, a nonprofit foundation, has a home page on the World Wide Web. Which of the following is the most likely address for its home page?

(A) http://www.charity.gov

(B) http://www.charity.edu

(C) http://www.charity.com

(D) http://www.charity.org

(E) http://www.charity.aca

40. A geographic information system must have which of the following characteristics?

I. Every record has an identified geographic location.

II. The system uses global positioning satellites.

III. The system provides results in a graphic format.

(A) I only

(B) I and II only

(C) I and III only

(D) II and III only

(E) I, II, and III

41. What is the term that refers to the downloading of live video, audio, or animation in such a manner that the user can begin to access the content before the download is complete?

    (A) Spooling

    (B) Streaming

    (C) Flaming

    (D) Spamming

    (E) Queuing

42. Which of the following is a set of protocols used to link different types of computers over the Internet?

    (A) HTML

    (B) HTTP

    (C) ERP

    (D) TCP/IP

    (E) Ethernet

43. A table called "Students" consists of the following records:

Name	Credits	GPA
Anderson	10	3.0
Chen	9	3.2
Gomez	12	3.1
Jones	12	3.0

A user entered the following SQL command:

Select Name;
From Students;
Where Credits > 9 and GPA > 3

How many names would meet criteria?

    (A) None

    (B) One

    (C) Two

    (D) Three

    (E) Four

44. Voice recognition can be included with which of the following systems?

    I. Office automation systems

    II. Security systems

    III. Batch-processing systems

    (A) I only

    (B) II only

    (C) I and II only

    (D) I and III only

    (E) I, II, and III

45. Which of the following is the software agent used by Internet search engines to generate search results?

    (A) Web bot

    (B) TCP filter

    (C) Auto responder

    (D) Worm

    (E) Indexer

46. Which of the following statements is (are) true concerning multiuser database management systems?

    I. They increase the standardization of data.

    II. They increase the need to store data in many different locations in the database.

    III. They can increase access to and availability of information.

    (A) I only

    (B) II only

    (C) I and II only

    (D) I and III only

    (E) I, II, and III

47. A manager of a small business wants to use a computer to store information about clients, vendors, inventory (item, number, price), and orders. The manager needs to be able to sort and group data for various reports. Which of the following types of software packages would be best for this task?

(A) Word processor
(B) Spreadsheet
(C) Database management system
(D) Presentation software
(E) System software

48. A business often identifies that its software has been trademarked by using a unique symbol or attaching the letters TM to its name. What is the purpose of the trademark?

(A) To eliminate unauthorized copying and distribution
(B) To identify the software as available for use, free of charge
(C) To identify and differentiate the product brand name
(D) To assure the user that the software is properly licensed and ready to use
(E) To assure the user that the software contains unique features not found in other products

49. Which of the following is (are) reasons to select a virtual team as opposed to an on-site team?

I. It works better when team members have different physical locations.
II. It works better when the team is trying to reach consensus.
III. It works better when there are personality conflicts among team members.

(A) I only
(B) III only
(C) I and II only
(D) I and III only
(E) I, II, and III

50. The maintenance phase of the system development process could include all of the following activities EXCEPT

(A) correcting errors in the software that were detected after implementation
(B) changing the heading on a printed report
(C) updating entries in the tax table to reflect changes in the tax rates
(D) adding a new function to an existing system
(E) performing a complete rewrite for an existing system

51. A company is planning to connect data communications devices in a new building by using either fiber-optic cable or twisted-pair cable. Which of the following is NOT true of fiber-optic cable when compared with twisted-pair cable?

(A) Fiber-optic cables have less electrical interference.
(B) Fiber-optic cables are less susceptible to corrosion.
(C) Fiber-optic cable connections are easier to install.
(D) Fiber-optic cables are less bulky.
(E) Fiber-optic cables support a higher transmission rate.

52. The ability of computerized systems to store and exchange information represents a potential threat to the individuals' right to

(A) free speech
(B) privacy
(C) equal access to information
(D) assembly
(E) consumer protection

53. http://www.mywebsite.com:8080/
homepage/mine/index.html

Which part of the URL above is the domain name?

(A) http

(B) www.mywebsite.com

(C) 8080

(D) homepage/mine

(E) index.html

54. The required components for a LAN include each of the following EXCEPT a

(A) networking protocol

(B) cabling standard

(C) media-sharing method

(D) unique address for each node

(E) print server

55. Which of the following statements concerning real-time processing is generally NOT true?

(A) A real-time system uses online processing methods.

(B) A real-time system uses sequential file access.

(C) A real-time system uses online files.

(D) A real-time processing operation processes all transactions as they occur.

(E) Real-time processing uses direct access storage.

56. The CEO of an employment agency is concerned about the imminent retirement of key associates and the resulting impact on the quality of service provided to the agency's customers as newer employees are brought into the firm. Which of the following types of systems is most likely to lessen the impact of changing demographics on the firm's performance?

(A) Work flow management system

(B) Groupware system

(C) Customer relationship management system

(D) Knowledge management system

(E) Data mining system

57. Data values A and B are stored in spreadsheet cells C1 and D2, respectively. After a cut operation on C1 followed by a paste operation on D2, which of the following will be true?

I. Data value B is overwritten.

II. Data value A is in location C1.

III. Data value A is in location D2.

(A) I only

(B) III only

(C) I and III only

(D) II and III only

(E) I, II, and III

58. Which of the following statements is true regarding client/server architecture?

(A) The server computer accepts commands from a number of computers that are its clients.

(B) The server computer manages a number of computers that it services.

(C) The server computer is connected to a number of computers that provide it with services.

(D) The client computer is connected to a number of computers that provide it with clients.

(E) The client computer manages a number of computers being served by it.

59. Which of the following is true of C++?

 (A) It is an object-oriented, real-time, general-purpose programming language.

 (B) It is a procedural programming language designed primarily for business applications.

 (C) It uses a noncomplicated syntax for ease of programming.

 (D) It is used primarily to develop applications that work across the Internet.

 (E) It is designed to operate only on organized databases.

60. Which of the following is a protocol used to route an e-mail message through the Internet?

 (A) TCP/IP
 (B) HTML
 (C) RISC
 (D) HTTP
 (E) SMTP

61. Which of the following is (are) true about customer relationship management systems?

 I. They focus on the connection between suppliers, manufacturers, and customers.

 II. They enable employees in all departments to have a consistent view of customers.

 III. They focus on customer retention.

 (A) I only
 (B) I and II only
 (C) I and III only
 (D) II and III only
 (E) I, II, and III

62. Which DBMS data model uses two-dimensional tables to display data structures?

 (A) Relational
 (B) Hierarchical
 (C) Network
 (D) Navigational
 (E) CODASYL

63. Which of the following network technologies allows secure transmission of data over an unsecured public network link between private networks?

 (A) Local area network
 (B) Wide area network
 (C) Virtual private network
 (D) Intranet
 (E) Extranet

64. Which of the following is NOT true of expert systems?

 (A) They are limited in scope to relatively narrow processes.

 (B) They can provide explanations of their reasoning processes.

 (C) They can use commonsense knowledge.

 (D) They can consider multiple hypotheses simultaneously.

 (E) They can perform the problem-solving work of humans.

65. The sharing of a computer's resources by allowing the running of two or more programs concurrently on a computer with a single CPU is called

 (A) booting
 (B) paging
 (C) multitasking
 (D) multiprocessing
 (E) thrashing

66. Which of the following is NOT an advantage of having an entire department using the same office software suite?

(A) Lower cost per application than if purchased individually

(B) Ease of moving data between suite applications

(C) Ease of moving data between users in the same department

(D) Ease of installation and maintenance

(E) Optimal functionality of individual application packages

67. The following pseudocode depicts the logic in a section of a computer program.

> SET A TO 1
> SET B TO 3
> SET A TO A + B
> WHILE A < 20
>   SET A TO (A*A)/2
> END WHILE

After execution of the program segment, what will be the value of variable A?

(A) 16
(B) 20
(C) 21
(D) 32
(E) 64

68. How many 8-bit characters (ASCII) could be placed in the same amount of memory as 300 16-bit characters (Unicode)?

(A)   150
(B)   300
(C)   600
(D) 32,768
(E) 76,800

69. A company is planning to automate the importation of data into its mainframe-based system. The data are to be received from several offices, each using PCs. This process will occur on a set schedule without any human intervention at either end. Which of the following is most likely to be used?

(A) FTP
(B) ANSI
(C) WWW
(D) VPN
(E) DVD

70. Which of the following is (are) true of HTML tags?

I. Tags are usually used in pairs.
II. Tags are visible when Web pages are displayed using browsers.
III. Tags are predefined.

(A) I only
(B) II only
(C) I and III only
(D) II and III only
(E) I, II, and III

Study Resources

Most textbooks used in college-level introductory business information systems or information technology courses cover the knowledge and skills in the outline given earlier. The approaches to certain topics and the emphases given to them differ; therefore, it is advisable to study one or more current college textbooks to prepare for the Information Systems and Computer Applications exam. When selecting a textbook, check the table of contents against the knowledge and skills required for this test.

Visit www.collegeboard.com/clepprep for additional study resources. You can also find suggestions for exam preparation in Chapter IV of the *Official Study Guide*. In addition, many college faculty post their course materials on their schools' Web sites.

Answer Key

1.	C	36.	C
2.	E	37.	D
3.	E	38.	A
4.	C	39.	D
5.	E	40.	C
6.	D	41.	B
7.	C	42.	D
8.	C	43.	B
9.	A	44.	C
10.	D	45.	A
11.	B	46.	D
12.	C	47.	C
13.	D	48.	C
14.	A	49.	A
15.	C	50.	E
16.	B	51.	C
17.	A	52.	B
18.	D	53.	B
19.	B	54.	E
20.	A	55.	B
21.	A	56.	D
22.	E	57.	C
23.	B	58.	A
24.	B	59.	A
25.	A	60.	E
26.	D	61.	D
27.	C	62.	A
28.	C	63.	C
29.	E	64.	C
30.	B	65.	C
31.	B	66.	E
32.	A	67.	D
33.	E	68.	C
34.	D	69.	A
35.	B	70.	C

Introductory Business Law

Description of the Examination

The Introductory Business Law examination covers material that is usually taught in an introductory one-semester college course in the subject. The examination places not only major emphasis on understanding the functions of contracts in American business law, but it also includes questions on the history and sources of American law, legal systems and procedures, agency and employment, sales, and other topics.

The examination contains approximately 100 questions to be answered in 90 minutes. Some of these are pretest questions that will not be scored. Any time candidates spend on tutorials or providing personal information is in addition to the actual testing time.

Knowledge and Skills Required

Questions on the test require candidates to demonstrate one or more of the following abilities in the approximate proportions indicated.

- Knowledge of the basic facts and terms (about 30–35 percent of the examination)
- Understanding of concepts and principles (about 30–35 percent of the examination)
- Ability to apply knowledge to specific case problems (about 30 percent of the examination)

The subject matter of the Introductory Business Law examination is drawn from the following topics. The percentages next to the main topics indicate the approximate percentage of exam questions on that topic.

5–10% History and Sources of American Law/ Constitutional Law

5–10% American Legal Systems and Procedures

25–35% Contracts
  Meanings of terms
  Formation of contracts
  Capacity
  Consideration
  Joint obligations
  Contracts for the benefit of third parties
  Assignment/delegation
  Statute of frauds
  Scopes and meanings of contracts
  Breach of contract and remedies
  Bar to remedies for breach of contract
  Discharge of contracts
  Illegal contracts
  Other

25–30% Legal Environment
  Ethics
  Social responsibility of corporations
  Government regulation/ administrative agencies
  Environmental law
  Securities and antitrust law
  Employment law
  Creditors' rights
  Product liability
  Consumer protection
  International business law

10–15% Torts

5–10% Miscellaneous
  Agency, partnerships, and corporations
  Sales

Sample Test Questions

The following sample questions do not appear on an actual CLEP examination. They are intended to give potential test-takers an indication of the format and difficulty level of the examination and to provide content for practice and review. Knowing the correct answers to all of the sample questions is not a guarantee of satisfactory performance on the exam.

Directions: Each of the questions or incomplete statements below is followed by five suggested answers or completions. Select the one that is best in each case.

1. The authority of a court to hear and decide cases is known as

    (A) jurisdiction
    (B) habeas corpus
    (C) demurrer
    (D) quo warranto
    (E) stare decisis

2. Law that is formed by a group of individuals, acting as representatives for other individuals, is best termed

    (A) criminal law
    (B) civil law
    (C) legislative law
    (D) adjective law
    (E) tort law

3. A contract will be unenforceable if

    (A) one party to the contract feels he or she has been taken advantage of
    (B) a statute declares such a contract illegal
    (C) performance becomes difficult
    (D) public authorities voice disapproval of the contract
    (E) the parties involved believe the contract to be illegal

4. Angela promises to work for Barbara during the month of July, and Barbara promises to pay Angela $600 for her services. In this situation, what kind of contract has been made?

    (A) Unilateral
    (B) Executed
    (C) Quasi
    (D) Bilateral
    (E) Bilingual

5. Which of the following is an essential element of fraud?

    (A) Injury to a business interest
    (B) Misrepresentation of a material fact
    (C) Destruction of property
    (D) Knowledge of the consequences of an act
    (E) Mistake about the identity of the subject matter

6. Clyde received the following letter from Joe: "I will sell you the books you examined yesterday for $10 each or $100 for the entire set." Clyde, not sure he would get much use from the books, told his brother, Michael, about the offer. Michael tendered Joe $100 for the books, but Joe refused to sell the books to Michael.

    If Michael sued Joe, the court would probably hold that Michael

    (A) can accept the offer because he is Clyde's brother
    (B) can accept the offer if he will do so within a reasonable period of time
    (C) cannot accept the offer until Clyde's rejection is communicated to Joe
    (D) cannot accept the offer because it was not made to him
    (E) cannot accept the offer unless he does so in writing

7. All of the following have the right to enforce a contract EXCEPT

   (A) an assignee

   (B) a transferee

   (C) a third-party creditor beneficiary

   (D) a third-party donee beneficiary

   (E) a third-party incidental beneficiary

8. A method of discharging a contract that returns each party to his or her original position is

   (A) an assignment

   (B) an accord

   (C) a revocation

   (D) a rescission

   (E) a novation

9. A contract clause that requires both parties to act simultaneously is called a

   (A) condition subsequent

   (B) condition concurrent

   (C) condition precedent

   (D) negative condition

   (E) restrictive condition

10. Benson, a seventeen-year-old college freshman, was adequately supplied with clothes by his father. Smith, a clothing merchant, learned that Benson was spending money freely and solicited clothing orders from him. Benson bought $750 worth of luxury clothing from Smith on credit. Benson failed to pay Smith.

If Smith sued Benson, the court would probably hold that

   (A) Benson is liable for the $750 because by accepting and wearing the clothes he ratified the contract

   (B) Benson is not liable for the reasonable value of the clothing because Smith solicited the sales

   (C) Benson can disaffirm the contract, return the clothing, and escape liability

   (D) Benson is liable for the $750 because under these circumstances the clothing was a necessity

   (E) Benson's father is liable to Smith for the $750

11. The enforcement of a contract may be barred, according to the operation of law, by

   (A) an assignment

   (B) a delegation

   (C) a material breach

   (D) the statute of limitations

   (E) a novation

12. A purchase from each of the following would be considered a purchase in the ordinary course of trade or business EXCEPT a purchase from a

   (A) pawnshop

   (B) department store

   (C) supermarket

   (D) discount department store

   (E) used car lot

13. Which of the following promises would be enforceable by the majority of courts?

    (A) Avery finds Bond's dog and returns it to Bond. Later, Bond promises to pay Avery a reward.

    (B) Husband, in consideration of the love and affection given him by Wife, promises to pay her $1,000.

    (C) Avery is extremely ill and placed in a hospital. Avery's neighbor, Bond, mows Avery's yard while Avery is recuperating. Later, Avery promises to pay Bond the reasonable value of his services.

    (D) Avery owes Bond $100, which debt is discharged in bankruptcy. Later, Avery writes Bond a letter promising to pay Bond the $100.

    (E) Daughter mows the family yard. In absence of an express agreement, Daughter can claim an implied promise on Father's part to pay for her services.

14. Base Electric Company has entered an agreement to buy its actual requirements of brass wiring for six months from the Valdez Metal Wire Company, and Valdez Metal Wire Company has agreed to sell all the brass wiring Base Electric Company will require for six months. The agreement between the two companies is

    (A) valid and enforceable

    (B) unenforceable because of lack of consideration

    (C) unenforceable because it is too indefinite

    (D) lacking in mutuality of obligations

    (E) illusory

15. Ordinarily an employer is liable for which of the following acts committed by an employee for the benefit of the employer and in the scope of the employment?

    I. Torts

    II. Contracts

    III. Misrepresentations

    (A) I only

    (B) II only

    (C) III only

    (D) II and III only

    (E) I, II, and III

16. Abbott was orphaned at the age of five. For the next fifteen years his material needs were met by his uncle, Barton. On his thirtieth birthday, Abbott wrote Barton and promised to pay him $100 per month as long as Barton lived. Abbott never made any payments. Barton died ten months later. If Barton's estate sued Abbott for the amount of the promised payments, the court would probably hold that Barton's estate is

    (A) not entitled to recover because past consideration will not support Abbott's promise

    (B) not entitled to recover because of the statute of limitations

    (C) not entitled to recover unless it can be shown that Barton's relatives were in desperate need

    (D) entitled to recover on the promise

    (E) entitled to recover because of Barton's previous aid to Abbott

17. An agreement among creditors that each will accept a certain percentage of his or her claim as full satisfaction is called

    (A) accord and satisfaction

    (B) creditor agreement

    (C) composition of creditors

    (D) liquidation

    (E) bankruptcy

18. Which of the following decisions could NOT be made by an appellate court?

   (A) Ordering a case to be tried in the appellate court

   (B) Affirming a decision of a lower court

   (C) Instructing a lower court to enter a judgment in accordance with the appellate court's opinion

   (D) Remanding a case for a new trial

   (E) Reversing the decision of a lower court

19. Upon delivery of nonconforming goods, a buyer may do which of the following?

   I. Reject all the goods.

   II. Accept all the goods.

   III. Accept those units that conform and reject the rest.

   (A) I only

   (B) III only

   (C) I and II only

   (D) II and III only

   (E) I, II, and III

20. All of the following are usual functions performed by judges of trial courts having general jurisdiction EXCEPT

   (A) issuing writs of habeas corpus

   (B) conducting pretrial conferences in civil cases

   (C) determining questions of fact in equity cases

   (D) guiding the jury on questions of law in criminal and civil cases

   (E) imposing pretrial settlements on parties who cannot agree

21. Which of the following will apply if the parties to a contract knew or should have known that a word has a customary usage in their particular trade or community?

   (A) No contract will result if the parties cannot voluntarily agree on the definition of the word.

   (B) The meaning of the word cannot be challenged once a contract is signed.

   (C) Parol evidence may be used to define the meaning of the word.

   (D) Courts will not impose a definition that is contrary to the meaning supported by one party.

   (E) A mistaken assumption regarding the definition by one of the parties will result in a voidable contract.

22. Webster insured her residence with Old Home Insurance Company. Assuming that the policy contained no provision with respect to assignment, which of the following statements is correct?

   (A) Webster may assign the policy to any person having capacity to contract.

   (B) If Webster suffers an insured loss, she may assign the amount due under the policy to anyone.

   (C) If Webster sells her residence, she must assign the policy to the purchaser.

   (D) If Webster suffers an insured loss, she may assign the amount due under the policy only to a party furnishing material or labor for repair of the residence.

   (E) Webster may assign the policy to any person having capacity to contract who agrees to pay the premium.

23. Recovery in quasi contract is based on a judgment that determines the presence of

    (A) an unjust enrichment
    (B) an express contract
    (C) an implied in fact contract
    (D) a violation of the statute of frauds
    (E) a mutual mistake

24. The commerce clause of the United States Constitution authorizes

    (A) Congress to tax corporations
    (B) Congress to regulate interstate commerce
    (C) courts to hear disputes between states and the federal government
    (D) states to regulate their own commerce
    (E) states to police the public anywhere

25. An employee is constantly subjected to extreme and unwanted sexual banter on the job. If this employee were to bring a suit to prevent this conduct or receive a damage award, which of the following would be the basis for the suit?

    I. Intentional infliction of emotional injury
    II. Negligence
    III. Title VII of the Civil Rights Act of 1964

    (A) I only
    (B) III only
    (C) I and II only
    (D) I and III only
    (E) I, II, and III

26. Acting in a manner that results in the greatest good for the greatest number is an ethical principle known as

    (A) utilitarianism
    (B) cost-benefit analysis
    (C) rights theory
    (D) the golden rule
    (E) Kantianism

27. Which of the following best defines the employment at will doctrine?

    (A) Employers can terminate employees for good cause only.
    (B) Employees can quit for good reason only.
    (C) Employers can terminate employees for any reason that is not discriminatory and employees can quit for any reason.
    (D) Employees can quit for any reason.
    (E) Employers can terminate employees for good cause and employees can quit for good reason.

28. Smith suddenly attacks Jones as Jones walks down the street. In this case, Smith has committed

    (A) negligence
    (B) a contractual act
    (C) a criminal act only
    (D) a tortious act only
    (E) a criminal act and a tortious act

29. Using nonpublic material information to buy or sell securities is known as

    (A) short-swing profits
    (B) insider trading
    (C) a "blue sky" transaction
    (D) an under-the-counter trade
    (E) an over-the-counter trade

30. Which of the following administrative agencies regulates unfair trade practices and the formation of monopolies that restrain competition?

    (A) The National Labor Relations Board
    (B) The Securities and Exchange Commission
    (C) The Federal Reserve Board
    (D) The Federal Trade Commission
    (E) The Consumer Protection Agency

31. Which of the following is a distinction that can be drawn between civil and criminal law?

   (A) Civil cases involve a jury and criminal cases do not.
   (B) The burden of proof in a civil case is "a preponderance of the evidence" standard, while the burden of proof in a criminal case is "beyond a reasonable doubt" standard.
   (C) Civil cases involve a wrong against society, while criminal cases involve a loss to only one specific victim.
   (D) Civil cases are all statutory, while criminal cases are based on statutes and case law.
   (E) There is no distinction between civil and criminal law.

32. Curtis is injured while performing his duties for his employer, Choice Banking Company. In most states, Curtis will be compensated for his injuries under which of the following?

   (A) Intentional tort
   (B) Negligence
   (C) Worker's Compensation
   (D) Common Law Contract
   (E) The Fair Labor Act

33. Barry sneaks up behind Caesar and hits him over the head with a bat. Caesar suffers a concussion and incurs damages exceeding $50,000.00. Under these facts, Caesar will most likely win a suit against Barry for

   (A) assault
   (B) battery
   (C) conversion
   (D) false imprisonment
   (E) negligence

34. Proximate cause means that the

   (A) defendant will be held liable for all the damages caused by his breach of duty
   (B) defendant will be held liable for only those damages that were reasonably foreseeable and a natural and probable consequence of his breach of duty
   (C) plaintiff's injury would not have occurred but for the defendant's breach of duty
   (D) plaintiff's injury would not have occurred unless the defendant's breach of duty was a substantial factor in bringing about the injury
   (E) plaintiff's injury occurred because of the defendant's breach of duty

35. Zack and Josh open a coffee shop. They have no written agreement, but intend to sell coffee and bagels together in order to make a profit. Which of the following describes Zack's and Josh's business relationship?

   (A) They are sole proprietors.
   (B) They are silent partners.
   (C) They are limited partners.
   (D) They are shareholders.
   (E) They are partners.

36. Fred is an attorney who wants to advertise that he is Austin's best lawyer. He buys a billboard and posts his message. The State Bar of Texas wants him to take down the billboard. Which of the following constitutional proposals best supports Fred's position?

   (A) The principles of the Fourth Amendment
   (B) The right against self-incrimination
   (C) The First Amendment
   (D) Freedom of assembly
   (E) The Declaration of Independence

37. Larry delivers newspapers for a living; he hires Fred to help with his route, paying him 5 cents per paper. Fred runs into a customer's car while delivering papers. Which of the following statements is true?

    (A) As partners, Larry and Fred are jointly liable for the damage.

    (B) If Larry does business as a corporation, he can be sued individually.

    (C) Since Fred was driving the car, he is the only one who can be responsible.

    (D) The facts suggest that the doctrine of respondent superior would apply.

    (E) If Fred does not have insurance, it means that the customer can never recover any of his damages to the car.

38. Al Katraz, a used car dealer, has a sports car for sale. A customer is interested in buying it. Al tells him, "It's a super car." Later, the customer discovers that his next-door neighbor's car can outperform his and he visits his attorney saying, "I want to sue Al." Which of the following would be the attorney's best answer?

    (A) Al cannot be sued successfully for fraud because the statement made was not in writing.

    (B) Al has engaged in fraud because the customer relied on his statement.

    (C) Fraud requires malice; therefore, Al cannot be held accountable.

    (D) Al's statement is probably considered an opinion; therefore, he cannot be held accountable.

    (E) Al cannot be successfully sued because fraud is only a criminal matter.

39. Which of the following is true of federal administrative agencies?

    (A) They occupy less importance today than they did in the nineteenth century.

    (B) They may investigate, but they cannot make rules.

    (C) They are all part of the executive branch.

    (D) Their actions are subject to judicial review.

    (E) They are not subject to constitutional scrutiny.

40. A bailment contract deals with which of the following?

    (A) The posting of a bond to guarantee that a defendant will appear in court when required

    (B) The establishment of a contract where one party tries to bail out of a bad situation

    (C) The owner of an article of personal property temporarily relinquishing possession and control of it to another

    (D) The leasing of unimproved land

    (E) The sale of personal property

41. Which of the following describes the relationship between law and ethics?

    (A) A law sets forth the highest ethical standard for society.

    (B) A law is enforceable in court, and it sometimes reflects society's standard of ethical conduct.

    (C) Laws are written to govern moral behavior, whereas ethics are designed to control civic behavior.

    (D) A law remains constant, whereas ethical values vary over time.

    (E) There is no relationship between law and ethics.

42. All of the following are foundations for business ethics EXCEPT

(A) religion

(B) philosophy

(C) law

(D) business practices of competitors

(E) cultural norms

43. In general, an appeal of an administrative decision to the courts must show that

(A) the case has been proved beyond a reasonable doubt

(B) administrative remedies have been exhausted

(C) a serious economic loss has been incurred

(D) the case has been proven by the greater weight of the evidence

(E) the administrative agency was unfair

44. The Civil Rights Act of 1964 protects victims of

(A) all forms of discrimination

(B) religious discrimination

(C) age discrimination

(D) discrimination on the basis of HIV-positive status

(E) discrimination based on sexual preference

45. Manuel is hired by Star Players Theater to design and maintain the theatre's Web site. Mango Theater learns of Manuel's work and convinces him to leave Star Players to come work for Mango. Mango Theater is probably liable for the tort of

(A) appropriation

(B) unfair competition

(C) breach of contract

(D) wrongful interference with a contractual relationship

(E) wrongful interference with a business relationship

46. Kate's corporation has accumulated a large number of accounts payable and lost its largest customer. Kate thinks that she can save the business by reorganizing it. Which of the following chapters of the bankruptcy code would she most likely use to protect the business from creditors while reorganizing?

(A) Chapter 1

(B) Chapter 7

(C) Chapter 11

(D) Chapter 13

(E) Chapter 14

47. Alexandra drops her credit card in a department store while looking in her purse for her car keys. Amanda finds Alexandra's card and uses it to charge $1,000.00 in merchandise. Alexandra does not discover the loss of her card until the following day, and she immediately notifies the credit company. The maximum amount for which Alexandra may be held liable to the credit card company is

(A) $1,000

(B) $ 500

(C) $ 100

(D) $ 50

(E) $ 10

48. All of the following are related to international business EXCEPT

(A) import quotas

(B) tariffs

(C) the World Trade Organization

(D) the North American Free Trade Agreement

(E) the Uniform Partnership Act

49. Yummy Soup Company broadcast a television commercial designed to show how thick its chicken soup was, implying that it was full of chunks of chicken. In fact, the soup in the commercial was loaded with potatoes so that it would look thicker than it really was. The Federal Trade Commission (FTC) prohibited use of the commercial. If Yummy Soup filed a suit against the FTC to continue the commercial, the suit would most likely

   (A) succeed because puffing in advertisements is an accepted practice

   (B) succeed because neither Yummy nor its advertising agency had the required intent to deceive the consumer

   (C) succeed because Yummy's First Amendment right of free speech supersedes the FTC's right to regulate marketing

   (D) fail because fairness in advertising is an implied responsibility under the commerce clause

   (E) fail because the FTC has statutory authority to regulate deceptive advertising

50. Which of the following is true about the concept of strict liability?

   (A) It requires proof of intent.

   (B) It does not require a showing of negligence.

   (C) It is a concept related to the sale of stock.

   (D) It does not apply to the third-party bystanders.

   (E) It requires privity of contract.

51. As a general rule, which of the following contracts CANNOT be rescinded?

   (A) A contract made by a minor

   (B) A contract based on a mutual mistake

   (C) A contract based on unilateral mistake

   (D) A contract in which one party makes a fraudulent misrepresentation

   (E) A contract in which one party lacks mental capacity

52. The concept of judicial review originated

   (A) as the result of a decision by the United States Supreme Court

   (B) as the result of a federal statute

   (C) as the result of a decision by a state supreme court

   (D) in the United States Constitution

   (E) in the Declaration of Independence

53. Oscar's neighbor built a tennis court with extremely bright lights to be able to play at night. The lights are so bright that they illuminate Oscar's house and keep everyone from sleeping. Oscar's repeated requests of his neighbor to turn down the lights have gone unheeded. Oscar could sue his neighbor to get a remedy under the legal theory of

   (A) assault

   (B) breach of warranty

   (C) nuisance

   (D) conversion

   (E) anticipatory breach

54. Juan hired Matt, a licensed architect and home builder, to build a house for him according to Matt's architectural plans. Matt built and delivered the house, but the house collapsed after 13 years due to defective design. Which of the following is true if Juan sued Matt for negligence?

   (A) Matt was negligent per se in constructing the house.

   (B) Juan could be successful in his suit if the state's statute of repose has not yet expired.

   (C) Juan may not sue Matt because Matt was not grossly negligent or willful in his conduct.

   (D) Juan will automatically win his suit against Matt if Juan can successfully invoke the doctrine of *res ipsa loquitur*.

   (E) Juan has no legal ground to sue Matt, since Juan has lived in the house for 13 years.

55. A contract is illusory and lacks mutuality when one party

(A) reserves the right to cancel the agreement at any time

(B) promises to perform on a specified day

(C) promises to pay a certain sum of money for the performance of a certain act

(D) promises to forbear a legal right in exchange for the promise of the other party

(E) gives a promise in exchange for the promise of the other party

56. John Roberts contracts to convey land to Sarah Simmons in consideration of Sarah's promise to pay $5,000 to his wife, Rhonda, to whom John wishes to make a settlement. Rhonda would have a contract claim against Sarah in Rhonda's status as

(A) wife

(B) obligee

(C) creditor

(D) intended beneficiary

(E) benefactor

57. Homeowner orally promises to sell her house to Mr. and Mrs. Youngpeople, who promise to buy it. The Youngpeoples then draft a letter containing the terms of the agreement, sign it, and send it to Homeowner. Under these circumstances the contract may be enforced against

(A) both Homeowner and the Youngpeoples

(B) the Youngpeoples only

(C) Homeowner only

(D) neither party because of the parol evidence rule

(E) neither party because of the statute of limitations

58. Ms. Jones was leaving class in a hurry and in the process knocked her friend Ms. Smith down a flight of steps, causing serious injury to Smith. Smith wishes to recover for her injuries. Smith's action would be brought in

(A) criminal law for assault and battery

(B) criminal law for trespass on a person

(C) criminal law for invasion of a person's privacy

(D) tort law on the grounds of negligence

(E) tort law on the grounds of assault and battery

59. ABC Company, incorporated under the laws of Delaware, has its principal place of business in the state of Georgia. ABC sells its merchandise at retail outlets located in all 50 states but sells the greatest percentage of its products in the five southern states of Alabama, Florida, Georgia, North Carolina, and South Carolina.

For purposes of diversity jurisdiction in the federal courts, ABC is considered to be a citizen of

(A) Georgia and Delaware

(B) Delaware only

(C) Georgia only

(D) the five southern states

(E) all 50 states

60. Statutory law is best defined as

(A) common law

(B) case decisions

(C) legislative enactments

(D) constitutional law

(E) administrative law

61. The process of selecting a jury in civil litigation is known as

    (A) voir dire
    (B) *res ipsa loquitor*
    (C) *causa mortis*
    (D) indictment
    (E) certiorari

62. Joe asks Bob to lend him $100. Bob says he will, but only if Joe repays him the $100 plus $50 interest in one month. Joe agrees, fails to repay, and Bob sues him. Which of the following is most pertinent to the lawsuit?

    (A) Bob cannot sue because the contract is not in writing.
    (B) Bob may be unable to recover because the contract is usurious.
    (C) Bob cannot prevail because of the statute of frauds.
    (D) Joe must rely on the defense of fraud.
    (E) The contract is not enforceable if Joe is only 18.

63. Alex bid on a used automobile at the Best Buy car dealership for seven thousand dollars. Alex negotiated a loan from Best Buy, made a down payment of five hundred dollars, and drove off with the vehicle without any kind of insurance. An hour later, while driving thirty miles per hour over the legal speed limit, Alex collided with a tree, and his car was totally demolished. Three months later, having received no payments from Alex and his loan, Best Buy tried to collect the loan. It will be able to collect UNLESS

    (A) Alex was drunk at the time of the accident
    (B) Alex is still hospitalized after the accident
    (C) Alex was one month short of his eighteenth birthday when he purchased the car
    (D) the book value of the car was only four thousand dollars when Alex bought it
    (E) the car came with a 90-day warranty

64. Marcus makes the following statement to Evan, while trying to sell Evan his boat: "This boat has the original engine!" By making such a statement, Marcus has most likely created

    (A) an express warranty
    (B) an implied warranty of fitness
    (C) an implied warranty of merchantability
    (D) a warranty that the boat is seaworthy
    (E) no warranty at all

65. It is common in international business contracts to include a clause that will excuse a party in the contract for nonperformance because of the occurrence of certain acts such as war, embargo, governmental restrictions, and labor strikes. This clause is known as

    (A) an exculpatory clause
    (B) a forum-selection clause
    (C) a force majeure clause
    (D) a choice-of-law clause
    (E) a sovereign immunity clause

66. Granny Smith told her grandson, Ned, that she was going to leave him $5,000 when she died because of all the things he had done for her over the years. After Granny died, Ned learned that she had not included him as a beneficiary in her will and had not left him any money. Ned sues her estate, claiming that he is entitled to the $5,000 she promised him.

    The court will probably hold that Ned is

    (A) entitled to the money
    (B) entitled to the money only if he can provide written evidence of the promise
    (C) entitled to be paid the fair value for the services rendered to Granny
    (D) is not entitled to the money, because there was no valid consideration exchanged
    (E) not entitled to the money, because the value of the services rendered was not equal to the value of the promise

67. Dr. Hidalgo was attending her son's soccer game when she heard a woman calling for help and asking that someone call 911. Dr. Hidalgo ran over to the woman and found that the woman's husband was unconscious on the ground and not breathing. Dr. Hidalgo rendered medical aid, saving the man's life. Can Dr. Hidalgo recover payment from the man for her services?

    (A) Yes; under quasi contract, the man must pay a reasonable amount for the medical services.

    (B) Yes; under implied-in-fact contract, the man must pay the current rate for the medical services.

    (C) Yes; under promissory estoppel, the man must pay a reasonable amount for the medical services.

    (D) No; the man never consented to the treatment and therefore there was neither a contract nor an obligation to pay.

    (E) No; there was no contract, and doctors are required to render medical aid in emergency situations.

68. Billy and Joey were playing baseball in Billy's front yard. Billy hit the ball hard and it flew into the neighbor's yard, breaking the neighbor's front window. Billy would be legally bound to pay for the broken window under the concept of

    (A) trespass
    (B) respondent superior
    (C) invasion of privacy
    (D) battery
    (E) assault

69. Cathie takes a bite of the burger she just purchased from Burger World Foods. The burger contains a piece of metal, and Cathie breaks one of her teeth, incurring substantial dental bills. Under which of the following theories can Cathie best recover for her injuries?

    (A) Breach of the implied warranty of fitness for a particular purpose

    (B) Breach of the implied warranty of merchantability

    (C) Breach of the express warranty

    (D) Breach of intentional tort law

    (E) Breach of contract

70. Under which of the following situations would a principal be liable for the tortuous act of its agent under the doctrine of respondent superior?

    (A) The agent had no authority (actual or apparent) to commit the act.

    (B) The agent's act was a criminal act against a third person, and the principal had not directed the act and had no knowledge of the agent's propensity to commit such an act.

    (C) The agent was an employee of the principal and the act was within the scope of the employee's duties.

    (D) The agent was an independent contractor acting without authority.

    (E) The agent, an employee of the principal, caused an automobile accident after he deviated greatly from his assigned delivery route.

Study Resources

Most textbooks used in college-level business law courses cover the topics in the outline given earlier, but the approaches to certain topics and the emphases given to them may differ. To prepare for the Introductory Business Law exam, it is advisable to study one or more college textbooks, which can be found in most college bookstores. When selecting a textbook, check the table of contents against the knowledge and skills required for this test.

Visit www.collegeboard.com/clepprep for additional business law resources. You can also find suggestions for exam preparation in Chapter IV of the *Official Study Guide*. In addition, many college faculty post their course materials on their schools' Web sites.

Answer Key

1.	A	36.	C
2.	C	37.	D
3.	B	38.	D
4.	D	39.	D
5.	B	40.	C
6.	D	41.	B
7.	E	42.	D
8.	D	43.	B
9.	B	44.	B
10.	C	45.	D
11.	D	46.	C
12.	A	47.	D
13.	D	48.	E
14.	A	49.	E
15.	E	50.	B
16.	A	51.	C
17.	C	52.	A
18.	A	53.	C
19.	E	54.	B
20.	E	55.	A
21.	C	56.	D
22.	B	57.	B
23.	A	58.	D
24.	B	59.	A
25.	D	60.	C
26.	A	61.	A
27.	C	62.	B
28.	E	63.	C
29.	B	64.	A
30.	D	65.	C
31.	B	66.	D
32.	C	67.	A
33.	B	68.	A
34.	B	69.	B
35.	E	70.	C

Principles of Management

Description of the Examination

The Principles of Management examination covers material that is usually taught in an introductory course in the essentials of management and organization. The fact that such courses are offered by different types of institutions and in a number of fields other than business has been taken into account in the preparation of this examination. It requires a knowledge of human resources and operational and functional aspects of management.

The examination contains approximately 100 questions to be answered in 90 minutes. Some of these are pretest questions that will not be scored. Any time candidates spend on tutorials and providing personal information is in addition to the actual testing time.

Knowledge and Skills Required

Questions on the Principles of Management examination require candidates to demonstrate one or more of the following abilities in the approximate proportions indicated.

- Specific factual knowledge, recall, and general understanding of purposes, functions, and techniques of management (about 10 percent of the exam)
- Understanding of and ability to associate the meaning of specific terminology with important management ideas, processes, techniques, concepts, and elements (about 40 percent of the exam)
- Understanding of theory and significant underlying assumptions, concepts, and limitations of management data, including a comprehension of the rationale of procedures, methods, and analyses (about 40 percent of the exam)
- Application of knowledge, general concepts, and principles to specific problems (about 10 percent of the exam)

The subject matter of the Principles of Management examination is drawn from the following topics. The percentages next to the main topics indicate the approximate percentage of exam questions on that topic.

15–25% Organization and Human Resources
Personnel administration
Human relations and motivation
Training and development
Performance appraisal
Organizational development
Legal concerns
Workforce diversity
Recruiting and selecting
Compensation and benefits
Collective bargaining

10–20% Operational Aspects of Management
Operations planning and control
Work scheduling
Quality management (e.g., TQM)
Information processing and management
Strategic planning and analysis
Productivity

45–55% Functional Aspects of Management
Planning
Organizing
Leading
Controlling
Authority
Decision making
Organization charts
Leadership
Organizational structure
Budgeting
Problem solving
Group dynamics and team functions
Conflict resolution
Communication
Change
Organizational theory
Historical aspects

10–20% International Management and Contemporary Issues

Value dimensions

Regional economic integration

Trading alliances

Global environment

Social responsibilities of business

Ethics

Systems

Environment

Government regulation

Management theories and theorists

E-business

Creativity and innovation

Sample Test Questions

The following sample questions do not appear on an actual CLEP examination. They are intended to give potential test-takers an indication of the format and difficulty level of the examination and to provide content for practice and review. Knowing the correct answers to all of the sample questions is not a guarantee of satisfactory performance on the exam.

Directions: Each of the questions or incomplete statements below is followed by five suggested answers or completions. Select the one that is best in each case.

1. Which of the following words is NOT logically related to the others?

(A) Planning

(B) Leading

(C) Producing

(D) Controlling

(E) Organizing

2. Program Evaluation and Review Technique (PERT) is a system for

(A) developing the organization chart for a company

(B) scheduling and finding the critical path for production

(C) evaluating the performance of workers

(D) reviewing the overall financial condition of the company

(E) programming a computer

3. Which of the following is a correct statement about controlling as a management function?

(A) It can be performed independently of planning.

(B) It is performed only by the controller of an organization.

(C) It is more prevalent in business than in government.

(D) It assumes a certain approach to motivating employees.

(E) It must be closely related to planning in order to work efficiently.

4. Decentralization tends to be encouraged by which of the following business trends?

I. Product diversification

II. Telecommuting

III. Geographical expansion of operations

(A) I only

(B) II only

(C) III only

(D) I and III only

(E) I, II, and III

5. Which of the following can be best determined by consulting an organization chart?

(A) The size of the company

(B) The distribution of company resources

(C) The nature of work performed

(D) The relationship of positions

(E) The quality of management of the firm

6. The number of subordinates who directly report to a superior refers to the manager's

(A) span of control

(B) organizational role

(C) organizational structure

(D) chain of command

(E) general staff

7. Which of the following best illustrates informal organization?

   (A) Line authority, such as that of the field marshal and battalion commander in the military
   (B) Staff authority, such as that of personnel or cost control in manufacturing
   (C) Functional authority, such as corporate supervision of the legal aspect of pension plans in branch plants
   (D) Groupings based on position titles
   (E) Groupings based on such factors as technical ability, seniority, and personal influence

8. The choice of organizational structure to be used in a business should be

   (A) made by mutual agreement among all the people affected
   (B) made by organization specialists rather than managers
   (C) subject to definite and fixed rules
   (D) based on the objectives of each individual business
   (E) based on consideration of the type of organizational structures used by competitors

9. The concept of hierarchy of needs attempts to explain which of the following?

   (A) Functional supervision
   (B) Unity of command
   (C) Line-staff conflict
   (D) Heuristic programming
   (E) Personal motivation

10. Frederick Taylor is considered a pioneer in the school of management referred to as the

    (A) management process school
    (B) empirical school
    (C) scientific management school
    (D) behaviorist school
    (E) social system school

11. Preparation of which of the following is the most logical first step in developing an annual operating plan?

    (A) A sales forecast by product
    (B) A production schedule by product
    (C) A flow-of-funds statement by product
    (D) A plant and equipment requirement forecast
    (E) A pro forma income statement and balance sheet

12. A large span of control throughout an organization invariably results in

    (A) low morale
    (B) high morale
    (C) an excess work load for each manager
    (D) a flat (horizontal) organizational structure
    (E) a tall (vertical) organizational structure

13. Which of the following is a conflict-resolution practice that seeks to satisfy both parties to a conflict?

    (A) Avoidance
    (B) Stipulation
    (C) Competition
    (D) Collaboration
    (E) Appeal to authority

14. Which of the following goals is most likely to produce the desired results?

    (A) Do your best.
    (B) Outproduce your competitor by 5%.
    (C) Introduce new products to the market at an unprecedented rate.
    (D) Increase the sales volume by 10% while maintaining the current rate of expenditures.
    (E) Reduce defects due to poor work habits.

15. The practice in large companies of establishing autonomous divisions whose heads are entirely responsible for what happens in the division is referred to as

(A) management by exception

(B) decentralization of authority

(C) delegation of authority

(D) integration

(E) informal organization

16. Which of the following control techniques is most likely to emphasize the importance of time?

(A) Break-even charts

(B) Physical standards

(C) Quality circles

(D) Variable budgeting

(E) PERT (Program Evaluation and Review Technique)

17. In a labor negotiation, if a third party has the power to determine a solution to a labor dispute between two parties, the negotiation is known as

(A) a grievance

(B) an arbitration

(C) a conciliation

(D) a mediation

(E) a concession

18. A type of control device for assessing the progress of planned activities and the expenditure of resources allocated to their accomplishments is referred to as

(A) a strategic plan

(B) an organizational chart

(C) a tactical plan

(D) a budget

(E) a proposal

19. Which of the following do managerial/leadership grids, team building, and sensitivity training have in common?

(A) They are crucial to operations management.

(B) They are tools for organizational development.

(C) They were developed by Peter Drucker.

(D) They are necessary to the budgeting process.

(E) They are the key elements of positive-reinforcement programs.

20. According to Maslow, the need to feel genuinely respected by peers, both in and out of the work environment, is included in which of the following need classifications?

(A) Physiological

(B) Safety

(C) Stability

(D) Esteem

(E) Self-actualization

21. Which of the following management activities is most typically described as a controlling function?

(A) Goal setting

(B) Purchasing

(C) Budgetary review

(D) Staffing

(E) Recruiting

22. Which of the following personality traits best describes individuals who can adapt and adjust their behavior to external factors?

(A) Low self-esteem

(B) External locus of control

(C) High self-monitoring

(D) Low authoritarianism

(E) High authoritarianism

23. A person who believes that "the ends justify the means" is best described as

(A) self-confident
(B) Machiavellian
(C) authoritarian
(D) having cognitive dissonance
(E) having an internal locus of control

24. In which of the following situations are groups most effective?

(A) Cohesive groups with groupthink
(B) Noncohesive groups without groupthink
(C) Cohesive groups in alignment with organizational goals
(D) Noncohesive groups in alignment with organizational goals
(E) Cohesive groups not in alignment with organizational goals

25. Which of the following is a view of conflict that argues that conflict must be avoided?

(A) Human relations
(B) Human resources
(C) Contemporary
(D) Traditional
(E) Interactionist

26. Which of the following best describes a team that brings together organizational members from various areas such as marketing, engineering, human resources, and production to work on a task?

(A) Command
(B) Self-managed
(C) Cross-functional
(D) Restrictive
(E) Informal

27. Which of the following is NOT an input, according to equity theory?

(A) Effort
(B) Experience
(C) Education
(D) Seniority
(E) Pay incentives

28. Which of the following terms best describes leaders who guide or motivate their followers in the direction of established goals by stressing rewards and the consequences of not conforming to expectations?

(A) Transactional
(B) Transformational
(C) Charismatic
(D) People-oriented
(E) Informal

29. Which of the following is the step that follows "measuring actual performance" in the control process?

(A) Establishing standards
(B) Obtaining employee inputs
(C) Reviewing performance standards
(D) Comparing results against standards
(E) Revising standards

30. Which of the following is best defined as a process that involves defining organizational objectives and goals, establishing an overall strategy, and developing a hierarchy of plans to integrate activities?

(A) Manipulating
(B) Leading
(C) Planning
(D) Managing by objectives
(E) Controlling

31. Which of the following terms best describes a corporation's sexual harassment policy?

(A) A single-use plan

(B) A standing plan

(C) A strategic plan

(D) A short-term plan

(E) A specific plan

32. The preparations that a small town might make for a visit by the President of the United States would be considered what type of plan?

(A) Strategic

(B) Directional

(C) Standing

(D) Long-term

(E) Single-use

33. Which of the following best describes a type of planning in which multiple scenarios are developed to test possible future outcomes?

(A) Queuing theory

(B) Simulations

(C) Linear regression

(D) Marginal profits

(E) Project management

34. Which of the following describes the critical path in a Program Evaluation and Review Technique (PERT) process?

(A) Parts that require the most costly materials

(B) The most time-consuming sequence of events and activities

(C) The shortest route to the project completion

(D) The central guideline for quality control

(E) The property insurance

35. Which of the following oversees the transformation process that converts inputs such as labor and raw materials into outputs such as goods and services?

(A) Operation management

(B) Control management

(C) Strategic management

(D) Human resource management

(E) Project management

36. The most evident change in organizational design caused by management information technology is that it makes organizations more

(A) formalized

(B) decentralized

(C) homogeneous

(D) centralized

(E) tightly controlled

37. The behavior of young athletes when they imitate the way they see professional athletes celebrate on television is most likely explained as

(A) classical conditioning

(B) operant conditioning

(C) cognitive learning

(D) social learning

(E) behavior modification

38. Which of the following best describes the situation in which an employee arrives for work on time in order to avoid being placed on probation for a second time?

(A) Positive reinforcement

(B) Negative reinforcement

(C) Extinction

(D) Intermittent reinforcement

(E) Cognitive learning

39. Which of the following are most likely to cause a team to avoid groupthink?

   I. The team holds a second chance meeting.

   II. Outside experts are invited to observe and react to the group process.

   III. The team leader expresses an opinion at the outset of the meeting to save time.

   (A) I only

   (B) I and II only

   (C) I and III only

   (D) II and III only

   (E) I, II, and III

40. If a manager announces a casual dress policy on Fridays and then comes to work dressed casually on the following Friday, this is an example of

   (A) planning

   (B) organizing

   (C) leading

   (D) controlling

   (E) negative reinforcement

41. Hillary finds that challenging tasks increase her level of job satisfaction. If she delegates challenging tasks to her direct reports to increase their job satisfaction, what error of perception is she exhibiting?

   (A) Stereotyping

   (B) Halo

   (C) Selective perception

   (D) Projection

   (E) Schema

42. If George blames new software for his group's poor performance in the most recent quarter, but attributes its success in the prior quarter to his outstanding managerial skills, he is most likely exhibiting

   (A) projection

   (B) selective perception

   (C) fundamental attribution error

   (D) self-serving bias

   (E) Pygmalion effect

43. Praise received from an employee's peers is best described as an example of

   (A) an extrinsic reward

   (B) an intrinsic reward

   (C) low valence

   (D) high instrumentality

   (E) high directive leadership

44. Which of the following procedures is (are) appropriate when disciplining an employee?

   I. Advise the employee on what he or she has done wrong.

   II. Advise the employee on what he or she does well.

   III. Discipline the employee in private.

   (A) I only

   (B) II only

   (C) I and II only

   (D) II and III only

   (E) I, II, and III

45. When a company adopts telecommuting, which core job characteristic is likely to be influenced the most?

   (A) Skill variety

   (B) Task identity

   (C) Task significance

   (D) Autonomy

   (E) Job feedback

46. If jobs are designed so that each worker assembles a different part of a product on an automated assembly line, the job design is most likely to

   (A) provide high levels of intrinsic rewards
   (B) be highly challenging
   (C) make it easy to train workers
   (D) be highly satisfying
   (E) demand creativity from the workers

47. If individual contributions in a group project are not evaluated, which of the following is likely to occur?

   (A) Synergy
   (B) Task significance
   (C) Social loafing
   (D) The Leavitt effect
   (E) Vertical loading

48. Determining whether membership of a group should be heterogeneous or homogeneous should be most influenced by which of the following factors?

   (A) The group size
   (B) Status congruence
   (C) The organizational setting
   (D) The goals, rewards, and resources
   (E) The nature of the task

49. Which of the following describes the most favorable situation for a leader of a group?

   (A) The group has high group cohesiveness and positive group performance norms
   (B) The group has high group cohesiveness and negative group performance norms
   (C) The group has low group cohesiveness and positive group performance norms
   (D) The group has low group cohesiveness and negative group performance norms
   (E) The group has both moderate cohesiveness and moderate performance norms

50. Which of the following actions is most appropriate for a group leader who believes the cohesiveness of a group is hurting its performance?

   (A) Rewarding individual results
   (B) Rewarding team results
   (C) Making the members feel secure
   (D) Establishing intrasender-role conflicts
   (E) Establishing person-role conflicts

51. If an investor buys a stock based on the recommendation of a broker because the broker's previous recommendations have been profitable, the broker possesses which type of power?

   (A) Referent
   (B) Legitimate
   (C) Informal authority
   (D) Charismatic
   (E) Expert

52. Which of the following styles of leadership is most likely to be effective with workers who have experience and are professionally oriented?

   (A) Supportive
   (B) Task-oriented
   (C) Achievement-oriented
   (D) Mentoring
   (E) Authoritarian

53.   "You are always late to meetings and this will have to change!"

   Which of the following best describes the comment above by a manager to an employee?

   (A) Proxemics
   (B) Constructive feedback
   (C) A general over-specific comment
   (D) A specific over-general comment
   (E) Nonverbal communication

54. The power base that relies on the use of knowledge to persuade is best described as

(A) rewards
(B) expert
(C) referent
(D) coercive
(E) legitimate

55. Which of the following is the most accurate description of a grapevine in an organization?

(A) It is a constant source of disruptive information.
(B) It follows the chain of command.
(C) It can be suppressed once it is recognized.
(D) It plays an important role in organizations.
(E) Most managers believe that it is a positive source of information.

56. Which of the following business situations is most appropriate for telecommuting?

(A) Workers thrive on competition.
(B) Decisions and actions are predetermined.
(C) Decisions rely on negotiation and social interaction.
(D) There is an oversupply of workers.
(E) Individual productivity is of primary importance.

57. Empowerment opportunities are LEAST likely to be found in which of the following?

(A) Participative goal setting
(B) Serving as a messenger
(C) Delegation of work
(D) Self-managed teams
(E) Freedom to experiment

58. Which of the following pairs of functions of management are most closely interdependent?

(A) Staffing and organizing
(B) Staffing and controlling
(C) Planning and leading
(D) Planning and controlling
(E) Disciplining and recruiting

59. Which of the following is the primary concern of employees responsible for strategic planning in a company?

(A) Monitoring daily cash flow
(B) Determining the contribution each subunit should make to the overall corporation
(C) Determining how to accomplish specific tasks with available resources
(D) Determining how to pursue long-term goals with available resources
(E) Preparing the annual statement

60. Which of the following is most likely to result from the use of flowcharts in planning?

(A) A guarantee that work will progress according to schedule
(B) A visual sequencing of activities
(C) A chart useful for comparing cash flow during two different quarters
(D) A scheduling process
(E) A combined sequencing and scheduling plan

61. Which of the following is a deterrent to "escalation of commitment"?

(A) A desire to justify earlier decisions
(B) Organizational politics
(C) An efficiency "reality check"
(D) The Abilene paradox
(E) A cultural emphasis on persistence

62. Which of the following is most likely to be a major advantage of group-aided decision making?

(A) Social pressure can drive the decision.

(B) Goal displacement and hidden agendas can occur.

(C) Groupthink may occur.

(D) The likelihood that the decision will be accepted increases.

(E) It frequently saves both time and money.

63. Which of the following basic leadership styles most closely matches the "high structure, low consideration" of the Ohio State leadership studies?

(A) Country club

(B) Team

(C) Selling

(D) Relationship motivated

(E) Telling

64. According to Fiedler's contingency studies, for organizations that were considered "moderately favorable" in terms of leaders' authority, task definition, and leader-member relationships, the most effective style for the leader to have was

(A) country club

(B) team

(C) selling

(D) relationship motivated

(E) telling

65. Large organizations are likely to structure their work operations and personnel in any of the following ways EXCEPT

(A) accounting

(B) divisional

(C) geographic

(D) market

(E) product

66. The span of control most appropriate in a given organization is primarily influenced by which of the following?

(A) Types of services or products being produced

(B) Amount of supervision needed by subordinates

(C) Amount of authority given to a supervisor

(D) Number of hierarchical levels within the organization

(E) Presence of work teams

67. The extensive use of work teams in an organization is most likely to occur under which of the following circumstances?

(A) Control is centralized by top management.

(B) The management style is primarily autocratic.

(C) Employees are unmotivated.

(D) Supervisors have a narrow span of control.

(E) Employee involvement is a management goal.

68. Management control systems are used to monitor all of the following EXCEPT

(A) financial results

(B) employee productivity

(C) operational effectiveness

(D) recruiting and selecting

(E) quality achievement

69. Outsourcing allows an organization to have which of the following?

(A) Higher employee motivation

(B) Improved labor-management relations

(C) Lower accident rates

(D) Greater flexibility in staffing

(E) Increased control over employees

70. Requiring a prospective employee to demonstrate the ability to do a specific task during the screening process is defined by which type of test?

(A) Achievement

(B) Aptitude

(C) Assessment

(D) Work sampling

(E) Spatial

71. Intrinsic rewards can be classified as rewards that do which of the following?

(A) Allow the employee to establish flexible working hours.

(B) Provide a sense of achievement and accomplishment.

(C) Create work coordination among all employees.

(D) Improve communication effectiveness.

(E) Allow greater span of control.

72. The best tangible measurement of leadership effectiveness is which of the following?

(A) Financial success

(B) Turnover ratios

(C) Training and development rates

(D) Employee job performance

(E) Employee morale

73. The use of transactional leadership is based on the concept of which of the following?

(A) Using rewards and coercive power

(B) Stressing intrinsic motivators

(C) Creating team-based goal setting

(D) Using peer-based performance evaluations

(E) Implementing employee involvement plans

74. Group or team cohesiveness is usually influenced by which of the following?

(A) Employee incentive systems

(B) Goal-setting processes

(C) Identification with the group by its members

(D) Size of the organization

(E) Type of organizational structure

75. Resolving conflict through collaboration requires that parties do which of the following?

(A) Work cooperatively

(B) Have a third party intervene

(C) Involve a supervisor in the process

(D) Establish predetermined outcomes

(E) Prepare written plans

76. Coaching as a leadership technique is most likely to work when which of the following exists?

(A) Employees are well trained.

(B) Job descriptions are valid.

(C) Performance development needs are known.

(D) A performance appraisal process is used.

(E) Training programs are offered.

77. All of the following criteria could be used to evaluate decision-making alternatives EXCEPT

(A) ethicality

(B) economic feasibility

(C) legality

(D) practicality

(E) popularity

78. All of the following are considered steps in the planning process EXCEPT

(A) determining the organization's mission

(B) establishing goals and objectives

(C) formulating strategies

(D) implementing strategies

(E) measuring performance

79. Job enrichment can be an effective tool to achieve which of the following?

(A) Better communication

(B) Increased job responsibility

(C) Improved work relations

(D) Teamwork

(E) Shared decision making

80. Examples of intrinsic motivators include all of the following EXCEPT

(A) achievement

(B) pay and benefits

(C) recognition

(D) self-esteem

(E) responsibility

81. Which of the following best describes managerial ethics?

(A) It is the social obligation that the individual manager has to fulfill.

(B) It is a statement of the social responsibility of the organization.

(C) It is the standard of conduct that guides a person's decisions and behavior.

(D) It is the mission statement of the organization.

(E) It is a behavior that conforms to legal principles of justice.

82. A manager decides to lay off 10 percent of the workforce and justifies the action by noting that 90 percent still have jobs and the company will remain solvent. This manager has utilized which view of ethics?

(A) Rights view of ethics

(B) Theory of justice view of ethics

(C) Integrative social contracts view of ethics

(D) Utilitarian view of ethics

(E) Golden rule view of ethics

Questions 83–84 are based on the following information.

Ruth has been the chief executive officer of her company for 15 years. Ten years ago, Ruth utilized the Internet to augment the traditional way of doing business, but she did not intend the Internet to replace her company's main source of revenue. Five years ago, Ruth's company began to use the Internet to perform traditional business functions better but did not sell anything on the Internet. Also, the company began to utilize an intranet as an internal organizational communication system. Last year, Ruth decided that her company's total existence must revolve around the Internet, leading to a seamless integration between traditional and e-business functions.

83. Ten years ago, Ruth's company would have been classified as which type of e-business?

(A) Total e-business organization

(B) E-business enhanced organization

(C) E-business enabled organization

(D) E-business committed organization

(E) E-business learning organization

84. Five years ago, Ruth's company would have been classified as which type of e-business?

(A) Total e-business organization

(B) E-business enhanced organization

(C) E-business enabled organization

(D) E-business committed organization

(E) E-business learning organization

85. According to Hofstede, the degree of individualism found in a country is most closely related to which of the following characteristics?

(A) Age

(B) Wealth

(C) Religion

(D) Location

(E) Democracy

86. A multinational company expands its operation to Brazil and hires Brazilians to manage the operation of the new branch. The company is using which type of approach to expand its operations?

(A) Ethnocentric

(B) Polycentric

(C) Monocentric

(D) Geocentric

(E) Egocentric

87. Knowledge management involves encouraging members of an organization to

(A) create educational programs targeted at the average employee

(B) develop new training programs to help new employees learn their jobs

(C) develop a corporate university to provide educational solutions in-house

(D) systematically gather information and share it with others

(E) retrain top managers through traditional MBA programs

88. Which of the following is the type of team that is made up of experts in various specialties working together on various organizational tasks?

(A) Functional

(B) Cross-functional

(C) Self-directed

(D) Vertical

(E) Autonomous

89. Which of the following types of questions would be the best to use during a job interview?

(A) Open-ended

(B) Rotational

(C) Technology-ended

(D) Prodding

(E) Hypocritical

90. In one stage of group development, group members come to accept and understand one another; differences are resolved and members develop a sense of team cohesion. This stage of group development is known as

(A) Adjourning

(B) Performing

(C) Storming

(D) Norming

(E) Forming

91. Solomon is reviewing the types of power the company has provided him for his job as a department head. A certain degree of authority comes with his position. He will directly exercise authority through which form of power?

(A) Referent

(B) Information

(C) Expert

(D) Legitimate

(E) Decision making

92. A performance appraisal method that utilizes evaluation information from supervisors, employees, and coworkers is known as

(A) paired-comparison feedback

(B) programmed feedback decision

(C) behaviorally anchored rating scale

(D) 360-degree feedback

(E) graphic rating scale

93. Which of the following refers to gender-related problems in the career advancement of employees?

(A) Flextime

(B) Glass ceiling

(C) Job enrichment

(D) Job sharing

(E) Career anchor

94. The breakeven point is defined as the level of production at which

    (A) fixed costs are covered by revenue
    (B) variable costs are covered by revenue
    (C) total revenue is sufficient to cover total costs
    (D) marginal revenue equals marginal cost
    (E) the law of diminishing returns is activated

95. Needs-based approaches of motivation focus on

    (A) understanding the individual's cognitive processes, which influence behavior
    (B) examining how consequences of actions mold behavior
    (C) specific factors within a person that energize, direct, or stop behavior
    (D) events that are internal and external to a person
    (E) expectancies and valences of outcomes

96. The Hawthorne studies are examples of which management approach?

    (A) Classical management
    (B) Behavioral management
    (C) Modern management
    (D) Administrative management
    (E) Scientific management

97. A Gantt chart is a visual depiction of the time frame planned for completing specific tasks as compared to which of the following?

    (A) The delivery date promised to the customer
    (B) The actual progress made on each task
    (C) The manager's projected task completion
    (D) The budgeted task completion
    (E) The weighted-average task-completion score

98. A manager who outlines a problem to employees, accepts suggestions, and makes a decision is said to be following what style of leadership?

    (A) Free reign
    (B) Democratic
    (C) Charismatic
    (D) Autocratic
    (E) Laissez-faire

99. Which of the following is first in the decision-making process?

    (A) Implementing a decision
    (B) Assigning the problem to qualified personnel
    (C) Considering all alternatives
    (D) Knowing when to decide
    (E) Defining the problem

100. Which of the following can best be described as a planning function?

    (A) Monitoring operations
    (B) Determining objectives
    (C) Acquiring necessary resources
    (D) Controlling inventory
    (E) Coordinating interdepartmental activities

Study Resources

Most textbooks used in college-level principles of management courses cover the topics in the outline given earlier, but the approaches to certain topics and the emphases given to them may differ. To prepare for the Principles of Management exam, it is advisable to study one or more college textbooks, which can be found in most college bookstores. When selecting a textbook, check the table of contents against the knowledge and skills required for this test.

Visit www.collegeboard.com/clepprep for additional management resources. You can also find suggestions for exam preparation in Chapter IV of the *Official Study Guide*. In addition, many college faculty post their course materials on their schools' Web sites.

Answer Key

1.	C	26.	C	51.	E	76.	C
2.	B	27.	E	52.	C	77.	E
3.	E	28.	A	53.	C	78.	E
4.	E	29.	D	54.	B	79.	B
5.	D	30.	C	55.	D	80.	B
6.	A	31.	B	56.	E	81.	C
7.	E	32.	E	57.	B	82.	D
8.	D	33.	B	58.	D	83.	B
9.	E	34.	B	59.	D	84.	C
10.	C	35.	A	60.	B	85.	B
11.	A	36.	B	61.	C	86.	B
12.	D	37.	D	62.	D	87.	D
13.	D	38.	B	63.	E	88.	B
14.	D	39.	B	64.	D	89.	A
15.	B	40.	C	65.	A	90.	D
16.	E	41.	D	66.	B	91.	D
17.	B	42.	D	67.	E	92.	D
18.	D	43.	A	68.	D	93.	B
19.	B	44.	E	69.	D	94.	C
20.	D	45.	D	70.	D	95.	C
21.	C	46.	C	71.	B	96.	B
22.	C	47.	C	72.	D	97.	B
23.	B	48.	E	73.	A	98.	B
24.	C	49.	A	74.	C	99.	E
25.	D	50.	A	75.	A	100.	B

Principles of Marketing

Description of the Examination

The Principles of Marketing examination covers the material that is usually taught in a one-semester introductory course in marketing. Such a course is usually known as Basic Marketing, Introduction to Marketing, Fundamentals of Marketing, Marketing, or Marketing Principles. The exam is concerned with the role of marketing in society and within a firm, understanding consumer and organizational markets, marketing strategy planning, the marketing mix, marketing institutions, and other selected topics, such as international marketing, ethics, marketing research, services and not-for-profit marketing. The candidate is also expected to have a basic knowledge of the economic/demographic, social/cultural, political/legal, and technological trends that are important to marketing.

The examination contains approximately 100 questions to be answered in 90 minutes. Some of these are pretest questions that will not be scored. Any time candidates spend on tutorials and providing personal information is in addition to the actual testing time.

Knowledge and Skills Required

The subject matter of the Principles of Marketing examination is drawn from the following topics in the approximate proportions indicated. The percentages next to the main topics indicate the approximate percentage of exam questions on that topic.

8–13% **Role of Marketing in Society**
Ethics
Nonprofit marketing
International marketing

17–24% **Role of Marketing in a Firm**
Marketing concept
Marketing strategy
Marketing environment
Marketing decision system
- Marketing research
- Marketing information system

22–27% **Target Marketing**
Consumer behavior
Segmentation
Positioning
Business-to-business markets

40–50% **Marketing Mix**
Product and service management
Branding
Pricing policies
Distribution channels and logistics
Integrated marketing communications/Promotion
Marketing application in e-commerce

Sample Test Questions

The following sample questions do not appear on an actual CLEP examination. They are intended to give potential test-takers an indication of the format and difficulty level of the examination and to provide content for practice and review. Knowing the correct answers to all of the sample questions is not a guarantee of satisfactory performance on the exam.

Directions: Each of the questions or incomplete statements below is followed by five suggested answers or completions. Select the one that is best in each case.

1. A manufacturer of car batteries, who has been selling through an automotive parts wholesaler to garages and service stations, decides to sell directly to retailers. Which of the following will necessarily occur?

   (A) Elimination of the wholesaler's profit will result in a lower price to the ultimate consumer.

   (B) Elimination of the wholesaler's marketing functions will increase efficiency.

   (C) The total cost of distribution will be reduced because of the elimination of the wholesaler.

   (D) The marketing functions performed by the wholesaler will be eliminated.

   (E) The wholesaler's marketing functions will be shifted to or shared by the manufacturer and the retailer.

2. Which of the following strategies for entering the international market would involve the highest risk?

   (A) Joint ventures

   (B) Exporting

   (C) Licensing

   (D) Direct investment

   (E) Franchising

3. For a United States manufacturer of major consumer appliances, the most important leading indicator for forecasting sales is

   (A) automobile sales

   (B) computer sales

   (C) educational level of consumers

   (D) housing starts

   (E) number of business failures

4. Which of the following is an example of a societal marketing approach?

   (A) Revamping the sales force training program

   (B) Making constant product improvements

   (C) Recalling voluntarily a product that is rumored to be defective

   (D) Implementing a marketing information system

   (E) Increasing efficiency by improving production facilities

5. In contrast to a selling orientation, a marketing orientation seeks to

   (A) increase market share by emphasizing promotion

   (B) increase sales volume by lowering price

   (C) lower the cost of distribution by direct marketing

   (D) satisfy the needs of targeted consumers at a profit

   (E) market products that make efficient use of the firm's resources

6. All of the following are characteristics of services EXCEPT

   (A) intangibility

   (B) heterogeneity

   (C) inseparability

   (D) perishability

   (E) inflexibility

7. A fertilizer manufacturer who traditionally
   markets to farmers through farm supply dealers
   and cooperatives decides to sell current
   products to home gardeners through lawn and
   garden shops. This decision is an example of

   (A) market penetration
   (B) market development
   (C) product development
   (D) diversification
   (E) vertical integration

8. A manufacturer who refuses to sell to dealers its
   popular line of office copiers unless the dealers
   also agree to stock the manufacturer's line of
   paper products would most likely be guilty of
   which of the following?

   (A) Deceptive advertising
   (B) Price discrimination
   (C) Price fixing
   (D) Reciprocity
   (E) Tying contracts

9. Prior to consumption by a final consumer, the
   last member in an indirect distribution channel
   is the

   (A) retailer
   (B) wholesaler
   (C) manufacturer
   (D) factor
   (E) freight forwarder

10. In which of the following situations is the
    number of buying influences most likely to be
    greatest?

    (A) A university buys large quantities of paper
        for computer printers on a regular basis.
    (B) A computer manufacturer is building a new
        headquarters and is trying to choose a line
        of office furniture.
    (C) A consumer decides to buy a different brand
        of potato chips because they are on sale.
    (D) A retail chain is searching for a vendor of
        lower-priced cleaning supplies.
    (E) A purchasing manager has been asked to
        locate a second source of supply for
        corrugated shipping cartons.

11. Roy Smith sells sets of encyclopedias door-to-
    door to families in low-income neighborhoods.
    Although the encyclopedias are priced above
    $300, they can be purchased for weekly
    installments of only $3. Roy's favorite sales
    pitch is "Would you deny your child a chance to
    become President of the United States someday
    just to save $3 per week?" Roy's selling
    approach appears to be an example of

    (A) deceptive advertising
    (B) questionable ethics
    (C) trade promotion
    (D) bait-and-switch pricing
    (E) mass-selling approach

12. Cooperative advertising is usually undertaken
    by manufacturers in order to

    (A) secure the help of the retailer in promoting a
        given product
    (B) divide responsibilities between the retailers
        and wholesalers within a channel of
        distribution
    (C) satisfy legal requirements
    (D) create a favorable image of a particular
        industry in the minds of consumers
    (E) provide a subsidy for smaller retailers that
        enables them to match the prices set by
        chain stores

13. A marketer usually offers a noncumulative quantity discount in order to

(A) reward customers for repeat purchases

(B) reduce advertising expenses

(C) encourage users to purchase in large quantities

(D) encourage buyers to submit payment promptly

(E) ensure the prompt movement of goods through the channel of distribution

14. A toy manufacturing firm sold its product through a toy wholesaler, who in turn sold to appropriate retailers. The manufacturer's price is $20 to the wholesaler, whose markup is usually 20 percent on the selling price to the retailer. If the retailer's markup on the selling price to the customer is 50 percent, what is the price to the customer?

(A) $24.00

(B) $30.00

(C) $36.00

(D) $37.50

(E) $50.00

15. Missionary salespersons are most likely to do which of the following?

(A) Sell cosmetics directly to consumers in their own homes

(B) Take orders for air conditioners to be used in a large institution

(C) Describe drugs and other medical supplies to physicians

(D) Secure government approval to sell heavy machinery to a foreign government

(E) Take orders for custom-tailored garments or other specially produced items

16. The demand for industrial goods is sometimes called "derived" because it depends on

(A) economic conditions

(B) demand for consumer goods

(C) governmental activity

(D) availability of labor and materials

(E) the desire to make a profit

17. Behavioral research generally indicates that consumers' attitudes

(A) do not change very easily or quickly

(B) are very easy to change through promotion

(C) cannot ever be changed

(D) can only be developed through actual experience with products

(E) are very accurate predictors of actual purchasing behavior

18. A channel of distribution refers to the

(A) routing of goods through distribution centers

(B) sequence of marketing intermediaries from producer to consumer

(C) methods of transporting goods from producer to consumer

(D) suppliers who perform a variety of functions

(E) traditional handlers of a product line

19. A major advantage of distributing products by truck is

(A) low cost relative to rail or water

(B) low probability of loss or damage to cargo

(C) accessibility to pick-up and delivery locations

(D) speed relative to rail or air

(E) ability to handle a wider variety of products than other means

20. If a firm is using penetration pricing, the firm is most likely trying to achieve which of the following pricing objectives?

    (A) Product quality leadership
    (B) Market-share maximization
    (C) High gross margin
    (D) Status quo
    (E) Geographic flexibility

21. The marketer of which of the following products would be most likely to use a promotional mix with a heavy emphasis on personal selling?

    (A) Life insurance
    (B) Pencils
    (C) Transistor radios
    (D) Bread
    (E) Crackers

22. Marketing strategy planning includes

    (A) supervising the activities of the firm's sales force
    (B) determining the most efficient way to manufacture products
    (C) selecting a target market and developing the marketing mix
    (D) determining the reach and frequency of advertising
    (E) monitoring sales in response to a price change

23. A brand that has achieved brand insistence and is considered a specialty good by the target market suggests which of the following distribution objectives?

    (A) Widespread distribution near probable points of use
    (B) Exclusive distribution
    (C) Intensive distribution
    (D) Enough exposure to facilitate price comparison
    (E) Widespread distribution at low cost

24. Market segmentation that is concerned with people over 65 years of age is called

    (A) geographic
    (B) socioeconomic
    (C) demographic
    (D) psychographic
    (E) behavioral

25. The XYZ Corporation has two chains of restaurants. One restaurant specializes in family dining with affordable meals. The second restaurant targets young, single individuals, and offers a full bar and small servings. The XYZ Corporation uses which form of targeted marketing strategy?

    (A) Mass marketing
    (B) Differentiated marketing
    (C) Undifferentiated marketing
    (D) Customized marketing
    (E) Concentrated marketing

26. The marketing director of a manufacturing company says, "If my wholesaler exceeds the sales record from last month, I agree to give him a paid trip to the Bahamas." This technique is a form of

    (A) sales promotion
    (B) advertising
    (C) personal selling
    (D) direct marketing
    (E) public relations

27. Using a combination of different modes of transportation to move freight in order to exploit the best features of each mode is called

    (A) conventional distribution
    (B) developing dual distribution
    (C) selective distribution
    (D) intermodal transportation
    (E) freight forwarding

28. Which of the following is a major disadvantage associated with the use of dual distribution?

(A) It is usually very expensive.

(B) It can cause channel conflict between members.

(C) It provides limited market coverage.

(D) It is only appropriate for corporate channels.

(E) Some distribution channel functions are not completed.

29. The three strategic options of distribution intensity are

(A) concentrated, exclusive, and intensive

(B) intensive, extensive, and selective

(C) intensive, exclusive, and selective

(D) extensive, concentrated, and selective

(E) extensive, integrated, and concentrated

30. Which of the following would be considered a nonprofit organization?

(A) A homeless shelter that charges a fee for its services and uses the proceeds for the upkeep of the shelter

(B) A drug rehabilitation center in which revenues in excess of cost go to the owners

(C) A vaccination clinic owned by an individual entrepreneur

(D) A bookstore open to the public for business

(E) A hospital that has a publicly traded common stock

31. Which of the following approaches for entering international markets involves granting the rights to a patent, trademark, or manufacturing process to a foreign company?

(A) Exporting

(B) Franchising

(C) Licensing

(D) Joint venturing

(E) Contract manufacturing

32. Reference groups are more likely to influence a consumer's purchase when the product being purchased is

(A) important

(B) expensive

(C) familiar

(D) intangible

(E) socially visible

33. Which of the following is true of the product life cycle?

(A) It can accurately forecast the growth of new products.

(B) It reveals that branded products have the longest growth phase.

(C) It cannot be applied to computer products that quickly become obsolete.

(D) It is based on the assumption that products go through distinct stages in sales and profit performance.

(E) It proves that profitability is highest in the mature phase.

34. The best way to segment consumer markets is by

(A) age, gender, income, and geographic area

(B) a combination of psychographic and geographic variables

(C) product benefits

(D) selecting important target groups

(E) the variables affecting purchase and consumption behavior of the target group

35. A marketing expert said that he could have advertised a brand of soap as a detergent bar for men with dirty hands, but instead chose to advertise it as a toilet bar for women with dry skin. This illustrates the marketing principle known as

(A) product positioning

(B) sales promotion

(C) cannibalization

(D) deceptive advertising

(E) undifferentiated marketing

36. The process of ensuring that people or companies may have a need for a salesperson's product is known as

    (A) cold calling
    (B) presenting
    (C) approaching
    (D) prospecting
    (E) targeting

37. Which of the following is a primary disadvantage of direct marketing?

    (A) It is difficult to measure response.
    (B) It is not personal.
    (C) It is poorly targeted.
    (D) It tends to have high costs per contact.
    (E) It has a fragmented audience.

38. A formal statement of standards that governs professional conduct is called a

    (A) customer bill of rights
    (B) business mission statement
    (C) corporate culture
    (D) code of ethics
    (E) caveat emptor

39. Maxine suddenly realizes that she is out of paper towels. She remembers that she last bought Max Dri Towels, so she stops at the store and picks up another roll of Max Dri on her way home from work. In this example, Maxine uses what form of information search in her decision process?

    (A) Limited problem solving
    (B) Extended problem solving
    (C) Internal information search
    (D) Compensatory information search
    (E) Information search by personal sources

40. The ability to tailor marketing processes to fit the specific needs of an individual customer in Internet marketing is called

    (A) customization
    (B) community building
    (C) standardization
    (D) mediation
    (E) product differentiation

41. Which of the following would most likely be considered a form of direct marketing?

    (A) Mail-order catalogs
    (B) Convenience stores
    (C) Department stores
    (D) Warehouse clubs
    (E) Supermarkets

42. ABC Company agrees to pay a certain amount of a retailer's promotional costs for advertising ABC's products. This is an example of

    (A) cooperative advertising
    (B) reminder advertising
    (C) comparison advertising
    (D) slotting allowance
    (E) a premium

43. To save time and money, a marketing research team uses data that have already been gathered for some other purpose. Which type of data is the team using?

    (A) Sample
    (B) Primary
    (C) Secondary
    (D) Survey
    (E) Experiment

44. Positioning refers to

    (A) the perception of a product in customers' minds

    (B) the store location in which a marketing manager suggests a product be displayed

    (C) where the product is placed on the shelf

    (D) which stores will distribute a company's product

    (E) where the new product is first advertised

45. A toothpaste company introduces a new flavor of a brand that it already sells. This is an example of

    (A) new product line

    (B) category extension

    (C) line extension

    (D) product improvement

    (E) repositioning

46. Companies tend to spend more on advertising when a product is at which level of brand loyalty?

    (A) Brand recognition

    (B) Brand preference

    (C) Brand insistence

    (D) Brand equity

    (E) Brand aversion

47. When a company markets services, as opposed to products, the characteristics of the services affect the marketing program. Which of the following best describes these differentiating characteristics of services?

    (A) Cost, time, quality, and value

    (B) Uncertainty, variability, and standardization

    (C) Intangibility, durability, and standardization

    (D) Intangibility, perishability, and variability

    (E) Tangibility, variability, and uncertainty

48. For a marketer of long-distance phone cards, which of the following methods of seeking new customers is LEAST likely to be considered Internet marketing?

    (A) Sending e-mail to addresses acquired from a list vendor

    (B) Having banner advertising on Web sites and portals

    (C) Having a Web site featuring all the marketer's phone cards

    (D) Publicizing the marketer's Web address on billboards and buses

    (E) Buying keyword-based advertising space on search engine pages

49. Which of the following is the fastest growing nonstore retail segment in the United States?

    (A) Television home shopping

    (B) Automatic vending

    (C) Online retailing

    (D) Catalog marketing

    (E) Direct-response marketing

50. While writing a marketing plan, Melanie decides that the marketing objective should be "to increase market share by 5 percent." A weakness in this objective is that

    (A) it is not measurable

    (B) it should be related to brand image rather than market share

    (C) it does not specify a time period

    (D) if the product is an industrial product, the objective should specify product quality

    (E) it does not address all elements of the business plan

51. Which of the following is the first step in the sales process?

(A) Prospecting

(B) Sales presentation

(C) Gaining commitment

(D) Approach

(E) Precall planning

52. Which of the following is an example of business-to-business buying?

(A) John buys a new home stereo.

(B) Hannah pays for a new television by monthly installment.

(C) Daniel decides on which college to attend.

(D) Avery purchases a new office desk for his company.

(E) Corey buys a soft drink from a vending machine.

53. President John F. Kennedy's assertion that consumers have certain rights led to legislation that guaranteed all of the following EXCEPT the right to

(A) be informed

(B) be heard

(C) choose

(D) bargain

(E) safety

54. Harmony Households is the largest home improvement retailer in China. Because of its size and market power, the firm can insist upon desired product features, delivery schedules, and price points from its suppliers. Harmony Households is

(A) a primary intermediary

(B) an agent retailer

(C) a multilevel distributor

(D) a channel captain

(E) a dominant distributor

55. Which of the following is NOT a segmentation criterion or consideration used for choosing a target market?

(A) Market accountability

(B) Market identifiability and measurability

(C) Market substantiality

(D) Market accessibility

(E) Market responsiveness

56. Rachel Terry, regional manager at Wilcon Solvents, Inc., compares last quarter's sales with the levels projected in the firm's marketing plan. She identifies three solvent brands whose sales are below projections and initiates a series of inquiries to discover the reasons for the shortfall. Ms. Terry is engaged in which stage of the strategic marketing process?

(A) Environmental scanning

(B) Opportunity analysis

(C) Planning

(D) Implementation

(E) Control

57. Richard Weiss, SA, is a Swiss watch manufacturer. One of its two major brands offers ruggedness, reliability and durability to active sports enthusiasts. The other offers elegance and stylishness to fashion conscious consumers. Which of the following segmentation approaches is this firm using?

(A) Demographic

(B) Geographic

(C) Usage

(D) Benefits sought

(E) Socioeconomic

58. Compared with agent intermediaries, merchant intermediaries

(A) sell only to organizational customers

(B) sell only in export markets

(C) are employees of the manufacturer

(D) are compensated by a commission on sales

(E) take title to the goods they sell

Directions: Select a choice and click on the blank in which you want the choice to appear. Repeat until all of the blanks have been filled. A correct answer must have a different choice in each blank.

59. Place the four steps in the marketing research process in the correct order.

Determine the research design.

Define the problem.

Collect data.

Choose the data collection method.

_____

_____

_____

_____

Directions: Choose among the corresponding environments in the columns for each entry by clicking on your choice. When you click on a blank cell a check mark will appear. No credit is given unless the correct cell is marked for each entry.

60. For each of the following events, indicate which kind of environment it belongs to.

	Sociocultural Environment	Economic Environment	Technological Environment
The development of new production techniques			
The growing Latino population			
Rising mortgage rates			

Study Resources

Most textbooks used in college-level principles of marketing courses cover the topics in the outline given earlier, but the approaches to certain topics and the emphases given to them may differ. To prepare for the Principles of Marketing exam, it is advisable to study one or more college textbooks, which can be found in most college bookstores. When selecting a textbook, check the table of contents against the knowledge and skills required for this test. Please note that textbooks are updated frequently; it is important to use the latest editions of the textbooks you choose. Most textbooks now have study guides, computer applications, and case studies to accompany them. These learning aids could prove useful in the understanding and application of marketing concepts and principles.

You can broaden your understanding of marketing principles and their applications by keeping abreast of current developments in the field from articles in newspapers and news magazines as well as in business publications such as *The Wall Street Journal*, *Business Week*, *Harvard Business Review*, *Fortune*, *Ad Week*, and *Advertising Age*. Journals found in most college libraries that will help you expand your knowledge of marketing principles include *Journal of Marketing*, *Marketing Today*, *Journal of the Academy of Marketing Sciences*, *American Demographics*, and *Marketing Week*. Books of readings, such as *Annual Editions— Marketing*, also are sources of current thinking.

Visit www.collegeboard.com/clepprep for additional marketing resources. You can also find suggestions for exam preparation in Chapter IV of the *Official Study Guide*. In addition, many college faculty post their course materials on their schools' Web sites.

Answer Key

1.	E	31.	C
2.	D	32.	E
3.	D	33.	D
4.	C	34.	E
5.	D	35.	A
6.	E	36.	D
7.	B	37.	D
8.	E	38.	D
9.	A	39.	C
10.	B	40.	A
11.	B	41.	A
12.	A	42.	A
13.	C	43.	C
14.	E	44.	A
15.	C	45.	C
16.	B	46.	A
17.	A	47.	D
18.	B	48.	D
19.	C	49.	C
20.	B	50.	C
21.	A	51.	A
22.	C	52.	D
23.	B	53.	D
24.	C	54.	D
25.	B	55.	A
26.	A	56.	E
27.	D	57.	D
28.	B	58.	E
29.	C	59.	See below
30.	A	60.	See below

59. Define the problem.
Determine the research design.
Choose the data collection method.
Collect data.

60.

	Sociocultural Environment	Economic Environment	Technological Environment
The development of new production techniques			√
The growing Latino population	√		
Rising mortgage rates		√	

CollegeBoard
inspiring minds™

What Your CLEP® Score Means

In order to reach the total score you see on your score report, two calculations are performed.

First, your "raw score" is calculated. This is the number of questions you answered correctly. Your raw score increases by one point for each question answered correctly, and no points are gained or lost when a question is not answered or is answered incorrectly.

Second, your raw score is converted into a "scaled score" by a statistical process called *equating*. Equating maintains the consistency of standards for test scores over time by adjusting for slight differences in difficulty between test forms. This ensures that your score does not depend on the specific test form you took or how well others did on the same form. Your raw score is converted to a scaled score that ranges from 20, the lowest, to 80, the highest. The final scaled score is the score that appears on your score report.

To see whether you attained a score sufficient to receive college credit, compare your score to the score in the table shown. The scores that appear in this table are the credit-granting scores recommended by the American Council on Education (ACE). **Each college, however, reserves the right to set its own credit-granting policy, which may differ from that of ACE.** If you have not already done so, contact your college as soon as possible to find out the score it requires to grant credit, the number of credit hours granted and the course(s) that can be bypassed with a satisfactory score.

Please note that CLEP® examinations are developed and evaluated independently and are not linked to each other except by the program's common purpose, format and method of reporting results. For this reason, direct comparisons should not be made between CLEP examinations in different subjects. CLEP scores are not comparable to SAT® scores or other test scores.

Test scores are kept on file for 20 years. During this period, score reports may be sent to an institution, but only at the request of the candidate. A Transcript Request Form and instructions for having a transcript sent to an institution can be downloaded from the CLEP Web site (www.collegeboard.com/clep) or obtained by contacting CLEP.

Candidates may not repeat an examination of the same title within six months of the initial testing date. If the candidate retakes the examination within the six-month period, the administration will be considered invalid, the score will be canceled and any test fees will be forfeited. DANTES-funded military examinees: The U.S. government will not fund CLEP examinations that are repeated within a 180-day period.

If you have a question about your score report, about a test question or about any other aspect of a CLEP examination that your test center cannot answer, write to CLEP, P.O. Box 6600, Princeton, NJ 08541-6600 or e-mail clep@info.collegeboard.org.

Visit CLEP on the Web: www.collegeboard.com/clep

2009-10 CLEP® Credit-Granting Recommendations

	Computer-Based Testing (CBT) and Paper-and-Pencil Testing	
	ACE Recommended Score[1]	Semester Hours[1]
Business		
Financial Accounting	50	3
Information Systems and Computer Applications	50	3
Introductory Business Law	50	3
Principles of Management	50	3
Principles of Marketing	50	3
Composition and Literature		
American Literature	50	6
Analyzing and Interpreting Literature	50	6
College Composition[2]	50	6
College Composition Modular[2]	50	3/6
English Composition with Essay[3]	50	6
English Composition Without Essay[3]	50	6
English Literature	50	6
Freshman College Composition[3]	50	6
Humanities	50	6
Foreign Languages		
French Language, Level 1	50	6
French Language, Level 2	59	12
German Language, Level 1	50	6
German Language, Level 2	60	12
Spanish Language, Level 1	50	6
Spanish Language, Level 2	63	12
Level 1 — equivalent to the first two semesters (or 6 semester hours) of college-level foreign language course work		
Level 2 — equivalent to the first four semesters (or 12 semester hours) of college-level foreign language course work		
History and Social Sciences		
American Government	50	3
History of the United States I: Early Colonization to 1877	50	3
History of the United States II: 1865 to Present	50	3
Human Growth and Development	50	3
Introduction to Educational Psychology	50	3
Introductory Psychology	50	3
Introductory Sociology	50	3
Principles of Macroeconomics	50	3
Principles of Microeconomics	50	3
Social Sciences and History	50	6
Western Civilization I: Ancient Near East to 1648	50	3
Western Civilization II: 1648 to Present	50	3
Science and Mathematics		
Biology	50	6
Calculus	50	3
Chemistry	50	6
College Algebra	50	3
College Mathematics	50	6
Precalculus	50	3
Natural Sciences	50	6

1. The American Council on Education's College Credit Recommendation Service (ACE CREDIT) has evaluated CLEP processes and procedures for developing, administering and scoring the exams. The scores listed above are equivalent to a grade of C in the corresponding course. The American Council on Education, the major coordinating body for all the nation's higher education institutions, seeks to provide leadership and a unifying voice on key higher education issues and to influence public policy through advocacy, research and program initiatives. For more information, visit the ACE CREDIT Web site at www.acenet.edu/acecredit.

2. These exams will be available to students on July 1, 2010. If the college does not require a supplemental essay for the Modular version of the examination, the ACE credit-granting recommendation is 3 credits. If the college does require a supplemental essay, the credit-granting recommendation is 6 credits.

3. Beginning July 1, 2010, these exams will no longer be available to students. They will be replaced by College Composition and College Composition Modular.

www.collegeboard.com/clep

751680